6.30
D

# BLUE GUIDE **ISTANBUL**

43,500 = c£30

10.30
8.40
6.40
7.15
7.30    Turkish airline
1 hr

D1574991

*The crown of the dome of Haghia Sophia soars 56m above the floor, about the height of a 15-storey building. (Ergun Cagatay)*

BLUE GUIDE

# ISTANBUL

John Freely

*With maps, plans and atlas*

**A. & C. Black**
London

**W. W. Norton**
New York

Second edition 1987

Published by A & C Black (Publishers) Limited
35 Bedford Row, London WC1R 4JH

© Copyright A & C Black (Publishers) Limited 1987

Published in the United States of America by
W W Norton & Company, Incorporated
500 Fifth Avenue, New York, NY 10110

Published simultaneously in Canada by
Penguin Books Canada Limited,
2801 John Street, Markham, Ontario L3R 1B4

**British Library Cataloguing in Publication Data**

Freely, John
  Istanbul.—2nd ed.—(Blue guide)
  1. Istanbul (Turkey)—Description—
  Guide-books
  I. Title    II. Series
  915.63    DR718

  ISBN 0–7136–2830–8


ISBN 0-393-30082-X    USA

Printed and bound in Great Britain by
William Clowes Limited, Beccles and London

# PREFACE

Istanbul, with a population of more than seven million, is by far the
largest city in Turkey. Few cities in the world can compare with it in
the beauty of its setting or in the number and grandeur of its ancient
monuments. This Blue Guide is designed to be the most comprehensive guide to Istanbul in any language, giving not only a complete and
accurate description of its antiquities, but also providing all of the
background and practical information that travellers will need to
enjoy all aspects of their stay in this extraordinary city.

Like the other Blue Guides, this book is divided into routes, all of
which can be followed in a day or less. The four principal monuments
of the city are treated as separate routes; these are: Haghia Sophia,
Topkapí Sarayí, the Süleymaniye, and Kariye Camii. There are 21
routes in all; 16 of them go through Stamboul, the old city, while the
last five deal with other parts of the city and its suburbs: Eyüp, a
religious shrine up the Golden Horn; Galata and Pera, the Levantine
quarters on the left bank of the Horn; the Bosphorus, the incomparable strait that separates the European and Asian parts of the city;
Üsküdar and Kadíköy, the suburbs on the Asian shore; and the
Princes' Isles, the suburban archipelago on the Sea of Marmara.

The *Background Information* in the first section of the guide
provides an introduction to the history, architecture and art of
Istanbul, so that one can more fully appreciate the ancient
monuments of the city. This is followed by a section on *Practical
Information*, which includes, among other things, a brief introduction
to the Turkish language. Travellers to Istanbul are urged to learn a
few words and phrases of basic Turkish, because it will make their
stay in the city more interesting and enjoyable.

# EXPLANATIONS

**Type.** The main routes are described in large type. Smaller type is used, in general, for historical, background and practical information, as well as for the description of sub-routes and diversions.

**Asterisks** (*) indicate places of special interest or excellence. **Double asterisks** (**) denote monuments of extraordinary interest, those that should not be missed on a visit to Istanbul.

**Abbreviations.** In addition to generally accepted and self-explanatory abbreviations, the following occur in the Guide:

Blv   *Bulvar* (Boulevard)
c     *circa* (about, concerning a date)
C     Century
Cd    *Caddesi* (Avenue)
m     metres
m.    miles
Md    *Meydan* (Square)
Pl    Atlas Plan
R     Room (as in a Museum, etc.)
Rte   Route
Sk    *Sokak* (Street)
SS.   Saints
TL    Turkish Lira

# CONTENTS

# 8 CONTENTS

## MAPS AND PLANS

# BACKGROUND INFORMATION

## A. Introduction to Istanbul

Istanbul is the only city in the world that stands upon two continents. The main part of the city, which is located at the SE tip of Europe, is separated from its suburbs in Asia by the Bosphorus, the beautiful and historic strait that cuts through from the Black Sea to the Sea of Marmara, the ancient Pontus and Propontus. The European part of the city is bisected by the Golden Horn, a stream that has its origins in the hills to the NW of the city. The oldest section of the city, Stamboul, is on the right bank of the Golden Horn; on the left bank is the port quarter of Galata, with the more modern neighbourhoods stretching out along the hills above the Bosphorus. (The words Istanbul and Stamboul are corruptions of the Greek *stin poli*, meaning 'in the city', or 'to the city', phrases that are still used by Greeks when referring to the imperial capital once known as Constantinople, and before that as Byzantium.) Stamboul itself forms a roughly triangular promontory, bounded on the N by the Golden Horn, on the S by the Sea of Marmara, and on its landward side by its ancient defence-walls. At Saray Burnu, the point that forms the apex of this promontory, the Bosphorus and the Golden Horn meet and flow together into the Marmara, together forming what a Byzantine poet referred to as the city's 'garland of waters'.

## B. History

**The Ancient City of Byzantium.** There is archaeological evidence of a settlement on the acropolis above Saray Burnu in the late Mycenaean period, dating to c the 13C BC. However, virtually nothing is known of this Mycenaean settlement, and the history of the city really begins with the founding of Byzantium in the 7C BC. According to tradition, the eponymous founder of Byzantium was Byzas the Megarian, who established a colony of Megarians and Athenians on the acropolis above the confluence of the Bosphorus and the Golden Horn in 667 BC. Before setting out, Byzas had consulted the Delphic oracle, which advised him to settle 'opposite the Land of the Blind'. The oracle was referring to the residents of Chalcedon, a Greek colony established a few years earlier on the Asian side of the strait. The implication is that the earlier settlers must have been blind not to have seen the much greater advantages of the site on the European side. A city built there would be more defensible, since the steep acropolis was bounded on two sides by deep waters, and its short landward exposure could be protected by strong walls. The city would then be in a position to control all shipping passing between the Aegean, the Propontus and the Pontus, while its situation on the principal crossing-point between SE Europe and Asia Minor would put it astride the main land routes that developed between the continents.

*One of the reliefs on the base of the Egyptian Obelisk at the N end of the Hippodrome. It shows Theodosius I in the royal enclosure. (Sedat Pakay)*

Byzantium soon became a centre for trade and commerce, acquiring wealth from its fisheries and the customs fees it charged on shipping through the Bosphorus. But despite great prosperity, Byzantium never distinguished itself culturally, as did so many contemporary Greek cities in Asia Minor. Histories of ancient Greece mention only one man from Byzantium in connection with the development of Greek thought; this was Hero the Younger (so-called to distinguish him from the more famous Hero of Alexandria), a physicist and inventor of hydraulic devices.

Nor did its strategic location make Byzantium a leading power in the ancient Greek world, for through most of its history it was dominated by other city-states or empires. Byzantium was taken by Darius in 512 BC, when he crossed the Bosphorus in his campaign against the Scythians. When the Emperor returned to Asia after his campaign, Byzantium and other Greek cities in the region rose in revolt, hoping for assistance from Sparta. But Sparta made no move, and by 509 the Persian army had put down the revolt and punished Byzantium and the other rebellious cities. Byzantium remained in Persian hands until 478, when an allied Greek force under the Spartan general Pausanius freed the city. Pausanius was recalled to stand trial after his campaign, and when he departed Byzantium and other cities in the region placed themselves under the protection of Athens. When Pausanius was exiled from Sparta after his trial he returned to Byzantium and set himself up as a tyrant, intriguing with the Persians. But in 475 the Athenians and their allies drove him out. In 441–440 Byzantium joined Samos and other Greek cities in Asia Minor in a revolt against Athenian domination, but in the following year they gave up the attempt and resumed their tributary status.

In 411, during the Peloponnesian War, Byzantium revolted once again against Athens, allying itself with Sparta, but three years later the Byzantines and their Spartan allies were defeated in a naval battle in the Hellespont. Alcibiades, who commanded the Athenian fleet, soon afterwards took control of Byzantium and then returned in triumph to Athens. In 403, after the final defeat of Athens and the end of the Peloponnesian War, Byzantium surrendered to the Spartan commander Lysander. Shortly afterwards Xenophon and the survivors of the Ten Thousand arrived in Byzantium, on the last stage of their march back from the heart of Persia. They were treated so inhospitably by the Byzantines that they took control of the town and threatened to sack it, leaving only after they had exacted a large bribe from the city council. In 392 Byzantium joined a coalition of Ionian city-states which in 377 became a member of the Second Athenian Alliance. But the Byzantines soon grew restive under the growing power and domination of Athens, and in 362 they placed themselves under the command of the great Boetian leader, Epaminondes, joining him in his war against the Athenians. A decade later Byzantium entered into an alliance with King Philip of Macedon, after which the Byzantines annexed Chalcedon and Selembria gaining complete control over the Bosphorus and its environs. Ten years later Philip began a systematic campaign to conquer Thrace, during the course of which he advanced toward Byzantium. At his approach the Byzantines appealed for help to the Athenians, who responded with a contingent of hoplites and a naval squadron. In the summer of 340 King Philip's army attacked Byzantium, but the Byzantines and their Athenian allies withstood a year-long siege and eventually forced the Macedonians to withdraw. A few years later, however, the Byzantines resumed their alliance with King Philip, for without the protection of what was then the most powerful state in Greece they would have fallen easy prey to the Persians.

Despite their spirited resistance to King Philip, the Byzantines were completely overawed by his son and successor, Alexander the Great. Immediately after Alexander's victory at the Battle of the Granicus in 334, Byzantium surrendered without a struggle and opened its gates to the Macedonians. Later, after Alexander's death in 323, Byzantium was involved in the events following on the collapse and dismemberment of his empire and the subsequent eastward expansion of Rome. In 179 Byzantium was captured by the combined forces of Rhodes, Pergamum and Bithynia. Then in 133 the last ruler of Pergamum bequeathed his kingdom to Rome, and within four years all of western Asia Minor was organised into the Roman Province of Asia, Byzantium included. During the period 88–63 BC, Byzantium was a pawn in the struggle between Rome and Mithridates, King of Pontus. After the final victory of Rome, Byzantium once again became part of the Province of Asia, and for more than 250 years afterwards it enjoyed a respite from war, sheltered by the mantle of the *Pax Romana*.

In the closing years of the 2C AD Byzantium was swept up once again in the tides of history when it became involved in the civil war between the Emperor Septimius Severus and his rival, Pescennius Niger, supporting the latter. After the Emperor defeated and killed Pescennius in 194 he returned to punish the Byzantines, putting their city under siege. After finally taking Byzantium in 196, the Emperor tore down the city walls, massacred all those who had supported his rival, and burned the city to the ground. A few years afterwards, however, Septimius realised the imprudence of leaving so strategic a site undefended, and rebuilt the city on an enlarged scale, enclosing it on its landward side with a new line of walls. The walls of Septimius Severus are thought to have begun at the Golden Horn a short distance downstream from the present Galata Bridge, and to have ended at the Marmara somewhere near where the lighthouse now stands. The area thus enclosed was twice as great as in the original town of Byzantium, which had comprised little more than the Acropolis itself.

At the beginning of the 4C AD Byzantium played an extremely important role in the climactic events then taking place in the Roman Empire. After the retirement of Diocletian in 305, his successors in the Tetrarchy, the two co-emperors and their caesars, fought bitterly with one another for control of the Empire. This struggle was eventually won by Constantine, Emperor of the West, who in 324 defeated Licinius, Emperor of the East. The final battle took place in the hills above Chrysopolis, just across the Bosphorus from Byzantium, where Licinius had his last base. On the following day Byzantium surrendered and opened its gates to Constantine, now sole ruler of the Roman Empire.

During the first two years after his victory Constantine conceived and put into operation a scheme that profoundly influenced the world for the next millennium: reorganising the Roman Empire and shifting its capital to Byzantium. This move had been considered even before Constantine's rise to power. Diocletian (284–305), the founder of the Tetrarchy, chose to rule as Emperor of the East, and established his capital at Nicomedia on the Sea of Marmara. This choice reflected the growing importance of the eastern part of the Empire. It was also based on the fact that the warrior emperors from Diocletian to Constantine had little use for Rome as a capital. They ruled from their headquarters, and a capital in the East would put them closer to the two vital imperial boundaries: the Rhone–Danube line and the Euphrates. Thus a new and more defensible capital on the Bosphorus would put them in a much better position to defend their frontiers in Europe and Asia.

After Constantine made his momentous decision he set out to rebuild and enlarge the old town of Byzantium to suit its imperial role.

The project began on 4 November 326, when the Emperor personally traced out the limits of the new city. The defence walls with which Constantine enclosed the capital extended in a great semi-circle from the Golden Horn to the Sea of Marmara, quadrupling the area of the city. The imperial building programme proceeded rapidly, and in less than four years the new capital was completed. On 11 May 330, in a ceremony in the Hippodrome, Constantine dedicated the city of New Rome and proclaimed that thenceforth it would be the capital of his empire. However, in popular speech the new capital soon came to be called Constantinople, the city of Constantine.

**Constantinople, Capital of the Byzantine Empire.** The new state created by Constantine turned out to be quite different to the old Roman Empire, although it was two centuries before its changed character fully emerged. One of the most important changes of this period involved the role of religion in the state, a development that began even before Constantine became sole ruler. In 313 Constantine and Licinius jointly issued the so-called Edict of Milan, in which for the first time the practice of Christianity was tolerated in the Empire. In 325, the year after he became sole emperor, Constantine convoked the First Ecumenical Council of the Christian Church in Nicaea. Although Constantine was not yet a Christian (according to tradition, he was baptised on his death-bed), he presided over meetings of the Council, using his enormous influence to force bishops from all over his empire to agree on what would be the orthodox religious doctrine of the Church. It would take several more stormy church councils before the final doctrine was decided upon, at the Council of Chalcedon in 451, and in the process irreparable rifts were created between the Greek Orthodox Church and those dissident churches that did not accept their dogma. But one fact clearly emerged during this period, that in Byzantium the Emperor was head of both Church and State. Though the Patriarch of Constantinople acted as First Minister in matters of religion, the Emperor was his master as Christ's regent on Earth, the 'Thirteenth Apostle', as he was hailed in court ceremonies. Modern historians refer to this concept as 'Caesaropapism', in that the Emperors from Constantine onward played the roles of both Caesar and Pope.

Despite Constantine's espousal of Christianity, Christians were still a distinct minority in the Empire during his reign. And the unification of the Empire that he had achieved at such great cost in men and wealth did not survive him, for when he died in 337 power was divided between his sons, with Constantius ruling in Constantinople as Emperor of the East, and Constantine II reigning as Emperor of the West in Rome. This division of rule continued through most reigns until 476, when the last Emperor of the West was deposed by the barbarians who had overrun most of Europe. By that time a series of imperial edicts had brought about the triumph of Christianity over paganism. The most important of these were an edict of Theodosius I in 380, which officially established Christianity as the state religion, and edicts of Theodosius II in 426 and 435, which closed pagan shrines and forbade pagan practices throughout the Empire.

By the time of Theodosius II the capital had grown considerably in population, expanding well beyond the limits established by Constantine. Because of this, and also because of the threat of barbarian invasions, the Emperor decided to build a new and stronger line of walls a mile further out into Thrace. The first phase of these walls was completed in 413 and the final phase in 447, just in time to turn aside the advancing hordes of Attila.

It is interesting to note that these walls enclosed seven hills, the same number as in Rome. The First Hill, so called, is the acropolis above Saray Burnu. The next five hills are low and broad peaks on the undulating ridge that runs from the acropolis out to the Theodosian walls, while the Seventh Hill has its peak far off in the SW corner of the old city, sloping down to the Marmara shore. Although the contours of these hills have been obscured by modern roads and buildings, they can still be discerned and form convenient reference-points for studying the old city.

Theodosius II also built a splendid new cathedral dedicated to Haghia Sophia, the Divine Wisdom. Completed in 415, it replaced an earlier church of the same name which may have been founded by Constantine, but was completed by his son Constantius in 360 and burned down during a riot in 404. The Theodosian church of Haghia Sophia was much larger than its predecessor, reflecting the fact that the Christian population of the city was now far greater than it had been in the time of Constantine. This process of conversion continued during the half-century after the death of Theodosius II, so that by the beginning of the 6C Constantinople was a predominantly Christian city. By that time the population was mainly Greek, with a small Jewish minority and some Gothic contingents in the army. Although Latin continued as the official language of the court for another few decades, its popular use had almost completely died out in the capital by the 6C.

A new epoch in the history of the city and the Empire began in 518, when Justin I became Emperor. Justin was a simple and uneducated soldier from the Balkans, and so early in his reign he came to rely more and more on the advice of his brilliant and highly-cultured young nephew, Justinian, who soon became the power behind the throne. Justinian became Consul in 521, Caesar in 525, and in 527 his uncle raised him to the throne as co-Emperor. During those years Justinian laid the foundation for the grand design that would be carried out during his reign, the reconquest of the lost dominions of Rome so as to make it once more a universal empire. He was fortunate to have in his service one of the greatest generals in military history, Belisarius, who in 526 began his illustrious career by leading Justin's army against the Persians. This campaign was prosecuted with even greater vigour the following year, when Justinian succeeded his uncle as Emperor.

A few years before becoming Emperor Justinian fell in love with a reformed courtesan named Theodora, and in 525 he married her. When he succeeded to the throne Theodora became his Empress; through her great influence on him she wielded more power than any woman in the history of the Empire. She had very strong and conservative views on religion and on more than one occasion she is known to have swayed the Emperor's decision on clerical affairs. She may very well have been influential in Justinian's decision, in 529, to close all the schools of pagan philosophy still functioning in the Empire, including the ancient Platonic Academy in Athens. This represented the final triumph of Christianity over paganism, just as it was the last step in the transition from what had been the old pagan Roman Empire to the medieval Greek Christian realm that later historians came to call the Byzantine Empire, one that combined Roman political concepts, Greek culture, and the Christian religion.

In 532 Justinian was very nearly overthrown in a revolt that broke out among the factions in the Hippodrome. This insurrection is known as the Nika Revolt, from the rallying-cry of 'Nika' (Victory) that the mobs shouted as they stormed the royal palace on the First Hill, confident that they would succeed in overthrowing the Emperor. At the height of the rebellion, when the rebels were almost in control of the capital, Justinian was on the point of giving up his throne and fleeing for his life. But Theodora persuaded him that it would be nobler to stay and fight on, even if it meant their death. After five days of bloody fighting the revolt was put down by Belisarius, who trapped and slaughtered 50,000 of the rebels in the Hippodrome.

When the revolt ended most of the buildings on the First Hill were in ruins, including the royal palace and the church of Haghia Sophia. Justinian immediately began a programme of reconstruction, taking the opportunity to rebuild on an even grander scale than before. Five years later Constantinople was the greatest city on earth, the subject of legends throughout medieval Europe and Asia. And the crowning glory of this metropolis was the new church of Haghia Sophia, which the Emperor dedicated on 26 December 537.

During the course of Justinian's long reign, 527–65, Belisarius and his other generals succeeded in regaining much of the former territory of the Roman Empire. By 565 the borders of Justinian's realm extended around the Mediterranean, including Palestine, Syria, Asia Minor, Greece, the Balkans, Italy, southern Spain, the North African littoral, Egypt, and the Mediterranean islands, an area only slightly smaller than that of the Roman Empire in the time of Augustus. But the strength of the Empire had been sapped by the enormous expenditure of wealth and manpower in the campaign of reconquest. Taxation had been exorbitant and the lives of many young men had been lost in the endless wars of Justinian's reign. Justinian's successor, the feeble-minded Justin II, made matters worse by rashly renewing the war with Persia, which dragged on for another 20 years and brought the Empire to the point of insolvency. And no sooner had a peace treaty been signed with Persia than a new menace appeared, an invasion of the Balkans by hordes of barbaric Slavs driven southward by the onslaughts of tribes of Avars, a warlike nomadic people from central Asia. By the beginning of the 6C the situation had grown so bad that there was deep unrest in the Empire, and finally in 602 a popular rebellion overthrew the reigning emperor, Maurice, who was brutally killed with all of his sons. The army put in his place their commanding general, Phocas, whom modern historians consider to be the very worst man to have held the throne of Byzantium. He began his reign by eliminating all of the leaders in the civil aristocracy who had opposed him, further weakening the Empire when its very existence was being threatened. The Persians took advantage of the situation and in 605 they invaded, sweeping almost unopposed as far as the Bosphorus. Finally in 610 all factions among the people and in the army united to overthrow Phocas, who was publicly burned to death in one of the main squares of the capital. The populace then unanimously chose as their new emperor Heraclius, son of the Byzantine governor of Carthage, who had appeared in the port of Constantinople in command of his father's fleet.

When Heraclius assumed power the Empire was in ruins; the government and the army completely disorganised, the treasury empty, the capital and the countryside in a state of anarchy and the morale of the people abysmally low, barbarians ravaging Thrace right up to the walls of Constantinople, the Persians controlling most of

Asia Minor. The situation was so bad that Heraclius at one point considered moving the capital from Constantinople to Carthage, but the populace opposed this so strongly that he changed his mind. After he came to this decision he began the long and slow process of restoring the fortunes of the country. The climax came in the summer of 626, when Heraclius was on campaign in the Caucasus. A Persian army outflanked the Emperor's forces and swept across Asia Minor to the Bosphorus, while at the same time the Avars and their Slav and Bulgar allies attacked the capital by land and sea. At one point the Avars actually broke through the Theodosian walls near the Golden Horn and very nearly succeeded in taking the city. But the Byzantine defenders withstood the attack (aided by the miraculous intervention of the Blessed Virgin, according to tradition), driving the barbarians out of the city. The Byzantine forces then counterattacked and defeated the barbarians on both land and sea, after which both their forces and those of the Persians withdrew. Heraclius, who was in the Caucasus through all of this, continued his campaign in Asia until he finally inflicted a decisive defeat on the Persians in 628, after which he returned in triumph to Constantinople. As a result of these successes, the Empire regained Armenia, Roman Mesopotamia, Syria, Palestine and Egypt, as well as winning a respite from invasions in Asia Minor and the Balkans. So when Heraclius died in 641, he left behind him a strong and healthy Empire, one that was able to function efficiently and to cope with its enemies for nearly four centuries to come.

The period from 610 to 1025, from the accession of Heraclius to the death of Basil II, is referred to by some historians as the heroic age of the Byzantine Empire. During this period a series of great warrior emperors led their armies against the enemies that continued to beset the Empire on all sides, retreating behind the Theodosian walls when invaders penetrated through Asia Minor or the Balkans, returning to the field to counterattaflck when the enemy sieges failed, as they inevitably did.

After the final defeat of the Persians the next enemies to appear were the Arabs, who first swept across Asia Minor in 674, putting Constantinople under siege for four years. The Byzantines withstood this siege, driving off the Arab fleet with their flame-throwers spewing the terrible 'Greek Fire'. The Arabs besieged the capital a second time in 717–18, but once again they were driven off with heavy losses. The next threat came from the Bulgars, who rose to dominance in the Balkans early in the 9C, besieging Constantinople unsuccessfully in 814, 913 and 924. The climax of this heroic age came with the campaigns of Basil II, who ruled from 976 till 1025, the longest and most illustrious reign in the history of the Byzantine Empire. In 995–1001 Basil defeated the Arabs and drove them out of southern Asia Minor for ever, and in 1014 he annihilated the Bulgar army and permanently ended their threat to Byzantium, a feat for which he received the title of Bulgaroctonus, the 'Bulgar-Slayer'. (Basil's punishment of the Bulgars after his final victory was meant to discourage them from ever again taking the field against him: he blinded all but ten of the 10,000 captives taken in battle, leaving the ten with one eye each to lead their comrades home. When the mutilated survivors finally reached the Bulgar capital the sight so shocked their leader, Csar Samuel, that he dropped dead on the spot, thus bringing the medieval Bulgarian Kingdom to an end.)

When Basil died in 1025 he left behind him an Empire that stretched from the Caucasus and Persia to the Adriatic and from the Holy Land to the Danube. This represented the zenith of Byzantine power in the late medieval period, for thenceforth its fortunes inexorably declined.

Even during the heroic age Byzantium was troubled by internal strife, civil wars, and palace coups, during the course of which several emperors were deposed, either losing their lives or ending them in exile, often after having been blinded or otherwise mutilated. By far the most serious of the internal disputes that took place in Byzantium during this period was the so-called Iconoclastic Crisis. This controversy began in 726, when Leo III delivered his first sermon warning against the veneration of icons and their display in homes and churches, holding that this was tantamount to idolatry. He took an even stronger position in 730, when he issued an imperial edict banning icons, ordering the destruction of all figurative representations in the Empire, including mosaics and frescoes in churches and monasteries. The ensuing crisis split the empire into two factions, the Iconoclasts, who supported this policy, and the Iconodules, who wanted sacred images restored to the churches and homes of Byzantium. The dispute grew so serious that at times it led to bloody battles in the streets of Constantinople, and on several occasions it brought the Empire to the brink of civil war. The Iconodules came briefly to the fore during the reign of the Empress Eirene, an ardent supporter of icon veneration. Eirene had seized the throne from her son, Constantine VI, and to prevent him from regaining it she had him blinded, mutilating him so badly that he died a few days later. But Eirene's rule was so weak that the Iconodules were unable to bring about the restoration of images, and the Iconoclasts regained power after she was deposed. The Iconoclastic Crisis did not end until 843, the first year in the reign of Michael III, when a synod of the Greek Orthodox Church in Haghia Sophia solemnly declared the restoration of icons, settling the question for the rest of Byzantine history. But although the crisis itself was over, irreparable damage had been done to the artistic heritage of Byzantium, for virtually all of the mosaics and frescoes had been destroyed in the churches and monasteries of the Empire. Consequently, there are very few works of Byzantine figurative art surviving from the pre-Iconoclastic Period, and none at all in the former capital of the Empire.

The death of Basil II in 1025 marked a turning-point in the history of the Byzantine Empire. His passing was followed by a half-century of steady decline, in which a series of weak and ineffective emperors proved unable to deal with the mounting internal troubles of the Empire, at a time when new and stronger enemies were appearing on all sides and threatening the very existence of Byzantium. The nadir of this decline came in 1071, when a Byzantine army led by the Emperor Romanus IV Diogenes was annihilated by the Selcuk Turks at Manzikert in eastern Asia Minor. This opened up all of Asia Minor to the Selcuks, who went through the country unopposed as far as the Sea of Marmara. And with them came hordes of nomadic Turcoman tribesmen, who divided up the former Byzantine territory in Asia Minor into a mosaic of Turkish *beyliks*, or principalities. In the same year, 1071, the Normans captured Bari, thus ending Byzantine rule in Italy.

Although the Empire had now lost forever its possessions in Italy, the Byzantines still maintained close political and economic ties with several Italian city-states, particularly Venice. (Until the 10C the Doges of Venice were subject to ratification by the Byzantine Emperor.) During the reign of Basil II, Doge Pietro Orseolo (991–1008) obtained commercial concessions for Venice in Constantinople, a development that had important consequences. These concessions included reduced customs fees for Venetian traders, and also gave them a small strip of territory extending from the Golden Horn, where they could build docks for their ships, warehouses for their goods, and houses for their merchants. The Byzantines later gave similar concessions to Amalfi, Pisa and Genoa. Amalfi and Pisa acquired strips of territory on the Golden Horn beside those of the Venetians, while the Genoese were given Galata. The Byzantines derived some commercial and political advantage from these concessions at first, but later the Italians and other Latins in Constantinople became virtually independent of the Empire. This was particularly true in Galata, which became a semi-autonomous city-state governed by an official sent out from its mother-city. With their stronger fleets the Italians were able to flout the laws and regulations of the Empire with impunity. Thus the Byzantines lost whatever benefits they formerly obtained from the concessions, and found increasingly aggressive and rapacious foreigners firmly settled right in their capital. This led to a great deal of friction between the Byzantines and the Latins, and was a contributory factor in the eventual downfall of Byzantium.

In 1081, a decade after the catastrophic defeat at Manzikert, Alexius I Comnenus became Emperor of Byzantium. Throughout the next century he and his son and grandson, in turn, successfully defended the Empire against the incursion of the forces that were hemming it in on all sides, using diplomacy and an enlightened foreign policy to great advantage. When Alexius first came to the throne, the Selcuk Turks and their Turcoman vassals were in complete control of virtually all Asia Minor, with their capital at Nicaea. When the armies of the First Crusade reached Constantinople in 1096, on their way to the Holy Land, Alexius took the opportunity to use their help in regaining the territory that Byzantium had lost to the Turks. He came to an agreement with the Latin leaders, promising to provide them with soldiers, weapons, supplies and transport for their crusade against the Moslems. In turn, he persuaded the Crusader leaders to swear an oath of allegiance to him as Emperor of Byzantium, vowing that they would return to the Empire any of its former cities that they might recapture. After reaching this agreement the Crusaders and their Byzantine allies crossed the Bosphorus into Asia Minor, marching toward the Holy Land. Their first success came in June 1097, when they captured Nicaea, the Selcuk capital. The Crusader leaders returned the city to Alexius and marched on, while the Emperor and his troops hastened to occupy all of the former Byzantine cities abandoned by the fleeing Turks. By the time the Crusaders reached Syria all of western Asia Minor was once more in the possession of the Byzantines, along with the Black Sea littoral. But then in June 1098 the Crusaders captured Antioch and refused to return it to the Byzantines, making it the capital of an independent principality ruled by the Norman Count Bohemund of Taranto. This violation of their agreement led to a bitter conflict between Alexius and the Crusader leaders, intensifying the feeling of enmity that was building up between the Greeks in the Byzantine Empire and the Latins in the West.

Alexius I died in 1118 and was succeeded by his son John II, who has been acclaimed by both his contemporaries and by modern historians as the finest ruler in the illustrious dynasty of the Comneni. John continued his father's foreign policy, applying clever diplomacy and the judicious use of military force against his opponents. When John died in 1143 all of the Empire bequeathed to him by his father was intact, and in addition he had regained southern Asia Minor, extending the borders of the Empire in that direction as far as Syria. John was succeeded by his son, Manuel I, who in a reign of 37 years (1143–80) preserved the Empire he had inherited aflnd added to it Dalmatia, Croatia and Bosnia. When he died the borders of the Empire stretched from Syria to Hungary and from central Asia Minor to the Adriatic, including Cyprus, Crete and the Aegean isles. But this was to be the last great resurgence of Byzantium, for the enormous effort that the Comneni had made during the century of their rule had fatally weakened the Empire, just when the forces were gathering that would ultimately destroy it.

Manuel Comnenus was succeeded by his 12-year-old son, Alexius II. Since Alexius was too young to rule in his own right his mother, the Empress Mary of Antioch, acted as regent. Mary was from a noble Latin family, and under her regency the government pursued a pro-Western policy. This caused growing resentment among the Greek populace, who saw the Empress giving preferential treatment to the wealthy Latin merchants and the western mercenaries who made up the mainstay of her army, particularly the palace guard. Leadership of the popular opposition to the regime was assumed by Andronicus Comnenus, younger brother of the late Emperor Manuel, who was serving as governor of the Pontus. Andronicus assembled a small army and marched across Asia Minor, and in spring 1182 his forces encamped across the Bosphorus from Constantinople. As soon as he appeared, the street mobs of the capital rose up in revolt, killing the Empress Mary's First Minister and slaughtering all of the Latins who had not fled the city. Andronicus marched into the capital and took control, posing as the young Emperor's protector. He forced Alexius to sign an order for the execution of his mother and her supporters. When this was done Andronicus became regent, and in September 1183 he was crowned as co-Emperor with Alexius. Two months later Andronicus had Alexius murdered and became sole Emperor. Then, to strengthen his claim to legitimacy, Andronicus married the 13-year-old widow of his murdered nephew, the Princess Agnes-Anna, a daughter of King Louis VII of France.

On becoming sole ruler, Andronicus set out to solve the problems that had arisen during the three years since his brother's death. These problems arose principally from widespread corruption and a breakdown of the authority of the central government. However, the harsh measures employed by Andronicus to bring about his reforms developed into a reign of terror. Finally, in 1185, Andronicus was overthrown in a rebellion, after which he was imprisoned, cruelly tortured, and finally executed publicly in the Hippodrome. His successor was Isaac II Angelus, a totally incompetent ruler who gave free play to the corrupt and divisive elements that Andronicus had so vigorously opposed. Consequently, during the decade of Isaac's first reign (he ruled again briefly in 1203–04), the Empire was irreparably weakened.

In 1195 Isaac II was deposed by his elder brother, Alexius III, who imprisoned him along with his eldest son, Prince Alexius, and blinded him so that he would not be tempted to try to regain power. Then in 1202 Prince Alexius escaped and fled to the West, where he sought help in restoring his father and himself to the throne. He went first to Pope Innocent II, who earlier that year had declared another Crusade,

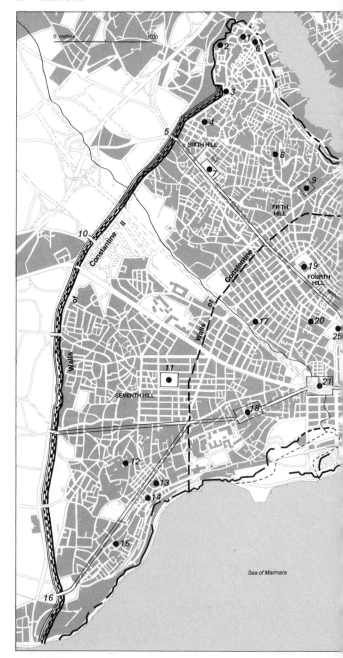

# MEDIEVAL CONSTANTINOPLE

Medieval Constantinople,
1. St. Mary of Blachernae
2. Blachernae Palace
3. Palace of the Porphyrogenitus
4. St. Saviour in Chora
5. Gate of Charisius
6. SS. Peter and Mark
7. Aetios cistern
8. St. Mary Pammakaristos
9. Aspar cistern
10. St. Romanus gate
11. St. Mocius cistern
12. St. Andrew in Crisei
13. St. Mary Peribleptos
14. SS. Karpos and Papylos
15. St. John of Studius
16. Golden Gate

17. Monastery of Lips
18. 1st Forum of Arcadius
19. Church of the Holy Apostles
20. Column of Marcian
21. Forum Bovis
22. Christ Pantepoptes
23. Christ Pantocrator
24. Aqueduct of Emperor Valens
25. St. Polyeuktos
26. St. Theodore
27. Church of the Kyriotisse
28. Philadelphion
29. Myrelaion
30. Tetrapylon
31. Forum Tauri
32. Galata Tower
33. Forum of Constantine

34. SS. Sergius and Bacchus
35. Binbir Direk cistern
36. St. Euphemia
37. Hippodrome
38. Bucoleon
39. Basilica
40. Milion
41. St. Mary Chalkoprateia
42. Haghia Eirene
43. St. George of Mangana
44. Haghia Sophia
45. Augustaion
46. Senate House
47. Chalkè
48. Baths of Zeuxippus
49. Imperial Palace
50. Nea Ekklesia

the Fourth, to free the Holy Land from the Moslems. When the Pope appeared unwilling to help him he went to the court of Philip of Swabia, his brother-in-law. Philip agreed to support him, and suggested that Alexius should present his case to the leaders of the Fourth Crusade; Henricus Dandolo, Doge of Venice, and Count Boniface of Montferrat. After the Pope's proclamation, the Crusaders had assembled in Venice, whence the Doge's fleet would transport them to Egypt to begin their campaign. But the Crusaders proved unable to pay for their passage, and there was an impasse until Dandolo suggested that they might make good the deficiency by helping the Venetians recapture the Dalmatian seaport of Zara (the modern Zadar), a former possession of theirs that had gone over to the Hungarians. The Crusaders agreed, and in November 1202 began their sacred mission with the capture and sack of the Christian city of Zara, an outrage for which they were all excommunicated by the Pope. The Latins were wintering in Zara when a messenger arrived from the court of Philip of Swabia, carrying Alexius's appeal that the Crusaders restore his father and him to the throne of Byzantium. Alexius promised enormous sums of money to the Latins for their support, conciliated the Pope by holding out the possibility of a union between the Greek Orthodox and Roman Catholic churches, and swore that he would take the cross himself if he were made co-Emperor with his father. Dandolo persuaded the Crusaders to agree, motivated both by the desire for wealth and by the vengeance which he sought for the thousands of Venetians who had been slaughtered by the Byzantines 20 years before. But his strongest motivation was his knowledge that Constantinople was now ripe for the plucking. And he had probably already formulated the plan that he proposed to the Crusaders two years later, the destruction of Byzantium and the creation in its place of a new Latin Empire of the East.

The Latins, accompanied by Alexius and his blind father, set sail from Zara in spring 1203, arriving in the port of Constantinople on 24 June of that year. As soon as their fleet appeared, Alexius III fled with the imperial treasury and the crown jewels, leaving the Byzantine government penniless. The Crusaders captured Galata and encamped outside the land walls of Constantinople, while Dandolo and the other Latin leaders negotiated with the Byzantines. Threatened by the vastly superior force of the Crusaders, the Byzantines agreed to restore Isaac II and to make his son co-Emperor as Alexius IV. Immediately after his coronation, Alexius tried to pay the indemnity that he had promised the Crusaders, but he found that the treasury was empty. Under pressure from Dandolo, Alexius attempted to raise the money by imposing confiscatory taxes on the Greek population of the capital. But this lost him what little public support he had, and in January 1204 he and his father were deposed and lost their lives in a popular revolt. They were replaced by Alexius V Ducas Murtzuphlos, who repudiated the agreement that Alexius IV had made with the Crusaders. This decided the matter as far as Dandolo was concerned, and in March 1204 he informed the Crusader leaders that the time had come to destroy Byzantium and to set up their own empire on its ashes. The Latins attacked Constantinople by land and sea, and on 13 April 1204 they breached the sea-walls along the Golden Horn and took the city by storm. They proceeded to sack the capital, stripping it of its wealth, its art treasures and its sacred relics, sending their loot back to western Europe and leaving the city a burned-out ruin. This catastrophe was so terrible that the surviving Greeks believed that their fate had been inflicted upon them by God, as punishment for their sins. As Nicetas Choniatis was to write in his lament on the fall of Constantinople to the Crusaders: 'Oh city, city, eye of all cities, subject of narratives all over the world, supporter of churches, leader of faith and guider of orthodoxy, protector of education, abode of all good. Thou hast drunk to the dregs the cup of the anger of the Lord, and hast been visited with fire fiercer than that which in days of yore descended upon the Pentapolis'.

**The Latin Occupation and the Empire of Nicaea**. Soon after their capture of Constantinople, the Latins divided up the territory they had seized from the Byzantines. The Venetians were awarded three-eighths of the capital and the church of Haghia Sophia, along with various ports and islands. (Dandolo ruled over the Venetian quarter of Constantinople with the title of Despot, grandiloquently styling himself 'Lord of a quarter and a half of all of the Roman Empire'.) Half of the conquered Byzantine territory outside the capital was given to various Crusader knights as fiefs, while the other half and the remaining five-eighths of Constantinople became the property of Count Baldwin of Flanders. On 16 May 1204 Baldwin was crowned in Haghia Sophia, now a Roman Catholic cathedral, and took the title of Emperor of Rumania, as the Latins called their new empire. The territory of this empire originally consisted of Thrace and the NW corner of Asia Minor, as well as a few Aegean isles. But in the subsequent half-century the Latin Empire steadily lost territory to its neighbouring states in Europe and Asia, so that by the middle of the 13C it was so small and weak that it lay open to conquest by those around it.

When Constantinople fell to the Latins in 1204, fragments of the Byzantine Empire continued in existence in several parts of Greece and Asia Minor, ruled by various members of the former royal families of Byzantium. As the Latin Empire progressively weakened, these Byzantine principalities contended with one another for the great prize, the recapture of Constantinople and the restoration of the Byzantine Empire. The most fortunately-placed of these states was the Empire of Nicaea, which was founded in 1204 by Theodore I Lascaris, a son-in-law of Alexius III Angelus. Nicaea, the capital, was only a short distance from Constantinople, and the Empire shared a common border to its N with the Latin Empire. Under the extremely able leadership of Theodore I (1204–22) and his son-in-law and successor, John III Ducas Vatatzes (1222–54), the Empire of Nicaea flourished and its boundaries expanded, so that by the middle of the 13C they included all of western Asia Minor from the Black Sea to the Aegean, including all of the offshore islands. By that time the Latin Empire had shrunk to little more than Constantinople and the European littoral of the Sea of Marmara, the Bosphorus and the Dardanelles.

When John III died in 1254 he was succeeded by his son Theodore II (1254–58). Theodore was a very effective ruler and a highly cultured man, a student of the scholar Nicephorus Blemmydes. During Theodore's brief but brilliant reign Nicaea became a cultural centre of such importance that scholars of the time referred to it as a second Athens. The cultural revival that started there later gave rise to a renaissance of learning in Byzantium, which in turn gave impetus to the European renaissance. But Theodore died of epilepsy at the age of 37. He was succeeded by his seven-year-old son, John IV, for whom a regent, George Muzalon, had been appointed by Theodore on his death-bed. But Muzalon was extremely unpopular with the aristocracy, and nine days after his appointment he was murdered, and the aristocracy appointed as regent the ablest and most distinguished man among them, Michael Palaeologus. Early in 1259 Michael became co-Emperor, taking the title of Michael VIII, the young John IV by then being a virtual prisoner. Two years later, on 25 July 1261, Michael's commanding general captured Constantinople with a small force and with hardly any opposition, for the Latin Empire had been moribund and was now dead. On 15 August Michael VIII made his triumphal entry into Constantinople with his court and army, after which he rode at the head of a joyous procession to Haghia Sophia, where a service of thanksgiving was held. The legitimate Emperor, the young John IV, took no part in the celebrations connected with this great event, for he remained a prisoner, and a few weeks later Michael had him blinded and sequestered in a monastery, where he spent the rest of his days in obscurity. Such were the events that led to the revival of the Byzantine Empire in its ancient capital.

**The Last Centuries of Byzantium.** The cultural renaissance that had started in Nicaea continued in Constantinople during the reigns of Michael VIII and his successors, the Palaeologi, the last dynasty to rule Byzantium. This renaissance gave birth to great scholars like Gemisthus Plethon, who were important influences on the Italian Renaissance, and it also produced masterpieces of art far surpassing anything created in the history of the Empire. But the Empire under Michael VIII was merely a fragment of what it been in its prime, comprising only western Asia Minor, Thrace, Macedonia, parts of the Peloponnesus, and a few of the Aegean islands.

At the beginning of the 14C a new power arose in western Asia Minor, one which would eventually destroy the Byzantine Empire and all of the other surviving medieval states in western Asia and SE Europe. These were the Osmanlí Turks, better known to Westerners as the Ottomans. The Osmanlí were named after their first leader, Osman Gazi (Gazi was an honorific title meaning 'Warrior for the Faith'). Between 1288 and 1326 Osman Gazi headed a small tribe of nomadic Turks from central Asia who had been settled in western Asia Minor by the Selcuks in the first half of the 13C. At that time the Osmanlí controlled a few square miles of farmland and pasturage as vassals of the Selcuks, and their little *beylik* shared a common border with the Empire of Nicaea, whose capital was only a day's ride from their territory. The Osmanlí gained their independence when the power of the Selcuks was broken by the Mongols in the second half of the 13C. By that time the Byzantines had recaptured Constantinople, and in resuming a more imperial foreign policy they paid less attention to the very minor Osmanlí *beylik* on their eastern frontier. As a result, the Osmanlí under Osman Gazi began to expand their borders westward, and by the time he died in 1326 their forces were besieging the Byzantine city of Brusa (the modern Bursa), a few miles from the Sea of Marmara. Shortly after Osman's death Brusa was captured by his son and successor, Orhan Gazi, who established his capital there. Historians generally mark this year, 1326, as the birth-date of the Ottoman Empire, and Orhan Gazi is considered to be the first Ottoman Sultan, for during the 36 years of his reign the Osmanlí forces conquered most of western Asia Minor and penetrated Europe as far as Bulgaria.

The Byzantines could do little to stop this expansion; when the Turks began to penetrate Europe the Empire was engaged in the most serious civil war in its history. In this struggle, which lasted from 1341 to 1347, the forces of the legitimate Emperor, John V Palaeologus, were arrayed against those of the usurper, John Cantacuzenos, who actually brought the Turks over into Europe as his allies. John V eventually emerged victorious, but by that time the Turks had established a permanent foothold in Thrace and were beginning to move northward. In 1361, the year before Orhon Gazi died, his son Murat captured the Byzantine city of Adrianople on the border between Thrace and Bulgaria. Murat succeeded his father as Sultan in 1362 and soon afterwards shifted his capital from Brusa to Adrianople (which in Turkish became Edirne), for the Thracian city now became the base for the annual campaigns in which the Ottoman armies penetrated ever deeper into SE Europe. Every new success brought the Sultan hordes of recruits from the Turcoman tribes of Asia Minor, eager for the spoils that they received after each victory. The situation grew so grave that in 1366 Pope Urban V proclaimed a Crusade against the Turks, but later that year, at the battle of the Maritza, Murat crushed an allied army from Hungary, Bulgaria, Serbia and Wallachia. He then continued his push northward until by 1389 he had advanced into Hungary, decisively defeating another allied Christian army at the battle of Kossova. Murat was killed at the end of the battle and was succeeded as Sultan by his son, Beyazit I. The Ottoman expansion continued under Beyazit, who extended the boundaries of his Empire in a series of annual campaigns in both Europe and Asia. In 1396 Pope Boniface IX called for another Crusade against the Turks, but later that year Beyazit annihilated the Crusader army at the battle of Nicopolis on the Danube.

By this time the Byzantines were so weak that they had been forced to become vassals of the Turks, and on several occasions the Emperor was ordered to send contingents of his troops to campaign with the Ottoman forces against Christian armies and towns. Constantinople was now completely cut off from the rest of the Christian world except by sea, and it seemed that it would be only a matter of time before it fell to the Turks who already controlled the Dardanelles. In 1394 Beyazit constructed a fortress on the Asian shore of the Bosphorus, as a first step in controlling that strait. The Sultan then blockaded Constantinople and the Byzantines braced themselves for a siege, but they were saved when the Sultan withdrew his forces to face the Crusader army at Nicopolis. Beyazit appeared ready to resume his blockade of Constantinople in 1400, but he was once again forced to withdraw his forces from the capital. This time it was to defend his Asian dominions against a Mongol invasion led by Tamerlane. The two powerful forces met near Ankara in central Asia Minor in August 1402 and the Mongols totally destroyed the Ottoman army, the first serious defeat it had ever experienced. Beyazit himself was taken prisoner by Tamerlane and died in captivity a few months later.

His death and the devastating defeat at Ankara caused a sudden collapse of Ottoman power, and for the next decade Byzantium and the other Christian states in SE Europe enjoyed a reprieve while Beyazit's four sons fought a war of succession for the throne. The eldest, Prince Mehmet, outlasted the others and in 1413 he became sole ruler of the Ottoman Empire. During the eight years of his reign, 1413–21, Mehmet began the slow process of reorganising the Empire and of regaining the territory lost during the interregnum. The process of recovery continued during the long reign of his son and successor, Murat II (1421–51), who was perhaps the greatest of all the warrior-sultans of the Osmanlí dynasty. As Murat led the Ottoman forces on their second invasion of the Balkans, the Christian leaders in their path fought valiantly to stop their advance, but vainly. In 1443 the Pope called for still another Crusade against the Turks, and in October of that year an allied army led by John Hunyadi of Transylvania set out to do battle with the Ottoman forces. In the winter of 1443–44 Hunyadi won two notable victories over Turkish armies in the Balkans, and in June 1444 Sultan Murat was forced to sign an armistice agreeing to a ten-year cessation of hostilities. But the Crusaders felt that the tide had turned in their favour, and in the autumn of 1444 they impetuously resumed their campaign against the Turks. When Sultan Murat heard the news he mustered his army in Edirne and set out after the Crusaders, although winter had already set in. He finally caught up with them on the Black Sea coast at Varna on 10 December 1444, annihilating their army in a brief battle. Hunyadi, who had been campaigning elsewhere in the Balkans, fought on, trying to rally his fellow Christians in one last desperate effort against the Turks. Murat took the field against him, and in the summer of 1448 the two armies met at Kossova, on the same field where the Ottomans had won their great victory in 1389. The result was the same in the second battle of Kossova, for Murat's army inflicted a decisive defeat on Hunyadi's forces, sealing the fate of the Balkans for the next 450 years.

During the first half of the 15C Byzantium made several futile attempts to obtain help from western Europe, but crushing defeats inflicted on most of the European armies that faced the Turks made the situation look increasingly hopeless. Nevertheless, in 1437 the Emperor John VIII Palaeologus made one more attempt, journeying to the West to ask for help from the Pope and the princes of western Europe. In the past the price asked by the Pope for his assistance had always been that the Emperor agree to a union of the Greek Orthodox and Roman Catholic churches, which meant that the Byzantines would have to give in to the Latins on all of the doctrinal and political issues that divided them. At the Council of Ferrara-Florence, which met from April 1438 until July 1439, the Emperor John and his Patriarch agreed to the Pope's terms, promising to bring the Greek people and clergy with them into union with Rome. But the Emperor gained nothing from this surrender, for not only did help for Byzantium never materialise in the West, but his own people and clergy completely repudiated the agreement. So when John died in 1448 he left behind him a dying Empire that was weakened further by religious dissension, just when it faced the greatest threat in its history.

John died childless and was succeeded by his younger brother Constantine XI Dragases (a name he derived from his mother's family). At the time of his accession Constantine was Despot of the Morea (the Peloponnesus), the only remaining Byzantine possession outside the capital. He was crowned Emperor of Byzantium in Mistra on 6 January 1449, after which he set out for Constantinople by sea, arriving there two months later. He took up the hopeless task that had occupied his late brother all through his long reign, attempting to gain help from the West to save Byzantium from the Turks who encircled it. He tried to persuade the people and clergy of the capital to agree to union with Rome, but the Greek hatred of the Latins was so great that this only turned the populace against him. As one of his highest court officials said to Constantine at the time, when asked to support the Emperor's policy of union with Rome: 'I would rather see the Moslem turban in the midst of the city than the Latin mitre'.

Sultan Mehmet I died on 13 February 1451 and was succeeded by his son, Mehmet II, then only 19 years old. The old Sultan had twice in the past retired from the throne and given power to young Mehmet, but the youth on both occasions had proved unable to handle the military emergencies that arose, and his father had been forced to resume control. But now that he was Sultan in his own right Mehmet acted quickly and decisively, immediately beginning preparations for the long-awaited siege of Constantinople. After organising his government and his military forces, Mehmet set up his military headquarters in Thrace, just a few miles from Constantinople. He then demanded and received from Constantine a plot of land on the European shore of the Bosphorus, just opposite the fortress that Beyazit I had built in 1394 in preparation for his abortive blockade of the city. There in the summer of 1452 Sultan Mehmet proceeded to build an enormous fortress; he called it Rumeli Hisarí, the Castle of Europe, while the smaller one across the way became known as Anadolu Hisarí, the Castle of Asia. These two fortresses enabled him to control the Bosphorus and cut off Constantinople from the Black Sea, depriving the city of the shipments of corn that were its main food supply.

In March 1453 the Ottoman navy sailed through the Dardanelles and the Sea of Marmara and anchored within sight of Constantinople, which was now completely cut off from the outside world. In the first week of April Sultan Mehmet massed his forces in Thrace and marched them into position before the Theodosian walls, beginning the siege of the city with a tremendous bombardment from his artillery park of giant cannon. The siege continued for seven weeks, with almost continual bombardment and with frequent attacks on the walls by the Turkish infantry. The Byzantines and their Genoese allies, outnumbered more than ten to one, defended the city valiantly, commanded by the Emperor and his Genoese general, Giustiniani. In the early weeks of the siege the Byzantines were able to keep the Turks out of the Golden Horn by stretching an enormous chain across its entrance, but one night the Sultan had the ships of his fleet placed on rollers and pulled across the ridge above Galata, so that by morning they were all in the Golden Horn. This put the Byzantines at an even greater disadvantage, for they were now forced to take men from their already inadequate ranks on the Theodosian walls to defend the sea-walls along the Golden Horn. But they fought on, though the walls were breached in many places, repelling attacks that often took the Janissaries, the elite corps of the Turkish army, into the inner line of defences. The Sultan decided to make a final all-out attack in the early morning hours of Tuesday, 29 May. The attack began with the heaviest artillery barrage of the siege, followed by repeated attacks by waves of Turkish infantry who hurled themselves against the walls, but still the defenders managed somehow to repel them. The Sultan then threw in his main reserve, the Janissaries, one contingent of which managed to scale the walls at their weakest point. During the fighting there Giustiniani received a fatal wound and was carried away by his men. This proved to be the turning-point in the battle, for the defenders now became disheartened and were no longer able to hold back the Janissaries, who poured through a breach in the walls. Constantine fought on with his men until he was killed beneath the walls of his fallen city.

**Istanbul, Capital of the Ottoman Empire.** All resistance ceased within a few hours, and by noon the city was completely in Turkish hands. Then, in keeping with Moslem practice, the Sultan turned his soldiers loose to loot the city for three days, as they stripped it of all its wealth and took as slaves most of the young and able Greeks who had survived the siege. Early in the afternoon Sultan Mehmet rode triumphantly into the city, acclaimed by his soldiers as Fatih, or the Conqueror, the name by which he would thenceforth be known. He rode to Haghia Sophia, which was filled with terrified refugees who were being carried off into slavery by Turkish soldiers. Fatih had the building cleared and ordered that it be converted into a mosque at once. This was done, and on the following Friday the Sultan attended the first Moslem service in what the Turks now called Aya Sofya Camii, the Mosque of Haghia Sophia.

Soon after his capture of Constantinople Fatih began to repair the damage it had sustained during the siege and in the decades of decay before the Conquest. A year or so later he transferred his government from Edirne to Constantinople, which thus became the capital of the Ottoman Empire. At about that time he constructed a palace on the First Hill of the city, in the quarter later known as Beyazit. Some years later he built a second and more extensive palace, Topkapí Sarayí, on the acropolis above the confluence of the Bosphorus and the Golden Horn. By 1470 he had completed the great mosque that bears his name, Fatih Camii, the Mosque of the Conqueror. This mosque, comparable in size to Haghia Sophia, was the centre of a külliye, a whole complex of pious foundations, religious and philanthropic institutions of various kinds. Many of Fatih's vezirs followed his example, building mosques and pious foundations of their own, each of which soon became the centre of its neighbourhood, together developing into the new Ottoman city that the Turks came to call Istanbul. (The name Constantinople continued to be used by Greeks and even some Turks until the establishment of the Turkish Republic in 1923, and even for some time afterwards.) Fatih also repeopled the city, which had lost much of its population in the decades preceding the Conquest, bringing in Turks, Greeks and Armenians from Anatolia. (Anatolia, the Greek word for East, denotes the Asiatic part of modern Turkey.) In the last decade of the 15C large numbers of Sephardic Jewish refugees from Spain were welcomed to the Empire, and many settled in Galata and Stamboul. By the end of the 15C Istanbul was a thriving and populous city, once again the capital of a empire.

Within two years of the Conquest, Fatih led the Ottoman army on his first campaign into Europe, and for the next quarter of a century he and his generals extended the boundaries of the Ottoman Empire in all directions, conquering most or all of southern Greece and the Peloponnesus, Moldavia, Wallachia, Bosnia, and the Crimea, while in Anatolia they conquered Karamania, the last of the Turcoman *beyliks*.

When Fatih died in 1481 he was succeeded by his son Beyazit II (1481–1512). At the beginning of his reign Beyazit was forced to fight a difficult war of succession with his brother, the fabulous Prince Cem. When Beyazit emerged victorious, he led the Ottoman army in a campaign into Moldavia. But he spent the remainder of his reign in the capital, leaving military operations to his generals and admirals. Instead, Beyazit concentrated on consolidating the resources of the Empire and developing its trade and commerce, which as a result increased greatly during his reign. Beyazit's reign also saw the emergence of the Ottomans as a major sea-power in the Mediterranean. The Ottoman navy won its first major victory at the battle of Navarino in 1499, when they defeated the combined fleets of Venice, Austria and the Pope. This had great significance for the future, for the navy opened a new avenue for the expansion of the Ottoman Empire, making it an even greater threat to Christian Europe.

In 1512 Beyazit was forced into retirement by his eldest son, Selim I, and he died soon afterwards in a way that led many to suspect that he had been poisoned. Selim spent the first year of his reign fighting a war of succession against his younger brothers, whom he defeated and killed. During the second year of his reign he put down a revolt in eastern Anatolia fomented by Shah Ismail of Persia. When the revolt had been crushed he marched against the Shah, decisively defeating the Persian army in 1514 at the battle of Çaldíran in eastern Anatolia, a victory that extended the borders of the Ottoman Empire into the Caucasus and western Persia. Selim then went to war against the Mamelukes, who ruled an empire that stretched from Egypt through Palestine and Syria into southern Anatolia. In 1516 Selim defeated the Mamelukes in Syria and captured Aleppo, and in the following year he defeated them again outside Cairo, a victory that added Egypt to the Empire. Cairo was at that time the seat of the Caliphate, and soon after his capture of that city Selim took the title of Caliph, and thereafter he and his successors in the Ottoman dynasty were officially the titular leaders of the Islamic people. (But it is a moot point as to whether the people of Islam ever took this title seriously.) The Sultan was known to his people as Yavuz Selim, or Selim the Grim, and he beheaded his Grand Vezirs at the rate of one a year. The last two years of his reign were spent preparing for a great campaign into Europe, which was cut short by his sudden and premature death in 1520. For long afterwards a cynical Turkish proverb maintained that 'Yavuz Selim died of an infected boil and Hungary was spared'.

Selim was succeeded by his eldest son, Süleyman, who came to be known in the West as Süleyman the Magnificent. During Süleyman's long reign, 1520–66, the Ottoman Empire reached the peak of its fortunes and became the most powerful state in the world. As the 17C Turkish chronicler Evliya Çelebi wrote of him: 'During the forty-six years of his reign he subdued the world and made eighteen monarchs his tributaries. He established order and justice in his dominions, marched victoriously through the seven quarters of the globe, embellished all the countries that were vanquished with his arms, and was successful in all undertakings'. Süleyman personally led his armies in a dozen victorious campaigns, failing only in his attempt in 1529 to take Vienna, which thereafter set the limit to Ottoman expansion into Europe. At the same time his fleet, commanded by pirate-admirals like Kílíç Ali Paşa and Barbarossa, was conquering the Aegean islands and extending the borders of the Empire along the coast of North Africa as far as Tunis and Algiers. Loot from these campaigns, and tribute and taxes from conquered territories enormously enriched the Empire, and much of this wealth was used by Süleyman and his vezirs to adorn Istanbul with palaces, mosques and pious foundations. The grandest of the structures built during this epoch is the Süleymaniye, the mosque complex completed for the

Sultan in 1557 by his Chief Architect, the great Sinan. The Süleymaniye stands today as the symbol of the splendour of Istanbul in the days of Süleyman the Magnificent, just as Haghia Sophia the golden age of Constantinople in the time of Justinian.

During Süleyman's reign a subtle but important change took place in the character of the sultanate, one that had serious consequences for the future of the Empire. Like all his ancestors in the Osmanli dynasty Süleyman was a warrior-sultan, and not only led his army in the field but personally directed the affairs of his government. The personal lives of Süleyman and his predecessors reflected the fact that they were primarily warriors, usually spending the summer months with their army on campaign, and in the winter retiring to their palace to rest and to attend to affairs of state. Until the reign of Süleyman the palace was modest in size, for the early sultans did not have a large number of women in their harem. (The harem was the women's quarter of a Turkish home or palace.) According to Moslem law, the Sultan and any other Moslem was allowed four wives, though he could have as many concubines as he wished. The two women who headed the Sultan's harem were his mother, the Valide Sultan, and his chief wife, the First Kadín. Early in Süleyman's reign he took as his First Kadín a woman whom he called Haseki Hürrem, the Joyous Favourite, who is better known in the West as Roxelana. Süleyman was so in love with her that he put aside all the other women in his harem and lived with her alone. The Italian Bassano, a palace page at the time, thus describes Süleyman's feelings toward Roxelana: 'He bears her such love and keeps such faith in her that all his subjects marvel and say that she has bewitched him'. Roxelana's rival for Süleyman's affections was his Grand Vezir, Ibrahim Paşa, a Greek convert to Islam who had been the Sultan's intimate companion since the early years of his reign. So Roxelana set out to eliminate Ibrahim, persuading Süleyman that his wealthy and powerful Grand Vezir was taking on airs of royalty and had designs on the throne. In the year 1536, after an intimate supper in the palace with his beloved friend, Süleyman gave orders to his mutes to strangle Ibrahim in his sleep. Roxelana's sinister influence over Süleyman continued until her death in 1558. During her last years Roxelana was concerned because her eldest son, Selim the Sot, was not first in line to succeed Süleyman as sultan. The heir-apparent was Prince Mustafa, an extremely able and immensely popular young man. Roxelana plotted with her son-in-law, the Grand Vezir Rüstem Paşa, and they convinced Süleyman that Mustafa was planning to overthrow him and usurp the throne. Süleyman had Mustafa strangled by his mutes, while he himself looked on through a screen. Thus Selim became the heir-apparent, succeeding Süleyman as Sultan on his death in 1566. Historians consider this to be the turning-point in the history of the Ottomans, for with Selim's reign the Empire began its long and steady decline.

During Selim's reign, 1566–74, the Sultan left all affairs of state to his Grand Vezir, Sokollu Mehmet Paşa, while he himself caroused with his women and his favourites in the Harem. Sokollu Mehmet, who had become Grand Vezir in the last year of Süleyman's reign, was one of the most capable men who ever held that office. And it was because of his leadership that the Empire still continued to expand during Selim's alcoholic reign, in the course of which the Turks conquered Cyprus and Georgia.

Selim's First Kadín was a woman called Nur Banu, who used his drunkenness to take complete charge of the Harem, running its affairs and those of the palace to her own advantage. Historians refer to this as the beginning of the 'Rule of the Women', a period in which a series of strong and determined women in the Harem took over control of the palace from their weak and dissolute sultans. The two most powerful women in the Harem were invariably the Valide Sultan and the First Kadín, the mother of the reigning sultan and his principal wife, between whom there were often violent struggles for power. When Selim died on 21 December 1574, after falling in his bath while in a drunken stupor, Nur Banu had all but one of his five sons strangled so that her own child, Murat III, would succeed him as Sultan. Nur Banu corrupted her son by supplying him at a very early age with all of the beautiful women that she could buy in the Istanbul slave market, so that while he spent his time with them she would be free to run the palace. Sokollu Mehmet Paşa continued to serve as Grand Vezir during the early years of Murat's reign, but when he was assassinated in 1578 Nur Banu became the power behind the throne. She eventually lost power to her son's First Kadín, a Venetian girl named Safiye, whose influence over Murat was so great that she persuaded him to adopt a more favourable policy toward her native city. When Murat died, on 16 January 1595, Safiye had all but one of his 19 brothers strangled so that her son, Mehmet III, would become Sultan. Safiye ruled the palace as Valide Sultan until 1602, when she was strangled by one of her rivals in the Harem. Mehmet III died the following year and was succeeded by his eldest son, Ahmet I, this time without bloodshed. Ahmet, who was only 13 years old at the time he became Sultan, soon fell under the influence of his First Kadín, a Greek girl named Kösem, who was herself only in her early teens when she first entered the Harem. Kösem, the most powerful and fascinating woman in the history of the Ottoman Empire, ruled in the Harem until Ahmet's premature death in 1617. She was then banished from Topkapí Sarayí to the Old Palace in Beyazit, the traditional fate for the women of departed sultans other than the Valide Sultan. She remained sequestered there until 1623, when her eldest son, Murat IV, became Sultan, at which time she made her triumphant return to Topkapí Sarayí as Valide Sultan. She ruled the Harem throughout Murat's reign and that of her second son, Crazy Ibrahim (1640–48). Kösem even managed to cling to power during the early years in the reign of her grandson, Mehmet IV (1648–87), but in 1652 she was strangled on the orders of the Sultan's mother, Turhan Hadice. This ended the Rule of the Women, and thenceforth the Harem ceased to play a dominant role in the history of the Ottoman Empire.

Another turning-point in Ottoman history came in 1683, when the Turks failed in their second attempt to take Vienna. The tide of Ottoman expansion had turned, and thereafter the Turks began to lose more battles against their European foes than they won. By the end of the 17C the fortunes of the Ottoman Empire had declined to the point where its basic problems could no longer be ignored, even in the palace. The Empire gave up large parts of its Balkan territories after losing wars with European powers. Within, the Empire was weakened by anarchy and rebellion, particularly among the subject Christians in the Balkans, who now began to nourish dreams of independence.

During the second half of the 18C the Ottoman Empire was strongly influenced by developments in western Europe, particularly by the liberal ideas that brought about the French Revolution. Which eventually led to a movement of reform in the Ottoman Empire. The first Sultan to be deeply influenced by these western ideas was Selim III, who ruled from 1789 until 1807. Selim attempted to improve and modernise the Ottoman army by reorganising it along European lines. By this means he hoped to protect the Empire from further encroachments on the part of foreign powers and from anarchy and rebellion within its own borders. But Selim's efforts were resisted and eventually frustrated by the Janissaries, who felt that their privileged position was being threatened by the reforms. The Janissaries were finally crushed in 1826 by Sultan Mahmut II (1808–39), who instituted an extensive programme of reform in all the basic institutions of the Ottoman Empire, remodelling them along Western lines. This programme continued for a time during the reigns of Mahmut's immediate successors, Abdül Mecit (1839–61) and Abdül Aziz (1861–76) . The reform movement (Tanzimat, in Turkish) culminated in 1876 with the promulgation of the first Ottoman constitution and the establishment of a parliament, which convened on 19 March 1877. But these reforms came too late to prevent the dismemberment of the Ottoman Empire, which in the 19C lost considerable territory as the Christian peoples of the Balkans fought wars of national liberation to free themselves from Turkish domination. Between 1804 and 1878 five independent states came into being on what had been Ottoman territory in the Balkans: Serbia, Greece, Montenegro, Romania, and Bulgaria. The Ottoman Empire was the Sick Old Man of Europe and it seemed to be just a matter of time before it would pass on.

Abdül Hamit II came to the throne in 1876 and set out to halt the reform movement, feeling that it was weakening the government at a time of national crisis. In 1878 he dissolved parliament and revoked the constitution, and for the next three decades he ruled the Empire with an iron hand. Nevertheless, the forces of reform had now grown too strong to be held down permanently. In 1909 the Young Turks deposed Abdül Hamit and restored parliament and the constitution. But this second experiment in Ottoman democracy lasted little longer than the first, for the Young Turks under the leadership of Enver Paşa set up a military dictatorship in which neither the Sultan, Mehmet V (1909–18), nor the people had any voice in the government. In 1912 the Greeks, Serbs and Bulgars inflicted a severe defeat on the Turks in the First Balkan War, in which the Ottoman Empire lost virtually all of Macedonia and Thrace, its last remaining territories in Europe. In 1913 the Balkan allies fell to fighting among themselves, and in the process the Turks regained eastern Thrace.

In 1914 Enver Paşa brought the Ottoman Empire into the First World War on the side of Germany, a decision that proved to be a fatal mistake. For when the war ended the Ottoman Empire was in ruins, its armies defeated in Palestine and the Caucasus, and with Istanbul occupied by an Allied army. A Greek army landed in Smyrna (modern Izmir) in May 1919 with the approval of the USA, France and Great Britain, and soon afterwards began advancing into western Asia Minor as far as the Sea of Marmara. The defeated Ottoman army was in no position to resist them, and so on 10 August 1919 Sultan Mehmet VI (1918–22), a puppet of the Allies, was forced to agree to an armistice. In doing so he put his signature to the Treaty of Sevres, by which the Ottoman Empire lost all of its territory except Istanbul and that part of Anatolia which was not occupied by the Greeks and the other Allies. However, the great mass of the Turkish people in

Anatolia refused to comply with the terms of the armistice or of the Treaty of Sevres. They rallied to the banner of Turkish Nationalism under the leadership of Mustafa Kemal Paşa, later to be known as Atatürk, who in 1919, in a conference in Sivas, called upon his fellow Turks to embark upon their own war of national liberation. In the following year Atatürk presided over a meeting in Ankara of the new Turkish National Assembly, which formed a government in opposition to the Sultan's puppet regime in Istanbul. The Turkish Nationalists then defeated the over-extended Greeks in several engagements, and by September 1922 the Greek army was forced to withdraw from Anatolia under circumstances which were catastrophic for their people, both in Asia Minor and in Greece itself. During the following year more than a million Greeks were forced to leave Asia Minor and to resettle in mainland Greece, part of a population exchange for Turks living in Greek territory. This was one of the results of the Treaty of Versailles, signed in July 1923, which established the boundaries of Turkey essentially as they are today. Meanwhile, the Turkish National Assembly had on 1 November 1922 declared that the Osmanlí sultanate no longer existed, whereupon Mehmet VI fled from Istanbul aboard a British warship. His younger brother Abdül Mecit (II) succeeded him as Caliph, an institution that was abolished in 1924, when he too was forced to flee from Turkey. The climax of these developments came on 29 October 1923, when the Turkish National Assembly proclaimed the founding of the Turkish Republic, with Atatürk as its first President. At the same time the Assembly declared that Ankara would be the capital, as in fact it had been in the formative years of Turkish Nationalism. Soon afterwards the embassies of the great European powers packed up and moved to new quarters in Ankara, leaving their old mansions along the Grande Rue de Pera in Istanbul. And so for the first time in sixteen centuries Istanbul was no longer the capital of an empire.

**Modern Istanbul.** The modern city of Istanbul has changed greatly since the days when it was the capital of the Ottoman Empire. Atatürk's programmes of modernisation and Westernisation did away with the colourful native costumes of the Turks, and the ethnic composition of the city has changed greatly, for the departure of most of the Greeks and other minorities has made the city more Turkish and less Levantine than it was half-a-century ago. The transfer of the great embassies to Ankara has made Istanbul less cosmopolitan and glittering than it was in its days as a world capital. And each year Istanbul becomes less European and more Asian, as hundreds of thousands of poor Anatolians flock there in search of work, settling into ramshackle dwellings in the slums that abound in and around the city, quadrupling its population in the past 20 years, with a consequent increase in social and political problems. Despite these changes Istanbul continues to be one of the most beautiful and interesting cities in the world, with the monuments of two vanished empires crowning its seven hills, still adorned with its encircling garland of waters.

# C.  List of Byzantine Emperors

| | |
|---|---|
| 324–337 | Constantine the Great |
| 337–361 | Constantius |
| 361–363 | Julian the Apostate |
| 363–364 | Jovian |
| 364–378 | Valens |
| 379–395 | Theodosius the Great |
| 395–408 | Arcadius |
| 408–450 | Theodosius II |
| 450–457 | Marcian |
| 457–474 | Leo I |
| 474 | Leo II |
| 474–491 | Zeno |
| 491–518 | Anastasius I |
| 518–527 | Justin I |
| 527–565 | Justinian the Great |
| 565–578 | Justin II |
| 578–582 | Tiberius II |
| 582–602 | Maurice |
| 602–610 | Phocas |
| 610–641 | Heraclius |
| 641 | Constantine II |
| 641 | Heracleonas |
| 641–668 | Constantine III |
| 668–685 | Constantine IV |
| 685–695 | Justinian II |
| 695–698 | Leontius |
| 698–705 | Tiberius III |
| 705–711 | Justinian II (second reign) |
| 711–713 | Phillipicus Bardanes |
| 713–715 | Anastasius II |
| 715–717 | Theodosius III |
| 717–741 | Leo III |
| 741–775 | Constantine V |
| 775–780 | Leo IV |
| 780–797 | Constantine VI |
| 797–802 | Eirene |
| 802–811 | Nicephorus I |
| 811 | Stauracius |
| 811–813 | Michael I |
| 813–820 | Leo V |
| 820–829 | Michael II |
| 829–842 | Theophilus |
| 842–867 | Michael III |
| 867–886 | Basil I |
| 886–912 | Leo VI |
| 912–913 | Alexander |
| 913–959 | Constantine VII Porphyrogenitus |
| 919–944 | Romanus I Lecapenus (co-Emperor) |
| 959–963 | Romanus II |
| 963–969 | Nicephorus II Phocas |
| 969–976 | John I Tzimisces |
| 976–1025 | Basil II |
| 1025–1028 | Constantine VIII |
| 1028–1034 | Romanus III Argyrus |
| 1034–1041 | Michael IV |
| 1041–1042 | Michael V |
| 1042 | Theodora and Zoe |
| 1042–1055 | Constantine IX |
| 1055–1056 | Theodora (second reign) |
| 1056–1057 | Michael VI |
| 1057–1059 | Isaac I Comnenus |
| 1059–1067 | Constantine X Ducas |
| 1067–1071 | Romanus IV Diogenes |
| 1071–1078 | Michael VII Ducas |
| 1078–1081 | Nicephorus III Botaniates |
| 1081–1118 | Alexius I Comnenus |
| 1118–1143 | John II Comnenus |
| 1143–1180 | Manuel I Comnenus |
| 1180–1183 | Alexius II Comnenus |
| 1183–1185 | Andronicus I Comnenus |
| 1185–1195 | Isaac II Angelus |
| 1195–1203 | Alexius III Angelus |
| 1203–1204 | Isaac II Angelus (second reign) |
| 1203–1204 | Alexius IV Angelus (co-Emperor) |
| 1204 | Alexius V Ducas |
| 1204–1222 | •Theodore I Lascaris |
| 1222–1254 | •John III Ducas Vatatzes |
| 1254–1258 | •Theodore II Lascaris |
| 1258–1261 | •John IV Lascaris |
| 1261–1282 | Michael VIII Palaeologus |
| 1282–1328 | Andronicus II Palaeologus |

(•Reigned in Nicaea)

1328–1341 Andronicus III Palaeologus
1341–1391 John V Palaeologus
1347–1354 John VI Cantacuzenos
1376–1379 Andronicus IV Palaeologus
1390 John VII Palaeologus

1391–1425 Manuel II Palaeologus
1425–1448 John VIII Palaeologus
1448–1453 Constantine XI Dragases

## D. List of Ottoman Sultans

1288–1326 Osman Gazi (Chieftain, but not Sultan)
1326–1362 Orhon Gazi
1362–1389 Murat I
1389–1403 Beyazit I
1403–1413 *Interregnum*
1413–1421 Mehmet I
1421–1451 Murat II
1451–1481 Mehmet II, the Conqueror
1481–1512 Beyazit II
1512–1520 Selim I
1520–1566 Süleyman the Magnificent
1566–1574 Selim II
1574–1595 Murat III
1595–1603 Mehmet III
1603–1617 Ahmet I
1617–1618 Mustafa I
1618–1622 Osman II
1622–1623 Mustafa I (second reign)

1623–1640 Murat IV
1640–1648 Ibrahim the Mad
1648–1687 Mehmet IV
1687–1691 Süleyman II
1691–1695 Ahmet II
1695–1703 Mustafa II
1703–1730 Ahmet III
1730–1754 Mahmut I
1754–1757 Osman III
1757–1774 Mustafa III
1774–1789 Abdül Hamit I
1789–1807 Selim III
1807–1808 Mustafa IV
1808–1839 Mahmut II
1839–1861 Abdül Mecit I
1861–1876 Abdül Aziz
1876 Murat V
1876–1909 Abdül Hamit II
1909–1918 Mehmet V
1918–1922 Mehmet VI
1922–1924 Abdül Mecit (II) (Caliph only)

## E. Byzantine Architecture and Art

The oldest surviving church in Istanbul is St. John of Studius, built in 463. The church is a basilica, a plan that was developed in Hellenistic and Roman times, and which in the early Byzantine period was the one most widely used for ordinary churches. The typical basilica is a long, rectangular building divided by two rows of columns into three parts, a wide central nave flanked by an aisle on either side, while at the E end of the nave a semicircular projection forms the apse. The entrance, at the W end opposite the apse, is generally preceded by a vestibule, or narthex, and sometimes by an outer vestibule, the exonarthex, which in turn opens into a large arcaded courtyard, the atrium.

The early Byzantine basilicas had pitched roofs and flat ceilings. Later, most notably in the reign of Justinian, a major innovation was made by introducing a dome. Two outstanding examples of the domed basilica survive in Istanbul, the churches of Haghia Eirene and Haghia Sophia, both completed in 537. In Haghia Eirene the nave is covered on the E by a large dome, and on the W by a smaller and slightly elliptical domical-vault; otherwise it is a very typical basilica. In Haghia Sophia the enormous central dome is supported to E and W by two semidomes of equal diameter, and there are other modifications that superficially conceal its basic plan, which is that of a basilica.

The other type of classical building sometimes used for early Byzantine churches was of a centralised plan, either round or polygonal. In Istanbul the most famous and beautiful example of this type is the church of SS. Sergius and Bacchus, built by Justinian in 527. In form it is an octagon inscribed in a rectangle with a projecting apse and a large central dome. Between the eight piers supporting the dome there are pairs of columns on both the ground floor and the gallery level, thus creating continuous ambulatories except in front of the apse. SS. Sergius and Bacchus closely resembles in its design the contemporary church of St. Vitale in Ravenna.

The period from the beginning of the 7C to the middle of the 9C may be called the Dark Ages of Byzantium. Little or no building of new churches was done, and virtually all the existing figurative mosaics and frescoes in the churches and monasteries of the Empire were destroyed because of the Iconoclastic movement. When Byzantine architecture began to revive in the second half of the 9C, a new type of church building came into being, one generally known as the cross-domed church. In this type a central dome is surrounded on the axes of the building by four long barrel vaults resting on four strong corner piers, thus forming an internal cross; on three sides there are aisles and galleries, so that the exterior is rectangular. At the E end the wide central apse is flanked by two smaller side apses; thenceforth three apses became the rule, required by the developed ritual; and at the W there is the usual narthex. In Istanbul the finest example of this type is the church of St. Theodosia (Gül Camii) probably dating from the 9C.

Another type is known as the four-column church, though some authorities consider this to be a mere development of the cross-domed type. Its most striking internal features are the four columns that here take the place of the corner piers of the earlier types as supports for the dome. These churches are all small and tall, more-or-less square externally, but preserving the cruciform plan within. There are no galleries, except sometimes over the narthex, but the four corners of the cross are occupied by domed bays or by domical vaults on high drums; these, together with the central dome, form a quincunx, by which name this type is sometimes known. The four-column church appeared in Constantinople in the 9–10C and thereafter became almost standard; its small size was suitable to the declining revenues of the shrinking Empire, while its internal form provided ample areas for mosaic and fresco decoration. In Istanbul no less than eight examples of this type have survived, of which perhaps the most typical are the two churches that form parts of the complex building of St Saviour Pantocrator (Zeyrek Camii).

All the Byzantine churches in Constantinople are built of brick, including Haghia Sophia, and they are generally little adorned on the exterior, depending for their effect on the warm brick colour of the walls. Toward the end of the Empire, in the 13–14C, exteriors were

*The mosaic portrait of the Virgin and Christ-Child flanked
by Justinian (left) and Constantine (right) over the doorway
leading into the narthex of Haghia Sophia, dating to the last
quarter of the 10C. (Ergun Cagatay)*

sometimes enlivened by polychrome decoration in brick and stone, a
style seen at its best and most elaborate in the facade of the outer
narthex of St. Theodore (Kilise Camii) or in that of the Palace of the
Porphyrogenitus (Tekfur Saray).

As if to compensate for the relative austerity of the outside, the
interior of the churches blazed with colour and life. The lower parts of
the walls up to the springing of the vaults were sheathed in marble,
while the vaults, domes and upper walls were covered in gold mosaic.
The most magnificent example of marble revetment is that in Haghia
Sophia, where a dozen different kinds of rare and costly marbles are
used, the thin slabs being sawn in two and opened out to form
intricate designs. Haghia Sophia was of course unique, though there
may have been a few other churches of Justinian equally lavishly
covered with marble. But even the humbler and smaller churches of a
later period had their revetment, largely of the common but attractive
greyish-white marble from the nearby quarries on the Isle of Proconnesus in the Marmara. Most of the churches surviving in Istanbul
have lost this decoration, but an excellent example survives almost
intact in St. Saviour in Chora (Kariye Camii).

The mosaics of the earlier Byzantine period seem to have consisted
chiefly of a gold ground round the edges of which, emphasising the
architectural forms, were wide bands of floral decoration in naturalis-
tic designs and colours; at appropriate places there would be a simple
cross in outline. Large areas of this simple but effective decoration
survive from Justinian's time in the dome and the aisle vaults of
Haghia Sophia. It appears that in Haghia Sophia, at least, there were
originally no pictorial mosaics. In the century following Justinian's
death, however, picture mosaics became the vogue and an elaborate
iconography was worked out which regulated which parts of the Holy

Story should be represented and where the various pictures should be placed in the church building. Then came the Iconoclastic Age (711–843) when all of these pictorial mosaics were ruthlessly destroyed, so that none survives in Istanbul from before the mid-9C. From then onwards there was a revival of the pictorial art, still in the highly stylised and formal tradition of the earlier period, and all the great churches were again filled with holy pictures. A good idea of the stylistic types in favour from the 9–12C can be seen in examples uncovered in Haghia Sophia.

But in Istanbul the most extensive and splendid mosaics date from the last great flowering of Byzantine culture before the Turkish Conquest in 1453. At the beginning of the 14C were executed the long cycles of the life of the Blessed Virgin and of Christ in St. Saviour in Chora, which have been so brilliantly restored in recent years by the Byzantine Institute. To this date also belong the glorious frescoes in the side chapel of that church, and the series of mosaics in the side chapel of the church of St. Mary Pammakaristos (Fethiye Camii), which although less extensive than those in Kariye Camii are no less impressive. The art of these pictures shows a decisive break away from the hieratic formalism of the earlier tradition, breathing the very spirit of the Renaissance as it was beginning to appear at the same date in Italy. In Byzantium it had all too short a life.

# F. Ottoman Architecture and Art

The mosques of Istanbul fall into a small number of fairly distinct types of increasing complexity. The simplest of all, used at all periods for the less costly buildings, is simply an oblong room covered by a tiled pitched roof; often there was an interior wooden dome but most of these have perished in fires and have been replaced by flat ceilings. Second comes the square room covered by a masonry dome resting directly on the walls. This was generally small and simple but could sometimes take on monumental proportions, as in the mosque of Selim I. Occasionally, as there, mosques had side rooms used as tabhanes, or hospices for travelling dervishes. Later, in the 18–19C, a more elaborate form of this type was adopted for the baroque mosques, usually with a small projecting apse for the mihrab, the niche that orients the faithful toward Mecca.

The next two types of mosque both date from an earlier period and are rare in Istanbul. Third is the two-domed type, essentially a duplication of the second, forming a large room divided by an open arch, each unit being covered by a dome. It is derived from a style common in the Bursa period of Ottoman architecture, and hence is often known as the 'Bursa type' (see the plan of Mahmut Paşa Camii). A modification occurs when the second unit has only a semidome. Mosques of this type always have side-chambers. A fourth type, of which only two examples occur in Istanbul, also derives from the earlier Selcuk and Ottoman periods: a rectangular room covered by a multiplicity of domes of equal size supported on pillars; this is often called the great-mosque or Ulu Cami type.

The mosques of the classical period (c 1500–1650)—what most people think of as 'typical' Ottoman mosques—are rather more elaborate than their predecessors. They derive from a fusion of a native Turkish tradition with certain elements of the plan of Haghia Sophia. The great imperial mosques have a vast central dome supported to E and W by semidomes of equal diameter. (All mosques face in the direction of Mecca, which in Istanbul is approximately SE, but for simplicity this Guide will follow the convention that they face East.) This strongly resembles the plan of Haghia Sophia, but there are significant differences, dictated partly by the native Turkish tradition, partly by the requirements of Islamic ritual. In spite of its domes Haghia Sophia is a basilica, clearly divided into a nave and side aisles by a curtain of columns, on both ground floor and gallery level. The mosques suppress this division by getting rid of as many of the columns as possible, thus making the interior almost open and visible from all parts. Moreover, the galleries, which in Haghia Sophia are as wide as the aisles, are here reduced to narrow balconies against the side walls. This is the plan of Beyazit Camii and the Süleymaniye. Sometimes this centralisation and opening-up is carried even farther by adding two extra semidomes to N and S, as at the mosques of the Şehzade, Sultan Ahmet I, and Yeni Cami. A further innovation of the mosques is the provision of a monumental exterior in attractive grey stone with a cascade of descending domes and semidomes balanced by the upward thrust of the minaret or minarets. The smaller mosques have a single minaret which is almost always on the right side of the entrance, while the larger imperial mosques may have two, four, or even six, as Sultan Ahmet I Camii, in which case they rise from the corners of the building and/or the courtyard. These minarets often have elaborately sculptured şerefes, or müezzin's balconies. Almost all mosques of whatever type are preceded by a porch of three or five domed bays and generally also with a monumental courtyard, the avlu. This is usually surrounded on three sides with a domed arcade and with a monumental gateway opposite the main doorway to the mosque. In the centre of the courtyard there is usually a şadırvan, or ablution fountain, where the faithful perform their abdest, or ritual washings, before going into the mosque to pray. The stone platform on the side of the courtyard next to the mosque is called the son cemaat yeri, literally the place of last assembly. When the mosque is full on the occasion of the Friday noon prayer, latecomers perform their devotions on this porch, usually at one of the niches flanking the doorway leading into the mosque.

The interior furnishings of all mosques are essentially the same. The most important element is the mihrab, a niche set into the centre of the wall opposite the main entrance. In the imperial mosques of Istanbul the mihrab is invariably quite grand, with the niche itself made of finely carved marble and with the wall around it sheathed in ceramic tiles. To the right of the mihrab is the mimber, or pulpit. At the time of the noon prayer on Friday the imam, or preacher, mounts the steps of the mimber and gives the weekly sermon, or hutbe. To the left of the mihrab, often standing against the main pier on that side, is the Kuran kürsü, where the imam sits cross-legged while he reads the Kuran to the congregation. And to the right of the entrance in the larger mosques there is usually a raised platform, the müezzin mahfili, where the müezzins kneel when they are chanting the responses to the prayers of the imam. In the imperial mosques there is always a hünkar mahfili, or royal loge, a chamber screened off by a gilded grille so that the Sultan and his party would be shielded from the public gaze when they attended services. This royal enclosure is usually in the far left corner of the gallery as one faces the mihrab, and it often had its own entrance from outside the mosque.

All imperial mosques and most of the grander ones of the great men and women of the Empire form the centre of a külliye, a whole complex of religious and philanthropic institutions comprising a vákíf, or pious foundation, often endowed with great wealth. The founder invariably built his türbe, or mausoleum, in the garden or graveyard behind the mosque; these are simple buildings, square or polygonal, covered by a dome and with a small entrance porch, sometimes beautifully decorated inside with tiles. Of the utilitarian institutions, almost always built around four sides of a central arcaded and domed courtyard, the commonest is the medrese, or college. The students' cells, or hücre, each had its dome and fireplace. The cells opened off the courtyard, which usually had a central fountain, and in the middle of one side of the portico was the large domed dershane, or lecture hall. Sometimes the medrese formed three sides of a mosque courtyard, while elsewhere it was an independent building, occasionally with an unusual shape, such as in the octagonal medrese of Rüstem Paşa. These medreses functioned at several academic levels, some being mere secondary schools, others teaching more advanced subjects, while still others were colleges for specialised studies such as law, medicine, and the hadis, or traditions of the Prophet. There were also primary schools, or sibyan mektebi (sometimes simply called a mektep), which were usually small buildings with a single domed classroom and sometimes an apartment for the teacher, or hoca.

The larger imperial foundations included a hospital, or darüşşifa, a caravansaray, and a public kitchen or imaret. The hospital closely resembled the medrese in structure, but the domed cells were used as the patients' rooms and the large domed chamber was used as a clinic and examining room. Large institutions like the Süleymaniye also included an insane asylum, or timarhane. The caravansaray was built to the same general plan as the medrese, with the domed rooms around the central courtyard serving to house and feed travellers, a service provided free of charge for three days when one first arrived in the city. The imarets had vast domed kitchens with very distinctive chimneys and large vaulted refectories. They provided free food for all the people associated with the külliye, as well as for the poor of the neighbourhood. All of the other institutions were free too, and in the great days of the Ottoman Empire they were very efficiently managed. In recent years many of them have been restored and are again serving the people of Istanbul, with Ottoman hospitals operating as clinics, schoolhouses functioning as children's libraries, and medreses being used as research centres, libraries, and student dormitories.

Sometimes these pious foundations were not part of a mosque complex, but were independent institutions. One example was the Ottoman library, or kütüphane, of which three charming examples from the 18C are still functioning in the city. Another such institution was the tekke, or dervish monastery, of which there were more than 300 housing the members of the 17 different religious orders represented in Istanbul. All of these were closed when the dervish orders were banned in the early years of the Turkish Republic, and most of the buildings have since been destroyed or have fallen into ruins. But a few tekkes have survived because of their status as religious shrines, in which some of the departed dervishes are venerated as saints by the people of Istanbul. One of them, the tekke of the Mevlevi dervishes in Tünel, has recently been restored and is now open to the public, revealing yet another aspect of the life of old Istanbul.

Another very important institution was the han, whose function closely paralleled that of the caravansaray. Like so many Ottoman structures, the han was built around one or more courtyards, but in two or three storeys, with the lower chambers used as stables for the horses and camels of the caravans that brought goods to Istanbul and the upper ones serving as guest-rooms for the merchants and as storage places for the wares that they sold there. These hans were virtually self-sufficient institutions, complete with kitchens, dining-halls, baths, toilets, blacksmith, and a mosque, and they were the mainstay of Istanbul's commercial life all through the Ottoman period. There are scores of these monumental old Ottoman hans still operating in Istanbul, some of them as much as five centuries old, and they are among the most picturesque sights in the old city.

One of the most important of these Ottoman foundations was the hamam, or public bath, whose revenues were often used to pay for the upkeep of the other institutions in a külliye. There are well over one hundred of these old Ottoman hamams still functioning in Istanbul. Since only the very wealthiest Ottoman homes had private baths, the vast majority of people in Istanbul used bathed in these hamams. In fact, the present fuel shortage, together with the lack of proper housing for so many of the city's poor, has made the hamams of Istanbul as popular today as they were in Ottoman times.

Turkish hamams are built to the same general design as the baths of ancient Rome. Ordinarily, a hamam has three distinct sections. The first chamber that one enters is the camekan, the Roman apoditarium. This is a reception chamber and dressing-room, a place in which one can relax and sip tea after bathing. Next comes the soğukluk, anciently known as the tepidarium, a chamber of intermediate temperature that serves as an anteroom to the bath, keeping the cold air out on one side and the hot air in on the other. Finally there is the hararet, or steam-room, the Roman calidarium. The camekan is usually the most monumental chamber in a Turkish hamam. It is typically a vast square room covered by a dome on pendentives or squinches, with an elaborate fountain in the centre; round the walls there is a raised platform where the bathers undress and leave their clothes. The soğukluk is almost always a mere passageway, which usually contains the lavatories. In most Turkish baths the most elaborate chamber is the hararet, perhaps the most beautiful example of which is that in the Cağaloğlu Hamamí. In the centre of the hararet there is usually a large marble platform, the göbek taşí, which is heated below by a wood fire in the furnace room, the külhan. The patrons lie on the belly stone to sweat and to be massaged before bathing at one of the wall-fountains in the side chambers.

Turkish fountains, or çeşme, are ubiquitous; there are more than 700 in Istanbul dating from Ottoman times, and even one or two that may date from before the Turkish Conquest. The most monumental of these are the imperial street-fountains, such as the splendid çeşme of Ahmet III beside the main entrance to Topkapí Sarayí. This huge structure is really a composite of the two basic types of fountains to be seen all over Istanbul. These are the sebil, or fountain house, which occupy the four corners of the structure, and the çeşme, the wall-foun-tains on each of the four sides. The sebil, which is often used to adorn the corner of a mosque precinct, is usually a domed structure with three or more grilled openings in its facade. In Ottoman times these sebils were staffed with attendants who passed out cups of water free to thirsty passers-by. There are scores of these old Ottoman sebils still standing in Istanbul, and although none of them is still serving its original purpose, they remain an adornment to the city. The most common type of Turkish fountain is the simple çeşme. In its most basic form a çeşme may consist of a mere niche set into a wall, with water flowing from a spout into a marble basin. The water-spout is set into a marble tablet called the mirror-stone, which is often decorated with floral or geometrical designs in low relief. The niche is usually framed in an arch, while the facade of the surrounding wall is decorated in the same design as the mirror-stone. At the top of this facade there is always a calligraphic inscription giving the name of the donor and the date of construction. The older inscriptions are often in the form of chronograms, in which the numerical values of the Arabic letters give the date of foundation. These chronograms became a favourite art form for Ottoman poets, and they vied with one another in composing clever and original epigrams, which would not only give the name of the donor and the date of foundation but would also advertise the poetic talents of the composer.

**Ottoman Architectural Forms.** In Ottoman architecture there are no 'orders' as these are understood in the West, such as the Doric, Ionic and Corinthian orders in ancient Greek architecture. Nevertheless, in the great period of Ottoman architecture there were two recognised types of capital: the stalactite and the lozenge. The stalactite is an elaborate geometrical structure composed chiefly of triangles and hexagons, which is built up so that it resembles a stalactite formation or a honeycomb. It is derived directly from Selcuk architecture and is used not only for capitals but often for portal canopies, cornices, and even pendentives and squinches. The lozenge capital, apparently introduced by Sinan or anyhow not much used before his time, is a simple structure of juxtaposed lozenges. Neither capital is very satisfactory compared with those of the ancient Greek orders, because both, especially the lozenge, give a too-smooth and weak transition from the cylinder of the column to the square of the impost. In the baroque period of Ottoman architecture bad imitations of western types of capitals came into vogue, almost all of them hopelessly weak. And until the baroque period all Turkish arches had not been round like the Roman ones but pointed like the Gothic, and sometimes of the ogive or 'broken' type that is often so effectively used by Sinan. It should also be noted that the Ottoman dome resembles the hemispherical Roman, Byzantine, and Syrian type, not the more common western ovoid type created by Brunelleschi, which is structurally double. Even when Ottoman domes are double, as in some türbes, each dome is structurally independent.

**Turkish Tiles.** Of decoration applied to architecture, far and away the most brilliant and striking is Turkish ceramic tiling. Only fairly recently have the full importance and uniqueness of Turkish tiles been recognised: they used often to be called Rhodian ware or else lumped together with Persian pottery. Even though the potters were sometimes Persian—as well as Greek, Armenian, and Turkish—the Ottoman tiles were altogether different from Persian ceramics. They were manufactured chiefly at Iznik, the ancient Nicaea, but also sometimes at Kütahya and Istanbul. Broadly speaking, there are three periods of Turkish ceramics represented in Istanbul. In the early period, from the Conquest to the mid-16C, the tiles were extremely plain and without design. These early Turkish tiles were usually hexagonal, a deep blue or a lighter green or turquoise, and sometimes overlaid with an unfired pattern in gold. More interesting are the tiles in the *cuerda seca* technique. Here, instead of a painted design covered by a transparent glaze, the glazes themselves were coloured and the colours were prevented from running into each other by a hair-like dividing line of permanganate of potash outlining the design (hence the name *cuerda seca*, dry cord); if visible at all this line is deep purple or black. The predominating colours of these tiles are apple-green and bright yellow with subordinate blues and mauves. They are very beautiful and very rare in Istanbul, and the only extensive examples are in the türbe of Prince Mehmet at the Şehzade Camii and in the porch of the Çinili Köşk.

About 1550 this lovely technique gave place to the no less beautiful and more famous Iznik style, where the design is painted on the clay and covered with an absolutely transparent glaze. Here the predominant colours are: on the purest, most unblemished white ground, deep blue, light blue, shades of green, and above all the matchless tomato red. This was made with a clay known as Armenian bole, found near Erzurum in central Anatolia. It has to be laid on very thickly so that it protrudes from the surface of the tile like sealing-wax. The technique of using it successfully is extremely tricky, so much so that it was only completely mastered toward 1570 and lost again in about 1620, so that the absolutely perfect tiles of this type are confined to this half-century. In tiles before or after this period the bole tends to be a bit muddy and brownish and lacking in clear outline. But at their best the Turkish tiles in the period 1550–1620 are incomparably beautiful.

After that the quality of Turkish tiles began to decline, like most other things in the Empire. A short revival was made about 1720 at Tekfur Saray in Istanbul, but this hardly outlasted the first generation of craftsmen. Thereafter inferior European tiles or even more inferior imitations of them became the vogue. There has been a considerable and praiseworthy revival of the old style in recent years, so that really good modern tiles (now made at Kütahya) are sometimes hard to distinguish, at first glance, from the great ones.

**Sinan the Architect.** No discussion of Ottoman architecture would be complete without at least a brief biography of the great Sinan, who created most of the masterpieces founded by Süleyman and his immediate successors. Sinan was born of Christian parents, presumably Greek, in the Anatolian province of Karamania in about 1491. When he was about 21 he was caught up in the *devşirme*, the annual levy of Christian youths who were taken into the Sultan's service. As was customary, he became a Moslem and was sent to one of the palace schools in Istanbul. He was then assigned to the Janissaries as a military engineer and served in four of Süleyman's campaigns. Around 1538 Süleyman appointed him Chief of the Imperial Architects, a post he held for half a century, continuing to serve under Süleyman's two immediate successors, Selim II and Murat III. Sinan built his first mosque in 1538, in Aleppo, and the following year he erected his first mosque in Istanbul; this was Haseki Hürrem Camii, commissioned by Süleyman for his wife Roxelana. In the following half-century he was to adorn Istanbul and the other cities of the Empire with an incredible number of mosques and other structures. The 'Tezkere-ül Ebniye', the official list of

Sinan's accomplishments, credits him with 81 large mosques, including 42 in Istanbul, 50 mescits, or smaller mosques, 55 medreses, 7 Kuran schools, 19 mausoleums, 15 public kitchens, 3 hospitals, 6 aqueducts, 32 palaces, 6 storehouses, 22 public baths, and 2 bridges, a total of 323 structures, of which 84 still remain standing in Istanbul alone. He was nearly 50 when he completed his first mosque, 66 when he completed the Süleymaniye, the crowning glory of Ottoman architecture in Istanbul, and he was 85 when the Selimiye mosque complex in Edirne was completed, a work that is generally agreed to be the supreme masterpiece in the history of Ottoman architecture. Sinan did not pause even then, but continued to work as Chief Architect, and built a half-dozen of Istanbul's finer mosques for the Sultan's vezirs. Koca Mimar Sinan, or Great Sinan the Architect, as the Turks call him, died in 1588 at the age of 97 (100, according to the Islamic calendar) just a few days after completing his last project, a new gate in the Byzantine sea-walls along the Golden Horn. He was then buried in a mausoleum that he had constructed himself in the shadow of the Süleymaniye, his greatest work in Istanbul. Sinan was the architect of the golden age of the Ottoman Empire, and his monuments are the magnificent buildings with which he adorned its capital.

# G.  Glossary of Architectural Terms

AMBO A raised pulpit from which the Epistle and the Gospel were read.

AMBULATORY A covered passageway, or synthronon, that led around behind the altar of a church.

APSE The circular or polygonal termination of a church sanctuary.

ARCADE A range of arches supported on piers or columns.

ARCHITRAVE The beam or lowest division of the entablature, which extends from column to column.

ATRIUM The forecourt of a church.

AVLU The forecourt of a mosque.

BARBICAN An outwork of a fortress, designed to protect a gateway.

BARREL VAULT A continuous vault of semicircular cross-section.

BEMA A raised stage reserved for the clergy in a Byzantine church.

BEDESTEN A domed building, usually in the centre of a Turkish market, where valuable goods are stored and sold.

BUTTRESS A mass of masonry built up against a wall to resist the outward pressure of an arch or vault.

CAMEKAN The reception or dressing room of a Turkish bath.

CAMI A mosque.

CAPITAL The crowning feature of a column or pilaster.

ÇARŞI A Turkish market.

ÇEŞME A Turkish fountain.

CIBORIUM A canopy supported by columns over an altar, also called a baldachino.

CORBEL A block of stone or wood, oftencarved or moulded, projecting from a wall, and supporting the beams of a roof, floor, vault or other architectural member.

CORNICEThe crowning or upper portion ofthe entablature.

CRENELLATIONS The indentations in the parapet of a fortress wall.

CROSS VAULT or GROIN VAULT Vaults characterized by arched diagonal groins, which are formed by the intersection of two barrel vaults.

CUPOLA or DOME A spherical roof,

placed over a circular, square, or polygonal chamber.

CURTAIN WALL A defence wall linking towers in a fortress.

DADO The portion of a pedestal between its base and cornice. The term also applies to the lower portion of walls when decorated separately.

DARÜLHADIS A college of advanced studies in the religious law (Şeriat) of Islam.

DARÜŞŞIF An Ottoman hospital.

DERSHANE The lecture hall of a medrese.

DOMICAL VAULT A dome rising direct on a square or polygonal base, the curved surfaces separated by groins.

ENTABLATURE The upper part of an Order of architecture, comprising architrave, frieze and cornice, supported by a colonnade.

EXEDRA A semicircular niche.

EXONARTHEX The outer vestibule of a church.

EXTRADO The outer curve of an arch.

FAIENCE Glazed earthenware, often ornamented, used for pottery or as revetment on the walls of a building.

FRESCO The term originally applied to painting on a wall while the plaster is still wet, but often used for any painting not in oil colours.

FRIEZE The middle division of a classical entablature, often decorated with carvings in low relief.

GROIN The curved edge formed by the intersection of two vaulting surfaces.

HAMAM A Turkish bath.

HAN An Ottoman inn for travellers.

HARARET The steam room of a Turkish bath.

HAREM The female quarter of a Turkish home or palace.

HISAR An Ottoman fortress.

HÜNKAR MAHFILI The Sultan's loge in an imperial Ottoman mosque.

HÜCRE A student's cell in a medrese.

ICONOSTASIS The screen between the nave and chancel of a Greek church, invariably decorated with icons, or holy pictures.

IMARET The public kitchen in an Ottoman pious foundation.

IMPOST The member, usually formed of mouldings, on which an arch rests.

INTRADO The inner curve of an arch.

KIBLE The direction of Mecca.

KONAK An Ottoman mansion.

KÖŞK A Turkish kiosk or pavilion.

KÜLLIYE An Ottoman mosque complex or pious foundation.

KÜRSU or KURAN KÜRSÜ The chair on which the imam, or preacher, sits when he is reading the Kuran to the congregation.

LINTEL The horizontal timber or stone, also known as the architrave, that spans an opening.

LUNETTE A semicircular window or wall-panel let into the inner base of a concave vault or dome.

MEKTEP An Ottoman primary school.

MESCIT A small mosque.

MIHRAB The niche in the wall of a mosque that indicates the kíble, the direction of Mecca.

MIMBER The pulpit in a mosque.

MINARET The spire, beside a mosque, from which the müezzin, or chanter, gives the call to prayer.

MOSAIC Decorative surfaces formed by small cubes (tesserae) of stone, glass, or marble.

MÜEZZIN MAHFILI The raised platform where the müezzins chant their responses to the prayers of the imam.

MUVAKITHANE The house of the müneccim, or mosque astronomer.

NAMAZGAH An outdoor place of prayer.

NARTHEX, The arcaded entrance porch of a Byzantine church.

OCAK, A Turkish fireplace.

ODA In Turkish, room or chamber.

OGIVE ARCH A pointed arch.

OPUS ALEXANDRINUM A mosaic inlaid in a stone or marble paving.

ORDER An Order in ancient Greek architecture comprised a column, with base (usually), shaft and capital, the whole supporting an entablature.

PENDENTIVE The triangular curved overhanging surface by means of which a circular dome is supported over a square or polygonal chamber.

PERISTYLE A range of columns surrounding a courtyard.

PIER A mass of masonry, as distinct from a column, from which an arch springs.

PILASTER A rectangular feature in the shape of a pillar, but projecting only about one-sixth of its breadth from a wall.

PORPHYRY, A hard, red or purple rock.

PORTICO A colonnaded space, with a roof supported on at least one side by columns.

REFECTORY The dining-hall in a monastery, convent, or college.

REVAK In Turkish, a domed or vaulted colonnade enclosing a porch

REVETMENT A facing of stone, marble, or ceramic tile upon a wall.

ŞADIRVAN An ablution fountain in the courtyard of a mosque.

SARAY An Ottoman palace

SEBIL An Ottoman fountain-house from which water is distributed free to passersby.

SELAMLIK The male quarters of an Ottoman home or palace.

ŞEREFE The balcony of a minaret, where the müezzin gives the call to prayer.

SIBYAN MEKTEBI See *mektep*.

SÖGUKLUK The chamber of intermediate temperature in a Turkish bath.

SOFFIT The ceiling or underside of any architectural member.

SON CEMAAT YERI The raised front porch of a mosque where late-comers pray.

SQUINCH A small arch, bracket, or similar device built across each angle of a square or polygonal structure to form an octagon or any appropriate base for a dome.

SURBASE A moulding at the base of a pedestal, podium, or wall.

SUTERAZI A Turkish water-control tower.

SYNTHRONON See *ambulatory*.

TABHANE A hospice for traveling dervishes.

TAKSIM A Turkish water-distribution system.

TEKKE A dervish monastery.

TIMARHANE An Ottoman insane asylum.

TÜRBE An Ottoman mausoleum.

TYMPANUM The space enclosed by an arch.

VAKIF The deed of an Ottoman pious foundation.

VAULT An arched covering in stone or brick over any building.

VOUSSOIRS The truncated wedge-shaped blocks forming an arch.

YALI An Ottoman mansion on the Bosphorus.

# H.  Bibliography

The following is a selective list of books in English about Istanbul. This is not meant to be a definitive bibliography, but rather an introduction to the history, archaeology, art, architecture and folklore of the city. Some of the books listed below are out of print. The *Hellenic Bookservice*, 122 Charing Cross Road, London WC2, specialises in books about Turkey and Greece and has many out-of-print books on Istanbul.

PRIMARY SOURCES *Procopius,* The Secret History; Procopius was the personal secretary of Belisarius, Justinian's commanding general, and the Secret History is a scandalous and sometimes unbelievable attack on the Emperor and his wife Theodora. Nevertheless, it is very interesting and sometimes quite amusing. *Michael Psellus,* The Chronographia; Psellus was court chamberlain of Michael VII, and his work is a lively and fascinating history of the emperors and empresses of the Macedonian dynasty, who ruled Byzantium in the period 843–1025. *Anna Comnena,* The Alexiad; Princess Anna was the eldest daughter of Alexius I Comnenus, and her work is a sympathetic account of her father's reign. *Geoffrey de Villehardouin,* The Conquest of Constantinople; a description of the Latin sack of the Byzantine capital in 1204, written by a Crusader knight who later set up his own principality in the Peloponnesus. *George Phrantzes,* History; Phrantzes was a Byzantine aristocrat and a very close friend of Constantine XI, last Emperor of Byzantium; his History is an eye-witness account of the last siege of Constantinople and of its aftermath, an extremely dramatic and moving account of the Conquest. *Kritovoulos of Imbros,* History of Mehmet the Conqueror; Kritoboulos was an aristocratic Byzantine who survived the Conquest; afterwards, to please his new masters, he wrote a sympathetic account of the early years of Fatih's reign; his work covers the period 1451–67, and a large part of it deals with the siege and capture of Constantinople. *Evliya Çelebi,* A Narrative of Travels (*Seyahatname*) ; Evliya was a Turk born in Istanbul in 1611, and much of his narrative is a description of his native city as it was in the mid-17C, an extremely interesting, lively, and humorous depiction of life in the Ottoman capital as it neared the end of its golden age.

EARLY HISTORIES OF THE OTTOMAN EMPIRE. *Richard Knolles,* History of the Othman Turks (1603). *Sir Paul Rycaut,* The History of the Present State of the Ottoman Empire, 3 vols (1670). *Demetrius Cantemir,* The History of the Growth and Decay of the Ottoman Empire .

EARLY TRAVELLERS. *S.H. Weber* (editor), Voyages and Travels in Greece, the Near East and Adjacent Areas Made Previous to the Year 1801. *John Sanderson,* Travels in the Levant, 1584–1602. *G. Sandys,* A Relation of a Journey An. Dom. 1610. *O.G. Busbecq,* Turkish Letters (1633). *Thévenot,* The Travels of Monsieur de Thévenot into the Levant (1687). *Aubrey de la Motraye,* Travels Through Europe, Asia, and into Part of Africa, 2 vols. (1723). *Lady Mary Wortley Montague,* Letters (1763). *Dalloway,* Constantinople, Ancient and Modern (1797).

MODERN HISTORIES OF THE BYZANTINE AND OTTOMAN EMPIRES. *Georg Ostrogorski,* History of the Byzantine State. *A.A. Vasiliev,* History of the Byzantine Empire, 2 vols. *Joan Hussey* (editor), The Byzantine Empire I, Byzantium and its Neighbours (The Cambridge Medieval History IV). *Sir Steven Runciman,* Byzantine Civilization; The Fall of Constantinople; A History of the Crusades, 3 vols. *Glanville Downey,* Constantinople in the Age of Justinian. *Romilly Jenkins,* Byzantium, the Imperial Centuries. *Charles Diehl,* Byzantine Empresses. *Andre Grabar,* Byzantium: From the Death of Theodosius to the Rise of Islam. *Paul Wittek,* The Rise of the Ottoman Empire. *Halil Inalcik,* The Ottoman Empire: The Classical Period, 1300–1600. *Stanford J. Shaw* and *Ezel Kural Shaw,* History of the Ottoman Empire and Modern

**48** BIBLIOGRAPHY

Turkey. *Stanford J. Shaw*, Between Old and New, the Ottoman Empire under Selim III. *Lord Kinross*, The Ottoman Centuries; Atatürk, The Rebirth of a Nation. *Bernard Lewis*, The Emergence of Modern Turkey; Istanbul, The Civilization of the Ottoman Empire. *Geoffrey Lewis*, Turkey. *Raphaela Lewis*, Everyday Life in Ottoman Turkey. *A.D. Alderson*, The Structure of the Ottoman Dynasty. *Joan Haslip*, The Sultan: The Life of Abdül Hamit II. *H.A.R. Gibb* and *H. Bowen*, Islamic Society and the West. *H.A.R. Gibb*, Mohammedanism, An Historical Survey. *A.H. Lyber*, The Government of the Ottoman Empire in the Time of Süleiman the Magnificent. *Carl Brockelmann*, History of the Islamic People.

ANTIQUITIES, ART AND ARCHITECTURE. *Pierre Gilles (Petrus Gyllius)*, The Antiquities of Constantinople (1550, English translation 1729). *Ernest Mamboury*, The Tourist's Istanbul. *Hilary Sumner-Boyd* and *John Freely*, Strolling Through Istanbul; Istanbul, A Brief Guide to the City. *Alexander van Millingen*, The Walls of Constantinople; Byzantine Churches in Istanbul: Their Ottoman Centuries; History and Architecture. *W.R. Lethaby* and *H. Swainson*, The Church of Sancta Sophia. *E.H. Swift*, Haghia Sophia. *Lord Kinross*, Haghia Sophia. *Thomas F. Matthews*, The Early Churches of Constantinople. *Barnette Miller*, Beyond the Sublime Court; The Palace School of Mohammed the Conqueror. *N.M. Penzer*, The Harem. *Fanny Davis*, The Palace of Topkapí in Istanbul. *Richard Krautheimer*, Early Christian and Byzantine Architecture. *Cyril Mango*, Byzantine Architecture; The Brazen House. *Godfrey Goodwin*, A History of Ottoman Architecture. *Oktay Aslanapa*, Turkish Art and Architecture. *Aptullah Kuran*, The Mosque in Early Ottoman Architecture. *Richard Ettinghausen*, Turkey: The Ancient Miniatures. *A. Lane*, Early Islamic Pottery; Later Islamic Pottery.

FOLKLORE AND LOCAL COLOUR. *J. Pardoe* The City of the Sultan (1838), Beauties of the Bosphorus (1839). *E.A. Grosvenor*, Constantinople, 2 vols (1896). *Alexander van Millingen*, Constantinople (1909). *H.G. Dwight*, Constantinople, Old and New (1915). *John Freely*, Stamboul Sketches.

# PRACTICAL INFORMATION

## I  Approaches to Istanbul

In view of the great distance, nearly 2000 miles, the most direct, practical, and comfortable way to reach Istanbul from Britain is by air. Those travelling by surface transport must allow six days for a return journey by train, eight days by bus, and eight to ten days by automobile, unless several people share the driving and continue in shifts throughout the day and night. Hardy souls can save money if they have plenty of time and are willing to sleep sitting up in a bus or train, but it is hardly worth it, except for the young and adventurous.

*General Information* on travel to Turkey can be obtained from the Turkish Tourism and Information Office at 49 Conduit Street, London W1. There is also an office in the USA at 821 United Nations Plaza, NY, NY 10017.

*Travel Agents.* There are many accredited travel agencies and tour operators in the UK and the USA who sell travel tickets to Istanbul and book accommodations there. For information contact the Association of British Travel Agents, 50–54 Newman Street, London W1, or the American Association of Travel Agents, 711 Fifth Avenue, NY, NY 10022.

Regular *Air Services* between London and Istanbul (once daily) are provided by both British Airways (BA) and Turk Hava Yollari (THY), the Turkish national airline. Information can be obtained from BA, Dorland House, Lower Regent St, London SW1, and from THY, 11/12 Hanover St, London W1. From North America only Pan Am has direct flights to Istanbul.

*Passenger Ships and Car Ferries.* Turkish Maritime Lines (in Turkish, Denizcilek Bankasi; DB) operates two regularly-scheduled passenger ships between Mediterranean ports and Istanbul. The Akdeniz and Karadeniz call at Barcelona, Marseilles, Naples, and Piraeus (the political situation permitting) before landing in Istanbul. (On some runs they also call at Izmir.) DB also operates a car-ferry, the Truva, which sails to Istanbul from Venice, Ancona and Split. Information can be obtained from DB's agents: Watford Lines, Ltd, St. Mary Axe House, London, EC3.

*Railway Service.* The following express trains terminate in Istanbul: The Marmara Express from London and Paris via Lausanne, Milan, Venice, Trieste, Belgrade, and Sofia; the Istanbul Express and the Tauren Orient Express from Vienna via Graz, Zagreb, Belgrade and Sofia. For information, contact the British Railway Travel Centre, Rex House, Lower Regent St, London SW1.

*Bus Service.* There is no direct bus service from London to Istanbul, but there are buses from Brussels, Milan, Salzburg and Vienna. For information and reservations, contact British Rail, Europabus Office, 50 Liverpool Street, London EC2.

*Motorists* usually take four or five days to drive from London to Istanbul, depending on the route and pace. The shortest route, which covers 3000km (c 1875 miles), is via Ostend, Nurnberg, Munich, Salzburg, Lbubjlana, Belgrade, Niş, Sofia, Plovdiv, Haskova, Svelenograd, and Edirne. No visa for Yugoslavia is required for citizens of the UK. Citizens of the USA require a transit visa, which can be obtained at the border. No visa is required in Bulgaria for citizens of the UK or the USA staying in the country more than 24 hours; otherwise a transit visa must be obtained at the border. The Green-Card insurance is valid only for European Turkey, so those planning to travel in Asiatic Turkey should purchase another policy in Istanbul. Motorists planning a tour in Turkey are advised to apply for membership in one of the following organisations: The Automobile Association, Fanum House, Leicester Square, London WC2; the Royal Automobile Club, 83 Pall Mall, London SW1; the American Automobile Association, 8111 Gate House Road, Falls Church, Virginia. These clubs will provide all of the necessary documents, as well as information about rules of the road in force in the countries of transit, advice on routes, and arrangements for repairs and spare parts and assistance in case of emergencies.

*Student Travel.* Accredited students under the age of 28 can stay at youth hostels in Turkey and are entitled to reductions on Turkish airlines, trains, and buses. In order to qualify for these accommodations and reductions, one must produce an International Student Identity Card. For information on student travel in general, contact CIEE, the Council on International Educational Exchange, 777 United Nations Plaza, NY, NY 10017. For information on student travel and accomodations in Turkey, contact either of the following organizations: The Turkish Tourism Organization of Students and Youths, Samanyolu Sk 62/8, Şişli, Istanbul; or The Tourist Department of the Turkish National Youth Organization, Istiklal Cd 471/2, Istanbul.

# II Formalities and Customs

*Passports* are necessary for all foreigners entering Turkey. Citizens of the UK and the USA do not require visas to enter Turkey, but if they wish to remain in the country for more than three months they must apply for an extension at an office of the Tourist Police (see VI Useful Addresses, below).

*Health Regulations.* Vaccination and innoculation are not required for travellers entering Turkey from Europe and North America.

*Currency Regulations.* There are no restrictions on the amount of sterling that a traveller may take out of Great Britain. When entering Turkey, foreign currency and travellers' cheques may be exchanged for Turkish currency at exchange bureaux (*Cambio*). When exchanging money, retain your receipt, for this will allow you to exchange your unused Turkish currency when you leave the country.

*Money.* The monetary unit is the Turkish Lira (TL), divided into 100 *kuruş* (kr). The Turkish Government issues banknotes of 10, 20, 50, 100, 500, 1000, 5000, and 10,000 TL, as well as nickel coins of 5, 10, 25 and 50 TL.

*Turkish Customs.* On entering Turkey you are allowed to bring in your personal belongings, sporting, camping, and photographic equipment, 250gm of coffee, a litre of alcohol, 200 cigarettes, and 50 cigars. If you are carrying a portable radio, tape-recorder or electric typewriter they may be recorded in your passport, in which case you must have these in your possession when you leave the country. Antiquities may not be taken out of Turkey under any circumstances, so if you buy anything old (and here the definition of what is an antique is quite vague) be sure to have it validated by the merchant from whom you purchase it. It is also necessary to do this when purchasing Turkish rugs and carpets. Private cars may be brought into Turkey for up to four months without a *carnet de passage*, although trailers and caravans require a customs document. The licence and engine number of your car will be recorded in your passport, and you will not be able to leave the country without it unless you have it officially sealed in a customs warehouse. The baggage of most foreigners entering and leaving Turkey is examined cursorily, and customs and immigration authorities are invariably reasonable and courteous.

# III  Hotels and Pensions

*Hotels* in Istanbul range from luxurious establishments with international standards to simple inns used by Anatolian peasants. The hotels listed below are some of those that cater largely to foreign travellers. *Omission of a hotel from this list does not imply any adverse judgement, nor does inclusion imply any guarantee of satisfaction.* Hotels are required to list their prices, including taxes and service charges. It is also compulsory for hotels to have a book in which guests can register remarks, suggestions, and complaints. These establishments and their complaint books (*sikayet defteri*) are regularly inspected by officials of the Ministry of Tourism. Complaints may also be made directly to the Ministry of Tourism and Information, Gazi Mustafa Kemal Blv 33, Ankara.

Hotels that are licensed and controlled by the Ministry of Tourism are officially categorised, according to their accommodations, as Deluxe, First, Second, Third, and Fourth Class. There are also a few Pensions, which are rated as First, Second, and Third Class. The following is a list of establishments in Istanbul and its environs. (There are also perfectly satisfactory hotels that are licensed and controlled by the Municipality of Istanbul; information concerning these establishments can be obtained at any of the Municipal Bureaux of Information.) Most major hotels are in atlas squares 7,2; 7,3 and 7,4.

DELUXE HOTELS: *Büyük Tarabya*, Tarabya (on the Bosphorus); *Çinar*, Yeşilköy (near the airport); *Divan*, Cumhuriyet Cd 2, Şişli; *Etap Marmara*,Taksim; *Hilton*, Cumhuriyet Cd, Harbiye; *Sheraton*, Taksim.

FIRST-CLASS HOTELS: *Dragos*, Sahil Yolu 12, Cevizli-Maltepe;*Etap Istanbul*, Meşrutiyet Cd, Tepebaşi;*Istanbul Dedeman*, Yildi Posta Cd 50, Esentepe;*Maçka*, Eytam Cd 35, Teşvikiye; *Pera Palas*,Meşrutiyet Cd 98/100.

SECOND-CLASS HOTELS: *Akgün*, Ordu Cd–Haznedar Sk 6; *Anka*, M. Gürani Cd 46,Finidikzade; *Dilson*, Siraselviler Cd 49,Taksim; *Kalyon*, Sahil Yolu, Sultanahmet;*Keban*, Siraselviler 51, Taksim; *Oktay*, Millet Cd 187, Topkapi; *Sözmen*, Millet Cd 104,Çapa; *T. M. T.*, Büyükdere Cd 84, Gayrettepe;*Washington*, Gençtürk Cd 12, Laleli.

THIRD-CLASS HOTELS: *Bale*, Refik Saydam Cd62, Tepebaşi; *Barin*,Fevziye Cd 25, Sehzadebaşi; *Büyük Keban*, Gençtürk Cd 47, Aksaray; *Büyük Londra*,Meşrutiyet Cd, Tepebaşi; *Cidde*, Aksaray Cd 10,Laleli; *Çirağan*, Müvezzi Cd 3, Beşiktaş;*Doru*, Gençtürk Cd 44, Laleli; *Gezi*, Mete Cd 42, Taksim; *Hamit*, Gençtürk Cd 57,Saraçhane; *Harem*, Ambar Sk 1, Selimiye-Üsküdar; *Imparator*, Anadol Sk, Beyoğlu; *Ipek Palas*,Orhaniye Cd 9, Sirkeci; *Nevizade Sk 35*, Galatasaray; *Ipek Palas*, Orhaniye Cd 9, Sirkeci; *Kavak*, Meşrutiyet Cd 201, Tepebaşi;*Konak*, Cumhuriyet Cd, Nispet Sk 9, Elmadağ;*Malkoç*, Mesih Paşa Cd 41, Laleli;*Maya*, Fevziye Cd 19, Şehzadebaşi;*Opera*, Inönü Cd 38–42, Taksim; *Plaza*, Arslan Yatağī 19 (The Street of the Lion's Bed!); *Santral*, Siraselviler Sk—Billurcu Sk 26, Taksim;*Star*, Sağlik Sk 11/13, Gümüşsuyu-Taksim;*Suadiye*, Plaj Yolu 51, Suadiye; *Şahinler*,Koska Cd 10, Laleli; *Topkapi*, Oguzhan Cd 20, Findikzade;Roro, Koska Cd 24, Laleli; *Yenişehir Palas*,Meşrutiyet Cd, Balyoz Sk 113, Tepebaşi;*Zarih*, Vidinli Tevfik Paşa Cd, Harikzadeler Sk 37,Laleli.

FOURTH-CLASS HOTELS: *Ağan*, Saffettin Paşa Sk 6, Sirkeci; *Astor*, Laleli Cd, Aksaray; *Avrupa*, Topçu Cd 32, Talimhane-Taksim; *Aygün*,Azimkar Sk 95, Laleli; *Babaman*, Laleli Cd 19, Aksaray; *Bebek*, Cevdetpaşa Cd 113 Bebek(on the Bosphorus); *Bern*, Muratpaşa Sk, Aksaray; *Burç*, Gençtürk Cd 18, Laleli;*Cinardibi*, Bagdat Cd 326/A, Kadiköy;*Desen*, Şair Haşmet Sk 58, Laleli;*Ebru*, M. Kemal Paşa Cd 29, Aksaray; *Engin*, Tayyareci Sami Sk 17, Kadiköy;*Ensar*, Yeşil Tulumba Sk 39, Laleli; *Eriş*,Demirkapí Cd 17, Sirkeci; *Evren*, Dullar Çilmazi 3,Topkapí; *Eyfel*, Kurultay Sk 19, Laleli; *Florida*, Kemal-paşa Mah. Fevziye Cd 38, Laleli; *Geçit*, Aksaray Cd 5, Aksaray; *Hakan*, Gençtürk Cd 9, Laleli; *Hislon*, Mollagürani Cd 1,Findikzade; *Inka*, Meşrutiye Cd 225, Tepebaşí; *Istanbul*, Gençtürk Cd 38,Laleli; *Karatay*, Sait Efendi Sk 42, Laleli;*Kent*, Haznedar Sk 12, Beyazit; *Kilim*,Millet Cd 85/A, Findikzade;*Metin*, Namik Kemal Cd 25; *Mini Harem*,Iskele Cd 20; *München*, Gençtürk Cd 55, Laleli; *Nazar*, Yeşiltulumba Sk 17, Aksaray; *Nobel*, Aksaray Cd 23, Laleli;*Ons*, Gençtürk Cd—Mimarbaşi Sk 7, Laleli;*Oran*, Harikzadeler Sk 40; *Oriental*, Cihangir Cd 60, Taksim; *Pamukkale*, Ordu Cd, Selimpaşa Sk 8, Aksaray; *Saruhan*, Mesihpaşa Cd 56, Laleli; *Side*, Koska Cd 33; *Sözer*, Topkapí Cd 8; *Tahran*, Mehmet Lütfi ŞekerciSk 21, Aksaray; *Tebriz*, Muratpaşa Sülüklü Sk 7, Aksaray; *Terminal*, Iskender Cd 60, Şişhane-Karaköy; *Tura*, Valide Camii Sk30, Aksaray; *Ulubat*, Kalburcu Mehmet Çeşme Sk 5, Topkapí; *Ulubat*, Kalburcu Mehmet Çeşme Sk 5, Topkapi; *Uzay*, Şair Fitnat Sk 20, Laleli; *Yaşmak*, Ebussuut Cd 18, Sirkeci; *Yilmaz*, Valide Camii Sk 79, Aksaray.

FIRST-CLASS PENSIONS: *Omür Pansiyon*,Zeynep Kamil Sk 39, Beyazit; *Petek Pansiyon*,Alptekin Sk 4, Fenerbahče.

THIRD-CLASS PENSION: *Villa Rifat*, Yilmaz Türk Cd 80, Büyükada (The Princes' Isles).


# IV Restaurants


Istanbul, with its cosmopolitan atmosphere and its rich mixture of ethnic backgrounds, is particularly well-endowed with excellent restaurants (*lokanta*), which cater to every taste and social class. The gastronomic spectrum includes: the deluxe western-style restaurants in the modern sections of the city, the excellent kebab lokantas in the old city, the famous fish-restaurants along the Bosphorus, and the simple little working-men's cookshops found all over the city. It would be impractical to list all of the good restaurants in the city, for there are so very many in every category, so what follows is just a selection. The list is arranged topographically, and does not include the restaurants in the deluxe and first-class hotels. These are often excellent, but travellers wishing to experience something of the flavour of Turkey are advised to eat in those restaurants which the Turks themselves frequent.

RESTAURANTS IN THE MODERN CITY: *Bab Kafeterya*, Yeşilcam Sk 24, Beyoğlu; *Bar Servis*, Tünel Cd 2, Karaköy; *Doğu*, Istiklal Cd 231, Beyoğlu; *Dört Mevsim* (Four Seasons), Istiklal Cd 509, Tünel; *Galata Kulesi* (on top of the Galata Tower); *Geçit* (above the square in Karaköy); *Hací Baba*, Istiklal Cd 49, Taksim; *Hací Salih*, Sakízağací Sk 19, Beyoğlu; *Hallo Pub Cafe*, Halaskargazi Cd 331, Şişli; *Liman Lokantasi* and *Liman Kafeterya*, Yolcusalonu (Maritime Passenger Terminal), Galata;*Malta Köşkü*, Yíldíz Parkí, Beşiktaş; *Pandrossa*, Cumhuriyet Cd 6, Taksim; *Piknik*, Istiklal Cd 40, Beyoğlu; *Rejans*, (The Old Russian Restaurant),Olivio Çíkmazi 17, Galatasaray; *Restaurant 1001*, Síraselviler Cd 61, Taksim, *Restoran 29*, Nisbetiye Cd 29, Etiler; *Sempati Pub*, Halaskargazi Cd 27, Pangaltı; *Suisse Pub*, Cumhuriyet Cd 14, Taksim; *Şamdan*, Harbiye Eytam Cd 12,Şişli; *Şamdan 2*, Nisbetiye Cd 30, Etiler;*Zibni*, Bronz Sk 21, Tesvikiye; *Ziya*,Kemal Cd 21, Nişantaş; *Ziya Turistik Tesisleri*,Muallim Naci Cd 109, Ortaköy.

RESTAURANTS IN THE OLD CITY: *Pandelis*, Eminönü Meydaní (in the upper level of the gatehouse of the Spice Bazaar); *Old Pandelis*, Zindankapí Cd 35, Eminönü; *Konyalí Lezzet*,in the Fourth Courtyard of Topkapí Sarayí;*Canli Balík*, on the shore road beside the fishing-port in Kumkapí; *Havuzlu Lokantasi*, in the Covered Bazaar; *Karíşma Sen*,(in Turkish, this means Mind Your Own Business!), on the Marmara shore road below the Blue Mosque;*Deutsches*

*Cafe*, Teceddüt Sk 66, Aksaray; *Karides*, on the Marmara shore road in Yenikapí;*Piyerloti Kahvesi*, in the Eyüp cemetery above the Golden Horn; *Omür Lokantasí*, Yeni Londra Asfaltí, Bakirköy, on the airport road outside the old city; *Beyti*, Orman Sk 33, Florya, on theMarmara coast near the airport.

RESTAURANTS ALONG THE BOSPHORUS: Arnavutköy: *Kuyu, Kaptan, Şölen*, Yeni Köşk;Bebek: *Yeni Güneş* ; Rumeli Hisar: *Karaca*; Emirgan: *Abdullah's, Sarıköşk*;Istinye: *Fondüç*; Yeniky: *Iskele*;Tarabya: *Garaj, Gemi, Kösem, Balıkçil, Haluk, Palet, Façyo, Zarifler*; Kireçburnu: *Bízím*; Büyükdere: *Andoni, Şamdan 1*; Sariyer: *Canli Balík, Sahil Aile Lokantasí* (on the quay behind the mosque, in an extremely picturesque location); Rumeli Kavağí: several good and inexpensive restaurants near the ferry-station; Anadolu Hisar: *Yalí*.

RESTAURANTS IN THE PRINCES' ISLES: Heybeliada: *Yeni Park*; Büyükada: *Akasya, Kapri, Neptün*.

**Turkish Food and Drink** The Turkish cuisine is one of the best and most varied in the world, and in Istanbul you can dine like a Sultan, if you know how and what to order. This is no problem in a *lokanta*, the simple restaurants where the working-class people eat, for there you simply walk up to the counter and choose what you want from the pots on the steam table. But in higher-class restaurants the procedure is more complex. Traditionally, one begins with cold hors d'oeuvres (*soğuk meze*), selected from a huge tray. Then, if one wishes to, one can order a few hot hors d'oeuvres (*sícak meze*). After that comes the main course, which may be followed by a sweet (*tatlí*) and a cup of Turkish coffee (*kahve*).

The *Menu* below includes most of the popular dishes that are served in Istanbul restaurants:

**Soğuk Meze**, Cold Hors d'Oeuvres

*Beyaz peynir*, White goat cheese; *Kaser peynir*, Hard cheese resembling cheddar; *Zeytin*, Olives *Lakerda*, Salted bonito; *Tarama*, Carp roe; *Beğendi*, Aubergine puree; *Yaprak dolması*, Stuffed green peppers; *Biber dolmasí*, Stuffed green peppers; *Domates dolmasí*, Stuffed tomatoes; *Lahana dolmasí*, Stuffed cabbage; *Beğin*, Brain; *Cacík*, Chopped cucumbers with yogurt and garlic; *Imam bayíldí* (literally, 'The Imam Fainted'), Aubergines with parsley; *Midye pilakísí*, Mussels cooked with olive oil and served cold

**Salata**, Salads

*Domates salatasí*, Tomato salad; *Yeşil salata*, Green salad; *Salatalík salatasí*, Cucumber salad; *Çoban salata* (Shepherd's salad), Chopped peppers, tomatoes, lettuce, cucumbers, and celery; *Fasulye ezmesi*, Dried kidney bean salad; *Pancar salatasí*, Beet salad; *Piyaz*, Dried white kidney bean salad; *Patates ezmesi*, Mashed potato salad; *Patlícan salatasí*, Aubergine salad; *Marul*, Romaine lettuce; *Ispanakökü salatasí*, Spinach root salad; *Yoğurtlu kabak salatasí*, Zucchini salad with yogurt

**Sícak Meze**, Hot Hors d'Oeuvres

Among the most popular hot *meze* dishes are the various types of *börek*, thin layers of pastry with various fillings, such as the following: *Peynerli börek, Börek* with cheese filling; *Etli börek, Börek* with minced meat filling; *Pastírmíli börek, Börek* with filling of dried spiced beef; *Tavuklu börek, Börek* with chicken filling; *Ispanaklí börek, Börek* with spinach filling; *Mantarlí börek, Börek* with mushroom filling

Other popular hot *meze* dishes are the following: *Arnavut ciğer*, Chopped liver and onions; *Midye tavasí*, Fried mussels; *Midye dolmasí*, Fried mussels served in the shell and stuffed with *pilav*; *Beğin tavasí*, Fried brain; *Koç yumurtasí*, Fried sheep's testicles; *Et sauté*, Thin slices of meat sauteed in tomato and pepper sauce; *Menemen*, Eggs scrambled with green and red peppers and white cheese; *Kabak kízartmasí*, Fried zucchini; *Patlícan kízartmasí*, Fried aubergines; *Izgara köfte*, Grilled meat balls; *Patates köfte*, Potato crocquets; *Patates kízartmasí*, Fried potatoes

**Etler**, Meat Dishes

Meat (and fish) may be prepared in several ways: grilled (*ízgara*), fried (*tava*), roasted (*kízartma*), in casserole (*güveç*), grilled on a skewer (*şiş*). The general types of meat are the following: *Sığír*, Beef; *Dana*, Veal; *Kuzu*, Lamb; *Pirzola*, Lamb chops; *Kuzu budu rostosu*, Roast leg of lamb; *Kíyma*, Minced meat; *Ciğer*, Liver; *Yaban domuz*, Wild boar; *Tavşan*, Rabbit

Among the most popular meat dishes are the various types of *kebabs*. *Şiş kebab*, Lamb skewered on a spit with tomatoes and onions and grilled over a charcoal fire; *Tas kebab*, Lamb stew with rice and vegetables; *Çöp kebab*, Same ingredients as in *tas kebab*, but cooked in a wax-paper envelope; *Döner kebab*, Pressed lamb cooked on a rotating spit over a charcoal fire and carved off in thin slices; *Bursa kebab*, Döner kebab served with yoğurt and tomato sauce, sometimes called *Iskender kebab*; *Kâğít kebab*, Meat, vegetables, and herbs in a wine sauce, and cooked in a wax-paper envelope; *Bahçevan kebabí*, Meat cooked with all of the vegetables one would find in typical kitchen garden; *Islim kebabí*, Meat and aubergines cooked in a covered casserole

Other popular meat dishes are: *Hünkar beğendi* ('The Sultan's Favourite'), Puréed aubergine served with chicken or meat; *Kadín budu* ('The Lady's Thigh'), Ground meat and rice first formed into oval patties and then dipped into beaten eggs and fried; *Karníyarik* ('Belly Split-Open'), Ground meat cooked together with aubergines; *Güveç*, Meat or poultry baked together with vegetables in a casserole; *Kíş Türlüsü*, A winter (kíş) dish cooked with meat, carrots, celery, potatoes, and leeks

**Balík**, Fish

*Lüfer*, Bluefish; *Levrek*, Bass; *Üskümrü*, Mackerel; *Kílíç*, Swordfish; *Kílíç şişte*, Swordfish skewered on a spit and cooked over a charcoal fire; *Barbunya*, Red mullet; *Tekir*, Small red mullet; *Palamut*, Bonito; *Kalkan*, Turbot; *Mercan*, Bream; *Dil*, Sole; *Çínakok*, A species of small bluefish; *Som balíğí*, Salmon; *Alabalík*, Trout

**Tavuk**, Poultry

*Tavuk*, Chicken (it also means poultry in general); *Piliç*, Young chicken; *Piliç kağítta*, Chicken cooked in a waxed-paper envelope; *Tavukklu beğendi*, Chicken in egg purée; *Piliç dolmasí*, Stuffed roast chicken; *Tavuklu güveç*, Chicken casserole; *Çerkaz tavuk* (Circassian chicken), Chicken with walnut sauce; *Hindi dolmasí*, Stuffed turkey; *Ördek*, Duck; *Kaz*, Goose; *Çulluk*, Woodcock; *Sülün*, Pheasant; *Bíldírcín*, Quail; *Keklik*, Partridge

**Sebze**, Vegetables

*Patates*, Potatoes; *Domates*, Tomatoes; *Pirinç*, Rice (*Pilav* when cooked); *Bezelye*, Peas; *Havuc*, Carrots; *Lahana*, Cabbage; *Patlícan*, Aubergine; *Pancar*, Beets; *Salatalík*, Cucumbers; *Çalí fasulye*, Green string beans; *Fasulye*, Green beans; *Fasulye plakisi*, White beans; *Bamyas*, Okra; *Enginar*, Artichoke; *Karníbahar*, Cauliflower; *Kabak*, Zucchini; *Biber*, Green pepper; *Soğan*, Onion; *Ispanak*, Spinach; *Pírasa*, Leeks; *Kuşkonmaz*, Asparagus; *Maydonoz*, Parsley; *Kereviz*, Root celery; *Híyar*, Cucumber

**Çorba**, Soup

*Tavuk çorbasí*, Chicken soup; *Domateslí çorbasí*, Tomato soup; *Domateslí pirinç çorbasí*, Tomato and rice soup; *Mercimek çorbasí*, Lentil soup; *Kírmízí mercimek çorbasí*, Red lentil soup; *Işkembe çorbasí*, Tripe soup; *Dügün çorbasí* (Wedding Soup), Soup with meat, vegetables, eggs, and paprika; *Yayla çorbasí*, Beef soup with yogurt

**Meyva**, Fruit

*Elma*, Apple; *Portakal*, Orange; *Grepfrut*, Grapefruit; *Üzüm*, Grapes; *Kavun*, Melon; *Karpuz*, Watermelon; *Muz*, Banana; *Şeftali*, Peach; *Kiraz*, Cherry; *Vişne*, Sour cherry; *Erik*, Plum; *Çilek*, Strawberry

**Tatlí**, Sweets and Puddings

*Sütlaç*, Rice pudding; *Muhallebi*, Pudding made from milk, rice, and rose-water; *Baklava*, Many-layered pastry filled with walnuts, baked and soaked in syrup; *Lokma*, Flour dessert fried in oil and soaked in syrup; *Kadín gobeği*, ('The Lady's

Navel'), Doughnut soaked in syrup; *Gül receli*, Rose jam; *Ayva marmaladí*, Quince marmalade; *Ayva kompostu*, Stewed quince; *Aşure* ('Noah's Pudding'), Sweet pudding with walnuts, raisins, and peas; *Dondurma*, Ice cream; *Bal kabağí tatlísí*, Pumpkin dessert; *Helva*, Dessert made with farina and flour mixed with nuts and served with cinnamon; *Yoğurt tatlísi*, Pudding made with yogurt and eggs; *Portakal peltesi*, Orange pudding; *Revani*, Dessert made with farina, flour, and eggs soaked in syrup; *Sarığí burma*, Rich, flaky dessert with nut filling; *Tulumba tatlísi*, Rich flour dessert with almond flavouring; *Ekmek kadayífí*, Crumpet in syrup; *Bülbül Yuvasí*, ('The Nightingale's Nest'), Shredded wheat with pistachios and syrup

**Beverages.** When dining, Turks like to imbibe *rakí*, a strong (87 proof) anis-flavoured drink. They rarely drink it straight, mixing it half-and-half with water, when it turns milky white. *Rakí* is definitely an acquired taste, but when one gets used to it it goes very well with Turkish food. In recent years Turks have begun to drink more wine (*şarab*) with their meals. Most restaurants have a wide selection of red (*kírmízí şarab*), white (*beyaz şarab*), and rosé (*pembe şarab*) wines. The best-known brands are Doluca (red and white), Kavak (white), Trakya (white), Dikmen (red and white), Yakut (red), and Lal (rosé). There are three brands of bottled beer, Tuborg, Efes, and Tekel, which can occasionally be found on tap. Tekel, the government monopoly, also puts out vodka (*votka*) and cognac (*kanyak*), neither of which is recommended, as well as a variety of liqueurs, all of which are very sweet. Soft drinks include Fruko, a lemon drink, as well as the local varieties of Coca Cola and Pepsi Cola. Turks wash down their food with copious quantities of bottled water (*su*) and mineral water (*maden suyu*), which is excellent and cheap. They also drink *ayran*, a kind of liquid yogurt, which goes very well with Turkish foods. Here and there in the old city one can find a *bozahane*, a café that sells *boza*, a delicious drink made from grain and slightly fermented. And an excellent breakfast drink, particularly in winter, is *salep*, a thick beverage made from wheat and served piping hot. *Salep* goes very well with a *simit*, a kind of ring-shaped pretzel, which are carried in huge stacks by itinerant vendors. They are quite delicious, and make an excellent snack when strolling around town.

All Turkish meals end with coffee (*kahve*), served in a small cup with varying amounts of sugar (*şeker*). If you want no sugar in your coffee say *sade*, a little sugar: *az şekerli*, medium-sweet: *orta şekerli*, sweet: *şekerli*. You can also order tea (*çay*), which is served in a small bell-waisted glass with several cubes of sugar on the side. The tea is usually bitter and of very inferior quality, but you will probably end up drinking it anyway, because it is such a basic element in the Turkish way of life.

# V  Transport

*Automobile.* Travellers motoring in Turkey can obtain free assistance and advice from the Turkish Touring and Automobile Society (Türkiye Turing ve Otomobil Kurumu, or тток. Their main office in Istanbul is at Halaskargazi Cd 364, near Şişli Square (Tel: 407127). тток publishes a quarterly pamphlet in English entitled *Istanbul: A Handbook for Tourists*, which contains, among other things, a list of recommended car-repair shops in Istanbul.

*Buses.* The city has an extensive network of buses, many of which go out to the suburbs along the Marmara and both the European and Asian shores of the Bosphorus. Buses bear signs showing their route and destination; when you get aboard let the conductor know where you are going and he will tell you the price of the ticket and inform you when you have reached your stop. Buses are usually packed, and unless one gets on at the first stop it is usually impossible to find a seat.

*Taxis* are designated either by a sign or by a striped border around the chassis. All taxis have meters and are required to use them,so that it is not necessary to bargain about fares. There are taxi-ranks all over town,the most popular being at Taksim, Galatasaray, Beşiktaş, Karaköy, Eminönü, and Beyazit.

*Public taxis (dolmuş).* A *dolmuş* is a public taxi that travels a fixed route. You pay only for the seat that you occupy, and fares are posted at designated *dolmuş* stands. The *dolmuş* is a venerable Istanbul institution, and these often aged automobiles are the best and cheapest form of public transport in the city.

*Car Rental.* For those courageous enough to venture into Istanbul traffic on their own, here are the addresses of a few car-rental agencies: Genco, Şehit Muhtar Cd 13; Gökaltay, 44/4 İnönü Cd; Kayhan Turizm, Mete Cd 26/4. All three of these agencies are in the vicinity of Taksim Square.

*Train Service.* A commuter train from Sirkeci Station runs out along the Marmara coast to the beach resort at Florya. Service is frequent and inexpensive.

*Tünel.* This is the venerable funicular railway that ascends from Karaköy (near the Galata end of the Galata Bridge) to the lower end of Istiklal Cd. The fare is extremely cheap and the ride takes just two minutes. This is a tremendous saving in time and energy, for the climb up from Karaköy is exhausting and takes at least half-an-hour.

*Ferries* leave from on and around the Galata Bridge to all parts of the city and its suburbs. Locations of the various lines are posted on the bridge and on the quays on both banks of the Golden Horn; schedules and itineraries are posted at all ferry stations. (For help in reading ferry-schedules see IX The Turkish Language, below). Ferries on the upstream side of the Galata Bridge go up the Golden Horn (Haliç), calling at various stations on both shores before reaching the last stop at Eyüp. Ferries for the Princes' Isles (Adalar) and the Asiatic suburbs on the Marmara shore leave from the landing on the downstream side of the bridge, while Bosphorus (Boğaziçi) ferries depart from the quay on the right bank of the Golden Horn, downstream from the Galata Bridge. The large maritime station in Galata, at the confluence of the Bosphorus and the Golden Horn is the terminus for longer-range ferries to ports in the Sea of Marmara, the Marmara islands, the Dardanelles, and the Turkish Aegean islands of Imbros and Boz-caada, the ancient Tenedos. The fares are very low and the ferries are quite comfortable and usually not too crowded. And there is no more exciting way to see the city, particularly when steaming up the Bosphorus on a fine day.

# VI Useful Addresses

*Information Bureaux (Danışma)*. Ministry of Tourism Regional Directorate, Meşrutiyet Cd 57; information offices in the Hilton Arcade, the Covered Bazaar, the Hippodrome, the Maritime Passenger Terminal (*Yolcu Salonu*) in Galata, at Sirkeci Station, and at Yeşilköy Airport.

*Tourist Police*. Headquarters (*Emnivet Karakol*) in Bahçekapí (near Sirkeci Station); also offices at Alemdar Karakol, near the Blue Mosque; the Maritime Passenger Terminal in Galata; Sirkeci Station; and at Yeşilköy Airport.

*Airlines and Travel Agents*. Almost all airlines and travel agents have their offices on Cumhuriyet Cd between the Hilton and Taksim Square. BA is at No.10; THY is at No.131; Cooks/Wagon-Lits at No.22; Pan Am and Türk Express (the local affiliate of American Express) are in the Hilton Arcade.

*Shipping Lines*. Turkish Maritime Lines (*Denizcelik Bankasí*) and Italian Adriatic have representatives at the Maritime Passenger Terminal in Galata.

*Post Offices* (PTT). Central Post Office, Yeni Postahane Sk 25 (near Sirkeci Station) (open 8 am–9 pm daily, including Sunday); branch post offices on Istiklal Cd just off Galatasaray Square (open 9 am–5 pm, Mon–Fri, 9 am–1 pm, Sat), and just off Taksim Square (open 9 am–7 pm, Mon–Fri, 9 am–1 pm Sat).

*Hospitals (Hastahane)*. American Hospital (Amiral Bristol Hastahane), Güzelbahçe, Nişantaş; German Hospital, Síraselviler Cd, Taksim; French Hospital, behind the Divan Hotel, Taksim; Beyoğlu First-Aid Hospital, Síraselviler Cd, Taksim.

*Religious Services*. Protestant: St. Helena's Church (Anglican), Meşrutiyet Cd 34 (in the grounds of the British Consulate); Dutch Chapel (non-denominational), Postacilar Sk 4 (behind the Dutch Consulate). Roman Catholic: St. Espirit, Cumhuriyet Cd (across from the Hilton); St. Antoine, Istiklal Cd (near Galatasaray Square); St. Louis des Francais, Istiklal Cd (on the grounds of the French Consulate). Jewish: Neve Shalom Synagogue, Büyük Hendek Sk 61 (near the Galata Tower); Beth Israel Synagogue, Şişli Square. Greek Orthodox: Aghia Trianda, Meşelik Sk (just off Taksim Square).

*Consulates*. UK, 26 Meşrutiyet Cd (just off Galatasaray Square); USA, 106 Meşrutiyet Cd (next to the Pera Palas Hotel).

*Banks*. Any bank with a 'Kambiyo' sign will change money or cash travellers' cheques. For foreign travellers, the most convenient and efficient bank is the *Türk Díş Ticaret Bankasí*, which is affiliated with the Bank of America; its main office is at Cumhuriyet Cd 207 (just across from the Hilton).

# VII Museums and Monuments

The table below gives the hours of admission to the various museums and monuments in Istanbul. (The mosques of Istanbul are not included on this list; they are open during the period of the five occasions of daily prayer, that is, from just before sunrise until dusk. The larger mosques are open throughout the day. The smaller ones may be closed between the hours of prayer, but if you stand patiently by the front door someone inevitably will fetch the caretaker, who will open up the mosque for you.) The opening hours listed below may vary by half-an-hour or an hour depending on the season. All museums and monuments are closed on the following national holidays: 23 April, 1 May, 19 May, 27 May, 30 August, 29 October. They are also closed during the religious holidays of Şeker Bayram and Kurban Bayram, whose dates are regulated by the Islamic lunar calendar.

HOURS OF ADMISSION TO THE MUSEUMS AND MONUMENTS OF ISTANBUL

**Haghia Sophia** (*Aya Sofya*): 10–5 every day except Mon.
**Topkapí Sarayí**: 9:30–5:30 every day except Tues.
**Archaeological Museum** (*Arkeoloji Müzesi*): 10–5 every day in summer, closed Mon in winter.
**Çinili Köşk**: 10–5 every day except Mon.
**Museum of the Ancient Orient** (*Eski Şark Eserleri Müzesi*): 9:30–12, 1–5 every day except Mon and Tues.
**Mosaic Museum** (*Mozayik Müzesi*): closed for repairs.
**Basilica Cistern** (*Yerebatansaray*): closed for repairs.
**Museum of Turkish and Islamic Art** (*Türk ve Islam Eserleri Müzesi*): 10–5 every day except Mon.
**Municipal Museum** (*Şehir Müzesi*): 10–12, 1:30–4:30 every day, closed on the fifth day of the month.
**Church of the Pammakaristos** (*Fethiye Camii*): 9:30–4:30 every day except Wed.
**Church of St. Saviour in Chora** (*Kariye Camii*): 9:30–5 every day except Tues.
**Castle of the Seven Towers** (*Yedikule*): 9:30–5 every day except Mon.
**Galata Tower** (*Galata Kulesi*): 9–6 every day; upper floors open in evening.
**Military Museum** (*Askeri Müze*): 9:30–12, 1:30–5 every day except Mon and Tues.
**Atatürk Museum**: 10–12, 1:30–5:30 every day except the 15th of the month.
**Yíldíz Sarayí**: 9–11, 1:30–4 every day except Mon and Tues.
**Dolmabahçe Sarayí**: every day 9:30–11,1:30–4:30 except Mon and Sat.
**Naval Museum** (*Deniz Müzesi*): 9–12, 1:30–5 every day except Mon and Tues.
**Rumeli Hisari**: 10–4:30 every day
**Church of Haghia Eirene** (*Aya Irene*): 9:30–4:30 every day except Mon and Tues.
**Ibrahim Paşa Sarayí**: every day 9:30–5except Mon.
**Beylerbey Sarayí**: every day 9:30–12, 1:30–4:30except Mon and Sat.
**Mevlevi Tekke, Tünel**: every day 9:30–12, 1:30–4:30except Mon.
**Aynalíkavak Kasrí**: every day 9:30–4:00except Mon and Thur.

# VIII Entertainment

*The Istanbul Festival.* From mid-June through mid-July each year there is an international cultural festival in Istanbul, in which outstanding artists from all over the world give performances in the city. Many of these performances are held in settings of great beauty and historic interest, as was the case when Mozart's 'Abduction from the Seraglio' was put on in Topkapí Sarayí, where the composer originally set the opera. For information and tickets consult the office of the Istanbul Festival at the Atatürk Kültür Merkezi in Taksim Square.

*The Opera House* (Atatürk Kültür Merkezi) puts on a full season of opera, ballet and symphonic music, featuring both Turkish and foreign artists. Check with the box-office of the Opera House for information and tickets.

*Folk-Dancing.* The Turkish National Folk-Dance Group is one of the best ethnic dance-groups in the world. The number and variety of Turkish folk-dances reflects the great depth and diversity of the cultures that have flourished in Anatolia and that have been assimilated by the people of Turkey. The Group performs in the colourful native costumes of the various regions of Anatolia where the dances originate and they are accompanied by the lively music from those areas. Performances are given at both the Açík Hava Tiyatrosu (Open-Air Theatre) near the Hilton, and also in Rumeli Hisarí, the ancient Ottoman fortress on the European shore of the Bosphorus. There can be few more beautiful settings, watching the performance against the background of the castle and the Bosphorus flowing by it, while across the strait the lights twinkle in the seaside villages on the Asian shore.

*Cinemas.* There are a number of cinemas that exhibit European and American films in their original language, with subtitles in Turkish. The best of these cinemas are the *Site* and the *Kent*, which are on Halaskargazi Cd near Şişli Square, and the *Konak*, which is on Vali Konak Cd in Nişantaş.

*Night Clubs and Shows.* The *Hilton*, the *Sheraton* and the *International* all have night-clubs with dancing, as does the Kervansaray, which is on Cumhuriyet Cd between the Hilton and Taksim Square. All of these night-clubs have shows featuring Turkish folk-dance groups and belly-dancers. For a typically Turkish night-club go to the *Taksim Belediye Gazinosu*, just off Taksim Square. The only legal gambling in the city is at the *Istanbul Casino*, in the basement of the Hilton. The casino is open only to foreigners, so passports must be shown to gain admittance.

*The Galata Tower.* There is a night-club on the top floor of the Galata Tower, and visitors ought to go there at least once to enjoy the view of the city lights sparkling on the shores of the Golden Horn and the Bosphorus.

*The Bosphorus by Night.* Perhaps the best way to spend an evening in Istanbul is to stroll down to the Galata Bridge at sunset, when the polluted air of Stamboul crowns the old city in a roseate glow and when the foul waters of the Horn are indeed golden. Then board a ferry going up the Bosphorus and sit out on the fantail, watching the lights of the Bosphorus villages on the European and Asian shores, the soaring arc of the Bosphorus Bridge, and the brooding fortresses of Rumeli and Anadolu Hisar. It is an unforgettable sight, particularly under the light of a full moon.

# IX  The Turkish Language

**A Turkish Primer.** Although Turkish may look and sound a bit strange at first, it is not really a difficult language. With a little work and practice, a visitor can soon learn enough basic Turkish to communicate with the people of Istanbul. (An excellent primer is 'Teach Yourself Turkish' by Geoffrey Lewis, Hodder & Stoughton, London.)

**The Sounds of Turkish.** All letters have one and only one sound; no letters are silent. Vowels have their short continental value; i.e. *a* as in father (the rarely used *â* sounds rather like *ay*), *e* as in get, *i* as in sit, *o* as in doll, *u* as in bull; *ı* (undotted) is between *i* and *u*, somewhat as the final *a* in Anna; *ö* is as in German or the *u* in further; *ü* is as in German or the French *u* in tu. Consonants are as in English except for the following: *c* as *j* in jam, *ç* as *ch* in church; *g* is always hard as in give, never soft as in gem; *ğ* is almost silent, tending to lengthen the preceding vowel; *s* is always unvoiced as in sit, never like *z*; *ş* is as *s* in sugar. Turkish is very lightly accented, most often on the last syllable, but all syllables should be clearly and almost evenly articulated.

**Numbers.** 1 – *bir*; 2 – *iki*; 3 – *üç*; 4 – *dört*; 5 – *beş*; 6 – *altı*; 7 – *yedi*; 8 – *sekiz*; 9 – *dokuz*; 10 – *on*; 11 – *on bir*; 12 – *on iki*; 13 – *on üç*; 14 – *on dört*; 15 – *on beş*; 16 – *on altı*; 17 – *on yedi*; 18 – *on sekiz*; 19 – *on dokuz*; 20 – *yirmi*; 21 – *yirmi bir*; 30 – *otuz*; 40 – *kırk*; 50 – *elli*; 60 – *altmış*; 70 – *yetmiş*; 80 – *seksen*; 90 – *doksan*; 100 – *yüz*; 101 – *yüz bir*; 200 – *iki yüz*; 300 – *üç yüz*; 1000 – *bin*; 1001 – *bin bir*; 1,000,000 – *bir milyon*; one-half – *yarım*; one and one-half – *bir büçük*, zero – *sıfır*;

**Clock and Calendar:** Day – *gün*; Sunday – *Pazar*; Monday – *Pazartesi*; Tuesday – *Salı*; Wednesday – *Çarşamba*; Thursday – *Perşembe*; Friday – *Cuma*; Saturday – *Cumartesi*; month – *Ay*; January – *Ocak*; February – *Şubat*; March – *Mart*; April – *Nisan*; May – *Mayıs*; June – *Haziran*; July – *Temmuz*; August – *Augustos*; September – *Elül*; October – *Ekim*; November – *Kasím*; December – *Aralık*; week – *hafta*; hour, time – *saat*; What time is it? – *Saat kaç?*; one o'clock – *saat bir*; ten past two – *ikiyi on geçiyor*; twenty to five – *beşe yirmi var*; at six o'clock – *saat altıda*; morning – *sabah*; noon – *öğle*; afternoon – *öğleden sonra*; evening – *akşam*; night – *gece*; today – *bügun*; yesterday – *dün*; tomorrow – *yarín*; year – *yil, sene*.

**Everyday Words and Expressions.** Hello – *merhaba*; I – *ben*; we – *biz*; you – *sen* (singular), *siz* (plural); he, she, it – *o*; they – *onlar*; this – *bu*; that – *şu* (near), *o* (remote); Where? – *Nerede?*; here – *burada*; there – *şurada* (near), *orada* (remote); When? – *Ne zaman?*; Why? – *Niçin?*; What? – *Ne?*; Yes – *Evet*; No – *Hayır*; very, much – *çok*; little – *az*; large – *büyük*; small – *küçük*; and – *ve*; good – *iyi*; very good – *çok iyi*; bad – *fena*; very bad – *çok fena*; now – *şimdi*; later – *sonra*; before – *evvel*; fast – *çabuk*; slow – *yavaş*; open – *açık*; closed – *kapalí*; forbidden – *yasak*; please – *lütfen*; Thank you – *Teşekkürederim* (or simply *merci*); What do you want – *Ne istiyorsunuz?*; I want tea. – *Çay istiyorum.*; I don't want tea. – *Çay istemiyorum*; Is there any tea? – *Çay var mí?*; There isn't any tea. – *Çay yok.*; Do you understand? – *Anlıyormusun?*; I understand. – *Anlıyorum.*; I don't understand – *Anlamiyorum.*; How are you? – *Nasílsíníz?*; I'm fine. – *Iyiyim.*; Not so good – *Şöyle böyle.*; nice, pretty – *güzel*; very nice – *çok güzel*; Good morning. – *Gün aydín.*; Good evening. – *Iyi akşamlar.*; Good night. –

*Iyi geceler.*; Sir – *Efendim*; Mr. – *Bay*; Mrs. – *Bayan*; man – *adam*; men – *adamlar*; woman – *kadín*; What is your name? – *Isminiz ne?*; Where are you from? – *Nerelísíníz?*; I'm English/American. – *Ben Ingliz/ Amerikalí.*; Welcome – *Hoş geldiniz* (In response one says *Hoş bulduk.*); Goodbye. – *Allahísmarladík* (said by the person leaving). *Güle güle* (said by the person who remains).

**Getting Around Town.** Street – *Sokak*; Road – *Yol*; Avenue – *Cadde*; Boulevard – *Bulvar*; Square – *Meydan*; Bus – *Otobüs*; Taxi – *Taxi*; Train – *Tren*; What time does the train leave/arrive? – *Tren ne zaman kalkíp/varíyor?* automobile – *oto*; petrol – *benzin*; station – *istasyon*; ticket – *bilet*; right – *sağ*; left – *sol*; straight ahead – *doğru*; mosque – *cami*; church – *kilise*; museum – *müze*; cinema – *sinema*; theatre – *tiyatro*.

**At the Hotel.** Hotel – *Otel*; room – *oda*; Do you have a room? – *Oda var mí?*; Yes, there is a room. – *Oda var.* There is no room. – *Oda yok.* For how many people? – *Kaç kişi?*; One person – *Bir kişi*; Two people – *Iki kişi*; For how many days/nights? – *Kaç gün/gece?*; How many rooms/beds? – *Kaç oda/yatak?*; single room – *tek oda*; double room – *çift oda*; toilet – *tuvalet*; bath – *banyo*; with bath – *banyolu*; without bath – *banyosuz*; shower – *duş*; hot water – *sícak su*; soap – *sabun*; towel – *havlu*; toilet paper – *tuvalet kâğít*; key – *anahtar*; The bill, please. – *Hesap, lütfen.*

**At the Restaurant.** Restaurant – *lokanta*; meal – *yemek* (it also means "to eat"); menu – *yemek listesi*; waiter – *garson*; What is there to eat? – *Yemek ne var?*; knife – *bíçak*; fork – *çatal*; spoon *kaşík*; plate – *tabak*; napkin – *pecete*; glass – *bardak*; cup – *fincan*; bottle – *şişe*; water – *su*; milk – *süt*; bread – *ekmek*; salt – *tuz*; pepper – *biber*; without oil – *yagsíz.* (A more detailed vocabulary is given in the section on Turkish food.)

**In the Market.** Market – *Pazar*, or *Çarşí*; Shop – *Dukkan*; How much is this? – *Bu, ne kadar?*; Too much – *Çok pahalí*; Cheap – *Ucuz*; How many? – *Kaç tane?*; One item. – *Bir tane*; One more. – *Bir tane daha.*; Bigger. – *Daha büyük*; Smaller. – *Daha küçük.*; Half a kilo. – *Yarím kilo.*; 250 grams – *iki yüz elli gram*; Money – *Para*; eliminate. – Do you have change? – *Bozuk para var mi?*

**Emergencies.** Hospital – *Hastahane*; doctor – *doktor*; pharmacy – *eczane*; first aid – *Ilk sihhi imdad*; sick – *hasta*; I'm sick. – *Hastayím.*; I want a doctor. – *doktor istiyorum.* There's a fire – *Yangín var.*

**Reading a Ferry Schedule and Purchasing a Ticket.** Timetables are posted on all ferries and ticket booths. There are two sets of timetables, one for Sundays and holidays (*Pazar Günü ve Tatil Günü*) and one for weekdays (*Pazardan Başka*). The timetables give the stations and arrival and departure times for the three lines that terminate on or around the Galata Bridge (*Köprü*), with separate listings for each direction. The lines are: 1. Up and down the Golden Horn (*Halíç*); 2. To and from Usküdar, Kadiköy, the Princes' Isles (*Adalar*) and Yalova; 3. Up and down the Bosphorus (*Boğaz* or *Boğaziçi*). The names and times for the ferry-stations on the European shore of the Marmara are printed in black, while those on the Asian shore are printed in red. In purchasing a ticket, simply tell the clerk the name of your destination, the class of ticket, and whether you want a one-way or round-trip ticket. The following vocabulary will enable you to read the timetables and to purchase a ticket.

*Köprüdan Boğaza* From the Galata Bridge to (up) the Bosphorus; *Boğazdan Köprüye* From (down) the Bosphorus to the Galata Bridge; *Köprüdan Haliça* From the Galata Bridge to (up) the Golden Horn; *Haliçdan Köprüye* From (down) the Golden Horn to the Galata Bridge; *Köprüdan Adalara* From the Galata Bridge to the Princes' Isles; *Adalardan Köprüye* From the Princes' Isles to the Galata Bridge; *Kalkiş* (K.) Departure time; *Variş* Arrival time; *Hat, Hattî* Itinerary; *Günleri yapílí* Days operating; *Günleri yapílmaz* Days not operating; *Hergün* Daily; *Expres* Express; *Birinci sínif* First class; *Ikinci sínif* Second class; *Gidiş* One-way ticket; *Gidiş-Geliş* Round-trip ticket; *Iyi yolculuklar* Have a pleasant journey.

# X  General Information

**National Holidays.** The Turkish National Holidays, when all offices, shops, schools, banks and museums are closed, are as follows: 23 April (National Sovereignty Day and Children's Day), 1 May (Spring Day), 19 May (Sport Day), 27 May (Constitution Day), 30 August (Victory Day), and 29 October (Republic Day). There are also two religious holidays when all of the above places are closed; these are Şeker Bayram (3 days) and Kurban Bayram (4 days); the dates of these holidays are regulated according to the Moslem lunar calendar and thus occur 12 days earlier each year.

**Working Hours.***Offices*: Weekdays 9–12, 1:30–5; Sat. 9–1; Closed Sun. & Holidays.
*Shops* (varies): Weekdays 9–1, 2–7; Sat. 9–12, 1–7; Closed Sun & holidays.
*Banks*: 9–1, 2–5 (9–2 in summer); Sat 9–12.
*Covered Bazaar*: 8–6:30 every day except Sun.

**Telephones and Postal Information.** Stamps (*Posta pulu*) are sold only at Post Offices (for location see VI Useful Addresses, above). Special delivery is called *expres* and registered mail is *taahhütlü*. Telegrams may also be sent at Post Offices. There are numerous telephones (*telefon*) all over the city, particularly at kiosks, and also in Post Offices. They are operated by metal discs called *jetons*, which may be purchased at Post Offices. Most cities in the USA and Europe can now be dialled direct from Istanbul; this can be done most conveniently at the larger hotels, where there are English-speaking telephone operators.

*Newspapers (Gazete) and Books (Kitap).* Most British newspapers and the 'International Herald Tribune' are on sale in the deluxe and first-class hotels and at a few kiosks around Taksim Md and Galatasaray Md. There is also an English-language newspaper,'The Daily News', which is published in Ankara. There are half-a-dozen bookshops (*kitabevi*) that have a fairly large stock of books in English: *Sander*, Halaskargazi Cd, Şişli, and at Istiklal Cd 178, Galatasaray; *Haşet*, Istiklal Cd 469, Tünel, and in the lobby of the Hilton. By far the largest and best selection of books in English is that of the *Redhouse Kitabevi*, Riza Paşa Yokuşu 50 (in the Old City, just below the Vezir Han). There is also a small but excellent bookshop, *Yalter Kitabevi*, in the village of Bebek on the Bosphorus.

*Barbershop (Berber) and Hairdresser (Küafor)*. The best barbershop and hair-dressing salon in Istanbul is in the Divan Hotel.

*Toilets. (Tuvalet)*. Signs read WC or OO. Men is *Baylara* or *Erkeklere*; Women is *Bayanlara* or *Kadinlara*. There are also large public toilets under the Galata Bridge, in the Karaköy pedestrian underpass, in the Hippodrome, next to the Galatasaray Lise, and behind the water-distribution building in Taksim Md. There are public toilets in most mosque courtyards.

**Weather**. The weather in Istanbul is generally pleasant and quite temperate. In summer the prevailing wind, which blows down the Bosphorus from the Black Sea, keeps the city pleasantly cool, except on the few days when the infamous *lodos* blows in from the Marmara. Spring is the best time of year, particularly along the Bosphorus, when the hills on both sides of the strait are adorned with flowering judas trees and one is serenaded by nightingales. In winter, the rainy season, the temperature seldom drops below freezing; there may be one or two snowstorms, but these usually melt away in a day or two.

**Plan of Visit**. The 21 itineraries in this Guide are designed so that each takes a day or less. To follow all of them in some detail would require several weeks. For those with only a short time at their disposal the following places should not be missed:
1. The Galata Bridge and the Golden Horn (Rte 1).
2. Haghia Sophia (Rte 2).
3. Topkapí Sarayí (Rte 3).
4. Haghia Eirene, The Archaeological Museum, and the Museum of the Ancient Orient (Rte 4).
5. The Hippodrome, the Mosque of Sultan Ahmet I, the Mosque of Sokollu Mehmet Paşa, and the Church of SS. Sergius and Bacchus (Rte 5).
6. The Basilica Cistern, the Column of Constantine, and the Mosque of Sultan Beyazít II (Rte 6).
7. The Covered Bazaar (Rte 7).
8. The Mosque of Rüstem Paşa (Rte 8).
9. The Süleymaniye (Rte 9).
10. The Church of St. Saviour in Chora (Kariye Camii; Rte 13).
11. The Theodosian Walls (Rte 16).
12. The Shrine and Cemetery of Eyüp (Rte 17).
13. The Galata Tower (Rte 18).
14. The Bosphorus and Rumeli Hisarí (Rte 19).
For those who can only spend a long weekend in Istanbul, the sights that should not be missed are Haghia Sophia, Topkapí Sarayí, the Covered Bazaar, the Süleymaniye, Kariye Camii, and the Bosphorus.

Note: Because of the extremely high inflation rate and frequent currency devaluations, it has been impossible to quote prices or exchange rates in this Guide. For information on prices and exchange rates consult your travel agent or bank before leaving for Turkey.

# STAMBOUL–THE OLD CITY

The name Stamboul generally refers to that part of the city which was once called Constantinople; that is, the area bounded on the S by the Sea of Marmara, on the N by the Golden Horn, and on the landward side by the Theodosian walls. Modern Istanbul extends far beyond those limits, including within its boundaries the European and Asian suburbs along the Marmara coast, as well as both shores of the Bosphorus out almost as far as the Black Sea. Stamboul is connected to the more modern sections of the city by two bridges: the Galata Bridge, which crosses the Golden Horn 1km above its confluence with the Bosphorus, and the Atatürk Bridge, which is about another km upstream. (A third bridge spans the Horn just outside the Theodosian walls, forming part of the highway that runs from Yeşilköy Airport to the Bosphorus Bridge.)

*The Galata Bridge, dominated at its far end by Yeni Cami, the New Mosque, completed in 1663. (S.P. Fay, Jr)*

# 1   From the Galata Bridge to the Summit of the First Hill

The **Galata Bridge** (Pl 11,1) is the focal point of Istanbul's colourful and turbulent daily life. Throughout the day and early evening a steady stream of pedestrians and traffic pours across the bridge between Karaköy and Eminönü, the busy squares at its Galata and Stamboul ends. Both squares are thronged with people shopping at the fish markets along the quays or dining in simple restaurants set up among the stalls and barrows of the fishmongers. There are restaurants on the lower level of the bridge as well, along with cafes and teahouses, all of them crowded with commuters waiting for the ferries that will take them home to the maritime suburbs of the city.

The upper level of the Galata Bridge is an excellent vantage-point from which to orient oneself before setting out to explore the city. Looking towards the eastern tip of Stamboul one sees **Saray Burnu** (Pl 11,4), the point where the Golden Horn and the Bosphorus meet and flow together into the Marmara. Above Saray Burnu, on what was once the acropolis of ancient Byzantium, there are the pavilions and gardens of **Topkapí Sarayí** (Pl 11,4), the imperial residence of the Sultan and his court in Ottoman times. To the right of the Saray, on the summit of the First Hill, is the majestic edifice of **Haghia Sophia** (Pl 11,5), the former cathedral of Byzantine Constantinople. The most prominent monument on the Second Hill is **Nuruosmaniye Camii** (Pl 10,6), a baroque mosque framed by a pair of minarets. The Third Hill is crowned by the **Süleymaniye** (Pl 10,4), the great mosque complex of Süleyman the Magnificent, which dominates the skyline of the old city as seen from the bridge. On the foreshore between these two hills stands **Yeni Cami** (Pl 10,4), the large mosque that looms over the Stamboul end of the Galata Bridge, while farther off to the right, in the midst of the market quarter, is the smaller **Mosque of Rüstem Paşa** (Pl 10.4). The Fourth Hill is surmounted by **Fatih Camii** (Pl 9,2), the Mosque of the Conqueror, whose dome and four minarets can be seen in the middle distance, some way in from the Golden Horn. Atop the Fifth Hill, on the edge of the ridge above the Golden Horn, stands the **Mosque of Selim I** (Pl 5,6), flanked by a pair of minarets. Just visible in the distance are the dome and two minarets of **Mihrimah Camii** (Pl 4,6); this marks the summit of the Sixth Hill, some 2km in from the Golden Horn and just inside the Theodosian walls. Across the Golden Horn the skyline is dominated by the huge, conical-capped **Galata Tower** (Pl 7,5), the last remnant of the medieval Genoese town of Galata.

The right bank of the Golden Horn between the two bridges was known in Byzantine times as Perama. Perama was the principal commercial port and market quarter of Constantinople, a characteristic that it still retains. During the latter period of the Byzantine Empire this part of the city was given over to various Italian city-states, some of which had obtained trading and commercial concessions as early as the 11C. The area to the right of the Galata Bridge was the territory of the Venetians, which included piers, warehouses, and the residences of the merchants and their families. The area to the left of the bridge belonged to the Amalfians; beyond that was the concession of the Pisans, followed by that of the Genoese, who also controlled the town of Galata. The Italians, particularly the Venetians and the Genoese, fought several wars with one another and with the Byzantines, striving to extend their maritime empires. During the final siege in 1453, the Genoese in Constantinople fought valiantly alongside the Byzantines, but their compatriots in Galata surrendered to the Turks without a struggle. After the Turkish Conquest the Italian concessions were eliminated on the right bank of the Golden Horn, but the Genoese in Galata retained some measure of autonomy for about a century longer.

The area at the Stamboul end of the Galata Bridge, where Yeni Cami now stands, was in earlier centuries a Jewish quarter, wedged in between the concessions of the Venetians and the Amalfians. The Jews who resided here were members of the schismatic Karaite sect, who broke off from the main body of Orthodox Jewry in the 8C. The local community of Karaites seem to have settled on this site as early as the 10C, at least a century before the Italians first obtained their concessions in Constantinople. The Karaites continued to live in this quarter until 1597, when they were evicted to clear the area for the construction of the first mosque on this site. They returned for a time in the first half of the following century, after construction of the mosque had been interrupted, but they left again in 1660, when the whole quarter was destroyed by fire. Soon afterwards Sultan Mehmet IV resettled them on the left bank of the upper reaches of the Golden Horn, in a new community called Hasköy, or the Royal Village. About fifty Karaite families remain in Hasköy to the present day.

**Yeni Cami**, the New Mosque, is one of the most familiar landmarks in the city, standing as it does at the Stamboul end of the Galata Bridge. It was the last large mosque to be built in the city during the classical period of Ottoman architecture. Although it cannot stand comparison with the great imperial mosques built earlier in that era, it does possess a certain grandeur, an effect that is enhanced by its dramatic setting beside the Golden Horn.

HISTORY. The name of the building is an abbreviation of Yeni Valide Camii, the New Mosque of the Valide Sultan. (The Valide Sultan was the mother of the reigning Sultan.) The first stage in the construction of the mosque began in 1597, under the sponsorship of the Valide Sultan Safiye, mother of Mehmet III. The original architect was Davut Ağa, a former apprentice of the great Sinan, the architect who built most of the imperial mosques in the city during the classical period of Ottoman architecture. Davut Ağa died in 1599, however, and was replaced by Dalgíç Ahmet Çavuş. Dalgíç Ahmet Çavuş remained chief architect until 1603, when the death of Mehmet III halted construction of the mosque, for his mother then lost her power in the Saray. The new Sultan, Ahmet I, showed no interest in completing the mosque, nor did his immediate successors. For more than half a century it stood unfinished, gradually falling into ruins, until it was destroyed by fire in 1660. Later in that year the fire-blackened ruins of the mosque attracted the attention of the Valide Sultan Turhan Hadice, mother of Sultan Mehmet IV, who decided to rebuild it as an act of piety. The architect Mustafa Ağa was placed in charge of the project, which was completed according to the original design in 1663.

EXTERIOR. Like all of the imperial mosques in Istanbul, Yeni Cami is preceded by an avlu, a monumental courtyard on its W side. The ceremonial entrance to the courtyard, now unused, is at the centre of the W end of the avlu, where a grand flight of steps leads up to an ornate portal. A calligraphic inscription over the gateway reads: 'Health be with you; should you be worthy, enter in for eternity.'

Today one enters the courtyard through smaller gateways at its NE and SE corners. The courtyard is square in plan, measuring 39m on a side along its outer walls. The interior of the courtyard has along its periphery a peristyle of 20 columns, with six along each of the four sides, counting corner columns twice. This peristyle borders a portico covered by 24 small domes of equal size, and in the centre of the courtyard there is a pretty octagonal şadírvan. But here the şadírvan serves merely a decorative function, and the ritual ablutions are performed at water-taps along the S wall of the mosque. The facade of the mosque under the porch is decorated with tiles and faience inscriptions forming a frieze. The two centre columns of the portico that frame the entrance to the mosque are of a most unusual and beautiful marble not seen elsewhere in the city.

The external form of the mosque reflects its internal plan. The central area of the interior is defined by four great piers that ultimately support the central dome. This central dome is flanked by semidomes along both axes of the mosque, with smaller domes at each corner of the building and still smaller domes beside these, two each at the NE and SE corners, and three each above the NW and SW corners. The N and S sides of the mosque have two storeys of porticoed galleries that produce a charming effect. Notice how the four great piers are continued above the building as tall octagonal turrets. Smaller turrets rise in steps on either side of the semidomes, producing with them and the central dome a symmetrical cascading impression. The two minarets, which are entered from within the mosque, rise from the NW and SW corners of the building. Both of them have three şerefes with superbly sculptured stalactite parapets. In Ottoman times the call to prayer in Yeni Cami was given by six müezzins, one on each şerefe, but now only one müezzin gives the call, and in some instances it is broadcast from a tape-recorder.

At the NE corner of Yeni Cami there is a very interesting and unusual building, through the centre of which a great arched portal allows one to pass around behind the mosque. This is a kasír, or royal pavilion, entered by the ramp beside the mosque. This ramp leads to a suite of rooms (not open to the public) built over the archway, and from there a door leads to the royal loge within the mosque. This suite of rooms included a salon, a bedchamber and a toilet, with kitchens on the lower level, and served as a *pied-à-terre* for the royal family when they attended services. There is reason to believe that this royal pavilion was the first part of the mosque complex to be completed, and that Turhan Hadice used it as a vantage point to observe the construction of her mosque.

INTERIOR. The floor plan of the mosque is a square 41m on a side. On the sides and rear there is a colonnade of slender marble columns connected by alternating large and small arches, which vary in shape from ogee to pointed to round. This colonnade supports the upper gallery, which has a fine marble parapet.

The central area of the interior is defined by the four huge piers that are the main support of the dome. From these piers rise four great arches, and between them four squinches make the transition from square to circle. Upon the circle so formed rests the dome, which is 17·5m in diameter and has its crown 36m above the floor. The interior space is extended by the semidomes along the E–W axis of the mosque, with smaller domes above each corner of the nave and still smaller domes above the corners of the galleries, features already seen on the outside of the mosque.

The royal loge is at the NE corner of the gallery; this is screened off by a gilded grille to shield the Sultan and his family from the public gaze when they attended services. This loge is connected by a long passageway to the royal pavilion at the NE corner of the mosque.

The general appearance of the mosque interior is somewhat disappointing, partly because of the accumulation of soot on its windows from the smoke of ferry boats in the Golden Horn. The blue, green and white tiles on the walls add to the sombre effect; they are of inferior quality, since the great age of Turkish ceramics ended half-a-century before the mosque was completed. Nevertheless, the interior furnishings of the mosque are quite elegant in detail, particularly the mihrab, which is decorated with gilded stalactites, and the mimber, which is surmounted by a conical canopy carried on marble columns.

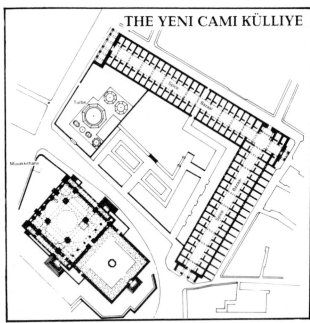

THE YENI CAMI KÜLLIYE

PRECINCTS. Yeni Cami, like all of the imperial mosques of the Ottoman Empire, was the centre of a külliye, a whole complex of religious and philanthropic institutions. The original külliye of Turhan Hadice included the mosque, a hospital, a primary school, a mausoleum, two fountains, a public bath, and a market, with the proceeds of the latter two institutions contributing to the support of the rest of the foundation. The hospital, the public bath, and the primary school have been destroyed, but the other institutions remain, although only the market is now open to the public.

The market of the Yeni Cami complex is the handsome L-shaped building to the S and W of the mosque. It is called the *Mísír Çarşísí*, the Egyptian Market, because it was originally endowed with the Cairo imposts. In English it is more commonly known as the Spice Bazaar, because it was famous for selling spices and medicinal herbs. Spices and herbs are still sold there, but the bazaar now deals in a wide variety of other commodities making it, perhaps, the most popular market in the city. There are 88 vaulted rooms in all, as well as chambers above each of the entryways at the ends of the two halls. The main entrance is through the monumental gatehouse near the SW corner of Yeni Cami, an impressive building that gives an imperial Ottoman touch to the busy market square outside.

The domed building at the E end of the mosque garden is the *türbe* of the Yeni Cami külliye. Turhan Hadice, foundress of the mosque, is buried there. Buried beside her is her son, Mehmet IV, and five later sultans: Mustafa II, Ahmet III, Mahmut I, Osman III and Murat V.

The small building to the W of the türbe is the *library*; this was built by Turhan Hadice's grandson, Ahmet III. Ahmet III was known in his lifetime as the Tulip King, and the period of his reign, 1703–30, is called the Lale Devrisi, the Age of Tulips, because a fabulous tulip festival was held each April in the palace gardens.

Across the street from the türbe, at the corner of the wall enclosing the garden of the mosque, is a tiny polygonal building with a quaintly-shaped dome. This was the *muvakithane*, the house and workshop of the müneccim, the mosque astronomer.

The müneccim regulated the times for the five occasions of daily prayer and fixed the exact times of sunrise and sunset during Ramazan, beginning and ending the daily fast which was required during that period. It was also his duty to determine the day on which each month of the Moslem lunar calendar commenced, beginning with the appearance of the first sickle moon in the western sky just after sunset. The müneccim, like most astronomers of that period, also served as an astrologer and was expected to cast the horoscopes of the Sultan and other notables. In more recent times the müneccim also repaired clocks and watches for people in the neighbourhood of the mosque.

Hamidiye Cd begins behind Yeni Cami and leads one on the first stretch of the route from the Galata Bridge to the summit of the First Hill. On the first corner to the right along Hamidiye Cd is the *sebil* of the Yeni Cami külliye. This is the only sebil in Istanbul still serving something like its original purpose; bottled spring water is sold there, whereas in Ottoman times it would have been handed out in cups to passersby.

The next turning to the right on Hamidiye Cd is a narrow alley that leads to the *hamam of Yíldíz Dede.* (Yíldíz means star in Turkish, and Dede means Grandfather, a name often given to Moslem holy men.) Yíldíz Dede was court astrologer in the reign of Mehmem II, and won fame by predicting that the young Sultan would conquer Constantinople in 1453. According to tradition, Yíldíz Dede built his hamam on the site of an ancient synagogue, perhaps one belonging to the Karaite Jews, since it stood in their quarter. However, the present structure is thought to date only from the first half of the 18C. It is now known as the Yíldíz Hamamí, but of old it was called Çífit Hamamí, the Bath of the Jews.

At the next corner on the right of Hamidiye Cd stands the *türbe of Abdül Hamit I.* This türbe was part of a small külliye that also included a sebil and a medrese. The medrese is still in existence, adjoining the türbe, but the sebil was displaced when Hamidiye Cd was widened some years ago. (It is now on Alemdar Cd; see below.) Buried alongside Abdül Hamit I is his son, the mad Mustafa IV. In 1807 the Janissaries overthrew Selim III and placed his brother Mustafa IV on the throne. Selim was soon afterwards murdered on Mustafa's orders, leaving the Sultan and his young nephew Prince Mahmut as the only surviving males in the imperial Ottoman dynasty. The following year, to strengthen his hold on the throne, Mustafa ordered that Mahmut be murdered. But before his orders could be carried out a counter-revolt deposed Mustafa and raised his nephew to the throne as Mahmut II. Shortly afterwards Mustafa himself was executed and buried here beside his father.

A short distance beyond the türbe Hamidiye Cd intersects Ankara Cd, a broad avenue that leads uphill from the Golden Horn to the ridge that joins the First and Second Hills. Ankara Cd follows approximately the course of the defence-walls that Septimius Severus built encircling the town of Byzantium in around AD 200.

To the left of the intersection is *Sirkeci Station*, the last stop for trains from Europe to Istanbul. The station was built in 1889 as the terminus for the Orient Express, which that year made its first through run from Paris to Istanbul. In front of the station are a number of antique railway cars, including one that was the Sultan's private carriage.

THE CAĞALÖGLÜ BATHS

Ankara Cd curves uphill for about half a km, at which point its name changes to Babíali Cd. At that intersection Hilaliahmer Cd leads off to the left, heading directly to the summit of the First Hill. About 100m along on the left is the entrance to the men's section of the *Caĝaloĝlu Hamamí (Pl 11,5), the most famous and beautiful Turkish bath in Istanbul. (The entrance to the women's section of the bath is down the street that leads off Hilaliahmer Cd to the left just past the baths.) This hamam was built in 1741 by Mahmut I, who used the revenues from the baths to pay for the upkeep of the library that he endowed in the nave of Haghia Sophia. The layout of the men's baths is conventional, in that the bathers pass from the camekan through the rather small soĝukluk into the hararet, with all three chambers laid out in a straight line. But in the women's baths the camekan is not in line with the other two chambers but set off to the side, with one of its corners joining a corner of the soĝukluk. This peculiar arrangement was undoubtedly dictated by the requirement that the entrances to the men's and women's baths be on different streets, so as to give the women more privacy. As in most Turkish baths, the most elaborate chamber is the hararet, which has the same form in both the men's and women's sections. This is an open cruciform chamber, with its central dome supported by a circlet of columns and with domed side-chambers in the arms of the cross. In the lobby of the men's section there is an enlarged reproduction of a print by Thomas Allom, showing the hararet of the men's bath as it was in about 1835. There is also a small but interesting display of objects used in the baths in Ottoman times. Notice in particular the extremely high-platformed shoes worn by Ottoman ladies in their bath.

The first turning left past the Cağaloğlu Hamamí is Alay Köşkü Cd, which runs downhill as far as the outer walls of Topkapí Sarayí. At the last turning on the left before reaching the avenue that runs along the walls there is a small mosque raised on a platform. This is *Beşir Ağa Camii* (Pl 11,5), built in 1745 by the Chief Black Eunuch in the reign of Mahmut I. In addition to the mosque, the külliye consisted of some shops, which occupied the vaults in the platform beneath the building, a medrese, and a dervish tekke. The tekke is no longer occupied by dervishes, since their various orders were disbanded in the early years of the Turkish Republic. The former dervish monastery is now the headquarters of the Turkish Folklore Group, one of the finest ethnic dance companies in Europe. The pretty baroque sebil on the corner was also part of Beşir Ağa's foundation.

A block further along Alay Köşkü Cd intersects Alemdar Cd, the avenue that skirts the outer wall of Topkapí Sarayí. Just to the left at the intersection there is a large ornamental gateway with a projecting canopy in the Turkish rococo style. This is the famous *Sublime Porte*, which in former times led to the palace and offices of the Grand Vezir, the Ottoman equivalent of the Prime Minister. The first palace on this site was built by Sokollu Mehmet Paşa when he became Grand Vezir in 1564, during the last years of Süleyman's reign. From that time onwards most of the business of the Ottoman Empire was conducted here, behind the Sublime Porte. Hence the gateway came to stand for the government itself, and ambassadors were accredited to the Sublime Porte rather than to the Ottoman Empire, just as to this day ambassadors to Great Britain are accredited to the Court of St. James. The present gateway was built early in the reign of Abdül Mecit, dating to about 1840. It now leads to various offices of the Vilayet, the governorate of the Istanbul Province, the main entrance to which is on Ankara Cd. The only structure of any interest within the precincts is to be seen just inside the Sublime Porte and to the right. This is the dershane, or lecture-room, of a medrese built in 1565, just after Sokollu Mehmet Paşa established the Grand Vezirate here. It is a pretty little building in the classical style of that period.

Across the avenue from the Sublime Porte there is a large polygonal gazebo built into a defence tower of the Saray wall. This is the *Alay Köşkü*, the Review Pavilion, originally constructed in about 1565 and rebuilt in 1819. The interior consists of several rooms reached by a ramp rising from just inside the gate of Gülhane Park. From the latticed windows of this kiosk the Sultan could observe the comings and goings at the palace of his Grand Vezir across the way. The kiosk also served as a pavilion from which the Sultan could review military parades or the fabulous Processions of the Guilds that were held from time to time in the earlier centuries of Ottoman rule in Istanbul.

The Turkish chronicler Evliya Çelebi, author of the 'Seyahatname', or 'Narrative of Travels', gives a vivid description of the Procession of the Guilds that took place in 1638, during the reign of Sultan Murat IV. According to Evliya, the Procession was divided into 57 different sections, and in his Seyahatname he gives detailed descriptions of no less than 735 different guilds as they passed before the Sultan and his court in the Alay Köşkü. Representatives of each of these groups paraded by, either marching, riding on horseback, or on floats pulled by horses or oxen. They all dressed in their characteristic costumes and tried to outdo one another in entertaining the Sultan and the other spectators, in a joyous festival which could last for a month. These processions were a favourite subject for Turkish painters of the period, and the Topkapí Sarayí Museum has several volumes of miniatures depicting the various guilds described by Evliya.

The Alay Köşkü has recently been restored and is now open to the public. It is presently used as a museum to exhibit the Kenan Özbel collection of Turkish embroideries and carpets.

Alemdar Cd leads uphill to the summit of the First Hill, curving away to the right, leaving the outer walls of the Saray. Just around the bend, on the right side of the avenue, there is a small baroque mosque, *Zeynep Sultan Camii* (Pl 11,5). This mosque was built in 1769 by the architect Tahir Ağa for Princess Zeynep, a daughter of Ahmet III. In form the mosque is merely a square room covered by a dome, with a square projecting apse to the E and a porch with five bays to the W. The walls are built with alternating courses of brick and stone, and the cornice of the dome undulates to follow the exadroes of the round-arched windows, all of which makes the building look more like a Byzantine church than an Ottoman mosque. The külliye also included a primary school, which stands at the corner of the street just below the mosque, and the picturesque little cemetery where the foundress and members of her family and household are buried. The elaborate rococo sebil outside the cemetery gate is not an original part of the foundation. It was built in 1778 as part of the külliye of Abdül Hamit I and was moved to its present location when Hamidiye Cd was widened some years ago.

One block beyond Zeynep Sultan Camii and on the same side of the street there is a short stretch of wall next to a cinema. This is the apse of the former Byzantine church of the *Theotokos in Chalkoprateia*, of which only this and a fragment of the N wall remain. This shrine of the Theotokos, the Mother of God, received its second name from the fact that it stood in the Chalkoprateia, the Copper Market, which in the early Byzantine period occupied this slope of the First Hill. There is a tradition that the church was built on the site of an ancient synagogue that served the Jewish artisans who worked in the Chalkoprateia, but no evidence has been found to support this claim. Most scholars now agree that the church was founded in about 450 by Pulcheria, wife of the Emperor Marcian, and was finished about a decade later by Verina, wife of Leo I. This was the most important shrine of the Virgin in Constantinople, since it housed her most sacred relic, the Holy Girdle; it was either the starting-point, or goal, of all processions celebrating her feast-days. The church fell into ruins after the Turkish Conquest and later a small mosque named Acem Ağa Mescidi was built in the apse, thereby preserving that part of the structure. The mosque was destroyed early in the present century, after which the remains of the church were rediscovered and identified in 1912 by Mamboury.

The handsome though sombre building that occupies most of the opposite side of the street is the *Soğuk Kuyu Medresesi* (Pl 11,5). This theological school was founded in 1559 by Cafer Ağa, Chief Black Eunuch in the reign of Süleyman the Magnificent, and the architect was Sinan. The hillside slopes quite sharply here, so Sinan first erected a vaulted brick substructure to support the medrese and its courtyard. The main entrance to the medrese is on the street running parallel to the W end of Haghia Sophia, but one can also enter it from Alemdar Cd by a stairway that goes up through the substructure to the courtyard. The interior of the medrese is now in a sorry state but it remains an interesting and unusual building.

Alemdar Cd now leads to the summit of the First Hill, which in the early centuries of the Byzantine Empire was the imperial quarter and the centre of the political and religious life of the city. The long park to the right, the *Atmeydani*, occupies the site of the Hippodrome, the huge arena that played such an important and dramatic role in the public life of Byzantine Constantinople. The area immediately to the E of the Atmeydani is dominated by the huge Sultan Ahmet I Camii (Pl 11,5), better known to foreigners as the Blue Mosque. The area between the Blue Mosque and Haghia Sophia was the site of the Augustaeum, the principal square of ancient Constantinople. The long park beyond the far end of the modern square here was the site of the Byzantine Senate, which formed the E side of the Augustaeum. At the SE corner of the Augustaeum stood the Chalke, or Brazen House, the monumental vestibule of the Great Palace. Nearby were the Baths of Zeuxippus, the largest public bathing establishment in the ancient city. The Baths stood on about the same site as the Hamam of Roxelana, the handsome Ottoman building that forms the E side of the park between the Blue Mosque and Haghia Sophia. On its N side the Augustaeum gave access to the church of Haghia Sophia and the Patriarchal Palace, the centre of the religious life of the Byzantine Empire. Just to the W of the Augustaeum there was another large square, the Basilica, a porticoed stoa surrounded by some of the most important public institutions in the city, including the University of Constantinople, the central law-courts of the Byzantine Empire, the principal public library, and a large outdoor book-market. Thus the Augustaeum and its immediate neighbourhood were at the hub of life in Byzantine Constantinople. Today the square is no longer a civic centre, but it is still a central starting-point for visiting the monuments on the First Hill of the city.

# 2   Haghia Sophia

**\*\*HAGHIA SOPHIA** (in Turkish, *Ayasofya*; Pl 11,5) is one of the most extraordinary buildings in the history of architecture, and a monument to the golden age of the Byzantine Empire. Some of the most important events in the history of Byzantium are connected with this venerable edifice, and it played such a central role in the life of the city that it has become the enduring symbol of Byzantine Constantinople.

ADMISSION. The museum and its precincts are open 9–5:30 every day except Mon. A separate ticket must be purchased to gain admission to the galleries.

HISTORY. The present edifice of Haghia Sophia is the third church of that name to stand upon this site. The first church was completed on 15 February 360, in the reign of Constantius, son and successor of Constantine the Great, and was dedicated to Haghia Sophia, the Divine Wisdom, an attribute of Christ. This building was probably comparable in size to the present structure, for it was also called Megale Ekklesia, the Great Church, a name that it passed on to its successors. This church was burnt down on 9 June 404 during a riot by the supporters of St. John Chrysostom, the Patriarch, who had been removed from his see by the Empress Eudoxia, wife of the Emperor Arcadius. A new church was later built on the same site by Theodosius II, son and successor of Arcadius, and dedicated on 10 October. This structure, which is known to archaeologists as the Theodosian church, was destroyed by fire on 15 Jan 532, the first day of the Nika Revolt. Justinian began work on the present church just a month after the end of the rebellion, on 23 February The Emperor appointed as head architects Anthemius of Tralles and Isidorus of Miletus, the two greatest mathematical physicists of the age. Anthemius died during the first year of construction, but Isidorus carried the project through to completion late in 537 and it was dedicated on 26 December of that year.

During the construction a number of structural crises had occurred, due partly to the rapidity with which the building had been erected, and also because of the enormous stresses caused by the vast and shallow dome. Then the structure was weakened by a series of earthquakes that shook the city between 553 and 557, and on 7 May 558 the eastern part of the dome collapsed, along with the arch and semidome on that side of the church. Isidorus of Miletus was no longer alive, so

Justinian entrusted the task of rebuilding the church to the architect's nephew, Isidorus the Younger. Isidorus decided to change the design of the dome, making it less shallow so as to reduce the lateral stresses. The reconstruction project was completed late in 563 and the church was rededicated on Christmas Eve of that year. Justinian presided at the ceremony, as he had at the original dedication 26 years before. But this would be the last great occasion of state that he would attend, for he died a little more than a year later, ending the most illustrious reign in the history of the Byzantine Empire.

A series of earthquakes in the 9–10C damaged the building and caused cracks to appear in the dome, until finally in 989 part of the dome and the eastern arch collapsed. Basil II entrusted the reconstruction to Trdat, an Armenian architect, and on 13 May 996 the church was once again reopened. The church interior suffered grievously in the Latin sack of Constantinople in 1204, when it was stripped of all of its sacred relics and other precious objects. During the Latin Occupation Haghia Sophia served as the Roman Catholic cathedral of the city, and a campanile was erected near the NW corner of the building. Following the recapture of Constantinople by the Byzantines in 1261 Haghia Sophia was reconsecrated as a Greek Orthodox sanctuary, after which the campanile was taken down and the church refurbished and redecorated. The dome suffered another partial collapse on 19 May 1346, and the church was closed until the reconstruction was completed in 1355. But during the last century of Byzantine rule Haghia Sophia was allowed to fall into serious disrepair, sharing in the general decay of the dying city, and travellers to Constantinople in that period report that the church was partially in ruins.

The last Christian liturgy in Haghia Sophia began shortly after sunset on Monday, 28 May 1453, the day before Constantinople finally fell to the Turks. The church was filled with those who were not manning their posts on the Theodosian walls, and throughout the night they prayed for divine deliverance. The Emperor Constantine XI Dragases paid a last visit to the church an hour or so before midnight, marching in at the head of his Greek and Italian knights, and there he made his peace with God before returning to his command post on the ramparts. The prayers continued in Haghia Sophia until dawn, but shortly after sunrise word came that the defence walls had been breached and that the city had fallen. The congregation in Haghia Sophia barred the doors, but within an hour the vanguard of the Ottoman army forced their way in, slaughtering those who resisted them and leading the others off into bondage. And with that the long history of Byzantium came to an end.

Sultan Mehmet II entered the city late in the afternoon of that same day and rode directly to Haghia Sophia. After inspecting the building he ordered that it should be converted into a mosque immediately, and the following Friday he attended the first Moslem service to be held in Ayasofya Camii, the Mosque of Haghia Sophia. This conversion required some structural additions and changes, including the erection of a minaret at the SE corner of the building and the construction of a mihrab and mimber, along with other furnishings used in Moslem services. Mehmet II and his successors continued to keep Haghia Sophia in good repair throughout the Ottoman period, for it was one of the principal imperial mosques of the city and was always held in great veneration. The last and most thorough of these restorations was commissioned by Abdül Mecit I and was carried out in 1847–49 by the Swiss architects Gaspare and Giuseppe Fossati. During the course of this restoration, the surviving figurative mosaics were cleared of the whitewash and plaster with which they had been covered earlier in the Ottoman period. When the project was complete the mosaics were covered over once again, in order to protect them from further damage. In April 1932 Thomas Whittemore and other members of the Byzantine Institute began the task of uncovering and restoring the mosaics, many of which had disappeared since the Fossati restoration, and at that time Haghia Sophia was closed to prepare the building for its reopening as a museum in 1934. Restoration of the mosaics was not completed until 1964, when the galleries of Haghia Sophia were for the first time opened to the public.

EXTERIOR. Haghia Sophia was laid out so that its apse faced in the direction of sunrise at the time of the winter solstice; thus it is oriented some 33 degrees S of E. In order to simplify the description of its plan, it will be assumed that its apse faces due E.

The main ground plan of the building is a rectangle, approximately 70m in width and 75m in length. At the centre of the E wall there is a projecting apse, semicircular within and three-sided on the exterior, while to the W the church is preceded by a narthex and exonarthex. Above the central part of the rectangular area there is an enormous dome, with smaller semidomes to E and W and conches over the apse and the four corners. These cover the central area of the nave, which is flanked by side aisles with galleries above that extend around the S side of the church above the narthex. This was the basic form of the church as it was originally planned, but structural crises during the construction and subsequent damage due to earthquakes necessitated the erection of buttresses on all sides of the building. The oldest of these are the two pairs of very tall buttresses built against the N and S walls of the church. These were built during Justinian's reign, either in the latter part of the original construction or in the rebuilding of the dome in 558–63. The pillar-like outer parts of these buttresses were added in 1317 by Andronicus II to provide additional support for the building, which had seemed in imminent danger of collapse. The four massive flying-buttresses against the W gallery were added in the second half of the 9C. The arch buttresses and retaining walls at the E side of the church were erected by Mehmet II soon after the Conquest. The Conqueror also built the brick minaret at the SE corner of the building; this replaced a temporary wooden minaret which had been erected over the SE buttress in the first three days after the Conquest, when Haghia Sophia was being converted into a mosque. Selim II built the stone minaret at the NE corner in 1574, and the two stone minarets at the NW and SW corners were added a year or so later by his son and successor, Murat III. All three of these stone minarets are works of Sinan, who also restored all of the buttresses and the fabric of the building. In addition to these repairs and additions, a number of subsidiary structures were erected in the precincts of Haghia Sophia during both the Byzantine and Ottoman periods; these minor monuments will be examined after visiting the church itself.

Justinian's church was preceded on its W side by an atrium, a porticoed arcade that enclosed an area 47·7m wide and 32·3m deep; this has now completely disappeared and its site is occupied by the garden to the W of Haghia Sophia. The E side of this atrium was formed by the exonarthex, which was entered through the three doors at the centre and one each at the N and S ends of the portico, with great arched windows piercing the other four bays. There were also large portals at the E ends of the side aisles, as well as a smaller door in the NE corner of the SE bay. In addition, there were entryways at the N and S ends of the narthex, both of which were preceded by vestibules, the one to the N being a Turkish addition.

VESTIBULE, NARTHEX AND EXONARTHEX. The present entrance to Haghia Sophia is through the central gate of the exonarthex, while the exit is through the vestibule at the S end of the narthex. In Byzantine times this entryway was reserved for the use of the Emperor and his party, because of its proximity to the Great Palace. It was called the Vestibule of the Warriors, since the troops of the Emperor's bodyguard waited there for him while he was in the church. The vestibule is a long and narrow chamber of somewhat irregular plan, being some 0·6m wider at the S than at the N. It is roofed by three cross-vaults of unequal size that bear no relationship to the room below, a fact that has led some scholars to suggest that the vestibule was added after the original construction of the church. If so, the addition must have been made soon afterwards, perhaps during the reconstruction of 558–63, because the gold mosaics on the vaults of the vestibule are from Justinian's reign. According to Paul the

Silentiary, who wrote a long poem describing Haghia Sophia at the time of its rededication in 563, this mosaic decoration covered the great dome, the semidome, the N and S tympanum walls, and the vaults of the narthex, aisles, vestibules and galleries, a total area of more than four acres. This decoration, much of which has survived, consists of large areas of plain gold ground adorned around the edges of architectural forms with bands of geometrical or floral designs in various colours. Simple crosses in outline on the crowns of vaults and the soffits of arches are constantly repeated, and, according to the Silentiary, there was a cross of this kind on the crown of the great dome. It is clear from the Silentiary's description that in Justinian's time there were no figurative mosaics in the church. The figurative mosaics that have survived are all from after the Iconoclastic period, which ended in 843. The panel in the lunette above the doorway at the inner end of the vestibule was the first figurative mosaic to be uncovered in the restoration project that began in 1932. The mosaic depicts the Blessed Virgin enthroned in an hieratic pose, holding the Christ-Child in her lap, as she receives two crowned and haloed figures. The figure on the right, identified by an inscription as 'Constantine, the great Emperor among the Saints', offers the Virgin a model of a walled town representing

Constantinople. The figure on the left, identified as 'Justinian, the illustrious Emperor', offers her a model of a church symbolising Haghia Sophia. The mosaic is dated to the last quarter of the 10C, and is thought to have been commissioned by Basil II.

When entering the narthex, do not fail to notice the huge doors sheathed in bronze, with the forms of crosses still visible on the upper and lower panels. These doors are from Justinian's church, as are most of the other doors in the building. The embossed medallions on the middle panels of both doors were once adorned with imperial monograms in damascened silver, giving the names of the Emperor Theophilus, his wife Theodora, and their son Michael; the inscription also bore the date 839, three years before Theophilus died and was succeeded by his son, who became Michael III. Unfortunately, these beautiful monograms were stolen during a restoration in the 1960s.

The narthex consists of nine cross-vaulted bays separated by arches springing from the right wall to massive engaged pillars on the left. Five doors to the left open off from alternate bays into the exonarthex, which is about half the height and width of the narthex; this also has nine cross-vaulted bays separated by arches. Doors open off from the right of each bay of the narthex into the nave, with the largest one at the centre, flanked by a pair of somewhat smaller portals, and with

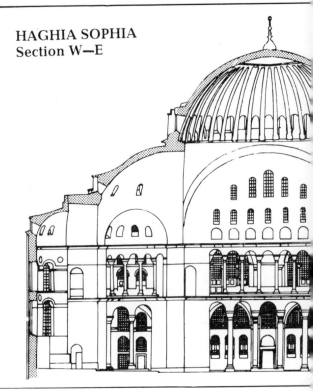

HAGHIA SOPHIA
Section W—E

two pairs of still smaller doors to either side. The monumental central
door from the narthex into the nave was known as the Imperial
Gate; this was reserved for the use of the Emperor and the Patriarch and those who accompanied them in processions. Above the
centre of the brass cornice of this door there is an embossed
decoration in very low relief showing a dove flying straight down
above an open book, which rests upon a throne framed by two
pillars and an arch. The book is inscribed with these words from
the tenth chapter of the Gospel according to St. John, in which
Jesus addresses the Pharisees: 'Our Lord spoke: "I am the door of
the sheep; by me, if any man enter he shall be saved, and shall go
in and out, and shall find pasture"'. In the lunette above the
Imperial Gate there is a figurative mosaic, the second of those
uncovered in 1932. The mosaic shows Christ seated upon a jewel-
led throne, his feet resting upon a stool. He raises his right hand in
a gesture of blessing, and in his left hand he holds a book with this
inscription: 'Peace with you, I am the Light of the World'. At the left
a crowned figure prostrates himself before the throne, his hands
outstretched in supplication. Above, on either side of the throne,
there are two roundels, the one on the left containing a bust of the
Blessed Virgin and the other an angel carrying a staff or wand. It is

thought that the imperial figure depicts the Emperor Leo VI, the Wise, and the mosaic is dated to the period of his reign, 886–912.

THE NAVE. Here one enters the nave, inevitably pausing to look upon the vast interior of the church, particularly the fabled dome. The main support for the dome is provided by four enormous and irregularly-shaped piers standing in a square approximately 31m on a side. From these piers rise four great arches, between which four pendentives make the transition from the square to the circular base of the dome. Upon the cornice of this circular base rests the slightly elliptical dome, of which the E–W diameter is about 31m and the N–S approximately 33m, with the crown soaring 56m above the floor, about the height of a fifteen-storey building. The dome has 40 ribs which intersect at the crown, separated at the base by 40 windows. To the E and W smaller pairs of subsidiary piers support the two great semidomes, each pierced by five windows, which give the nave its vast length. The central arches to N and S are filled with tympanum walls pierced by 12 windows, seven in the lower range, five in the upper. Between the great piers on the N and S four monolithic columns of verd antique support the galleries, while above six columns of the same marble carry the tympanum walls. At the four corners of the nave there are semicircular exedrae covered by conches, in each of which there are two massive columns of porphyry below and six of verd antique above. At the E, beyond the subsidiary piers, a semicircular apse projects beyond the E wall of the church, covered by a conch. To the N and S of the main piers there are lateral piers, which are joined structurally with the four main buttresses on those sides, consolidating the fabric of the church. These divide the side aisles and the galleries above into six large compartments on each floor, three on either side, joined to one another by great arches springing between the piers. The N and S compartments on either side consist of a single bay and those at the centre have two bays each, all of them domical cross-vaults surrounded by half-barrel vaults. These vaults are supported internally by a double colonnade within each aisle, with pairs of rectangular pillars at the ends of each aisle and verd antique columns in between.

The capitals of the columns are unique and famous. There are several different types, but they are all alike in having the surface decoration of acanthus leaves and palm foliage so deeply undercut that they produce an effect of white lace on a dark ground. Most of the capitals are of the bowl type, including all of those in the nave and gallery arcades. There, Ionic volutes support a decorated abacus beneath which the bowl-shaped body of the capital is adorned with acanthus leaves. In the centre of these capitals, at both front and back, there are the imperial monograms of Justinian and Theodora. The capitals of the 16 verd antique columns of the aisles are of similar type but smaller in scale. Those of the eight pillars at the ends of the aisles are much the same, only there the bowl, instead of becoming circular towards its base, remains rectangular throughout.

One of these pillars, that which is sheathed in brass at the NW corner of the aisle, is the subject of a medieval legend that still has believers today. Antony of Novgorod, who visited Haghia Sophia in 1200, reports it thus: 'One sees at the side of the church the column of St. Gregory the Miracle-Worker. St. Gregory appeared near this column, and the people kiss it and rub their breasts and shoulders against it to be cured of their pains'. Credulous pilgrims have worn a hole in the brass plate and into the pillar itself, for the moisture contained in the cavity has always been considered a cure for eye diseases and a nostrum for fertility. It is often said that the moisture in this little hole is drawn up through the column from cisterns that are supposed to underlie the church. However, a recent study has shown that the cisterns do not exist.

There are also many legends concerning the provenance of the various columns in the church, but there is every reason to believe that most or all of them were specially quarried for Haghia Sophia. From Silentiary's description there can be little doubt that the verd antique columns in the nave and galleries were expressly hewn for Haghia Sophia from the famous quarries near Molossis in Thessaly. But there is a possibility that the eight porphyry columns in the exedrae, which differ from one another in height and diameter, may have been taken from an ancient building, but if so there is no evidence as to its identity.

The only other kind of marble used for columns in the church comes from the ancient quarries on the isle of Proconnesus in the Marmara. This is a soft white stone streaked with grey or black, and is used for the 24 aisle columns of the gallery and the eight rectangular pillars at the ends of the aisles on the ground floor. The pavement of the church, the frames of the doors and windows, and parts of the wall surfaces are also made of this marble.

A great variety of rare and beautiful marbles was used for the superb revetment of the piers and walls; according to the Silentiary's poem, these came from quarries all over Justinian's empire. In order to obtain the elaborate symmetrical patterns of each panel, the thin blocks of marble were cut in two, sometimes in four, and opened out like a book so that the natural veining of the stone was duplicated and quadruplicated, giving the unique natural designs that add so much to the beauty of the interior.

Other types of decoration in rare marbles are also found in the church. The great square of *opus Alexandrinum* in the pavement toward the SE of the nave is the most noteworthy of these. This is made up mostly of circles of granite, red and green porphyry, and verd antique. According to Antony of Novgorod, the Emperor's throne stood upon this square at the time of his coronation, surrounded by a bronze enclosure. There are also some interesting marble panels above the inner side of the Imperial Gate, in which slabs of verd antique alternate with inlaid panels of various marbles. At the top is an elaborate ciborium with drawn panels revealing a cross on an altar; lower down are other panels with ovals of porphyry, those at the bottom surrounded by pairs of stylized dolphins with foliate tails gobbling up tiny squid with waving tentacles. In the spandrels above the nave there is a superb frieze of sectile work with scrolls of trees and flowers, with the figures of birds perched on the twigs.

THE CHURCH OF HAGHIA SOPHIA. Virtually nothing now remains of the structures and furnishings associated with the Christian liturgy in Haghia Sophia, but from the Silentiary's poem the main features of the church can be established. The raised eastern end of the nave constituted the bema, the inner sanctum reserved for the clergy. (The Emperor, in his role of God's regent on Earth, could also enter the bema.) The bema was separated from the western part of the nave by the iconostasis, a marble screen with twelve engaged columns; according to the Silentiary, this was completely sheathed in silver. This screen, which was pierced by three portals, is believed to have extended between the E corners of the two main E piers. Behind the iconostasis, probably ,just to the W of the subsidiary piers at that end, was the hieron trapeza, the main altar, which was sheathed in gold and silver studded with precious stones. The altar was surmounted by the ciborium, an octagonal silver canopy carried on four silver columns and arches. Around the periphery of the apse ran the synthronon, seven tiers of marble benches where the clergy sat, and at its centre was the cathedra, or patriarchal throne. The bema was flanked by two side chambers, which were located in the exedrae; the one to the N served as the prothesis, or sacristy, while the one on the S was the metatorium, an enclosure set aside for the Emperor and the Patriarch when they were participating in the liturgy. Extending westward from the central portal of the iconostasis was a raised walkway called the solea, with a low parapet of marble slabs. This led to the ambo, a monumental pulpit that stood under the great dome somewhat to the E of its centre, probably next to the square of *opus Alexandrinum*. The ambo, which was raised on marble columns and had a golden dome adorned with designs in semi-precious stones, was approached by two long flights of steps to N and S. It is thought that the final stage in imperial coronations was carried out on the ambo, particularly because of the statement by Antony of Novgorod that during these ceremonies the Emperor's throne stood on the square of *opus Alexandrinum*. At other times the Emperor attended services in the royal loge, which was located just to the S of this square, abutting the SE pier. (Notice the markings in the pavement where the columns of the loge were located.)

THE MOSQUE OF HAGHIA SOPHIA. When Haghia Sophia was converted into a mosque, the mihrap and mimber were oriented toward Mecca, which is some 10 degrees S of the main axis of the church. These undistinguished structures date from the Fossati restorations of 1847–49, as does the Sultan's loge against the NE pier. The Fossatis were also responsible for the six huge green levhas, or painted wooden plaques, that hang from the piers at gallery level. These were done by the calligrapher Mustafa Izzet Efendi and bear in golden letters the Sacred Islamic Names, those of Allah, the Prophet Mohammed, and the first four Caliphs: Abu Bekr, Umar, Othman, and Ali. The

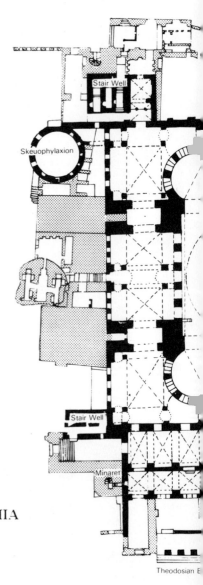

HAGHIA SOPHIA
Plan

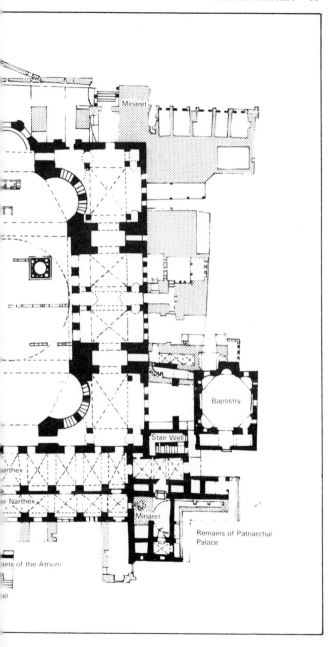

Minaret

Baptistry

Stair Well

arthex

r Narthex

Minaret

Remains of Patriarchal
Palace

ains of the Atrium

all

inscription in the dome is also by Mustafa Izzet Efendi. This is a
quotation from the Koran, reading: 'In the name of God the Merciful
and Pitiful; God is the light of Heaven and Earth. His light is Himself,
not that which shines through glass or gleams in the morning star or
glows in the firebrand'.

The oldest objects now remaining in Haghia Sophia from the
Ottoman period are the two beautiful lustration urns of Proconnesian
marble in the W exedrae. These are late Classical or early Byzantine
urns to which have been added Turkish lids. According to Evliya
Çelebi, these were gifts of Murat III, who also built the large müezzin
mahfili beside the SE pier and the smaller enclosures for chanters
against the other three piers. The marble Kuran kürsü in the N arcade
was presented to the mosque by Murat IV, and the very elegant
library in the S aisle was built by Mahmut I in 1739. The library, which
was endowed with the revenues of the Çağaloğlu Baths (see above,
Rte 1), consists of several domed rooms enclosed with metal grilles.
These rooms, housing some 5000 Ottoman books and manuscripts,
are revetted with superb Iznik tiles of the 16C, which the Sultan found
stored in the Saray.

THE MOSAICS IN THE NAVE. Little remains of the mosaics which once
adorned the nave of Haghia Sophia. The largest and most beautiful of
those which survive appears in the conch of the apse. This *mosaic
depicts the Virgin Mary with the Christ-Child on her knees; she is
dressed in flowing robes of blue with a small cross on the fold of the
mantle over her head and one on each shoulder; her right hand rests
upon her son's shoulder and her left upon his knee. Jesus is dressed in
gold and wears sandals on his feet; his right hand is raised in blessing
while his left hand holds a scroll. The Virgin sits on a simple bench-
like throne adorned with jewels. Beneath her are two cushions, the
lower one green, the upper one embroidered with clubs like those on
playing-cards, while her feet rest upon a plinth-like stool, also
bejewelled. At the bottom of the arch that frames the apse there is a
colossal figure of the Archangel Gabriel; he wears a divitision, an
undergarment, over which is thrown a chlamys, a cloak of white silk;
his great wings, reaching nearly to his feet, are of brightly-coloured
feathers, mostly green, blue and white. In his right hand he holds a
staff, in his left a translucent globe through which can be seen his
thumb. Although the upper part of his left side and the top of his wings
are lost, he is, a fine and striking figure. Opposite, on the N side of the
arch, there are only a few feathers remaining from the wings of the
Archangel Michael. On the face of the apse conch there remain the
first three and the last nine letters of an inscription in Greek, of which
the whole of the middle part is now missing. The inscription was an
iambic distich that once read in full: 'These icons the deceivers once
cast down the pious emperors have again restored'. The apse mosaic
was unveiled by the Patriarch Photius on Easter Sunday 867; this was
a most momentous occasion, for it signified the final triumph of the
Orthodox party over the Iconoclasts and celebrated the permanent
restoration of sacred images to the churches of Byzantium. The two
pious sovereigns referred to here are Michael III, the Sot, and his
protégé, Basil I, whom Michael had made co-Emperor the previous
May and who would the following September murder his benefactor
and usurp the throne for himself.

Three other mosaic portraits are located in niches at the base of the
N tympanum wall and are visible from the nave. In the first niche from

the W there is St. Ignatius the Younger, who was twice Patriarch of Constantinople (847–58, 867–77); in the central niche is St. John Chrysostom, once Patriarch of Constantinople (398–404); and in the fifth niche from the W is St. Ignatius Theophorus of Antioch. All three figures are nearly identical except for the faces: St. Ignatius the Younger is a youthful man with a very ascetic countenance; St. John is in early middle age; and St. Ignatius Theophorus is an old man with white hair and a beard. They are all clad in the same sacerdotal robes, the most striking article of which is the omorphion, or stole, with two large crosses below the shoulders and a third just below the knee. Each of them holds in his left hand, which is concealed below his cloak, a large book with bejewelled binding; the younger St. Ignatius appears to be touching the top of the book with his right hand, while the other two have their right hands raised in blessing. All three of these mosaics are dated to the last quarter of the 9C.

The only other mosaics that are visible from the nave are the six-winged angels in the E pendentives. (Those in the W pendentives are imitations in paint done by the Fossatis at the time of their restoration in 1847–49.) These are the only figurative mosaics that were not plastered over during the Ottoman period, although during their restoration the Fossatis did cover the faces with gold-starred medallions, which are still in place. The E pendentives were probably destroyed when that side of the dome collapsed in 1346; the mosaics would therefore date to the restoration of 1346–55.

THE GALLERIES. The public entryway to the galleries is at the N end of the narthex, where a door leads into the N vestibule. From there an inclined ramp leads up to the NW corner of the galleries. (At present the galleries are not open to the public.)

The Silentiary and other ancient sources write that the galleries in Haghia Sophia served as the gynaceum, the women's quarters. However, there is reason to believe that the two eastern bays of the S gallery were reserved for the use of the royal family and, on occasion, for synods of the Greek Orthodox Church. The N and S galleries have the same plan as the side aisles below them, with a series of four cross-vaulted bays in succession with smaller barrel-vaulted bays, while the W gallery, which is above the narthex, is a broad barrel-vaulted hall with nine windows on the W framed by pillars. The throne of the Empress of Byzantium was located just behind the balustrade at the centre of the W gallery; the spot is marked by a disc of green Thessalian marble set into the pavement, framed by a pair of coupled columns of green marble.

Three of the four surviving mosaics in the galleries are located at the far end of the S side, beyond the first bay. That part of the S gallery is partially screened off by two pairs of false doors of marble with elaborately ornamented panels, the so-called Gates of Heaven and Hell. Between them is the actual doorway, surmounted by a slab of translucent Phrygian marble, above which a wooden beam carved with floral designs in low relief forms a cornice to the whole gateway. This gateway is certainly not an original part of the church but a later addition, and it was probably erected to close off the far end of the S gallery when it was used for synods of the Greek Orthodox Church.

The latest in date of the mosaics in the gallery is located to the right of the entrance to the bay beyond the marble screen, on the E wall of the lateral pier. This is the *Deesis, an iconographic type in which Christ is flanked by the Blessed Virgin and St. John the Baptist, who are shown interceding with him on behalf of mankind. Here John is shown to the right, an expression of agonised grief on his ascetic face, and on the left the young and wistful Virgin casts her gaze shyly downward, while between them Christ holds up his right hand in a gesture of blessing. Although two-thirds of the mosaic is now lost, the features of the three figures in the portrait are still completely unmarred. This superb mosaic is dated to the second half of the 13C, and is one of the finest extant works of art from the Palaeologian renaissance.

Set into the pavement just opposite the Deesis there is a sarcophagus lid inscribed in Latin capital letters with the name Henricus Dandolo. Dandolo, Doge of Venice, was one of the generals of the Fourth Crusade, and though nearly 90 years old and almost blind he led the charge that broke through the Byzantine defences on 13 April 1204. Afterwards the Venetians were awarded three-eighths of Constantinople, including Haghia Sophia, whereupon Dandolo added the title of Despot to his name and styled himself 'Lord of the fourth and a half of all :the Roman Empire'.Dandolo died in Constantinople on 16 June 1205, after which he was buried here in the gallery of Haghia Sophia. After the Conquest, according to tradition, Dandolo's tomb was broken open and his bones thrown to the street dogs.

The other two mosaics in the S gallery are located on the E wall of the church, at the far end of the last bay. The oldest of these is on the left, next to the apse, where Christ is shown between the figures of an Emperor and Empress of Byzantium. Christ is shown enthroned, his right hand raised in a gesture of benediction, his left holding the book of Gospels. At the left of the scene the Emperor is shown offering a money-bag, and on the right the Empress is holding an inscribed scroll. Above the Emperor's head an inscription reads: 'Constantine, in Christ, the Lord Autocrat, faithful Emperor of the Romans, Monomachus'. Above the head of the Empress there is this inscription: 'Zoë, the most pious Augusta'. The scroll in her right hand has the same legend as that over the Emperor's head, save that the words Autocrat and Monomachus are omitted for want of space. It is evident that all three heads and the two inscriptions concerning Constantine have been altered. This has led to the identification of the imperial figures as the Empress Zoë, daughter of Constantine VIII and one of the few women to rule Byzantium in her own right (1042), and her third husband, Constantine IX Monomachus (1042–55). It has been suggested that Constantine is the third imperial figure to be shown with Zoë in the mosaic, replacing her second husband, Michael IV (1034–41), who in turn replaced her first husband, Romanus III Argyrus (1028–34), with the Emperor's head and the identifying inscription being changed on each accession. The heads of Christ and the Empress are thought to have been defaced during the brief reign of Zoë's adopted son, Michael V (1041–42). Michael loathed his foster mother and exiled her in 1042, at which time he may have taken the opportunity to destroy her portrait in Haghia Sophia. But he was shortly afterwards overthrown and Zoë was placed on the throne, ruling with her spinster sister Theodora until her marriage later that year to Constantine IX Monomachus. The mosaic in its present state is thus dated to 1042 or shortly afterwards.

The third of the mosaics in the S gallery is located on the wall to the right of the Zoë mosaic, separated from it by a window. In the centre of this mosaic the Blessed Virgin is depicted holding the Christ-Child; to the left an emperor is shown offering a bag of gold, while on the right a red-haired empress holds forth a scroll. The imperial figures are identified by inscriptions as: 'John, in Christ the Lord, faithful Comnenus', and 'Eirene, the most pious Augusta'. The mosaic extends onto the narrow panel of side wall at right-angles to the main composition; here is the figure of a young prince, identified by an inscription as 'Alexius, in Christ, faithful Emperor of the Romans, Porphyrogenitus'. These are portraits of the Emperor John II Comnenus; his wife, the Empress Eirene, daughter of King Ladislaus of Hungary; and their eldest son, Prince Alexius. The main panel has been dated to 1118, the year of John's accession to the throne, and the portrait of Alexius to 1122, when at the age of 17 he became co-Emperor with his father. Alexius did not live to succeed John, he died not long after his coronation; in fact one can detect the signs of his last illness in this mosaic, his face is pale and lined. The Emperor was known in his time as Kalo John, or John the Good. The Byzantine historian Nicetas Choniates wrote of John that 'he was the best of all the emperors from the family of the Comneni who ever sat upon the Roman throne'. Eirene was noted for her piety and her kindness to the poor, for which she is revered as a saint in the Greek Orthodox Church.

The fourth of the surviving mosaics in the galleries is located high on the E face of the NW pier. This panel represents the Emperor Alexander, who ascended to the throne in May 912, succeeding his elder brother, Leo VI. 'Here comes the man of thirteen months', said Leo with his dying breath, as he saw his despised brother coming to pay his last respects. This cynical prophecy was fulfilled in June of the following year, when Alexander died of apoplexy during a drunken game of polo. The mosaic portrait of Alexander, the last to be uncovered during the restoration of 1932–64, is dated to the brief period of his reign. The portrait shows him standing full-length, wearing the gorgeous ceremonial costume of a Byzantine emperor: crowned with a camelaucum, a conical, helmet-shaped coronet of gold with pendant pearls; draped in a loros, a long gold-embroidered scarf set with jewels; and shod in gem-studded crimson boots. Four medallions flanking the imperial figure bear the legend: 'Lord help the servant, the orthodox and faithful Emperor Alexander'.

THE PRECINCTS OF HAGHIA SOPHIA. There are a number of minor monuments of some interest in the precincts of Haghia Sophia, some of them dating from Byzantine times and others from the Ottoman era. These precincts are open during the same hours as the museum, except for the buildings and grounds in the restricted area just to the N of the church.

*The Theodosian Church.* The garden to the W of Haghia Sophia is lined with columns and other ancient architectural fragments unearthed in Istanbul in the course of construction projects since World War Two. Outside the NW side of the exonarthex there are visible some remains of the Theodosian church of Haghia Sophia, excavated in 1935. What remains *in situ* is chiefly the foundation of a monumental entrance-porch. It is essentially in the classical manner: a colonnaded porch with the traditional entablature and coffered ceiling above the columns; although at least above the central columns over the main door the entablature appears to have been arched instead of trabeated (i.e., with a horizontal lintel), as was always the case in classical buildings. Vast fragments of this superstructure can examined close at hand as they lie scattered here and there in front of the building, and it is interesting to see the predominantly Hellenistic decorative motifs giving place occasionally to some distinctively Christian symbol.

Through the temple-like porch one entered a great basilical church, probably with five aisles rather than the usual three. Such a plan, with a wide central nave flanked on either side by two rows of columns forming a double aisle, was occasionally used in early times for the largest churches. It can be seen, for example, at the Lateran and San Paolo fuori le Mura in Rome or at St. Demetrius in Thessalonica. The remaining fragments of the Theodosian church show that this too was a building of monumental proportions, comparable in size and grandeur to Justinian's church.

*The Imperial Ottoman Tombs.* The domed buildings in the garden to the S of Haghia Sophia are all imperial Ottoman tombs. The building just to the right of the present entrance to the church, an octagonal structure with a low dome, is the former Baptistery of Justinian's church (this is not open to the public). In 1623 it was converted into a mausoleum to house the remains of the mad Sultan Mustafa I, who died shortly after he was deposed by the Janissaries on 10 September of that year. A quarter of a century later the mad Sultan Ibrahim was interred there too, on 10 September 1648, after he had been deposed and executed on the orders of his mother, the Valide Sultan Kösem.

The other imperial tombs, or türbe, are located at the E end of the garden to the S of Haghia Sophia. The earliest in date is that of Selim II, which wàs completed in 1577. This türbe is important because it is a work of Sinan, and also because both the exterior entrance facade and the whole of the interior are revetted with superb Iznik tiles. The building is square, with an outer dome resting directly on the exterior walls, while within, a circlet of columns supports the inner dome. The largest of the catafalques in the türbe covers the grave of Selim II, the Sot, son and successor of Süleyman the Magnificent. Selim died in 1574 at the age of 54, after having fallen in his bath while in a drunken stupor. Beside Selim's catafalque is that of his favourite wife, Nurbanu. Arrayed around them are the tiny catafalques covering the graves of five of Selim's sons, three of his daughters, and 32 children of his son and successor, Murat III. Selim's sons were all strangled on the night of 21 December 1574, executed, according to Ottoman law, to ensure the peaceful accession of Murat III, his eldest son.

The türbe of Murat III stands just beside that of his father; this fine building was completed in 1599 by Davut Ağa, the successor to Sinan as Chief of the Imperial Architects. It is hexagonal in plan, also with a double dome, and is revetted with Iznik tiles comparable in quality to those in Selim's türbe. The türbe contains the remains of Murat III as well as those of his favourite wife, Safiye, along with four of his concubines, 23 of his sons, and 25 of his daughters. (According to the official records of Topkapí Sarayí, Murat III fathered a total of 103 children.) Nineteen of these princes were strangled on the day that Murat died, 16 January 1595, in order to ensure the peaceful succession of his eldest son, Mehmet III. This was the last instance of this bloody Ottoman custom; thenceforth the younger brothers of a succeeding sultan was confined in the Kafes, a royal prison in Topkapí Sarayí, rather than being executed.

Built up against Murat's türbe is the little building called the Türbe of the Princes, which contains only the tiny catafalques of five infant sons of Murat IV. These five princelings died natural deaths, perishing during one of the many plagues that ravaged the Harem.

The latest in date of the türbes in the garden beside Haghia Sophia is that of Mehmet III, son and successor of Murat III. The türbe was completed in the year of the Sultan's death, 1603; it is octagonal in plan, with a double dome, and is also revetted with superb Iznik tiles. Buried beside the Sultan is his favourite wife, Handan, and nine of his children, all of whom died natural deaths. Also interred here are 16 daughters of Murat III, all victims of the plague in the same year, 1598.

MINOR OTTOMAN STRUCTURES. The other Ottoman structures in the courtyard of Haghia Sophia are of very minor importance. The building just to the left of the entrance is a primary school built by Mahmut I in 1740. It is very typical of the little Ottoman one-room schoolhouses of that period, consisting of just a porch and a square chamber covered by a dome. This schoolhouse was used for the education of the children of the clergy and staff of the Haghia Sophia Mosque. To the right of the entrance there is a little domed structure built by the Fossatis in 1847–49. This was the muvakithane, the house and workshop of the mosque astronomer, whose sundial can still be seen on the facade of Haghia Sophia to the left of the entrance. In the centre of the courtyard, to the left, is the mosque şadirvan, built for Mahmut I in about 1740. The şadirvan is designed in the Turkish rococo style and is one of the most attractive mosque fountains in the city, with its widely-projecting roof gaily painted in floral motifs, its fine bronze grilles, and its marble panels carved in low relief.

*The Hamam of Roxelana* is located on the E side of the park between Haghia Sophia and the Blue Mosque; this is outside the precincts of Haghia Sophia, but it was closely connected to it, having been built principally to serve the clergy, staff and congregation of that mosque. This splendid public bath was commissioned by Süleyman the Magnificent in the name of his wife Haseki Hürrem, better known in the West as Roxelana. The hamam was designed by Sinan and was completed by him in 1556. It is a double hamam, one end being for men and the other for women. Each end of the building consists of a great entrance hall covered with a vast dome; from there one passes through a corridor with three small domes to the hararet, the steam-room, which is also domed and surrounded by a series of little chambers for bathing. Note the charming symmetry of the building

*The fountain of Sultan Ahmet III was built in 1728 and is a particularly fine example of Turkish rococo architecture.*

and its gracious lines; it is one of the most attractive and elaborate of the Turkish baths in the city. It has been well restored in recent years and there are plans to open it as a museum.

The street that runs past the E end of Haghia Sophia was known in Byzantium as the Embolos of the Holy Well. This was a porticoed way by which the Emperor could walk from the Chalke, the monumental vestibule of the Great Palace of Byzantium, to the Holy Well, a sacred spring that issued forth near the SE corner of Haghia Sophia. From there the Emperor could enter the metatorium of Haghia Sophia directly, passing through the large portal that can still be seen in the E bay of the S aisle.

Farther along this street, at the NE corner of the church, there is a large Turkish gateway in the rococo style. This is the rear entrance to the garden N of Haghia Sophia (closed to the public). The gateway leads to a building known in Byzantium as the skeuophylakion, the treasury of Haghia Sophia, where all the precious objects and sacred vessels of the church were kept. This two-storey building, which stands just to the E of the NE buttress, is circular in plan and covered with a dome. Archaeological studies have indicated that the skeu-phylakion is older than Justinian's church, and some authorities believe that it served as the treasury of the original church of Haghia Sophia which was completed by Constantius. There is another domed building S of the skeuphylakion, built in between the two N buttresses. This dates to the 16C and was an imaret, or free kitchen, which served the clergy and staff of the Mosque of Haghia Sophia.

Just opposite the rear gate of Haghia Sophia is the monumental •street-fountain of Ahmet III, which stands just to the right of the outer entrance to Topkapí Sarayí. This is one of the most beautiful and elaborate of the monumental Ottoman fountains in Istanbul, and is a particularly fine example of Turkish rococo architecture. It is a square structure with an overhanging roof surmounted by five small domes. On each of the four sides there is a çeşme, or wall-fountain, and at each of the four corners there is a sebil. Each of the wall-fountains is set into a niche framed in an ogival archway. The voussoirs of the arches are in alternating red and pink marble and the facade is richly decorated with floral designs in low relief. The corner sebils are semicircular in form, each having three windows framed by engaged marble columns and enclosed with ornate marble grilles. The curved wall above and below each sebil is elaborately decorated with relieved designs and ornate inscriptions. Above each of the four fountains there is a long and beautifully written calligraphic inscription in gold letters on a blue-green ground. The words were written by the poet Seyit Vehbi Efendi in praise of Sultan Ahmet's fountain, in which he compares it to the sacred cascade fountains of Paradise.

# 3 Topkapí Sarayí

**••Topkapí Sarayí** (Pl 11,4), which for more than four centuries was the imperial residence of the Ottoman sultans, is the most extensive and fascinating monument of Turkish civil architecture in existence. In addition to its historical and architectural interest, it houses extraordinary collections of porcelains, armour, fabrics, jewellery, miniatures, calligraphy, and many precious objects and works of art that once belonged to the sultans and their court.

ADMISSION. Topkapí Sarayí is open 9:30–5:30 every day except Tues. Tickets are purchased in the gateway to the Second Court. A separate ticket must be purchased to gain admission to the Harem.

HISTORY. When Sultan Mehmet II captured Constantinople in 1453, he found the palaces of the Byzantine emperors in such ruins as to be uninhabitable. He then chose a large overgrown area on the broad peak of the Third Hill as the site of his first imperial residence. Here he constructed an extensive complex of buildings and gardens which later came to be known as Eski Saray, the Old Palace. Only a few years later he decided to build a new palace on the N side of the First Hill, on what had been the acropolis of ancient Byzantium. He began by ringing the acropolis with a massive wall, which extended from the Byzantine sea-walls along the Marmara to those along the Golden Horn. (The new palace eventually took its name from the main sea-gate in this wall; this was Topkapí, the Cannon Gate, so-called because it was flanked by two enormous cannon that threatened all shipping approaching Saray Burnu. This twin-towered gateway was destroyed in the 19C.) The Conqueror constructed the palace buildings on the high ground of the acropolis, while on the slopes of the hill and along the shore he laid out extensive parks and gardens. This was done during the period 1459–65, after which the Sultan and his court took up residence in Topkapí Sarayí, leaving the Old Palace as a residence for the women of his departed father's harem. The Harem in Topkapí Sarayí in its present state dates largely from the reign of Murat III (1574–95), with extensive reconstruction and additions chiefly under Mehmet IV (1648–87) and Osman III (1754–57), while the isolated pavilions of the Fourth Court date from various periods. In 1574, 1665 and 1856 serious fires devastated large sections of the palace, so that many of the older buildings have disappeared, particularly those in the First Court. Nevertheless the three inner courtyards and the buildings around them remain much the same as they were in the 15–16C.

Topkapí Sarayi was much more than just the private residence of the Sultan and his court. It was the seat of the supreme executive and judicial council of the Empire, the Divan, and it housed the largest and most select of the training schools for the imperial civil service, the Palace School. In fact, the Saray was laid out to accommodate these various institutions, each in their own courtyard. The First Court, which was open to the public, was the service area of the palace. It contained a hospital, a bakery, an arsenal, the state mint, a branch of the treasury, and various storage places, as well as dormitories for guards, labourers and domestics in the Outer Service, those whose duties did not bring them into the inner palace. The Second Court was the seat of the Divan, devoted to the public administration of the Empire, and was open to anyone who had business to transact with the Council. Beyond this court to right and left were certain other service areas, principally the kitchens and privy stables. The Third Court was strictly reserved for members of the Sultan's household and government officials, and was largely given over to the various divisions of the Palace School. Beyond this was the Fourth Court, a large enclosed garden on several levels, in which there were a number of pavilions. The residential section of the palace extended along the W side of the three inner courts, with the Harem, the women's quarters to the S and the Selamlík, the residence of the Sultan and the royal princes, to the N. During the great days of the Ottoman Empire the population of the palace is estimated to have been between 3–4000. Topkapí Sarayí continued as the principal imperial residence for four centuries, until in 1853 Sultan Abdül Mecit I moved into the new palace of Dolmabahçe on the Bosphorus. The old palace on the First Hill was thereafter used to house the women of departed sultans, and their servants, and continued to do so until 1909, when the imperial harem was officially disbanded. After that, a few old servants and eunuchs remained there as squatters until 1924, when Topkapí Sarayí was converted into a museum. In the years since then the Saray has undergone a continuous process of renovation and restoration; the high-point came in the 1960s with the opening of part of the Harem to the public.

THE FIRST COURT. The main entrance to the palace grounds, now as in Ottoman times, is through Bab-í Hümayün, the Imperial Gate, opposite the NE corner of Haghia Sophia. This monumental gateway was erected by Mehmet the Conqueror in 1478. Originally there was a second storey, demolished in 1867 when Sultan Abdül Aziz surrounded the gate with the present marble frame and lined the niches on either side with marble. In Ottoman times these niches often displayed the severed heads of rebels or those convicted of serious crimes. The rooms in the gateway housed the Kapícís, or guards, of whom 50 were on watch at all times of the day and night. The older part of the arch contains four beautiful calligraphic inscriptions, one recording the erection of the gate by the Conqueror and the other three quotations from the Kuran. The tuğra, or imperial monogram, is that of Mehmet II, and other calligraphic inscriptions record the reconstruction of the gateway by Abdül Aziz in 1867.

The Imperial Gate leads to the FIRST COURT of Topkapí Sarayí. This was sometimes called the Courtyard of the Janissaries, as they assembled here when on duty in the palace. During the decline of the Ottoman Empire in the 17–18C, the Janissaries lost most of their effectiveness as a military force and kept the town and the palace in constant terror from their outrages and violence. Several sultans lost their thrones in Janissary insurrections and two reigning monarchs were murdered by them. The Janissary Corps was finally annihilated by Mahmut II in 1826, the first step in the Sultan's attempt to reform the Ottoman Empire.

The First Court formed the outer grounds of Topkapí Sarayí, and was not considered to be part of the palace proper. To the right of the entryway there once stood the palace infirmary. Farther off to the right a road leads down to what was once part of the outer gardens of the Saray (not open to the public), and before that the grounds of the Great Palace of Byzantium. The rest of the right side of the First Court consists of a blank wall behind which were the palace bakeries, famous for the superfine white bread baked for the Sultan and the chosen few upon whom he bestowed it. These buildings, several times burned down and reconstructed, now serve as workrooms for the Topkapí Sarayí museum.

To the left of the entryway stands the Byzantine church of Haghia Eirene, which most travellers visit after completing a tour of Topkapí Sarayí (see below, Rte 4A). Until 1826 the church served as an arsenal for the Janissaries, and later in the 19C it served as a storehouse for antiquities, principally old Ottoman armaments.

During Ottoman times the area between Haghia Eirene and the Saray defence-walls was the site of a quadrangle that housed the Straw Weavers and the Carriers of Silver Pitchers, with a central courtyard where the palace firewood was stored. Still standing behind a high wall N of Haghia Eirene are the buildings once used as the Imperial Mint and the Outer Treasury. Just to the N of these buildings a road leads down to Gülhane Park and the museums that stand on its upper terrace (see below, Rte 4); during Ottoman times this area also formed part of the lower gardens of the palace.

Near the far right-hand corner of the First Court there is a fountain known as Cellad Çeşmesi, the Executioner's Fountain, so named because the Chief Executioner of the palace cleaned his hands and sword there after performing his duties. The fountain is flanked by two truncated pillars called by the Turks 'Example Stones'. The examples were the severed heads of executed criminals and rebels.

At the far end of the First Court is *Bab-üs Selam*, the Gate of Salutations, better known as Orta Kapí, or the Middle Gate. This was the entryway to the Inner Palace, through which only authorised persons could pass, and only on foot. This is a much more impressive entryway than the Imperial Gate and it preserves its original appearance to a greater extent. The gateway is typical of the military architecture of the Conqueror's time, with its twin octagonal towers capped with conical roofs. The gatehouse itself is surmounted by a crenellated parapet with sloping merlons, concealing a patrol-walk broad enough to hold several cannon. The double-arched doorway is closed by two pairs of splendid doors, the outer one of which bears the Islamic date AH (after the Hegira, Mohammed's flight to Mecca) 931, or AD 1524–25. Above the outer gate is the tuğra of Süleyman the

Magnificent and a calligraphic inscription giving the Islamic creed: 'There is no God but God, and Mohammed is his Prophet'. Between the two doorways there is a large central chamber, which now serves as the entrance to the Topkapí Sarayí museum. To the right of this chamber there are several rooms that once housed the head gate-keepers; one of these chambers was used as a waiting-room for for-eign ambassadors or other foreign visitors who had an audience with the Grand Vezir or the Sultan (a very rare occurrence). To the left are smaller rooms for the lower-ranking gatekeepers, along with a cubicle for the Chief Executioner and a tiny cell for prisoners awaiting execution.

THE SECOND COURT. The enormous Second Court, some 130m long and 110m in width at its S end, appears much as it did when it was first laid out in the time of the Conqueror. The main path through the court is flanked by ancient cypresses and plane trees, with rose bushes growing alongside the other pathways, giving it a tranquil park-like atmosphere. In Ottoman times this was known as the Court of the Divan, the Imperial Council, which met in the domed chambers at the far left corner of the courtyard. The Divan and the Inner Treasury beyond it are the only buildings in the courtyard, with the remainder of its periphery consisting simply of blank walls faced by colonnaded porticos with antique marble columns and Turkish capitals. Beyond the colonnade the whole of the right side of the courtyard is occupied by the kitchens of the palace, while beyond the wall to the left are the Privy Stables, a mosque, and some dormitories (see below).

The Court of the Divan seems to have been designed essentially for the pageantry connected with the transaction of the public business of the Empire. Here, four times a week, the Divan met to deliberate on administrative matters or to discharge its judicial functions. On such occasions the whole courtyard was filled with a vast throng of magnificently dressed officials and the corps of palace guards and Janissaries—at least 5000 people on ordinary days, but more than twice that number when some special ceremony was being held. Even at such times an almost total silence prevailed throughout the courtyard, a fact commented upon with astonishment by the travellers who witnessed it.

*The Divan.* From the Middle Gate five paths radiate to various parts of the courtyard, with the second from the left leading to the Divan. This building, together with the Inner Treasury, projects from the NW corner of the courtyard and is dominated by the square tower with a conical roof that is such a conspicuous landmark of the Saray. This complex dates in essentials from the time of the Conqueror, though much altered in subsequent periods. The tower was originally lower and had a pyramidal roof; the present structure with its Corinthian columns was built for Mahmut II in 1820.

The Divan complex consists of the Council Chamber (the first room on the left), the Public Records Office, and the Office of the Grand Vezir. The first two rooms, both of which are square and covered by a dome, open widely into one another under a great arch. Both chambers were badly damaged by fire in 1574, and were immediately afterwards restored by Murat III, probably under the supervision of Sinan. During the reign of Ahmet III they were redecorated in a rather charming rococo style, but in 1945 the Council Chamber was restored to appear as it was after the repairs by Murat III. The lower walls are revetted in Iznik tiles of the best period, while the upper parts of the walls, as well as the vaults and the domes, retain faded traces of their original arabesque painting. Around three sides of the room there is a low couch covered with Turkish carpets, the divan from which the

Council took its name. Here sat the members of the Council: the
Grand Vezir in the centre opposite the door, the other vezirs on either
side of him in strict order of rank. Over the Grand Vezir's seat there is
a grilled window looking into a small room in the tower; this was
called the Eye of the Sultan because from his hiding-place he could
witness the proceedings of the Council without being observed. The
Records Office, which has retained its 18C decor, served as an archive
for Divan records and for documents that might be needed at Council
meetings. From here a door led to the Grand Vezir's office, though the
present entrance is from under the elaborate portico with its richly-
painted rococo ceiling.

The Records Office chamber is now used to exhibit some of the
Saray's large and fascinating *Clock Collection*, which includes
priceless timepieces from all periods in the history of the palace, only
a portion of which are on display. The most splendid clock on display
is one that was presented by Napoleon I as a gift to Mahmut II. This
masterpiece, which was made in Paris by A.L. Breguet c 1810, is set
with rubies and emeralds and is decorated with enamel panels with
painted landscapes of the Bosphorus and its shores, along with a

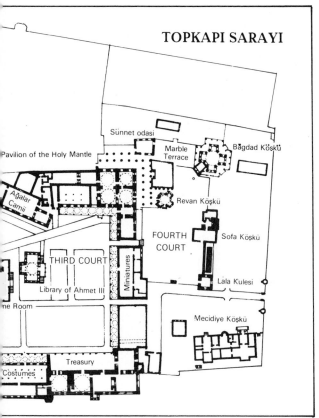

TOPKAPI SARAYI

Sünnet odasi

Pavilion of the Holy Mantle

Marble Terrace

Bâgdad Köskü

Ağalar Camii

Revan Köşkü

FOURTH COURT

Sofa Köşkü

THIRD COURT

Miniatures

Library of Ahmet III

Lala Kulesi

ne Room

Mecidiye Köşkü

Treasury

Costumes

cameo portrait of the Sultan. In the various cabinets there are a
number of superb clocks made in England and on the Continent in the
18C. The oldest of these is in Cabinet 4 (No.730); this is a table clock
with chimes made by the Marwick Markham Borrell firm in London c
1740.

*The Inner Treasury.* Adjacent to the three rooms of the Divan complex
is the *Inner Treasury, a long chamber with eight domes in four pairs
supported internally by three massive piers. This building dates from
the late 15C or the early 16C, and was most recently restored in 1926.
Here, and in the vaults below, were stored the tax receipts and tribute
money as they arrived from all over the Empire. These funds were
kept here until the quarterly pay-days for the use of the Council in
meeting the expenses of government, and at the end of each quarter
what remained unspent was transferred to the Imperial Treasury in
the Third Court.
    The Inner Treasury is now used to display the Saray's *Collection of
Arms and Armour.* As one would expect, this is especially rich in
Turkish arms and armour of all periods, including many objects that

belonged to the sultans themselves. Among the latter there are bows
made by several sultans for their own use, including a particularly fine
one made by Beyazit II. (All of the sultans were forced to learn a trade
in their youth, and many of them chose to become bow-makers.) There
are also a large number of superb swords that formerly belonged to the
Ottoman sultans and other Moslem rulers, the latter taken as booty by
the Turks during their conquests in Asia and Africa. Among these, the
finest are the weapons belonging to the Mameluk sultans of Egypt,
seized by Selim I when he took Cairo in 1517, and the sword of the
Caliph Muawija (7C), which is displayed in a case near the entrance.
Besides these there are other weapons, armour, banners, and military
emblems of all kinds; the most unusual of these are the three pieces of
frontal armour for horses, one of which was worn by the steed which
Selim I rode on his victorious campaigns in Egypt and Persia. Also, one
should not fail to notice the Executioner's sword, a cleaver-like
weapon which shows signs of considerable use, exhibited here along
with its fine scabbard. Altogether there are 364 items exhibited in this
room, only a tiny fraction of the Saray's collection of arms and armour,
estimated to be in excess of 11,000 pieces.

Around the corner from the Divan, directly under the S side of the
Divan Tower, is the Carriage Gate, one of the two main entrances to
the Harem. Guided tours of the Harem start here; check at the
Information Desk for scheduled departure times of tours led by
English-speaking guides. Most visitors on a fi; it visit to Topkapí
Sarayí prefer to postpone their tour of the Harem until they have seen
the rest of the palace, returning to the Carriage Gate from the Fourth
Court.

The remainder of the W side of the Second Court is occupied by a
long portico where various inscriptions in old Turkish script are
displayed; they have been assembled from demolished Ottoman
buildings all over Istanbul. A small door (not open to the public) in the
wall near the Carriage Gate leads to the quarters of the Halberdiers-
with-Tresses, so called because they wore headdresses in which two
tufts of horse-hair hung down before their eyes, designed to prevent
them from getting a good look at the women when they delivered
firewood to the Harem.

*The Privy Stables.* (Not open to the public at present.) At the S end of
this portico there is a door known as *Meyyit Kapísí*, the Gate of the
Dead, because those who died in the Inner Palace were carried
through it for burial outside; this leads down to the area of the Privy
Stables on the lower slope of the hill. The Privy Stables occupy the W
side of a long and narrow courtyard, with the barracks of the
Halberdiers-with-Tresses at the N end and at the S the mid-18C
mosque of Beşir Ağa, Chief Black Eunuch in the reign of Mahmut I.
(Neither of the latter buildings are open to the public.) The mosque
has a curious minaret corbeled out from a corner of the building; the
minaret has no balcony but, instead, an enclosed space at the top with
openings for the müezzin to make the call to prayer.

The *Privy Stables were built by Mehmet II not long after the
Conquest; they housed only 20 to 30 horses for the use of the Sultan
and his favourite pages. The building consists of two parts, the long
stables themselves and at the far end two smaller rooms, that of the
Imrahor, or Master of the Horse, and the Raht Hazinesi, the Harness
Treasury. These are very pretty rooms, one with a charming 18C
painted ceiling, the other domed and with a quaint gallery. In both,

the valuable imperial harnesses are now displayed, while the long stable building houses carriages used by the sultans, most of them from the late 18C and the early 19C. The finest of these is the Aynalı Araba, the Mirrored Carriage, decorated with diamond-shaped pieces of glass and inlaid mother-of-pearl and sea-tortoise shell; this belonged to Selim III and is dated c 1790. There are also some charming old sedan chairs which were used by the leading ladies of the Harem on their excursions into town. One interesting exhibit is a tombstone that Osman II erected for his favourite horse Süslü Kara, Fancy Black, who died in 1622.

Returning to the Middle Gate, one now takes the right-hand path towards the Saray kitchens. On the way notice the enormous Byzantine capital lying near the portico; this was dug up in the courtyard some years ago, along with another capital of the same type that is now in the corridor of the kitchen area, near the southernmost gateway. Both capitals, which are dated 5–6C AD, obviously bore honorific statues, but who these works represented and why they happened to be standing on this part of the First Hill is not known.

*The *Palace Kitchens.* Beyond the three gateways in the E portico a long, narrow courtyard runs the entire length of the area. The palace kitchens open off from this on the right, as one faces N, while the rooms on the left served as storerooms, except for two that were used as mosques by the kitchen staff. The kitchens consist of a long series of ten spacious chambers with lofty domes on the Marmara side—a conspicuous feature of the Istanbul skyline — and equally lofty dome-like chimneys on the side of the courtyard. The two southernmost domes go back to the time of the Conqueror, the other eight to that of Beyazit II, while the cone-like chimneys in front of them are additions by Sinan, who reconstructed much of this area after the devastating fire of 1574. Each kitchen had a separate use: for the Sultan, the Valide Sultan, the Chief Black Eunuch, the other eunuchs, the women of the Harem, the Divan, etc.; but the assignments varied from time to time.

*The **Porcelain Collection.* Today the kitchens are used for the display of the Saray's incomparable collection of Chinese porcelain and other china and glassware. The Chinese collection, which is housed in the three southernmost rooms, is considered to be the third richest and most varied in the world, surpassed only by those at Peking and Dresden. The collection, of which 4584 pieces are exhibited out of a total of 10,512, was begun by Beyazit II, and augmented by Selim I and above all by Süleyman the Magnificent. The pieces date from the wonderful celadons of the Sung and Yuan dynasties (AD 960–1368) to the later Ming of the 18C. The European specimens: Limoges, Sèvres, Meissen, and others, are less impressive. The last two kitchens at the N end have been restored to their original appearance and are used for a fascinating display of antique Turkish cooking utensils, including platters, bowls, ladles and kazans, bronze cauldrons of prodigious size, all of which were once used in the Saray kitchens. The small building with three domes at the N end of the courtyard is variously identified as the confectioner's mosque or as an olive-oil refinery and soap-factory; doubtless it served different purposes at different times. It now houses an interesting collection of Turkish glass from the Beykoz and other Istanbul factories of the 18–19C, some of it very lovely.

Leaving the kitchen precincts, one approaches *Bab-üs Saadet*, the Gate of Felicity. This is the entryway to the Third Court and to the strictly private and residential areas of the palace, which in Ottoman times was called the House of Felicity. The gateway itself was originally built in the time of the Conqueror, though it was reconstructed in the late 16C and thoroughly redecorated in the rococo style in the 18C. At the time of his accession and on holidays, the Sultan sat before the gate on his gold and emerald Bayram Throne to receive the homage of his subjects and officials.

THE THIRD COURT. Just beyond the inner threshold of the Bab-üs Saadet stands the *Arz Odasí*, the *Throne Room. Although this structure is in the Third Court, it belongs by function and use rather to the Second, for here was played out the last act of the ceremonies connected with the meetings of the Divan. Here, at the end of each session of the Council, the Grand Vezirs and the other high officials of the realm waited on the Sultan and reported to him upon the business transacted and the decisions taken, which could not be considered final until they had received the royal assent. Here also the ambassadors of foreign powers were presented to the Sultan upon their arrival and departure. Among the very few private citizens ever allowed to enter here was Lord Byron, who in 1811 had an audience with Mahmut II in the company of the British Ambassador, Stratford Canning.

The Throne Room occupies a small building with a heavy and widely overhanging roof supported on a colonnade of antique marble columns. The foundations date from the time of the Conqueror, but most of the superstructure dates to the reign of Selim I; inscriptions record restorations by Ahmet III and Mahmut II. The room was restored yet again in more recent times, after having been badly damaged in the fire of 1856. On either side of the entrance portal there are panels of yellow and green tiles done in the charming *cuerda seca* technique of the early Iznik period in the 16C, and nearby is a fountain placed there by Süleyman. The building is divided into a small antechamber on the right and the throne room proper on the left. The magnificent canopy of the throne, dated by an inscription to AH 1005 (AD 1596), and the gilt-bronze ocak, or chimney-piece, are the only parts of the decoration that survived the fire in 1856. The throne was hung with magnificent bejewelled embroideries for different occasions; some of these are on display in the Treasury.

*The Palace School.* Apart from the Throne Room, the Treasury, and the Pavilion of the Holy Mantle, all the buildings in and around the Third Court were devoted to the various branches of the Palace School. The School was organised in six divisions, or Halls; the two introductory schools, Küçük Oda (Small Hall) and Büyük Oda (Large Hall), occupied the entire S side, to left and right respectively, of the Bab-üs Saadet. Here also were the quarters of the White Eunuchs, and their Ağa, who were in charge of the administration and discipline of the School. If a boy was talented in any field, he would pass from this introductory school to one of the four vocational Halls. The Seferli Koğuşu, or Campaign Hall, stands on the raised part of the E side of the Court. The N side of the Court, opposite the Bab-üs Saadet, was occupied by the Hasine Koğuşu, the Hall of the Treasury, on the right, next to the Treasury itself, and the Kiler Koğuşu, the Hall of the Commissariat. Finally, the last and highest of the vocational schools, the Has Oda Koğuşu, the Hall of the Privy Chamber, occupies a large

building on the W side of the Court between the Pavilion of the Holy
Mantle and Ağalar Camii, the principal mosque of the School.

This elaborately organised school for the training of the Imperial Civil Service
appears to be unique in the Islamic world. It was founded and its principles laid
down by the Conqueror, though later sultans added to and modified it. The pages
who attended the school came from the Christian subjects of the Empire and
likely youths captured in war. They entered at various ages from 12 to 18 and
received a vigorous training, intellectual and physical, which in contrast to the
usual Islamic education was largely secular and designed specifically to prepare
the students for the administration of the Empire. There can be no doubt that the
brilliant success of the Ottoman state in the earlier centuries of its existence was
to a large extent due to the training its administrators received in the Palace
School.

*The Imperial Costume Collection*. Turning to the right from the
Bab-üs Saadet, one passes the building which was once the Büyük
Oda. This building burned down in 1856 but has since been reconstructed and is now used for museum offices. One then comes to
the Seferli Odasí, which is preceded by a domed colonnade supported
by a row of very handsome Byzantine columns in verd antique. The
Hall is a long room divided into three aisles by two rows of pillars
supporting barrel-vaults. It houses the Imperial Wardrobe, a fascinating collection of costumes of the Ottoman sultans from the time of
the Conqueror onwards. There are over 1300 of them in the Saray's
collection, of which the most splendid and interesting are on display.
All of the older ones are of the kaftan type, a long robe reaching to the
feet made of silk, satin or velvet brocade in brilliant colours and bold
design, often lined or trimmed with fur; many are of outstanding
beauty and nearly all are in perfect condition. Notice the kaftan of
Osman II, bespattered with blood at the time of his assassination by
the Janissaries in 1622. In the inner room there are displayed some
costumes worn in the Saray by the little princelings and princesses in
the early Ottoman period.

**The Treasury*. The rest of the E side of the court is taken up with the
rooms, on a slightly lower level, of the pavilion of the Conqueror,
which served him and several later sultans as a selamlik, or suite of
reception rooms. The vaults below were used as the Privy Treasury
and gradually the rooms themselves were turned over to the Treasury
as storerooms. It is curious that these rooms, some of the finest in the
palace and with an unrivalled view, should from the 17C onward have
been used as mere storerooms, even the superb open loggia at the
corner having at one time been walled in. The loggia has been opened
again and the rooms are used for the display of the palace treasures; it
is altogether an astonishing collection, admirably mounted and
displayed.

  **R1** (the farthest to the right): The most notable exhibit here is an
*ebony throne inlaid with ivory and mother-of-pearl, made for Murat
IV. Also of interest are: narghilahs, or water-pipes, with cut-crystal
bases and mouthpieces set with diamonds; little coffee-cup holders,
including one set with small rose-coloured diamonds; and an enamel-
led gold pen-box encrusted with gems. **R2:** The *Eve Throne, so called
because it was used in ceremonies that took place on the eve of
festivals, made for Ahmet I; the famous *Topkapí Dagger, with three
great emeralds on the sides and one on the top that opens to reveal a
watch, the property of Mahmut I; a set of armour that belonged to
Murat IV; robes, turbans and aigrettes belonging to various sultans,
including one made for his own use by Süleyman, who was an

accomplished goldsmith. **R3:** the so-called *Throne of Shah Ismail
(now believed to have been presented by Nadir Shah to Mahmut I), an
elaborate oval seat plated with gold and set with emeralds, rubies and
pearls in an enamel base; a Kuran case encrusted with gems, and with
a floral design in diamonds on the cover, the property of Mehmet III;
Shah Ismail's gold-plated belt, armlet and goblet, part of the loot taken
by Selim I in his victorious Persian campaign in 1514; golden reli-
quaries for supposed fragments of the skull and hand of St. John the
Baptist.

The loggia beyond forms an antechamber between R3 and R4; it has
in its centre a pretty fountain and basin carved from a single piece of
marble, and on two sides it opens out onto balconies with sweeping
views out over the Marmara.

**R4** contains some of the most valuable objects in the Treasury. Many
of these were part of the sürre, the gifts that were sent annually by the
Sultan to the holy cities of Mecca and Medina; these were returned to
Istanbul during World War I by the Ottoman governor of the Hejaz, in
order to prevent them from falling into enemy hands. One of the
celebrated exhibits here is the golden Bayram Throne (see above); this
was presented by the Governor of Egypt to Murat III at the time of his
accession to the throne in 1574, and was used on state occasions down
to the last days of the Empire. Another famous exhibit is Kaşíkçí
Elmasí, the Spoonmaker's Diamond (Case 4). An 86-carat diamond, it
is the fifth largest in the world. It belonged to Mehmet IV, who wore it
in the aigrette of his turban at the time of his accession to the throne in
1648. Also on exhibition here is an 80-carat diamond that belonged to
Ahmet I, along with jewel-studded pendants, aigrettes and other
precious objects belonging to various sultans.

In the centre of the Court, standing by itself, is the Library of Ahmet
III, erected in 1719 near the site of an older pavilion with a pool. It is an
elegant little building of Proconnesian marble consisting of three
domed areas flanked by three loggias with sofas and cupboards for
books; although 18C, the decoration is still almost wholly classical.

*The **Exhibition of Miniatures.** The two main buildings on the N side
of the Court were both damaged in the fire of 1856; the nearest one
was entirely reconstructed and now serves as offices for the Director of
the Museum. The farther one, beyond a passage leading to the Fourth
Court, houses the Exhibition of Turkish and Persian Miniatures. From
an artistic point of view this is perhaps the supreme treasure of the
Saray; the collection of miniatures is said to number more than 13,000,
of which only a few are exhibited at any one time.

The oldest of the miniatures shown here are contained in the three
so-called Fatih (the Conqueror) Albums; these contain miniatures and
specimens of calligraphy cut from various other books and albums.
These works have no connection with the Conqueror, but were
apparently brought to Istanbul by Selim I after his Persian campaign of
1514, and derive mainly from the 15C Persian court. They are ascribed
(with considerable uncertainty) to a painter called Mohammed Siyah
Kalem, Mohammed of the Black Pen, and have been dated variously,
from earlier than the 13C, to the second half of the 15C. Their place of
origin is unknown, but the scenes depicted suggest the vast hinterland
of central Asia, perhaps in Turkish-speaking lands. They are original
and powerful masterpieces of primitive art, and there is nothing quite
like them anywhere in the world.

The oldest Ottoman miniatures in the collection are by Matrakci

Nasuh, court-painter in the reign of Süleyman the Magnificent, who was also famous in his time as a calligrapher, mathematician, scientist, historian and soldier. The most interesting of Matrakci's works is his Description of the Stages of Sultan Süleyman's Campaign in the Two Iraqs. This marvellous work, completed in 1537, shows in a series of 132 miniatures the progress of Süleyman's march from Istanbul to Baghdad in his Persian campaign of 1534–35, depicting all of the places where the Ottoman army stopped along the way. The first miniature in this series has great historical importance in addition to its artistic merit, for in showing the Sultan's fleet sailing down the Golden Horn it gives an astonishingly accurate picture of Stamboul and Galata as they were at that time, so much so that one can recognise individual monuments and even streets and squares.

Other celebrated manuscripts exhibited here are the 'Hünername' (The Book of Accomplishments), the 'Shahanshahname' (The Book of the King of Kings), and the 'Surname' (The Book of Festivals). All three works were commissioned by Murat III (1574–95); they were written in Persian (the court language of literature) by Lokman bin Hüseyin al-'Ashur, the court poet and historian, and illustrated by the court-painter Osman. The first two of these are works glorifying the sultans and their exploits, particularly Süleyman the Magnificent, showing them leading their armies in victorious battle, surrounded by their pages in hunting, archery and polo, receiving dignitaries in audience. The 'Surname' represents a completely new and original development in Turkish painting, principally because of the novel subject matter, but also because of the new departure in artistic style. The theme of the 'Surname' was the lavish celebration of the circumcision feast of the Sultan's first son, Prince Mehmet, in 1583. The festivities were held in the Hippodrome and lasted for 57 days and nights, and the miniatures by Osman depict the guilds of the city entertaining the Sultan and the other spectators.

The latest in date of these manuscripts is a 'Surname' composed in 1720 to commemorate the circumcision feast of four sons of Ahmet III, a festival that lasted for two weeks and where the entertainment was once again provided by the guilds of the city. Here the text was written by the celebrated poet Vehbi, and the miniatures were done by Levni, perhaps the greatest painter in the history of Ottoman art.

Compared with the earlier 'Surname' of Murat III, the figures are shown far more realistically and with more verve and colour, and the whole scene evokes a greater sense of life and activity. Levni also painted a large number of portrait miniatures: the finest of those exhibited here is that of a dancing-girl in the Harem, a charming and bewitching figure.

In the last building on the N side of the courtyard, beyond another passage leading to the Fourth Court, there are exhibited a royal tent and throne used by the sultans when on campaign; also a mounting-block sheathed in silver.

The W side of the Court is occupied by the following buildings, going from N to S: the Pavilion of the Holy Mantle, the Hall of the Privy Chamber, the Mosque of the Ağas, and Kuşhane Kapísí, the Brigade Gate, the second of the two main entrances to the Harem. The first and last of these will be visited presently; meanwhile, a few words will suffice for the two middle ones. The Has Oda, the Hall of the Privy Chamber, was the highest of the vocational divisions of the Palace School. It was limited to 40 pages in immediate attendance upon the Sultan, and included the highest of the officials in the Inner Palace. Here is displayed a part of the collection of manuscripts, not miniatures this time, but admirable calligraphy, of all periods and all schools. Beyond the Has Oda, the building that juts out at an angle is Ağalar Camii, the Mosque of the Ağas, the principal place of worship of the Palace School. Though dating from the time of the Conqueror, it has been much remodelled and now houses the Library of the Saray.

*The Pavilion of the Holy Mantle.* A gateway leading to the left from the NW corner of the courtyard gives entrance to *Hírka-i Saadet Dairesi,* the chambers where the relics of the Prophet Mohammed and other sacred objects are preserved. These relics, of which the Prophet's mantle is the most sacred, were brought from Egypt by Selim I after his conquest of that country in 1517, when he assumed the title of Caliph. For centuries these relics were guarded here and displayed on state occasions only to the Sultan, his family, and his immediate entourage; in 1962 the present exhibit was arranged and opened to the public. The Pavilion itself consists of four domed rooms forming a square, with a fifth domed room opening off to the left of the SW chamber. The foundation and plan of the Pavilion date to the reign of the Conqueror; at that time and until the mid-19C it formed part of the Has Oda, or Selamlík. Murat III partly reconstructed the rooms and revetted them with tiles, and Mahmut II added some rather unfortunate embellishments.

One enters a room with a pretty fountain under the dome, which opens by a huge arch into the second room. Here are displayed the bow of the Prophet Mohammed and the swords of the first four Caliphs: Abu Bekr, Umar, Othman and Ali; farther on is one of the doors of the great mosque at Mecca. In the room to the left are some beautiful ancient Kurans; the solid gold covering for the Hacer-i Esved, the meteorite that is built into the Kaaba at Mecca; also water-gutters from Mecca of chased and moulded silver-gilt, and other precious objects. Returning to the room with the fountain, one passes into another chamber where the more personal relics of the Prophet are preserved: hairs from his beard, one of his teeth, his footprint, and his seal. Through a grilled door in this room one looks into the enclosure where the Holy Mantle is preserved in a golden coffer under a magnificent golden baldachino. In another coffer is the Holy Standard, unfurled when a cihad, or holy war, was declared against the infidel. This room has the most superb tiles of the greatest Iznik period, but it has been marred somewhat by the heavy rococo fireplace added by Mahmut II.

*The Kiosks in the Portico of Columns.* A door in the right wall of the NE room of the Pavilion leads into the open L-shaped Portico of Columns. This portico adjoins two sides of the Pavilion of the Mantle, with kiosks opening off from the E and W ends. The one to the E is the *Rivan Köşkü,* built in 1636 by Murat IV to commemorate his capture of Rivan (modern Erivan), in the Caucasus. It is a cruciform room entirely revetted in Iznik tiles dating from just after the greatest period, but still beautiful, while the outside has a polychrome revetment of marble. The kiosk at the W end of the portico is the *Sünnet Odasí,* the Circumcision Room; this was built for Sultan Ibrahim in 1641, and for the next two centuries the circumcision rites of young Ottoman princes were carried out here. Both the interior and exterior of the kiosk are covered with ceramic tiles; none of these is from Ibrahim's own time but they range in date from the earliest Iznik style in *cuerda seca* technique through the great period in the second half of the 16C and the early 17C.

THE FOURTH COURT. The Sünnet Odasí stands at the S end of a broad marble terrace overlooking the Golden Horn. This terrace forms the W end of the Fourth Court, which is not really a courtyard but a garden on several levels, adorned with a number of pavilions. At the

SE corner of the terrace there is a large marble pool with a cascade fountain at its centre, once the scene of aquatic revels staged for Crazy Ibrahim by the women of his harem. On the left side of the terrace there is a curving balustrade of white marble carved in openwork design. At the centre of this balustrade, hanging high out over the lower gardens of the Saray, there is a charming little balcony covered by a domed canopy in gilded bronze carried on four slim bronze pillars. An inscription on the canopy records that the balcony is called Iftariye and was made in 1640 for Sultan Ibrahim. The balcony takes its name from the Iftar, the festive meal taken after sunset in the holy month of Ramazan, which ends the daily fast. According to palace tradition, Ibrahim partook of the Iftar on this balcony, and a miniature in one of the 'Surnames' shows him seated there watching his children playing on the terrace.

At the N end of the terrace stands the *Baghdad Köşkü*, built in 1638 by Murat IV to commemorate his capture of Baghdad the previous year. The kiosk is cruciform in plan and its wide overhanging eaves are carried by an arcade of slender marble columns. The columns are crowned with lotus capitals and the voussoirs of the arches are in alternating white and coloured marble with serrated edges. The walls inside and out are sheathed in ceramic tiles, chiefly blue and white. The interior is furnished with carved wooden cabinets and coffee-tables inlaid with mother-of-pearl, and the window-recesses on four sides are lined with embroidered divans. One of the eight walls is taken up with a splendid bronze chimney-piece, while the other seven are graced by stained glass windows in two courses. The dome of the kiosk is adorned with elaborate arabesques on a crimson ground, painted on leather.

A staircase beside the pool leads down into what was once the garden of Ahmet III, the site of his fabulous Tulip Festivals. At the centre of the garden there is a charming pavilion known as the *Sofa Köşkü*. (This is sometimes called, though incorrectly, the Kiosk of Kara Mustafa Paşa.) The pavilion is believed to have been built for Ahmet III, probably as a pied-à-terre for his use during the Tulip Festival; in 1752 the building was redecorated in the rococo style by Mahmut I. Farther on there is a low tower called variously *Başlala Kulesi*, the Tower of the Head Tutor, or *Hekimbaşí Odasí*, the Chamber of the Head Tutor; it doubtless served different purposes at different periods. Across a road that leads down to the outer gardens there is a pavilion standing on a marble terrace; this is the *Mecidiye Köşkü*, the last building to be erected in the Saray before it was abandoned as an imperial residence. This kiosk was erected in about 1840 for Abdül Mecit I, and is entirely western in style. In recent years its lower floor and terrace have been converted into a restaurant, the Lezzet, from which there is a panoramic view out across the Marmara to the Asian suburbs of the city.

**\*\*The Harem**. One now returns to the Court of the Divan to visit the Harem. The Harem is a veritable labyrinth of passages, courtyards, gardens, staircases and rooms—some 300 chambers in all, almost all of them surprisingly small—on half-a-dozen different levels. It included not only the women's quarters, or Harem proper, but also the quarters of the Black Eunuchs, who were in charge of the Harem, along with rooms for the young princes and the Sultan's private apartments. To inspect it all, even cursorily, would take many days of arduous exploration. At present only about a score of rooms, passageways and

courtyards are open to the public, including most of the
more important and impressive chambers.

HISTORY. The Harem was not an original part of the palace as laid out by
Mehmet II. The Conqueror seems to have designed Topkapí Sarayí primarily as
the administrative centre of his Empire, reserving the Old Palace on the Third
Hill for his court and his harem. This arrangement was maintained by his three
immediate successors: Beyazit II, Selim I, and Süleyman the Magnificent, at least
during the early years of his reign. According to tradition, Süleyman allowed
Roxelana to install herself in Topkapí Sarayí, but probably only in wooden
pavilions, and his son Selim II seems to have followed this. The first permanent
structures in the Harem appear to have been built during the reign of Selim's son
Murat III (1574–95).

The Carriage Gate took its name from the fact that the Harem ladies
entered their carriages here when they were allowed to go for an
outing. Above the gateway is an inscription giving the date AH 996
(AD 1588). The gateway opens into a small, dark vestibule called
*Dolaplí Kubbe*, the Dome with Cupboards (1); this is followed by a
larger chamber revetted with fine tiles, which served as a guardroom
(2). On the left a door opens to a long passage leading down to the
gardens of the Saray, and another gives access to the mosque of the
Black Eunuchs; while on the right a door opens into the Divan tower.
Straight ahead is the long, narrow *Courtyard of the Black Eunuchs* (3).
The left side of the courtyard is bordered by an arcade of ten marble
columns with lotus capitals, above which hang wrought-iron lamps
that once lighted the way to the Carriage Gate. The building to the
rear of the porch, which is revetted in ceramic tiles, was the barracks
of the Black Eunuchs (4); an inscription in the courtyard bears the date
AH 1079 (AD 1668–69), indicating that this part of the Harem was
rebuilt by Mehmet IV after the great fire of 1665. The living quarters
of the Black Eunuchs are arranged around an inner covered courtyard
in three storeys with a tall fireplace at one end. There are about a
dozen little rooms on each floor; these must have been very crowded
since there were several hundred Black Eunuchs on duty in the
palace; doubtless they served in watches and slept in relays.

Returning to the outer Courtyard of the Black Eunuchs, one passes on the left a
staircase that leads up to the Schoolroom of the Princes, where the young sons of
the Sultan received their primary education; these are pretty rooms with good
tiles, but they are not open to the public. Just beyond the Schoolroom a door
leads to the apartments of the Kízlar Agasí, the Chief Black Eunuch; these too
are closed to the public.

At the far end of the Courtyard of the Black Eunuchs is the *Cümle
Kapísí*, the Main Gate (5), which opens into the Harem proper. This
leads to a second guard-room (6), from the left. side of which a long,
narrow corridor stretches to the open *Courtyard of the Cariyeler* (7), or
women servants. On the right side of this courtyard there are three
suites of rooms for the chief women officials of the Harem: the Head
Stewardess, the Treasurer, and the Chief Laundress. Their domed
and tiled rooms are very attractive, particularly as they overlook the
lower gardens of the Saray. (One of these suites is open to the public.)
The long staircase just beyond the three suites leads down to a large
courtyard on a much lower level, once the site of the Harem hospital.
The site is very picturesque; unfortunately it is not open to the public.
   Just beyond the Cümle Kapísí a gateway opens onto a wide corridor
which extends the entire E side of the Harem; this is the *Altín Yol*, the
Golden Way, a name which often appears in the history of the palace.
At the very beginning of the corridor an opening on the left leads to

*Ahead is Cümle Kapísí, the main entrance to the Harem. To the left is the former barracks of the Black Eunuchs. (Sedat Pakay)*

the large open *Courtyard of the Valide Sultan* (8). The Valide Sultan reigned over the Harem and frequently dominated her son, the Sultan, and through him the Empire. Her ˙apartments, which occupy most of the W side of the courtyard on two levels, were well placed for her to exercise her often nefarious influence, for they are in the centre of the Harem. The rooms of the Valide's apartment are small but quite attractive, with tiled walls and painted ceilings; unfortunately they are not yet open to the public.

At the NW corner of the courtyard a doorway leads into the ˙*Ocaklí Oda*, the Room with a Hearth (9), a beautifully tiled chamber

# THE HAREM

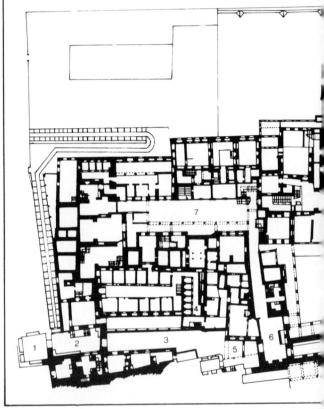

dominated by a large and splendid bronze chimney-piece. On the right a door leads to the suites of the First and Second Kadíns, the two highest ranking women in the Sultan's harem. On the left a door opens into a smaller chamber called *Çeşmeli Oda*, the Fountain-Room (10). The pretty çeşme, or wall-fountain, after which the room is named, bears the date AH 1077 (AD 1665–66). On the wooden door leading out of this room there is a superb Cufic inscription with letters of mother-of-pearl on a background of sea-tortoise shell; it reads: 'O Sultan, let your friends be joyful and happy and your enemies be full of woe'. The inscription is dated the same year as the fountain, and so it appears that both this room and the Ocaklí Oda are part of Mehmet IV's reconstruction after the fire of 1665. The two rooms served as antechambers between the Harem and the Sultan's own apartments.

A doorway leads from the Çeşmeli Oda into the *Hünkar Sofasí*, the

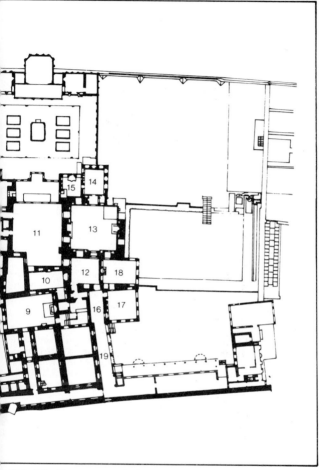

Hall of the Emperor (11), the largest and grandest room in the palace. Divided by a great arch into two unequal sections, the larger section is domed and the smaller, slightly raised, had a balcony above. The upper part of the room—dome, pendentives and arches—has been restored to its original appearance. However, the lower part retains the unfortunate baroque decorations added by Osman III (1754–57). This Hall was a reception room where the Sultan gave entertainments for the women of the Harem: the balcony was used by the musicians. This splendid chamber is believed to have been constructed for Murat III (1574–95), in which case the architect would surely have been Sinan.

A door at the NE corner of the Hünkar Sofasí leads into a small but lavishly-tiled antechamber (12). This once-elegant little room was badly disfigured during a reconstruction in the late 16C or the early

17C, when it was cut in half right through the dome to make space for an adjacent apartment (see below). This antechamber leads into the **\*\*Salon of Murat III** (13), the most splendid room in the palace. The Salon is dated, by an inscription, 1578, and, unlike the Hünkar Sofasí, it has retained the whole of its original decoration. The walls are sheathed in Iznik tiles from the greatest period of their manufacture; the panel of plum blossoms surrounding the elegant bronze chimney-piece is especially noteworthy, as is the calligraphic frieze which runs around the room. Opposite the fireplace there is an elegant three-tiered cascade fountain of carved polychrome marble set in a marble embrasure.The beauty of the decoration and the perfect and harmonious form of the room identify it as a work of Sinan.

Opening off the W side of the Salon there is a small chamber known as the *\*Library of Ahmet I,* (14) built in 1608–09. This is one of the most delightful rooms in the palace. The library is adorned with finely-carved wooden book-shelves and cabinets inlaid with sea-tortoise shell and mother-of-pearl, and its walls are revetted with blue and green tiles almost as beautiful as those in the salon. The room is lighted by windows on two sides, affording sweeping views across the Marmara and up the Bosphorus and the Golden Horn. Flanking each of the windows there are little fountains, designed to cool the summer breezes that enter the room.

A marble doorway in the S wall of the library leads to an even lovelier chamber, the **\*\*Dining-Room of Ahmet III,** (15) constructed in 1705–06. Its walls are panels of lacquered wood decorated with paintings of brightly-coloured flowers in garlands and vases, of heaped bowls of fruit, and, in one corner, a group of yellow-feathered ducklings following their mother. These decorations are charactistic of the Tulip Period, when European rococo art and architecture made its first appearance in Istanbul.

To the E of the Salon of Murat III there are a pair of very handsome rooms known as the **\*\*Double Kiosk** (17 and 18). Until recently these were thought to be the infamous Kafes, or Cage, the place where the younger brothers of a reigning sultan were confined after his accession to the throne, to avoid the possibility of a war of succession. However, the Kafes has now been identified as a suite of small rooms on the upper floor of the Harem just to the E of these apartments. It is not known exactly when or for what purpose the apartments in the Double Kiosk were built, but they must date from the end of the 16C, or the first years of the 17C, as their tiles are of the very greatest period and perhaps the most beautiful in the palace. The first room has a dome magnificently painted on canvas, while the ceiling of the inner room is flat but also adorned with superb painted designs. The second room also has a wonderful brass-gilt fireplace, on each side of which, above, are two of the most gorgeous tile panels in existence. Beyond the fireplace the paving stones have been removed to reveal, at a depth of about 30cm, another pavement and a surbase of tiles, also of the greatest period, but of a totally different design and colour from those that now revet the two rooms. This was the level of the Salon of Murat III, which was cut in half to provide space for the first of the two rooms in the Double Kiosk.

The colonnaded corridor that runs past the Double Kiosk is called, for some unknown reason, the *Consultation-Place of the Jinns* (19). This leads out to an open courtyard known as *Gözdelere Taşlíğí,* the Terrace of the Favourites, which overlooks the lower gardens of the palace. On the right side of the terrace is a long wooden building in

*The Dining-Room of Sultan Ahmet III, perhaps the most charming room in Topkapí Sarayí, constructed in 1705–06. (Turkish Ministry of Tourism)*

two storeys which once housed the Sultan's favourite women. These rooms are not open to the public, for they have not been changed or reconstructed since the last women of the Harem left the palace in 1909.

At the far end of the colonnaded corridor the Golden Road (20) leads off to the right. A short way along the Golden Road, one passes on the right, a staircase where in 1808 the slave-girl Cevri Khalfa fought off the assassins who were trying to kill Prince Mahmut, the future Sultan Mahmut II. Then one comes to *Kuşhane Kapísí*, the Birdcage Gate (21), where in 1651 the Valide Sultan Kösem was killed by the Chief Black Eunuch, Tall Süleyman. Guided tours of the Harem end at this point, after which those who have seen the rest of Topkapí Sarayí can make their way back to the Middle Gate, leaving the House of Felicity.

# 4 The Lower Gardens of the Saray

The lower gardens of Topkapí Sarayí extended from the outer walls of the palace down to the shores of the Marmara and the Golden ' Horn. The gardens on the Marmara side of the palace have long since vanished, but those on the slope of the First Hill leading down to the Golden Horn and Saray Burnu have been preserved in Gülhane Park. The main entrance to the park is on Alemdar Cd, beside the Alay Köşkü, but one can also enter the grounds through a gate in the W wall of the First Court of Topkapí Sarayí, just beyond the church of Haghia Eirene. The latter entrance is the most convenient for those who have just completed a tour of the Saray, for it enables one to visit Haghia Eirene and then go on to tour the museums that are located on the upper terrace of Gülhane Park: the Archaeological Museum, the Museum of the Ancient Orient, and the *Çinili Köşkü*.

## A. Haghia Eirene

**\*\*Haghia Eirene** (Pl 11,5) is the second largest medieval Christian sanctuary in the city, surpassed in size only by Haghia Sophia. It is one of the most beautiful Byzantine churches in existence, and a landmark in the history of Christian architecture.

ADMISSION. The church is open 9:30–4:30 every day except Mon. Tickets may be purchased at a booth beside the NW corner of the church.

HISTORY. According to tradition, the original church of Haghia Eirene was one of the first Christian sanctuaries in the old town of Byzantium. This sanctuary was dedicated to Haghia Eirene, the Divine Peace, an attribute of Christ, complementary to his personification of the Divine Wisdom. The church was rebuilt on a larger scale by Constantine the Great or his son Constantius, and it served as the patriarchal cathedral until the completion of the first church of Haghia Sophia. During the reign of Constantius Haghia Eirene was at the centre of the violent disputes then taking place between the Arians and the Orthodox party, the upholders of the Nicene Creed: in 346, 3000 people were killed in a religious riot in the courtyard of the church. The final triumph of the Orthodox party occurred in Haghia Eirene in 381, when the Second Ecumenical Council reaffirmed the Nicene Creed and condemned the Arians as heretics. Haghia Eirene came into prominence again after the destruction of Haghia Sophia in 404, when, for a decade, it served as the patriarchal cathedral once more. But then, after the completion of the Theodosian church of Haghia Sophia, Haghia Eirene took its accustomed second place and seldom played a leading role in the religious life of the city. At the time of the Nika revolt, in 532, Haghia Eirene and Haghia Sophia were totally destroyed by fire. After the revolt was put down Justinian began a project to rebuild both churches; the new church of Haghia Eirene was probably completed at about the same time as Haghia Sophia, in 537. The new churches of the Divine Wisdom and the Divine Peace were thenceforth closely linked and formed two parts of what was essentially one religious establishment, both of them administered by the Patriarchate and served by the same clergy. Haghia Eirene was almost destroyed in 564, when a fire ruined the atrium and part of the narthex, but it was immediately restored by Justinian, then in the last year of his life. In October 740 the church was severely damaged by an earthquake, after which it was restored, either by Leo III or his son, Constantine V. It appears that since that date no other major catastrophes have befallen the church, therefore the building one sees today dates from Justinian's time, with the exception of 8C repairs and minor Turkish additions. After the Conquest Haghia Eirene was enclosed within the outer walls of Topkapí Sarayí, serving as an arsenal for the Janissaries. In the late 19C, half a century or so after the dissolution of the Janissaries, the building became a storehouse for antiquities, principally old Ottoman armaments. In recent years these were removed and are now exhibited in the Military Museum in Harbiye (see Pera, Rte 18), after which the church was restored to its present condition. During the summer months it is now used for musical productions connected with the Istanbul Festival.

EXTERIOR. In plan the church is a rectangle, 42·2m long and 36·7m wide, with a five-sided apse projecting from the E wall, and to the E a narthex preceded by an atrium. The central area of the nave is covered by a dome carried on a high drum, with peaked roofs to its N, E and S, and a lower domical vault to the W.

INTERIOR. The ground around the church has risen some 5m above its original level and the present entry is through a Turkish porch and outbuildings outside the W end of the N aisle. From there a stone ramp leads down to the level of the interior.

In plan the church is a basilica, but a basilica of a very unusual type, as can be seen from an examination of its plan. The central nave is flanked by a pair of side aisles, above which there is a gallery that also surmounts the narthex. The central area of the nave is covered by the great dome, some 15·5m in diameter, about half the size of that in Haghia Sophia. The dome is supported primarily by four huge piers standing on the corners of a square. Between these piers there are four great circular arches; pendentives then make the transition to the circle on which the drum carrying the dome rests. Barrel-vaults open off from these arches to the N, E and S, with a conch covering the apse. Another pair of piers at the W end of the nave support an elliptical domical vault, from which barrel-vaults open off to the N and S. The wide nave is separated from the side aisles by the usual colonnade: there are four monoliths on either side between the main piers, and another one on either side between the W piers, and a pair of subsidiary piers which help to support the W ends of the N and S galleries. Around the periphery of the semicircular apse there is a synthronon, the only one in the city to have survived from the Byzantine period. This has six tiers of seats for the clergy, with doors at either side leading to an ambulatory which runs beneath the fourth tier.

In the conch of the apse a mosaic cross in black outline stands on a pedestal of three steps, against a gold ground with a geometric border. The inscription here is from Psalm lxv, 4 and 5; that on the bema arch is from Amos ix, 6, with alterations. In both cases parts of the mosaic have fallen away and letters have been painted in by someone who was indifferent to both grammar and sense. There is some difference of opinion concerning the dating of these mosaics; one theory is that they date from the reconstruction after the earthquake of 740, the other, that they are from Justinian's reign. The decorative mosaics in the narthex, which are similar to those in Haghia Sophia, are almost certainly from Justinian's period.

At the W end of the nave a rather attractive Turkish wooden staircase leads to the galleries. At the W end of the nave five doors lead from the church into the narthex, a vestibule of five bays. The central bay of the narthex and those at either end are groin-vaulted; the two in between are barrel-vaulted. From the narthex five doors originally led into the atrium, but three of these have been blocked up. This atrium and the scanty remains of that at St. John of Studius are the only examples, in Istanbul, surviving from the Byzantine period. Unfortunately, the atrium in Haghia Eirene has been rather drastically altered; the whole of the inner peristyle is Turkish, as well as a good many bays of the outer. However, most of the outer walls date from the Byzantine period: they are curiously irregular, the N portico is

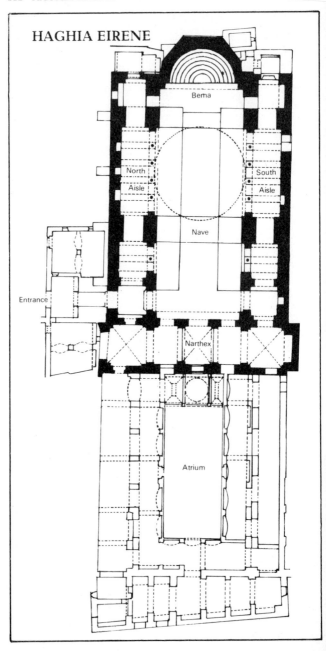

**HAGHIA EIRENE**

Bema

North
Aisle

South
Aisle

Nave

Entrance

Narthex

Atrium

considerably longer than the S, thus the W wall of the atrium is not parallel to the narthex. In the SE corner of the courtyard a short flight of steps and a door (now closed off) led to buildings S of Haghia Eirene. The ruins of these can be examined after leaving the church.

The ruins to the S of Haghia Eirene, between the church and the outer walls of the Saray, are off-limits to the public, but it is possible to give them a cursory examination by peering through the gateway. Excavated in 1946, they are almost certainly the remains of the Hospice of Samson. Procopius, Justinian's court chronicler, writes that between Haghia Eirene and Haghia Sophia 'there was a certain hospice, devoted to those that were at once destitute and suffering from serious illness, namely those that had lost their property and their health. This was erected in early times by a certain pious man, Samson by name'. Procopius goes on to report that the Hospice of Samson was destroyed by fire during the Nika Revolt—along with the two great churches on either side of it—and that it was rebuilt and considerably enlarged by Justinian. Unfortunately, the excavations were never carried out far enough to reveal the plan of the Hospice but one can make out a courtyard opposite the atrium of Haghia Eirene, where some columns and capitals have been re-erected. To the E there is a complex series of rooms including a nymphaeum, or ornamental fountain, with some of the chambers paved with *opus sectile* mosaic. There is a broad corridor between the Hospice and Haghia Eirene, while to the E a vaulted ramp exists which may have given access to the galleries of the church. From an observation of the masonry and capitals, it would appear that the structure dates principally from the time of Justinian. It is clear that the Hospice connected directly with the atrium of Haghia Eirene and was undoubtedly part of the complex formed by that church and Haghia Sophia.

From Haghia Eirene a path leads off to the left to a gate in the W wall of the First Court of the Saray. In Ottoman times this was called *Kíz Bekciler Kapísí*, the Gate of the Guardian of the Girls, presumably because an official with that title was in charge of security at the gate, which opened onto a road leading down to the lower gardens of the Saray. The narrow lane which leads downhill from here is flanked on both sides by ancient columns, capitals, sarcophagi and architectural fragments, an overflow from the museums on the terrace below. On the way down, on the right, is a large building under construction, which will house the new Archaeological Museum. One then comes to the entrance of the courtyard shared by the present Archaeological Museum, which occupies the right side and the two ends; the Museum of the Ancient Orient, which is to the left of the entrance; and the Çinili Köşkü, which stands at the far corner to the left. Around these buildings, as well as in the gardens to the left of the courtyard, antiquities of all sorts are displayed. The most noteworthy of these are the huge porphyry sarcophagi in front of the Archaeological Museum; these date from the 4–5C AD, and once contained the remains of Byzantine emperors and empresses of that period.

# B. The Archaeological Museum

**The Archaeological Museum** (Pl 11,5) has one of the world's richest collections of Graeco-Roman antiquities, including an extraordinary collection of sarcophagi. Besides these, there are a number of antiquities from the first two millennia in the history of Byzantium-Constantinople, including some objects dating from the Latin Occupation of 1204–61.

ADMISSION. The Museum is open every day 9:00–5:30 except Mon.

HISTORY. The first systematic attempt in the Ottoman Empire to collect and preserve the nation's antiquities began in 1846, during the regime of Abdül Mecit I. The project was initiated by Fethi Ahmet Paşa, son-in-law of Mahmut II, who contacted governors all over the Ottoman Empire and directed them to collect all of the moveable works of art from within their provinces and send them off to Istanbul. These antiquities were at first stored in Haghia Eirene, and when that was full the Çinili Köşkü was used as a storehouse, beginning in 1874. During the next decade attempts were made to identify and catalogue the museum's collection and to control the outflow of antiquities from Turkey. The modern history of the Museum really dates from 1881, when Hamdi Bey was made director. Over the next three decades, until his death in 1910, Hamdi Bey succeeded in establishing the museum.The most dramatic event in Hamdi Bey's career occurred in 1887, during his excavation of the royal necropolis at Sidon, in Syria, when he unearthed the superb group of sarcophagi which is the pride of the museum's collection. Since the Çinili Köşkü was too small to house these new acquisitions, the central building of the present museum was erected directly opposite and opened to the public in 1896. Later discoveries by Turkish and foreign archaeologists soon filled this building and it became necessary to build the N and S wings, the first of which was opened in 1902 and the second in 1908. The process of expansion continues, and work is currently underway on a new museum building behind the present structure. The excavations for this unearthed a large amount of Mycenaean pottery, as well as a number of Byzantine substructures and foundations, including the ruins of an early Christian sanctuary. Unfortunately, these antiquities were not carefully studied before being removed and, therefore, were neither identified nor dated.

THE LEFT WING. The rooms on the ground floor of the museum are numbered I through XX, starting at the far end of the left wing. The entrance lobby is between RRVIII and IX. The most natural way to begin the tour is to turn left from the entrance lobby into **RVIII**; exhibited there is the most famous work of art in the museum; this is the so-called **\*\*Alexander Sarcophagus** (#370), one of the funerary monuments discovered by Hamdi Bey in 1887 in the royal necropolis at Sidon. The sarcophagus was originally believed to have been that of Alexander the Great himself, for it is adorned with sculptures in deep, almost round relief, showing the Emperor in scenes of hunting and battle. But Alexander is known to have been buried in Alexandria. The sarcophagus has now been identified as that of an unknown

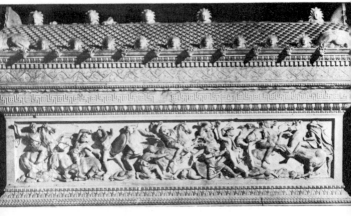

*The Alexander Sarcophagus, named from the reliefs of Alexander the Great hunting and in scenes of battle. It dates to the last quarter of the 4C B C. (Turkish Ministry of Tourism)*

ruler of the Seleucid dynasty, founded by the Emperor Seleucus I, who in 312 BC established an empire that included most of Alexander's Asian conquests. This magnificent sarcophagus, one of the masterpieces of Hellenistic art, is dated to the last quarter of the 4C BC. Just beyond it there is another funerary monument of almost equal beauty, the *Sarcophagus of the Mourners (#368), so named because of the figures in high relief of the mourning maidens that adorn its sides. This splendid sarcophagus, which is dated c 350 BC, was also found in the royal necropolis at Sidon by Hamdi Bey, as were the three small sarcophagi (#371, 372, 373) exhibited elsewhere in the room. To the right of the door leading to RVII there is a bronze bust of Hamdi Bey.

**RVII** is the Sidonian Salon, where there are more of the sarcophagi from the necropolis at Sidon on display. These are works of the late Roman period (2–4C AD).

**RVI** is the Salon of Sepulchral Monuments, which contains still more sarcophagi from the necropolis at Sidon. The most beautiful of these are the *Meleager Sarcophagus (#2100) and the *Sarcophagus of Phaedra and Hippolytus (#508), which take their names from the mythological scenes represented in relief on their sides. Both of these date from the 2C AD.

From **RVI** turn left into **RIII** (RRV and IV are storage areas, and are not open to the public), the Sidamara Salon, named after the splendid *Sidamara Sarcophagus (#1179), so called because it was found near the ruins of the ancient city of Sidamara in central Asia Minor. This is the most elaborately decorated sarcophagus in the museum. On the lid there are the reclining figures of a headless couple, man and wife, with Cupids at their head and feet, and below that a frieze showing naked youths in scenes of hunting and battle. On the two sides there are spirited scenes showing mounted warriors in battle; on the end nearest the window there are the figures of two deities, perhaps Apollo and Artemis. On the other end Castor and Pollux are shown holding the bridle of a horse and in another scene a young woman approaches the door of a tomb. Around the base of the sarcophagus a frieze shows naked athletes in training and competition. This marvellous work is dated to the 2–3C AD, as are most of the other sarcophagi in the room. The two stone lions flanking the staircase once stood on either side of the Imperial Marine Gateway of the Palace of Bucoleon, a seaside pavilion of the Great Palace of Byzantium (see below, Rte 5); these dated c 6C AD. The medallion head of Medusa on the wall of the landing above was found in Istanbul near the Column of Constantine and dates to the 4C AD.

The stairway leads to the second floor of the museum (now closed for restoration), which contains the museum's collection of ancient pottery, statuettes and bronzes. The room of greatest interest on that floor is the Treasury, which has a small but superb collection of ancient gold, silver and bronze ornaments and jewellery, including a few pieces unearthed at Troy by Schliemann.

The most interesting exhibits in **RII** are on the two side walls; these are panels from sculptured friezes found by Hamdi Bey in 1890 at two sites in western Asia Minor. On the right wall there are fragments from the frieze of the temple of Artemis Leucophriene at Magnesia on the Meander, on which are represented scenes of combat between Greeks and Amazons. (There is a model of the temple on the right side of the room.) On the left wall are fragments from the frieze of the temple of Hecate at Lagina, showing scenes connected with the cult of that goddess of the Underworld. Notice also in the centre of the room the Aeolian or proto-Ionic capitals in the form of branches springing from a tree-trunk and bending down on each side; this form was later to develop into the stylised volutes of the true Ionic capital. Capital #704 was found at Neandria, in the Troad, and #1924 is from Larissa, just N of Izmir; both are dated to the 6C BC. There are also a number of mosaics, all of them found in Istanbul and dating to the late Roman period: #4607 is a representation of four young women personifying the seasons; #1642 shows Eros surrounded by wild animals and sea-monsters; #2464 depicts two of the labours of Hercules, in the first of which he is gathering the golden apples of the Hesperides, and in the second he is slaying the Nemean lion; #1606 shows Orpheus seated on a rock playing the lyre to an enchanted audience of animals and birds.

The most noteworthy exhibits in **RI** are the funerary stelai to the left. These were discovered in Istanbul in the 1950s and date from the 4C BC to the end of the 3C AD. The area in which they were found, the valley between the Third and Fourth Hills, was apparently the necropolis of ancient Byzantium, lying outside the walls of the town. After Constantine the Great erected his new defence-walls in 326–330, this area was built over and the necropolis was no longer used. These stelai are particularly interesting because they are decorated with reliefs showing the deceased surrounded by the objects that they used in their daily life: the stele of the sailor Heris (#4205) represents his weapons and the prow of an ancient ship-of-war; the scholar son of Hecatadorus (#4206) is shown with his book, pen and inkpot; the physician Musa (#5024) with her surgical instruments and medical book; the astronomer Theodotus (#4845) with his globe and sundial; while the lady Lollia Salbia is shown lying on her couch attended by her maids, who bring to her a bronze mirror and vials of perfumes and cosmetics. One stele (unnumbered) represents a nude youth holding a small bird in his hand, with his faithful dog lying at his feet. On the other side of the room there are a number of statues discovered in 1950 just outside the Theodosian walls. The two finest of these are a head of Hercules and a charming statue of Artemis (both unnumbered), in which the goddess is shown as a young girl with her dog, symbolic of her role as the Protectress of Animals.

THE RIGHT WING. The right wing of the museum begins with **RXX**, the Salon of the Tabnit Sarcophagus. This *sarcophagus (#800) is in the form of an alabaster mummy-case; it once held the remains of Tabnit, father of the Pharaoh Eshmounazar II, whose mummy is now exposed in a case elsewhere in the room. The sarcophagus dates to the beginning of the 6C BC. Also on exhibition here are two of the most splendid sarcophagi in the museum: the *Satrap Sarcophagus (#367) and the *Lycian Sarcophagus (#369). The first of these is decorated with scenes from the life of the deceased, an unknown prince who ruled Syria as a satrap under the Persians (5C BC). The second, which is from Lycia, on the SW coast of Asia Minor, is decorated on its sides with a lion-hunt and a boar-hunt, and on its ends with the figures of centaurs and sphinxes (c 400 BC).

**RX** is the Finike (Turkish for Phoenicia) Salon, the exhibits are sarcophagi and funerary stelai from Sidon and other archaeological sites along what is now the Mediterranean coast of Lebanon and Syria, the ancient Phoenicia. Most of the sarcophagi exhibited here are of the anthropoid type, resembling mummy-cases; these date to the 5–4C BC.

**RXI** is the Salon of Archaic Sculpture. The finest work of art here is #1142, a funerary stele of a young man, represented naked in the customary pose of an ephebe, or military recruit; this was found on the

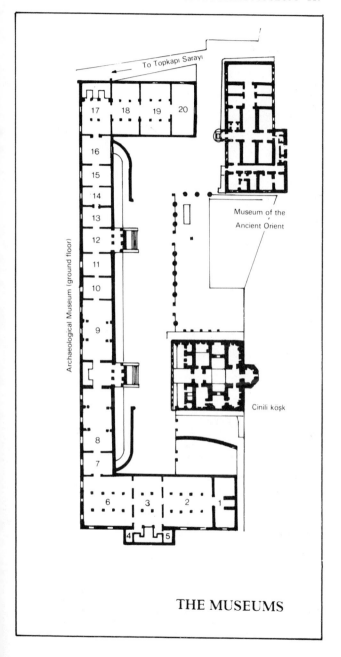

To Topkapı Sarayı

Museum of the
Ancient Orient

Archaeological Museum (ground floor)

Cinili köşk

**THE MUSEUMS**

Aegean isle of Nisyros and is dated to the 5C BC. #1502 is a funerary stele from Bandirma on the Sea of Marmara; the upper half of the front face is decorated with a scene showing the deceased on horseback about to spear a boar, while in the lower half he is shown on his funeral bier bidding farewell to his loved ones (5C BC). #1945: a headless statue of a seated male figure, found in Miletos (6C BC). #1645: head of an archaic statue of a kouros, an idealised representation of a young man personifying Apollo, discovered on the Aegean isle of Samos (6C BC).

**RXII** is the Assos Salon, named after the ancient city of Assos in the NW corner of Asia Minor. Displayed on the walls of this room are fragments (#257–268) from the frieze of the temple of Athena (c 530 BC) in Assos, the only archaic Doric sanctuary extent in Asia Minor. Also exhibited here is the most striking work of art in the museum, a colossal statue of Bes (#3317), the Cypriot Hercules, who is holding up a headless lioness by her hind legs; the gaping hole in his loins was probably the site of a phallic fountain (6C BC).

**RXIII** is the Salon of Attic Sculpture; exhibited here are statues and reliefs of the 5–4C BC, some of them original works of art and others copies of classical sculpture. #1189 is a Caryatid, similar to those in the Erechtheion on the Acropolis, where a kore, or maiden, supports on her headdress the architrave of a porch. #1427 is a Herm, a statue of the god Hermes in which only his head and genitals are represented on a stele. An inscription on the stele states that it is a copy of the famous Herm by Alkamenes, which stood just outside the Propylaia on the Athenian Acropolis; this was discovered in Pergamum and is dated to the 2C AD. #435: a fine statue of Athena from Trablus (5C BC).

**RXIV** is the Philiskos Salon, named after a Rhodian sculptor who flourished in the late 3C BC. The statues exhibited here are all copies of his works, except for one fragment (#2155) bearing his signature. The most noteworthy of the copies is the Apollo Kitharados (#2000), in which Apollo is shown playing a lyre (in Greek, kithara).

**RXV** is the Ephebos Salon; this is named after what is perhaps the most beautiful work of art in the Museum, the **Ephebos of Tralles (#1191). This statue represents a youth resting after exercise; he is shown standing in a relaxed attitude with a cape draped over his shoulders, a wistful smile on his face (3C BC). To the right of the Ephebos there is a superb *head of Alexander the Great (#1138), a 3C BC copy of an original by Lysippos. Directly behind that there is an outstanding life-size *statue of Alexander (#709), an original work dating from the 4C BC. On the wall directly opposite there is a relief honouring Euripides (#1242); there the dramatist is being presented with a tragic mask by Skene, the personification of the theatre, while Dionysus looks on with approval. #363: a fine statue of Hermaphroditus, the bisexual offspring of Hermes and A̤hrodite, an original from Pergamum (3C BC). #685: a colossal head of Zeus from Troy (3–2C BC). #764: a fine relief depicting a dancing Maenad (5C BC).

**RXVI** is the Attis Salon; this room is named for Attis, the Phrygian god of vegetation and fertility, whose statue (#3302) stands to the left of the entryway: this work, which was found in Cyzicus, on the Marmara, dates from the Roman period. #601: headless statue of a woman dressed in flowing robes, from Manissa (2C BC). #2645: fine statue of a lovely young woman, from Antiocheia ad Pisidium (2C BC). #3980: funerary stele of a warrior, decorated with a relief showing his helmet, armour, weapons, personal belongings, and three wreaths signifying his victories in athletic competitions. This was found in Kadiköy, the ancient Chalcedon, just across the Bosphorus from Saray Burnu, and is a work of the Roman period.

**RXVII** is the Aphrodisias Salon. This room takes its name from the ancient city of Aphrodisias, in W Asia Minor, which during the Hellenistic period was one of the artistic centres of the Greek world, exporting sculptures all over Asia Minor and the eastern Mediterranean. However, the only works from Aphrodisias exhibited here are the capitals and reliefs (#2270, 2271) on either side of the entryway, and the three large sculptured corbels (#2275, 2279, 2274), all of which date from the first half of the 2C AD. Prominent to the right of the entryway is a colossal statue (#4281) of the river-god Kaystros, from Ephesus (2C AD). To the left is a large statue (#4410) of Tyche, the Goddess of Fortune, who is shown holding the child Plutos, the God of Wealth, while above them there is a profusion of fruits and flowers; this is from Prusias ad Hypium and is tentatively dated to the 2C AD. To the left of the stairway there is an interesting statue (#1494) of Leda and the Swan in flagrante delicto.

**RXVIII**, the Roman Salon, exhibits statues of Roman emperors, empresses, philosophers and high officials of the Empire, along with the figures of Roman deities and mythological figures. The finest of these is a superb ˙head of the Emperor Arcadius (#5028) found in Beyazit Square in Istanbul. Arcadius is here represented as a young man with delicate features, crowned with a simple diadem formed from two circlets of large pearls; this is dated to the period AD 395–408, when Arcadius was ruler of the eastern part of the Roman Empire. The other imperial statues and busts exhibited here are also dated to the period of the particular emperor's reign; #4864: Diocletian (284–305); #5555 and #385: Tiberius (14–37); #124 and #406: Marcus Aurelius (161–180); #2646: Lucius Verus (161–169); #506: Nero (54–68); #2264: Valentinian II (375–392); #50: Hadrian (117–138); #87: Augustus (27 BC–AD 14); #5296: Constantine the Great (324–337). Among the statues of deities and mythological figures, the most noteworthy is a figure of Silenus (#1222), a satyr who˙followed Dionysus in his revels; this is a Roman copy of an original from the Hellenistic period, found in Nablus.

**RXIX** is the Salon of Christian Art. This exhibition is particularly interesting, since it includes antiquities from Byzantine Constantinople as well as from the medieval Genoese town of Galata. Just inside the door there is a pair of marble panels (unnumbered) decorated with the figures in low relief of two gorgeous peacocks, with traces of the original colour still adhering to their feathers; these are thought to have formed part of the facade of a large street-fountain, and are tentatively dated to the 6C AD. The most beautiful of the exhibits in this room is the ˙Sariğüzel Sarcophagus (#4508), named after the Istanbul neighbourhood where it was unearthed in 1950. This is decorated on both of its long sides with a pair of angels in flight, carved in high relief, while at each of the ends a pair of bearded apostles support a tall cross. The sarcophagus is believed to have been the last resting-place of a young Byzantine prince, and is dated to the 5C BC. Next to the sarcophagus there is a very interesting funerary stele (#755), which is inscribed with the name Kefalo. Kefalo was obviously a comic actor, for the reliefs on the two sides of his stele depict him in two of his roles, on one side wearing a wolf's head and on the other the head of a dog. Also of interest is #3914, a headless marble icon of the Blessed Virgin, who is shown with her arms raised in benediction; this was found in Istanbul and is dated c 11–12C. The left side of the room is taken up mostly with gravestones from Genoese Galata. Many of these stones were discovered in 1912 in Arab Camii, the former Roman Catholic church of SS. Paul and Dominic. Several of these tombstones bear the date 1347, the year when the Black Death first struck Galata and Constantinople, spreading from there to the rest of Europe a few months later.

**RXX** is the Salon of Byzantine Art. The most prominent objects here are the pair of large *marble pedestals which stand either side of the mosaic pavement. The pedestal to the right (#2995) was discovered in 1845 and that to the left (#5560) in 1963, both of them unearthed in the Second Court of the Saray. These pedestals once stood in the Hippodrome of Constantinople, placed there by the Emperor Anastasius I (491–518) to honour the famous charioteer Porphyrios. He is shown racing in his chariot in a relief on one of the faces and on another he is receiving the wreath of victory from the Emperor. The mosaic pavement (#1642) has a border of foliage in which the figures of animals, with human faces are depicted in the four corners. In the centre Orpheus is shown playing a lyre and Pan is holding a flute, while around them are the figures of two women, a Centaur, and an assemblage of wild beasts, all of them listening entranced to the god's music. This work, which was found in Jerusalem, is dated to the 5–6C AD. Another interesting exhibit here is a sarcophagus (#5423), found in Istanbul and dated to the 5C AD. The sides of the sarcophagus are decorated with a relief in the form of a colonnade, with Christ seated enthroned in the centre of one long side with the twelve Apostles around him.

# C. The Çinili Köşkü

The **Çinili Köşkü** (Pl 11,5), or Tiled Pavilion, is the very oriental-looking structure at the NE corner of the courtyard opposite the Archaeological Museum. This is one of the oldest secular Turkish buildings in Istanbul, and is one of the most beautiful monuments ever created by Ottoman architecture.

ADMISSION. The Çinili Köşkü is open 9–5:30 every day except Mon.

HISTORY. The Çinili Köşkü was built by Sultan Mehmet II in 1472 as an outer pavilion of Topkapí Sarayi, serving as a pied-à-terre for the Sultan on occasions when he wanted to escape the crowded confines of the Inner Palace. At the time when the Çinili Köşkü was built, a large level area was cleared in front of it so that the young princes and palace pages could play cirit, a form of polo, and enabling the Sultan to look on from the elevated front porch of the pavilion. The pavilion continued in use until 1856, when the imperial residence was shifted to Dolmabahçe Palace. It was abandoned until 1874, when it was converted into a storehouse for antiquities. During the 1950s the Çinili Köşkü was thoroughly restored to its original condition and converted into a museum of Turkish tiles.

EXTERIOR. The kiosk is laid out in two almost identical storeys, cruciform in plan with chambers in the corners of the cross. It has a deeply recessed entrance alcove on the main floor entirely revetted in tiles of various kinds, most of them tile mosaic in turquoise and dark blue. On the back wall these form simply geometrical designs, but in the deep soffit of the arch there is an inscription in a geometricised form of Cufic calligraphy. On the three faces of the vault at the height of the lintel of the door there is a long double Persian inscription in the beautiful *cuerda seca* technique. The main inscription is in white letters on a dark blue ground. Above and entwined with this is a subordinate inscription in yellow, with the tendrils of a vine meandering in and out between the letters, the whole encased in a frame of deep mauve with flowers of dark blue, turquoise and white.

INTERIOR. The interior consists of a central salon in the shape of an inverted Latin cross with a dome over the crossing. The cross is extended by a vestibule at the entrance end, an apse-like room at the far end, and two eyvans or open alcoves (now glassed in) at the ends of the shorter arms, with additional chambers at the corners of the cross. All of these rooms were once tiled and many of them still are, with triangular and hexagonal panels of turquoise and deepest blue, sometimes with superimposed gold designs.

In the first room, to the left of the entrance vestibule, there is a small selection of Selcuk Turkish tiles—mostly wall tiles of enamel and majolica ware—of the 12–14C. The principal exhibit in the central salon is the superb mihrab from the mosque of Ibrahim Bey at Karaman, in central Anatolia, one of the most splendid works from the height of the great Iznik period. Also in this room are two lunette panels in the *cuerda seca* technique; these are from the medrese of the mosque of Haseki Hürrem in Istanbul and are dated 1539. The second room, to the left, has tiles of the transitional period from Selcuk to Ottoman, i.e., 14–15C. The third and fourth rooms contain some of the best Iznik ware of the 16C and early 17C. Notice in the third room a charming 18C baroque fountain, partly tiled and partly painted, set into a niche in the wall. These last two rooms also contain a pair of magnificent kandils, or mosque candles, one in **R3** and the other in **R4**; these are both from Sokollu Mehmet Paşa Camii in Istanbul, and are dated to 1577. The last two rooms contain ceramics from the 18–19C, some of it pretty but Europeanised and lacking the brilliance and superb craftsmanship of the earlier work. The best of these are exhibited in the last room; these are charming plates made in the 19C in Çanakkale, on the Dardanelles. They are painted with a very restricted palette in an expressionist style, representing gay seascapes with boats, fish and birds.

# D. The Museum of the Ancient Orient

The **\*\*Museum of the Ancient Orient** (Pl 11,5) contains a distinguished collection of objects from all over the Middle East, including artifacts and works of art from the ancient Egyptian, Sumerian, Akkadian, Babylonian, Hittite, Urartian, Aramaic and Assyrian cultures, as well as unique antiquities from Arabia and Nabatea in the pre-Islamic period.

ADMISSION. Open 9–5:30 every day except Monday.

HISTORY. The building was erected in 1883 and originally housed the Institute of Fine Arts, but in 1917 it was converted into a museum. Many of the objects exhibited here were shipped to Istanbul during World War One by Turkish governors in the Middle East, in order to prevent them from falling into enemy hands. During the 1960s the building was restored and the collection re-organised, creating today's very attractive exhibition halls.

The entrance to the museum is flanked by two huge Hittite lions (c 14C BC). After passing through the entrance lobby one ascends the stairs to the first floor, turning left to enter RI.

**RI** contains an exhibition of objects from Arabia and Nabatea in the Pre-Islamic period, with most of the Arabian antiquities coming from the S part of the peninsula. Flanking the entryway there are the torsos of two red sandstone statues representing kilted male figures (#7805, #7806), as well as the detached head of one of the statues: these are dated to the 3–1C BC. #7611: a superb relief with a floral design below and the heads of five bulls above, flanked by two giraffe heads (2C AD) #7608: Arabic inscription of the 6C AD in which the name of Christ is mentioned, evidence for the spread of Christianity in Arabia before the rise of Islam in the 7C. Case 1 contains tombstones, funerary offerings, tomb furnishings and other objects. The most interesting object here is the marble head of a clean-shaven young man, with plaster-of-Paris eyes in which coloured stones once formed the irises (1C BC–1C AD). Also of interest are a number of statuettes representing seated figures in hieratic pose, probably idols of some unknown Arabian deities (1C BC–1C AD). In addition, there are some vine bronze vases, arrow-heads and a statuette of a horse, all from the 4–1C BC. On the wall nearby there is a panel decorated with the figure in relief of a mythological beast with the body of a winged lion and the head of a bearded man (4–1C BC). This once decorated a grave, as did the other relief close by, which shows a warrior dressed in a long robe, with a spear in his right hand and a sword strapped to his waist (4–1C BC). In a niche in the wall is a sundial in red sandstone (#7664), at the base of which there is an inscription in Aramaic, the language of Christ.

**RII** is devoted to ancient Egyptian objects, ranging in date from the rise of the First Dynasty to the beginning of the Ptolemaic Dynasty (c 3200–305 BC). These works include sphinxes, stelai, tombstones, mummy-cases, funerary pottery, tomb furnishings, votive offerings, statuary and architectural fragments. Most of these objects came from Egypt, but a number came from other places to which they had been shipped from Egypt in the past, including one antiquity found in Istanbul. The latter is a headless granite sphinx (#10929); this was unearthed in the district of Samatya, in the SW corner of the old city. This sphinx was probably brought from Egypt to Constantinople by Theodosius II (379–395), along with the great obelisk that now stands in the Hippodrome (see below, Rte 5). #10956: Limestone statue of a sphinx. #10942: Stele with inscription recording a victory of the Pharaoh Setos I (1318–1299 BC), with a relief showing Setos presenting a gift to the god Amon and his wife Mut. #10859: Funerary stele from a common grave of the guild of carpenters. #10860: Tombstone, decorated with reliefs, with an inscription recording that it marked the grave of a priestess of the cult of the deified Queen Hathor (c 2100 BC). #10966: Sandstone statue of a squatting female figure who is holding in her right hand the sign of Ankh, the life-symbol. Case 2 contains mummy-cases and other funerary objects. Three mummy cases (#10891, #10892, #10866) bear inscriptions identifying the deceased as priests and priestesses of Amon. The small jars with lids in the form of animal heads contain the various internal organs of the deceased, in which the heads symbolise the several gods that will protect those parts until they are reunited with the body in the next world; e.g. the monkey-god Hapi protecting the bowels, the jackal-god Dua Mute the lungs, the falcon-god Kebindemut the liver, etc. Case 3 contains more funerary objects, of which the most interesting are some statuettes in the form of mummy-cases.

#357: statuette of a kilted male figure in hieratic pose, representing Ka, the spirit of the deceased. Case 3 contains still more funerary objects. Under the window there are two tables used for holding funerary objects in the tomb (c 550 BC). #10930: a funerary stele dating to the second half of the second millennium BC.

**RIII**, which is merely one end of a corridor, has on its walls the most striking exhibits in the museum, colourful *tile panels with the figures in relief of lions and mythological beasts. These panels are from Babylon, dating from the reign of Nebuchadnezzar II (605–562 BC); they formed part of the monumental processional way that led from the Ishtar Gate to the sanctuary where the New Year's festival was held. Case 4 contains antiquities from three different periods in Mesopotamian history: the Halaf Culture (fifth millennium BC); the Fifth Cultural Period in Nineveh (third millennium BC); and the Old Sumerian Period (fourth to third millennium BC). At the right of the doorway leading into R IV there is a colossal head atop a cast of the original body; this is a representation of Lamassu, a demon who guarded Assyrian doorways and gates (9C BC).

**RIV** contains antiquities from Mesopotamia and Urartu, a culture that flourished in Eastern Anatolia at the beginning of the first millennium BC. Case 5a has finds from Adap, a site in the Fertile Crescent midway between Baghdad and Basra, among them is a statuette of a male figure identified as the Sumerian King Lugal-da-lu (c 2500 BC). #401: a relief showing male figures in the typical kilted costumes of the Old Sumerian Period; an inscription identifies one larger-than-life figure as King Urnanshe of Lagash (c 2520 BC). Also of interest are some bronze fibulae whose heads are in the form of human figures (c 2600 BC); a clay seal of Urukagina, King of Lagash (c 2355 BC); and a fine bronze bull-head, a figure that had great religious significance in Mesopotamia and Anatolia during the Bronze Age, dated to the middle of the third millennium BC. Case 5 has objects from Nippur, including a wooden plaque with an inscribed decoration showing gifts being presented to a king and queen (c 2600 BC). Cases 6 and 7: objects from Fara, another site in the Fertile Crescent between Baghdad and Basra, including an unusual double marble vase resting on the figures of two pairs of bulls. Case 8: antiquities from Akkad, including an inscribed stele (#1027) with the figure in relief of the Akkadian King Naramsin (c 2650 BC). The most important exhibits here are several **tiles with stamped inscriptions dating from the period 2222–2198 BC; these are the oldest-known examples of printed writing in existence.

Case 9 (actually an alcove, with a glassed-in niche in the centre) exhibits objects from the New Sumerian period (2144–2000 BC), many of them associated with King Gudea, the most powerful ruler of that era. At the left side of the alcove is a statue of Gudea, a bald and beardless man with a broad face and large eyes, clad in a long gown. The most interesting exhibit in the alcove is #5555, a casket-shaped votive vessel, with a relief showing angels pouring water into vases held by a line of maidens clad in long robes, and with the overflow pouring onto the ground and forming a subterranean stream beneath them. This is a representation of the ancient Mesopotamian cosmology, in which the world was surrounded above and below by water. This was a belief that the Hebrews acquired during their Babylonian captivity, and which forms the basis of the Biblical story of the Flood. Case 10: antiquities from the Old Babylonian Period. On the right: a fine diorite statue (#7183) of a bearded male figure identified as

Puzur Ishtar, Governor of Mari (c 2000 BC), a site on the Euphrates midway between Aleppo and Babylon. (The head is a copy of the original, now in the East Berlin museum.) To the right of this there is a similar statue (#7814) of the Governor's father, Tura Doğan. Between the two statues there is the basalt *figure of a duck (#7878), with an inscription stating that it belongs to a priest named Musallim Marduk. The inscription also identifies this as an official standard weight, equal to about 30 kilograms; it has been dated to c 2000 BC, and is thus the oldest-known example of a standard measure in history. Case 10: objects from the Kassite or Middle Babylonian Period (c 1600–900 BC). The most interesting objects here are a number of fired clay statuettes; these are votive offerings representing deities, sacred weddings between gods and goddesses, and sacred and mythological beasts. Case 11: antiquities from the Old Assyrian (c 1350–1200 BC), Mittanian (c 1500–1300 BC), and Middle Assyrian (c 1200–1000 BC) periods from Ashur, a site on the Tigris S of Mosul, among which one notices a statuette of a god with a horned helmet. The most interesting objects in this case are fired clay representations of male and female organs, and within each of the latter there is an insignia of Ishtar, the goddess of love and fertility. To the right of Case 11 there is a fine sandstone relief showing a male figure in an attitude of prayer, flanked by two priests holding tall staffs surmounted by divine standards. Case 12: objects from the beginning of the New Assyrian Period (9C BC), including a reconstructed copper door from the palace of Shalmaneser III (858–824 BC), with an inscription recording one of the King's victories. Standing in the middle of the room in front of the case there is a large basalt statue (#5630) of Shalmaneser III, and on the side walls at the end of the room there are reliefs from the palace of Ashurnasirpal II (third quarter of the 9C BC) at Nimrud, on the Tigris near Mosul.

**RV** is devoted mostly to antiquities from the New Assyrian period, all dating to the 8C BC, but there is also exhibited here an extremely important collection of very old inscriptions. Case 13, to the right of the entryway, contains small objects from Assyrian sites, dated 8C BC, including some fine bronze and marble vases and a number of talismans for warding off evil spirits. In front of the case are stelai which once stood in the main square of Ashur, on the Tigris S of Mosul: these commemorate various high officials who gave their names to civic years of the Assyrian state. The large marble stele in the middle of the room (#1326) was erected in honour of Bel-Harran-Beli-Usur, who was prime minister during the reigns of both Shalmanasar IV (781–772 BC) and Tiglath-Pileser III (745–727 BC). He founded the city of Tel-Abda near Ashur, commemorating that feat by setting up this stele in a temple that he erected there. Cases 14 and 15 contain examples of the museum's extraordinary collection of cuneiform inscriptions, including samples from virtually all of the cultures that flourished in the Middle East and Anatolia during the Bronze Age. The oldest of these inscriptions date to c 2700 BC, the earliest known examples of writing. The most historic of the inscriptions on exhibition here is the famous **Code of Hammurabi (#Ni 2358), the world's oldest recorded set of laws (1750 BC). Also of great interest is *tablet #U93 103, dated c 320 BC, one of the earliest records of systematic astronomical observations, evidence of a science that began in Babylonia as early as c 2000 BC. On the wall above and below the cases there are reliefs from the palace of Tiglath-Pileser III at Nimrud.

**RVI** has exhibits from several historical periods and cultures in the early part of the first millennium BC. Opposite the entrance to the room there is a sacrificial table (#7761), and beside it a fragment of a floor mosaic (#7760); both of these date to the 7C BC, and are from a Urartian temple at Toprakkale, near Lake Van in eastern Anatolia. Case 16: Mesopotamian cylinder-seals of bronze, ivory and wood. Case 17: Small objects of Urartian manufacture, including cylinder-seals, fibulae with heads in the form of human figures, kitchenware, reliefs, votive offerings and architectural fragments. On the wall there are orthostats from the palace of Tiglath-Pileser III at Hadatu, NW of Aleppo; one shows the King driving a chariot, accompanied by his bodyguard, with a mounted warrior bringing up the rear. On the same wall there are reliefs from the palaces of Sennacherib (705–688 BC) and Ashurbanipal (669–629 BC). There are also two stelai commemorating victories by Sennacherib; these once stood in the main street leading to the royal palace in Nineveh.

From RVI a doorway leads into the museum lounge, at the right side of which one passes into RVII, the first of three rooms devoted to an exhibition of ancient Anatolian antiquities.

The oldest of the antiquities in these three rooms are works of the Hatti, whose culture flourished in Anatolia c 3000–c 1700 BC. The Hatti were supplanted by invaders known to historians as the Hittites, who were the dominant power in Anatolia in the period c 1700–c 1200 BC. In 1200 the Hittite Empire was destroyed by another wave of invaders, but their influence lingered on as the so-called Neo-Hittite culture for another five centuries in SE Anatolia, before that the area was overrun by the Assyrians.

**RVII** is devoted to an exhibition of Hatti works and objects from the Hittite Empire. Case 19: works of the Hatti from the early Bronze Age (third millennium BC), including bronze axes and arrow-heads, and the earliest known example of a bronze sun-disc, with the figures of two stags outlined in a braided halo. These sun-discs formed the top of sacred standards used in religious rites, and are among the most distinctive works of art produced in Bronze Age Anatolia. #9875: fragment of a vase with a relief showing a monstrous fertility god; this is dated to c 3000 BC, and is the oldest work of art in the museum's collection. Case 20 contains the most historic item in the museum, a clay tablet with a cuneiform inscription recording the ••Treaty of Kadesh; this is the world's oldest peace-treaty, dated to 1269 BC, signifying the end of a war between the forces of Ramses II of Egypt and Hattusilas, the Hittite Empire . Case 21: Clay pottery from the Old Hittite Kingdom (c 1700–1450 BC). Libation vessels from' Boğazköy, ancient Hattusas, the capital of the Hittite Empire. Case 23: Anatolian cylinder-seals, ranging in date from the Chalcolithic Period (c 5500–3000 BC) to the Late Hittite Period (c 1200–700 BC). #7775, #7776: Bases of limestone stelai decorated with reliefs; these were found in Boğazköy and are dated to the period of the Hittite Empire (1450–1200 BC). #7868: Reconstructed fragments of a sphinx that once stood beside one of the citadel gates at Bögazkoy (13C BC). #7739: basalt stele with a Hittite relief found near Polatíl, 100km W of Ankara, evidence of how far westward Hittite culture spread (14C BC). #7736: Hittite votive offering with hieroglyphic inscription and monogram of the Hittite Emperor Tudhaliyas IV (1250–1220 BC). #7693: limestone relief with Hittite hieroglyphics, found near Maraş in S Anatolia. On two walls of the room there are orthostats from the citadel gates at Zincirli, a Hittite site S of Maraş; these are decorated with lively reliefs showing the figures of gods, kings, and armed warriors marching and riding in chariots, along with representations of bulls, lions and mythological creatures (10–9C BC).

**RVIII** continues the exhibition of ancient Anatolian works. At the centre of the wall to the right of the entryway there is the Ivriz Kaya relief (#7869), named after the site in S Anatolia where it was found. This is one of the most striking exhibits in the museum, a colossal work showing the diminutive figure of a king presenting gifts of grain and fruit to a gigantic god, who is represented wearing boots and an elaborate head-dress. This is a plaster-of-Paris copy of the original relief, found near Konya and now in the local museum there; it dates to the 8C BC. To the right of this relief there is a basalt stele with the figure in relief of a bearded man wearing a long robe and a tall head-dress; an inscription on the robe identifies the figure as the Assyrian King Tiglath Pileser III. At the corner of the room to the left of the Ivriz Kaya relief there is the basalt statue of a small, snarling lion (#7699), and also a pair of basalt sphinxes (#7731) with archaic smiles. The lion once guarded the entrance to a Hittite palace in Maraş (8C BC). The sphinxes guarded a palace gateway in Zincirli during the time of the Aramaean dynasty (9C BC), and are considered to be among the finest extant examples of Late Hittite sculpture. Opposite the Ivriz Kaya relief is the colossal basalt statue of a bearded male figure (#7768) in hieratic pose, probably a king of the Late Hittite Period. At the base of the statue are the figures of two snarling lions held in check by their keeper (9C BC). #7967: An orthostat with the figure in relief of a bearded man: the long inscription to his right identifies him as the Aramaean King Barrakab, a vassal of the Assyrian King Tiglath Pileser III. Elsewhere in the room there are other orthostats from the palace of King Barrakab; the most interesting of these (#7723) shows four musicians in procession, the two in front playing lyres, the two behind slapping tambourines. #7772: The torso of a statue of the Hittite King Halparundu II, who ruled in Maraş in the 9C BC. Next to this is a fragmentary basalt stele (#7785) showing a man and woman seated at a dinner table being waited on by a servant. This charming relief, which undoubtedly depicts a Hittite king and his queen partaking of a ceremonial banquet, was found in Maraş, and dates to the 9C BC. #12874: A similar relief of the same provenance, showing the royal couple offering one another a toast. At the left side of the room there is another figure of a small, snarling lion (#7698); this is a companion of the one (#7699) to the right of the room. Just beyond the lion, in the entryway to RIX, there is a stele with the figure in relief of a bearded warrior wearing a kilt and shoes with upturned toes; he has a sword at his waist, holds aloft a torch in his left hand, and in his right hand he brandishes a battle-axe. This is a representation of Teshub, the Hittite Storm God and the principal deity, here serving as guardian of a gateway (9C BC).

**RIX** forms the opposite end of the corridor that began as RIII, and its walls exhibit more of the panels from the processional way that lead to the Ishtar Gate in Babylon. To the right there is a basalt stele (#7786) with a relief showing a Hittite warrior with a sword at his waist, a spear in his right hand, and a bow slung over his left shoulder; this fine work is from the Aramaean dynasty and is dated to the 9–8C BC. On the wall opposite is a fragmentary stele (#7754), decorated with a relief showing a bearded figure wearing a crown-like head-dress, he raises his right hand in a gesture of benediction (9C BC). #7754: a tile decoration surmounting a wooden column, with a relief and an inscription in Aramaic, dating to the 5C BC.

*Gülhane Park.* The road from the First Court of Topkapí Sarayí continues downhill to the S end of Gülhane Park, where the Soğuk Çeşme Gate leads out to Alemdar Cd. The S end of the park is largely given over to the Istanbul Zoo, which has little to interest a foreign visitor. A road leads past the Zoo towards the N end of the park, with the outer walls of the Saray on the left and on the right the retaining walls of the Inner Palace. The kiosk which juts out over the retaining wall is that of Osman III, built in 1754–57 in the baroque style. Once past the walls of the Inner Palace a path leads off to the right to a hill overlooking Saray Burnu. On top of the hill stands one of the very oldest but least known monuments in the city; this is the so-called *Goth's Column*, a granite monolith 15m high surmounted by a Corinthian capital. The name of the column comes from the laconic inscription in Latin on its base: 'To Fortune, who returns by reason of the victory over the Goths'. Some scholar have ascribed this column to Claudius II Gothicus (268–70) and others to Constantine the Great, both of whom won notable victories over the Goths, but there is no firm evidence either way. According to the Byzantine historian Nicephorus Gregoras, the column was once surmounted by a statue of Byzas the Megarian, the eponymous founder of Byzantium.

A path leads down from the column to the N exit of Gülhane Park. Just before it reaches the road through the park the path passes the ruins of, what appears to be, an early Byzantine structure, consisting of a series of small rooms fronted by a rather irregular colonnade. These ruins have never been thoroughly investigated, and so the identity and date of the site have not been established. One clue is furnished by a fragmentary inscription in Latin on an architectural fragment; it reads simply CONST.... Latin was not used in Constantinople after the first half of the 6C, so this suggests that the structure dates from either the reign of Constantine the Great or his son Constantius, since they were the only two emperors in that period whose names began with the five letters in the inscription.

There is a small park on Saray Burnu, at the confluence of the Bosphorus and the Golden Horn. From here there is a splendid view up the Bosphorus and across to the suburbs and seaside villages on the Asian shore. In the centre of the park there is a large bronze *statue of Kemal Atatürk* (1871–1938), the Father of modern Turkey and the first President of the Turkish Republic. This monument, made in 1926 by the Austrian sculptor Kripple, was the first statue of a Turk ever to be erected in this country.

A few hundred metres up the right bank of the Golden Horn there is a handsome Ottoman structure built directly at the water's edge. This is the recently-reconstructed *Sepetçiler Köşkü*, the Kiosk of the Basket-Weavers. Built in 1647 by Sultan Ibrahim, it served as a sea-pavilion and boat-house for Topkapí Sarayí. From here the Sultan and his entourage would board one of his barges to be rowed up the Bosphorus or the Golden Horn for a day's outing. Until the end of the last century the right bank of the Golden Horn between Saray Burnu and the end of the outer palace walls was lined with imperial pavilions such as this, but today only the Sepetçiler Köşkü remains.

From the Sepetçiler Köşkü one can walk along the shore road back to the Galata Bridge. The first part of this walk is rather difficult, passing lines of buses and lorries, but then the rest of the way lies along the quays past the ferry terminal, one of the liveliest places in the city, with a magnificent view up the Golden Horn.

# 5  Around the Hippodrome

**••Sultan Ahmet Camii** (Pl 11,5), the Blue Mosque, is one of the most
prominent landmarks in Istanbul, particularly when viewed from the
First Hill or from along the Marmara shore of the old city. It is thought
by many to have the most splendid exterior of the imperial mosques in
the city, with its graceful cascade of domes and semidomes, its six
slender minarets accentuating the corners of the building and the
courtyard, and its generally imposing but harmonious proportions.

HISTORY. The Blue Mosque was founded by Sultan Ahmet I, who in 1609
directed the architect Mehmet Ağa to begin construction. The mosque and all of
its associated pious foundations were completed in 1616, just a year before the
Sultan's death at the age of 27. For the next 250 years most reigning sultans
chose to perform their Friday noon prayers at the Blue Mosque, because of its
proximity to Topkapí Sarayí, and the imperial processions to and from the
mosque were the high-point of Istanbul life during that period. Even after
Topkapí Sarayí was abandoned as the imperial residence. Sultan Ahmet Camii
continued to hold pride of place as one of the two supreme imperial mosques of
the city, sharing that honour with the Süleymaniye, an eminence that both
mosques retain today.

EXTERIOR. Sultan Ahmet Camii is preceded by a courtyard as large in
area as the mosque itself, with monumental entryways at each of the
three sides. The gate at the centre of the W side is the grandest of
these; its outer facade is decorated with a calligraphic inscription by
Dervish Mehmet, the father of Evliya Çelebi. The courtyard is in the
classic style, bordered by a peristyle of 26 columns forming a portico
covered by 30 small domes. At the centre of the courtyard there is a
handsome octagonal şadírvan which, like the one at Yeni Cami, now
serves only a decorative purpose. The ritual ablutions are actually
performed at water taps in the outer courtyard, beneath the graceful
arcade which forms part of the N and S walls of the avlu.
   The four minarets at the corners of the mosque each have three
şerefes, while the pair at the far corners of the courtyard have two
each. The minarets are fluted and the şerefes have sculptured
stalactite parapets.
   The central dome of the mosque is flanked by semidomes on all four
sides, with those to N and S surrounded by three smaller semidomes
and those to E and W by two each, and with small full domes above
the four corners of the building. The four piers supporting the main
dome continue above the building as tall octagonal turrets capped
with domes, while smaller round turrets flank each of the corner
domes, all of which creates a harmonious cascade from the main
dome down through the clustering semidomes, turrets and smaller
domes. The N and S facades of the building have two storeys of
porticoed galleries.
   At the NE corner of the mosque there is a royal pavilion, rebuilt a
decade ago after having been damaged in a fire. The pavilion is
approached by a ramp leading up to a platform and an open loggia,
from which access is gained to a suite of two rooms that connect with
the royal loge inside the mosque. This very attractive and interesting suite of rooms is now used to display old Turkishcarpets, an
exhibition which continues in the old Ottoman stable at the rear of the
mosque *külliye*.

The main entrance to the mosque itself is at the E end of the courtyard, with smaller entrances from the outer courtyard beside the central minarets on the N and S sides. (During the busy summer season tourists are asked to enter through the N door and are restricted to that corner of the mosque.)

INTERIOR. The interior plan of Sultan Ahmet Camii, like that of Yeni Cami and the other imperial mosques of the city, recalls in a general way that of Haghia Sophia; although in this case there are also great differences. It is very nearly a square (51m long by 53m wide) covered by a dome (23·5m in diameter and 43m high) resting on four pointed arches and four smooth pendentives. To E and W there are semidomes which are themselves flanked by smaller semidomes. Thus far, the plan is not unlike that of Haghia Sophia. But in the Blue Mosque, instead of tympanic arches to N and S, there are two more semidomes, each surrounded by three smaller semidomes, making a quatrefoil design. The main support for the great dome comes from four colossal free-standing columns, 5m in diameter, which are divided in the middle by a band and ribbed above and below with convex flutes.

The mosque is flooded with light from its 260 windows. These were once filled with Turkish stained-glass of the early 17C which would have softened the in-coming sunlight. The original windows have been lost because of lack of maintenance during the latter years of the Ottoman Empire; now they are slowly being replaced by inferior modern imitations. The painted arabesques in the domes and the upper parts of the building are feeble in design and crude in colouring. This is almost always the case in these modern imitations of a type of decoration that was in the 16–17C richly elaborate in design and sombrely magnificent in colour. Here the predominant colour is an overly-bright blue, from which the building derives its popular name of the Blue Mosque. What is original and very beautiful in the decoration of the interior is the revetment of tiles on the lower part of the walls, especially in the galleries. These are Iznik tiles of the best period and they merit close observation. The magnificent floral designs display the traditional lily, carnation, tulip and rose motifs, as well as cypresses and other trees; these are all in exquisite colours, subtle blues and greens predominating. The mihrab and mimber, of white Proconnesian marble, are also original; they are fine examples of the carved stonework of the early 17C. Of equal excellence is the bronzework of the great courtyard doors, and also the woodwork of the doors and window-shutters of the mosque itself, encrusted with ivory, mother-of-pearl and sea-tortoise shell. Under the sultan's loge, which is in the upper gallery to the left of the mihrab, the wooden ceiling is painted with floral and geometrical arabesques in that exquisite early style in rich and gorgeous colours, of which so few examples remain.

PRECINCTS. The mosque and its courtyard were surrounded by an outer precinct wall, of which only part of the N section remains. This wall separated the mosque from its dependent associations in the külliye. The külliye of Sultan Ahmet Camii was extensive, including a medrese, türbe, hospital, kervansaray, primary school, public kitchen and a market; the rents from these helped defray the expenses of the other pious foundations in the mosque complex. The hospital, kervansaray and market were destroyed in the 19C, and the public kitchen is now incorporated into the structure of the School of Industrial Arts, which stands at the S end of the Hippodrome. The primary school, which has recently been restored, is elevated above the N wall of the outer precinct of the mosque. The large medrese, dwarfed somewhat by the scale of the mosque

# THE MOSQUE OF SULTAN AHMET I

itself, is just outside the precinct wall toward the NW, near the very large square türbe. Ahmet I is buried here, along with his wife Kösem and three of his sons: Osman II, Murat IV, and Prince Beyazit. All these institutions were closed to the public, but quite recently the türbe has been opened; it contains a small but interesting collection of Ottoman antiquities dating from the period of Sultan Ahmet I.

The square in front of the Blue Mosque is located on the site of the ancient **Hippodrome** (Pl 11,5), one of the most famous monuments in Byzantine Constantinople.

HISTORY. The original Hippodrome was constructed c AD 200 by the Emperor Septimius Severus, when he rebuilt the town of Byzantium. When Constantine the Great chose Byzantium as his new capital he reconstructed and considerably enlarged the Hippodrome, adorning it with works of art from all over the Roman Empire. It has often been remarked that just as Haghia Sophia was the centre of the religious life of Constantinople, so was the Hippodrome the focal point of its civil activities. Many of the great events in the history of the Byzantine Empire took place here, beginning with the solemn inaugural rites of the new capital on 11 May 330. The triumphs of victorious generals and emperors were celebrated here, and on several occasions the remains of deposed rulers were exposed for public abuse in the amphitheatre. But the Hippodrome functioned primarily as a sports centre, where the regular programme of chariot races and circuses served as a diversion for the people of the city for more than a thousand years.

The turbulent mobs of the Hippodrome were originally divided into four factions: the Greens, Blues, Whites and Reds. The origins of these factions went back to very early Roman times, and each of them was said to be associated with one of the four elements of nature: green–earth, blue–water, white–air and red–fire. The factions were intimately linked with the various craft and market guilds, and each had its traditional part to play in the civic and religious life of the city. In the early centuries of Constantinople the Blues and Green factions began to achieve dominance, and eventually the Whites and Reds were absorbed by the other two groups. Traditionally, the Blues were recruited from the upper and middle classes and were orthodox in religion and conservative in politics, while the Greens were lower class and radical both in their religious beliefs and in their politics. The social, religious and political polarisation between the two factions was the source of constant dissension during the early history of the Byzantine Empire. The worst of these disturbances was the Nika Revolt in 531, which resulted in the death of some 30000 partisans in the Hippodrome itself. This broke the political power of the popular factions in the Hippodrome, and they were never again a serious problem for the reigning emperor.

STRUCTURE. The Hippodrome was 480m long and 117·5m wide: according to one estimate it could seat about 100,000 spectators. Down the long central axis of the arena there was a raised terrace called the *spina*, or spine; this was adorned with a line of statues, obelisks, and columns, three of which are still standing *in situ*. The royal enclosure, the Kathisma, was probably at the middle of the E side of the amphitheatre, where the Emperor and his party could enter directly from the Great Palace. The straight N end of the arena, where chariots, performers and spectators entered through vaulted passageways, was at the N end of the present park. The semicircular S end, the *sphendone*, is today concealed by buildings at that end of the square. At the top of the outer wall an arcade of columns, with an epistyle in the classical manner, ran around the structure. Many of these columns were still standing a century after the Turkish Conquest, but in 1550 they were pulled down and used for building material. The final destruction of the Hippodrome occurred in 1609, when what remained of the amphitheatre was demolished to make way for the mosque of Sultan Ahmet I. The site of the arena became a public square, as it is still today, and was given the appropriate name of At Meydaní, the Square of Horses.

Excavations carried out in the 1960s at the NE corner of the At Meydaní unearthed some remains of that part of the Hippodrome. The site has not been protected and has suffered considerable deterioration in the interim, but one can still see several sustaining arches, remains of staircases leading to the seats, and a few of the seats themselves.

Across from this archaeological site, near the N end of the At Meydaní, there is a domed structure known as the Fountain of Kaiser Wilhelm II. The Kaiser donated the funds to build this fountain in 1895, on the occasion of his visit to Abdül Hamit II, and it was completed three years later.

*The majestic interior of the Blue Mosque, with the great
dome hovering over the vast prayer-room. (Ergun Cagatay)*

The first of the ancient monuments on the spina, beginning at the N
end of the Hippodrome, is the **Egyptian Obelisk*. This was
originally commissioned by the Pharaoh Thutmose III (1549–1503
BC), who erected it at Deir el Bahri opposite Thebes in Upper Egypt to
commemorate one of his campaigns in Syria and his crossing of the
Euphrates River. The obelisk was originally about 60m tall and
weighed some 800 tons, but it broke apart during shipment to
Constantinople in the 4C AD, and only the upper third survived. This
fragment lay on the seashore where it was unloaded for some years,

until it was finally erected on its present site by Theodosius I in 390. The obelisk is mounted on four brazen blocks resting on a marble base with sculptured reliefs. The scenes on the four sides of the base represent Theodosius I and his family in the Kathisma, as they look down at various events taking place in the arena below. On the N side of the base the Emperor is shown supervising the erection of the obelisk, with the operations shown on the lower block. On the W he is depicted with his family as he receives homage from a group of kneeling captives; standing beside Theodosius is his nephew Valentinian II, ruler of the western part of the Roman Empire, and flanking them are the Emperor's two eldest sons, Honorius and Arcadius, who would themselves later become Emperors of West and East, respectively. On the S side the royal family are shown watching a chariot race, and on the E Theodosius is represented standing between Honorius and Arcadius, holding a laurel wreath in his hand as he prepares to crown the winner of the race. Below the Kathisma, in this last scene, one can see the faces of the crowd in the stadium; their faces, like those of the royal family, have been badly eroded by the elements. At the bottom of the panel there are dancing maidens, in a line, accompanied by three musicians.

At the centre of the spina stands the so-called **‘‘Serpentine Column**. The three intertwined bronze serpents that form the column were the base of a trophy which once stood in the Temple of Apollo at Delphi, dedicated to the god by the 31 Greek cities who defeated the Persians at Plataea in 479 BC. The base of the column was uncovered in 1920, revealing the names of the cities inscribed on the lower coils of the serpents. The column was brought from Delphi by Constantine the Great; it seems to have stood at first in the courtyard of Haghia Sophia and was erected in the Hippodrome only at a later date. There are several stories about what became of the missing serpent heads, but the most likely one is that they were chopped off by a drunken member of the Polish Embassy, one night in April 1700. The upper part of one of the serpent heads was found in 1847 and is now in the bronze collection of the Archaeological Museum. Like the serpents themselves, it is a very beautiful and finished piece of bronze sculpture, characteristic of Greek art of that period.

The third of the ancient monuments on the spina is a roughly-built ‘pillar of stone 32m high that stands near the S end of the At Meydaní. The 16C French traveller Petrus Gyllius called it the *Colossus*, but most modern writers refer to it, incorrectly, as the *Column of Constantine Porphyrogenitus*. Both names stem from the Greek inscription on its base, where the pillar is compared to the Colossus of Rhodes, and where it is recorded that the pillar was restored and sheathed in bronze by the Emperor Constantine VII Porphyrogenitus (912–59). But the inscription also states that the pillar was decayed by time; thus it must date from an earlier period, perhaps to that of Theodosius I or Constantine the Great.

Most of the W side of the At Meydaní is taken up by a vast structure of the early Ottoman period, which is partly concealed by an ugly 19C building. This huge edifice is what remains of the palace of Ibrahim Paşa, completed in 1524. Ibrahim Paşa was a Greek convert to Islam who became an intimate companion of Süleyman the Magnificent during the early years of his reign. In 1523 Ibrahim was appointed Grand Vezir and the following year he married Süleyman's sister Hadice, at which time his palace on the At Meydaní was completed. Some idea of the enormous wealth and influence that Ibrahim had at this time can be gained from even a casual view of the palace, the grandest private residence ever built in the Ottoman Empire, far greater in size than any of the buildings in Topkapí Sarayí itself.

*The Egyptian Obelisk and the Hippodrome before it was tidied-up.*

The very magnitude of this wealth and power was the ultimate cause of Ibrahim's downfall. When Süleyman fell under the nefarious influence of his wife Roxelana, during the latter part of his reign, the Sultan was persuaded that Ibrahim must be eliminated for taking on the airs of royalty. Thus one night in 1536, after having dined alone with the Sultan, Ibrahim retired to an adjacent room in the Saray and was murdered while he slept. Immediately afterwards all of Ibrahim's wealth and possessions were confiscated by the State, including the palace on the At Meydaní. For a time Ibrahim's palace seems to have been used as a dormitory and school for the apprentice pages in Topkapí Sarayí. The great hall, that part of the palace which fronts on the At Meydaní, was in Ibrahim's time the Audience Room for the Grand Vezir, and afterwards it was probably the site of the High Court of Justice. In later times it seems to have been used as a barracks for unmarried Janissaries and also as a prison.

By the beginning of the present century much of the palace was in ruins, but in recent years it has been undergoing repairs. The restoration has recently been completed, and the palace has been opened as a museum of Turkish and Islamic art.

At the SW corner of the At Meydani a narrow street named Şehit Mehmet Paşa Yokusu leads off to the S, winding down towards the Marmara. At the second turning on the left, the street passes on the right, the remains of *Helyací Camii*, a mosque founded in 1546 by one Iskender Ağa. Unfortunately, this has fallen into ruins and is no longer of any interest.

Farther down the street on the left there is a very interesting dervish monastery, whose entrance is half way down the side street and on the right. This was built in 1692 by Ismail Bey and is known as the *Özbekler Tekkesi*. It is rather crudely designed, but its form is unique because of the steep descent of the hill on which it is built. The little domed gatehouse leads to an anteroom, opposite which there is the large and handsome mescit-zaviye, the room where the dervish ceremonies took place. On the right is a small porticoed courtyard with the cells of the dervishes; on the left is another courtyard of cells on two storeys, the lower level being reached by a staircase behind the zaviye. Both courtyards are rather low and dark with square pillars instead of columns, which gives them a rather forbidding appearance; nevertheless, the arrangement as a whole is ingenious and attractive. The building has been rather summarily restored, and is now being used as a hostel for university students.

Şehit Mehmet Paşa Yokuşu continues downhill past the walled garden of a mosque, after which it turns left to continue past the lower wall of the enclosure. This brings one to the entrance of **Sokollu Mehmet Paşa Camii** (Pl 10,6), which is perhaps the most beautiful of the smaller mosques in Istanbul, a minor masterpiece by Sinan.

HISTORY. The mosque was built by Sinan in 1571–72 for Sokollu Mehmet Paşa, one of the most outstanding Grand Vezirs in the history of the Ottoman Empire. Sokollu Mehmet, the son of a Bosnian priest, was taken into the Janissary Corps as a youth and was educated in the Palace School at Topkapí Sarayí. His outstanding genius brought him early preferment and he rose rapidly in the Ottoman hierarchy, becoming Grand Vezir under Süleyman the Magnificent in 1565. He continued to hold that post under Süleyman's son and successor, Selim II, and married the Sultan's daughter, the Princess Esmahan, in whose honour he built this mosque. (The mosque is officially named after Esmahan, but it is more commonly associated with her more famous husband.) After Selim's death in 1574, Sokollu Mehmet Paşa served as Grand Vezir under Murat III until 1579, when he was murdered by a mad soldier in the Divan. He was a man of great vision and served his country well, holding off for a few years the forces that would eventually ruin the Empire. Posterity owes him three of the most beautiful Ottoman monuments in Istanbul: the present structure, another mosque across the Golden Horn in Azap Kapí, and a splendid külliye in Eyüp where he lies buried with his wife Esmahan.

EXTERIOR. The courtyard of the mosque is enchanting in design. It served, as in the case of many mosques, as a medrese, with the scholars living in the little domed cells under the portico. Each cell had a single window, a fireplace, and a recess for storing bedding, books and personal belongings. Instruction was given in the dersh-ane, the large domed room over the staircase in the W wall, and also in the mosque itself. Notice the charming ogive arches of the portico and the fine şadírvan in the centre. The porch of the mosque forms the fourth side of the court; in the lunettes of the windows there are some striking and elegant inscriptions in blue and white faience.

INTERIOR. Entering the building, one is delighted by the harmony of its lines, the lovely soft colour of the stone, the marble decoration, and, above all, by the tiles. In plan the mosque is a hexagon inscribed in an

# THE MOSQUE OF SOKOLLU MEHMET PAŞA

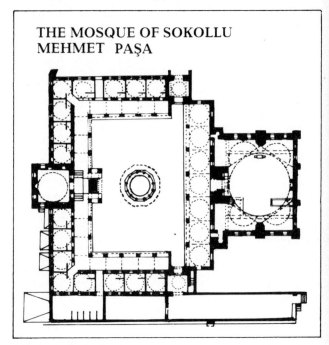

almost square rectangle, and the whole is covered by a dome, counter-balanced at the corners by four small semi-domes. There are no side aisles, but around three sides there is a low gallery supported on slender marble columns with typical Ottoman lozenge capitals. The polychrome of the arches, whose voussoirs are of alternate green and white marble, is characteristic of the period.

The tile decoration of the mosque has been used with singularly charming effect. Only selected areas of the walls have been sheathed in tiles: the pendentives below the dome, a frieze of floral design, and the exquisite central section of the E wall. The latter panel frames the mihrab with tiles decorated in vine and floral motifs in turquoise on a background of pale green, interspersed with panels of fine calligraphy with white letters on a deep blue field. The fine marble mimber is surmounted by a tall conical cap, sheathed in the same turquoise tiles that frame the mihrab. Above the mihrab the framed arch in the E wall is pierced by elegant stained-glass windows, whose bright spectrum of colours complements the cool tones of the faience flowers below. Above the entrance portal a small specimen of the wonderful painted decoration of the classical period can be seen. It consists of very elaborate arabesque designs in rich and varied colours. Also above the door, surmounted by a design in gold, there is a fragment of black stone from the Kaaba in Mecca; other fragments can be seen in the mihrab and mimber.

After leaving the mosque courtyard by the main gateway, turn left and then right at the next corner onto Kadirga Liman Cd. This picturesque old street soon leads to a large open square, much of which is now given over to a park and playground. This is the pleasant area known as *Kadirga Liman*, which means literally the Galley Port. As its name suggests, this was originally a seaport, long since silted up and built over. The port was originally dug and put in shape by the Emperor Julian the Apostate in 362. In about 570 Justin II redredged and enlarged the port and named it after his wife Sophia. It had to be continually redredged but remained in use until after the Turkish Conquest. By about 1550, when the French traveller Petrus Gyllius saw it, only a small part of the harbour remained, and now even this is gone. Today only bits and pieces of the inner fortifications of the harbour are left, cropping up here and there as parts of houses and garden walls in several of the streets between here and the Marmara.

In the centre of the square, Kadirga Liman Meydaní, there is a very striking and unique monument. This is the *namazgah of Esma Sultan*, daughter of Ahmet III, which was built in 1779. It is a great rectangular block of masonry. On two faces there are fountains with calligraphic inscriptions; the corners have ornamental niches, while the third side has a staircase leading to the platform on top. This is the only surviving example in Stamboul of a namazgah, or outdoor place of prayer, in which the direction of Mecca is indicated by a niche, but otherwise entirely without furniture or decoration.

At the S end of Kadirga Liman Meydaní there is a large open area next to the railway line; this is known as *Cinci Meydaní*, the Field of the Genii. The field is named after Cinci Hoca, a favourite of Sultan Ibrahim, who once owned land on this site. When Ibrahim first came to the throne in 1640 there were serious doubts about his sexual potency. This gave rise to alarm, since he was the last surviving male in the Ottoman dynasty, so his mother, Kösem, sought out Cinci Hoca, who had acquired a considerable reputation as a quacksalver. Cinci Hoca's wizard remedies apparently worked, for Ibrahim soon afterwards began fathering children, including half-a-dozen sons. But when Ibrahim was deposed and executed in 1648 Cinci Hoca fell too, and he and his friend, Pezevenk (the Pimp), were torn to pieces by a mob in the At Meydaní.

At the E end of Cinci Hoca Meydaní a path leads along the railway line. About 100m to the E the path ends at the courtyard of the former church of **\*\*SS. Sergius and Bacchus**, one of the most beautiful and historic of the surviving Byzantine churches in the city.

HISTORY. The church was begun by Justinian in 527, the first year of his reign. He dedicated the church to SS. Sergius and Bacchus, two Roman soldiers martyred for their faith and later the patron saints of Christians in the Roman army. During the reign of his uncle, Justin I, an old soldier, Justinian had been accused of plotting against the throne and had been sentenced to death. But SS. Sergius and Bacchus appeared to the Emperor in a dream and told him that his nephew was innocent of the charges against him. The next morning Justin ordered that Justinian be freed and restored to his former rank of Caesar. Justinian then vowed that he would show his gratitude to the saints by building a church dedicated to them, and when he succeeded to the throne he did so. This church, the first of several splendid sanctuaries with which Justinian adorned Constantinople, was probably finished before work began on the new Haghia Sophia in 532. It thus belongs to that extraordinary period of prolific and fruitful experiment in architectural forms which produced, in Constantinople, buildings so ambitious and so different as the present church, Haghia Sophia itself, and Haghia Eirene—to name only the surviving monuments— and in Ravenna, S. Vitale, the Baptistery, and S. Apollinare in Classe. It is as if the architects were searching for new modes of expression suitable to a new age. The domes of this period are especially worthy of note: the great dome of Haghia Sophia is of course unique, but the dome of SS. Sergius and Bacchus is no mere small-scale version of it, being quite different in design and very extraordinary on its own account.

SS. Sergius and Bacchus served as a Christian sanctuary for nearly a thousand years, until it was finally converted into a mosque in the first decade of the 16C.

The man responsible for its conversion was Hüseyin Ağa, Chief Black Eunuch in the reign of Beyazit II, whose tomb can be seen in the garden to the N of the mosque. The building continues to serve as a place of Islamic worship; in Turkish it is called Küçük Aya Sofya Camii, the Mosque of Little Haghia Sophia, because of its supposed resemblance to the Great Church.

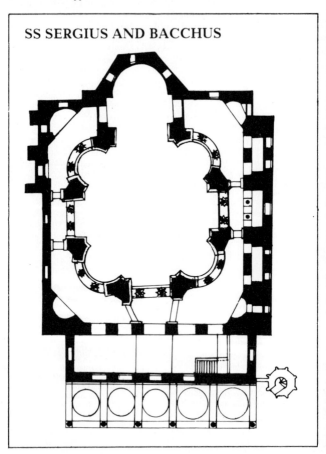

## SS SERGIUS AND BACCHUS

INTERIOR. In plan the church is an irregular octagon crookedly inscribed in a very irregular rectangle. It is difficult to account for these irregularities but they may be partly due to the fact that SS. Sergius and Bacchus was one of a pair of contiguous churches and had perhaps to be slightly deformed to accommodate its neighbour. The neighbouring church is thought to have been that of SS. Peter and Paul, which was probably located just to the S of the present building.

The method of transition from the octagon to the dome is astonishing: the dome is divided into sixteen compartments, eight flat sections alternating with eight concave ones above the angles of the octagon. This gives the dome the oddly undulatory or corrugated effect that is so distinctive when the building is observed from the heights of the First Hill. The octagon has eight polygonal piers with pairs of columns in between, alternately of verd antique and red Synnada marble, both above and below, arranged straight on the axes but curved out into the exedrae at each corner. The space between this brightly-coloured, moving curtain of columns and the exterior walls of the rectangle becomes an ambulatory below and a spacious gallery above. (The gallery is reached by a staircase at the S end of the narthex; do not fail to make the ascent, for the view of the church from above is very impressive.) The capitals and the classic entablature are exquisite specimens of the elaborately carved and deeply undercut style of the 6C, similar to those in Haghia Sophia. On the ground floor the capitals are of the 'melon' type, in the gallery 'pseudo-Ionic'; a few of them still bear the monogram of Justinian and Theodora, though most of these have been effaced. In the gallery the epistyle is arcaded in a way that became traditional in later Byzantine architecture. On the ground floor, the entablature is still basically classical, trabeated instead of arched, with the traditional architrave, frieze and cornice, but it is very different in effect from anything classical, the impression is of lace. The frieze consists of a long and beautifully carved inscription in twelve Greek hexameters honouring Justinian and Theodora, the two founders, and also St. Sergius, although for some reason St. Bacchus is not mentioned.

Nothing remains of the original interior decoration of the church. The walls, like those of Haghia Sophia, were revetted with veined and variegated marbles, while the vaults and domes glittered with mosaics. As described by Procopius, Justinian's court chronicler: 'By the sheen of its marbles it was more resplendent than the sun, and everywhere it was filled profusely with gold'.

Just NE of the church, on Küçük Aya Sofya Cd, there is an old Turkish bath known as Çardaklı Hamam. An inscription on the bath records that it was built in 1503 by an unnamed Kapíağası, or Chief Black Eunuch, who served under Beyazit II. The date of the bath and its proximity to SS. Sergius and Bacchus suggest that its founder was probably Hüseyin Ağa, who converted the church into a mosque. The hamam has been abandoned and is falling into ruins, but from what remains it can be seen that it was once quite grand.

A winding lane leads from the outside courtyard of SS. Sergius and Bacchus and passes under the railway line, after which a few steps takes one out onto the Marmara highway. Turn left here to follow a well-preserved stretch of the ancient **Byzantine sea-walls** along the Marmara.

HISTORY. The Byzantine sea-walls along this part of the Marmara shore were originally constructed by Constantine the Great, ending where his land-walls met the sea at Samatya. When the Theodosian walls were built in the following century, the sea-walls along the Marmara and the Golden Horn were extended to meet them. During the 9C the Marmara walls were almost completely rebuilt by the Emperor Theophilus, who sought to strengthen the city's maritime defences against the Arabs. The Marmara defences consisted of a single line of walls 12–15m high with 188 towers at regular intervals. These walls stretched from Saray Burnu to the terminus of the Theodosian walls on the Marmara, a total distance of 8km, and were pierced by 13 sea-gates. Although much of the fortifications along the Marmara have been destroyed in modern times, particularly during the building of the railway in the 1870s, that which remains is still grand and impressive, particularly the walls and towers below the First Hill.

Almost immediately in front of SS. Sergius and Bacchus there is a small postern gate, undoubtedly designed for the use of the monastery that was once attached to the church. Closer inspection shows that the posts of the gateway are carved with a long inscription in Greek, containing a conflation or cento from Habakkuk and Psalms. It

is believed that these doorposts once formed the base of the celebrated equestrian statue of Justinian that stood in the Augustaeum.

A short distance beyond this gate there are the ruins of a larger and
much grander postern, whose Turkish name is Çatladí Kapí, or the
Cracked Gate. The marble sides and archway of the gate are finely
carved with acanthus-leaf decorations as well as a large monogram of
Justinian. This postern is probably the one that was called the
Imperial Marine Gate, since it appears to have been one of the
entrances to the Great Palace from Porta Leonis, the Emperor's
private harbour. This port took its name from the statues of the two
lions that flanked the Imperial Marine Gate. These are the lions now
in the Archaeological Museum. The Gateway gave entrance to the
Palace of Bucoleon, one of the seaside pavilions of the Great Palace.
The remains can be seen just beyond the next tower in the sea-walls;
here one sees the E loggia of the palace, with its three huge
marble-framed windows and a vaulted room behind them. Below the
windows some projecting corbels indicate that a balcony ran along
the facade, suspended over a marble quay below. Notice the curious-
looking row of large square marble slabs built into the lower part of
the wall; these are the bottoms of Doric capitals of the 5C BC,
doubtless from some ancient temple that stood nearby.

HISTORY. These ruins are virtually all that remains of the Great Palace of
Byzantium whose pavilions and gardens covered the Marmara slopes of the First
Hill. The Palace was first built by Constantine the Great when he founded his
new capital. Much of the Palace was destroyed during the Nika Revolt in 532,
but it was rebuilt and considerably enlarged by Justinian soon after. Several
later emperors restored and extended the Palace, adorning it with works of art,
most notably Basil I (867–86). The Great Palace was divided into several
different establishments: the Sacred Palace and the Palaces of Daphne and
Chalke, which were located near the present site of the Blue Mosque; the
Palaces of Magnaura and Mangana, which stood to the SE of Haghia Sophia, on
the slope of the First Hill leading down to the Marmara; and the seaside Palace of
Bucoleon. In its time the Great Palace had no equal in the world, and medieval
travellers have left awed descriptions of its splendours. The Great Palace served
as the imperial residence until the sack of Constantinople by the Crusaders in
1204. After the recapture of the city in 1261 the Great Palace was found to be in a
state of advanced decay and was never afterwards restored. Instead, the later
emperors abandoned the palaces by the Marmara and took up their residence in
the Palace of Blachernae, in the NE corner of the city. At the time of the Turkish
Conquest the Great Palace was completely in ruins. Shortly after he entered the
city, Sultan Mehmet the Conqueror walked through the ruined halls of the
palace and was so saddened that he recited a melancholy distich by the Persian
poet Saadi: 'The spider is the curtain-holder in the Palace of the Caesars. The
owl hoots its night call on the Towers of Aphrasiab'.

The tower that forms the angle in the defence-walls just to the E of
Bucoleon was once the *Pharos*, the lighthouse of Constantinople. (In
modern times the lighthouse has been relocated farther to the E along
the sea-walls, near the SE corner of the old city.) About 400m E of the
lighthouse is an ancient entryway in the sea-walls. The Byzantine
name of this gateway is unknown, but in Ottoman times it was called
*Ahír Kapísí*, the Stable Gate, because it led to the imperial mews in
the lower gardens of the Saray. Perhaps it was also called by the same
name in Byzantine times, for Michael III is known to have built some
marble stables in the same area in the mid 9C. Ahír Kapísí is the main
entrance to the old city from the Marmara shore below the First Hill,
and the starting-point for the last stage of the present itinerary. Those
wishing to proceed farther along the sea-walls (see below) can return
to Ahír Kapísí after having completed that diversion.

There are two minor monuments of some historic interest along the walls past Ahir Kapisi. The first of these is about 500m along, just beyond the modern lighthouse. This is a marble structure called *Incili Köşkü*, the Kiosk of the Pearl, the only Ottoman sea-pavilion still standing along the Marmara shore. An inscription on the wall-fountain built into this kiosk gives the name of its founder as Sinan Paşa and the date 1578.

A short distance beyond the Incili Köşkü there is the facade of an ancient church built into the sea-walls, with blocked-up doors, window niches, and a huge arch rising to the top of the wall. These are the substructures of the church of *St. Saviour Philanthropus*, built in the first half of the 12C by Alexius I Comnenus. There is a tradition that the Emperor was buried in this church, but no trace of his tomb has been found.

In returning to the Stable Gate, notice the huge vaults in the lower part of the sea-walls just beyond the Incili Köşkü; these are probably part of the substructure of the Palace of Mangana, one of the divisions of the Great Palace of Byzantium. Beyond these substructures there are several small posterns that once gave access to the area which in Ottoman times was part of the lower gardens of the Saray. This whole area is a honeycomb of subterranean vaults, crypts and passageways that once formed part of the substructures of the various pavilions, churches and monasteries that covered this part of the First Hill, all of them part of the Great Palace of Byzantium. Unfortunately, the area has never been systematically excavated to establish the topography of the Palace, nor is it open to the public.

After passing through the Stable Gate turn immediately left onto Ahír Kapí Sk; then take the first right onto Keresteci Hakkí Sk, following this street around a bend to the right until it reaches Ak Bíyík Meydaní, the Square of the White Moustache. There are two street-fountains in the square worthy of notice, particularly the one to the left. This is an attractive example of a Turkish baroque fountain, with its rich decoration of flowers and cypress trees in relief. When deciphered the calligraphic chronogram on the facade of the fountain gives the date 1734 and records that the founder was the mother of Ali Paşa, a vezir in the reign of Mahmut I.

The street opposite the baroque fountain, Ak Bíyík Cd, leads under the railway line, after which it turns right and goes uphill until it intersects Mimar Mehmet Ağa Cd, a broad street that heads up towards the At Meydaní. The first turning on the left takes one onto Torun Sk, a quiet street that runs directly behind and below the Blue Mosque. Halfway along this street on the right is the entrance to the *Mosaic Museum. This is not so much a museum as an archaeological site, in which some interesting remnants of the Great Palace of Byzantium are exhibited. (The museum is open 9–5:30 every day except Tues.)

EXTERIOR. The architectural fragments visible outside the museum and in its outer courtyard were excavated during an archaeological study that began in 1935. These, together with the mosaic pavements inside the museum, were once part of the Great Palace of Byzantium, and the only parts of that fabled institution to have survived, aside from the facade of Bucoleon. The remains here were part of the Mosaic Peristyle, an open courtyard surrounded on four sides by a portico. This portico formed an antechamber between the Emperor's private apartments, which extended from here to the Marmara, and the more public sections of the Palace to the N.

INTERIOR. The entryway heads into a quaint little alley with booths on either side. This is all that remains of a Turkish bazaar street of the early 17C, still shown on official city maps as Kaba Sakal Sk, the Street of the Bushy Beard. The booths that line the street were part of

*The street-fountain in the Square of the White Moustache,
built in 1734. (Sedat Pakay)*

the Külliye of Sultan Ahmet Camii, housing shops whose rent went
toward the upkeep of the mosque and the other pious foundations in
the complex. In some of the booths panels of the mosaic pavement of
the Great Palace are displayed; these were found under Torun Sk and
are from the S side of the Mosaic Peristyle. At the end of the alley a
shed has been erected to preserve a section of the pavement *in situ*, it
is the stretch which formed the floor of the NE portico of the Mosaic
Peristyle. This pavement is decorated with several interesting scenes,
the most notable of which shows two hunters confronting a charging
lion. There has been considerable discussion about the date of these

mosaics, but pottery found on the site indicates that they are from the second quarter of the 6C AD: the Mosaic Peristyle would therefore have been part of the reconstruction programme instituted by Justinian after the Nika Revolt in 532.

After leaving the museum, walk back along Torun Cd and turn left onto Mimar Mehmet Ağa Cd., which leads uphill to the N end of the At Meydaní, passing between the Blue Mosque and Haghia Sophia.

# 6  From the Hippodrome to Beyazit Square

The itinerary from the Hippodrome to Beyazit Square follows the route of the ancient Mese, or Middle Way, the main thoroughfare of Byzantine Constantinople. This continued to be the principal artery of the city in Ottoman times because it led from the vicinity of Topkapí Sarayí to the centre of Stamboul. Consequently, the modern avenue here is lined with monuments of the imperial Ottoman centuries, along with some ruined remnants of the Byzantine Empire.

The first stretch of the avenue is called Divan Yolu, the Road of the Divan, for it was the principal approach to Topkapí Sarayí for the thousands who attended the tri-weekly meetings of the Divan in earlier Ottoman times. At the very beginning of Divan Yolu on the right there is a suterazi, or water-control tower, one of the very few that remain from the extensive water-distribution system built by the Ottomans in the century after the Conquest. Recent excavations at the foot of the suterazi have revealed ancient substructures identified as belonging to the Miliarium Aureum, the Golden Milestone. This was a triumphal archway that stood at the beginning of the Mese; it served as the reference point for all milestones on the Roman roads that led out of Constantinople into Thrace. It was also known as the Milion.

Yerebatan Cd leads off to the right from the beginning of Divan Yolu. A short way down this street, on the left, there is a small building that serves as the entrance to an enormous underground cistern called **Yerebatan Saray**, the Underground Palace, which is one of the most extraordinary monuments in Istanbul.

ENTRANCE. Yerebatan Saray is open every day from 9–5.

HISTORY. The structure was known in Byzantium as the Basilica Cistern because it lay beneath the Stoa Basilica, the great public square on the First Hill. The Basilica Cistern was built by Justinian after the Nika Revolt in 532, possibly as an enlargement of an earlier cistern constructed by Constantine the Great. Throughout the Byzantine period the Basilica Cistern was used to store water for the Great Palace and the other buildings on the First Hill. After the Conquest it served Topkapí Sarayí and the palace gardens. Nevertheless, general knowledge of the cistern's existence seems to have been lost in the century after the Conquest, and it was not rediscovered until 1545. In that year Petrus Gyllius, while engaged in his study of the surviving Byzantine antiquities in the city, learned that the people in this neighbourhood obtained water by lowering buckets through holes in their basement floors; some even caught fish from there. Gyllius made a thorough search through the neighbourhood and finally found a house through whose basement he could go down into the cistern, probably at the spot where the modern entrance is located.

INTERIOR. Yerebatan Saray is a magnificent structure, the largest and most beautiful of the many ancient underground cisterns in the city. It is 140m long (the longitudinal axis is in the direction of the street above) by 70m wide. Its 336 columns are arrayed in 12 rows of 28 each

(90 of these columns in the SE corner of the cistern were walled off at the end of the 19C, about 4m apart and 8m high). The columns are topped by Byzantine Corinthian capitals; these have imposts above them that support little domes of brick in a herring-bone pattern. But only a small part of this vast cistern is visible from the landing at the bottom of the stairway that leads down from the entrance above, leaving the rest in total darkness.

*Yerebatan Saray, built by Justinian in c 532, is by far the largest underground cistern in the city. (Bizans Caği)*

At the beginning of Divan Yolu on the right, just beyond the water-control tower, a bronze bust honours one of the heroines of modern Turkey, Halide Edib Adívar. Halide Edib, a novelist and political activist, was the most prominent woman among the Turkish Nationalists during the War of Independence, and was the first of her sex to play a leading public role in the life of the new Republic. She is the only woman ever to have been honoured by a public monument in Turkey.

100+m or so up Divan Yolu on the left is a small mosque, one of the oldest in the city. This was constructed in 1491 for Firuz Ağa, Chief Treasurer in the reign of Beyazit II. *Firuz Ağa Camii* is of interest mainly because it is one of the few examples in Istanbul of a mosque of the 'pre-classical' period, that is, of those built before 1500. This is the architectural style that flourished principally in the city of Bursa when it was the capital of the Ottoman Empire, in the century before the Conquest. Firuz Ağa Camii is quite simple in form, consisting merely of a square room covered by a windowless dome resting on the walls, the so-called single-unit type of mosque. The building is preceded by a little porch of three bays, while the minaret, unusually, is on the left side. The tomb of the founder, in the form of a marble sarcophagus, is on the terrace beside the mosque. Firuz Ağa Camii is an elegant little building, perhaps the most handsome of the early mosques of its type in the city.

Just beyond Firuz Ağa Camii a little park borders an open area excavated in the 1950s. The ruins exposed in these excavations are so fragmentary that it is difficult to determine their identity. It is thought that they are the ruins of two adjacent palaces, those of Antiochus and Lausus, noblemen of the early 5C AD. The grander of these is the palace of Antiochus, an hexagonal building with five deep semicircular apses, between each pair of which there are circular rooms. Early in the 7C the palace of Antiochus was converted into a martyrium for the body of St. Euphemia of Chalcedon, a Christian maiden who was martyred for her faith in the year 303. The martyrium is elaborately decorated with frescoes representing scenes from the life and martyrdom of St. Euphemia, along with a striking picture of the Forty Martyrs of Sebaste; these are preserved in rather poor condition under a shed at the rear of the site. (This is not open to the public.) The frescoes were at first ascribed to the 9C, but the latest study dates them to the late 13C. The silver-plated casket of St. Euphemia is preserved in the church of St. George in the Greek Orthodox Patriarchate in the Fener (see below, Rte 14).

Once past these ruins continue along Divan Yolu for a short distance and then take the second street on the left, Işík Sk, which leads uphill to a large open square. On the S side of the square there is a little building which serves as the entrance to another ancient underground cistern; this is known in Turkish as **\*\*Binbirdirek**, the Cistern of a Thousand-and-One Columns.

ADMISSION. The cistern is not officially open to the public. However, if one waits by the entrance the local children will usually fetch the watchman, who for a small tip will unlock the door and turn on the lights in the cistern.

INTERIOR. A flight of steps leads down from the entryway into the cistern. Unlike Yerebatan Saray, the cistern is dry and completely illuminated, and so one can walk about and appreciate the grandeur of this extraordinary structure. The cistern was originally about 19m high from the floor to the top of the little brick domes in herring-bone design, but over the centuries mud has accumulated to a depth of some 4·5m. The columns are in two tiers bound together by curious stone ties. There were originally 224 double columns in 16 rows of 14 each, but 12 of these were walled in not long after the cistern was completed. The impost capitals are plain except that some of them are inscribed with the monograms of the stonemasons. The dimensions of Binbirdirek are 64m by 56·4m, giving it a floor area of some 3610 square m; this makes it the second largest underground cistern in the city, but still only about a third of the area of Yerebatan Saray. It is thought that the cistern was originally built by Philoxenus, a Roman senator who came to the city with Constantine the Great, although there is evidence that some of the structure dates to the 5–6C. During the 19C the cistern was used as a spinning-mill and more recently as a storehouse.

On emerging from the cistern turn right and then right again onto the street at the W side of the square, Klot Farer Cd (named after the French novelist Claud Farrere), then a short way along turn left onto the main avenue, which now becomes Yeniçeriler Cd, the Avenue of the Janissaries.

At the first intersection on the left the avenue crosses Piyer Loti Cd (named after the French novelist Pierre Loti). On the other side of the avenue stands the *türbe of Sultan Mahmut II*, enclosed by a long garden wall. The türbe was built in 1838, the year of Mahmut's death; it was designed in the Empire style then popular in Europe, and is thus a little pompous and formal. Mahmut's son and grandson, Sultans Abdül Aziz and Abdül Hamit II, together with a large number of princes and imperial consorts are also buried here.

Directly opposite the türbe of Mahmut II, on the left side of Yeniçeriler Cd, is an elegant Ottoman library. This is one of the buildings of the *Köprülü külliye*, whose other institutions are scattered about in the immediate neighbourhood. These buildings were erected in 1659–60 by two members of the illustrious Köprülü family, Mehmet Paşa and his son Fazil Ahmet Paşa. The Köprülüs are generally considered to have been the most distinguished family in the history of the Ottoman Empire. During the second half of the 17C and the early years of the 18C five members of the family served as Grand Vezir, some of them among the most able of those that ever held that post. The library of the Köprülü külliyesi is a handsome little building with a columned porch and a domed reading-room, constructed in a mixture of brick and stone. The library contains an important collection of books and manuscripts, many of which are state papers and other documents belonging to the two founders.

One block beyond the library and on the same side of Yeniçeriler Cd are two other institutions belonging to the Köprülü külliyesi; these are the mosque and the türbe of Mehmet Paşa. The türbe is roofed unusually, with a metal grille. The mosque is a few steps beyond the türbe, projecting out onto the sidewalk of the avenue. The mosque, which is octagonal, was once the lecture hall of the Köprülü medresesi, most of which has now disappeared.

Directly across the avenue from the Köprülü mosque stands the *Çemberlitaş Hamamí, one of the finest extant examples of a classical Turkish bath. This hamam was founded some time before her death in 1583 by the Valide Sultan Nur Banu, wife of Selim II and mother of Murat III. The bath was originally double, but the women's section was destroyed when the avenue was widened some years ago. In general, the plan of the hamam follows the usual form, with a great domed camekan leading to a small three-domed soğukluk, which in turn opens into a square hararet. The hararet has a rather charming arrangement, similar to that seen earlier in the Çağaloğlu Hamamí, with a circlet of columns supporting an arcade on which the dome rests. In the corners there are little washing-cells, each with a dome and an attractive door, the pavements decorated with geometric designs.

Just beyond the hamam, at the corner of Yeniçeriler Cd and Vezirhaní Cd, stands one of the most venerable monuments in the city, the **Column of Constantine. This is known locally as Çemberlitaş, the Hooped Column, a name that it has given to the adjacent bath and the surrounding neighbourhood.

HISTORY. The column was erected by Constantine the Great to commemorate the dedication of the city as capital of the Roman Empire on 11 May AD 330. The dedication ceremony was a curious mixture of pagan rites and Christian rituals, with priests of both religions taking part. During the ceremony sacred objects of the old Roman religion as well as Christian relics were immured in the base of the column. These included the Palladium of Troy, the wooden icon of Athena that Aeneas brought with him on his journey to Italy; the sun-rays of Apollo's crown; the nails of Christ's Passion; and fragments of the True Cross discovered in Jerusalem by St. Helena, Constantine's mother.

The column stood at the centre of the Forum of Constantine, an oval colonnaded portico which is thought to have been similar to that which Bernini later built in front of St. Peter's in Rome. Around the Forum, which was adorned with statues of pagan deities, Roman emperors, and Christian saints, there stood several large public buildings, temples, and churches. All that remains of this grandeur now lies buried beneath 3m of earth, with only the battered column itself surviving.

The column, whose present height is 34·8m, originally had a square pedestal standing on five steps; above this there was a porphyry plinth and column base supporting a shaft of seven porphyry drums. In 416 the column was damaged during an earthquake. As it seemed in imminent danger of collapse, iron hoops were bound around the junctions of the drums to stabilise the shaft. At the summit of the shaft there was a large capital, presumably Corinthian, upon which stood a colossal statue of the Emperor Constantine in the guise of Apollo, with a sceptre in his right hand, the globe of the world in his left, and a crown of brazen sun-rays glittering in his helmet. The statue fell down and was destroyed during a hurricane in 1106, and some 50 years later Manuel I Comnenus replaced the capital with the present masonry courses and marble block, with a large cross above, which was removed after the Conquest. In 1779 the column was damaged during a great fire that destroyed most of the surrounding neighbour-hood, leaving the black scars that one sees today. The column was soon afterwards repaired by Abdül Hamit I, who enclosed the base of the column in its present masonry casing, which conceals the lowest porphyry drum. The column was restored during the 1970s, when the ancient iron hoops were replaced.

A short way down the right side of Vezirhani Cd is the entrance to another institution of the Köprülü külliye, the *Vezir Han*. Along with the other buildings in the külliye, the Vezir Han was erected in 1659–60 by Mehmet Paşa and his son Fazíl Ahmet Paşa. It served as a hostel for travelling merchants and was also equipped with stables for their animals as well as shops and storerooms for their goods. The Vezir Han was also the principal slave-market in Istanbul, until the abolition of slavery in the Ottoman Empire in 1855.

The entrance to the han is through a monumental gateway with very strong doors of thick wood bound with iron, which are locked and barred at night. The vast rectangular courtyard is surrounded with porticoes on two floors. The windowless chambers on the ground floor housed the stables, storerooms, shops, toilets, as well as the kitchen and dining-hall. A passageway led from the courtyard to the Çemberlitaş Hamamí, so that those staying in the han could go there to bathe. Staircases on each side of the courtyard led up to the gallery on the first floor, where the sleeping-quarters were located, along with additional shops for finer and more expensive goods; these chambers were brighter and more open than the ones below.

Today, with the replacement of the horse and camel by motorised transport, the character of the Vezir Han and the other old caravan-sarays in Istanbul has changed considerably, and they are given over to every conceivable form of industry and commerce. Most of them, like the Vezir Han, are in a shocking state of dilapidation and near ruin. Nevertheless, they are still grand and picturesque structures, evoking something of the now almost vanished Oriental atmosphere of old Ottoman Stamboul.

Just beyond the Column of Constantine, on the same side of Yeniçeriler Cd, there is an interesting old mosque, *Atik Ali Paşa Camii*. This is one of the oldest mosques in the city, built in 1496 by the Hadím (Eunuch) Atik Ali Paşa, Grand Vezir of Beyazit II.Surrounded

*The Beyazidiye, constructed in 1501–06, is one of the most
beautiful imperial mosque courtyards in Istanbul.*

by a quiet garden off the busy street, it is an attractive little mosque,
particularly from the outside. Its plan is somewhat unusual, it consists
of a rectangular room divided into two unequal parts by an arch. The
larger W section is covered by a dome, the E by a semidome under
which is the mihrab, as if in a sort of great apse. The W section is also

flanked to N and S by two rooms with smaller domes. The semidome and the four small domes have stalactite pendentives, a common feature in Ottoman mosques of early date.

Atik Ali Paşa Camii originally had several dependencies: a tekke, an imaret, and a medrese. Of these only a part of the medrese remains; this is across Yeniçeriler Cd from the mosque, the remainder having been destroyed some years ago when the road was widened. This building, though mutilated, is interesting as being one of the very few medreses of the pre-classical period that survive in the city.

A short distance beyond Atik Ali Paşa Cd, on the same side of the avenue, there is the *külliye of Koca Sinan Paşa*, enclosed by a picturesque marble wall with iron grilles. The külliye consists of a medrese, a sebil, and the türbe of Koca Sinan Paşa, who died in 1595. Koca Sinan Paşa was Grand Vezir under both Murat III and Mehmet III, and was the conqueror of the Yemen. Perhaps the most outstanding element in this very attractive complex of buildings is the türbe, a fine structure with 16 sides. It is built of polychrome stonework, white and rose-coloured, and with a rich cornice of stalactites and handsome window mouldings. The medrese, which is entered through a gate in the alley alongside, has a charming courtyard with a portico in ogive arches. The sebil, too, is an elegant structure with bronze grilles separated by little columns and surmounted by a hanging roof. The külliye was built in 1593 by Davut Ağa, the successor to Sinan as Chief Architect of the Ottoman Empire; it has recently been restored.

On the other side of the alley across from the sebil a marble wall with grilles encloses another complex of buildings, the *külliye of Ali Paşa of Çorlu*. This Ali Paşa was a son-in-law of Mustafa II and served as Grand Vezir under Ahmet III, on whose orders he was beheaded in 1711 on the Aegean island of Mytilene. Ali Paşa's head was later brought back to Istanbul and buried in the cemetery of his külliye, which had been completed three years earlier. This külliye, consisting of a small mosque and a medrese, belongs to the transitional period between the classical and baroque styles. Though attractive, there is nothing outstanding about these buildings, although one might notice how essentially classical they still are. The only very baroque features are the capitals of the columns on the porch. The külliye has recently been restored, and the medrese now serves as a hostel for university students.

Directly across the avenue stands the octagonal *mosque of Kara Mustafa of Merzifon*. This unfortunate Grand Vezir also lost his head, executed by Mehmet IV after the second unsuccessful siege of Vienna in 1683. The buildings were begun in 1669 and finished by the Paşa's son in 1690. This mosque is of the transitional type between classical and baroque; it is of interest as being one of the few mosques with an octagonal plan. This külliye has also been restored in recent years; the medrese has been converted into a research institute commemorating the Turkish poet Yahya Kemal, who died in 1958.

The street beyond this little külliye is called Gedik Paşa Cd; this leads to a hamam of the same name on the second turning on the left. This is one of the very oldest baths in the city (c 1475), and it is still in operation. Its founder was Gedik Ahmet Paşa, one of Mehmet the Conqueror's Grand Vezirs (1470–77), commander of the Ottoman fleet at Azof and conqueror of Otranto. This hamam has an unusually spacious and monumental soğukluk consisting of a large domed area flanked by alcoves and cubicles; the one on the right has a very elaborate stalactited vault. The hararet is cruciform except that the lower arm of the cross has been cut off and made part of the soğukluk; the corners of the cross form domed cubicles. The bath has recently been restored and now glistens with bright new marble; it is much patronized by the inhabitants of this picturesque quarter.

At the first cross street beyond Gedik Ahmet Cd the avenue reaches Beyazit Square (the official name is Hürriyet Meydani, but everyone refers to it by its original name, Beyazit Meydani), one of the busiest intersections in the old city. A pedestrian subway makes it possible to cross safely to the other side of the avenue, from where one can walk through the crowded market area to the **Beyazidiye**, the mosque complex of Sultan Beyazit II.

HISTORY. The Beyazidiye was the second great mosque complex to be erected in Istanbul after the Conquest, the first being that of Mehmet II himself (see Rte 11, Fatih Camii). The külliye was built between 1501 and 1506, and consists of the great mosque itself, along with a medrese, primary school, public kitchen, public bath, and several türbes. Heretofore the architect's name has variously been given as Hayrettin or Kemalettin, but a recent study has shown that the külliye is due to a certain Yakub-şah bin Sultan-şah, who also built a caravansaray at Bursa. His background is unknown and his origin uncertain, but he may have been a Turk. Whatever his origin, he created a work of the very greatest importance, both in its excellence as a building and in its historic significance in the development of Ottoman architecture. The Beyazit mosque marks the beginning of the great classical period that continued for more than two centuries. Before this time Ottoman architects had been experimenting with various styles of mosques and had often produced buildings of great beauty, as in Yeşil Cami at Bursa or Üç Şerefli Cami at Edirne; but no definite style had been evolved that could produce the vast mosques demanded by the capital of a world empire. The original mosque of the Conqueror was indeed a monumental building, but as that was destroyed by an earthquake in the 18C, Beyazit Camii remains the earliest extant example of the great imperial mosques of Istanbul.

EXTERIOR. Beyazit Camii is entered through what is perhaps the most charming of all the mosque courtyards in Istanbul. A peristyle of 20 ancient columns—porphyry, verd antique, and Syenitic granite—upholds an arcade with red-and-white or black-and-white marble voussoirs. The colonnade is roofed with 24 small domes and three

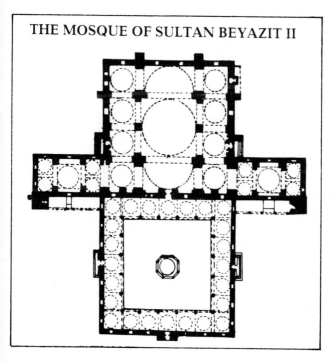

THE MOSQUE OF SULTAN BEYAZIT II

magnificent entrance portals give access to it. The pavement is of polychrome marble and in the centre stands a beautifully decorated şadírvan. (The encircling colonnade of stumpy verd antique columns supporting a dome appears to be a clumsy restoration.)Capitals, cornices, and niches are elaborately decorated with stalactite mouldings. The harmony of proportions, the rich but restrained decoration, the brilliance of the variegated marbles, give this courtyard a quite unique charm.

INTERIOR. An exceptionally fine portal leads into the mosque, which in plan is a greatly simplified and much smaller version of Haghia Sophia. As there, the great central dome and the semidomes to E and W form a kind of nave, beyond which to N and S are side aisles. The arches supporting the dome spring from four huge rectangular piers; the dome has smooth pendentives but rests on a cornice of stalactite mouldings. There are no galleries over the aisles which open wide into the nave, separated only by the piers and by a single antique granite column between them. This is an essential break with the plan of Haghia Sophia: in one way or another the mosque architects all tried to centralise their plan as much as possible, so that the entire area is visible from any point. At the W side a broad corridor, divided into domed or vaulted bays and extending considerably beyond the main body of the mosque, creates the effect of a narthex. This is a transitional feature, retained from an older style of mosque; it appears only rarely later on. At each end of this corridor rise the two fine minarets, their shafts picked out with geometric designs in terracotta; they stand far beyond the main part of the building in a position which is unique and gives a very grand effect. At the end of the S arm of the corridor a small library was added in the 18C by the Şeyh-ül Islam Veliyüttin Efendi. An unusual feature of the interior of the mosque is that the Sultan's loge is to the right of the mimber instead of to the left. The loge is supported on columns of very rich and rare marbles. The central area of the building is approximately 40m on a side, and the diameter of the dome is about 17m.

THE MOSQUE PRECINCTS. Behind the mosque is the türbe garden; Beyazit II is buried here in a simple, well-proportioned türbe of limestone picked out in verd antique. The even simpler türbe of his daughter Selçuk Hatun is nearby. Behind these a third türbe, in a highly ornate Empire style, is that of the Grand Vezir Koca Reşit Paşa, the distinguished leader of the Tanzimat (Reform) Movement, who died in 1857. Below the E side of the türbe garden facing the street is an arcade of shops originally erected by Sinan in 1580; it had almost disappeared long ago but it was restored during the 1960s.

Just beside these shops is the large double síbyan mektebi with two domes and a porch; this is the oldest surviving primary school in the city, since that belonging to the külliye of the Conqueror has disappeared. The school has recently been restored and now houses the *hakki tarík us Research Library*. (hakki tarík us was a journalist who, like the poet e. e. cummings, had an aversion to capital letters.) Between this building and the N minaret is a very pretty courtyard called *Sahaflar Çarşísí*, or the Market of the Secondhand Booksellers.

Almost opposite the N minaret stands the extremely impressive imaret of the külliye. The imaret, in addition to serving as a public kitchen, seems also to have been used as a caravansaray. The various rooms of the imaret line three sides of the courtyard (now roofed in), with the fourth side pierced by the monumental entrance portal. The first room on the right housed an olive press, the second was a grain storeroom, and the third, in the right-hand corner, was the bakery, equipped with two huge ovens. The large domed chamber at the far corner of the courtyard was the kitchen and dining-room. The even larger domed chamber beside it, forming the left third of the complex, served as a stable for the horses and camels of the travellers who were guests at the imaret, while the chamber between the stable and the courtyard was used as a dormitory. The imaret was converted into a library by Abdül Hamit II in 1882; it now houses the *State Library*. This library is an important one, with 120,000 volumes and more than 7000 manuscripts, and the imaret makes a fine home for it.

The medrese of the Beyazidiye is at the far W end of the square. It is of the standard form; the cells where the students lived and studied are ranged around four sides of a porticoed courtyard, while the lecture-hall is opposite the entrance portal. This building now serves as the *Municipality Library*; unfortunately, the restoration and conversion were rather badly done, a lot of cement having been used instead of stone, and with the portico very crudely glassed in. Nevertheless, the proportions of the building are so good and the garden in the courtyard so attractive that the general effect is still quite charming.

Beyond the medrese, facing on the main avenue (which here takes the name Ordu Cd), are the splendid remains of *Beyazit's hamam*. This must have been the most magnificent Turkish bath in the city, and deserves restoration, for the fabric of the building still seems to be essentially in good condition. It was a double hamam; the two sections were almost identical, except that the women's bath was slightly smaller than the men's. Apart from the monumental facade of the two camekans with their great domes, the best view of the hamam may be had from the second floor of the new University building just beyond; from there one can see the elaborate series of domes and vaults, now overgrown with moss and wild plants, that cover the two soğukluks and hararets. Before leaving the hamam, do not fail to notice the reliefs built into the lower part of the facade near the street corner, including a line of marching soldiers placed upside down in the wall. These are fragments of the triumphal arch of Theodosius the Great, which stood in the centre of the Forum Tauri. Some remnants of the archway and the forum can be seen on the opposite side of Ordu Cd (see below, Rte 8).

On the N side of Beyazit Square stand the main buildings of the **University of Istanbul**, the oldest and largest institution of higher education in Turkey.

HISTORY. Without any undue stretching of continuity, the University of Istanbul can be shown to have been in existence since the time of the Conquest. Immediately after the Conquest Mehmet II founded a university and a few years later installed it in the eight great medreses which were attached to his mosque (see Rte 11, Fatih Camii). Later, other such institutions were added by Beyazit II, Selim I, and, above all, by Süleyman, who surrounded his own mosque with seven medreses. At all of these medreses, which together can be said to constitute the University of Istanbul, there were Faculties of Theology, Philosophy, Law, Medicine and Science. But the decline of the Ottoman Empire was accompanied by a corresponding decline of the University. During the mid-19C several attempts were made to modernise the University and reorganise it along European lines, but these efforts were for the most part frustrated by the reactionary conservatism of the ulema, the religious hierarchy. After the establishment of the Turkish Republic the University was finally reformed and

modernised, at which time it was installed in its present building, till then the
Seraskerat or Ministry of War. The main part of the building was constructed by
the French architect Bourgeois in 1866, in the sumptuous style then thought
appropriate to ministerial edifices. During the last two decades or so various
wings have been added, equally styleless but not nearly so sumptuous.

The area on which these central buildings of the University stand
formed part of the site where Mehmet the Conqueror built Eski Saray,
the Old Palace, immediately after the Conquest. Somewhat later he
began to build Topkapí Sarayí on the First Hill, and the Old Palace
was gradually abandoned as the official residence of the sultans.
Some of its buildings were used as a place of claustration for the
women of departed sultans, others as private palaces of distinguished
vezirs; later a large part of its grounds was appropriated by Süleyman
for his great mosque complex. In the end the whole of the Old Saray
disappeared, and there is not a single trace of it to be seen today.

In the courtyard of the University stands the *Beyazit Tower*, a
familiar landmark on the skyline of the old city. There had long been a
wooden tower at this point for fire-watchers, but it was not until 1828
that Mahmut II caused the present tower to be built. It is some 50m
high and is made largely of Proconnesian marble. There is a
fire-watch station at the top, reached by a winding staircase of 180
steps. This is open to the public, and although the climb is an arduous
one it is well worth the effort, for the magnificent view includes almost
the whole of Istanbul and its surrounding waters.

# 7  The Market Quarter

The lively and colourful area between Beyazit Square and the
Golden Horn is the principal market quarter of Istanbul. It is also the
industrial centre of the old city, with innumerable small and
primitive factories, forges, workshops, ateliers and stores, along with
warehouses and depots. Many of these establishments are housed in
old Ottoman hans, as picturesque as they are ruinous; among them
are the most splendid extant examples of Ottoman civil architecture.

A number of outdoor markets are to be found in and around the outer
courtyard of the Beyazidiye, including the fascinating *Bit Pazar*, or
Flea Market. This is located at the NE corner of the courtyard, just
outside the walls of Istanbul University. The Bit Pazar spills over into
Bakírcílar Cd, the Avenue of the Copper-Workers, where most of the
coppersmiths in the city make and sell their wares. Many of the streets
in this quarter are named after the artisans, tradesmen and merchants
who carry on their activities there, just as they have for centuries past.

Just N of the Beyazit mosque there is an open courtyard entered
through a stone portal known as *Kaşíkcí Kapísí*, the Gate of the
Spoonmakers. This is *Sahaflar Çarşísí*, the Market of the
Secondhand Booksellers. The Sahaflar Çarşísí is one of the most
interesting and picturesque spots in the city, with bookshops and
stalls around the vine-shaded courtyard exhibiting everything from
rare and beautifully bound tomes to paperback trash and secondhand
magazines, including works written in every language of the Middle
East and Europe. The courtyard is always crowded, particularly with
students and professors from the University. There is a constant

stream of pedestrians passing through it between the outer courtyard of the Beyazidiye and the nearby Kapalí Çarşí, the Covered Bazaar (see below).

HISTORY. The Sahaflar Çarşísí is one of the most ancient markets in the city; it occupies the site of the Chartoprateia, the book and paper market of Byzantine Constantinople. After the Conquest this became the market for the spoon-makers (hence the name of the entryway from the outer courtyard of the Beyazidiye), turban-makers, and metal-engravers, at which time it was called Hakkaklar Çarşísí, after the guild of the latter. At the beginning of the 18C the booksellers set up shop there too, moving from their old quarters inside the Kapalí Çarşí. In the second half of the 18C, with the legalisation of printing and publishing in the Ottoman Empire, the booksellers greatly increased their trade and came to dominate the market; from that time it was named after them. During the 19C and early 20C, the Sahaflar Çarşísí was one of the principal centres in the Ottoman Empire for the sale and distribution of books. However, in the past half-century, the establishment of university libraries and modern bookshops elsewhere in the city has somewhat diminished its importance, although it is still the centre of Istanbul's book trade, particularly for old, rare, and scholarly works. The owners of the bookshops in the market are all members of the guild of booksellers. This guild is one of the oldest in Istanbul, its origins, like those of most other craft-guilds in the city, dating back to Byzantine times.

At the far end of the courtyard a stairway leads down to an ancient stone portal known as *Hakkaklar Kapísí*, the Gate of the Engravers, a name that goes back to the time when that guild carried on its activities here. After passing through the gateway, turn right on the narrow street outside, and then a short way along turn left into an entryway of the Kapalí Çarşí, the Covered Bazaar.
   **The Kapalí Çarşí** is one of the most fascinating and picturesque markets in the world, and an irresistible attraction for all visitors to Istanbul, Turks and foreigners alike.

HISTORY. The Kapalí Çarşí was established on its present site by Mehmet II soon after the Conquest, when it occupied about the same area that it does today. Although it has been destroyed several times by fire, most recently in 1954, the Bazaar is essentially the same in structure and appearance as when it was first built, although much of the fabled Oriental atmosphere of the market has vanished in the past half-century.

INTERIOR. The Kapalí Çarşí is a small city in itself: according to a survey made in 1880, the Bazaar contained at that time 4399 shops, 2195 ateliers, 497 stalls, 12 storehouses, 18 fountains, 12 mescits or small mosques, as well as a larger mosque, a primary school, and a türbe. The number of commercial establishments would appear to be about the same today, in addition to which there have been added half-a-dozen restaurants, innumerable cafés and teahouses, two banks, plus a public toilet and an information centre for tourists.
   At first the Kapalí Çarşí seems a veritable labyrinth, but the plan reveals that most of the streets form a fairly regular grid, particularly in the central area of the market, and it is not too difficult to find one's way about. Shops selling the same kind of merchandise tend to be congregated in their own streets: thus there is a handsome colon-naded street of oriental rug-merchants, whose wares range all the way from magnificent museum pieces to cheap modern imitations. There is also a glittering street of jewellers and dealers in silver and gold ornaments, whose merchandise spans the spectrum from tawdry costume jewellery to priceless heirlooms. Every conceivable type of goods is sold somewhere or other in the Bazaar: one has but to wander, shop and bargain. Almost all of the dealers speak several languages and there is little difficulty in communication. But time is

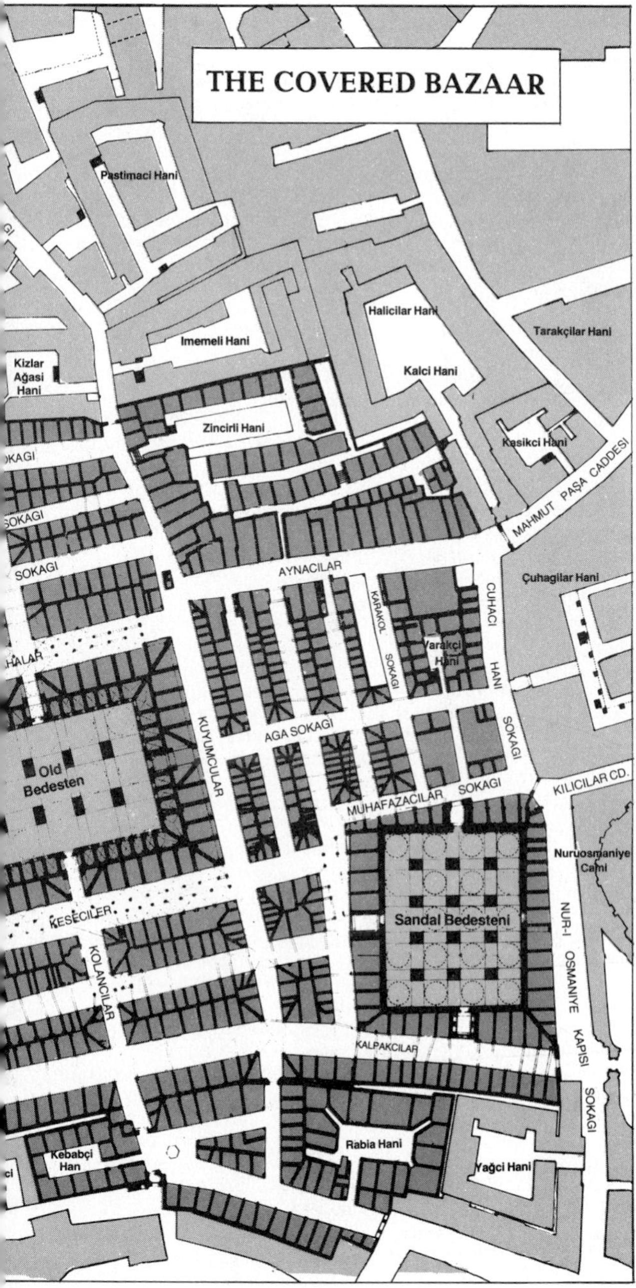

# THE COVERED BAZAAR

Pastimaci Hani

Halicilar Hani

Tarakçilar Hani

Imemeli Hani

Kizlar Ağasi Hani

Kalci Hani

Zincirli Hani

Kesikci Hani

SOKAGI

MAHMUT PAŞA CADDESI

SOKAGI

SOKAGI

AYNACILAR

Çuhagilar Hani

HALAR

KARAKOL SOKAGI

CUHACI HANI

Yarakçi Hani

KUYUMCILAR

AGA SOKAGI

SOKAGI

Old Bedesten

MUHAFAZACILAR SOKAGI

KILICILAR CD.

KESECILER

Nuruosmaniye Cami

Sandal Bedesteni

NUR-İ OSMANIYE KAPISI

KOLANCILAR

KALPAKCILAR

SOKAGI

Kebabçi Han

Rabia Hani

Yağci Hani

essential: a good bargain can rarely be struck in a few moments; often it requires a leisurely cup of Turkish coffee, readily provided by the dealer.

In the centre of the Bazaar is the great domed hall known as the ··OLD BEDESTEN. This is one of the original structures surviving from the time of the Conqueror. Then, as now, it was used to house the most precious wares, for it can be securely locked and guarded at night. Some of the most interesting and valuable objects in the Bazaar are sold here: brass and copper of every description, often old and fine; ancient swords and other weapons; antique coins, jewellery and costumes; classical and Byzantine pottery and figurines. As one might expect, not all of the antiquities sold in the Bedesten are authentic. Nevertheless, many of the imitations are of excellent workmanship: the craftsmen often belong to the same guild as the makersof the originals, and use the same kinds of tools and techniques as their predecessors.

The E portal of the Bedesten is known as *Kuyumcu Kapísí*, the Gate of the Goldsmiths. Above the outer part of the gateway there is the figure in relief of a single-headed Byzantine eagle, the date and origin of which are unknown. The single-headed eagle was the imperial emblem of the Comneni dynasty, who ruled over Byzantium in the 11–12C. (The Palaeologus dynasty, who ruled in the period 1261–1453, had a double-headed eagle as their emblem.) This has led some scholars to suggest that the Old Bedesten was originally of Byzantine construction, but most authorities reject this and agree that the building was erected soon after the Conquest.

The Gate of the Goldsmiths opens into Inciciler Sk, the Street of the Pearl-Merchants. The third turning on the right from this street leads to the Sandal Bedesten, whose main entrance is a few steps down the second turning on the left.

The *Sandal Bedesten* is a great hall that is thought to have been built early in the 16C, probably during the reign of Beyazit II, when the great increase in Ottoman trade and commerce required an additional market and storehouse for valuables in the Kapalí Çarşí. The Sandal Bedesten is far quieter and less colourful in its activities than the rest of the Bazaar, for it is almost empty most of the time. But for that reason one can examine its splendid structure more easily, particularly since it is largely unencumbered with shops and stalls. The internal support for the lofty roof is provided by twelve massive piers, in four rows of three each, supporting 20 brick domes. The best times to visit the Sandal Bedesten are Monday and Thursday at one o'clock in the afternoon, when the rug-auctions are held. These auctions take place in what looks like a little odeum in the centre of the hall, where rug-merchants sit and bid upon the rugs and carpets which the sellers exhibit on the floor.

The gateway at the far end of the Sandal Bedesten leads out of the Kapalí Çarşí. Turn right here and then take the first turning on the left just opposite Çarşí Kapí, one of the main entrances to the Kapalí Çarşí. This brings one into the outer courtyard of **Nuruosmaniye Camii** This is one of the most picturesque mosque courtyards in the city, shaded by plane trees and horse chestnuts, with the mosque on the left and the various buildings of the külliye—the medrese, library, türbe, and sebil—scattered here and there irregularly. The courtyard is always very busy, for it is one of the principal approaches to the Kapalí Çarşí; thus it attracts a colourful collection of beggars, itinerant peddlars, and an occasional Aşík, or wandering Anatolian minstrel.

HISTORY. Nuruosmaniye Camii was begun in 1748 by Mahmut I and completed in 1755 by his brother and successor, Osman III, from whom it takes its name, the Mosque of the Sacred Light (Nur) of Osman. The architect seems to have been a Greek by the name of Simeon, who had probably studied in Europe prior to designing the mosque. For Nuruosmaniye Camii is the first large and ambitious Ottoman building to exemplify the new baroque architectural style then prevalent in western Europe.

EXTERIOR. The whole structure is erected on a low terrace to which irregularly-placed flights of steps give access. On the W the mosque is preceded by a porch with five bays, and this is enclosed by a very unusual courtyard with nine domed bays arranged in a semicircle. The two minarets rise from outside the ends of the porch. At the NE corner of the mosque an oddly-shaped ramp supported on wide arches leads to the Sultan's loge. (Note that the arches here, and most of those elsewhere in the building, are semicircular—they are generally pointed in earlier mosques.) Do not fail to notice the porphyry sarcophagus that lies behind this ramp; this is an imperial Byzantine sarcophagus dating from the 4–5C, but how it came to rest here is a mystery.

INTERIOR. The mosque consists essentially of a square room covered by a large dome resting on four circular arches in the walls; the form of these arches is strongly emphasised, particularly on the exterior, where the great wheel-shaped arches constitute the most characteristic feature of the building. There is a semicircular apse for the mihrab at the centre of the E wall and side chambers at the NE and SE corners. The Sultan's loge, which is screened off by a gilded metal grille, is in the gallery above the NE corner.

Nuruosmaniye Camii is an extremely unusual building. It has a certain perverse genius but its proportions are awkward and ungainly and its oddly-shaped members seem to have no organic unity. Also, the stone from which it is built is harsh and steel-like in texture and dull in colour. All things considered, the mosque must be pronounced a failure, although a charming one.

A gateway at the far end of the outer courtyard leads out to Vezirhaní Cd. Turn left here and then at the first cross-street, Kílíççílar Sk, turn right into a picturesque little square, from which a gateway leads into the courtyard of a large and venerable mosque. This is *Mahmut Paşa Camii, one of the very oldest mosques in the city. Mahmut Paşa Camii is interesting not only because of its great age, but also because it is a very fine example of the so-called 'Bursa style' of mosque architecture, of which very few examples survive in Istanbul.

HISTORY. Mahmut Paşa Camii was built in 1462, the first large mosque to be erected in Istanbul after that of the Conqueror himself. The founder was one of the Conqueror's Grand Vezirs, the most distinguished of those who held that post during his reign. Mahmut Paşa was of Greek origin, descended from one of the leading aristocratic families of the latter years of the Byzantine Empire. During the second quarter of the 15C his paternal grandfather, Philaninos, had been ruler of what remained of the Byzantine possessions in Greece, with the rank and title of Caesar. Mahmut Paşa was one of several Greeks from aristocratic families who threw in their lot with the Turks after the Conquest, becoming Moslems and rising rapidly in the Ottoman hierarchy because of their natural talents and superior education. After he became Grand Vezir, Mahmut Paşa proved to be a very capable general and administrator. He was also a great patron of learning and the arts, particularly poetry. But he was beheaded by the Conqueror, in 1474, after an army led by the Grand Vezir suffered a serious defeat in Anatolia.

EXTERIOR. To the W the mosque is preceded by a porch of five bays. Unfortunately, this has been ruined by a clumsy modern restoration,

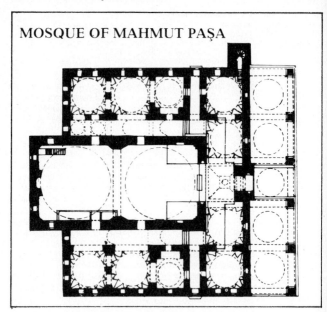

## MOSQUE OF MAHMUT PAŞA

in which the original columns have been replaced by, or encased in, ungainly octagonal piers. Over and beside the entrance portal there are several calligraphic inscriptions in Arabic and Osmanli (Old Turkish) verse giving the date of foundation and of two restorations, one in 1755 and the second in 1828. The ugly piers undoubtedly belong to the latter restoration, since they are characteristically baroque. The entrance portal itself is also clearly restoration work of the 19C. The single minaret of the mosque rises from the SW corner of the building, just behind that end of the porch.

INTERIOR. The entryway leads into a narthex; this is a most unusual feature, which in Istanbul mosques is found only here and in the Beyazidiye. The vaults of the narthex are interesting and different from one another. The central bay has a square vault heavily adorned with stalactites. In the first two bays on either side smooth pendentives support domes with 24 ribs; while in the two end bays the domes are not supported by pendentives at all, but by a very curious arrangement of juxtaposed triangles so that the dome rests on a regular sixteen-sided polygon. Other examples of this odd and not unattractive expedient are found in Istanbul only in the W dome of Murat Paşa Camii and in one or two other mosques that belong to the same early period.

The mosque itself consists of a long rectangular room divided in the middle by an arch, thus forming two square chambers each covered by a dome of equal size. On each side of the main hall there is a narrow barrel-vaulted passage that communicates both with the hall and with three small rooms on either side. The two large domes of the great hall of the mosque have smooth pendentives, rather than the stalactited ones usually found in these early mosques. The mihrab and mimber are inferior works of the 18C or later, as are most of the other decorations and mosque furniture. This is a pity, since it spoils the appearance of the mosque interior, making it difficult to recapture its original charm. In the small side-chambers some of the domes have smooth pendentives while others are stalactited. The side-chambers were called tabhanes, and were used as hostels by travelling dervishes, a feature found only in early Ottoman mosques.

The külliye of Mahmut Paşa also included a hamam and the founder's türbe. The hamam is some distance away (see below), but the türbe is just behind the mosque, in a little graveyard at the end of Kılıççılar Sk. This magnificent and unique *türbe is dated by an inscription to 1474, the year Mahmut Paşa was executed. It is a tall octagonal building with a blind dome and two tiers of windows. The upper part of the fabric on the outside is entirely encased in a mosaic of tile-work, with blue and turquoise predominating. The tiles make a series of wheel-like patterns of great charm; they are presumably of the first Iznik period (1453–1555), and there is nothing else exactly like them in Istanbul.

Kılıççılar Sk, the Street of the Sword-Makers, is one of the most picturesque byways in the city, and is one of the very few surviving examples of an old Ottoman bazaar street. The left side of the street is lined with an arcade of 18C shops that were once part of the külliye of Nuruosmaniye Camii. (The shops on the side street facing the Kapalı Çarşi are also part of this complex; these have been very attractively restored and are now open for business.) On the right side of the street the shops and ateliers are part of the *Çuhacılar Hanı*, the Han of the Cloth-Dealers, which takes up the whole block to the right. This han was built in the early 18C by Damat Ibrahim Paşa, Grand Vezir in the reign of Ahmet III. It is not as grand as some of the other old hans in this neighbourhood; nonetheless it adds to the distinctively Ottoman attraction of the quarter. The main entrance to the han is through an arched gateway halfway down the street on the left; this brings one into the cluttered inner courtyard, which is lined with an arcade of shops and ateliers.

A portal in the far left-hand corner of the courtyard takes one out to the street running past the E side of the Kapalı Çarşi. A short way down this street and to the right there is an arched gateway that opens onto Mahmut Paşa Yokuşu, one of the principal market streets of the old city. The *Mahmut Paşa Hamamı is about 250 m down the street, an imposing domed building standing off a little to the left.

HISTORY. The Mahmut Paşa Hamamı is one of the two oldest Turkish baths in the city. It is dated by an inscription over the entrance portal to 1476, two years after the Grand Vezir's death. (The Gedik Ahmet Paşa Hamamı, seen on the previous Rte, may possibly be a year or two older, but it is not positively dated by an inscription.) The hamam was built by Mahmut Paşa's family after his death, so that its revenues would help pay for the upkeep of his mosque and türbe. Like most of the great Ottoman hans, it was originally double, but the women's section was torn down to make way for the adjacent han. For a time the men's hamam fell into disuse and then served as a storage depot, but in recent years it has been restored and now once again serves as a public bath.

INTERIOR. One enters through a large central hall of square plan, 17m on a side, covered by a high dome on stalactited pendentives; the impressive size of this camekan is hardly spoiled by the addition of a modern wooden balcony. The soğukluk is a truly monumental room covered by a dome with spiral ribs and a huge semidome in the form of a scallop shell, while on each side there are two square cubicles with elaborate vaulting. The hararet is octagonal with five shallow oblong niches, and in the cross-axis there are two domed eyvans, each of which leads to a pair of more private bathing cubicles in the corners. Like all of the other buildings in Mahmut Paşa's külliye, the hamam is a very handsome and well-built structure.

On leaving the hamam a complicated detour leads to an interesting monument. Take Sultan Mektebi Sk (this is also called Sultan Oda Sk), the street that leads off to the right from Mahmut Paşa Yokuşu directly opposite the hamam; follow it for about 200m to its end then turn left onto Cahaní Sk and continue for another 50m. This brings one to the **medrese of Rüstem Paşa**, Süleyman's son-in-law and for a time his Grand Vezir. This fine building was designed by Sinan, and an inscription records that it was completed in 1550. It has a unique plan for a medrese. The courtyard is octagonal, with a şadirvan in the centre and a colonnaded portico of 24 domes. Behind the portico the cells are also arranged in an octagonal plan, but the building is made into a square on the exterior by filling in the corners with auxiliary rooms, which served as baths and lavatories. One side of the octagon is occupied by the lecture-hall, a large domed room that projects from the square on the outside like a great apse. The medrese has been beautifully restored in recent years, and it is now used as a dormitory for university students.

From here the detour can be extended to another interesting monument nearby. Go back along Cahaní Sk for a few steps and take the first turning on the left into hakkı tarík us Sk (named after a famous Turkish journalist). At the bottom of the steps turn left on Cemal Nadír Sk, the left side of which is formed by a massive retaining wall with two iron doors and barred windows. (Ask the proprietor in the office just opposite for the key.) Entering through one of the doors, one finds oneself in a very impressive Byzantine substructure consisting of a congeries of rooms and passages, 12 in all, of every size and shape. There is a great central hall, 16m by 10·5m in plan and about 6m high, whose roof is supported by two rows of six columns each, with simple but massive bases and capitals. From this another great room opens, 13m by 6·7m, ending in a wide apse. A series of smaller chambers, one of them oval in shape, opens from each of these large rooms and from the passages that lead off in all directions. The whole thing is like an underground palace and must clearly have underlain some very grand building indeed. However, all attempts to identify this structure with some building mentioned in Byzantine sources have been inconclusive.

After returning to the hamam, continue in the same direction down Mahmut Paşa Yokuşu. Many of the buildings on this and the adjacent streets are old Ottoman hans, perhaps several score of them in all. Evliya Çelebi mentions by name more than 25 that already existed by the middle of the 17C, and many others were built during the following century; some go back to the time of the Conquest and many are built on Byzantine foundations.

About 100m downhill from the Mahmut Paşa Hamamí there is an arched gateway on the left side of the street; this is the entrance to the *Kürkçü Haní*, the Han of the Furriers. This, too, is a benefaction of Mahmut Paşa and was built at about the same time as his mosque, making it the oldest surviving han in the city. Unfortunately, part of it is in ruins and what remains is quite dilapidated. Originally the han consisted of two large courtyards. The first, nearly square, was 45m by 40m, and had about 45 rooms on each of its two floors; in the centre there was a small mosque, now replaced by an ugly block of modern flats. The second courtyard to the N was smaller and very irregularly shaped because of the layout of the adjacent streets. It had about 30 rooms on each floor and must have been very attractive; unfortunately it is now almost completely ruined.

After leaving the Kürkçü Haní, continue down Mahmut Paşa Yokuşu and turn left at the next corner onto Çakmakçílar Yokuşu. Just beyond the first turning on the left there is a massive gateway that leads to another Ottoman han. This is the *Büyük Yeni Han*, which means literally the Big New Han. It is called new because it was built in 1764, just a youngster in this ancient town, and big because it is the second largest han in the city. Its tall and very narrow courtyard is over 100m in length. Unfortunately, it has been divided in the middle by what appears to be a later construction that detracts from its grandeur. Nevertheless, its three storeys of great round-arched arcades are very picturesque. It was built by Mustafa III and is one of the finest extant examples of a baroque Ottoman han.

Just beyond the Büyük Yeni Han is a much smaller one of about the same date. This is the *Küçük Yeni Han*, or the Small New Han, also a work of Mustafa III. Looking up at this point, one sees a small mosque perched on the roof of the han. This curious little mosque, which bears Sultan Mustafa's name, has an almost Byzantine-looking dome and a pretty minaret. It is much frequented by the merchants and workers in the market quarter.

A little farther up Çakmakçilar Yokuşu, and on the opposite side, is the monumental arched entrance to the grandest and most interesting of all the hans in the city, the **\*Valide Hani**. This han was built by the Sultan Valide Kösem shortly before her death in 1651, apparently on the site of an older Ottoman palace founded by Cerrah Mehmet Paşa. A great double gateway leads into the first courtyard, which is small and irregularly shaped because of the alignment of the han relative to the street outside. From here another arched passage leads into the main court, a vast square area 55m on a side, surrounded by a two-tiered arcade. Behind the arcade on each floor there are 50 vaulted chambers, most of which are now used as workshops or storerooms. Although the entire han is now in a state of appalling squalour and disrepair, it is still impressive and extremely colourful.

In the centre of the courtyard there is a little mosque (recently rebuilt) belonging to Persian Turks working in the han, all of whom are members of the Shiite sect of Islam. (Most Turks are members of the Sunni sect, particularly those living in the western part of the country.) Each year, on the 23rd day of the Islamic month of Murarrem, the Shiites used to congregate in the courtyard of the Valide Hani in mournful commemoration of the battle of Kerbala in 638. They wept and flagellated themselves while the imam recited the tragic story of the martyrdom of Hüseyin, grandson of the Prophet. However, in recent years these emotional outbursts have been banned by the authorities, and the ceremony is confined to the interior of the mosque.

A vaulted tunnel leads from the far left-hand corner of the main courtyard into the inner court, which because of the lie of the land is set at a lower level than the rest of the han. The chambers around the two floors of this court house a weaving-mill. At the back of the courtyard are the remains of a Byzantine tower which is built into the structure of the han. This has traditionally been called the *Tower of Eirene* and is thought to date from the middle Byzantine period, although the evidence for this is very uncertain. The tower appears as a prominent feature of the city skyline in the drawing made by Melchior Lorichs in 1559; it is much taller in the drawing than it is today. The lower part of the tower is now part of the weaving-mill, while the upper room is fitted out as a mosque with a pretty ribbed dome; unfortunately the mosque is now disaffected and is used as a storeroom.

At a corner of the inner court, on its upper floor, an archway leads to an open area to the rear of the han. Just opposite stands the large *mosque of Ibrahim Paşa*, one of the most ancient in the city. This mosque was founded in 1478 by Çandarli Ibrahim Paşa, Grand Vezir

under Beyazit II, who was killed during the siege of Lepanto in 1499.
The mosque was in ruins for many years and has only recently been
restored. However this restoration was so poorly done that it destroyed all that was original in the structure.

A path between the han and the mosque leads out to another
bustling market street named Uzun Çarşí Cd, the Avenue of the Long
Market. This follows the course of the ancient Byzantine street called
Makros Embolos, which led from the Forum of Constantine to the
Golden Horn, down the valley between the Second and Third Hills.
The Greek name means Great Colonnade, and the street was indeed
lined with colonnaded porticoes on both sides. But today the street is
mean and squalid, although always lively and picturesque. For this is
the site of the infamous *Secondhand Clothing Bazaar*, where the poor
of the city sell one another clothes.

About 200m down Uzun Çarşí Cd, on the right just past the second
cross-street, there is a little mosque known as Yavaşça Şahin Camii.
This is one of several insignificant but very ancient mosques that are
found in this neighbourhood, which, apparently, was the first Turkish
quarter to be established in the city after the Conquest. Yavaşça Şahin
Paşa was a captain in the fleet of Mehmet II at the time of the
Conquest; he built this mosque soon afterwards, but the exact date is
unknown. It was badly damaged in the great fire of 1908 but was
restored in 1950. It is one of a small group of early mosques that form a
distinct type: the front porch has only two domed bays, with the
entrance portal shifted off centre under the S dome. Within, a square
chamber with a blind dome resting on an octagonal drum is supported
by a series of triangles making a sixteen-sided base. It is an odd type
but not unattractive; unfortunately the porch was not restored
because of the intrusion of an adjacent shop.

Just opposite Yavaşçfla Şahin Camii a street named Agízlíkçi Sk leads steeply
uphill. At the first corner on the left is a very ancient mosque in an advanced state
of decay. This is *Samanveren Camii*, founded soon after the Conquest by a
certain Sinan Ağa, an inspector of straw. (In Turkish, Sinan Ağa's title as
inspector of straw was Samanveren, hence the name of his mosque.) Though in a
very ruinous condition, this is a quaint and interesting building of brick and
stone construction; what is left of the minaret has some curious leaf-like
decorations in brick. The mosque itself was on the first floor and was entered by a
staircase that has now disappeared; a little courtyard led to the prayer-room,
which was covered by a wooden roof.

Directly across from Samanveren Camii a street with the bizarre name of
Devoğlu Yokuşu, the Path of the Giant's Son, rambles downhill to the N. At the
second turning on the left a side street leads to another ruined Ottoman building.
This is the *medrese of Siyavuş Paşa*, a very irregular structure wedged in an
angle of the hill above. The medrese is presently inhabited by old rag-pickers
who ply their trade in the ruins of the courtyard, where a modern ramshackle
warehouse now stands. Round about are the cells of the medrese, most of them
with their domes more-or-less intact, but the colonnade in front of them has
disappeared. The dershane, unusually, is in the corner immediately to the right
of the once-handsome entrance portal. This medrese was constructed some time
before his death in 1601 by Siyavuş Paşa, brother-in-law of Murat III and thrice
his Grand Vezir. Siyavuş Paşa also had a magnificent palace close by, built by
Sinan in the last quarter of the 16C, but this has vanished without a trace.

The Path of the Giant's Son continues down to the shore highway
along the Golden Horn, but a short way past the last detour its name
changes to Ord. Prof. Cemil Bilsel Cd. (The Municipality has a
regrettable tendency to change some of Istanbul's wonderful old
Ottoman names to more prosaic modern ones.) After about 100m the
street crosses Kantarcílar Sk, the Street of the Scale-Makers, where at

the near corner to the right there stands another ancient mosque. This is *Timurtaş Camii*, which has been completely restored in recent years. It is very like Samanveren Camii; it is built over a vaulted ground floor with the same brick and stone construction, and has a large wooden porch in front. Its minaret is unusual; instead of having a balcony it is entirely enclosed, with four small grilled openings toward the top through which the müezzin gives the call to prayer. It is thought that Samanveren Camii originally had the same type of minaret, since they seem to be almost twin mosques. The exact date of these mosques is unknown, but both are believed to date from the reign of the Conqueror.

Kantarcílar Sk runs past the N side of the mosque, intersecting Uzun Çarşi Cd at the next corner. At the near corner to the left there is an enormous double bath known as the *Tahtakale Hamamí*, which also dates from the reign of the Conqueror. Unfortunately, it is no longer a public bath but is used for cold-storage. The camekan, which from its great size must have been very impressive, has been divided into two storeys by a low wooden floor and is stacked with packing cases, so that one can get very little idea of what it looked like. The hararet, which is also large and has a high dome, is not so cluttered. This is a very interesting building, and one hopes that it will be restored as a public bath.

Uzun Çarşi Cd runs past the E wall of the hamam and at the next corner intersects Kutucular Cd, the Avenue of the Box-Makers. This picturesque lane is the main E–W street of the industrial and market area to the S of the shore highway and along the Golden Horn between the two bridges, and it is lined on both sides with shops and stalls selling every conceivable type of merchandise.

At the far corner, to the right of the intersection, stands the great \*\*mosque of Rüstem Paşa, one of the most beautiful of the smaller mosques of Sinan. This mosque was built in 1561 by Rüstem Paşa, twice Grand Vezir under Süleyman and husband of the Sultan's favourite daughter, the Princess Mihrimah.

EXTERIOR. The mosque is built on a high terrace over an interesting complex of vaulted shops, the rent from which went to maintain the rest of the külliye. Interior flights of steps lead up from the corners of the platform to a spacious and beautiful courtyard, unique in the city. The mosque is preceded by a curious double porch: first the usual type of porch consisting of five domed bays, and then, projecting from this, a deep and low-slung penthouse roof, its outer edge resting on a row of columns. This arrangement, although unusual, is very pleasant and has a definite architectural unity.

INTERIOR. The plan of the mosque consists of an octagon inscribed in a rectangle. The dome is flanked by four small semidomes in the diagonals of the building. The arches of the dome spring from four octagonal pillars, two on the N, two on the S, and from piers projecting from the E and W walls. To the N and S there are galleries supported by pillars and by small marble columns between them.

Rüstem Paşa Camii is especially famous for the very fine tiles which almost cover the walls, not only on the interior but also on the facade of the porch. One should also climb to the galleries to see the tiles there, which are of a different pattern. Like all the great Turkish tiles, those of Rüstem Paşa came from the kilns of Iznik in its greatest period (c 1555–1620), and they show the tomato-red or 'Armenian bole' which is characteristic of that period. These exquisite tiles, in a wide variety of floral and geometric designs, cover not only the walls, but also the columns, the mihrab, and the mimber. Altogether they make this one of the most beautiful and striking mosque interiors in the city.

Just to the E of Rüstem Paşa Camii, a few steps down Kutucular Cd and on the same side of the street, there is a very ancient han. This is *Hurmali Han*, the Han for Dates, which has been ascribed to early Byzantine times, perhaps the 6–7C. The oldest part of the structure is the long and narrow courtyard, which is believed to be part of the original structure, while the remainder of the building probably dates from Ottoman times, with modern reconstructions. There are a great many ancient hans in this neighbourhood, but they are for the most part decayed and cluttered, and almost nothing is known about them except their names.

Continuing E along Kutucular Cd, take the next right and then in the middle of the block turn left into a large open courtyard. This is the Balkapan Han, the Han of the Honey-Store, of which there remains only the courtyard and the extensive vaults beneath it. Evliya Çelebi, in his 'Narrative of Travels', writes that in his time this was the storehouse used by the Egyptian honey-dealers, hence the name of the han. Access to the vaults is gained through the small building at the centre of the courtyard, where a flight of steps leads down into the vast Byzantine dungeons below. There one can see the ranks and columns of great rectangular pillars of brick supporting massive brick vaulting in the usual Byzantine herringbone pattern. Unfortunately, the basement is so cluttered with boxes and crates that only a small part of the total area of some 2000 square metres is visible, but even this is extremely impressive. The vaults undoubtedly belong to one of the many granaries and storage-depots which are known to have existed on this site from as early as the 4–5C AD.

Returning to the main market street, whose name here changes to Hasírcilar, the Street of the Mat-Makers, continue in the same direction. At the next corner the street comes to the W gate of the Spice Bazaar, from where one can return to the great square at the Stamboul end of the Galata Bridge.

# 8 The Third Hill

The broad summit of the Third Hill comprises the area bounded on the E by Beyazit Square, on the S by Ordu Cd, on the N by Şehzadebaşi Cd, and on the W by Atatürk Blv, which runs along the valley separating the Third and Fourth Hills. This region, and the upper part of the slopes leading down to the Marmara and the Golden Horn, contains more than a score of ancient monuments, including some very impressive structures from the late Roman era as well as the Byzantine and Ottoman periods. The most convenient way to see these monuments is to begin at the SW corner of Beyazit Square, where Ordu Cd heads W to its intersection with Atatürk Blv, and then walk around the Third Hill in a great arc so as to return in the end to Beyazit Square.

At the beginning of Ordu Cd, flanking both sides of the avenue as it leaves Beyazit Square, one sees the stupendous remains of the **Forum Tauri**, unearthed when the square was redesigned in the 1950s.

Tauri, the Forum of the Bull, took its name from a large, hollow bronze statue of a bull that once stood in the centre of the square. In late Roman times the statue served as an oven to roast sacrificial animals and, on occasion, to cremate convicted criminals. According to one authority, the Emperor Phocas was roasted to death in the bronze bull after his deposition in 610. In Byzantine times the square was known as the Forum of Theodosius I, after the great emperor who rebuilt it on a more monumental scale in 393. The Forum of Theodosius was the largest of the great public squares of Byzantine Constantinople. It contained, among other things, a gigantic triumphal arch in the Roman fashion, and a commemorative column showing the victories of Theodosius I, like that of Trajan in Rome. Colossal fragments of the triumphal arch can be seen just opposite the hamam of Sultan Beyazit. Notice the columns curiously decorated with the peacock-eye or lopped branch design, also the enormous Corinthian columns.

At the very beginning of Ordu Cd on the left side, just behind the ruins of the triumphal arch of Theodosius, there are the remains of two Ottoman hans of some interest. The first is called Şimkeşhane and was originally built as a mint by Mehmet the Conqueror. The mint was later transferred to Topkapí Sarayí, after which Şimkeş-hane was used to house the spinners of silver thread. The han was damaged by fire and then rebuilt by Rabia Gülnuş Ümmetullah, wife of Mehmet IV and mother of Mustafa II and Ahmet III. Its front half was demolished during the 1950s when the avenue was widened and since then it has fallen into ruins. The same fate befell the han next to it, which was built in about 1740 by Seyyit Hasan Paşa, Grand Vezir in the reign of Mahmut I. This is a pity, for both were handsome and interesting buildings, particularly the latter. It is still worthwhile to walk around them to see the astonishing and pictures-que irregularity of their design, with great zigzags built out on corbels following the crooked line of the streets. A corner of the *Hasan Paşa Haní* has recently been rebuilt, and it is hoped that this restoration will be extended to what remains of these two fine old hans.

Some 150m down the left side of Ordu Cd is the ornate entryway to a small *külliye*. This delightful little complex was founded in 1762 by Ragíp Paşa, Grand Vezir in the reign of Mustafa III. The architect seems to have been Mehmet Tahir Ağa, whose mas-terpiece, Laleli Camii, can be seen farther down the avenue on the other side. Above the entryway there is a room which was once a primary school, and which is now used as a children's library. Across the courtyard, surrounded by an attractive garden, is the main library; this has been restored in recent years and is now once again serving its original purpose. From the courtyard a flight of steps leads to a domed lobby which opens into the reading-room. This is square in plan, the central space is covered by a dome supported on four columns; between these, beautiful bronze grilles form a kind of cage in which the books and manuscripts are kept. Round the sides of this vaulted and domed room are chairs and tables for reading. The walls are revetted in blue and white tiles, either of European manufacture or Turkish tiles strongly under European influence, but charming nevertheless. In the garden, which is separated from the courtyard by fine bronze grilles, is the pretty open türbe of the founder. Ragíp Paşa, who was Grand Vezir from 1757 until 1763, is considered to have been the last of the great figures to hold that post, comparable in stature to men like Sokollu Mehmet Paşa and the

Köprülüs. Ragíp Paşa was also the best poet of his time, and composed some of the most apt and witty of the chronograms inscribed on the street-fountains in Istanbul. His little külliye, though clearly baroque in detail, has a classic simplicity which recalls that of the Köprülü complex on the Second Hill.

After leaving the library, continue along Ordu Cd and take the second turning on the left, just opposite Laleli Camii. Then turn right at the next corner and at the end of the street ascend a flight of steps onto a large open terrace, now used as a playground. Just beyond the left corner of this terrace stands a former Byzantine church known locally as *Bodrum Cami or the Subterranean Mosque, because of the vast crypt that lies beneath it.

HISTORY. The church was originally identified by Gyllius as that of the monastery of the Myrelaion, mentioned frequently in Byzantine sources. The church and the monastery to which it was attached were founded by Romanus I Lecapenus, an Armenian who in 919 became co-Emperor with Constantine VII Porphyrogenitus. Romanus built the church next to his palace, which he converted into a nunnery after the completion of the sanctuary. His wife Theophano spent her last years in the Myrelaion, and when she died in 922 she was buried there. The church was converted into a mosque late in the 15C by Mesih Paşa, a descendent of the Palaeologues, who led the Ottoman forces in their first and unsuccessful attack on Rhodes in 1479. The building was several times gutted by fire and is now a mere shell, no longer in use. In recent years the Myrelaion has been excavated, and the church was given a partial and not very successful restoration.

The recent excavations revealed that the building is actually a double church, with one sanctuary on the level of the terrace and the other in a crypt below. The lower sanctuary was undoubtedly built as a funerary chapel for the Empress Theophano. Studies have shown that the two superimposed churches were built during the period 919–23, and that both of them were of the same design, namely the four-column type so common in the 10–11C. On the terrace beside the church stood the palace of Romanus, with the outline of the walls still visible in the pavement. Below the terrace there is an enormous rotunda, originally designed in the 5C AD as the reception hall of a great palace, but apparently never finished. It was later roofed over and used as a cistern. The roof was supported by a colonnade of 75 columns, and the palace of Romanus was built on top. The whole structure is extremely interesting and well worth a visit.

After returning to Ordu Cd one is confronted by the imposing edifice of *Laleli Camii, the Lily Mosque. This is a charming building, the finest of all the baroque mosques in the city. It was founded by Mehmet III and built between 1759 and 1763 by Mehmet Tahir Ağa, the greatest and most original of the Turkish baroque architects.

EXTERIOR. The mosque is built on a high terrace, beneath which there is a veritable labyrinth of winding passages and vaulted shops. In the centre, directly underneath the mosque, there is a great hall supported by eight enormous piers, with a fountain in the centre and a café and shops round about. It has been suggested that this subterranean arcade is a *tour de force* of Mehmet Tahir, designed to show that he could support his mosque virtually on thin air.

The mosque itself is constructed of brick and stone, but the superstructure is of stone only; and the two parts do not appear to fit together very well. Along the sides there are amusing but pointless galleries, with the arcades formed of round arches; a similar arcade covers the ramp leading to the imperial loge.

INTERIOR. The plan of the interior is an octagon inscribed in a rectangle. All but the W pair of supporting columns are engaged in the walls; those at the W support a gallery along the W wall. All the walls are heavily revetted in variegated marbles—yellow, red, blue and other colours—which give a gay if somewhat gaudy effect. In the W wall of the gallery there are medallions of opus sectile which incorporate not only rare marbles but also semi-precious stones such as onyx, jasper and lapis lazuli. A rectangular apse contains the mihrab, which is made of sumptuous marbles. The mimber is fashioned from the same materials, while the Kuran kürsü is a rich work of carved wood heavily inlaid with mother-of-pearl.

MOSQUE PRECINCTS. Like all of the other imperial mosques, Laleli Camii was surrounded by the many attendant buildings of a civic centre, some of which, unfortunately, have disappeared. On Ordu Cd there still remains the pretty sebil with bronze grilles, and the somewhat sombre octagonal türbe in which are buried Mustafa III and his son, the unfortunate Selim III. On the terrace inside the enclosure is the imaret, an attractive little building with a very unusual plan. The other institutions in the külliye—the medrese and the hamam—have disappeared.

The street just to the E of the mosque, Fethi Bey Cd, leads at the second turning on the left to a fascinating han that probably belongs to the Laleli complex. This was formerly known as Çukur Çeşme Hani, the Han of the Sunken Fountain, but now it is called *Büyük Taş Hani*, the Big Stone Han. One enters through a very long vaulted passage, with rooms and a small court leading from it; it emerges into a large courtyard, in the middle of which a ramp descends into what were once the stables. Around this porticoed courtyard open rooms of most irregular shape, and other passages, lead to two additional small courts with even more irregular chambers. One seems to detect in this the ingenious but perverse mind of Mehmet Tahir Ağa, and the disappearance of his medrese and hamam is greatly to be regretted.

After leaving the han, continue in the same direction along the side street and take the third turning on the right onto Selim Paşa Sk. This soon reaches the back of the huge office building that houses the Belidiye, or Municipality, the headquarters of the civil government of Istanbul.

Just behind the Belidiye stands the quaint little medrese of the *Şeyh-ül Islam Ankaravi Mehmet Efendi*, founded in 1707. This has recently been restored and is now used as a research centre by the Economics Faculty of Istanbul University. It is a small and attractively irregular building, chiefly of red brick, with a long narrow courtyard, at the far end of which is the lecture-hall, reached by a flight of steps.

After walking around the Belidiye to the left, one finds oneself at the intersection of Atatürk Blv and Şehzadebaşi Cd, with splendid views of the Mosque of the Conqueror to the left, Valens Aqueduct straight ahead, and the Şehzade mosque complex to the right.

Crossing to the opposite side of Şehzadebaşi Cd, in front of the W wall of the Şehzade precinct is a pretty little mosque, recently restored, called *Burmali Cami*. This was built in about 1550 by the Kadi (Judge) of Egypt, Emin Nurettin Osman Efendi. Although of the very simplest type—a square room with a flat wooden ceiling—it has several peculiarities that give it a *cache* of its own. Most noticeable is the brick minaret with spiral ribs, from which the mosque gets its name (in Turkish, *burmali* means spiral); this is unique in Istanbul and is a late survival of an older tradition, of which a few examples survive in Anatolia. The porch is also unique: its roof, which is pitched, not domed, is supported by four columns with Byzantine Corinthian capitals. (Bayan Cahide Tamer, the architect who so ably restored the mosque, found the original Corinthian capitals in such bad condition that they could not be used in the restoration, but she was able to find, in the Archaeological Museum, four others of the same type with which she replaced the originals.) Finally, the entrance portal is not in the middle but on the right-hand side. This is usual in mosques with porches supported by only three columns— to prevent the door from being blocked by the central column—but here there seems to be no reason for it. The interior of the mosque has no special features.

After leaving Burmalí Cami, return to Şehzadebaşí Cd and walk down the avenue to the left for about 100m. This brings one to the main entrance of the precincts of **•Şehzade Camii**, one of the great imperial mosque complexes in the city.

HISTORY. Şehzade Camii, the Mosque of the Prince, was built by Süleyman in memory of his eldest son, Prince Mehmet, who died of smallpox in 1543, when he was only 21 years old. Süleyman was heartbroken at the death of his beloved son, and he sat beside Mehmet's body for three days before he would permit burial to take place. When Süleyman recovered from his grief he determined to commemorate Prince Mehmet by the erection of a great mosque complex dedicated to him. Sinan was commissioned to design and build the külliye, which was completed in 1548. Sinan himself called this his 'apprentice work', but it was the work of an apprentice of genius, his first imperial mosque on a truly monumental scale.

EXTERIOR. The Şehzade complex is surrounded by an outer courtyard wall, enclosing the mosque and the other institutions of the külliye, which includes a medrese, a tabhane or hospice, a public kitchen, a primary school, and several splendid türbes.

Şehzade Camii is preceded by a handsome inner courtyard whose area is equal to that of the mosque itself, with the monumental entrance portal at the centre of the W side. The courtyard is bordered by a portico with five domed bays of equal height on each side, counting corner báys twice, with the voussoirs of the arches in alternating pink and white marble. At the centre of the courtyard there is a şadírvan which, according to Evliya Çelebi, was a gift of Murat IV. The two minarets are exceptionally beautiful: notice the elaborate geometrical sculpture in low relief, the intricate tracery of their two şerefes, and the use of occasional terracotta inlay. The cluster of domes and semidomes, many of them with fretted cornices and bold ribbing, crowns the building in an arrangement of repetition and contrast that is nowhere surpassed. It was in this mosque that Sinan first adopted the brilliant expedient of placing colonnaded galleries along the entire length of the N and S facades in order to conceal the buttresses. This is certainly one of the very finest exteriors that Sinan ever created; one wonders why he later abandoned, or at least greatly restrained, these decorative effects.

INTERIOR. Sinan wanted a centralised plan and so he adopted an expedient,extending the area not by two but by four semidomes. Although this is the most obvious and logical way of both increasing the space and of centralising the plan, the identical symmetry along both axes has a repetitive effect that tends toward dullness. Furthermore, the four great piers that support the dome are stranded and isolated in the midst of the vast space and their inevitably large size is unduly emphasised. These drawbacks were obvious to Sinan once he had tried the experiment, and he never repeated it.

The vast and empty interior is very unusual among the imperial mosques; it has not a single column, nor are there any galleries. Sinan succeeded in minimising the size of the great piers by making them very irregular in shape: contrast their not unpleasing appearance with the gross 'elephant's feet' columns in the Blue Mosque. The general effect of the interior is of an austere simplicity that is not without charm.

THE ŞEHZADE TÜRBES. Behind the mosque there is the usual walled garden of türbes. These türbes are quite extraordinary, for they constitute a veritable museum of the two best periods of Turkish tiles, the first extending from the time of the Conquest up until about 1555, while the second and greatest ran from 1555 to 1620. The türbes in the precincts of Haghia Sophia are larger and grander than those at the Şehzade, but their tiles, magnificent as they are, are all much of the same date and style, as are those at the Süleymaniye. Here, on the other hand, the buildings are of quite different dates and span the whole of the great age of the Iznik kilns, together with a few of those produced at a later period at Tekfur Saray.

The first and largest türbe in the centre of the garden is that of the **Şehzade Mehmet** himself. It is octagonal, the faces separated by slender engaged columns; the stonework is polychrome, panels of verd antique being inset here and there in the facades, while the window frames and arches are picked out in terracotta. The dome, which is double and carried on a fluted drum, is itself fluted. The small entrance porch has a fine pavement of opus sectile. Altogether it is a very handsome building in the ornately decorated style of the mosque itself.

The inscription in Persian verse over the entrance portal, which gives the date of the Prince's death, suggests that the interior of the türbe is like a garden in Paradise. It is sheathed in tiles from the floor to the cornice of the dome, all apple-green and vivid lemon-yellow. These are almost the last and by far the most beautiful flowering of the middle period of Iznik tiles, done in the cuerda seca technique. Tiles in this technique and in these colours are extremely rare. They were first manufactured at Iznik in about 1514, when Selim I brought back a group of Persian craftsmen after his conquest of Tabriz, while the latest known examples date from 1555. Thus the türbe of the Şehzade contains the most extensive and beautiful collection of tiles of this rare and beautiful type.

The tile decoration of the interior was clearly designed as a whole. Panels of floral design separate the lower tier of windows; in the lunettes above them are inscriptions framed in arch-shaped borders; in the spandrels between these appears an occasional boss in faience. Above, a continuous series of large panels, each spanning two windows, contains a long inscription; then comes the upper tier of windows framed in floral panels with a lovely medallion between each pair. The ground is in general apple-green, sometimes dark blue; on this are designs of leaves and flowers in lemon-yellow, turquoise, dark blue, white, and a curious unfired pinkish-mauve; the colours are separated by the thin, almost black line of the cuerda seca. The whole effect is lyrically beautiful, truly like a garden in Paradise, making this türbe a masterpiece unrivalled of its kind.

The beauty of the türbe is not limited to its tiles, for the upper row of windows contains some of the most perfect examples of Turkish stained glass in rich and brilliant colours. Unfortunately, some of these are broken and damaged, but many remain entire; only in the Süleymaniye is there so extensive and brilliant a display of Turkish

*Şehzade Camii was erected by Süleyman the Magnificent in
memory of his eldest son, Mehmet, who died at the age of 21
in 1543. Built by Sinan, it was completed in 1548.*

stained-glass of the 16C. The dome, supported on a deep cornice of
stalactites with a frieze of trefoils, preserves its original arabesque
painting: a great medallion in the crown with a circle of leaf-like forms
in rich brick-red from which a cascade of smaller medallions rains
down nearly to the cornice. Unquestionably, this is the very best
painted dome that survives in the city. Still another unique feature of
the türbe is the very curious baldachino over the Şehzade's cenotaph.
It is of dark walnut wood, supported on four legs beautifully inlaid
with ivory in a style that seems almost Indian; above this there is a sort
of open-work box of interlacing polygons, made of the same wood
without inlay. It has been suggested that the box-like structure may
have been intended to represent the Kaaba at Mecca, so as to give the
impression that the Prince had been buried in the most holy place on
earth. To the left of Mehmet's cenotaph is that of his daughter

Humuşah Sultan, and to the right that of his hunchbacked brother
Cihangir. Cihangir died in 1553 out of grief for his elder half-brother,
the unfortunate Prince Mustafa, put to death by their father
Süleyman.

Just to the left and behind the türbe of the Şehzade is that of the
*Grand Vezir Rüstem Paşa*. This türbe is also by Sinan and it too is
completely sheathed in tiles from floor to dome, but here everything is
a little wrong. The building is too high for its diameter and too small to
support the overwhelming quantity of tiles with which it is revetted, in
addition to which the tiles, though beautiful, are just too early to
display the full perfection of the Armenian bole technique. Rüstem
Paşa evidently had a passion for tiles, since both his türbe and his
mosque are entirely revetted with them. He died in 1561 and was,
therefore, unable to see the tiles when the new technique had been
completely mastered, just a decade later. Here the most gorgeous
panels are those between the lower windows: vases with a deep blue
mandorla of flowers rising out of them. Between the lower and upper

windows there is a continuous inscription—white on dark blue—and between the upper windows floral tiles without an overall pattern. The drawing and composition are firm and good, while the colours—on a white ground, dark blue, turquoise, red, and a little green—are clear and vivid (all but the red, which on many tiles is muddy or brownish). There is no doubt that this türbe suffers greatly by comparison with that of the Şehzade, and also with that of *Ibrahim Paşa, which is just opposite the SW precinct gate.

The Grand Vezir Ibrahim Paşa, son-in-law of Murat III, died in 1601 and his türbe was completed early in 1603, designed and built by the architect Dalgíç Ahmet Çavuş. This türbe almost equals that of the Şehzade in splendour and perfection. It is octagonal and fairly plain on the exterior, though two marble panels on either side of the entrance portal, carved with elaborate floral and arabesque designs in low relief, are unusual and lovely. Inside, there is again the effect of the paradisical garden, but with a very different colour scheme: white, intense blue, turquoise and scarlet. Here the walls to the top of the lower tier of windows are of marble with a surbase of flower tiles. Between the two rows of windows there are two continuous friezes of calligraphy, white on dark blue, divided by a deep band of interlaced polygons in scarlet on a white ground. The effect is astonishing but beautiful, and there is nothing quite like it. The upper windows are divided by superb floral panels which are predominately turquoise picked out in scarlet. All the tiles are absolutely perfect in technique, the Armenian bole standing out boldly in relief and displaying its scarlet colour at its most intense: notice the spots of it in the curliques of the calligraphy, appearing like drops of blood.

This türbe, too, has almost an *embarras de richesses*: between the lower windows there are cupboards with carved doors, with the interiors also lined with tiles. These were evidently added later, for some of them appear to be works from the Tekfur Saray kilns, but very good examples of that type. The two cupboards on either side of the door have tiles with an unusual and attractive Chinese cloud pattern; the others have the more ordinary floral designs. The dome also preserves its original painting, with elaborate arabesques and flowers on a terracotta ground; it is rather heavy and more cluttered than that of the Şehzade, but far finer than any modern imitation. Ibrahim Paşa's cenotaph is the usual wooden box draped with embroidered cloth, but beyond it there are two tiny sarcophagi of gaily painted marble, the tombs of his infant son and daughter.

There are three other türbes in the garden: those of *Prince Mahmut*, son of Mehmet III; *Hatice Sultan*, daughter of Murat III; and *Fatma Sultan*, granddaughter of Prince Mehmet, but these are unadorned. There is, however, one more remarkable türbe well worth a visit; this is outside the türbe garden by the main entrance to the mosque precincts. The türbe is that of **Destari Mustafa Paşa**, dated by an inscription to 1611. It has the unusual form of a rectangle, and is roofed with a low central dome flanked at each end by a shallow cradle-vault. The effect is very pretty. The walls between the windows are revetted with tiles which, though still of the best period, are perhaps not quite so stunning as those in Ibrahim Paşa's türbe; but they do contain a great deal of Armenian bole at its most brilliant. Unfortunately, the türbe is now quite shabby and neglected-looking.

OTHER INSTITUTIONS OF THE SEHZADE COMPLEX. The medrese of the Şehzade complex is at the far side of the precinct, near the NW corner of the outer courtyard wall. It is a handsome building of the usual form. The S side, facing the mosque, has a portico but no cells. Opposite the entrance, instead of the usual dershane, there is an open loggia. The lecture-hall itself stands in the centre of the E side. The building has been well restored and is now a residence for university students.

In line with the medrese but farther E is the caravansaray, which now serves as a science laboratory for the adjacent secondary school, Vefa Lisesi. This building is probably not by Sinan, although it is obviously contemporary with the rest of the complex. The structure is L-shaped, with the bottom stroke of the L consisting of a long, wide hall, roofed with eight domes supported on three columns down its length; perpendicular to this is a block of eight cubicles, with two spacious halls providing access to them. This interesting building is in good condition.

A gate in the E wall of the türbe garden of the Şehzade leads out into a side street, Dede Efendi Cd. Across this street to the left are the primary school and public kitchen of the complex. The primary school is of the usual type. The public kitchen consists of a spacious courtyard, on one side of which there are three double kitchens and a small refectory, its four domes supported on three columns. This is a charmingly proportioned and gracious building. It is now used as a storage place; but the fabric of the structure is in good condition and one hopes that a more worthy use will be found for it.

Turning back towards the main street, one finds on the left opposite a very pretty medrese with a sebil at the corner. This was built by the Grand Vezir Nevşehirli Ibrahim Paşa, son-in-law of Ahmet III. It is dated by its inscription to 1720 and thus comes just between the end of the classical period and the beginning of the baroque, so that it has pleasing characteristics of both eras. At the ends of the facade stand two large domed chambers surrounded by an attractive raised portico, with the entrance portal in the centre between them. The chamber to the left served as the library, that to the right was the lecture hall of the Dar-ül Hadis, or School of Sacred Tradition, the study of which was the main function of the medrese. Later, the lecture-hall was turned into a mescit, or small mosque, and a minaret was added. The far sides of the courtyard are partly lined with porticoes with cells beyond them, these are irregularly placed after the baroque fashion. The building is in good condition, and part of it is now used as a clinic. Outside, at the street corner, is the extremely handsome sebil, a favourite among painters and etchers; it was still in use up until recent years, but now it serves as a fruit-seller's shop. Behind the sebil there is a pretty little graveyard in which the founder of this fine small külliye is buried. Ibrahim Paşa served as Grand Vezir under Ahmet III from 1718 until 1730, during the golden years of the Tulip Period. That delightful epoch ended on 20 September 1730, when the Janissaries deposed the Tulip King and strangled Ibrahim Paşa.

Farther on down Dedi Efendi Cd, just past the precinct wall of the Şehzade complex, is the *Vefa Lisesi*, built during the 1920s by the architect Kemalettin Bey. In its precincts are two ancient buildings, one of which, the Şehzade tabhane, has already been described. The other is the library of Damat Şehit Ali Paşa, built early in the 18C. The founder, Ali Paşa, was called Damat (son-in-law) because he married Fatma Sultan, a daughter of Ahmet III, and Şehit (martyr), because he was killed in the battle of Peterwaredin in 1716. Fatma did not grieve long for Ali; shortly after she received news of his death she married Nevşehirli Ibrahim Paşa. Ali Paşa's library is raised on a high superstructure and approached by a long flight of steps; it consists of only two rooms, the larger one domed. At present it is not in use.

At the far left-hand corner of the next cross-street, Cemal Yener-tosyalí Cd, there is another ancient Ottoman building. This is the handsome medrese built sometime before his death, in 1618, by Ekmekçizade Ahmet Paşa, son of an Edirne baker, who rose to the rank of Defetedar (First Lord of the Treasury) and Vezir, and died one of the richest men in the Empire. Until recently the medrese was a ruin, inhabited by squatters, but it has now been partially restored. The right side of the courtyard of the medrese is occupied by the usual dershane, next to which, however, is a türbe of the same size, undoubtedly that of the founder: This is a unique arrangement, but it gives the courtyard a somewhat lopsided appearance. Both the dershane and the türbe still preserve remnants of rather good painted decoration in their domes and pendentives, a rich red with deep green meander patterns. Even in its half-restored condition this is an interesting monument and well worth a visit.

Turn left onto Cemal Yenertosyalí Cd and then right at the next corner onto Katip Çelebi Cd. At the corner to the left is the famous *Vefa Bozahanesi*. (Boza is a drink made from fermented millet, once a favourite of the Janissaries.) Notice the silver cup in a glass case on the wall inside the shop; it is preserved there because Atatürk once drank from it.

Just beyond the Vefa Bozahanesi, on the same side of the street, there is a little mosque called *Kovacílar Mescidi*. This was built in 1514 by a certain Revani Şuccağ Efendi, who was Sürre Emin, or official escort of the annual embassy to Mecca. It is a small, square building of brick with a dome; it is of no great interest, but it has a pretty minaret. The mosque has recently been restored.

At the next corner the street divides, with the right branch taking the name of Vefa Cd. The left side of this street is, for the most part, a vacant lot with heaps of rubble and architectural fragments. This is the site of Vefa Camii, the mosque from which the street and the surrounding neighbourhood take their name. The mosque has vanished and all that remains of the foundation is the türbe of the founder, Şeyh Muslihiddin Vefa, dated 1491.

In years past Şeyh Vefa was one of the most popular folk-saints in Istanbul, and even today a few old women occasionally come to pray at his türbe. (Officially there are no saints in Islam, but Istanbul abounds with the tombs and graves of holy men which are the objects of veneration.) Şeyh Vefa was one of the most renowned scholars and mystics of his time, numbering among his disciples Sultan Beyazit II; nevertheless, he decided quite early in life that he would devote himself entirely to the welfare of the poor. He therefore spent his fortune building a pious foundation which included a mosque, hamam, primary school, public kitchen, and caravansaray, where the poor of the city could be assured of food and shelter for as long as they were in need. All of these benefactions have now disappeared, although the poor of modern Stamboul are still in residence, constructing their shanties in the ruins around Şeyh Vefa's tomb.

Just beyond Şeyh Vefa's türbe, and on the same side of the street, stands the *Library of Atif Efendi*. Of all the Ottoman public libraries in the city this is the most charming and original. The library was founded in 1741–42 and constructed of stone and brick in the baroque style. The building consists of two parts, a block of houses for the staff and the library itself. The former faces the street and its upper storey projects *en cremaillère*, that is, in five zigzags supported on corbels. Three small doors lead to the lodgings, while a large gate in the middle opens into a courtyard, on the other side of which stands the library. This consists of an entrance lobby, a room for book storage, and a large reading-room of astonishing shape. This oblong area, cross-vaulted like the other rooms, is surrounded at one end by a series of five deep bays arranged like a fan. A triple arcade supported on two columns divides the two parts of the room; on the exterior this fan-like arrangement presents seven faces. Displayed near the entrance to the reading-room is the entire vakfiye, or deed of foundation, inscribed on a marble plaque.

The street just opposite the library entrance is called Tirendaz Sk, the Street of the Archer. At the far end of this street, on the left, there is a handsome *Byzantine church with a fluted minaret. This is known in Turkish as **Kilise Cami**, literally Church Mosque, a linguistic amalgamation of Christianity and Islam. It was identified by Gyllius as the church of St. Theodore, but nothing is known of its history other than the fact that it was converted into a mosque soon after the Conquest. The most attractive part of the building is the outer narthex with its facade. Constructed of stone, brick and marble, its elaborate design and decoration identify it at once as belonging to the last great flowering of Byzantine architecture in the early 14C. In the S dome of the outer narthex there are some fine mosaics in which the Mother of God is shown surrounded by Prophets; these are of the same date and type as those at St. Saviour in Chora. The inner narthex and the church itself, which is of the four-column type, are dated to some time between the 12–14C, when this style was predominant. The narthexes contain some handsome columns, capitals and door-frames which appear to be re-used material from an earlier sanctuary, probably of the 6C.

To reach the next stop on the itinerary one must follow a rather tricky but quite picturesque route. At the end of Tirendaz Sk turn right and then follow a winding cobbled lane that eventually leads to the rear of the medrese of Ekmekçi Ahmet Paşa. Returning to the corner of Dede Efendi Sk and Cemal Yenertosyalí Sk, turn left onto the latter street and follow it for about 200m before turning right on the first through street. This leads through a picturesque arched gateway under the Valens Aqueduct and out onto a large open area on the other side. There to the right is a large and handsome Byzantine church known locally as *Kalenderhane Camii*.

HISTORY. In the past this building had been identified by some scholars as the church of St. Mary Diaconissa; others thought that it was of St. Saviour Akataleptos. It was generally dated to the middle Byzantine period. But during the 1970s, when the building underwent a thorough archaeological investigation and restoration directed by Professor Lee Striker of the Dumbarton Oaks Society, the church was identified as that of the Kyriotissa and dated to the middle of the 9C, with extensive rebuilding in the Byzantine and Ottoman periods.

INTERIOR. The church itself, which is preceded by a narthex and exonarthex, is cruciform in plan with deep barrel-vaults over the arms and a dome with 16 ribs over the centre. The building still preserves some of its fine marble revetment and sculptured decoration. The recent study by Professor Striker brought to light a number of frescoes, including some very interesting ones depicting scenes from the life of St. Francis of Assisi, which were it seems painted only a few years after his death in 1226. These have been identified as works of the court painter of King Louis of Jerusalem, and have been dated to the latter part of the Latin occupation of Constantinople (1204–61).

After leaving the church, walk out to Sehzadebaşi Cd and turn left, crossing over to the other side at the next intersection. There one comes upon a medrese built into a triangular plot at the angle of two streets. This elegant little complex was built in 1606 by Kuyucu Murat Paşa, Grand Vezir in the reign of Ahmet I. (Murat Paşa received his nickname of *kuyucu*, or the pit-digger, from his favourite occupation of supervising the digging of trenches for the mass burial of the rebels he had slaughtered.) The apex of the triangle is formed by the columned sebil, a fine work with simple classical lines. Facing the street is an arcade of shops in the middle of which a doorway leads to the courtyard of the medrese. Entering, one finds the türbe of the founder in the acute angle behind the sebil, and at the other end the dershane, which, as so often, also served as a small mosque. This building has recently been taken over and restored by Istanbul University; the courtyard has been roofed in and is used as a small museum, while the dershane contains a library.

Continuing along and passing the new University annex, one turns right and soon comes on the left to another medrese complex, now the Istanbul University Institute of Turkology. This is a baroque building founded in 1745 by the Grand Vezir Seyyit Hasan Paşa, who built the han at the SW corner of Beyazit Square. It is curiously irregular in design and is raised on a high platform, so that on entering one mounts a flight of steps to the courtyard, now roofed in and used as a library. In one corner is the dershane-mescit, which has become the office of the Director of the Institute of Turkology; in another is a room designed as a primary school; and this and other cells of the medrese are used for special library collections or as offices. Outside in the street at the corner of the building is a fine rococo sebil with a çeşme beside it.

After leaving the medrese, continue walking along the street; it soon veers left and ends in a flight of steps beside the hamam of Sultan Beyazit. This brings one back to the SW corner of Beyazit Square, the point where this itinerary began.

# 9   The Süleymaniye

APPROACHES. From the Galata Bridge: enter the main gate of the Spice Bazaar and walk through to the street at the far end of the main hall, Sabuncuhaní Sk. Take the third turning to the right off this street onto Vasíf Çínar Cd. Follow this street and its continuations, Ismetiye Cd and Hesapçeşme Cd, to come to Tiryaki Çarşísí, the street that runs along the S side of the Süleymaniye mosque complex. From Beyazit Square: at the NE corner of the square take Bakírcílar Cd and turn left at the first corner onto Fuat Paşa Cd, the street that runs along the E side of the grounds of Istanbul University, then turning left at the first turning onto Hesapçeşme Cd (see above for continuation).

The **Süleymaniye** is the second largest but by far the finest and most magnificent of the imperial mosque complexes in the city. It is a fitting monument to its founder, Süleyman the Magnificent, and a masterwork of the greatest of Ottoman architects, the incomparable Sinan. The mosque itself, the largest of Sinan's many works, is unquestionably the most important Ottoman building in Istanbul. For four centuries it has excited the wonder and enthusiasm of all foreign travellers to the city.

HISTORY. The construction of the Süleymaniye began in 1550 and the mosque itself was completed in 1557, but it was some years before all the buildings of the külliye were finished. The mosque stands in the centre of a vast outer courtyard surrounded on three sides by a wall with grilled windows. On the N side, where the land slopes sharply down to the Golden Horn, the courtyard is supported by an elaborate vaulted substructure; from the terrace there is a superb view of the Golden Horn, the hills of Asia beyond. Around this courtyard on three sides the other buildings of the külliye are arranged with as much symmetry as the nature of the site would permit. Nearly all of these pious foundations have been well restored, and some of them are once again serving the people of Istanbul as they did in the days of Süleyman.

**The Mosque.** The mosque is preceded by the usual avlu, a porticoed courtyard of exceptional grandeur, with columns of the richest porphyry, marble and granite. The W portal of the court is flanked by a great pylon containing two storeys of chambers; according to Evliya

*The türbes of Süleyman and his wife Roxelana in the walled garden behind the Süleymaniye mosque.*

Çelebi, these served as the house and workshop of the mosque astronomer. At the four corners of the courtyard rise the four great minarets. These four minarets are traditionally said to signify that Süleyman was the fourth sultan to rule in Istanbul, while the ten şerifes denote that he was the tenth monarch of the imperial Ottoman line.

Entering the mosque, one finds oneself in a vast room, almost square in plan, surmounted by a huge and lofty dome. The interior is approximately 58·5m by 57·5m, while the diameter of the dome is 27·5m and the height of its crown above the floor is 47m. To E and W the dome is flanked by semidomes, and to N and S by arches with tympana filled with windows. The dome arches rise from four great irregularly shaped piers. Up to this point the plan follows that of Haghia Sophia, but beyond this—as at the Beyazidiye—all is different. Between the piers, to the N and S, triple arcades on two enormous porphyry monoliths support the tympana of the arches. There are no galleries here, nor can there really be said to be aisles, since the great porphyry columns are so high and so far apart that they do not in any way form a barrier between the central area and the walls. Thus the immense space is not cut up into sections, as at Haghia Sophia, but is centralised and continuous. The method used by Sinan to mask the huge buttresses required to support the four central piers is very ingenious, and here he has turned what is generally a liability in such a building into an asset. On the N and S he incorporated the buttresses into the walls of the building, allowing them to project about equally within and without. He then proceeded to mask this projection on both sides by building galleries with arcades of columns between the buttresses. On the outside the gallery is double, with twice the number of columns in its upper storey as in its lower; on the inside there is a single gallery only. In both cases—especially on the outside—the device is extremely successful, and is indeed one of the features that give the exterior its interesting and beautiful distinction. On the E and W facades the buttresses are smaller, for here the weight of the dome is distributed by the semidomes. On the E face, therefore, Sinan merely placed the buttresses wholly outside the building, where their moderate projection gives emphasis and variety to that facade. On the W side Sinan was not so successful. Here, in order to preserve the unity of the courtyard and the grandeur of the W facade, he chose to place the buttresses wholly within the building. Again he masked them with galleries, but in this case the device was inadequate. The great W portal, instead of being as impressive as it ought to be, seems squeezed by the deep projection of the buttresses, which, moreover, not only throw it into impenetrable shadow, but also abut in an unpleasing way on the two small domes on which the W semidome reposes. Sinan was rarely completely successful with the interior of his W walls; in almost every case, even in his smaller mosques, there is a tendency to squeeze the main portal. Nevertheless, his solution of the main problem was masterly.

The general effect of the interior is of a severely simple grandeur. Only the E wall is enlivened by some touches of colour: here the lovely stained-glass windows are by the glazier known as Sarhoş (the Drunkard) Ibrahim. The tiles, used with great restraint, are the earliest known examples of the new techniques of the Iznik kilns, leaf and flower motifs in turquoise, deep blue and red on a pure white ground. The mihrab and mimber in Proconnesian marble are of great simplicity and distinction, as is also the woodwork, inlaid with ivory and mother-of-pearl, of the doors, window shutters, and the preacher's chair. Throughout the building the inscriptions are by the most famous of Ottoman calligraphers, Ahmet Karahísarí and his pupil Hasan Çelebi.

THE TÜRBES. The türbes of Süleyman and his wife Haseki Hürrem, better known in the West as Roxelana, are in the walled garden behind the mosque. *Süleyman's 'türbe*, as is fitting, is the largest and grandest of Sinan's mausoleums, although not quite the most beautiful. Octagonal in form, it is surrounded by a pretty porch on columns. This türbe, like those at Haghia Sophia and elsewhere, has a double dome, with the inner dome supported by columns in the interior. This inner dome preserves its gorgeous painting in wine-red, black and gold. The walls of the interior are covered with Iznik tiles, twice as many in this small room as in all the vastness of the mosque itself. However, the grand effect has been marred, for the interior of the türbe is dark and overcrowded with cenotaphs; besides that of Süleyman there are also those of his favourite daughter, the Princess Mihrimah, and two later sultans, Süleyman II and Ahmet II. Nevertheless, this remains one of the most impressive monuments of its kind in the city. It is dated 1566, the year of Süleyman's death.

The *türbe of Haseki Hürrem* stands just to the E of Süleyman's; and although this is smaller and simpler than the Sultan's tomb, it is decorated with even finer Iznik tiles. In this türbe the cylindrical base of the dome, slightly recessed from the octagonal cornice of the building itself, is decorated with a long inscription forming a kind of sculptured frieze. This, and the türbe of the princes at the mosque of Selim I (see Rte 12), are the only ones to use this form and these decorations. For some reason this türbe is not included in the 'Tezkere', the list of Sinan's works, but it is almost certainly his creation. The türbe is dated 1558, the year of Haseki Hürrem's death.

*The Dar-ül Hadis*. Farther E along the N terrace, and beyond the wall of the türbe garden, stands the dar-ül hadis, or school of tradition, which runs off at an angle to the line of the terrace, following the direction of the street below. This is a medrese of most unusual form. It consists of 22 cells in a long straight line, rather than around a courtyard; opposite them is a plain wall with grilled openings enclosing a long, narrow garden. At the end of the line of cells nearest the mosque a staircase leads up to a sort of open loggia above, which appears to have served as the dershane. It was for summer use only since it would have been too cold in winter. Unfortunately, this unique and once charming building has been very badly restored.

From the outer edge of the terrace one can look down onto the street that borders the N wall of the outer precincts of the Süleymaniye. This was once an attractive arasta, or market street, with shops built into the retaining wall of the terrace and also opposite. The shops still serve the purpose for which they were designed four centuries ago, but they are now rather badly battered. However, it is planned to restore the entire arasta to its original condition.

*The Salis and Rabi Medreses*. Just across the street there are two medreses of the Süleymaniye külliye; these are presently closed to the public and can best be viewed from the terrace. They are by far the most elaborate, original and picturesque of all Sinan's medreses. The one to the W, farther down the street, is called Salis (Third), while that to the E is known as Rabi (Fourth). The two medreses form a group with another pair that stand opposite them on the S side of the külliye; these are called Evvel (First) and Sani (Second); each of them serving as a college in one of the four orthodox schools of Islamic law. There is still another medrese, the Mülazimler (Preparatory Students), which lies beneath the Salis and Rabi medreses. These three medreses were built on the steep northern slope of the Third Hill, and in order to use this almost precipitous site two expedients were necessary. The N side of the courtyard was raised on high superstructures, beneath which lies the Mülazimler medrese. Even so, the courtyard itself slopes downhill fairly sharply, and the cells along the sides are built on five different levels connected by four flights of six shallow steps each under the portico. On each level outside the cells there is a verandah with a low parapet. The dershane occupies most of the upper (S) side of the courtyard, but since it is at the highest level it is entered from the sides rather than from the facade on the court. Salis and Rabi are absolutely identical; between them there is a small court from whose lower level two staircases lead to the courtyard of the Mülazimler medrese. This medrese consists of 18 cells with barrel-vaults under the N side of the upper medreses. As a display of architectural virtuosity these medreses surely have no rival; their effortless charm and simple distinction show that they were no empty vaunting of ingenuity, but a genuine inspiration by a master architect. It is to be hoped that they will one day be opened to the public, for they are unique and interesting monuments of Ottoman architecture.

At the end of the street, just below the dar-ül hadis, there is a building that was originally the hamam of the Süleymaniye külliye. This fine building, of an original design and once elegantly decorated, has been restored in recent years, and it may soon be open to the public. Now used as a warehouse, it is seriously dilapidated; the owner is very reluctant to allow visitors to inspect it. Hopefully this building will soon be restored and opened to the public, for it is original in design and was once elegantly decorated.

*The Dar-ül Kura.* The far eastern end of the terrace, the area behind the türbe garden, is a large open area, triangular in shape because of the direction of the streets below. This was known in early Ottoman times as the Iron Wrestling Ground, because weekly wrestling matches were held there. (Wrestling has always been an honoured sport in Islam, and one with religious significance, particularly because the Prophet himself enjoyed wrestling with his companions.) At the western end of the area, set into the middle of the türbe garden wall, there is a handsome building that once served as the dar-ül kura, or school for the study of the Kuran. Such schools appear to have always been small buildings, rather like mekteps or the dershanes of medreses. Sometimes they were directly attached to a mosque and without accompanying living-quarters for students, since the course in Kuran reading was naturally ancillary to more general studies. The school consists of a large domed chamber of very lovely proportions; beneath it there is a small Byzantine cistern with four columns.

On the S side of the mosque, outside the precinct walls, there stretches a long and broad esplanade lined with institutions belonging to the Süleymaniye külliye. This attractive avenue is called Tiryaki Çarşísí, the Market of the Addicts, because in Ottoman times the cafés which stood outside the medreses here used to serve opium to their customers in addition to tea, coffee and tobacco.

At the E end of the esplanade stands the former *primary school of the külliye*, where the children of the clergy, faculty and staff of the Süleymaniye received their elementary education. This little building, whose entrance is around the corner, has recently been restored and is now in use as a very charming children's library.

The next two institutions along the esplanade are the *Evvel and Sani medreses*, forming a group with the other two schools of Islamic law on the N side of the mosque. The entrance to these twin medreses is at the far end of the narrow alley that separates them. The two medreses now house the celebrated Süleymaniye library; this is one of the most important in the city, with more than 32,000 manuscripts. The buildings are mirror-images of one another, and although the arrangement is typical enough—cells around a porticoed courtyard—there are interesting variations. For example, there is no portico on the N side, but, instead, the three cells are open, forming a kind of loggia; the portico on the S side is cut by the dershane. All of the porticoes have been glassed-in to accommodate the library; this has been done well and attractively, and there is a charming garden in the courtyard itself.

Just beyond the Sani medrese is the building that was originally the *Típ Medresesi*, or Medical College, once the foremost in the Empire. Unfortunately, all that remains of it now is the row of cells along the Tiryaki Çarşísí; the other three sides have long since disappeared. In their place a modern concrete structure has been built, and the building now serves as a maternity clinic.

Across the street from this to the W is the vast *dar-üs şifa*, now a military printing-house and closed to the public. Like most of the larger Ottoman hospitals, that of the Süleymaniye had a special section for the care of the insane. Foreign travellers to Istanbul were much impressed by these establishments and praised their number and size, charity and organization.

*The ˙Imaret.* The first building on the street bordering the W end of the mosque courtyard is the imaret, or public kitchen, now the *Museum of Turkish and Islamic Antiquities.* (Open 9:30-5:30 every day except Mon) The imaret is enormous, as well it might be, for it had to supply food not only for the poor of the district but also for the several thousand people directly dependent on the Süleymaniye: the clergy of the mosque, the faculty and students of the several medreses, the staff and patients of the hospital, and the travellers staying at the caravansaray. In the kitchens and refectories of this great building there is a display of Turkish and Islamic antiquities: pottery and glass, much of it Selcuk and early Ottoman; early Turkish carpets; metalwork and gold and silver jewellery; interesting Kuran cases with covers in the shape of mosque domes; calligraphy of all periods, many of the manuscripts containing miniatures; and in the courtyard Ottoman tombstones and lapidary inscriptions. The courtyard itself is charming, with its ancient plane trees and young palms and a lovely marble fountain in the centre.

*The Caravansaray.* Next beyond the imaret is the building that was once the caravansaray of the Süleymaniye. This included a kitchen, bakery, olive press, sleeping-quarters for travellers, stables for their horses and camels, and storage-rooms for their belongings. According to ancient Turkish tradition, all accredited travellers to the city were given free food and shelter for three days at this and other caravansarays in the Empire.

*The Türbe of Sinan.* The türbe of Sinan, the architect of the Süleymaniye, stands in a little triangular garden at the NE corner of the complex, just beyond the caravansaray. Sinan apparently built a house here when he began construction of the Süleymaniye, and he lived in it until his death in 1588; he was then buried in his garden, in a türbe that he had designed and built himself. At the apex of the

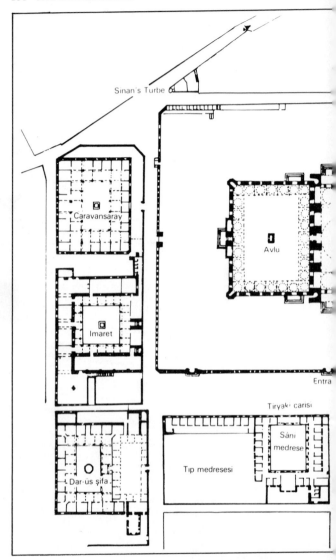

triangle is a sebil with six grilled openings and covered by a little
dome with projecting eaves. From this radiate the garden walls,
inside which stands the marble türbe. An arcade with six ogive arches
supports a marble roof which has a tiny dome over Sinan's marble
sarcophagus, with a turbaned tombstone at its head. Around the türbe
there are other tombstones, presumably marking the graves of

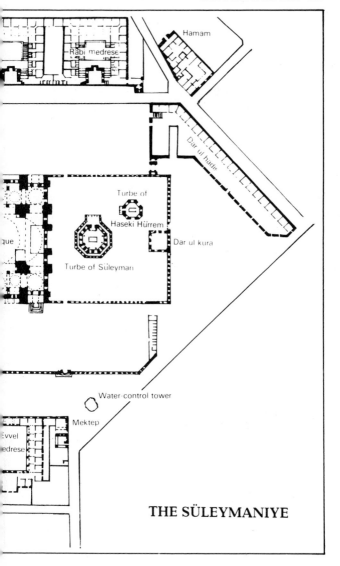

THE SÜLEYMANIYE

members of Sinan's family, but there are no inscriptions to identify them. On the S wall of the türbe garden there is a long inscription by Sinan's friend, the poet Mustafa Sa'i, which commemorates the architect's accomplishments. There could be no more appropriate place for Sinan's tomb, looking out toward the great mosque complex that he created, the crowning glory of Süleyman's golden age.

# 10   From the Galata Bridge to Şehzadebaşi

This itinerary follows a route that runs first along the Golden Horn
between the two bridges, then turns up the valley between the Third
and Fourth Hills to visit monuments on the slopes of both eminences,
and finally ends at Şehzadebaşí, on the crest of the ridge between
the Golden Horn and the Marmara.

The easternmost quarter of the market district between the shore
highway and the Golden Horn is known as *Zindan Kapí*, or the Prison
Gate. The quarter takes its name from the ancient tower visible
amongst the confused crowd of buildings that stand just beyond the
parking-lot beside the Golden Horn. The tower seems to have been
used for centuries as a prison, by both the Byzantines and the Turks,
hence the name of the surrounding quarter. Within the tower a certain
Cafer Baba is buried, who, according to tradition, came to Constantinople as the envoy of Haroun al-Rashid but was imprisoned here
and died. His grave was rediscovered and restored after the Conquest
and is still much venerated.

Just beside the tower, to the W, there are the shattered remains of
an arched gateway dating from the medieval Byzantine period. The
Byzantine name of this gate is uncertain, but in early Ottoman times
local Greeks referred to it as the *Porta Caravion*, the Gate of the
Caravels, because of the large number of ships that docked at the pier
nearby, the ancient Scala de Drongario. This pier, which in Ottoman
times came to be called *Yemiş Iskelesi*, the Fruit Pier, is still the
principal mooring-place for the picturesque caiques that bring
produce to the wholesale markets between the two bridges. This has
been a port and market area since the early years of Byzantine
Constantinople, and it continues to be one of the liveliest and most
colourful quarters in the city.

A short distance from the tower and gateway there is an ancient
mosque known as *Ahi Çelebi Camii*. This mosque was founded in the
early 16C by Ahi Çelebi ibni Kemal, who was Chief Physician at the
hospital attached to the Külliye of the Mosque of the Conqueror; he
died in 1523 while returning from a pilgrimage to Mecca and the
mosque can thus be dated to before that time. The mosque is of little
interest except for the fact that it was restored at one point by Sinan.

On the left side of the shore highway between the two bridges one
passes, in turn, three little mosques which are among the very oldest
in Istanbul, all of them built just after the Conquest. The first of these
is about 250m beyond the Byzantine tower; this is *Kantarcílar
Mescidi*, the Small Mosque of the Scale-Makers, named after the
guild whose artisans have had their workshops in this neighbourhood
for centuries. This mosque was founded during the reign of the
Conqueror by one Sarí Demirci Mevlana Mehmet Muhittin. It has
been reconstructed several times and is of little interest except for its
great age.

The second of these ancient mosques, which is about 250m beyond
the first, is called *Kazancílar Camii*, the Mosque of the Cauldron-
Makers, here again named after one of the ancient neighbourhood
guilds. It is also known as Üç Mihrablí Cami (literally the mosque with
the three mihrabs). Founded by a certain Hoca Hayrettin Efendi in

1475, it was enlarged first by the Conqueror himself and then by Hayrettin's daughter-in-law, who added her own house to the mosque, so that it came to have three mihrabs, and hence the name. The main body of the building, which appears to be original in form though heavily restored, consists of a square room covered by a dome resting on a high blind drum; this is worked in the form of a series of triangles so as to dispense with squinches or pendentives. In the dome there are some rather curious arabesque designs; these are not in the grand manner of the 16–17C nor yet in the degenerate Italian taste of the 19C; their date is uncertain but they are unique in the city and quite attractive both in design and colour. The deep porch has three domes only, the arches are supported at each end by rectangular piers and in the centre by a single marble column. The door is not in the middle, where it would have been blocked by the column, but on the right-hand side; this arrangement was common in the pre-classical period, but there are very few examples in the city. To the S of the main building there is a rectangular annexe with a flat ceiling and two mihrabs, and it is through here that one enters the mosque today. One authority has suggested that this might be the house added to Hayrettin's house by his daughter-in-law; if true, this would be the oldest dwelling-place in the city.

The third mosque is found about 150m farther along, a short distance before the Atatürk Bridge. This is *Sagrícílar Camii*, the Mosque of the Leather-Workers, named after another guild that has long had its workshops in this quarter. This building is of the simplest type, a square room covered by a dome, the walls of stone. It was restored in 1960 with only modest success. But although the mosque is of little interest architecturally, its historical background is fascinating. This is probably the oldest mosque in the city, founded in 1455 by Yavuz Ersinan, standard-bearer in the Conqueror's army during the final siege of Constantinople by the Turks. He was an ancestor of Evliya Çelebi and his family remained in possession of the mosque for at least two centuries, living in a house just beside it. Evliya Çelebi was born in this house in 1611, and 20 years later he began to write his 'Narrative of Travels' there, which contains a vivid and very comprehensive picture of life in Istanbul in the 17C. The founder is buried in the little graveyard beside the mosque. Beside him is buried one of his comrades-in-arms, Horoz Dede, one of the fabulous folk-saints of Istanbul. Horoz Dede, or Grandfather Rooster, received his name during the siege of Constantinople in 1453, when he made his rounds each morning and woke the troops of the Conqueror's army with his loud rooster call. Horoz Dede was killed in the final assault on the walls, and after the city fell he was buried here, with the Conqueror himself among the mourners. The saint's grave is venerated to this day.

Atatürk Blv begins at the Atatürk Bridge and runs uphill along the valley between the Third and Fourth Hills. About 300m up the avenue and on the left side there is a handsome baroque mosque, *Şebsafa Kadín Camii*. This was founded in 1787 by Fatma Şebsafa Kadín, one of the women in the harem of Abdül Hamit I. It is of brick and stone; the porch has an upper storey with a cradle-vault, and inside there is a sort of narthex, also of two storeys, covered with three small domes. These upper storeys form a deep and attractive gallery overlooking the central area of the mosque, which is covered by a high dome resting on the walls. To the N of the mosque there is a long mektep with a pretty cradle-vaulted roof.

Directly across the avenue from the mosque one can see the domes of an ancient church standing atop the bluff which lines that side of Atatürk Blv. This is the former church of the Pantocrator, one of the major monuments on the present itinerary. But before proceeding there a short detour might be made through the shopping-mall farther up the avenue beyond the mosque, to see two very minor sights of some historic interest.

In the centre of the shopping-mall there is an ancient little *Moslem graveyard* that has recently been restored. Among the handsome old Ottoman tombstones is one with a modern inscription bearing the illustrious name of Katip Çelebi and his dates, 1609–58. Katip Çelebi, one of the most enlightened Ottoman scholars of the 17C, was the author of at least 23 books, along with a large number of shorter treatises and essays, most of them on history and philosophy. His last and best-known work, 'The Balance of Truth', translated into English by Geoffrey Lewis, is the best contemporary Turkish work on the political and social condition of the Ottoman Empire in the mid-17C.

At the rear of the shopping-mall there is a small Greek chapel in the midst of a garden surrounded by a high wall. The gate to the garden is always locked; it is best seen from the balcony of one of the nearby buildings in the shopping-mall. The church is of interest only because of its association with an old Greek tradition, which holds that it was the burial-place of Constantine XI Dragases, the last Emperor of Byzantium, who was interred there after he died fighting in the last hours of the Turkish siege on 29 May 1453. However, there is no historical basis for this; in fact, an even older Greek tradition, equally baseless, places the Emperor's grave elsewhere in the city (see Rte 14).

On the other side of Atatürk Blv a stepped path leads up and to the right from the avenue to the bluff above. A short distance uphill, at the second turning, there is a small Ottoman primary school in a walled garden, the *Mektep of Zenbelli Ali Baba*. The founder was the Şeyh-ül Islam Ali bin Ahmet Efendi, better known as Zenbelli Ali Baba. Ali Baba died in 1525, so his mektep can be dated to some time prior to that year. The mektep has recently been restored and is now used as a children's library; it is a very pleasing example of the minor Ottoman architecture of the early 16C. The founder is buried beneath a marble sarcophagus in the garden.

Taking the street on the right past the entrance to the mektep, one comes almost immediately to a picturesque square dominated by the former **church of the \*Pantocrator** (Pl 10,1), known locally as Zeyrek Camii. It is one of the most important Byzantine sanctuaries surviving in the city.

HISTORY. The Pantocrator is a composite building that originally consisted of a monastery with two churches and a chapel between them; the whole complex was built within the period 1120–36. The monastery and the S church were founded by the Empress Eirene, wife of John II Comnenus, and dedicated to St. Saviour Pantocrator, Christ the Almighty. After Eirene's death in 1124 John decided to erect another church a few metres to the N of hers; this was dedicated to the Virgin Eleousa, the Merciful or Charitable. This chapel was designed to serve as a mortuary for the imperial Comneni dynasty. The first to be buried there was the Empress Eirene, who died in 1124. (Until about 1960 Eirene's verd antique sarcophagus stood in the square outside the Pantocrator, but then it was taken to the Archaeological Museum; today it stands in the exonarthex of Haghia Sophia.) John II was interred in the chapel after his death in 1143, and his son and successor, Manuel I was buried there in 1180, thus bringing to a close an illustrious century of rule by the Comneni family. During the first half of the 15C the chapel served as a mortuary for the imperial Palaeologus family, the last dynasty to rule Byzantium. Two of the last three Emperors of Byzantium were buried here: Manuel II in 1425 and John VIII in 1448. Buried alongside John was his wife, Maria of Trebizond, the last Empress of Byzantium (Constantine XI was a widower when he became Emperor, and he did not marry again), who had died a few years earlier.

The monastery to which these churches belonged was one of the most renowned in Byzantium. It was a very extensive foundation, including a hospice for old men, an insane asylum, and a famous hospital. All of these have long since disappeared, doubtless the source of the widespread ruins and substructures in the neighbourhood of the Pantocrator.

During the 57 years of Latin rule in Constantinople, the Pantocrator was taken over by the Roman Catholic clergy of the Venetians. Toward the close of the Latin occupation, the monastery of the Pantocrator became the official residence of the Latin kings, because the Great Palace by the Marmara had been so neglected that it was no longer habitable. The last Latin ruler in Constantinople, Baldwin II, fled from the Pantocrator on 25 July 1261, after he received news that the Byzantine army had entered the city. Immediately after the capture of the city by the Byzantines, their Genoese allies stormed the Pantocrator, where some of the Venetians were still holding out, and in the course of the fighting the monastery burned to the ground. The monastery was soon afterwards rebuilt, and during the latter Byzantine period it resumed its role as one of the most important religious centres in the city. The most famous resident of the monastery during this period was George Scholarius, better known as Gennadius. Gennadius accompanied John VIII Palaeologus and the Patriarch Joseph to the Council of Ferrara-Florence in 1438 when the Greek and Roman churches were officially reconciled. Gennadius bitterly opposed the union, however, and when he returned to Constantinople he vehemently denounced it; his view was shared by most people in the capital. After that Gennadius retired to his cell in the Pantocrator, emerging only after the city fell to the Turks. Shortly after the Conquest Gennadius was invited to meet Mehmet II, and after several cordial conversations the Sultan appointed him Patriarch, a post which, under Turkish rule, made him head of the entire Greek Orthodox population in the Ottoman Empire.

INTERIOR. In plan the S church erected by the Empress Eirene is of the four-column type, with a central dome, a triple apse, and a narthex with a gallery overlooking the nave. (The columns were removed in Ottoman times and replaced by piers.) This church preserves a good deal of its original decoration, including the marble pavement, the handsome door-frames of the narthex, and the almost complete marble revetment of the apse. Recent work by the Byzantine Institute has brought to light again the magnificent *opus sectile* floor of the church itself, arranged in great squares and circles of coloured marbles with figures in the borders. Notice also the curious Turkish mimber made from fragments of Byzantine sculpture, including the canopy of a ciborium. The investigations of the Byzantine Institute also discovered fragments of stained-glass from the E window, which seems to show that the art of stained-glass was a Byzantine rather than a western European creation.

The N church, erected by the Emperor John, is somewhat smaller than Eirene's but of essentially the same type and plan; here again the columns have been replaced by piers. Unfortunately, it has preserved none of its original decoration and is now in appalling condition. When this church was finished, the idea seems to have struck the Emperor to join the two churches by building a chapel between them. This is a structure without aisles and with only one apse, covered by two domes; it is highly irregular in form in order to make it fit between the two churches, which were not of exactly the same size. Parts of the walls of the churches were demolished so that all three sections opened widely into one another. John also added an outer narthex which must once have extended in front of all three structures, but which now ends awkwardly in the middle of the chapel.

In spite of the labours of the Byzantine Institute, the building is in a lamentable state of decay and squalour, and the three sections have been divided from each other by wooden partitions, so that it is quite impossible to form any idea of what it was originally like. A complete restoration of this important and unique building is urgently required.

What may perhaps be the only surviving part of the monastery of the Pantocrator stands about 150m to the SW of the church. To find it, return to the primary school of Zenbelli Ali Baba and turn right at the corner, then right again at the next corner. Near the end of the block and to the right one sees a small, tower-like building known locally as *Şeyh Süleyman Mescidi*. This building is obviously Byzantine in construction and may possibly have been one of the institutions associated with the Pantocrator monastery, perhaps a library or a funerary chapel. The lower part is square on the exterior and octagonal above; within it is altogether octagonal, with shallow niches in the cross-axes; below there is a crypt. This strange and interesting building has never been seriously investigated, so that neither its identity nor its date are known.

Continue past the mescit and turn right at the corner, then take the first left onto Hací Hasan Sk. At the end of this street and on the left about 100m along, there is a tiny mosque with a quaint and pretty minaret. The mosque is known locally as *Eğri Minare*, the Crooked Minaret, for obvious reasons. The minaret has a stone base at the top of which there is a curious rope-like moulding. The shaft is of brick and stone arranged to form a criss-cross or chequerboard design, unique in Istanbul. The şerefe has an elaborate stalactite corbel and a fine balustrade, partly broken; but the scale seems a little too big for the minaret. The mosque itself is rectangular, built of squared stones and with a wooden roof; in its present condition it is without interest. The founder was the Kazasker (Judge) Hací Hasanzade Mehmet Efendi, who died in 1505; therefore the mosque must be dated no later than that year.

Once past the mosque turn left and then right at the next corner onto Küçük Mektep Sk, at the end of which stands a handsome Byzantine church known locally as *Eski Imaret Camii* (Pl 10,1). This has been identified with virtual certainty as the church of •St. Saviour Pantepoptes, Christ the All-Seeing, one of the more important Byzantine churches in the city.

HISTORY. This church was founded in about 1185–90 by the Empress Anna Delessena, mother of Alexius I Comnenus and founder of the dynasty which ruled so brilliantly over Byzantium in the 11–12C. Anna ruled as co-Emperor with her son for nearly 20 years, and during that time she had a great deal of influence on the affairs of the Byzantine state. In the year 1100 the Empress retired to the convent of the Pantepoptes and spent the rest of her life in retirement there. She died in 1105 and was buried in the church that she had founded.

The church was converted into a mosque almost immediately after the Conquest. After the original Mosque of the Conqueror was erected nearby, the church was converted into a kitchen and dining hall for the students and faculty attending the medreses there, until the completion of their own imaret. Then the church of the Pantepoptes became a mosque again and was called Eski Imaret Camii. Recently it was been put to use as a Kuran school, and also serves as a dormitory for the youths who study there. Like the Pantocrator, the Pantepoptes is in a sad state of dilapidation, and hemmed in on three sides by mean wooden houses.

EXTERIOR. The exterior, though most of it is concealed by houses, is very charming and the fabric is in good condition. It is a very characteristic Byzantine church of the 11C, with its 12-sided dome, and its decorative brickwork in the form of blind niches and bands of Greek-key and swastika motifs, along with rose-like medallions.

INTERIOR. The interior is cluttered with wooden partitions and with the bedding-rolls of the youths who study at the Kuran school. Nevertheless, one can see that it is a quite perfect example of an 11C church of the four-column type, with three apses and a double narthex, where many of the doors retain their magnificent frames of red marble. Over the inner narthex there is a gallery that opens into the nave by a charming triple arcade on two rose-coloured marble columns. The church itself has retained most of its original characteristics, though the four columns have as usual been replaced by piers, and the windows of the central apse have been altered. The side apses, however, preserve their windows and their beautiful marble cornice. The dome, which has 12 windows between which 12 deep ribs taper out toward the crown, rests on a cornice which still preserves its original decoration, a meander pattern of palmettes and flowers. It is a beautiful church, and it is a pity that it is not restored to its original condition.

The little square in front of the Pantepoptes affords a sweeping view of the upper reaches of the Golden Horn. It was on this spot that the Emperor Alexius V pitched his vermilion tent during the last days of the siege of Constantinople by the Crusaders in April 1204. On the morning of 13 April the Emperor emerged from his tent and saw that the Crusaders had breached the sea-walls along the Golden Horn, whereupon he mounted his white charger and fled from the doomed city. (He was shortly afterwards captured by the Crusaders and executed.) That night, after the Crusaders had taken the city by storm, Count Badouin of Flanders, one of their leaders, spent the night in the former Emperor's tent outside the Pantepoptes.

The northern slope of the Fourth Hill in this area is rather thickly dotted with small mosques, many of them ancient but few of much interest. Some are in a state of ruin or near ruin; others have been restored, often quite badly. Two of these are in the vicinity of the Pantepoptes, but it should be understood that they are of relatively minor interest.

The first of these mosques is reached by taking Şair Baki Sk (named after a famous Turkish poet of the 17C), the continuation of Küçük Mektep Sk. The mosque is two blocks along on the right, at the corner of Esrar Dede Sk. This mosque, constructed of alternate rows of brick and stone, was built in 1564. It is called *Aşik Paşa Camii*, after a famous Turkish poet of the early 14C; it was built for the peace of his soul by one of the poet's descendants, Şeyh Ahmet Efendi. Beside it is a tekke, also named after Aşik Paşa; this was built somewhat earlier than the mosque—about 1522—by a man called Seyyidi-Velayet Efendi, but is in the same general style. Opposite the mosque is the grand türbe of Şeyh Ahmet Efendi. Although not actually planned as a külliye, these buildings in their walled garden nevertheless have an attractive unity.
    Returning to the Pantepoptes, turn right off Küçük Mektep Sk immediately after passing the church. Follow this street past the intersection and for two more blocks beyond; this brings one to an ancient mosque at the corner of Kadi Çeşme Sk and Şebnem Sk. This is *Yarhisar Camii*, the second oldest mosque in the city, apparently predated only by Sağrıcılar Camii. Yarhisar Camii may in fact be the older of the two, for its date is a matter of official record, while that of Sağrıcılar Camii is from unattested tradition. According to the register of pious foundations ('Hayrat Kaydi'), this mosque was built in 1461; its founder was Musliheddin Mustafa Efendi, Chief Judge of Istanbul during the reign of the Conqueror. It was once a handsome edifice, built entirely of ashlar stone; it consists of a square chamber covered by a dome on pendentives, preceded by a porch with two domes and three columns. It was burned in the great fire of 1917, which destroyed much of this district, but even in its ruined state it was a fine and dignified structure. In 1954–56 the building was restored, with a thin veneer of brick and stone, *à la Byzantine*, covering the original structure, and the interior was redecorated. The restoration was not a success; it obscures what is still attractive in the mosque and it is not true to the spirit of the original structure.

After returning to the Pantepoptes, retrace the route back past Şeyh Süleyman Mescidi and then turn right at the next corner. A short way along on the left is an old hamam of considerable interest. This is

**\*Çinili Hamam**, the Tiled Bath, an early work of Sinan. It was built in about 1545 for Süleyman's great admiral Hayrettin Paşa, better known in the West as Barbarossa. It is a double bath, the men's and women's sections standing side-by-side and with their entrances in the same facade, a rather unusual feature; the plans of the two parts are almost identical. In the centre of the great camekan is an elaborate and beautiful marble fountain with goldfish swimming in it. The narrow soğukluk with two little semidomes at each end leads to the cruciform hararet, where the open arms of the cross are covered with tiny domes; the rooms in the corners each have a larger dome. Here and there on the walls there are small panels of faience, and the floor is paved in *opus sectile*. In the camekan fragments of a more elaborate wall revetment of tiles of a later period may be seen. A half century ago this fine hamam was abandoned and fell into a state of decay, but in recent years it has been restored and is now once again in use.

Beyond the hamam the avenue, Itfaiye Cd, widens and becomes quite pretty, with a double row of plane trees shading the open stalls of a gay and colourful fruit and vegetable market. Follow Itfaiye Cd as far as Kovacílar Cd, the last street before the aqueduct, and turn left. At the right on the next corner, where the street intersects Atatürk Blv, there is a small classical külliye built up against the aqueduct. This is the **\*medrese of Gazanfer Ağa** (Pl 10,3), which now serves as the **Municipal Museum of Istanbul**.

ADMISSION. The museum is open 9–12, 1:30–5:30 every day except the fifth of the month.

HISTORY. The külliye was founded in 1599 by Gazanfer Ağa, Chief of the White Eunuchs in the reign of Mehmet III. Gazanfer Ağa was the last of the Chief White Eunuchs to head the civil hierarchy in the Inner Palace, for after his time the Chief Black Eunuch became the dominant figure; he was executed in 1603, after having involved himself too deeply in the politics of the Harem.

*The Külliye*. The külliye includes a small medrese, a charming sebil with handsome grilled windows, and the türbe of the founder, in the form of a marble sarcophagus. The külliye was restored in 1945, at which time the medrese was converted into the Municipal Museum of Istanbul.

*The Museum*. The cells of the medrese have had doors cut between them, forming suites of rooms. One such suite illustrates the life of Istanbul—past, present, and future—with paintings, old prints, maps, and models. Another suite has an exhibition of Istanbul manufactures, including a good collection of glassware, porcelain and crystal made at Beykoz, on the Asian side of the Bosphorus, and a small and not particularly good collection of puppets and figures used in Karagöz, the old Turkish shadow-plays. One interesting exhibit shows a recreated Turkish coffee-house of the early 19C, and in another suite there is an exhibition of costumes and other articles used by the various dervish orders that had tekkes in Istanbul.

After leaving the museum one might take the opportunity to examine more closely the **\*\*Aqueduct of Valens**,which has been dramatically in view throughout the whole of this and other itineraries.

HISTORY. The aqueduct was built by the Emperor Valens in about AD 375 as part of the new water-supply system that he constructed during his reign. The water, tapped from various streams and lakes outside the city, appears to have entered through subterranean pipes near the Adrianople Gate and to have passed through a large underground pipe along the ridges of the Sixth, Fifth and Fourth Hills to a point near the present site of the Conqueror's Mosque (see Rte 11). From there the water was carried by the aqueduct across the deep valley that divides the Fourth from the Third Hill. On the Third Hill, near the present site of Beyazit Square, the water was received in a huge cistern, the *nymphaeum maximum*, from which it was distributed to the various parts of the city. This ancient cistern seems to have been near the present *taksim*, the modern water-distribution centre, which is supplied from Lake Terkoz, some 60km NW of Istanbul, near the Black Sea. The aqueduct was damaged at various times but was kept in good repair by both the Byzantine emperors and the Ottoman sultans, the last important restoration being that of Mustafa II in 1697. The aqueduct continued in use until the late 19C, when it was replaced by the modern water-distribution system.

The length of the aqueduct was originally about 1000m, of which some 625m remain standing; its maximum height, where it crosses Atatürk Blv, is 18·5m. It consists of two superimposed series of arches; a portion of the eastern side of this was demolished by Süleyman to give a clear view of the Şehzade mosque after it was built. The effect of these double arches across the valley is grand and Roman and the aqueduct is one of the most impressive and characteristic landmarks on the skyline of the old city.

After passing through the aqueduct, Atatürk Blv continues to its intersection with Şehzadebaşi Cd at the crest of the ridge between the Third and Fourth Hills, where the present Rte ends and the next one begins.

# 11  The Fourth Hill

The area where Atatürk Blv and Şehzadebaşi Cd intersect coincides with the site of the ancient *Forum Amastrianum*, one of the main squares in Byzantine Constantinople. At this point the Mese, which ran along the same route as Şehzadebaşi Cd, divided into two branches, one of which continued in the same direction along what is now Macarkardeşler Cd (the continuation of Şehzadebaşi Cd), while the other branch ran S along the present route of Atatürk Blv to the Forum Bovis, the modern Aksaray.

When the ground was being cleared for the Atatürk Blv underpass in the mid 1960s the extensive remains of an ancient church were discovered, and its ruins are visible in the open area to the right of the boulevard. An excavation was taken in hand by Dumbarton Oaks under the supervision of Martin Harrison, a project that has now been completed and published. The church was built between 524 and 527 for the Princess Anicia Juliana, who dedicated it to St. Polyeuktos, and is thus one of the earliest sanctuaries erected in Justinian's reign. It was an enormous building, some 52m on a side (compare the Süleymaniye mosque, which is about 58m on a side); it was essentially basilical in form, but very probably domed. The fragments of columns, capitals, elaborately carved entablature, and parts of a long and beautifully written inscription, by which the building was identified, are very impressive indeed.

Just to the W of the ruins of St. Polyeuktos is the fine *küllïye of Amcazade Hüseyin Paşa (Pl 9,4). This is one of the most elaborate and picturesque of the smaller classical complexes, another foundation of the illustrious Köprülü family.

HISTORY. Hüseyin Paşa, the founder, was a cousin (in Turkish, *amcazade*) of Fazil Ahmet Paşa, and was the fourth member of the Köprülü family to serve as Grand Vezir. He held that post from 1697–1702, during which time he founded this külliye. In recent years it has been restored and now houses the *Museum of Turkish Architectural Works and Construction Elements.*

ADMISSION. The museum is open 9:30–12, 2–4:30 on Mon, Tues, Wed, and Sat.

*The Külliye.* The complex includes an octagonal dershane, which also served as a mosque; a medrese; a library; a large primary school over a row of shops; two little graveyards with open türbes; a şadírvan; a sebil; and a çeşme; all arranged with an almost romantic disorder. The street facade consists first of the open walls of the small graveyards, divided by the projecting curve of the sebil. All of these have fine brass grilles, those of the türbe nearest the entrance being quite exceptionally beautiful specimens of early 17C grillework. Next comes the entrance gate with an Arabic inscription giving the date 1698. The çeşme just beyond it, with its reservoir behind, is a somewhat later addition, for its inscription records that it was built in 1739 for the Şeyh-ül Islam Mustafa Efendi. Finally there is a row of four shops, with an entrance between them leading to the two large rooms of the mektep on the upper floor. On entering the courtyard, the first of the open türbes—with the exceptionally handsome grilles—is on the left; notice the columned portico of the mosque, which runs around seven of the eight sides of the building and frames it in a rectangle. The mosque itself is without a minaret, and its primary purpose was clearly as the lecture hall for the medrese. It is severely simple; its dome adorned only with some rather pale stencilled designs probably later than the building itself.

The far side of the courtyard is formed by the 17 cells of the medrese, with their domed and colonnaded portico. Occupying the main part of the right-hand side is the library building. There are two storeys, but the lower floor serves chiefly as a water reservoir; the upper floor is reached by a flight of outside steps around the side and back of the building, leading to a little domed entrance porch on the first floor. The medallion inscription on the front of the library records a restoration in 1755 by Hüseyin Paşa's daughter. (The manuscripts which were once in this library, many of them Hüseyin Paşa's state papers, were removed after the külliye was severely damaged by the earthquake of 1894, and are now in the library of the Süleymaniye.) The right-hand corner of the courtyard is occupied by the shops of the külliye and the mektep above them: note the amusing little dovecotes in the form of miniature mosques on the facade overlooking the entrance gate. A columned şadírvan stands in the middle of the courtyard. This charmingly irregular complex is made still more picturesque by the warm red of the brickwork alternating with buff-coloured limestone, and not least by the venerable trees—cypresses, locusts, and two enormous terebinths—that grow out of the open türbes and in the courtyard.

THE MUSEUM. On exhibition in the Külliye are various architectural fragments, sculptured stonework, calligraphic inscriptions, and old tombstones. Many of these were formerly stored in the Second Court of Topkapí Sarayí, where they had been placed for safe keeping after the buildings to which they belonged were either ruined or demolished. They make an interesting display of Turkish stonework throughout the Ottoman period in Istanbul.

Opposite the Amcazade complex there is a pretty little park with an ugly monument in the form of a broken-off column at its centre; this is dated 1922 and commemorates Turkish aviators killed during World War I.

Continuing along the avenue on the left side, one passes an ancient but not very interesting little mosque called *Dülgerzade Camii*; this was built by one of Mehmet the Conqueror's officials, Şemsettin Habib Efendi, some time before his death in 1482.

The side street to the left beyond the mosque leads to a monument known locally as Kíz Taşí, the Maiden's Column (Pl 9,2). This is actually the ancient **\*Column of Marcian**, one of three late Roman honorific columns that still stand in the city. The other two are the Goth's Column and the Column of Constantine; the base of a fourth Roman column survives in Samatya (see below, Rte 15).

HISTORY. This column, though known to Evliya Çelebi and described by him in his 'Narrative of Travels', escaped even the penetrating eyes of Gyllius and remained unknown to the West until rediscovered in 1675 by Spon and Wheler. The reason for its obscurity was that it stood in the garden of a tall house, which, together with its neighbours, hid it from view. However, in 1908 a fire destroyed the houses and opened up the column to view, and now it stands in the centre of a small square.

The base is formed by a pedestal of Corinthian marble on three steps; above this stands a granite column 10m high, surmounted by a battered Corinthian capital and a plinth with eagles at the corners; this once supported a seated statue of the Emperor Marcian (450–57). On the base fragments of sculpture remain, including a Nike, or Winged Victory, in high relief. There is also on the base an elegiac couplet in Latin which records that the column was erected by the Prefect Tatianus in honour of the Emperor Marcian. The Turkish name of the column is undoubtedly due to the figure of the Nike on the base. This has led them to confuse this column with the famous Column of Venus, which also stood in this neighbourhood, and which reputedly possessed the power of being able to distinguish true virgins from false ones.

Two blocks farther along Macarkardeşler Cd and on the same side is another little külliye. This is the medrese founded in 1700 by the Şeyh-ül Islam Feyzullah Efendi, a great scholar and one of the most enlightened men of his time; it now serves as the People's Library of Istanbul. The cells of the medrese surround two sides of the courtyard, in the centre of which a şadírvan stands in the midst of a pretty garden. The street side of the courtyard is wholly occupied by a most elaborate and original dershane building: a flight of steps leads up to a porch covered by nine domes of very different patterns; the arches of these are supported on four columns. The effect of this porch has been somewhat impaired by glazing-in a part of it, but its usefulness has doubtless been increased. To the right and left of the porch are the large domed lecture-rooms of the medrese, now used as library reading-rooms. The medrese was restored and converted into a library by Ali Emiri Efendi, a famous bibliophile who died in 1924; he donated to the people of Istanbul his valuable collection of books and manuscripts.

This brings one to the enormous \*mosque complex of Mehmet the Conqueror (Pl 9,2), known in Turkish as **Fatih Camii**. The massive walls along the right side of the avenue here are the backs of the medreses attached to the mosque complex; its main entrance is reached by taking the first turning on the right onto Islambol Cd, the street bordering the W side of the outer precinct wall. There one is confronted by the imposing edifice of Fatih Camii, flanked on either side by the great medreses and the other institutions of the külliye.

HISTORY. The huge mosque complex built by Sultan Mehmet the Conqueror was the most extensive and elaborate in Istanbul, and indeed in the whole of the Ottoman Empire. An inscription records that the architect was Atik Sinan, and that the complex was built in the period 1463–70. The identity of the architect is uncertain but he is believed to have been a Greek, from the European provinces of the Empire, who had been taken up in the devşirme, the annual levy of subject youths, and trained in an Ottoman school of architecture. In addition to the great mosque itself, the külliye consisted of eight medreses and their annexes, along with a hospice, public kitchen, hospital, caravansaray, primary school, public bath, and a graveyard with two türbes. The complex was laid out over a vast, almost square area—about 325m on a side—with almost rigid symmetry. The complex stood on the site of the famous Church of the Holy Apostles, in whose funerary chapel most of the earlier Emperors of Byzantium were buried, and which was exceeded in size in Constantinople only by Haghia Sophia. The church and its attendant buildings, which were already in ruins at the time of the last siege, served as a quarry to supply building material for the Conqueror's mosque complex, and today not a trace of them remains.

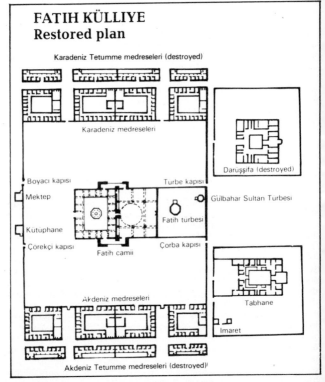

# FATIH KÜLLIYE
## Restored plan

Karadeniz Tetumme medreseleri (destroyed)

Karadeniz medreseleri

Daruşşifa (destroyed)

Boyacı kapısı

Mektep

Kutuphane

Çörekçi kapısı

Turbe kapısı

Fatih turbesi

Fatih camii

Gülbahar Sultan Turbesi

Çorba kapısı

Akdeniz medreseleri

Tabhane

Imaret

Akdeniz Tetumme medreseleri (destroyed)

The original mosque built by the Conqueror was completely destroyed by an earthquake on 22 May 1766. Mustafa II immediately undertook its reconstruction, and the present mosque, designed on a wholly different plan, was completed in 1771. What remains of the original mosque complex of the Conqueror is, most probably, the courtyard, the main entrance portal of the mosque, the mihrab, the minarets up to the first şerefe, the S wall of the graveyard and the adjoining gate. All of the other buildings in the külliye were badly damaged in the earthquake but were restored by Mustafa II, presumably in their original form. There has been considerable speculation about the original plan of the mosque, the first monumental Ottoman sanctuary to be erected in Istanbul. It is believed that the Conqueror's mosque had a very large central dome, some 26m in diameter (compare Haghia Sophia, where the diameter is 31m), with a semidome of the same diameter to the E; these were supported by two great rectangular piers on the E and by two enormous porphyry columns toward the W. The two porphyry columns also supported a double arcade below the tympanum walls of the great dome arches, while to N and S there were side aisles, each of which were covered with three small domes. Those who saw and described the mosque before it was destroyed, Turks and foreigners alike, compared it to Haghia Sophia. There is a curious tradition, repeated by Evliya Çelebi and other writers, that the architect was executed by the Conqueror soon after Fatih Camii was completed, because the Sultan was enraged that the dome of his mosque was smaller than that of the Great Church.

*The Mosque Courtyard.* Approaching the mosque from the W end of the outer courtyard, one finds that part of the W wall of the precinct has been demolished, together with the small library and primary school that once stood outside it. Trees and wooden houses have intruded but they make a picturesque enclave in this corner. Still visible are the remains of one of the original gateways to the outer courtyard; this is Boyací Kapísí, the Painter's Gate. There was a similar portal 75m to the S of this called Çörekçi Kapísí, the Gate of the Muffin-Maker; these two gates flanked the mektep (to the N) and the library (to the S). The inner courtyard of the mosque begins some 75m to the E; this, with its monumental entrance portal, is original. In the lunettes of the six W windows of the courtyard wall there are some of the most remarkable inscriptions in the city: the first Surah of the Kuran is written in white marble letters on a ground of verd antique. The effect is extremely lovely, and one wonders why this fascinating technique of calligraphy should occur only here. The calligrapher was Yahya Sufi, and it was his son Ali who wrote the inscriptions over the main portal of the mosque and also over the Bab-í Hümayun at Topkapí Sarayí. The dignified but simple portal has rather curious engaged columns at the corners. The convex flutes or ribs of their shafts become interlaced at top and bottom to form an intertwined snake pattern, while the columns end in a sort of hour-glass-shaped capital and base. This treatment is found elsewhere in the külliye, but otherwise it is unique in Ottoman architecture.

In the centre of this picturesque courtyard stands the şadírvan, with a gay witch's cap conical roof resting on eight marble columns and surrounded by tall cypress trees. In essentials it is original, even to the cypresses, which are constantly mentioned by travellers, though doubtless replanted from time to time. The antique marble columns of the portico have stalactite capitals of fine, bold workmanship. At either end of the mosque porch there are two more exquisite lunette inscriptions, this time in faience, showing a vivid yellow combined with blue, green and white in the cuerda seca technique typical of this early period. Similar panels are to be seen in the mosque of Selim I (see below, Rte 12), the türbe of the Şehzade Mehmet, and a few other early buildings. The W facade of the mosque itself belongs to the baroque reconstruction, except for the entrance portal. On the exterior it has the same engaged columns as the gate to the courtyard, and is surmounted by a stalactite canopy enclosed in a series of projecting frames that give depth and emphasis. On the sides and over the door are written in bold calligraphy the historical inscriptions, giving the names of the founder and the architect and the date of completion of the mosque. But the interior side of the portal is even more remarkable; its canopy is a finely-carved scallop shell supported on a double cornice of stalactites. Unfortunately, it is masked by a later baroque balcony built in front of it.

*The Mosque Interior.* The interior is of little interest. It is a copy of the type in which the central dome is flanked by four semidomes on the axes, invented by Sinan for the Şehzade and used again for the Blue Mosque and Yeni Cami. Here the exterior lines are still reasonably classical and pleasing, but the interior is at once weak and heavy. The painted decoration is fussy in detail and dull in colour; the lower part of the walls is sheathed in common white tiles of such inferior make that they have become discoloured with damp. In the right-hand corner is a curious fountain for drinking-water, the only one of its kind in the city, with an old-fashioned bronze pump and silver drinking-mugs; the water is cool and delicious. The mihrab, which is from the original building, resembles in style the entrance portal, though the gilt-framed panels in the lower part are perhaps a baroque addition. Certainly baroque but equally handsome is the mimber, an elaborate structure of polychrome marble. The sultan's loge is also baroque; its antechambers are now being used to house a school for imams. The window shutters in these rooms are fine examples of baroque intarsia work, while the small dome over the loge itself is gaily painted with *trompe l'oeil* windows.

*The Türbes.* In the graveyard behind the mosque stand the türbes of Mehmet II and his wife Gülbahar, the mother of Beyazit II. Both of these türbes were completely reconstructed after the earthquake, though on the old foundations. The Conqueror's türbe is very baroque and its interior extremely sumptuous in the Empire style. The türbe of Gülbahar is simple and classical and must resemble the original quite closely. The little library in the SW corner of the graveyard beside the mosque was built by Mahmut I and dates from 1742.

*The Medreses.* To N and S of the precinct are the eight great medreses; those to the N were known as the Karadeniz Medreseleri, the Medreses of the Black Sea, while those to the S were called the Akdeniz Medreseleri, the Medreses of the White Sea, i.e., the Mediterranean. These buildings, which date from the Conqueror's original construction, are severely symmetrical and are almost identical in plan. Each contains 19 cells for students and a dershane. The entrance to the dershanes is from the side, and beside each entrance is a tiny garden planted with trees; an effect as rare as it is pretty. Behind each medrese there was originally an annex about half as large; these have totally disappeared. Altogether there must have been about 255 hücres, or students' rooms, each housing perhaps four youths. Thus the establishment must have provided for about a thousand students in all, making it a university on a big scale. These fine buildings have recently been restored and are now again being used as residences by university students.

*The Hospice.* The **taphane, or hospice, stands outside the SE corner of the mosque precincts. It is approached by a gateway just beside that corner of the mosque graveyard; this is called Çorba Kapísí, the

Soup Gate, because of the proximity of the imaret. Çorba Kapísí is part of the Conqueror's original külliye; notice the elaborate and most unusual designs in porphyry and verd antique let into the stonework of the canopy, and also the 'panache' at the top in verd antique. After passing through this gate one comes to what is perhaps the finest building of the külliye, the tabhane, or hospice for travelling dervishes. It has a very beautiful courtyard and is in general an astonishing, indeed unique, building. The 20 domes of the courtyard are supported on 16 exceptionally beautiful columns of verd antique and Syenitic granite, doubtless from the Church of the Holy Apostles. At the E end a large square room (which has unfortunately lost its dome) originally served as the mescit-zaviye, the room where the dervish ceremonies were performed. On each side of this there are two spacious rooms opening out into two unenclosed eyvans. These are very interesting: each has two domes supported on a rectangular pillar that at first sight appears to be baroque. However, a closer examination shows the same engaged ribbed columns ending in intertwined designs and an hour-glass capital and base as those seen earlier on the entrance portals of the mosque itself. The rosettes too, and even the very baroque-looking mouldings can be paralleled in this and other buildings of the Conqueror's time. It is thought that the two open eyvans were used for meetings and prayers in summer, the two rooms adjoining the mescit zaviye for the same purpose in winter, and the two farther rooms in the corner as depositories for the guests' baggage. The two rooms at the W ends of the N and S sides do not communicate with the rest of the building in any way, but have their own entrances from the W forecourt; they were used as kitchens and bakehouses and doubtless depended on the adjacent imaret. This leaves only 10, or possibly 12, rooms for guests, for in the middle of the S side a passage leads through a small arched entryway to the area where the caravansaray and imaret stood; an adjacent staircase leads to a room with a cradle-vault above. Opposite on the N side a similar area was occupied by the lavatories; but here the dome and outer wall have fallen, and a very poor repair makes it difficult to see what was the original arrangement.

*The Caravansaray.* The great vacant lot to the S, now used as a playing-field by the children of the (modern) Fatih school, was the site of the caravansaray (to the E) and the imaret (to the W). Two fragments of the latter—small domed rooms, but ruinous now—remain in the SW corner. Evliya Çelebi writes that it had 70 domes; this would imply that it was a third again as big as the tabhane, which had 46 domes, but one can quite believe it. As it had to supply two meals a day to the thousand students of the medreses, along with the vast corps of clergy and professors of the foundation, the patients and staff of the hospital, the guests at the tabhane and the caravansaray, as well as the poor of the district, it is clear that the imaret must have been enormous. The caravansaray has wholly disappeared, but it too must have been very big, even if one discounts Evliya Çelebi's statement that it could hold 3000 horses and mules. This whole area to the S should be excavated; it is clear that the ground has risen considerably, presumably with the rubble of fallen buildings, and it should be possible to determine at least the extent and plan of the imaret and caravansaray. Another building of the külliye that has disappeared is the dar-üs şifa, or hospital. This was placed symmetrically with the tabhane on the N side of the graveyard; a street-name still recalls its site and bits of its wall may be seen built into the modern houses there.

*The Türbe of Nakşidil.* Opposite the tabhane is the türbe complex built in 1817–18 for the Valide Sultan Nakşidil, wife of Abdül Hamit I and mother of Mahmut II. Nakşidil's türbe is a very gay one in its baroque-Empire way, forming a pleasant contrast with the austerity of the classical structures of the Conqueror's külliye. At the corner stands the enormous türbe, which has 14 sides; of its two rows of windows the upper ones are oval, a unique and pretty feature. The 14 faces are divided from one another by very slender columns which bear, on top of their capitals at the first cornice level, tall, flame-like acanthus leaves carved almost in the round, giving a fine bravura effect. Nakşidil's türbe is altogether a very original and entertaining building.

The wall stretching along the street opposite the tabhane contains a gate and a grand sebil in the same flamboyant style as the türbe. The gate leads into an attractive courtyard from which one enters Nakşidil's türbe, whose interior decoration is rather elegant and restrained. Diagonally opposite at the far end of the courtyard is another türbe, round and severely plain. In this türbe are interred the Valide Sultan Gülüstü, wife of Abdül Mecit I and mother of Mehmet VI Vahdettin, the last Sultan of the Ottoman Empire, along with other members of the imperial family. Outside, the wall along the street running N ends in a building at the next corner which was once a sibyan mektebi and is now used as a sewing-school. Both the wall and the mektep building, constructed of brick and stone, seem to belong to an older tradition than Nakşidil's türbe, but the recurrence here and there of the flame-like acanthus motif shows that they are part of the same complex.

The street that runs along the E side of the mosque complex is called Aslanhane Sk, the Street of the Lion House, which suggests that the Conqueror may have had a menagerie near his külliye. After crossing the avenue, which is here called Fevzi Paşa Cd, the street takes on the more conventional name of Feyzullah Efendi Sk, after the library at the corner to the left. At the second intersection after the avenue turn right onto Sarígüzel Cd and continue for two blocks to come on the left to an ancient mosque, *Iskender Paşa Camii*. The mosque is dated by an inscription to 1505, but the identity of the founder is uncertain; he is thought to have been a vezir of Beyazit II who was governor of Bosnia. It is a simple dignified building with a blind dome on pendentives resting on the walls; the three small domes of the porch are supported on ancient columns with rather worn Byzantine capitals. The şerefe of the minaret has an elaborately stalactited corbel, but the curious decoration on top of the minaret probably belongs to an 18C restoration.

After leaving the mosque, continue along Sarígüzel Cd for another block and then turn left into Halícílar Cd. After a walk of nearly half a km one comes to the wide Vatan Cd, where at the corner to the left there stands a large and handsome Byzantine church known locally as **Fenari Isa Camii** (Pl 9,3), the Mosque of the Lamp of Jesus. This is the *monastery church of Constantine Lips, another of the surviving Byzantine sanctuaries in the city.

HISTORY. This complicated building, the various parts of which were construc-ted at different dates, consists of two churches, along with a double narthex and a side chapel; its original structure was altered in Ottoman times, when it was converted into a mosque. The first church on the site, the one to the N, was built in 907 by Constantine Lips, a high official in the reigns of Leo VI and Constantine VII Porphyrogenitus. This sanctuary was dedicated to the Theotokos Panachr-antos, the Immaculate Mother of God, and served the monastery that Const-antine Lips founded at the same time. The establishment apparently fell into disuse during the Latin Occupation of 1204–61, for soon after the recapture of the city by the Byzantines the monastery was refounded by the Empress Theodora, wife of Michael VIII Palaeologus. At the same time the Empress also added another church to the S, an outer narthex for both churches, and a chapel to the S of her new church dedicated to St. John the Baptist. The chapel of St. John was designed as a funerary chapel, and several members of the imperial Palaeologus family were interred there during the course of the next two centuries, beginning with the Empress Theodora herself in 1304. Other members of the family buried there include Theodora's sons, Prince Constantine and the Emperor Andronicus II (1282–1328), as well as the Princess Irene of Brunswick, first wife of Andronicus III (1328–41), and the Princess Anna, first wife of John VIII (1428–48). Neither Irene nor Anna lived to become Empress of Byzantium, for they died before their husbands were raised to the throne. Chronicles of the time tell how Anna was buried in the church in the dead of night, in a city terrified by the Black Death.

The church was converted into a mosque in 1496, and at that time the monastery was given over to a community of dervishes. The first head of this dervish tekke was called Isa, which is the Moslem name for Jesus, and the mosque thereafter was known as Fenari Isa Camii. The mosque was abandoned at the beginning of the present century after having been badly damaged in a fire, which utterly destroyed the monastery. The building has since been completely restored by the Byzantine Institute of America, and its structure is now in excellent condition. After the restoration it was rededicated as a mosque, and in recent years it has also been used to house a Kuran school.

INTERIOR. The original N church constructed by Constantine Lips was of the four-column type (the columns were replaced by arches in the Ottoman period), but quite unusually it had five apses, the extra ones to N and S projecting beyond the rest of the building. The northern apse is now demolished, while the southern one is incorporated into the S church. Another unusual, perhaps unique, feature is that there are four little chapels on the roof, grouped around the main dome. The S church erected by the Empress Theodora was of the ambulatory type; that is, its nave was divided from the aisles by a triple arcade to N, W, and S, with each arcade supported by two columns. (All this was removed in Ottoman times, but the bases of some of the columns still remain and one can see the narrow arches of the arcades above, embedded in the Turkish masonry.) Of its three apses, the northern one was the southern supernumerary apse of the older church. Thus there were in all seven apses, six of which remain and make the eastern facade of the building exceedingly attractive. On the interior walls a certain amount of good sculptured decoration survives in cornices and window frames, especially in the N church.

Vatan Cd runs along the ancient course of the Lycus River through a district called Yeni Bahçe, the New Garden. Until recently this was mostly garden land, and a certain number of vegetable gardens still survive, but now the district is rapidly being covered with apartment buildings.

About 100m W of Constantine Lips, on the other side of Vatan Cd, there is a large and handsome medrese, founded in 1562–63 by Süleyman and dedicated to the memory of his father, Selim I; the architect was Sinan. The 20 cells of the students occupy three sides of the courtyard; on the fourth side stands the large and handsome lecture-hall, which was at some point turned into a mosque. The original entrance, through a small domed porch, is behind the dershane and at an odd angle to it; the wall that encloses this whole side is irregular in a way that is hard to account for. Nevertheless, the building is very attractive, and once inside one does not notice its curious dissymmetry.

Just W of this medrese across a side street there is a small külliye consisting of a mektep and a türbe in a walled garden. The entrance to the gaily planted garden is through a gate in the N wall; on the left is

202 TOMB OF HÜSREV PAŞA

the octagonal türbe, that of Şah Huban Kadín, a daughter of Selim I,
who died in 1572. While there is nothing remarkable about the türbe
the mektep is a grand one. It is double: that is, it consists of two
spacious square rooms, each covered by a dome and containing an
elegant ocak, or fireplace. The wooden roof and column of the porch
are modern, part of a recent restoration. Both the mektep and the
türbe are works of Sinan, and they are dated to the year of Şah
Huban's death. The mektep now serves as an out-patient clinic for
mental illnesses.

Recrossing Vatan Cd, take the street just opposite, Akdeniz Cd, and
walk uphill as far as the fourth turning on the left, Hüsrev Paşa Sk.
One block down this street, at the far corner to the left, is a handsome
and elaborate türbe. This is the *tomb of Hüsrev Paşa* (Pl 9,1), built by
Sinan and dated by an inscription to 1545–46.

HISTORY. Hüsrev Paşa was a grandson of Beyazit II and had been one of the
leading generals in the great Ottoman victory of Mohacz in 1526, when the fate
of Hungary was decided in less than two hours. After that victory Hüsrev Paşa
governed Bosnia for a decade with great pomp and luxury, but also with severe
justice. Later he became governor of Syria, and in 1536–37 he commissioned
Sinan to build a mosque for him in Aleppo; this is the earliest dated building by
the great architect and it is still in existence. While governor of Rumelia in 1544
Hüsrev Paşa fell into disgrace through his complicity in a plot against the Grand
Vezir Süleyman Paşa. Despairing because of his fall from power, he took his own
life soon afterwards by literally starving himself to death, one of the very rare
incidents of suicide among the Ottomans.

EXTERIOR. The türbe of Hüsrev Paşa is octagonal in form. The eight
faces are separated from one another by slender columns that run up
to the first cornice, which is elaborately carved with stalactites; the
dome is set back a short distance and has another cornice of its own,
also carved. At the moment the türbe is made more picturesque by the
bushes that grow out of the cornice, but they are destroying the fabric
of the structure, and a careful restoration is in order.

Two blocks N on the side street that passes the türbe there is on the
left *Bali Paşa Camii*, a fine old mosque with a ruined porch. An
inscription over the portal records that the mosque was built in 1504
by Huma Hatun, daughter of Beyazit II, in memory of her late
husband, Bali Paşa, who had died in 1495. Since this mosque appears
in the 'Tezkere', the listing of Sinan's works, it appears that Sinan
must have built Bali Paşa Camii some time later, though whether on
its old plan or a new one it is impossible to say. The plan of the mosque
is simple and to a certain extent resembles that of Iskender Paşa
Camii, visited earlier on this Rte. The chief difference between these
two mosques is that in Bali Paşa Camii the dome arches to N, W, and S
are very deep, almost barrel vaults; thus room is left, on the N and S,
for shallow bays with galleries above. The mosque was severely
damaged in the earthquake of 1894 and again in the fire of 1917; it
was partially restored in 1935 and further work has been done on it in
recent years. But the five domes of the porch have never been rebuilt
and this gives the facade a somewhat naked look.

After leaving the mosque return to Hüsrev Paşa Sk and continue on
in the same direction; then take the second turning on the left, onto
Akşemsettin Cd, and walk one block downhill. There, at the corner to
the left is a very handsome minaret standing by itself in the middle of
a vacant lot. This is all that now remains of *Mimar Sinan Camii*, a little
mosque that Sinan himself endowed and built in 1573. The mosque
itself was rather irregular, consisting of two rectangular rooms with a

wooden roof; it was in ruins at the beginning of the present century and has now completely disappeared. The minaret is of a very rare type, perhaps the only one of its kind that Sinan ever built. It.is octagonal and without a şerefe; instead, at the top, a decorated window in each of the eight faces allowed the müezzin to give the call to prayer. Although a very minor antiquity indeed, this isolated minaret stands as a monument to the genius of the great Sinan.

Now walk back uphill along Akşemsettin Cd for about 250m to a square dominated to the left by a fine classical mosque. This is *Mesih Paşa Camii*, built by an unknown architect in 1585. (The mosque is popularly attributed to Sinan, but without any evidence.) The founder was the eunuch Mesih Mehmet Paşa, infamous for his cruelty as Governor of Egypt, who became Grand Vezir for a short time at the age of 90 in the reign of Murat III. The courtyard of the mosque is attractive but rather sombre. It consists of the usual domed porticoes under which, rather unusually, are the ablution fountains; this is because the usual place of the şadírvan in the centre of the courtyard has been taken up by the picturesque open türbe of the founder. The mosque is preceded by a double porch, but the wooden roof of the second porch has disappeared, leaving nothing for the arcades to support; the inner porch has the usual five bays. In plan the building is an octagon inscribed in a square with semidomes as squinches in the diagonals; to N and S are galleries. But the odd feature is that whereas in most mosques of this form aisles are under the galleries here they are turned into porches. That is, where one would expect an arcade of columns, one finds a wall with windows opening onto an exterior gallery which, in turn, opens to the outside by enormous arches, now glazed in. The mihrab and mimber are very fine works in marble, as are the grilles above the windows. Tiles of the best period complete the decoration of this interesting building.

The S side of the mosque opens onto a road that winds uphill, soon leading one to a mosque of a very different style indeed. This is *Hirka-i Şerif Camii*, the Mosque of the Holy Mantle, built in 1851 by Sultan Abdül Mecit I to house the second of the two mantles of the Prophet that are among Mohammed's chief relics in Istanbul. (The other is in its own treasury in Topkapí Sarayí; see above, Rte 3.) The mosque is in the purest Empire style and just misses being a great success, as do most buildings in that style; nevertheless it is very entertaining. A monumental gateway leads to a spacious paved courtyard, at the corners of which are the two tall minarets; these are extremely slender and have balconies in the form of Corinthian capitals. The facade is a little forbidding, more like a palace than a mosque, but the interior is very gay; it is in the form of an octagon with an outside gallery. The walls and dome, of a greenish brown, are covered with plaster mouldings of garlands and vines in buff, done with a certain bravura but also with elegance. The mihrab, mimber, and Kuran kürsü, elaborately carved, are of a deep purple conglomerate marble flecked with grey, green, blue, black and yellow, all highly polished. Part of the decoration consists of elegant inscriptions by the famous calligrapher, Mustafa Izzet Efendi; others are by Sultan Abdül Mecit I, who was himself an able calligrapher. This is a building which should not be missed by anyone who delights in the follies and oddities of architecture as long as they have a certain verve and charm.

Hirka-i Şerif Camii is built on a high terrace, partly artificial, to the S of which a long staircase leads to a lower monumental gateway opening onto the street below, Keçeciler Cd. About 500m to the right down this street, which runs through a pleasantly rural area, one finds on the left a small mosque that is of little interest save that its architect was Sinan. According to an inscription, the mosque was founded in 1560 by one Hürrem Çavuş, who was a messenger in Topkapí Sarayí. The mosque is of the rectangular type with wooden roof and porch. Other inscriptions record restorations to the mosque in 1844 and 1901. Perhaps because of these, the building has lost any charm that it might once have possessed.

# 12 The Fifth and Sixth Hills

This Rte leads from the Mosque of the Conqueror on a circuit around the Fifth and Sixth Hills of the old city. The itinerary begins at the W side of the outer courtyard of the mosque, where Daruşşafaka Cd leads off to the N, passing through the lively market quarter of Çarşamba.

Çarşamba, which in Turkish means Wednesday, is named after the picturesque street market that throngs its streets on that day each week, as it has for centuries past. This is a travelling market that sets up its stalls and barrows in various parts of the city on different days; thus there are neighbourhoods in Istanbul named after all the days of the week except Saturday and Sunday, the Moslem and Christian days of rest.

About 500m beyond Fatih Camii Daruşşafaka Cd intersects Yavuz Selim Cd; turn left here and 150m farther along turn right at the first through street. A short way along this street on the left is a mosque known as *Kumrulu Mescit*, the Little Mosque of the Turtle-Dove. The mosque takes its name from a fragment of Byzantine sculpture used in the adjoining çeşme, in which a relief represents two turtle-doves drinking from the Fountain of Life. This mosque is of interest principally because its founder and builder was Atik Sinan, the architect of the original Mosque of the Conqueror. Atik Sinan's tombstone is to be seen in the mosque garden, with an inscription recording that he was executed by the Conqueror in 1471; the mosque, therefore, is dated prior to that year.

Continuing along the same street, one soon sees on the left the beautiful *mosque of Nişanci Mehmet Paşa* (Pl 5,7), one of the finest classical mosques in the city.

HISTORY. This mosque is popularly ascribed to Sinan, but it does not appear in the best texts of the 'Tezkere', the list of his works; therefore it is probably not by him. Unfortunately, the identity of the architect is unknown. The mosque was built between 1584 and 1588 for Mehmet Paşa, who was Keeper of the Seal (in Turkish, Nişanci) in the reign of Murat III.

EXTERIOR. Even from a distance the elegance of line and the masterly arrangement of the upper structure of the mosque can be seen: the great dome surrounded by the eight little weight-turrets (the continuation of the columns that support the dome arches), the eight semidomes of two sizes, and the minaret unusually close to the dome base: an excellently proportioned distribution of curves and verticals. One enters through a very charming courtyard, where the arches are of the ogive type; under the porch of five bays an inscription with the imperial monogram of Mustafa III records a restoration in 1766, presumably after the very severe earthquake of that year.

INTERIOR. The plan of the mosque is an interesting variation of the octagon inscribed in a square. Eight partly-engaged columns support the dome arches; in the axes there are four semidomes, while in the diagonals four smaller semidomes serve as squinches instead of pendentives. The eastern semidome covers a projecting apse for the mihrab, while those to N and S also cover projections from the square. The western corners of the cross so formed are filled with small independent chambers; above on three sides there are galleries. The whole arrangement is original and masterly; and there are interesting details. In the corners of the E wall there are two charming little platforms, which can be reached by staircases built into the thickness of the wall from the recesses. In the voussoirs and balustrades of these platforms, in the window frames, and elsewhere throughout the mosque, an interesting conglomerate marble of pale violet and grey is used. For the columns that support both platforms and galleries there is another conglomerate marble of tawny brown flecked with yellow, grey, black and green. The arches of the galleries, like those of the courtyard, are of the ogive type. As a whole, the mosque is a masterpiece; it is as if the unknown architect, in the extreme old age of Sinan, had decided to play variations on themes invented by Sinan himself and to show that he could do them as well as the Master. In the little graveyard behind the mosque is the small and unpretentious türbe of Nişancí Mehmet Paşa.

Leaving the mosque and continuing in the same direction one soon comes to a small square called Üç Baş Meydaní, literally the Square of the Three Heads. The square takes its name from *Üç Baş Camii*, the tiny mosque to the right.

Evliya Çelebi writes that the mosque received this odd name 'because it was built by a barber who shaved three heads for a single copper coin, and, not-withstanding, grew so rich that he was enabled to build this mosque, which is small but particularly sanctified'. A more prosaic explanation is given in the 'Hadika', the comprehensive description of the mosques of Istanbul written in 1780; there it is recorded that the founder of this mosque, Nurettin Hamza ben Atallah, came from a village in Anatolia called Üç Baş. (But then where did the village get its name?) An inscription over the gate gives the date of foundation as 1532–33. The mosque is of no interest except for its name.

Opposite the mosque there is a ruined medrese founded in 1575 by a certain Halil Efendi; the decaying cells of the building are now used to house a boys' club. In the centre of the square there is an ancient çeşme, with a beautifully written inscription recording that it was founded in 1681 by a man called Mustafa Ağa.

Continuing on in the same direction, take the next turning on the left to come to a little mosque called *Zincirli Kuyu Camii*. This was built in about 1500 by Atik Ali Paşa, Grand Vezir of Beyazit II, whose larger and better-known mosque stands next to Constantine's Column. Zincirli Kuyu Camii is a small rectangular building of brick and stone, covered by six equal domes in two rows of three supported by two massive rectangular pillars; its original porch of three bays has disappeared, and the present porch is a poor reconstruction. The mosque is interesting as being a tiny example of the so-called Ulu Cami type borrowed from Selcuk architecture, which was fairly common during the period when the Ottoman capital was still in Bursa. The type consists of a square or rectangular space covered by a multiplicity of equal domes supported by pillars or columns; it can be very large and impressive, as in the Ulu Cami of Bursa with its 20 domes. On the very small scale of Zincirli Kuyu Camii it is rather heavy and oppressive.

Opposite the mosque there is a small late baroque türbe dated by an inscription to 1825. Here is buried the famous calligrapher Hattat Rakím Efendi who designed the beautiful inscriptions on the türbe and sebil of the Valide Sultan Nakşidil (see Fatih Camii, above). The interior of the türbe is decorated with photographs of his work.

Beyond the türbe on the main street there is an attractive medrese of the classical period, which has recently been restored and converted into a children's clinic. This medrese, also called *Zincirli Kuyu* (the name of the quarter), was founded by Semiz (the Fat) Ali Paşa, Grand Vezir in the reign of Süleyman the Magnificent. Ali Paşa was born of a Christian family in Dalmatia, and after having been taken up in the devşirme he was educated in the Palace School in Topkapí Sarayí. He rose rapidly in the Ottoman hierarchy, becoming in turn Ağa of the Janissaries, governor of Rumelia, Second Vezir, and finally Grand Vezir. Since he died in office in 1564, the medrese must have been built before that time. It is a work of Sinan, but presents no special features except the two symmetrical entrances on either side of the dershane.

About 100m past the medrese along the main avenue, Fevzi Paşa Cd, is a huge open cistern now used as a football stadium. This is one of the three Roman reservoirs in the city; its attribution was long in doubt but it has been identified with great probability as the reservoir constructed in about AD 421 by Aetios, Prefect of Constantinople in the reign of Theodosius II. Huge as it is, it is yet the smallest of the three Roman cisterns that still survive in the city, measuring 224m by 85m; its original depth was probably about 152m. Like the others, it was already dry in later Byzantine times and was used as a kitchen garden, until its recent conversion into a stadium. There are a number of very ruined Byzantine churches in the region behind the Cistern of Aetios, none of them of any significance. To find them, take the street that leads off Fevzi Paşa Cd to the right just before the cistern and then take the first through street to the left behind it. About 100m along on the right there is a vacant lot where one sees the many domes of a covered cistern, some of which have caved in and the others overgrown with grass and moss. In the NW corner of the lot are the remains of a Byzantine building converted into a very mean hovel; beyond and below this, across a narrow street, the even more exiguous remains of a Byzantine structure support a rather more respectable house. These are believed to be the ruins of a Byzantine monastery, which has been tentatively identified as the *Theotokos of Petra*, known to have been located in this area. Both structures were converted into mosques; the northern one was known as Odalar Camii and the southern one Kasím Ağa Mescidi; both were burned down earlier in this century.

More interesting than the vanishing remains of these buildings is the beautiful covered cistern. It has 28 columns in four rows of seven; they are of various sizes and are made of several different kinds of marble and granite; many have fine Corinthian capitals (some are stilted on overturned capitals to bring them to the right height). Unfortunately, many of the domes have fallen in and the cistern is used as a dump for the refuse of the neighbourhood.

A little farther down the valley, in the cross street called Draman, is yet another Byzantine building that has been converted into a mosque. This is called *Kefeli Camii*; it is in fairly good condition and is still in use. It is a long narrow building with two rows of windows and a wooden roof; the entrance is now in the middle of the W wall. The identification of this building is also uncertain; it may have belonged to the Monastery of the Prodromos in Petra, which is known to have been located in this area; but the building here was probably a refectory, not a church, since it has only one apse and is oriented N instead of E. It has been dated variously from the 9C to the 12C.

After leaving Kefeli Camii turn right onto Draman Cd and then take the first street to the left, which leads through a rural area to the ruined crypt of a tiny Byzantine building now a hovel. This is known as *Boğdan Saray*, the Moldavian Palace, because from the 16C to the 18C it served as a private chapel attached to the palace of the Hospodars of Moldavia, who ruled that semi-autonomous region under the Ottomans. It is thought to have been a funerary chapel dedicated to St. Nicholas, and it appears to date from the 12–13C. At the beginning of the present century it had an upper storey with a dome, but the owner of the building tore this down in order to sell the materials; what remains is a tiny barrel-vaulted room with a pretty little apse at the end.

About 200m along Draman Cd past Kefeli Camii one sees on the right a small mosque on a high terrace reached by a double staircase. This is **Draman Camii**, a minor work of Sinan.

HISTORY. Inscriptions show that the külliye was founded in 1541 by Yunus Bey, the famous interpreter (in Turkish, drağman, or dragoman) of Süleyman the Magnificent; according to Bassano da Zara, Venetian ambassador to the Sublime Porte, Yunus Bey was a Greek from Modon and 'possessed the Turkish, Greek, and Italian languages to perfection'. In collaboration with Alviso Gritti, bastard son of the Doge of Venice, he wrote in the Venetian dialect a brief but very important account of the organisation of the Ottoman government. He also seems to have served on at least two occasions as the representative of the Grand Vezir Ibrahim Paşa to the Venetian Republic.

*The Mosque.* Unfortunately, the mosque was badly restored a few years ago and has lost any interest it might have had. It was of the rectangular type, covered by a wooden roof and preceded by a wooden porch, now hideously rebuilt in concrete. Originally the mosque was the centre of a small complex consisting of a medrese and a mektep, both presumably by Sinan. The medrese has perished but the mektep remains, though in ruins; it is the fine domed building to the NE of the mosque. Although the mosque itself is disappointing, the high terrace, the mektep, and the wild garden and graveyard are attractive.

Continue in the same direction along the main avenue, whose name here changes to Fethiye Cd. About 200m past Draman Camii, just before the main avenue makes a sharp turn to the right, a short street named Fethiyekapísí Sk leads off to the left. A few steps further is a large and handsome Byzantine church standing on a terrace overlooking the Golden Horn; this is the former church of the **Theotokos Pammakaristos**, the Joyous Mother of God, known locally as **Fethiye Camii** (Pl 5,5).

ADMISSION. Fethiye Camii is open from 9:30–4:30 every day except Wed.

HISTORY. This complicated building consists of a central bay with a narthex; a small chapel, or parecclesion, on the S; and a curious perambulatory forming a side aisle on the N; with an outer narthex on the W; and two bays of an aisle on the S in front of the parecclesion. Each of these three sections was radically altered when the building was converted into a mosque. The work of the Byzantine Institute of America has at last cleared up many of the puzzles arising from the various periods of construction and transformation. It now appears that the main church was built in the 12C by an otherwise unknown John Comnenus and his wife Anna Doukaina, whose names indicate that they were related to the royal family. In form this church was of the ambulatory type, a triple arcade in the N, W, and S dividing the central domed area from the ambulatory; at the E end there were the usual three apses, and at the W a single narthex. Toward the end of the 13C the church was reconstructed by a prominent general named Michael Doukas Glabas Tarchaniotes. Then, in about 1310, a pareeclesion was added on the S side of the church, by Michael's widow, Maria Doukaina Comnena Palaeologina Blachena, as a funerary chapel for her husband. This chapel was of the four-column type and was preceded by a two-storeyed narthex covered by a tiny dome. In the second half of the 14C the N, W, and S sides were surrounded by a perambulatory, which ran into and partly obliterated the S chapel.

The church remained in the hands of the Greeks for some time after the Conquest; in fact, in 1456 it was made the site of the Greek Orthodox Patriarchate after the Patriarch Gennadius abandoned the Church of the Holy Apostles. It was in the pareeclesion of the Pammakaristos that Mehmet the Conqueror came to discuss questions in religion and politics with Gennadius. The Pammakaristos continued as the site of the Patriarchate until 1568; five years later Murat III converted it into a mosque. He then called it Fethiye Camii, the Mosque of Victory, to commemorate his conquest of Georgia and Azerbaijan.

When the building was converted into a mosque the main concern seems to have been increasing the available space. Most of the interior walls were demolished, including the arches of the ambulatory; the three apses were replaced by the present domed triangular projection; and the side chapel was made part of the mosque by removing the wall and suppressing the two N columns. As a result, the main area of the church has become a dark, planless cavern of shapeless hulks of masonry joined by low, crooked arches. After the restoration by the Byzantine Institute, this section was divided off from the side chapel and reconsecrated as a mosque, while the pareeclesion was converted into a museum to exhibit the surviving mosaics.

EXTERIOR. The exterior presents one of the best examples in the city of the fine stone and brick work of the Palaeologian renaissance. Because of the two-storeyed narthex, the chapel has a cubic form divided into three storeys of blind arcades; with a succession of wide and narrow arches, slender niches, and concave roundels.

INTERIOR. The side chapel has been most beautifully restored by the Byzantine Institute, its missing columns replaced, and its surviving mosaics uncovered and cleaned. (In the description that follows, the number in parenthesis before the name of a mosaic is keyed to the Plan.)

The mosaics in the dome were never concealed but now they once again gleam with their former brilliance. In the crown of the dome is (1) Christ Pantocrator, surrounded by twelve Prophets: (2) Moses; (3) Jeremiah; (4) Zephaniah; (5) Micah; (6) Joel; (7) Zachariah; (8) Obadiah; (9) Habakkuk; (10) Jonah; (11) Malachi; (12) Ezekiel; (13) Isaiah. In the conch of the apse is (14) Christ Hyperagathos, the All-Loving; on the left wall of the bema is (15) The Virgin; on the right wall is (16) St. John the Baptist; and in the domical vault above there are depicted the four archangels: (17) Michael; (18) Raphael; (19) Gabriel; (20) Uriel. In the conch of the side apse to the left is (34) St. James, Brother of Christ; to the left (35) St. Clement (?); to the right (36) St. Metrophanes of Constantinople. In the conch of the side aisle to the right is (22) St. Gregory the Theologian; to the left (23) St. Cyril; to the right (24) St. Athanasius. On the soffit of the arch between the NE pier and the pilaster to its E: (to the E) (25) St. Gregory the Miracle-Worker; (to the W) (26) St. Gregory of Agrigentum. On the soffit of the arch between the NE pier and the pilaster to its S: (to the N) (27) St. Antipas; (to the S) (28) St. Blasius. The only surviving scene mosaic is on the E section of the domical vault in the S aisle; this depicts (21) The Baptism of Christ. On the soffit of the arch between

# CHURCH OF THE PAMMAKARISTOS
## (Fethiye Camii)

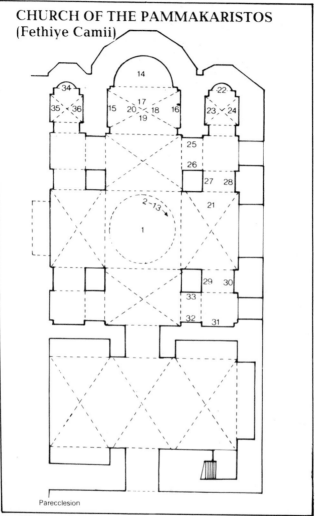

Parecclesion

the SE pier and the pilaster to its S: (to the N) (29) St. Sabas; (to the S) (30) St. John Climacus. On the soffit of the arch between the SE pier and the pilaster to its W: (to the W) (32) St. Chariton; (to the E) (33) St. Arsenius. At the W end of the S aisle: (31) St. Euthemius.

Between the marble facing on the lower part of the S wall and the mosaics on the upper part there is a long inscription in gold letters on a blue ground. This is a threnody written by the Byzantine poet Philes to commemorate the love which Maria, the founder of the funerary chapel, bore for her departed husband Michael Tarchaniotes.

The mosaics in the Pammakaristos are dated to the early 14C, and they are thus contemporary with those at Kariye Camii. Though the mosaics here are far fewer in number and less various than those at Kariye Camii, they are, nevertheless, an extremely precious addition to our knowledge of the art of the last Byzantine renaissance.

Returning to the main avenue, which now changes its name to Manyasízade Cd, follow it as it bends to the right and then take the first turning on the right. A short distance ahead is a tiny and forlorn Byzantine church in the angle between two streets; this is the former church of *St. John in Trullo*, known locally as *Ahmet Paşa Mescidi.*

HISTORY. Nothing whatever is known of the history of this church in Byzantine times. In 1456, when Gennadius transferred the Patriarchate to the Pammakaristos, he turned out the few nuns who still remained there and gave them this church instead. There were nuns in residence here until about 1586, when the church was converted into a mosque by Hirami Ahmet Paşa, from whom it takes its Turkish name.

THE CHURCH. This little building is a characteristic example of the four-column type of church with a narthex and three semicircular apses, evidently of the 11–12C. Until a few years ago it was ruined and dilapidated, but still showed signs of frescoes under its faded and blotched whitewash. Recently it underwent a partial and badly-botched restoration, which utterly destroyed whatever remained of the underlying frescoes. The original four columns, long since purloined, were replaced with poor columns and awkward capitals, and the restored brickwork is also wrong. The building is completely neglected and is once again falling into ruins.

Returning to the main avenue, take the first street to the right. At the end of the block to the left one sees a small mosque in its walled garden; this is **Mehmet Ağa Camii**, part of a small külliye that includes the mosque, a türbe, and a hamam.

HISTORY. Though of modest dimensions, this is a pretty mosque and interesting because it is one of the relatively few that can be confidently attributed to Davut Ağa, Sinan's colleague and his successor as Chief Architect to the Sultan. Over one of the gates to the courtyard there is an inscription naming Davut Ağa as architect and giving the date 1585, at which time Sinan was still alive. The founder, Mehmet Ağa, was Chief of the Black Eunuchs in the reign of Murat III.

In plan the mosque is of the simplest type: a square room covered by a dome, with a projecting apse for the mihrab and an entrance porch with five bays. But unlike most mosques of this simple type, the dome does not rest directly on the walls but on arches supported by pillars and columns engaged in the walls; instead of pendentives there are four semidomes in the diagonals. Thus the effect is that of an inscribed octagon, as in several of Sinan's mosques, but in this case without side aisles. The effect is unusual but not unattractive. The interior is adorned with faience inscriptions and other tile panels of the best Iznik period; but the painted decoration is tasteless; fortunately it is growing dim with damp. Mehmet Ağa's türbe is in the garden to the left; it is a rather large square building of little interest.

Just to the S outside the precincts stands a handsome double bath; this is part of Mehmet Ağa's külliye and presumably was also built by Davut Ağa. In the men's bath there is a large camekan whose dome is supported on squinches in the form of conches, and a cruciform hararet with cubicles in the corners of the cross. However, the lower arm of the cross has been cut off and turned into a small soğukluk which leads through the right-hand cubicle into the hararet. In the cubicles there are very small private washrooms separated by low marble partitions, a quite unique disposition. As far as one can judge from the outside, the women's section seems to be a duplicate of the men's.

Returning once again to the main avenue, continue along in the same direction and take the next left. Halfway down the block on the right side there is a handsome old Ottoman building standing in an extensive and very pretty walled garden. This is the *library of Murat Molla, founded in 1775 by a distinguished judge and scholar. The library is a large square building of brick and stone built on Byzantine substructures, fragments of which may be seen in the garden. The central area of the main reading-room is covered by a dome supported by four columns with re-used Byzantine capitals; the corners of the room also have domes with barrel-vaults over them. It is a very typical and very attractive example of an 18C Ottoman library, to be compared with those of Ragip Paşa and Atif Efendi, seen on previous tours; like these, it is constantly in use.

Returning to Manyasızade Cd, at the next corner on the left is a mosque known as *Ismail Efendi Camii*. This is a quaint and entertaining example of a building in a transitional style between the classical and baroque, founded in 1724 by the Şeyh-ül Islam Ismail Efendi. The vaulted substructure contains shops, with the mosque standing on a terrace above them; according to the Hadika, this was done in order to have the structure resemble the sacred Kaaba at Mecca. Above the main entrance to the courtyard there is a very characteristic sibyan mektebi of one room. To the right a long double staircase leads up to the mosque: the porch has been tastelessly reconstructed in detail but the general effect is pleasing except for the glazed-in portico. On the interior there is a very pretty—perhaps unique—triple arcade in two storeys of superposed columns repeated on the S, W, and N sides and supporting galleries, giving the dome an unusually high appearance. At the back of the courtyard there is a small dar-ül hadis, or school of tradition. It has been greatly altered and walled-in, so that it has little resemblance to the original structure. Nevertheless, it is once again being used for something like its original purpose, for it now houses a Kuran kürsü, a school for reading the Kuran. All-in-all this little külliye is quite charming, with its warm polychrome of brick and stone masonry; it was, on the whole, fairly well restored from near ruin in 1952.

Returning once again to Manyasızade Cd, walk one block and turn left onto Yavuz Selim Cd. There one is confronted with an extraordinary sight, the great mosque of Sultan Selim I standing in its walled courtyard, and directly in front of it a vast sunken area filled with houses, trees and gardens, a veritable subterranean village (Pl 5,6). The Turks call this place **Çukur Bostan**, the Sunken Garden. It has been identified as the *Cistern of Aspar, constructed by a Gothic general put to death in 471 by the Emperor Leo I. This is the largest of the three Roman reservoirs in the city; it is square, 152m on a side, and was originally 10m deep. Until recently one could still see its original construction in courses of stone and brick, with shallow arches on its interior surface. All this is difficult to detect today because of the houses and trees that conceal the walls. It is one of the most picturesque spots in the city, a little farm village whose trees and house-tops barely reach to the level of the surrounding streets. One of the residents of Çukur Bostan, whose house and garden are near the NE corner of the cistern, raises peacocks for sale, which adds further colour to this romantic scene.

The cistern is an appropriately grand foreground for the imperial
**\*\*mosque of Selim I**, which stands on a high terrace overlooking the
Golden Horn. This is one of the most beautiful buildings in Istanbul,
and its dramatic position on top of the Fifth Hill makes it a familiar
landmark on the skyline of the old city.

HISTORY. Sultan Selim I Camii is the second oldest imperial mosque in the city,
exceeded in age only by the Beyazidiye. The mosque was finished in 1522 under
Süleyman the Magnificent, but it may have been begun two or three years
earlier by Selim himself, as the Arabic inscription over the entrance portal would
seem to imply. Although the mosque is very often ascribed to Sinan, even by
otherwise reliable authorities, it is certainly not so: it is too early, and is not listed
in the 'Tezkere.' Unfortunately, the identity of the actual architect has not been
established.

EXTERIOR. The mosque, with its great shallow dome and cluster of little
domes on either side, is impressive and worthy of the site. The
courtyard is one of the most charming and vivid in the city, with its
columns of various marbles and granites, the polychrome voussoirs of
the arches, the very beautiful tiles of the earliest Iznik period in the
lunettes above the windows—turquoise, deep blue, and yellow—and
the pretty şadírvan surrounded by tapering cypress trees.

INTERIOR. The plan of the mosque is quite simple: a square room, 24·5m
on a side, covered by a shallow dome 32·5m in height under the
crown, with the cornice resting on the outer walls through smooth
pendentives. The dome, like that of Haghia Sophia, but unlike that of
most Ottoman mosques, is significantly less than a hemisphere. This
gives a very spacious and grand effect, recalling to a certain extent the
beautiful shallow dome of the Roman Pantheon. The room itself is vast
and empty, but saved from dullness by its perfect proportions and by
the exquisite colour of the Iznik tiles in the lunettes of the windows
and the variegated Turkish carpets on the floor. The mosque
furniture, though sparse, is quite fine, particularly the mihrab,
mimber, and sultan's loge. The border of the ceiling under the loge is
a quite exceptionally beautiful example of the painted and gilded
woodwork of the early 16C; notice the deep, rich colours and the
varieties of floral and leaf motifs in the five separate borders, like an
Oriental rug, only here picked out in gold. To N and S of the great
central room of the mosque are annexes consisting of a domed
cruciform passage giving access to four small domed rooms. These, as
in other early mosques elsewhere in the city, served as hospices for
travelling dervishes.

*The türbes.* In the garden behind the mosque is the grand türbe of
Selim I, externally octagonal. In the porch on either side of the door are
two beautiful panels of tilework, presumably from Iznik but unique in
colour and design. The interior has unfortunately lost its original
decoration, but it is still impressive in its solitude, with the huge
catafalque of the Sultan standing alone in the centre of the tomb,
covered with a sheet of embroidered velvet and with Selim's enormous turban at its head.

Facing Selim's türbe is another in which four children of Süleyman
the Magnificent are buried. This, too, has a pretty and unique feature:
the circular drum of the dome, set back a little from the octagon of the
building itself, is adorned with a long inscription carved in the
stonework. The porch also has panels of faience, hexagonal tiles with
stylised floral motifs set separately on the stone. This türbe was built
in 1556, probably by Sinan.

Standing in the garden near Selim's türbe is that of Sultan Abdül Mecit I, built some time before his death in 1861; for a building of this late date it is simple and has good lines. Abdül Mecit chose this spot for his türbe because of his admiration for his great warrior-ancestor, who in his time was called Selim the Grim.

The mosque of Selim I was formerly surrounded by the usual buildings of a külliye, which in this case included a public kitchen, a medrese, and a primary school. Of these only the last remains, a little domed building at the SW corner of the outer courtyard.

After leaving the mosque turn left and then right at the next corner onto Yavuz Selim Cd, the street that borders the Cistern of Aspar to the S. At the corner of this street and the first turning to the left, Ali Naki Sk, there is a little building with barred windows. If one peers through the windows it will be found that this is a superb **Roman basement**, with a colonnade of marble columns consisting of four rows of seven monoliths topped with Corinthian capitals and imposts. The date and identity of this structure are uncertain, although there is some reason to believe that it was built by the Empress Pulcheria, wife of the Emperor Marcian (450–57).

Now continue along Yavuz Selim Cd as far as Daruşşafaka Cd, which leads back to the outer courtyard of the mosque of the Conqueror.

# 13 Kariye Camii

APPROACHES. From the Mosque of the Conqueror: Take Fevzi Paşa Cd out almost as far as the Edirne Gate. Turn right there onto Hoca Çakır Cd, the street that runs just inside the Theodosian walls, and then take the third right onto Neşter Sk, which leads directly to Kariye Camii.

ADMISSION. Kariye Camii is open 9:00–5:30 every day except Tues.

Note: the present description of Kariye Camii is based almost entirely on the great publication of this work by *Paul A. Underwood*, in particular the following: Paul A. Underwood, *The Kariye Djami*, Vol. 1: *Historical Introduction and Description of the Mosaics and Frescoes*; Vol. 3: *The Frescoes/Plates 335–553*, Bollingen Series 70. Copyright 1966 by Princeton University Press. Excerpts, pp. 19–29, 43,adapted by permission of Princeton University Press.Figures 1–12 reprinted by permission of Princeton University Press.

**\*\*Kariye Camii** (Pl 5,7), the former church of St. Saviour in Chora, is, after Haghia Sophia, the most interesting Byzantine church in the city. This is not due to the building itself, pretty as it is, but because of the superb mosaics and frescoes that it contains, a magnificent heritage of Byzantine art that has no equal in the world.

HISTORY. The name of the church 'in Chora' means 'in the country', because the original church and monastery on this site were outside the walls of Constantine. Later, when it was included within the Theodosian walls the name remained (compare St. Martin in the Fields, London) but was given a symbolic sense: Christ as the 'country' or 'land' of the Living, and the Blessed Virgin as the 'dwelling-place' of the Uncontainable, as they are referred to in inscriptions on mosaics in the church.

No trace remains of the original ancient church, nor is anything certain known about its origin. The present building in its first form dates only from the late 11C. This church was founded by Maria Doukaina, mother-in-law of Alexius I Comnenus, between the years 1077 and 1081; it was probably of the four-column type so popular at that time. However, this church did not last long in its original form; the foundations at the E end appear to have slipped, causing the apses to fall in, and so the opportunity was taken to remodel the building. At the E the present wide central apse with its deep barrel-vault was erected; the walls of the nave were retained, but the piers were added in the corners as supports for the arches of a much larger dome. A narrow side-passage was added to the S, traces of which remain in the passages and gallery between the nave and the present parecclesion, which dates from a still later reconstruction. This elaborate remodelling was apparently carried out early in the 12C by Maria Doukaina's grandson, the Sebastocrator Isaac Comnenus, third son of Alexius I Comnenus.

A third period of building activity some two centuries later created the present church. At this time the nave area was left essentially unchanged except for redecoration. But the inner narthex was rebuilt, the outer narthex and the parecclesion were added, the small side apses reconstructed and the northern passage with its gallery was built in its present form. In addition to all these structural alterations, the church was completely redecorated, and the interior was adorned with the superb marble revetment, mosaics and frescoes that one sees today. All of this rebuilding and decoration was carried out in the period 1315–21.

The man responsible for all of this was Theodore Metochites, who served as both Prime Minister and First Lord of the Treasury during the reign of Andronicus II Palaeologus. Metochites was one of the greatest men of the age: a diplomat and high government official, theologian, philosopher, astronomer, poet and patron of the arts, a leader in the artistic and intellectual renaissance of the late Byzantine era. The peak of his career came in 1321, when he was appointed as

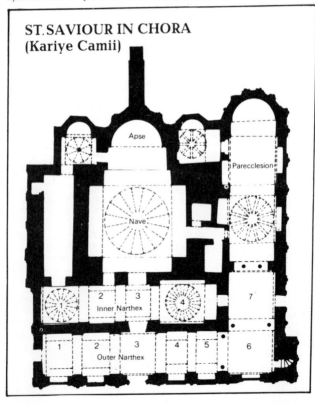

Grand Logothete, the highest-ranking official in the Byzantine Empire, an honour which was accorded him just weeks after he presided at the opening of the newly restored and redecorated church of St. Saviour in Chora. But his career ended just seven years later, when Andronicus III usurped the throne; Metochites was stripped of his power and possessions and sent into exile, along with most other officials of the old regime. He was allowed to return to the capital in 1330, on condition that he retire as a monk in the monastery of the Chora, where he died on 13 March 1332. Toward the end of his life Metochites wrote of his hope that the church of St. Saviour in Chora would secure for him 'a glorious memory among posterity till the end of the world'.

At the time of the last siege the Chora's proximity to the Theodosian walls placed it virtually in the front line. At that time the Chora was used to house the famous icon of the Virgin Hodegetria, the Guide, or Teacher. This icon, which according to tradition was painted by St. Luke, was the legendary protectress of the city, and during times of siege it was carried in procession along the Theodosian walls. When the Turks broke through the walls on the morning of 29 May 1453 the Chora was pillaged and the icon of the Hodegetria disappeared, never to be seen again.

Early in the 16C the Chora was converted into a mosque by the eunuch Atik Ali Paşa, Grand Vezir in the reign of Beyazit II. The mosaics and frescoes were never wholly obliterated, though in the course of time most were obscured by plaster, paint and dirt, and many were shaken down by earthquakes. The church and its extraordinary works of art were unknown to the scholarly world until 1860, when the Greek architect Pelopidas Kouppas brought it to the attention of Byzantinists in the West. In 1948 the Byzantine Institute of America, under the direction of Paul A. Underwood, began a project to uncover the surviving mosaics and frescoes and to restore them and the fabric of the church to their original conditon. After a series of eleven annual campaigns the project was carried through to completion in 1958, and today the church of St. Saviour in Chora stands as one of the greatest monuments of Byzantine art in existence.

EXTERIOR. The church is preceded by an exonarthex and a narthex, with the parecclesion to the right and the two-storeyed northern passageway to the left. The archways in the bays of the exonarthex, where the main entrance is located, were walled up in Ottoman times, when the minaret was erected at the SW corner of the building. The central area of the church is covered on a dome carried on a high drum. There are two smaller domes carried on lower drums above the first and fourth (numbering from left to right) bays of the narthex, as well as one above the westernmost bay of the parecclesion, with still smaller domes above the prothesis and diaconicon, the apsidal chambers that flank the main apse to N and S, respectively. (These latter domes are visible only from the rear of the church, where one can also see the large buttress supporting the apse and the earlier substructures of the building.)

*The Narthexes.* The exonarthex and narthex were entirely new constructions of Metochites. In the vertical walls and lunettes the masonry consists of bands of four courses of brickwork alternating with four courses of roughly dressed stone. The masonry in the arches and vaults is entirely of brick. The walls of both narthexes were faced with decorative slabs of Proconnesian marble and verd antique, but most of this revetment was stripped from the exonarthex in Ottoman times. Above the cornice in both narthexes all surfaces were covered with mosaics, including the arches, vaults and lunettes. The floor of the inner narthex, like that of the nave, is paved in marble, but that of the exonarthex also vanished in Ottoman times and has been replaced by a modern pavement.

The outer narthex extends across the entire width of the church in six bays, with a seventh bay extending at right angles to the E, so as to go around the S end of the inner narthex and open into the W end of the parecclesion. The third bay in the exonarthex, through which one passes into the narthex and then the nave, is square in plan and covered with a domical vault, as are the sixth and seventh bays, the two largest. The two pairs of bays on either side of the entryway are oblong in shape; thus to cover them with domical vaults it was necessary to reduce them to squares by constructing arches against the E and W walls, an expedient that was also necessary in the second and third bays of the inner narthex. In order to provide illumination for the inner narthex, the two end bays, the first and fourth, were covered by domes carried on high drums, the sides of which were pierced by circlets of windows. This was not necessary in the exonarthex, for that was illuminated by semicircular windows at the top of the arches of the bays to the W (these originally had marble balustrades below), while the seventh bay at the end of the parecclesion had a triple-arched window in its S wall. At some later time, slightly pointed reinforcing arches of roughly dressed stone were added within the original transverse arches of the sixth bay; these rest on squat granite shafts without bases and detract somewhat from the general appearance of the exonarthex.

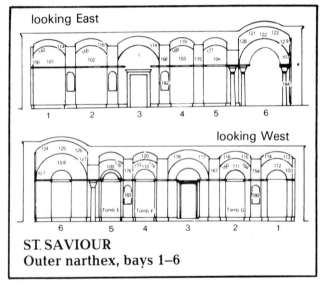

looking East

looking West

ST. SAVIOUR
Outer narthex, bays 1–6

*The Nave.* In Theodore Metochites's own description of the Chora, he states that little if any reconstruction was required in the nave. However, during the recent restoration it was discovered that Metochites had in fact rebuilt the dome and its supporting drum, along with parts of the pendentives and the crown of the W arch. The drum is supported on four huge pilasters that stand at the corners of the nave; four great arches spring from these and pendentives make the transition from them to the cornice. The present dome is Turkish, made of wood and covered with plaster, but the drum is from the reconstruction of 1315–21. The drum has 16 flutes, each pierced by a window. There are also great triple-arched windows in the apse and in the three tympanum walls, though those to the N have been blocked because of the intrusion of the upper floor of the N annexe. Nothing now survives of the liturgical furnishings of the bema; i.e., the altar, ciborium, and the iconostasis. However, excavations in the apse revealed the emplacement for the altar and the foundations for the columns of the ciborium. The excavations also unearthed, sunk beneath the altar, a large marble box filled with debris from the period when the church was converted into a mosque. Among the debris quantities of stained glass were found, similar to that discovered in the Pantocrator. This provides further evidence that stained glass was used in Byzantium prior to its development in Europe. Of the mosque furnishings of Kariye Camii, all that remains is the mihrab, which is tilted somewhat with respect to the axis of the church.

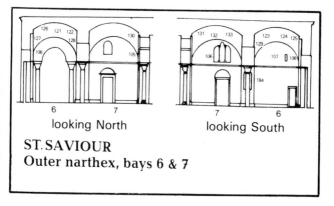

looking North    looking South

### ST. SAVIOUR
### Outer narthex, bays 6 & 7

As mentioned earlier, the apse was flanked to N and S, respectively, by two domed apsidal chambers that served as the prothesis and the diaconicon. In Byzantine churches the prothesis, which was generally, as here, to the left of the bema, was used for the preparation and storage of the species of the Eucharist, while the diaconicon served as the sacristy. In the 12C church of the Chora both of these chambers were connected to the apse by short passageways. The prothesis is still connected in this way but in the 14C restorations a passage was opened from it into the bema of the parecclesion. From the time of this alteration the prothesis apparently served as the sacristy for the main church and the diaconicon was used for the same purpose in the side chapel. There is also a passageway in the S wall of the nave leading to the W bay of the parecclesion. In the walls of this passageway doors open on either side into small enclosures which were apparently used as oratories.

*The Parecclesion.* The parecclesion was also a construction of Metochites, designed to serve as a funerary chapel. It lies parallel to the S side of the nave; the principal entryway is at its W end, where it is separated from the seventh bay of the exonarthex by two columns bearing a tympanum pierced by arches. The chapel consists of two square bays and at the E end a bema with a semicircular apse covered with a conch. The W bay is covered by a ribbed dome carried on a drum pierced by a circlet of windows; on the E and W the dome is

carried on transverse arches. The E bay is covered by a domical vault.
There are triple-arched windows in the conch of the apse and also in
the S tympanum walls of the two bays. Around the walls of the
parecclesion, at the springing level of the arches, there runs a cornice.
The N and S walls below this cornice are articulated into bays by
pilasters that receive the three transverse arches. Four recessed
niches (arcosolia) are built within the thickness of the walls, one on
each side of each of the two bays; these were designed to serve as
sepulchral monuments for Metochites and other important persons.

*The North Annexe.* Another structure built by Metochites is the
two-storeyed annexe adjoining the N side of the nave and parallel to
it. At the E end of the lower floor this annexe connected with the
prothesis, and at its W end with the first bay of the inner narthex. The
lower floor of this annexe is believed to have served as the skeuophylakion, or treasury, where all the precious objects and sacred
relics of the church were stored for safekeeping. It has been suggested that the second floor of the annexe was used to house
Theodore Metochites's celebrated collection of books and manuscripts.

**\*\*The Mosaics.** The mosaics and frescoes in the Chora are by far the
most important and extensive series of Byzantine paintings in the city
and among the most interesting in the world. They are of almost
exactly the same date as the work of Giotto in Italy, and though quite
unlike Giotto's work in detail they seem to breathe the same spirit of
life and reality, so typical of the dawn of the Renaissance.

To view the mosaics intelligently, as the artist intended them to be
seen, one must follow their iconographic order. They fall into seven
quite distinct groups: **I:** Six large dedicatory or devotional panels, in
the outer and inner narthexes; **II:** The Ancestry of Christ, in the two
domes of the inner narthex; **III:** The Cycle of the Life of the Blessed
Virgin, in the first three bays of the inner narthex; **IV:** The Cycle of the
Infancy of Christ, in the lunettes of the outer narthex; **V:** The Cycle of
Christ's Ministry, in the vaults of the outer narthex and the fourth bay
of the inner narthex; **VI:** Portraits of Saints; **VII:** The Mosaics in the
Nave.

The genealogy in the domes serves as a prelude to the narrative
cycles of the lives of the Blessed Virgin and Christ, which comprise
the major elements in the programme. These mosaic cycles are
closely linked together and form one continuous narrative, for the
cycle in the outer narthex takes up the account at the precise point in
Mary's life, as it is narrated in the apocryphal Protoevangelium of
James; where the Gospel accounts begin, they supersede the apocryphal account as the authority. However, while the mosaics depicting
the Infancy of Christ are based upon the Gospels and quote their texts
in inscriptions, at many points they illustrate events derived from the
Protoevangelium. In the account that follows the mosaics will be
described in the order in which they occur in the seven groups, with
each subject identified by a parenthetical number keyed to the plans.

### I. Dedicatory and Devotional Panels

(1) Christ Pantocrator (in lunette over door to inner narthex): The
inscription reads: 'Jesus Christ, the Land of the Living', with a play on
the name of the church and a reference to Psalm 116:9: 'I will walk
before the Lord in the Land of the Living'. (2) The Virgin Bla-

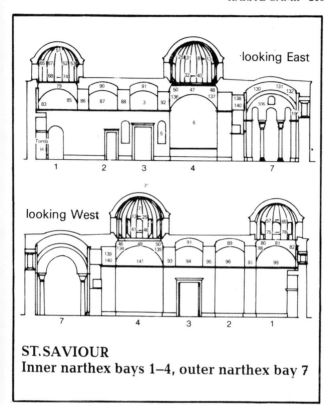

looking East

looking West

**ST. SAVIOUR**
**Inner narthex bays 1–4, outer narthex bay 7**

chernitissa and Angels (opposite the above, over entrance door to the building). The prominent position of this mosaic, facing that of Christ, indicates that the Church was dedicated to the Virgin as well as to her Son. Here she is shown praying in an attitude characteristic of the type known as the Blachernitissa, or the Theotokos of the Blachernae, who was venerated at a sacred spring near the Palace of Blachernae. The inscription reads: 'The Mother of God, the Dwelling-Place of the Uncontainable', with the same play on the name of the church and a reference to the mystery of the Incarnation. (3) The Enthroned Christ with the Donor (inner narthex in lunette over door to nave): Metochites offers a model of his church to the enthroned Christ. He is dressed in his official robes, wearing an extraordinary turban-like hat called a skiadon, literally a sunshade. Christ has the same inscription as in the outer narthex, while the figure of the Donor is thus identified: 'The Founder, Logothete of the Genikon (First Lord of the Treasury) Theodore Metochites'. (4) St. Peter and (5) St. Paul (to the left and right of the door leading into the nave): the two saints are represented here in standing, full-length poses as the two 'Princes of the Apostles'; in this context they too, as it were, assume the character of 'founders', in as much as they, more than any of the other Apostles, were most influential in bringing Christ's church into existence. (6) The Deësis (right of the door in E wall of S bay): (a Deësis is a representation of Christ with his Mother on his right and—usually, though not here—St. John the Baptist on his left). Here Christ is of the type known as *Chalkites*, from the famous icon over the main gate to the Great Palace of Byzantium. Below are the figures of two donors (very unusual in a deësis). At the Virgin's right stands 'The son of the most high Emperor Alexius Comnenus, Isaac Porphyrogenitus'; this is Isaac Comnenus, third son of Alexius I, who was probably responsible for the rebuilding of the church in the 12C. The inscription of the other figure is partly lost; what remains reads: '...of Andronicus Palaeologus, the Lady of the Mongols, Melane the nun'. This was either Maria, half-sister of Andronicus II, known as the Despoina of the Mongols, who founded the still-extant church of St. Mary of the Mongols; or else another Maria, an illegitimate daughter of Andronicus II, who also married a Mongol Khan. To add to the confusion, both of these women took the name of Melane when they became nuns, making it impossible to say which of them is represented in the mosaic.

## II. The Geneaology of Christ

These mosaics are contained in the two domes of the inner narthex. In the crown of the S dome there is a medallion of Christ Pantocrator and in the flutes two rows of his ancestors, from Adam to Jacob in the upper zone, and in the lower the 12 sons of Jacob and some others. In the crown of the N dome there is a medallion of the Blessed Virgin with the Christ-Child; below, in the upper zone 16 kings of the House of David, and in the lower 11 figures representing 'other ancestors in the genealogy'.

S dome (medallion): (7) Christ Pantocrator. S dome, upper zone; from Adam to Jacob: (8) Adam; (9) Seth; (10) Noah; (11) Cainan; (12) Maleleel; (13) Jared; (14) Lamech; (15) Sem; (16) Japeth; (17) Arphaxad; (18) Sala; (19) Heber; (20) Saruch; (21) Nachor; (22) Thara; (23) Abraham; (24) Isaac; (25) Jacob; (26) Phalec; (27) Ragau; (28) Mathusala; (29) Enoch; (30) Enos; (31) Abel. S dome, lower zone; the Sons of Jacob: (32) Reuben; (33) Simeon; (34) Levi; (35) Judah; (36) Zebulun; (37) Issachar; (38) Dan; (39) Gad; (40) Asher; (41) Naphtali; (42) Joseph; (43) Benjamin; (44) Pharez; (45) Zareh; (46) Esrom.

N dome (medallion): (51) The Theotokos, the Mother of God. N dome, upper zone; Kings of the House of David, David to Salathiel: (52) David; (53) Solomon; (54) Roboam; (55) Abia; (56) Asa; (57) Josophat; (58) Joram; (59) Ozias; (60) Joatham; (61) Achaz; (62) Ezekias; (63) Manasses; (64) Amon; (65) Josias; (66) Jechonias; (67) Salathiel. N dome, lower zone: 'Other ancestors outside the geneaology'. (68) Hananiah; (69) Azariah; (70) Mishael; (71) Daniel; (72) Joshua; (73) Moses; (74) Aaron; (75) Hur; (76) Samuel; (77) Job; (78) Melchizedek.

## III. Cycle of The Blessed Virgin

These mosaics are located in the first three bays of the inner narthex. The Cycle of the Life of the Virgin is based mainly on the Apocryphal Gospel of St. James, better known as the Protoevangelium, which dates back to at least the 2C. This gives an account of her birth and life from the rejection of the offerings of Joachim, her father, to the birth of Jesus. It was very popular in the Middle Ages and is the source of

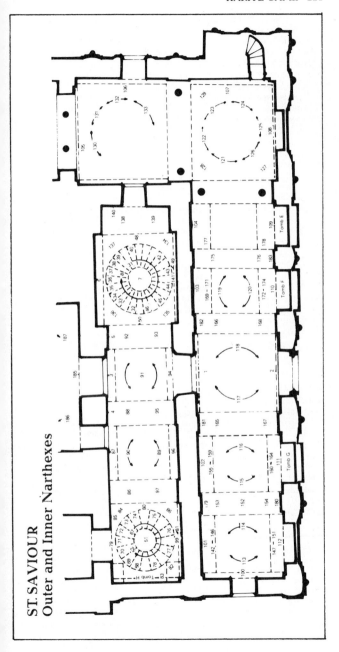

**ST. SAVIOUR**
Outer and Inner Narthexes

many cycles of pictures both in the East and the West. The most notable is Giotto's fresco cycle in the Arena Chapel at Padua, painted at a slightly earlier date and representing many of the same scenes. Here in Kariye Camii there were 20 scenes, of which 19 are either completely or partially preserved. (82) Joachim's Offerings Rejected (first bay, NW pendentive of dome): Zacharias, the High Priest before the altar, raises his hands in a gesture of refusal. (The rest of the scene in the NE pendentive is lost; it must have shown Joachim and his wife Anne bearing offerings. Their offerings were rejected because they had no children.) (83) Fragmentary Scene (in lunette of N wall): probably Joachim and Anne returning home; only a maid looking out of a doorway is preserved. (84) Joachim in the Wilderness (in SE pendentive): ashamed at the rejection of his offerings, Joachim goes into the wilderness to pray for offspring. (85) The Annunciation of St. Anne (in lunette of E wall, left half of scene lost): the right half of the scene shows the angel of the Lord announcing to Anne that her prayer for a child has been heard. (86) The Meeting of Joachim and Anne (in E soffit of arch between first and second bays): Anne informs Joachim on his return from the wilderness of the annunciation of the angel. The scene is inscribed: 'The conception of the Theotokos'. (87) The Birth of the Blessed Virgin (in E lunette of second bay). (88) The First Seven Steps of the Virgin (in E soffit of arch between second and third bays): she took her first seven steps when she was six months old. (89) The Virgin Blessed by the Priests (W side of domical vault in first bay). (90) The Virgin Caressed by her Parents (E side of domical vault in first bay). Note the two magnificent peacocks, representing incorruptibility, in the two pendentives. (91) The Presentation of the Virgin in the Temple (in domical vault of third bay): the scene is inscribed 'The Holy of Holies'. At the age of three the Virgin was presented as an attendant at the Temple, where she remained until she was about twelve. (92) The Virgin Receiving Bread from an Angel (in E soffit of arch between third and fourth bays): while the Virgin remained in the Temple she was miraculously fed by an angel. (93) The Instruction of the Virgin in the Temple (in W soffit of arch between third and fourth bays): the central figures of the scene, unfortunately, have been destroyed. (94) The Virgin Receiving the Skein of Purple Wool (in lunette above door from outer narthex): the priests decided to have the attendant maidens weave a veil for the Temple; the royal colours, purple, blue and scarlet, fell to Mary by lot. (95) Zacharias Praying before the Rods of the Suitors (in W soffit of arch between second and third bays): when the time came for the Virgin to be married, the High Priest Zacharias called all the widowers together and placed their rods on the altar, praying for a sign showing to whom she should be given. (96) The Virgin Entrusted to Joseph (in W lunette of second bay): when the rods were returned to the widowers, Joseph's rod began to sprout with green leaves and the Virgin was awarded to him. (97) Joseph taking the Virgin to his House (in W soffit of arch between first and second bays): here they are just leaving the Temple; the youth is one of Joseph's sons by his former wife. (98) The Annunciation to the Virgin at the Well (in SW pendentive of dome in first bay). (99) Joseph taking leave of the Virgin; Joseph reproaching the Virgin (two scenes in W lunette of first bay): Joseph had to go away for six months on business; when he returned he found the Virgin pregnant and was angry (until reassured by a dream, as in the first scene of the next cycle).

## IV. The Cycle of the Infancy of Christ

Each of the 13 extant or partly extant Infancy scenes occupies a lunette of the outer narthex, proceeding clockwise round all seven bays. In the soffits of the arches are saints, while in the domical vaults are the scenes of Christ's Ministry, which will be described later. The Infancy Cycle is largely based on the canonical Gospels, and most of the scenes are inscribed with quotations which sufficiently identify them. (100) Joseph Dreaming; The Virgin with Two Companions; The Journey to Bethlehem (three scenes in N lunette of first bay): first scene inscribed: 'Behold, the angel of the Lord appeared to him in a dream, saying: "Joseph, thou son of David, fear not to take unto thee Mary thy wife: for that which is conceived in her is of the Holy Ghost".' (Matt. 1:20); second scene uninscribed; third scene inscribed: 'And Joseph also went up from Galilee, unto the city of David, which is called Bethlehem...' (Luke 2:4). (101) The Enrolment for Taxation (in E lunette of first bay): inscription: '... (because he was of the House of David) to be taxed with Mary, his espoused wife, being great with child'. (Luke 2:4–5, continued from above). (102) The Nativity (in E lunette of second bay): inscription is simply the title 'The Birth of Christ'. To the shepherds the angel says:  Fear not; for behold, I bring you tidings of great joy, which shall be to all people'. (Luke 2:10). (103) The Journey of the Magi; the Magi before Herod (two scenes in E lunette of fourth bay): inscription: 'And behold, there came wise men from the East to Jerusalem, saying: "Where is he that is born King of the Jews?"' (Matt. 1:12). The second scene in the lunette is out of its proper chronological order, for, according to the texts, Herod consulted his priests and scribes (an incident illustrated in mosaic (104) in the next lunette) before consulting the Magi for information regarding the birthplace of Christ, whom he secretly wished to destroy. (104) Herod enquiring of the Priests and Scribes (in E lunette of fifth bay): partly destroyed; inscription (mutilated): 'And when he had gathered all the priests and scribes together he demanded of them where Christ should be born'. (Matt. 2:4).

Now turn the corner into the seventh bay. The lunette above the door to the inner narthex, now blank, probably contained the Adoration of the Magi. The lunette above the columns and arches that led to the parecclesion retains traces of (105) The Return of the Magi to the East. (106) The Flight into Egypt (in S lunette of seventh bay): main scene destroyed, only title remaining. On right of window scene of Fall of Idols from the Walls of an Egyptian Town as the Holy Family passes by (from an apocryphal source).

The mosaics in the W lunette of the sixth bay depict the Massacre of the Innocents. (107) (to the left): Herod Orders the Massacre; inscription: 'Then Herod. when he saw that he was mocked of the Wise Men, was exceeding wroth, and sent forth and slew all the children that were in Bethlehem, and in all the coasts thereof, from two years and under'. (Matt. 2:16). (108) (to the right) The Soldiers go forth to Slay the Children: central part and inscription destroyed. (109) Mothers Mourning their Children (in W lunette of fifth bay): inscription: 'In Rama was there a voice heard, lamentation and weeping, and great mourning'. (Matt. 2:18). (110) The Flight of Elizabeth (in W lunette of fourth bay): inscription is the title. The scene, from the Protoevangelium 22:3, depicts Elizabeth with her baby son, John the Baptist, born about the same time as Christ, seeking refuge from the massacre in the mountains which open up to receive her. (111) Joseph Dreaming; The Return of the Holy Family from Egypt (in W lunette of second bay): inscription: 'Being warned of God in a dream, he (Joseph) turned aside into the parts of Galilee: and he came and dwelt in a city called Nazareth'. (Matt. 2:22–23). (112) Christ Taken to Jerusalem for the Passover (in W lunette of first bay): inscription: 'Now his parents went to Jerusalem every year at the Passover'. (Luke 2:41).

## V. The Cycle of Christ's Ministry

This cycle occupies the domical vaults of all seven bays of the outer narthex as well as parts of the S bay of the inner narthex. Unfortunately, all but one of the vaults in the outer narthex are very badly damaged, many scenes being lost or reduced to mere fragments. The series begins in the vault of the first bay.

(113) Christ among the Doctors (in vault of first bay, N side, fragments only). (114) John the Baptist bearing witness of Christ I (in vault of first bay, S side, fragments only). (115) John the Baptist bearing witness of Christ II (in vault of second bay, N side): inscription: 'This was he of whom I spake, he that cometh after me is preferred before me: for he was before me'. (John 1:15). (116) The Temptation of Christ (in vault of second bay, S side). The four scenes of the Temptation are accompanied by a running dialogue between Christ and the Devil (from Matt. 4:3–10): 1. Devil: 'If thou be the Son of God, command that these stones be made bread'. Christ: 'It is written, Man shall not live by bread alone, but by every word that proceedeth out of the mouth of God'. 2. Devil: 'All these things will I give thee, if thou wilt fall down and worship me'. Christ: 'Get thee behind me, Satan' (the Devil has offered 'all the kingdoms of the world', represented by six kings in a walled town). 3. 'Then the Devil taketh him up to the holy city (and setteth him on a pinnacle of the temple)'. 4. Devil: 'If thou be the Son of God, cast thyself down'. Christ: 'It is written, thou shalt not tempt the Lord thy God'. (117) The Miracle at Cana (in vault of third bay, N side, badly ruined). (118) The Multiplication of the Loaves (in vault of third bay, S side, badly ruined). (119) Christ Healing a Leper (in vault of fourth bay, E side, fragments only). (120) Christ walking on the Water (in vault of fourth bay, W side, fragments only).

The fifth vault is completely empty. The vault of the sixth bay contains fragments of the following nine scenes, the identification of some of which are uncertain, at best: (121) Christ Healing the Paralytic at the Pool at Bethesda; (122) an unidentified scene showing the fragmentary figures of two disciples; (123) Christ Healing the Dropsical Man; (124) Christ Healing the Paralytic at Capernaum; (125) an unidentified scene, showing the fragmentary figures of nine disciples; (126) fragment showing the lower part of a barefooted figure; thought to be either the healing of the Gadarene Demoniac or the Healing of the Blind and Dumb Demoniac of Capernaum; (127) Christ and the Samaritan Woman at the Well (in the NW pendentive); (128) the Paralytic Carrying off his Bed (in the NE pendentive); (129) Christ Healing the Blind Born (in the SE pendentive).

In the seventh bay there are fragments of four scenes, three of which (130, 131, and 133) are so meagre that they cannot be identified; the fourth (132) has been identified as a representation of Christ calling Zacchaeus from the Sycamore Tree, with part of the inscription saying, 'Zacchaeus, make haste and come down'.

Now re-enter the inner narthex to see the eight scenes of Christ's Ministry, almost all of which are well preserved; these are to be found in the pendentives, vaults and lunettes under the southern dome. The inscriptions in this series are merely the titles of the scenes.

(134) Christ Healing the Blind and Dumb Man (in SW pendentive); (135) Christ Healing the two Blind Men (in NW pendentive); (136) Christ Healing Peter's Mother-in-Law (in NE pendentive); (137) Christ healing the Woman with the Issue of Blood (in SE pendentive); (138) Christ healing the Man with the Withered Hand (in soffit of S arch, E side); (139) Christ Healing the Leper (in soffit of S arch, W side); (140) an unidentified scene, showing a miracle of healing (in S lunette, inscription and half of the mosaic lost); (141) Christ Healing a Multitude Afflicted with Various Diseases (in the W lunette).

## VI. Portraits of Saints

The soffits of the arches in the outer narthex are decorated with the portraits of martyr-saints; there were originally 50, of which 37 still exist in whole or in part. The portraits were of two kinds: busts in medallions, and full-length standing figures. In addition to these there were also a dozen portraits of saints on the pilasters that receive the transverse arches in the outer narthex, of which only battered fragments of six have survived.

Martyrs in the arches: First bay, E arch, medallions (left to right, facing E): (142) St. Mardarius of Sebaste; (143) St. Auxentius of Sebaste; (144) St. Eustratius of Sebaste; (145) St. Eugenius of Sebaste; (146) St. Orestes of Sebaste. First bay, W arch, medallions (left to right facing W); (147) St. Anempodistus of Persia; (148) St. Elpidephorus of Persia; (149) St. Acindynus of Persia; (150) St. Aphthonius of Persia; (151) St. Pegasius of Persia. First bay, S transverse arch, one medallion and two full-length figures: (152) medallion of unidentified martyr, perhaps St. Probus of Cilicia; (153) St. Andronicus of Cilicia; (154) St. Tarachus of Cilicia. Second bay, E arch, medallions (left to right facing E): (155) St. Philemon of Egypt; (156) St. Leucius of Nicomedia; (157) St. Agathonicus of Nicomedia; (158) St. Thyrsus of Nicomedia; (159) St. Apollonius of Egypt. Second bay, W arch, medallions (left to right facing W): (160) St. Laurus of Illyria; (161) St. Florus of Illyria; (162) St. Menas of Phrygia; (163) St. Victor; (164) probably St. Vincentius. Second bay, S transverse arch, E side, full length figure: (165) probably St. George of Cappadocia. Third bay, S transverse arch, E side, full-length picture: (166) probably St. Demetrius of Thessalonica. Second bay, S transverse arch, W side, full-length figure: (167) an unidentified martyr. Third bay, S transverse arch, W side, full-length picture: (168) an unidentified martyr. Fourth bay E arch, medallions (left to right facing E): (169) St. Abibus of Edessa; (170) St. Gurius of Edessa; (171) St. Samonas of Edessa; (172) St Eugraphus of Alexandria; (173) St. Menas of Alexandria; (174) St. Hermogenes of Alexandria. Fourth bay, S transverse arch, full-length figures: (175), (176) unidentified martyrs. Fifth bay, E arch, medallion (left side of arch): an unidentified martyr. Fifth bay, W arch, medallion (right side of arch): St. Sergius or St. Bacchus.

*Saints in the wall panels.* The six panels in the first, second and third bays would seem to have been devoted to portraits of those who, by divine intervention, were precursors of the Incarnation. Facing one another across the exonarthex between the first and second bays are

(179) (to the E) St. Anne, with the infant Mary in her arms; and (180)
(to the W) her husband Joachim. Between the second and third is
(181) (to the E) the Virgin Mary and the Christ-Child; facing this (to
the W) there was in all probability the figure of Joseph, but this has
been entirely destroyed. On the E pilaster between the third and
fourth bays is a small fragment of (182) St. John the Baptist; across
from this there would have been a portrait of either John's father
Zacharias or his mother Elizabeth, but this too has disappeared. The
panels on the other six pilasters undoubtedly also bore portraits of
saints; of these only two fragments remain: (183) an unidentified
military saint (on the W pilaster between the fourth and fifth bays);
and (184) St. Euthymius, the Palestinian hermit (on the S pilaster
between the sixth and seventh bays).

## VII. The Panels in the Nave

(185) The Dormition (Koimesis) of the Virgin (over the central door
from the narthex). Here the Virgin is shown laid out on her bier.
Behind her Christ stands holding her soul, represented as a babe in
swaddling clothes, while over his head hovers a six-winged seraph.
Around the bier there stand apostles, evangelists and early bishops.
The theme is taken from an apocryphal work, *Concerning the
Koimesis of the Holy Mother of God*, ascribed to St. John the Divine.
(186) Christ (in panel at left of bema), with an inscription reading:
'Jesus Christ, the dwelling-place of the Living'. Christ holds the

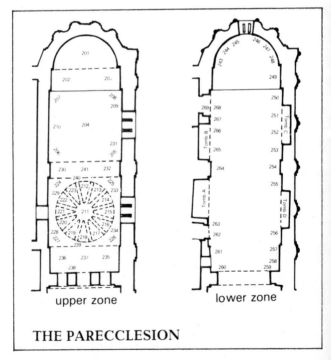

upper zone          lower zone

**THE PARECCLESION**

Gospels open to Matthew 11:28: 'Come unto me, all ye that labour and are heavy laden, and I will give you rest'. (187) The Virgin Hodegetria (in panel at right of bema), with an inscription reading: 'The Mother of God, the dwelling-place of the Uncontainable'.

## The Parecclesion: The Frescoes

The superb **fresco decoration of the parecclesion was the last part of Theodore Metochites's work of redecoration to be carried out, probably in 1320–21. The great but unknown master artist of these frescoes also, probably, created the mosaics in the rest of the church. The decoration of the chapel is designed to illustrate its purpose as a place of burial. Above the level of the cornice the paintings represent the Resurrection and the Life, the Last Judgement, Heaven and Hell, and The Mother of God as the Bridge between Earth and Heaven. Below the cornice there is a procession of saints and martyrs, interrupted here and there by tombs. The following account will deal first with the upper series of frescoes, beginning at the E, then with the portraits of the saints below cornice level, and finally with the tombs.

## I. Scenes of Resurrection

(201) **The Anastasis (Resurrection). This scene, called Anastasis in Greek, is better known in English as the Harrowing of Hell. The central figure in this scene is Christ, who has just broken down the gates of Hell, which lie beneath his feet, while Satan lies bound before him. With his right hand Christ pulls Adam out of his tomb; behind Adam stand St. John the Baptist, David, Solomon, and other righteous kings. With his left hand he pulls Eve out of her tomb; standing in it is

*The conch of the funerary chapel in Kariye Camii is decorated with a fresco of the Resurrection. Christ is shown raising Adam and Eve from their tombs. (Şemsi Güner)*

Abel and behind him another group of the righteous. This is surely
one of the greatest paintings in the world, and the apogee of
Byzantine art in its last renaissance. (202) Christ raising the Widow's
Son (N side of bema arch). (203) Christ raising the Daughter of Jairus
(S side of bema arch).

## II. The Last Judgement: Heaven and Hell

(204) The Second Coming of Christ (in vault of E bay). This vast scene
occupies the whole domical vault; the title is inscribed at the centre. It
represents the Doctrine of the Last Things: death, judgement, immor-
tality in Heaven or damnation in Hell. In the crown is the Scroll of
Heaven (Apocalypse 6:14). In the E half sits Christ in Judgement. To
the souls of the saved on his right he says: 'Come, ye blessed of my
Father, inherit the kingdom prepared for you from the foundation of
the world.' (Matt. 25:34). To the condemned souls on his left he says:
'Depart from me, ye cursed, into everlasting fire, prepared for the
Devil and his angels.' (Matt. 25:41). Below to the left a River of Fire
broadens into a lake in which are the damned. Below Christ is the
Etimasia, the empty throne prepared for the Second Coming, with
Adam and Eve prostrate before it. Below this is depicted the Weighing
and Condemnation of Souls. The W half of the vault is occupied by the
Choirs of the Elect in clouds. (205) The Land and the Sea giving up
their Dead (in SW pendentive). (206) An Angel conducts the Soul of
Lazarus to Heaven (NW pendentive). (207) Lazarus the Beggar in
Abraham's Bosom (NE pendentive). (208) The Rich Man in Hell (SE
pendentive). (209) The Torments of the Damned (in lunette of S wall,
E half). This scene consists of four rectangular panels, identified as:
(upper left) The Gnashing of Teeth; (upper right) The Outer
Darkness; (lower left) The Worm that Sleepeth Not; (lower right) The
Unquenchable Fire. (210) The Entry of the Elect into Paradise (in
lunette of N wall). The Elect are led by St. Peter toward the Gate of
Paradise, guarded by a Cherub; the Good Thief welcomes them and
points to the enthroned Mother of God.

## III. The Mother of God and her Prefigurations

This cycle, in the W dome and bay, represents the Blessed Virgin in a
series of five episodes from the Old Testament, which came to be
symbolically interpreted as prefigurations or 'types' of the Mother of
God and the Incarnation. (211–223) The Virgin and Child (211) in the
crown, surrounded by the heavenly court of angels (212–223) in the
spaces between the ribs. (224–227) Four Hymnographers (in the
pendentives of the dome). These poets were chosen because in their
hymns, verses of which are inscribed on their scrolls, they referred to
the prefigurations of the Virgin depicted below: (224) St. John
Damascene (NE); (225) St. Cosmas the Poet (SE); (226) St. Joseph the
Poet (SW); St. Theophanes (NW). (228) Jacob's Ladder; Jacob wrestling with the Angel (in W half of N lunette). This symbolises the
ladder or bridge to heaven as a prefiguration of the Virgin. The
inscription reads: 'And Jacob took one of the stones of the place, and
put it at his head, and dreamed; and behold, a ladder fixed on the
earth, whose top reached to heaven, and the angels of God ascended
and descended on it. And the Lord stood upon it.' (Genesis 28: 11–13).
Note that the Lord, here and elsewhere, is represented by the Virgin
and Child. The story of Moses and the Burning Bush is represented in
two scenes in the E half of the N lunette and on the soffit of the

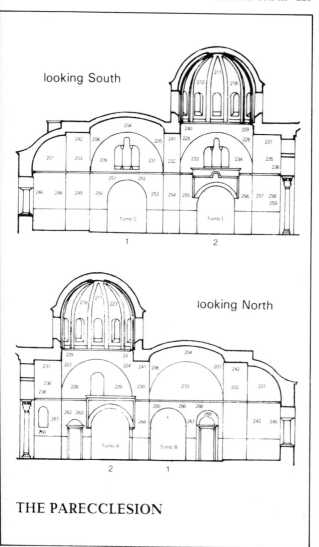

looking South

looking North

**THE PARECCLESION**

adjacent arch: (229) Moses before the Bush; Moses removes his sandals; (230) Moses hides his Face. The burning bush that was not consumed was another prefiguration of the Virgin. The first scene is inscribed: 'Now Moses came to the mountain of God, even to Choreb. And the angel of the Lord appeared to him in a flame of fire out of the bush... saying "Put off thy shoes from off thy feet, for the place whereon thou standest is holy ground".' (Exodus 3:1–2,5). The second scene, on the arch, is inscribed: 'And Moses hid his face; for he was afraid to look upon God.' (Exodus 3:6). Four scenes on the S wall depict the Dedication of Solomon's Temple: (231) The Bearing of the Ark of the Covenant; (232) The Bearing of the Sacred Vessels; (233) Solomon and all Israel; (234) The Installation of the Ark in the Holy of Holies. The Ark of the Covenant is here symbolized as a prefiguration of the Virgin. The first scene, in the W half of the S lunette, is inscribed: 'And it came to pass when Solomon was finished building the house of the Lord, that he assembled all the elders of Israel in Sion, to bring the Ark of the Covenant of the Lord out of the City of David, that is Sion, and the priests took up the Ark of the Covenant and the tabernacle of the testimony.' (I Kings 8:1–4). The inscription on the second scene, on the soffit of the arch, is lost, but it was probably a continuation of verse 4: 'and the holy vessels that were in the tabernacle of testimony'. The third scene, on the E half of the S lunette, is inscribed: 'And the King and all Israel were assembled before the Ark.' (v.5). The fourth scene, on the W half of the S lunette, is inscribed: 'And the priests bring in the Ark of the Covenant into its place, into the oracle of the house, even into the holy of holies, under the wings of the cherubim.' (I Kings 8:6). (235) Isaiah Prophesying; The Angels Smiting the Assyrians before Jerusalem (in S soffit of W arch). Here the inviolable city is a prefiguration of the Virgin. The inscription on Isaiah's scroll is almost illegible, but probably reads: 'Thus saith the Lord concerning the King of Assyria: "He shall not come into this city".' (Isaiah 37:33). (236) Aaron and his Sons before the altar (in N soffit of W arch). Here the altar is a prefiguration of the Virgin. The inscription, almost illegible, is perhaps: 'They draw nigh to the altar and offer their sin-offerings and their whole burnt-offerings.' (Leviticus 9:7). (237, 238) The Souls of the Righteous in the Hand of God (in crown of W arch). This scene is almost entirely lost, but one can make out part of the hand of God holding the souls of the righteous, represented as infants in swaddling bands.

*Medallion Portraits in the Arches.* The only portraits on the vaults still to be described are the four medallion portraits in the crowns of the transverse arches. (239) Melchizedek the Righteous (at the centre of the vertical face of the W arch, in the narrow space below the dome cornice, head missing in its entirety). (240) Jesus Christ (facing (239) in the corresponding position on the arch at the E side of the dome; the head is damaged but the essential features remain). These two portraits were placed in confrontation to illustrate that Melchizedek the Righteous, King of Salem and priest of the most high God, who offered bread and wine to Abraham and blessed him (Gen. 14: 18–19), was the foreshadowing of Christ. A second medallion portrait of Christ (241) is found on the same arch as (240), on the horizontal surface in the centre of the soffit. The fourth medallion portrait (242) is a bust of the Archangel Michael at the centre of the bema arch; this is larger than the other three medallions and is in a much better state of preservation. The large scale and prominent position of this portrait have led some scholars to suggest that Theodore Metochites may have dedicated the funerary chapel to the Archangel Michael.

*Portraits on the Walls.* a long frieze of portraits encircles the chapel on the walls below the cornice. In the apse there are the full-length figures of six Church Fathers; they are, from left to right: (243) Fragments of an unidentified bishop; (244) St. Athanasius; (245) St. John Chrysostom; (246) St. Basil; (247) St. Gregory the Theologian;

(248) St. Cyril of Alexandria. In the rectangular panel on the pier to the S side of the bema arch there is a life-size portrait (249) of the Virgin and Christ-Child. The portrait of the Virgin is of the type called Eleousa, the Merciful or Compassionate. There was originally a portrait of Christ on the opposite panel on the N side of the bema arch, but this has entirely disappeared.

Outside the bema, the frieze in the lower zone of the parecclesion consists mainly of portraits of martyrs and warrior-saints, the most prominent of them full-length military figures dressed in full armour. S wall, E bay: (250) St. George of Cappadocia; (251) St. Florus (medallion); (252) St. Laurus (medallion); (253) St. Demetrius of Thessalonica. S wall, pier between E and W bays: (254) St. Theodore Tiro. S wall, W bay: (255) St. Theodore Stratelates; (256) St. Mercurius. S wall, W pier: (257) St. Procopius; (258) St. Sabas Stratelates. W wall, S pier: (259) an unidentified saint. W wall, N pier: (260) St. David of Thessalonica. N wall, W pier: (261) St. Eustathius Plakidas. N wall, W bay: (262) St. Samonas of Edessa; (263) St. Gurias of Edessa. N wall, pier between W and E bays (264) inscription lost; either St. Artemius or St. Nicetas. N wall, E bay: (265) St. Bacchus (medallion); (266) St. Sergius (medallion); (267) an unidentified military saint; (268) an unidentified saint (medallion). N wall, soffit of arch: (269) an unidentified stylite saint (a stylite is one who lives out his life perched on a pillar).

*The Tombs.* There were four tombs in the parecclesion, each in a deep niche which originally held a sarcophagus with mosaics or frescoes above; some fragments of this decoration still exist.

Tomb A, the first in the N wall, has lost its identifying inscription. Nevertheless, it is almost certainly that of Theodore Metochites himself; it has an elaborately carved and decorated archivolt above. Tomb B is entirely bare, and there is no evidence to identify who was buried there. Tomb C has well-preserved paintings of a man and woman in princely dress, but there is no inscription to identify them.Tomb D is that of Michael Tornikes, a general who was a close friend of Metochites. The deceased is identified by a long inscription above the archivolt, which is even more elaborately carved than that of Metochites himself. Fragments of the mosaic and fresco decoration still exist. Tomb E, in the fifth bay of the outer narthex, is that of the Princess Eirene Řaoulaina Palaeologina, a connection by marriage of Metochites; it preserves a good deal of its fresco decoration. Tomb F, in the fourth bay of the outer narthex, is that of a member of the imperial Palaeologus family; however, it cannot be more definitely identified. Part of the fresco decoration of the tomb survives, showing the lower halves of a couple dressed in colourful princely costumes. Tomb G, in the second bay of the outer narthex, is the latest in the church, dating to the very last years before the Turkish Conquest, with fresco decoration showing strong influence of the Italian Renaissance. Unfortunately, the inscription has vanished and the identity of the deceased is unknown. Tomb H, in the N wall of the inner narthex, is that of the Despot Demetrius Doukas Angelus Palaeologus, youngest son of the Emperor Andronicus II, who died c 1340. Only a small part of the mosaic decoration has survived, and the only intact figure is that of the Virgin. Beneath her a fragmentary inscription reads: 'Thou art the Fount of Life, Mother of God the Word, and I, Demetrius, am thy slave in love'.

# 14 The Stamboul Shore Of The Golden Horn

The region along the Stamboul shore of the Golden Horn above the
two bridges is one which few tourists ever see. This is a pity, for it
has a distinctive atmosphere which is quite unlike that of any other
part of the city. Some of its quarters, particularly Fener and Balat,
are very picturesque and preserve aspects of the life of old Stamboul
which have all but vanished elsewhere in the modern city.

The main road along the right bank of the Golden Horn above the
Atatürk Bridge, which begins as Abdül Ezel Paşa Cd, follows the
course of the **ancient Byzantine sea-walls** which protected that side of
Constantinople. Here and there along the route are well-preserved
stretches of the fortifications, along with some of its gates and
defence-towers.

HISTORY. The sea-walls along the Golden Horn began on the shore below the
acropolis on the First Hill, there joining the maritime defence-walls along the
Marmara, and stretched out to meet the Theodosian land-walls at the NW corner
of Constantinople. The walls along the Golden Horn were repaired and
reconstructed many times during the Byzantine period, particularly by the
Emperor Theophilus in the 9C. These fortifications consisted for the most part of a
single line of walls 10m high and 5km long, studded by a total of 110 defence
towers placed at regular intervals. Considerable stretches of this wall still remain
standing, although almost all of it is in ruins. Much of this ruination was brought
about in the last great sieges of Constantinople, by the Crusaders in 1203–04 and
by the Turks in 1453. In both instances the besiegers lined up their warships
against the sea-walls along the Golden Horn and repeatedly assaulted them. And
the destruction wrought by these sieges and subsequent centuries of decay is now
being rapidly completed by the encroachment of modern highways and factories.

The sea-walls along the Golden Horn were pierced by about a score of
gates and posterns, many of them famous in the history of Byzantine
Constantinople. Of these only one or two remain, although the location
of the others can easily be determined, since the streets of the modern
town still converge where these ancient gates once opened, following
the same routes that they have for many centuries.

Walking along Abdül Ezel Paşa Cd from the Atatürk Bridge for about
450m, one sees on the left the first of these ancient gateways; this is
*Cíbalí Kapí*, known in Byzantium as the Porta Puteae. A Turkish
inscription beside the gate commemorates the fact that it was breached
on 29 May 1453, the day on which Constantinople fell to the Turks. This
gate also marks the point which stood opposite the extreme left wing of
the Venetian fleet in their final assault on 12 April 1204.

About 250m past Cíbalí Kapí on the left stands a little pink-walled
Greek church dedicated to *St. Nicholas*. This church dates to about
1720 and was originally the *metochion*, or private property, of the
Vathopedi Monastery on Mount Athos. The corbelled stone structure
in which the church is housed is one of the few Ottoman buildings of its
type still to be seen here and there along the Golden Horn, most of them
dating from the 17–18C. The principal treasure of the church is a very
rare portative mosaic icon dating from the 11C. Notice also in the
narthex of the church the model of an ancient galleon hanging from the
ceiling. Ship models such as this are to be found in many of the
waterfront churches of the city, placed there by Greek sailors in
gratitude for salvation from the perils of the sea. Also, one should walk

out into the courtyard behind the church, which is partly enclosed by a well-preserved stretch of the ancient Byzantine sea-walls.

Just beyond the church of St. Nicholas the shore road passes *Aya Kapí*, the Holy Gate, a small portal in the sea-walls. This was known in Byzantium as the Gate of St. Theodosia, since it led to a famous church of that name. After passing through the gate, walk straight ahead for about 50m before taking the second turning on the left; then proceed for another 50m to find an imposing but sombre Byzantine edifice. This is the former **\*church of St. Theodosia** known locally as **Gül Camii** (Pl 5,6).

HISTORY. The church is thought to have been built by the Emperor Basil I (867–86); it was originally dedicated to St. Euphemia of the Petrion, but when the very popular iconodule, St. Theodosia, was later buried there it came to be known by her name instead. The church was renowned for its collection of sacred relics, which were carried in procession twice a week and were reputed to have effected many miraculous cures. However, these were all stolen by the Crusaders when they sacked the city in 1204, and many of them still exist in the churches of western Europe. The church figured prominently in the final hours of Byzantine history, for the Emperor Constantine XI Dragases stopped to pray there after his final visit to Haghia Sophia. The church was adorned with roses to commemorate the feast-day of St. Theodosia, which was celebrated annually on 29 May. When the Emperor arrived, accompanied by the Patriarch and the Senate, he found the church packed with women, children, and old men, all of them praying to Theodosia to intercede with Christ and the Virgin to spare their city. After the Emperor and his entourage left the congregation remained, and they were captured there when the city fell to the Turks the following morning. The Turkish soldiers who stormed the church were evidently moved by the garlands of roses they found festooned there, for the tale became one of the enduring traditions of the Conquest. After the Conquest the church became a storehouse for the Ottoman navy, because of its proximity to the great arsenal on the Golden Horn (see Kasîm Paşa, Rte 17). Then, in the first decade of the 17C, it was converted into a house of Islamic worship, known since then as Gül Camii, the Mosque of the Roses. The Greeks of the city still call it the Church of the Undying Rose.

EXTERIOR. The upper parts of the church were considerably altered in Ottoman times, a reconstruction that gave it the appearance of a medieval fortress. The two side apses, nonetheless, are worthy of note, with their three tiers of blind niches and their elaborate brick corbels. Among the more pleasing aspects of the exterior is the minaret, which is handsomely proportioned and clearly belongs to the classical period of Ottoman architecture, when the church was converted into a mosque.

INTERIOR. The building is a cross-domed structure with side-aisles surmounted by galleries; the piers supporting the dome are disengaged from the walls, and the corners behind them form alcoves of two storeys. The central dome and the arches that support it are Ottoman reconstructions, as are most of the windows. A doorway in the SE pier gives access to a winding staircase leading up to a small chamber, within which there is a catafalque covered with a green shawl adorned with Turkish embroidery. This chamber, which has a small window overlooking the nave, was probably the tomb of St. Theodosia. An apocryphal Greek legend identifies this as the last resting-place of Constantine XI Dragases, a tradition that began long after the Conquest. An equally baseless Turkish legend identifies this as the tomb of Gül Baba, Father Rose, a Moslem saint who was the eponymous founder of Gül Camii. The confusion of legends is compounded by the Turkish inscription in gilt letters over the doorway in the SE pier, which identifies the chamber above as: 'The tomb of the Apostle of Christ—peace be to him'.

After leaving the church turn left, and then at the second turning turn left again. A short distance down the left side of the street there stands one of the oldest and grandest Turkish baths still in use in the city. It is now called **\*Küçük** (Little) **Mustafa Paşa Hamamí**, but it seems actually to have been founded by Koca Mustafa Paşa, Grand Vezir to Beyazit II, who built it some time before his death in 1512. The plan of the hamam and the incredibly varied and intricate structure of its domes would entirely bear out that early date. The camekan, about 14·5m on a side, is among the largest in the city, so that the later wooden galleries around it do not detract from its grandeur. The soğukluk, typically, is merely carved out of the hararet, consisting of its right-hand cubicle and the bottom arm of the cross. The hararet itself is very splendid, covered by a central dome with a deep cornice of elaborately-carved stalactites. Each of the three remaining cross-arms is covered by a vault of utterly different structure; the prettiest is perhaps that on the right, which has a semidome in the form of a deeply-ribbed shell. The two corner cubicles at the back have domes supported on a cornice of juxtaposed triangles, while the third cubicle has a very beautiful *opus sectile* pavement in a variety of brilliant coloured marbles. This delightful bath was in disuse half a century ago, but has since been restored and is in use once again.

After leaving the hamam turn right and walk along Küçük Mustafa Paşa Sk for about 100m, coming to an intersection with streets leading off in several directions. The street that veers off at about 45 degrees to the right leads to the fragmentary ruins of a small Byzantine church partly concealed by trees and houses. Only a portion of the apse survives, with an elaborate decoration in brickwork of meander and zigzag designs typical of the last period of Byzantine architecture. Attempts to identify the building with several churches known to have been in the area lack any serious evidence. The church, which is known locally as Sinan Paşa Mescidi, would appear to date from the 13–14C.

A short distance beyond Sinan Paşa Mescidi one comes to *Yeni Aya Kapí*, a gateway that leads out to the shore road along the Golden Horn. This portal is not one of the original gateways in the Byzantine sea-walls, but was constructed in 1582 by Sinan. The local residents had petitioned the government to open a gate there so that they could more easily make their way to a new bath which had been constructed outside the walls at that point. This bath, the *Havuzlu Hamam*, is probably also a work of Sinan, built by him for Nur Banu, wife of Selim II and mother of Murat III. Unfortunately, the hamam is now disaffected and in a state of advanced decay.

About 100m beyond this gate Sadrazam Ali Paşa Cd branches off at a slight angle to the left from the shore road along the Golden Horn. This was the site of the *Gate of the Petrion*, one of the portals in the Byzantine sea-walls. The quarter for which it was named was a walled enclave that comprised the lower slope of the Fifth Hill leading down to the Golden Horn.

HISTORY. The Petrion figured prominently in the assaults upon the sea-walls by the Crusaders and the Turks. On 13 July 1203 the Venetian galleys under Doge Dandalo pushed their prows up against the sea-walls of the Petrion and captured 25 defence towers. Though the Doge was nearly 90 years old and almost totally blind, he personally commanded the attack, carrying the banner of St. Mark as his men helped him from his galleon onto the ramparts. In the final Crusader assault upon the city on 12 April 1204 the Petrion was once again the centre of the action. It was here that two brave Crusader knights jumped from the flying-bridge of the galleon Pelerine onto a defence tower, and from there led the charge that breached the walls and brought about the capture of the city. On 29 May 1453 the Petrion withstood a sustained attack by the Turkish fleet, and the defenders surrendered only when they heard that the land walls were breached and that the city had fallen. Since the Petrion had surrendered rather than being taken by assault, the Conqueror decreed that the houses and churches in the quarter would be spared in the general sack of the city.

Leaving the main road and veering left along Sadrazam Ali Paşa Cd, one soon comes to the entrance to the *Greek Orthodox Patriarchate (Pl 5,6). On entering notice that the main gate is welded shut and painted black; this is the famous *Orta Kapí*, the Central Gate, which has become a symbol of Greek-Turkish intransigence: it was here that Gregory V, Patriarch of Constantinople, was hanged for treason on 22 April 1821, at the outbreak of the Greek War of Independence.

HISTORY. The Greek Orthodox Patriarchate has been on this site since about 1601, having moved around for a number of years after leaving the Pammakaristos in 1586. However, the present patriarchal church of St. George dates only from 1720. Within the enclosure there are also the administrative offices of the Greek Orthodox Patriarchate. During the Ottoman period the Ecumenical Patriarch of Constantinople, under the suzerainty of the Sultan, was the religious leader of all Christians in the Empire. The present Patriarch, Demetrius, is still the spiritual head of the Greek Orthodox Church; however, his real power only extends to the few thousand Greeks still resident in Istanbul and the Aegean isles of Imroz and Bozcaada (the ancient Tenedos).

INTERIOR. Like almost all of the post-Conquest sanctuaries in the city, the patriarchal church of St. George is a small basilica. This form was adopted partly because of its simplicity, but largely because the Christians in Istanbul were forbidden to build churches with domes or masonry roofs, so that the basilica with its timbered roof, a traditional Christian edifice, was the obvious solution. The earlier church of St. George seems to have had the same form, for an Italian traveller who saw it in 1615 described it as 'of moderate size, long in form, and with several aisles'. Among the many relics in the church are the bodies of St. Omonia, St. Theophano, and St. Euphemia of Chalcedon, whose remains were brought here after her martyrium near the Hippodrome was destroyed, probably in the early Ottoman period. On the right side of the central aisle is the patriarchal throne, which is thought to date from the late Byzantine period; however, the pious claim is that it is the original throne of St. John Chrysostom, who was Patriarch at the beginning of the 5C. The church also contains a very lovely portative mosaic of the Blessed Virgin, of the same type and date as the one in the church of St. Nicholas (see below).

PRECINCTS. Across the courtyard from the church are the other buildings of the Patriarchate. With the exception of the library, a pleasing old building, these are all modern structures erected after the disastrous fire of 1951, which gutted most of the buildings on this side of the courtyard. It was fortunate that the library was spared, because it houses an important collection of Byzantine manuscripts and documents.

After leaving the Patriarchate, continue along Sadrazam Ali Paşa Cd for a few paces to the next intersection. Just to the right, at this point, is the site of the famous *Fener Kapísí*, the ancient Porta Phanari, or the Gate of the Lighthouse. This gate, now vanished, long ago gave its name to the adjacent quarter, the Fener, so famous in the history of Istanbul during the Ottoman period.

HISTORY. Beginning in the early 16C, Greeks of this quarter, the Feneriotes, amassed considerable wealth in trade and commerce under the protective mantle of the Ottoman Sultan. Many Feneriotes achieved positions of great eminence in the Empire, and several families between them even gained control of the trans-Danubian principalities of Moldavia and Wallachia, client states of the Ottomans. The Feneriotes ruled there as Hospodars, or Princes, a position that allowed them to acquire enormous wealth. Much of this wealth was brought back to the Fener, where the Hospodars and other members of their family and court built magnificent mansions and palaces. The palaces of the Feneriotes have all vanished, but a few of their mansions have survived, although in very dilapidated condition. They can be seen here and there along the Golden Horn road, identified by their massive stone walls and their upper storeys projecting out on corbels.

Continuing along in the same direction for a few steps past the site of Fener Kapísí, take the first left and then almost immediately turn right into the next street, Vodina Cd. About 100m along this street one comes on the left to a high wall that encloses a large open area extending up the side of the hill. This area is the property of the Greek Orthodox Patriarchate, and within it are two churches of some historic interest. The gates to the enclosure are locked at all times but anyone wishing to enter can ask permission at the Patriarchate and a caretaker will be sent to open the outer gates and those of the two churches within.

The first of these is the *church of St. George*, just inside the walls along Vodina Cd; this is approached through the gate halfway along the walls on that street. The church has absolutely no architectural value, but it has interesting historical connections. The date of foundation of the original church on this site is unknown, though the present structure probably dates from the early 19C. Since the middle of the 17C this has been the Metochion of the Patriarchate of Jerusalem. The church was originally given to the Patriarch of Jerusalem by Michael Cantacuzenos, one of the first Feneriote plutocrats. The church of St. George also served as the private chapel of the Cantacuzenos family, whose magnificent palace stood at the centre of the walled enclosure. This palace, of which not a trace remains, was called Vlach Saray, or the Palace of the Wallachians, because several members of the Cantacuzenos family were Hospodars of Wallachia and Moldavia. Michael Cantacuzenos, whom the Turks called Şeytanoğlu, or the Son of Satan, used his enormous wealth to good advantage, acquiring a vast library that included a collection of most of the extant ancient Greek manuscripts in the city. Many of these manuscripts were later given to various monasteries on Mount Athos, where they can still be seen; some remained stored in the church of St. George until the early years of the present century. In 1906 a careful study of the manuscripts in the church was made by the German scholar Heiberg, who discovered in palimpsest a perfect and complete copy made in the 10C of a lost work of Archimedes. This is his 'Method of Treating Mechanical Problems, Dedicated to Eratosthenes', written in Alexandria in c 250 BC. This is considered to be the single most important work of the greatest mathematical physicist of antiquity, and its discovery represented an extremely important addition to our knowledge of ancient science.

The second church within the walled enclosure is approached by continuing along Vodina Cd to the next corner and following the street that leads uphill to the left, entering the grounds through an iron gate a short way along on the left. This is the *church of the Panaghia Paramithias* (St. Mary the Consoler), which dates from the mid-16C. It served as the Patriarchal church from 1586 until 1596, in the years just after the Patriarchate was shifted from the Pammakaristos. Unfortunately, the church was gutted in a disastrous fire in 1973 and has not been rebuilt. Notice the double eagle carved on the marble flagstone at the entrance to the church; this was the symbol of the imperial Palaeologus dynasty, and today it is the emblem of the

Greek Orthodox Church. The church is known locally as Vlach Saray, since it stood within the precincts of the palace of the Hospodars of Wallachia and Moldavia.

After leaving the church continue uphill and turn left at the corner; then take the second right. Straight ahead lies a rose-red Byzantine church, deformed in shape and with an unusually high drum. This is the church dedicated to the Theotokos Panaghiotissa, the All-Holy Mother of God, but it is more generally called the **Panaghia Mouchliotissa**, or St. Mary of the Mongols. This building has little to recommend it architecturally, but it is interesting historically as the only Byzantine sanctuary continuously in the hands of the Greeks since before the Turkish Conquest.

HISTORY. This church was either founded or rebuilt in c 1282 by the Princess Maria Palaeologina, an illegitimate daughter of the Emperor Michael VIII Palaeologus. In 1265 Maria was sent off by her father as a bride to Hulagu, the Great Khan of the Mongols. However, Hulagu died before Maria arrived at the Mongol court, so she was married instead to his son and successor Abagu. Maria lived at the Mongol court in Persia for about 15 years, and through her influence the Khan and many of his court became Christians. But then, in 1281, Abagu was assassinated by his brother Ahmet and Maria was forced to return to Constantinople. After Maria's return her father offered her as bride to another Khan of the Mongols, Charabanda, but this time she refused. At about this time she founded the present church, together with a convent, and dedicated it to the Virgin, the protectress of the Christian Mongols. Maria, the Despoina of the Mongols, as she was then known, then became a nun and spent her last years in retirement in her convent. After the Conquest Mehmet II, at the request of his Greek architect Christodoulos (who may be Atik Sinan, the architect of the original Mosque of the Conqueror), issued a firman, or imperial decree, confirming the right of the local Greeks to keep this church. The Greeks remain in possession of the church to this day, and what is claimed to be a copy of the Conqueror's firman is still displayed there.

INTERIOR. The plan of the church was originally quatrefoil internally and trefoil externally. That is, the small central dome on a high drum was surrounded by four semidomes along the axes, all but the western one resting on the outer walls of the building, which thus formed exedrae, with a narthex of three bays preceding the church to the W. But the entire southern side of the church was swept away in modern times and replaced by a squarish narthex, which is in every direction out of line with the original building. The effect is most disconcerting. The church is still adorned with one art treasure from its Byzantine period, a very beautiful portative mosaic of the Theotokos Pammakaristos, the All-Joyous Mother of God. The obvious similarity of this icon to those in St. Nicholas and St. George has led scholars to believe that they were all done by the same artist, working in the 11C. These are the only three portative mosaics that are left in the city, and there are only about ten others still known to exist elsewhere.

To the right of the church on leaving one sees a huge structure that dominates the skyline in this part of the city, an ugly red-brick building dating to 1881. This building formerly housed the Megali Scholea, the Great School, a secular institution of higher education for Greeks founded in c 1840. Prior to that time the Patriarchate had operated a school of higher learning on this site that offered both religious and secular studies, one of the very few such institutions in the Ottoman Empire. Here many of the Greek Voivodes (Governors) and Hospodars of Moldavia and Wallachia were educated, as well as most of the chief interpreters, who often wielded great influence at the Sublime Porte. This latter group includes men with the illustrious names of the Byzantine aristocracy: Palaeologus, Cantacuzenos, Cantemir, Mavrocordato and Ypsilanti. The school continued to operate until 1971, when a law was passed closing all foreign institutions of higher learning in Turkey.

Return now to the last turning before the church and take the street to the right. This almost immediately leads to a steep step-street that bounds the walled enclosure containing the churches of St. George and Vlach Saray. At the bottom of the steps turn left and then right at the next corner to return to Vodina Cd. Follow this for a few feet and take the first left; then after a few steps turn left again and continue in the same direction along the main road up the Golden Horn.

About 150m along the right there is an extraordinary church, that of *St. Stephen of the Bulgars*. This and the building opposite, the former Exarchate, were erected in 1871, at a time when the Bulgarian Church was asserting its independence from the Greek Orthodox Patriarchate of Constantinople. The astonishing thing about the church is that it is constructed entirely of cast iron, not only the structure itself but all of its interior decorations, and all is in the neo-Gothic style. The church was prefabricated in Vienna and shipped down the Danube and across the Black Sea in sections, after which it was erected here on the Stamboul shore of the Golden Horn. The church is actually rather handsome, both inside and out, and it is kept in excellent repair by the small community of Bulgarians who worship there. The church is surrounded by a pretty and well-tended garden in which several metropolitans of the Bulgarian Orthodox Church are buried.

About 250m farther along, on the right side of the road, just before a petrol station, there stands one of the oldest and grandest of the former **Feneriote mansions**, still impressive though it is in a very dilapidated condition. This is the finest extant example of a Greek residence in Istanbul of the Ottoman period, erected apparently in a continuation or modification of the Ottoman style. Its walls are constructed of alternate courses of stone and brick; the upper storey projects out over the street, corbelled out on elaborate consoles; with the cornice under the roof consisting of courses of brick in saw-tooth design. The mansion is very stoutly built, with massive walls and iron doors and window-shutters, more like a fortress than a dwelling-place. Unfortunately, its interior was badly damaged during the anti-Greek riots in 1955, and it is closed to the public.

HISTORY. The mansion here is of particular interest because it was for nearly three centuries the Metochion of the Monastery of St. Catherine on Mount Sinai. The Monastery of St. Catherine, first founded by Justinian, was for centuries a semi-autonomous church under the control of the Patriarchate of Alexandria. The Monastery, like many others, has always been represented in Constantinople by one of its archimandrites, who first took up residence in this mansion in 1686. It was abandoned in the mid-1960s and is now used as a factory and warehouse; it is rapidly falling into ruins.

Just beyond the mansion a gateway leads into the courtyard of a Greek church; this is dedicated to St. John the Baptist, and served as the chapel of the monastery which was once part of the metochion of St. Catherine. The church is probably Byzantine in foundation, but it has been burned down and reconstructed several times and the present structure dates from only 1830. It is of no interest except for its connection with the Metochion of Mount Sinai.

About 150m beyond the Metochion is *Balat Kapísí*, the site of another of the Byzantine sea-gates along the Golden Horn, of which only fragments now remain. This has been identified variously as the

Gate of the Kynegos (St. John the Hunter) or that of the Prodromus (St. John the Baptist). The Turkish name is a corruption of Palation or Palace, because this was one of the gates that lead to the Byzantine Palace of Blachernae, the ruins of which stand just inside the Theodosian walls (see below, Palace of Blachernae). Although the gate has now all but disappeared, its name survives in that of the surrounding quarter, the picturesque and venerable Balat.

HISTORY. Balat has been for many centuries one of the principal Jewish quarters of the city. Many of the people of the quarter were Greek-speaking Jews who had resided there since early Byzantine times, but these were later absorbed by the Sephardim who emigrated from Spain in 1492 and took up residence in the Ottoman Empire at the invitation of Beyazit II. There are still half-a-dozen ancient synagogues in the quarter, several dating in foundation from Byzantine times, although most of the present structures date from no earlier than the first half of the 19C. Although many in the Jewish community have now moved to more modern neighbourhoods in Istanbul or emigrated to Israel, some still remain in their old quarter in Balat, continuing to speak the medieval Ladino of their Spanish ancestors.

There are a few monuments of some minor interest in the immediate vicinity of Balat Kapísí. The first of these is found in the second street in from the Golden Horn road and somewhat to the left of the gate. (Although the gate no longer exists, there is no mistaking its former location, for all the local streets converge on it.) After a few twists and turns through the tortuous streets one comes to a rather handsome church, apparently dating to the 18C. This is the Armenian *church of Surp* (St.) *Reşdagabet*, which stands on the site of a Byzantine church of the 13–14C. This earlier sanctuary was dedicated to the Taxiarch Saints, the Archangels Michael and Gabriel, as chiefs (taxiarchoi) of the celestial militia, but when the Armenian community took possession of the church in 1629 they changed the name to its present one.

To the right of Balat Kapísí and on the same street as the church there is a small *mosque* which is a minor work of Sinan. A long and handsomely-written inscription, in Arabic over the fine entrance portàl, states that the mosque was built in 1562–63 by Ferruh Ağa, Kethüda (Steward) of the Grand Vezir Semiz Ali Paşa. The mosque is of the simple rectangular type; it probably once had a wooden ceiling with a little dome, but this has been replaced in a recent restoration by a flat concrete ceiling. The building is very long and narrow, with a shallow apse for the mihrab, which is adorned with tiles from the Tekfur Saray period. A wooden balcony runs along the W wall, but this is clearly not like the original, for it obstructs the windows in an awkward way. A deep porch precedes the mosque: this originally had a colonnade of eight columns, but these were removed so as to glaze in the porch. All the same, the porch is attractive, with its marble portal, two handsome niches with pretty conch tops, and at each end a curious sort of anta or projection of the mosque wall with windows above and below. This is the handsomest and most interesting of Sinan's many mosques of this simple type, and it deserves a more sympathetic restoration. From the courtyard of the mosque these is an excellent view of the great retaining wall of the Palace of Blachernae, the last monument on the present itinerary.

Before proceeding in that direction, one might glance at an ancient hamam just to the E of the mosque. This has been attributed to Sinan, but wrongly; it is not in the 'Tezkere', and furthermore it appears much earlier in a vakfiye, or deed of a pious foundation, of the Conqueror himself. However, it is not very impressive and is hardly worth a visit.

Now continue up the Golden Horn along the street that runs by the N side of the mosque, passing through a quiet and almost rural district of old wooden houses and kitchen gardens. About 150m beyond the mosque there is a little Greek church on the left side of the road. This is the *church of the Panaghia Balinu*, which is of no interest except for its great age.

HISTORY. Although the present structure dates only to 1730, with later alterations, the original church of the Panaghia Balinu was standing on this site as early as 1583. The evidence for this is a list of churches and monasteries in Istanbul made by Tryphon Karabeinikoff, who was sent by the Czar in 1583 and again in 1593 to distribute money to those institutions. Tryphon listed seven monasteries and 47 churches in the city which were functioning at that time, including the Panaghia Balinu.

About 100m farther along, just to the right past a bend in the road, there is another Greek church, that of *St. Demetrius Kanabu*. This also is of no architectural interest, but it does have some interesting historical associations.

HISTORY. The church of St. Demetrius Kanabu is also included in the list of Tryphon Karabeinikoff, although the present structure dates only to 1730 at the earliest. The origins of St. Demetrius go back to Byzantine times, for a church of that name is known to have existed on this site as early as 1334. It is suggested that the church may have been founded by the family of Nicholas Kanabu, who became emperor for a few days in April 1204, in the brief interval between the deposition of the co-Emperors Alexius IV and Isaac II and the later usurpation by Alexius V. (The rule of Nicholas Kanabu was so brief that he is not included among the list of Byzantine emperors.) St. Demetrius served as the Patriarchal church from 1597 until 1601, the period just before the Patriarchate was shifted to its present site.

Beyond St. Demetrius there stretches a long kitchen garden with a few fruit trees, an area which is very pretty and pastoral in spring. At the far end of the garden stands a small Byzantine church converted into a mosque known as *\*Atik Mustafa Paşa Camii* (Pl 5,3). Until recent years this was identified as the Church of SS. Peter and Mark; this designation has been generally abandoned but no convincing alternative has been proposed. The building appears to be the last in date of the 9C domed-cross churches, of which St. Theodosia and the Kyriotissa are earlier and grander examples. The wooden porch, the dome and its drum, and probably some of the roofs and many of the windows are Turkish restorations. For the rest, the church preserves its original plan, which is simple and, for a Byzantine structure, regular. A dome, doubtless originally on a fairly high drum with windows, covers the centre of the cross. The arms of the cross are barrel-vaulted, as are the four small rooms beyond the dome piers that fill up the corners of the cross: these are entered through high, narrow arches. The three apses, semicircular within, have three faces on the exterior. It must once have been an attractive little church, and it still has a faded charm.

After returning to the street by which the church was first approached, continue in the same direction as before. At the next corner on the left one comes to the entrance to the famous *ayazma of Blachernae*, a sacred spring enclosed by a little shrine surrounded by a garden.

HISTORY. This ayazma, like countless others in the city and elsewhere in the Greek world, has been venerated since pre-Christian times, and its waters are believed to possess healing powers. The ayazma at Blachernae was one of the most popular in the city and even the Emperor and Empress came here to partake of the life-giving waters. In 451 a great church was built over the spring by Pulcheria, wife of the Emperor Marcian. A few years later the church served to house the celebrated robe and mantle of the Virgin. These garments, which had been stolen from a Jewess in Jerusalem by two Byzantine pilgrims, were considered to be the most sacred relics in Constantinople, 'the palladium of the city and the disperser of all warlike foes'. The Blacherniotissa, as the Virgin was here called, was revered as the protectress of the city; according to tradition, she appeared on the walls to disperse the Avars when they almost broke into the city near the Golden Horn in 627. Thus Blachernae became the most important shrine in Constantinople and remained so throughout the history of Byzantium. The ancient church of the Blachernae was destroyed by fire in 1434, and it was subsequently rebuilt several times, most recently in the 1960s. The shrine is still a popular place of pilgrimage among the Greeks of the city; and each year, on the anniversary of the repulse of the Avars, they gather here to give thanks to the Blacherniotissa in a very moving liturgy.

After leaving the ayazma turn left and then right at the next corner onto Dervişzade Sk, the Street of the Dervish's Son, which winds uphill to a broad terrace just inside the ancient Byzantine land-walls. At the N end of the terrace, standing close to the ramparts, there is a very attractive mosque called *Ivaz Efendi Camii* (Pl 5,1).

HISTORY. Some scholars have attributed the mosque to Sinan, but it does not appear in the 'Tezkere' and there seems to be no definite evidence to identify the architect. There is no historical inscription, and the date of construction is given variously as 1581 or 1585, the latter being the year when Ivaz Efendi died. The founder had been Chief Judge of Istanbul in the reign of Murat III.

EXTERIOR. The W facade of the mosque is most unusual: instead of a central entrance-portal there are double doors at each end of the facade, the rest of it being filled in with windows, producing a very pretty effect. Another odd, indeed unique feature is that the minaret is at the SE corner of the building. Originally there was a porch, evidently with a sloping roof supported by columns, which ran around three sides of the building.

INTERIOR. The mosque is almost square in plan; the dome rests on four semidomes with stalactite cornices, while the mihrab, in a projecting apse, is decorated with Iznik tiles of the best period. The centre of the W wall is occupied by a gallery in two storeys supported on slender marble columns. There are also wooden galleries to N and S, but these are probably not original, certainly not in their present form. The interior is very elegant and gives a great sense of light: there are many windows in all its walls.

The terrace on which Ivaz Efendi Camii stands is the site of the famous *•Palace of Blachernae* (Pl 5,1), the imperial residence during the last centuries of Byzantine rule. Only a few ruined towers and some substructures of the palace remain; nevertheless, it is one of the most romantic and historic sights in the city.

HISTORY. The first palace on this site was built by the Emperor Anastasius in about 500. The palace was thenceforth used by the imperial family whenever they came to visit the nearby shrine of Blachernae (see above). Over the centuries the Palace of Blachernae was rebuilt and enlarged several times, particularly during the reign of the Comneni dynasty in the 11–12C. From that time on Blachernae became the favourite residence of the imperial family, gradually supplanting the Great Palace on the First Hill. The magnificence of the Palace of Blachernae particularly impressed the Crusaders, some of whom have left glowing accounts of its splendours. This may have heightened their desire to take the city for themselves in 1204. After the restoration of the Empire in 1261 the Great Palace on the Marmara was abandoned altogether, and for the remainder of the Byzantine period the imperial family lived exclusively at Blachernae. They were still in residence there when the city fell to the Turks on

29 May 1453. Because of its close proximity to the defence-walls, the palace suffered grievously during this campaign.

The two towers just behind Ivaz Efendi Camii are a part of the palace. The one to the left is traditionally called the *Tower of Isaac Angelus* and that to the right the *Prison of Anemas*, although there are scholars who would identify the latter with one of the towers closer to the Golden Horn. The Prison of Anemas appears frequently in the history of the last centuries of Byzantium. A half-dozen emperors were at one time or another imprisoned, tortured and mutilated in this tower and two of them were executed there: Isaac II Angelus and his son Alexius III, who were strangled shortly before the Crusader sack of the city in 1204.

The Tower of Isaac Angelus was probably built by that emperor in about 1188, during his first reign; it was perhaps designed as a private palace with its upper level serving as a belvedere. Certainly the upper storey of the tower, on a level with the terrace, commands a superb view of the Golden Horn and the surrounding countryside; notice outside the windows the shafts of columns that once supported a balcony.

A modern concrete stairway in the terrace leads down to the substructures of the palace. These are quite impressive, but visitors must be equipped with a flashlight. The penetralia consist of two nearly parallel walls some 60m long; the space between, which varies from 2–12m in width, is divided by arched cross-walls into three storeys of compartments, 42 in all. Since the wooden floors have long since decayed, these vast dungeons give an impression of immense height. From this passage one can enter the towers of Isaac Angelus and Anemas. From the latter tower a ramp leads down to a small entrance at the foot of the wall, from where there is a good view of the enormous towers from the outside, and also the curious counterfort by which they are surrounded at the bottom.

After leaving the palace, return along Dervişzade Sk to the main road along the Golden Horn. A short distance along to the left is the last stretch of the maritime fortifications along the Golden Horn, a massive wall and the impressive ruins of three defence towers. Just beyond that stretch the sea-walls on this side of the city came to an end, joining the great land-walls after their long march across the Thracian downs from the Sea of Marmara to the Golden Horn.

# 15  The Seventh Hill

The first six hills of the city march in an almost straight line above the right bank of the Golden Horn. The Seventh Hill stands by itself toward the Marmara shore, comprising most of the SW area of the old city. Its highest point is at the Gate of Romanus (Top Kapi), whence it slopes down to the N toward the valley of the Lycus, which divides it from the Sixth, Fifth and Fourth Hills. To the S it approaches the Marmara, leaving sometimes a wide, sometimes a narrow plain along the shore. The present itinerary goes along the Marmara slopes of the Seventh Hill, through one of the most pleasant and picturesque parts of the city. This region preserves something of the flavour of Ottoman Stamboul, with its winding cobbled streets lined with old wooden houses, its vine-shaded teahouses sitting under venerable plane trees, and its ancient mosque courtyards still serving as communal centres as they did in centuries past.

The itinerary begins in Aksaray Square (Pl 9,4), at the intersection of Ordu Cd and Atatürk Blv. Like Beyazit Square, Aksaray occupies the site of an ancient Roman forum, in this case the Forum Bovis. At the Forum Bovis the Mese once again divided into two branches, one leading off to the NW along the route of the modern Millet Cd, the other going to the SW, following approximately the course of Cerrah Paşa Cd. Until a decade ago Aksaray was a lively, colourful market square, but it has been utterly destroyed by a massive clover-leaf intersection.

Just to the N of the overpass stands *Valide Sultan Camii*, the last imperial mosque to be erected in Istanbul. It is generally ascribed to the Italian architect Montani, and was built in 1871 for Pertevniyel Valide Sultan, mother of Sultan Abdül Aziz. The foundress was a veritable Cinderella, for she was elevated in a single day from the palace kitchens to the bed of Sultan Abdül Mecit. She was not so fortunate in her mosque, a tasteless structure that combines elements of Moorish, Turkish, Gothic, Renaissance and Empire styles in a garish rococo hodgepodge. One authority on the monuments of Istanbul has described Valide Sultan Camii as the bitter end of Ottoman architecture.

At the W of the overpass, and to the left down the first cross street, there is a handsome *sibyan mektebi*. This was founded in 1723–24 by Ebu Bekir Paşa; it has recently been restored and is now in use as a children's library, like so many other old Ottoman one-room schoolhouses of its type.

Beyond the W end of the overpass the two new highways meet in an acute angle; the southern one, Millet Cd, runs up the back of the Seventh Hill to Top Kapí and is a very busy and important thoroughfare; the northern one, Vatan Cd, is needlessly wide and is hardly used, for it leads nowhere; it follows the course of the Lycus River, which is canalized beneath it.

In the angle between these two avenues stands **Murat Paşa Camii** (Pl 9,4), one of the oldest and most attractive vezirial mosques in the city.

HISTORY. The founder, Murat Paşa, was a convert to Islam from the imperial Palaeologus family; he became one of the Conqueror's vezirs and died in battle as a relatively young man. The date of construction of his mosque is given, in an intricate inscription in Arabic over the main door, as 1469. (The calligraphy in this inscription is exceptionally beautiful and is probably by Ali Sufi, who carved the fine inscription over the Imperial Gate to Topkapí Sarayí.)

*The Mosque.* Murat Paşa Camii is the second in date of the two mosques of the 'Bursa type' that still survive in Istanbul, built just seven years after Mahmut Paşa Camii. Murat Paşa's mosque is smaller and less elaborate than that of Mahmut Paşa, nevertheless, it resembles it in general plan. A long rectangular room is divided by an arch into two squares each covered by a dome, with two small side-chambers to N and S forming hostels for travelling dervishes. Of the two large domes the eastern one rests on pendentives, but the western one has the same curious arrangement of triangles seen on the smaller domes at Mahmut Paşa. The porch has five domed bays with six very handsome ancient columns, two of Syenitic granite, four of verd antique. The capitals are of three different kinds, arranged symmetrically, two types of stalactite and the lozenge capital. The walls of the building are in alternating courses of brick and stone. The pious foundation originally included a medrese and a large double hamam, but unfortunately these perished during the widening of the adjacent streets.

Just behind Murat Paşa Camii a large ancient catacomb was discovered in 1972 during excavations for a new sewer. A cursory exploration at that time revealed that there were eight vaulted chambers extending over an area roughly 30m on a side. It is thought that there is a second storey of comparable size beneath the first, but this has not yet been explored. The catacomb is believed to date from the 6C AD; unfortunately it is not open to the public.

A little farther up Millet Cd on the same side of the avenue, is an interesting *mosque* which has recently been reconstructed here. It was founded by Selçuk Hatun, daughter of Sultan Mehmet I (1413–21) and an aunt of Mehmet the Conqueror. Selçuk Hatun died in 1485, therefore, her mosque must be dated before 1485. In the 17C the mosque was partially destroyed in a fire and was later reconstructed by the Chief Black Eunuch Abbas Ağa. In 1956, when Millet Cd was widened, the mosque was demolished and re-erected not far from its original site. How far the reconstructed building follows the original plan is not clear; at all events the mosque is rather attractive and the rebuilding at least adequate.

Now cross Millet Cd and continue S for a short distance as far as Cerrah Paşa Cd, which leads westward parallel to the Marmara shore. A short way along on the left one comes to an imposing mosque surrounded by a walled garden. This is *Cerrah Paşa Camii (Pl 9,3),the fine mosque after which the avenue and the surrounding neighbourhood are named.

HISTORY. The founder, Cerrah Mehmet Paşa, served as Grand Vezir for a short time during the reign of Mehmet III (1595–1603). He had originally been a barber and surgeon (cerrah), and rose in the favour of Murat III after having performed the circumcision of the crown prince, the future Mehmet III. The latter in 1598 appointed him Grand Vezir and wrote him a letter warning that he would be drawn and quartered if he did not do his duty. But he was dismissed after about six months, without being drawn and quartered, after the failure of a military campaign that he led against Hungary.

INTERIOR. An Arabic inscription over the door of the mosque gives the date as 1593; the architect was Davut Ağa, Sinan's successor as Chief Architect of the Empire. Historians of Ottoman architecture generally rank Cerrah Paşa Camii among the half-dozen most successful of the vezirial mosques. Its plan presents an interesting modification of the hexagon-in-rectangle type. The four domes that flank the central dome at the corners, instead of being oriented along the diagonals of the rectangle, are parallel with the cross axis. This plan has the advantage that, for any hexagon, the width of the building can be increased without limit. Such a plan was never used by Sinan, and is seen elsewhere only in Hekimoğlu Ali Paşa Camii, which is a little farther W on the Seventh Hill (see below). The mihrab is in a rectangular apse which projects from the E wall. The galleries, which run around three sides of the building, are supported by pretty ogive arches with polychrome voussoirs of white stone and red conglomerate marble; in some of the spandrels there are very charming rosettes. In short, the interior is elegant in detail and gives a sense of spaciousness and light.

EXTERIOR. The exterior, too, is impressive in its proportions, despite the ruined state of the porch and the unfortunate restoration of the domes and semidomes. The porch originally had seven bays; its handsome antique columns are still standing: four of Proconnesian marble, two of Theban granite, and two of Syenitic granite. From the garden beside the mosque there is a delightful view of the kitchen gardens of the Vlanga district, which occupies the silted-up site of the ancient Byzantine harbour of Eleutherius. The türbe of the founder, a simple octagonal building, is in front of the mosque beside the entrance gate. Nearby there is a ruined şadírvan, and outside in the corner of the precinct wall there is set a pretty çeşme. The külliye originally included an interesting hamam, but unfortunately this has vanished.

Immediately across the street there is an interesting medrese which is not a part of Cerrah Paşa's foundation. This was built in the second half of the 16C by Gevher Sultan, daughter of Selim II and wife of the great admiral Piyale Paşa. This medrese, recently restored, has the standard form of a rectangular porticoed courtyard with cells beyond.

Continue along Cerrah Paşa Cd for another 100m and take the second turning on the right, Haseki Kadín Sk. A short distance up the street, on the right, are the shapeless remains of a massive column base wedged tightly between two houses. It is nearly as tall as the houses and is covered with ivy. This is all that is left of the famous **•Column of Arcadius**, erected by that emperor in 402 to commemorate his military triumphs. It stood in the centre of the Forum of Arcadius and was decorated with spiral bands of sculpture in bas relief representing the Emperor's victories, like Trajan's column in Rome. At the top of the column, which was more than 50m high, there was an enormous statue of Arcadius, placed there in 421 by his son and successor, Theodosius II. This statue was eventually toppled from the column and destroyed during an earthquake in 704. The column itself remained standing for more than another thousand years until it was deliberately demolished in 1715, when it appeared to be in imminent danger of collapsing on the neighbouring houses. Now all that remains are the mutilated base and some fragments of sculpture from the column that are on display in the Archaeological Museum. It is possible to enter the interior of the base through a side door in the house to the left. Inside the base, there is a stairway to the top of the ruin; there one sees a short stump of the column, with barely discernible remnants of the sculptured decoration.

After leaving the column, continue along Haseki Kadín Sk to the end of the street. There one finds the *külliye of Bayram Paşa*, which is divided by the street itself; on the right are the medrese and mektep, and on the left the mescit, tekke, türbe, and sebil. An inscription on the sebil gives the date of construction of the külliye as 1634. At that time Bayram Paşa was Kaymakan, or Mayor, of Istanbul; two years later he became Grand Vezir under Murat IV and soon afterwards he died on the Sultan's expedition against Baghdad. At the corner to the left is the handsome sebil, with five grilled openings; behind it is the really palatial türbe of the founder, looking rather like a small mosque. (It is said to be revetted inside with fine and original tiles; unfortunately it is shut up and inaccessible.) At the far end of the enclosed garden and graveyard stands the mescit, which is flanked on two sides by the porticoed cells of the dervish tekke. The mescit is a large octagonal building which served also as the room where the dervishes performed their mystical ceremonies, with music and dancing. The whole complex is finely built of ashlar stone in the high classical manner, and the very irregularity of its design makes it singularly attractive.

Turning left at the corner and passing the külliye of Bayram Paşa, one comes immediately to the **\*külliye of Haseki Hürrem** (Pl 9,3), which is contiguous with it to the W. This is the third largest and most magnificent mosque complex in the old city, surpassed only by those of the Conqueror and Süleyman the Magnificent.

HISTORY. This külliye was built by Süleyman for his wife, Haseki Hürrem, the famous Roxelana. The mosque and its dependencies were designed by Sinan and completed by him in 1539, making these the earliest known works by the great architect in Istanbul. According to tradition, Süleyman kept the project secret from Roxelana while the külliye was being built, and brought her to the site only on the day the mosque complex was completed and dedicated in her honour.

*The Mosque.* The mosque itself is disappointing, especially as it is a work of Sinan. Originally it consisted of a small square room covered by a dome on stalactited pendentives, preceded by a rather pretentious porch of five bays that overlapped the building at both ends. It may perhaps have had a certain elegance of form and detail in its original design. But in 1612 a second and identical room was added on the N: the N wall was removed and replaced with a great arch supported on two columns. The mihrab was then moved to the middle of the new extended E wall, so that it stands squeezed behind one of the columns. The result is distinctly unpleasing.

*The Pious Foundations.* The other buildings of the mosque complex are magnificent; comprising a medrese, primary school, public kitchen, and hospital. Moreover, most of the complex has been well restored during the last decade. The medrese is immediately across the street from the mosque. It is of the usual type: a porticoed courtyard surrounded by the cells of the students and the larger domed dershane; but apart from its truly imperial size, it is singularly well-proportioned and excellent in detail. Its 20 columns are of granite, Proconnesian marble, and verd antique; their lozenge capitals are decorated with small rosettes and medallions of various elegant designs, as well as here and there a sort of snaky garland motif—a unique design. Also unique are the two pairs of lotus flower capitals, their leaves spreading out at the top to support a sort of abacus; though soft and featureless, they make a not unattractive variation from the almost equally characterless lozenge. Two carved hemispherical bosses in the spandrils of the arcade call attention to the dershane, a monumental square room with a dome. The great charm of this courtyard must have been still greater when the faience panels with inscriptions were still in place in the lunettes of the windows; many years ago, when the building was abandoned and dilapidated, they were removed to the museum and are now on display at the Çinili Köşkü (see above, Rte 4C). Next to the medrese is the large and very oddly-shaped sibyan mektebi, which is in two storeys with wide projecting eaves.

The imaret, beyond the mektep, is entered through a monumental portal that leads to an alleyway. At the end of this one enters the long rectangular courtyard of the imaret, shaded with trees. Vast kitchens with large domes and enormous chimneys (better seen from outside at the back) line three sides of the courtyard.

Until a decade ago this was the only imaret in the old city still in use as a public kitchen. (There is another one still open in the suburb of Eyüp, that of Mihrişah Sultan; see below, Rte 17.) Here, once a day between 11 and 12 in the morning, food was distributed free to some 500 poor people from all parts of the city. But then, unfortunately, the imaret was closed when plans were made to convert it and the medrese into a modern tourist hostel. This grandiose plan was later abandoned and the project left half-finished, as a result of which the imaret is no longer in use and is presently closed to the public.

Haseki Hürrem's hospital is behind the medrese and entered from the street behind the külliye to the N. It is a building of most unusual form: the court is octagonal but without a columned portico. The two large corner-rooms at the back, whose great domes have stalactited pendentives coming far down the walls, originally opened to the courtyard through huge arches, now glassed-in; with these open rooms or eyvans all the other wards and chambers of the hospital communicated. Opposite the eyvans on one side is the entrance portal; this is approached through an irregular vestibule, like that found so often in Persian mosques. On the other side are the lavatories, also irregular in shape, while the eighth side of the courtyard forms the facade on the street with grilled windows. This building too has recently been well restored and is once again in use as a hospital.

Returning to the street outside Haseki Hürrem Camii, continue in the same direction for about 400m. Then on the left, set back from the road and partly concealed by trees and houses, is a fine but dilapidated old mosque. This is **Davut Paşa Camii** (Pl 8,4),dated, by an inscription over the door, 1485. Davut Paşa, the founder, was Grand Vezir under Beyazit II.

INTERIOR. In plan the mosque is of the simplest type: just a square chamber covered by a large blind dome. However, the mihrab is in a five-sided apse projecting from the E wall, and to N and S there are small rooms, two on each side, once used as hostels for travelling dervishes. What gives the building its distinction and harmony, is the beautiful shallow dome, quite obviously less than half a hemisphere. The pendentives of the dome are an unusually magnificent example of the stalactite form, here boldly incised and brought far down the corners of the walls. Unfortunately, they are in very bad condition, as is the interior in general. A small amount of very careful restoration is called for, because this mosque is one of the half-dozen of the earliest period which are most worthy of preservation. The five-domed porch, has been restored, and hopefully the interior will be treated soon.

Behind the mosque a delightfully topsy-turvy graveyard surrounds the founder's türbe, octagonal in form and with an odd dome in eight triangular segments. Across the narrow street to the N stands the medrese of the külliye, almost completely surrounded and concealed by houses. The courtyard is extremely handsome, with its re-used Byzantine columns and capitals, but it is in an advanced state of ruin and urgently needs restoration, especially as it is the only 15C vezirial medrese to survive in something like its original form. The külliye also once had an imaret and a mektep, but these have completely disappeared.

Some 200m beyond Davut Paşa Camii and on the same side of the street is a grand and interesting mosque, **\*Hekimoğlu Ali Paşa Camii** (Pl 8,4).

HISTORY. The founder of the mosque, Ali Paşa, was an Ottoman nobleman who was the son (*oğlu*) of the court physician (*hekim*), and was himself Grand Vezir for 15 years under Mahmut I. A long inscription in Turkish verse over the door to the mosque gives the date of construction as 1734–35; the architect was Ömer Ağa.

EXTERIOR. One can consider this complex to be either the last of the great classical buildings or the first in the new baroque style, for it has characteristics of both. At the corner of the precinct wall beside the N entrance is a very beautiful sebil of marble with five bronze grilles. Above this is an elaborate frieze with a long inscription and fine carvings of vines, flowers and rosettes in the new rococo style that had recently been introduced from France. The facade of the türbe along the street is faced in marble, corbelled out toward the top and with a çeşme at the far end. It is a large rectangular building with two domes dividing it into two equal square areas. This form was not unknown in the classical period (compare Sinan's Pertev Paşa türbe at Eyüp, see Rte 17) but it was rare, and the use of it here seems to indicate a willingness to experiment with new forms. Farther along the precinct wall stands the monumental gateway with a domed chamber above; this was the library of the foundation. Though the manuscripts have been transferred elsewhere, it still contains the painted wooden cages with grilles in which they were stored; an elegant floral frieze runs around the top of the walls and floral medallions adorn the dome. From the columned porch at the top of the steps leading to the library there is a good view of the whole complex, with its singularly attractive garden full of tall cypresses and aged plane trees, and opposite the stately porch and very slender minaret of the mosque.

INTERIOR. The mosque itself, raised on a substructure containing a cistern, is purely classical in form. Indeed, its plan is almost an exact replica of that at Cerrah Paşa, seen earlier on this itinerary. In contrast to Cerrah Paşa, the present building is perhaps a little weak; there is a certain blurring of forms and enervating of structural distinctions, an effect not mitigated by the pale colour of the tile revetment. The tiles are still Turkish, not manufactured at Iznik as formerly, but at the recently established kilns at Tekfur Saray in Istanbul. All the same, the general impression of the interior is charming if not exactly powerful. There is a further hint of the new baroque style in one of its less pleasing traits in some of the capitals of the columns, both in the porch and beneath the sultan's loge. The traditional stalactite and lozenge capitals have been abandoned there in favour of a very weak and characterless form like an impost capital, which seems quite out of scale and out of place.

PRECINCTS. The whole complex within the precinct wall is in the process of being very completely and very well restored. Outside the precinct, across the street to the NE, stands the tekke of the foundation, but little is left of it save a very ruinous zaviye, or room for the dervish ceremonies.

There are two minor monuments in the area to the N of Hekimoğlu Ali Paşa Camii. It is impossible to give precise directions for this detour, for the neighbourhood is a veritable maze of tiny gecekondus (hovels, literally shacks erected in a single night), with paths leading off in every direction.

Some 200m N of Hekimoğlu Ali Paşa Camii there are the ruins of a once handsome medrese, whose cells are now inhabited by squatters. It was built by Sinan for Nişanci Mehmet Bey, who served as Keeper of the Royal Seal (Nişanci) in the reign of Süleyman the Magnificent. The medrese was built before 1566, when Nişanci Mehmet Bay died on hearing the news of Süleyman's death.

About 350m N of Hekimoğlu Ali Paşa Camii is the third of the city's three surviving open Roman reservoirs. This is known locally as *Alti Mermer*, the Six Marbles; in Byzantium it was called the Cistern of St. Mocius, from a famous church of that name which stood in its vicinity. The cistern was constructed during the reign of the Emperor Anastasius (491–518); like the two other surviving Roman reservoirs, it fell into disuse in the later Byzantine period. Today it is used as a vegetable garden and orchard, with a few wooden houses at the E end. The cistern is a vast rectangle measuring 170m by 147m on the inside, with walls 6m thick; the present depth is about 10–5m. On the E and S sides the wall emerges, between 2m to 4m, from the surrounding earth. The walls are of good late Roman construction, they are composed of brick, alternating both inside and out with beds of dressed stone, 15cm to 20cm high. The interior of the cistern is most easily reached on the N side.

Returning to Hekimoğlu Ali Paşa Camii, take the street that runs past the N side of the mosque precinct, following this to its intersection with Koca Mustafa Paşa Cd (the continuation of Cerrah Paşa Cd). Then take the street opposite and slightly to the left; this immediately brings one to a pathetic ruin that is of interest only because of its association with Sinan.

This complex, which is known locally as *Isa Kapí Mescidi*, consists of two walls of a Byzantine church and the wreck of a medrese by Sinan. Of the church only the S and E walls remain. It was of the simplest kind: an oblong room without aisles ending at the E in a large projecting apse and two tiny side apses. In the southern side apse there could be seen till recently the traces of frescoes; these have now almost completely disappeared. The church is thought to date from the beginning of the 14C, but nothing is known of its history nor even the name of the saint to whom it was dedicated. In about 1560 the church was converted into a mosque by Hadím (the Eunuch) Ibrahim Paşa, who at that time was Süleyman's Grand Vezir, and who added to it a handsome medrese designed by Sinan. Both mosque and medrese were destroyed by the great earthquake of 1894, and they have remained abandoned ever since. The ruins of the medrese, which is unusual in plan, are rather fine; its large dershane still retains traces of plaster decoration around the dome, and the narrow courtyard beyond must have been very attractive. But the columns and domes of the porticoes have fallen, squatters live in the few remaining cells, and all is desolate and squalid. The name Isa Kapí means the Gate of Christ, and some scholars have suggested that it preserves the memory of one of the gates in the city walls built by Constantine the Great, which are thought to have been close by. This is possible, but the evidence is inconclusive.

The alley that goes round behind Isa Kapí Mescidi leads to the top of a steep hill overlooking the Marmara. There turn right onto Sancaktar Tekke Sk, which leads after several zigzags to another ruined Byzantine building, known locally as *Sancaktar Mescidi*. This has been tentatively identified, on very slender evidence, as one of the buildings of the Monastery of Gastria. The legend is that this monastery was founded in the 4C by St. Helena, mother of Constantine the Great, and that it derives its name of Gastria, which means vases, from the vases of flowers she brought back from Calvary, where she had discovered a fragment of the True Cross. This story has been refuted by the French scholar Janin, who shows that there is no trace of the existence of the monastery before the 9C. The present little building has the form of an octagon on the exterior with a projecting apse at the E end; the interior takes the form of a domed cross. It is thought that it was once a funerary chapel, and has been dated variously from the 11C to the 14C. It is now a wreck; its dome and most of the S wall have fallen, and the rest seems in imminent danger of collapse, although this does not seem to deter the squatters.

Leaving the church, walk straight ahead for a few paces to the next intersection and then turn right onto Marmara Cd. This leads back to Koca Mustafa Paşa Cd; turn left there and then take the second right onto Ramazan Efendi Cd. A short way along on the right one comes to a small but charming mosque with a pretty garden courtyard in front; this is *Ramazan Efendi Camii, a work of Sinan (Pl 8,4).

HISTORY. The mosque was founded by an official in the Ottoman court named Hoca Hüsref, but it soon took the name of Ramazan Efendi Camii, after the first şeyh of the dervish tekke that was part of the original külliye. The mosque was designed and built by Sinan, and a long inscription over the inner door by his friend, the poet Mustafa Sa'i, gives the date as 1586; thus this is undoubtedly the last mosque erected by the great architect, completed in his 95th year.

*The Mosque.* The mosque is a structure of the simplest type: a small rectangular room with a wooden roof and porch. It is thought that it was originally covered by a wooden dome and that it had a porch with three domed bays supported by four marble columns; the present wooden porch and flat wooden ceiling are botched restorations after an earthquake. The minaret is an elegant structure both in proportion and detail, while the small şadírvan in the courtyard is exquisitely carved. The great fame of the mosque comes from the magnificent panels of faience with which it is adorned. These are from the Iznik kilns at the height of their artistic production, and are thus some of the finest tiles in existence; the borders of 'tomato-red' or Armenian bole are especially celebrated.

After leaving the mosque return to Koca Mustafa Paşa Cd and continue in the same direction as before. A short way along the avenue forks to the right and soon comes to a very picturesque square shaded with trees and lined with teahouses. At the left side of the square is the entrance to the outer courtyard of *Koca Mustafa Paşa Camii (Pl 8,6), the popular religious shrine after which the avenue and the surrounding neighbourhood are named.

HISTORY. The central building of this picturesque complex is *Koca Mustafa Paşa Camii*, much earlier a church known as St. Andrew in Krisei. The identification and history of this church are, however, very obscure and much disputed. One may summarise the opinions of Byzantinists as follows: Koca Mustafa Paşa *may* have been one of the churches in this region dedicated to a St. Andrew; if it is, it is *probably* that dedicated to St. Andrew of Crete in c 1284 by the Princess Theodora Raoulaina. Also, the present building was almost certainly of the ambulatory type; it *may* have been built on the foundations of an earlier church dedicated to St. Andrew the Apostle; and it certainly re-used 6C materials, especially capitals. In any event, the church was converted into a mosque early in the 16C by Koca Mustafa Paşa, Grand Vezir in the reign of Selim I (1512–20).

INTERIOR. When the church was converted into a mosque the interior arrangements were re-oriented by ninety degrees because of the direction in which the building was laid out. Thus the mihrab and mimber are under the semidome against the S wall; and the entrance is in the N wall, in front of which a wooden porch has been added. One enters through a door at the W end of the N aisle into the narthex, from where one should proceed at once to the central bay of the narthex. This bay has a small dome supported by columns with beautiful 6C capitals of the pseudo-Ionic type. From here the central portal opens into a sort of inner narthex or aisle, separated from the nave by only two verd antique columns; this aisle is regrettably obstructed by a large wooden gallery. From this point the whole interior of the former church is visible; it now has a trefoil shape but was probably originally ambulatory: that is, there would have been a triple arcade supported by two columns to N and S, like the one that still exists on the W. To the E the conch of the apse is preceded by a deep barrel-vault; to the N and S the two later Ottoman semidomes open out. Even in its greatly altered form it is an extremely attractive building.

PRECINCTS. The dependencies of the mosque include a medrese, a tekke, a mektep, and two türbes; what survive of these are of a much later date than the conversion of the church into a mosque. The mosque is one of the most popular Moslem religious shrines in the city, for in one of the türbes in the courtyard the famous Istanbul folk-saint Sümbül (Hyacinth) Efendi is buried. Sümbül Efendi was the first şeyh of the dervish tekke established here in the early 16C, and in the centuries since then he has been prayed to by the people of the city for help in solving their problems. In the other türbe Sümbül Efendi's daughter Rahine is buried; she is generally prayed to by young women looking for husbands. The ancient tree tottering above her türbe is also said to possess miraculous powers.

After leaving the mosque precincts, return along Koca Mustafa Paşa Cd as far as the first right after the fork in the road. This street, Mudafaai Milliye Cd, leads down the slope of the Seventh Hill towards the Marmara shore. About 250m along turn left on Marmara Cd, a wide and pleasant avenue that runs along the heights parallel to the sea. A short way along one sees, on the right, the large Armenian church of *Surp Kevork* (St. George), known locally as Sulu Monastir; this is a modern structure of no interest, but the original church on this site has an interesting history.

HISTORY. The modern church is built on the site of the ancient Byzantine monastery of St. Mary Peribleptos, the All-Seeing, of which nothing but substructures remain. It was founded in the 11C by the Emperor Romanus III Argyros (1028–34), and it continued to serve as a Christian sanctuary after the Turkish Conquest. Heretofore, the generally accepted tradition is that the church remained in the hands of the Greeks until 1643, when it was given to the Armenians by Sultan Ibrahim under the influence of a favourite Armenian concubine. (This lady's name was Şeker Parça, or Piece of Sugar; she is said to have weighed more than 300 pounds.) But this story appears to be fictitious: in the recently published work of the Armenian traveller Simeon of Zamosc in Poland, who visited the city in 1608, it is recorded that the church was already in the hands of the Armenians and that it served as the cathedral for the Armenian patriarch.

Once past the church turn right and take the road that leads down toward the Marmara. In doing so one is confronted almost immediately with an interesting view of a vast double hamam. It is astonishing how many domes of all sizes, arranged apparently at random, these hamams have, and it is not often that one can get a good view of them from above. This one is called *Ağa Hamamí* and is a work of Sinan. Unfortunately, it is disaffected and ruinous, used partly for storage, partly as a depot for tempering copper. The workshop is installed in what was once the hararet of the bath, a typical cruciform room with cubicles in the corners, now much blackened by the smoke of the furnace.

After passing the hamam, turn right on Samatya Cd, which skirts the foot of the Seventh Hill not far from the sea. On the left one soon sees the courtyard wall of a very venerable Greek church, St. George of the Cypresses. This church is thought to have been founded in the 9C, and has remained in the hands of the Greeks ever since. However, the present building is dated 1830.

A little farther along the avenue, on the right, one sees on the heights above the tall campanile of a modern Greek church, *St. Menas:* The church itself is of no interest, but beneath it, though in no way structurally connected with it, there are some very important and ancient substructures. They are entered from Samatya Cd and are currently used as a carpenter's shop and storage place for lumber. These substructures, discovered only in 1935, have been identified as the crypt of the ***Martyrium of SS. Karpos and Papylos** (Pl 8,6) who perished in the Decian persecutions in the mid-3C. The crypt is a large, circular, domed chamber reminiscent of the tholos tombs at Mycenae, only constructed of brick rather than of stone, in the excellent late Roman technique of the 4–5C AD. At the E end is a deep apse, while completely round the chamber runs a vaulted passage, also of brick. (This passage can be entered through a door in the teahouse just beyond the carpenter's shop.) Since this appears to be one of the oldest Christian antiquities in the city, and also since it is unique in form, one hopes that it will be rescued from its commercial uses, so that it can be thoroughly investigated and restored.

Some 500m farther along the avenue, on the left, stands the modern Greek church of *SS. Constantine and Helena*. This church has been rebuilt in recent years, but its foundation goes back at least as far as 1563, the date of the earliest recorded reference to it. The profusion of Christian sanctuaries in this area indicates that this is a very old Greek quarter. The official Turkish name for the area is now Koca Mustafa Paşa, but local Greeks still refer to it as Samatya, a name by which this part of the city has been known since the 6C BC.

The second street to the left past SS. Constantine and Helena leads to the walled courtyard of a ruined but extremely impressive Byzantine church of obviously great age. This is the former monastic church of ***St. John the Baptist of Studius**, known in Turkish as **Imrahor Camii** (Pl 8,6). This is the oldest surviving Christian sanctuary in the city, and though in ruins is still one of the greatest monuments of architecture remaining from the days of Byzantium.

HISTORY. The church of St. John the Baptist was completed in 463 and its associated monastery was founded shortly afterwards. The church and monastery were benefactions of the Roman patrician Studius, who served as consul during the reign of the Emperor Marcian (450–7). The first monks in the Studion, as the monastery was called, were from an order known as the Akoimati, receiving this name because they perpetuated the divine service day and night throughout the year, praying in shifts around the clock and calendar. In its early years the Studion housed a full thousand monks, and was one of the richest and most populous monasteries in Byzantium. Later, however, during the Iconoclastic Period, the Studion and all other monasteries in the Empire were suppressed and then finally shut down altogether in 754 by Constantine V. They remained closed for the next generation but were reopened in 787, after the first restoration of icons by the Empress Eirene, mother of Constantine VI.

The golden age in the history of the Studion began in 799, when the great abbot Theodore arrived to take direction of the monastery. During the following generation Theodore made the Studion the most powerful and influential monastery in the Empire. He was a leader in the struggle to restore icon veneration, which was proscribed again in 815 during the reign of the iconoclast Leo V. Theodore was also an outspoken critic of court morals, an activity that brought him into conflict with four successive emperors in the first quarter of the 9C. Although he was reviled, beaten, deposed and exiled by each of them in turn, he held firm to his stern principles to the grave. Theodore died in exile on

*The former church of St.John of Studius was completed in 463. Converted to a mosque in the late 15C, it was ruined by an earthquake in 1894. (Sedat Pakay)*

the isle of Prinkipo in the Marmara on 11 November 826, but in 843 he was reburied in the garden of the Studion, after the final restoration of icons under Michael III. Today he is venerated in the Greek Orthodox Church as St. Theodore of Studion. Under the direction of St. Theodore, and his successors, the Studion flourished and became a centre for the first cultural and artistic renaissance of Byzantium in the early 9C. Many monks of the Studion won renown as composers of sacred hymns, painters of icons, and illuminators of manuscripts. The monastery was also noted for its scholarship and was one of the centres for the preservation and copying of ancient manuscripts, many of which would be carried to Europe by Byzantine scholars during the western renaissance in the 14–15C.

The most momentous hour in the long history of the Studion occurred on 15 August 1261, when Byzantium was officially restored in its ancient capital after the recapture of the city from the Latins. On that day Michael VIII Palaeologus entered in triumph through the Golden Gate and walked in procession to the Studion, following the sacred icon of the Hodegetria, which was being carried before the populace in a chariot. After reaching the Studion the icon was placed on the main altar of the church, and the Emperor joined the Patriarch in a ceremony of thanksgiving. Then the Emperor left the church and mounted his white charger in the square outside, after which he and his entourage rode off to Haghia Sophia for his formal recoronation.

The Studion continued as one of the spiritual and intellectual centres of the Empire right up to the Conquest. During the first half of the 15C the University of Constantinople was located at the Studion, and during that period some of the greatest scholars in the history of Byzantium taught and studied there, men who would later be influential figures in the Italian renaissance of the 15C. The Studion survived the fall of Byzantium and continued to function for nearly half a century after the Conquest, celebrating its millennium in 1463. But then at the close of the 15C the church of St. John was converted into a mosque, and the few monks that were still resident in the monastery were forced to seek shelter elsewhere. The founder of the mosque was Ilyas Bey, Master of the Horse (Imrahor) under Beyazit II, and so it came to be called Imrahor Camii. What was left of the monastery in modern times was utterly destroyed in the earthquake of 1894. The church itself was badly damaged in the earthquake, and from that time on it was abandoned and allowed to fall into ruins. Although several cursory studies have been made of the building, it still awaits a thorough archaeological and architectural investigation.

*The Church.* The church was preceded by an atrium, or courtyard, whose site is now occupied by the walled garden through which the building is approached. The narthex is divided into three bays; the wider central bay has a very beautiful portal consisting of four columns *in antis*, with magnificent Corinthian columns supporting an elaborate entablature with richly sculptured architrave, frieze and cornice. Two of the marble door-frames still stand between the columns. From the narthex five doors lead into the church. In form the church was a pure basilica, with a nave flanked by side aisles separated from the sanctuary by two rows of seven columns each. Six of these on the N side still stand; they are of verd antique, with capitals and entablature as in the narthex. The nave ends in a single semicircular apse where tiers of seats once rose, for the clergy, with the altar in front of them. Originally there was a second row of columns, above the entablature of the aisle colonnades, which supported the wooden roof. The interior was revetted with marble and the upper parts decorated with mosaics. The floor was also of mosaic in opus sectile design, and of this some portions may still be seen, although they are fast disappearing.

Leaving the church, turn left and follow the winding path that leads around to the SW corner of its outer precincts. Here, at the edge of a vacant lot, there is a small shed that gives access to a covered cistern that was once part of the Studion. It is quite impressive, containing 23 granite columns with handsome Corinthian capitals. The cistern is usually accessible, being used as a sort of iron-shop and storage-place for bedsteads. Beside it there is a holy well with two ancient columns, the identity of which is unknown.

After leaving the cistern, continue on in the same direction as far as the railway line. There turn left and follow the railway as far as the first underpass, from where a path leads out to the sea-walls. At this point turn right to come to an ancient portal called *Narlı Kapı*, the Pomegranate Gate, whence a path leads out past the modern Greek church of St. John to the Marmara highway.

HISTORY. In Byzantium this gateway was used by the Emperor when he went from the Great Palace to the Studion by sea. According to the Book of Ceremonies, the imperial visit to the Studion occurred annually on 28 August, the

*The Byzantine land-walls, mostly constructed in the first half of the 5C, extend from the Sea of Marmara to the Golden Horn, some 6.5km.*

feast day of the Decapitation of St. John. The Emperor landed at a quay before the gateway, he was received by the Abbot of the Studion, and the two led the procession to the church, walking between two long files of chanting monks holding lighted tapers. At the end of the service the Emperor was served refreshments in the monastery gardens, after which he returned in procession to the royal barge, passing once again through the portal which even then was known as the Pomegranate Gate.

From Narlí Kapí one can walk westward farther along the shore road to the city walls, where the next itinerary begins. Those who wish to follow that itinerary on another day can return to town by walking back along the shore road. This is a pleasant stroll on a fine day, and along the way stretches of the ancient Byzantine sea-walls and the remains of some of the massive defence towers can be seen. The walls and towers along this part of the Marmara shore were built by the Emperor Theophilus (829–42), at a time when the city was threatened by an Arab invasion fleet. But the fleet never appeared before the city at that time, undoubtedly because the Arabs were deterred by the great walls that ringed it both by land and by sea.

The most colourful spot on the Marmara shore of the city is **\*Kumkapí** (Pl 10,8), the picturesque harbour and fish-market that is reached after a walk of some 2·5km from Narlí Kapí. Kumkapí occupies the site of the ancient Kontoscalion, the principal Byzantine port on the Marmara shore of Constantinople. It is still the largest and busiest fishing-port in the city, and is used by the local fishermen who sail from here out into the Marmara, up the Bosphorus, and along the coasts of the Black Sea. The port is always filled with picturesque caiques and the quayside is often carpeted with brilliantly-dyed fishing-nets spread there to be dried and mended by the fishermen and their families. The fish-market is one of the most colourful in the city, as the fishmongers shout out in Turkish, Greek, Armenian, and even Laz, the language of the Pontic people who have moved to Istanbul in recent times.

From the port a cobbled road leads down under the railway line, passing through the now almost vanished *Porta Kontascalion*, one of the principal gateways in the Byzantine sea-walls. At the first intersection is *\*Kumkapí Meydaní*, an extremely lively and picturesque market square lined with some of the best fish-restaurants in the city.

city, as the fishmongers shout out in Turkish, Greek, Armenian, and even Laz, the language of the Pontic people who have moved to Istanbul in recent times.

From the port a cobbled road leads down under the railway line, passing through the now almost vanished *Porta Kontascalion*, one of the principal gateways in the Byzantine sea-walls. At the first intersection is *Kumkapí Meydaní*, an extremely lively and picturesque market square lined with some of the best fish-restaurants in the city.

# 16 Along The Land Walls

This itinerary begins at the Sea of Marmara and follows the land-walls to the Golden Horn, with several detours to visit places of interest inside and outside the ancient fortifications. For the most part, no specific directions will be given for proceeding along on this Rte, for in some stretches it is more convenient to walk inside the walls, in others outside, and sometimes one can stroll along the walls themselves.

The **Byzantine land-walls** extend from the Sea of Marmara to the Golden Horn, a distance of about 6.5km. These walls protected Byzantium from its enemies for more than a thousand years, and in that way had a profound effect on the history of medieval Europe. Although they are now in ruins, the walls of Byzantium are still a splendid and even awesome sight, with towers and battlements marching across the hills and valleys of Thrace. Although a hike along the land-walls can be somewhat arduous, it is nevertheless quite rewarding, for on and around them one often discovers aspects of the old city which are not evident elsewhere. And in springtime this stroll can be extremely pleasant, when the walls and towers are covered with ivy, the terraces carpeted with fresh grass, and the moat colourful with wild flowers and blossoming trees.

HISTORY. The land-walls were, for the most part, constructed in the first half of the 5C, during the reign of Theodosius II (408–50). The first phase of the Theodosian wall was completed in 413 under the direction of Anthemius, Prefect of the East. This consisted of a single wall studded with defence towers at regular

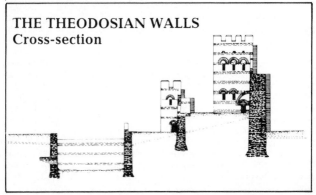

**THE THEODOSIAN WALLS**
Cross-section

intervals. However, in 447 a violent earthquake destroyed much of this wall, throwing down 57 towers. This happened at a very critical time, for Attila the Hun was then advancing on Constantinople. Reconstruction of the fortifications began immediately under the direction of the then Prefect of the East, Constantine. The circus factions of the Hippodrome all worked together in the project, each of them assigned a certain stretch of the circuit, and within two months the walls had been rebuilt and were far stronger than they had been before the earthquake. In addition to restoring and strengthening the original wall, Constantine added an outer wall and a moat, making the city virtually impregnable to assault by land. The new walls saved the city from Attila, the Scourge of God, who redirected his invasion against the western regions of the Roman Empire.

*Plan.* Even though large stretches of the fortifications are in ruins, enough remains of the Theodosian walls to reconstruct their original plan. The main element in the defence system was the inner wall, which was about 5m thick at the base and rose to a  height of 12m above the city. This wall was guarded by 96 towers, 18m to 20m high, at an average interval of 55m; these were mostly square but some were polygonal. Each tower was generally divided into two floors, which did not communicate with one another. The lower storeys were used either for storage or for guard-houses, and were entered from inside the city. The upper rooms were entered from the parapet walk, which was connected by staircases to the ground and to the tops of the towers, where engines were placed for hurling missiles or the terrible incendiary mixture known as Greek Fire. Between the inner and outer walls there was a terrace, called the peribolus, which varied from 15m to 20m in breadth, and stood at about 5m above the level of the inner city. The outer wall, the protichisma, was about 2m thick and 8·5m in height. This wall also had 96 towers, alternating in position with those of the inner wall; in general these were either square or crescent-shaped in turn. Beyond this there was an outer terrace called the parateichion, bounded on the outside by the counterscarp of the moat, which was a battlement nearly 2m high. The moat itself was originally about 10m deep and 20m wide, and was flooded when the city was threatened by invaders. Altogether it was a most formidable system of fortification, perhaps the most elaborate and unassailable ever devised in the medieval world.

Most of the inner wall and nearly all of its huge towers are still standing, although sieges, earthquakes, and the ravages of time have left their scars. While a few of the towers are still intact, most of them are split or cracked, or have half-tumbled to the ground. The outer walls have been almost completely obliterated in many places, and the fragmentary remains of only about half of the towers can still be seen.

**From the Marble Tower to Yediküle** (distance c 620m). The sea-walls along the Marmara joined the land-walls at the SW corner of the city, they are anchored by the *Marble Tower*, the handsome structure standing on a little promontory by the sea. This tower, 13m on a side, at its base, and 30m high; with its lower half faced in marble, is unlike any other structure in the whole defence system. It is thought that it may have been designed as an imperial sea-pavilion, a *pied-à-terre* for the Emperor and his party when they came by sea from the Great Palace to visit the shrine of Zoodochus Pege, which was outside the Theodosian walls. The tower also seems to have served, for a time, as a prison, and one can still see the chute down which the bodies of those executed were thrown into the sea.

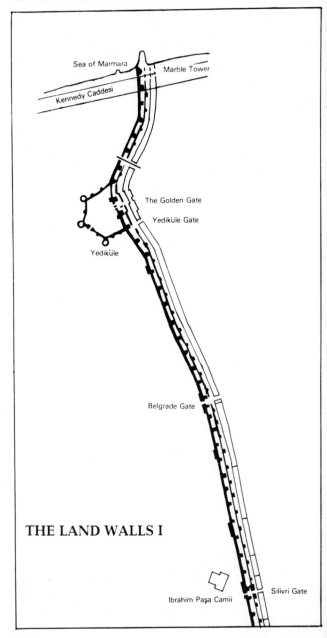

Sea of Marmara

Marble Tower

Kennedy Caddesi

The Golden Gate

Yediküle Gate

Yediküle

Belgrade Gate

Ibrahim Paşa Camii

Silivri Gate

# THE LAND WALLS I

A short way in from the shore highway, immediately to the N of the first tower of the inner wall, there is one of the ancient gateways of the city; this is called the *Gate of Christ* because of the laurate monogram XP (the first two Greek letters in His name) above it.

In the long line of the Theodosian walls there were only ten gates and a few small posterns. Five of the ten gates were public entryways and five were used exclusively by the military, such as the Gate of Christ (this was also called the First Military Gate). The distinction was not so much in their structure as in the fact that the public gates had bridges leading over the moat to the country beyond, while the military gates gave access only to the fortifications. Until the end of the last century Stamboul was still a walled town and these gates were the only entrances to the city from Thrace. However, in recent times the walls have been breached in several places to permit the passage of the railway and modern highways. Nevertheless, nearly all the ancient gates continue in use, as they have now for more than fifteen centuries.

The first stretch of the Theodosian walls is rather difficult to inspect because of the railway and the various unpleasant industries located just outside the city, particularly the reeking tanneries. Those able to make the effort will find that the wall around the Gate of Christ is in a remarkably good state of preservation, with hardly a stone out of place. The first small tower of the protichisma bears an inscription of John VIII Palaeologus (1425–48); the fourth tower in the inner wall (counting from the Marmara) has an inscription of Romanus I Lecapenus (919–44); and the seventh inner tower has one with the names of Leo III (717–41) and his son Constantine V (741–75); all of them recording repairs to the walls. There are 30, still legible, inscriptions recording imperial repairs on the towers, gates and ramparts that remain standing between the Marmara and the Golden Horn; they range over a period of more than a thousand years, evidence of how carefully the Byzantines maintained the great walls that stood between them and their enemies.

The railway cuts through the walls between the seventh and eighth towers of the inner wall. The ninth tower of the inner wall forms the NW corner of Yediküle, the Castle of the Seven Towers, while the ninth and tenth towers are marble pylons flanking the famous Golden Gate; these towers are also part of Yediküle, as is the eleventh and last tower in this first stretch of the Theodosian walls. Immediately beyond this last tower is *Yediküle Kapísí*, a small portal which was the public entryway to this part of the city in Byzantine times, the Golden Gate being reserved for ceremonial occasions. In the interior above the arch of this gate there is the figure of an imperial Byzantine eagle represented in white marble.

**Yediküle and the Golden Gate. **Yediküle** (Pl 8,7) is a curious structure, partly Byzantine and partly Turkish. The seven eponymous towers consist of four in the Theodosian wall itself, plus three additional towers built inside the walls by Mehmet the Conqueror. The three inner towers are connected together and joined to the Theodosian walls by four heavy curtain-walls, forming a five-sided enclosure. As has been seen, the two central towers in the Theodosian wall are marble pylons flanking the Golden Gate, and are actually older than the walls themselves. Yediküle was never used as a castle in the usual sense, but two of the towers served in Ottoman times as prisons; the others were used as storage places for a part of the State treasure.

The main entrance to Yediküle (open 9:30–4:30 every day except

Mon) is by a gate near the E tower; once inside the grounds turn left to enter the tower itself. This is sometimes called the Tower of the Ambassadors, since in Ottoman times foreign envoys were often imprisoned there. Many of these unfortunates have carved their names and dates and tales of woe upon the walls of the tower in half-a-dozen languages. An inscription in French gives this advice in verse; 'Prisoners, who in your misery groan in this sad place, offer your sorrows with a good heart to God and you will find them lightened'. The floors of the tower have fallen out, but a staircase in the thickness of the wall leads up to the top. When at the top it is worth while walking around the *chemin de ronde* as far as the Golden Gate, for there is a fine view of the castle and of the Theodosian walls down to the sea.

The pylon to the left of the Golden Gate was also used as a prison in Ottoman times, and it was also one of the principal places of execution in the city. On exhibition are the instruments of torture and execution that were used here in Ottoman times, as well as the infamous 'well of blood', down which the heads of those executed in the tower were supposed to have been thrown to be flushed into the sea. Sultan Osman II was one of the many executed here, strangled by the bowstring after he was deposed on 22 May 1622, when he was only 17 years old.

The much celebrated **\*\*Golden Gate** between the pylons was actually a Roman triumphal arch erected in about 390 by Theodosius I, the Great. At that time the present city walls had not yet been built and the triumphal arch, as was customary, stood by itself on the Via Egnatia, about 2km outside the walls of Constantine. The arch was of the usual Roman form, with a triple arcade consisting of a large central archway flanked by two smaller ones. The outlines of the arches can still be seen clearly although the openings were bricked up in later Byzantine times. The gates themselves were covered with gold plate—hence the name—and the facade was decorated with sculptures, the most famous of which was a group of four elephants, placed there to commemorate the triumphal entry of Thedosius the Great after his victory over Maxentius. When Theodosius II decided to extend the city walls two decades later, he incorporated the Golden Gate within his new land-walls. It was presumably in connection with this new wall that he built the small marble gate outside the triumphal arch; the arch itself would have had no gates, except for ornamental iron or bronze grilles, and would have been indefensible. The outer gateway is part of the general system of defence; together with the curtain walls that join it to the city walls near the polygonal towers, it forms a small courtyard in front of the Golden Gate.

HISTORY. After the time of Theodosius the Great, the Golden Gate was, on many occasions, the scene of triumphal entries by Byzantine emperors: Heraclius in 629 after he saved the Empire by defeating the Persians; Constantine V, Basil I, and Basil II after their victories over the Bulgars; John I Tzimisces after his defeat of the Russians; Theophilus and his son Michael III after their victories over the Arabs. Perhaps the most emotional of all these triumphal entries was that of 15 August 1261, when Michael VIII Palaeologus rode through the Golden Gate on a white charger after Constantinople was recaptured from the Latins. This was also the last time an Emperor of Byzantium rode in triumph through the Golden Gate. In its last two centuries the history of the Empire was one of continuing defeat, and by that time the Golden Gate had been walled up for defence, never again to open.

**From Yediküle to Belgrad Kapísí** (distance c 620m). From Yediküle to the next town gate, Belgrad Kapísí, it is possible to walk either on top of the great wall or on the terrace below, for the fortifications along this stretch are in quite good condition. All of the 11 towers that guard the wall along this line are still standing, as are all but one of those in the outer wall. An inscription on the eighth tower of the inner wall records repairs by Leo III and Constantine V in the years 720 to 741, and one on the tenth tower of the outer wall states that it was restored in 1434 by John VIII Palaeologus.

*Belgrad Kapísí* was known in Byzantium as the Second Military Gate. It was also called Porta tou Deuterou, because it led to the military quarter of Deuterou, where the Gothic soldiers had their barracks during the early Byzantine period. This was the largest of all the military gates and it may also have been used in Byzantium by the public, as indeed it has been since. The gate came by its Turkish name because Süleyman settled in its vicinity many of the artisans he brought back with him from Belgrade after his capture of that city in 1521.

**From Belgrad Kapísí to Silivri Kapísí** (distance c 680m). The stretch of walls from Belgrad Kapísí to the next town gate, Silivri Kapísí, is also in good condition, with all 13 towers still standing in the inner wall and only one missing in the outer. The third and fourth towers of the inner walls both bear inscriptions of Leo III and Constantine V; while the fifth, tenth, and twelfth towers of the protichisma have inscriptions of John VIII, the first dated 1440 and the second and third 1434.

*Silivri Kapísí* was known in Byzantium as the Porta tou Pege because it was near the famous shrine of Zoodochus Pege (see below). Like all of the larger gates, it is double, with entryways through both the inner and outer walls. On the S tower beside the gate there is an inscription dated 1438 and recording a repair by Manuel Bryennius, a nobleman in the reign of John VIII, and on the N tower there is an inscription of Basil II (976–1025) and his brother Constantine VIII (1025–8).

The most memorable day in the history of this gate was 25 July 1261. On that day a small body of Greek troops led by Alexius Strategopoulos overpowered the Latin guards at the gate and forced their way inside, thus opening the way to the recapture of Constantinople and the restoration of the Byzantine Empire in its ancient capital.

The ancient shrine of **Zoodochus Pege**, the Life-Giving Spring, is some 500m outside the walls in the vicinity of the Silivri Gate. It is approached by walking out from the gate along Seyitnizam Cd for a short distance and veering right along Silivrikapí Balíklí Cd. The shrine stands to the left of this road just before the first crossroads; it is known locally as Balíklí Kilesi, the Church of the Fish, a name it acquired because of the fish that have swum in the sacred spring since Byzantine times.

HISTORY. Like most shrines of the Zoodochus Pege, the ayazma here was probably a sanctuary of Artemis in ancient times, and became sacred to the Blessed Virgin with the triumph of Christianity in the Greek world. According to the Byzantine chronicler Nicephorus Caliste, the spring was first enclosed within a Christian shrine by the Emperor Leo I (457–74). Tradition has it that Justinian, while hunting on the Thracian downs one day, came upon a crowd of women at the sacred spring, who told him that its waters had been given therapeutic powers by the Blessed Virgin. Soon afterwards Justinian built a larger sanctuary to enclose the spring, using in its construction surplus materials from Haghia Sophia. This church was destroyed and rebuilt several times during the

Byzantine period, and it remained in the hands of the Greeks after the Conquest. The church was rebuilt again during the Ottoman period, and the present structure dates only from 1833.

*The Shrine.* The outer courtyard is particularly interesting because it is paved with old tombstones, many of which have inscriptions in the curious Karamanlí script; i.e., Turkish written in the Greek alphabet. This was the script used by those Anatolian Greeks who lost their mother language during the long centuries of Turkish domination, but who continued to use the Greek alphabet through their clergy. The inner courtyard has several elaborate tombs of bishops and patriarchs of the Greek Orthodox Church, and many still show the damage suffered during the anti-Greek riots of 1955. The entrance to the shrine is in the corner between the inner and outer courtyards. From there a long flight of steps leads down to a small chapel enclosing the sacred spring. The shrine is little frequented except on the feast day of the Blessed Virgin, 15 August, when the Greeks of the city come to spend the day picnicking there, just as they have for centuries past.

Just inside Silivri Kapísí there is a fairly large and charming mosque, *Ibrahim Paşa Camii*. This was built in 1551 by Sinan for Hadím Ibrahim Paşa, who at that time was Grand Vezir under Süleyman the Magnificent. The mosque has a fine porch with five domed bays and a portal surmounted by an elaborate stalactited baldachino. In form it is an octagon inscribed in a rectangle with galleries on each side; it has no columns, but in the angles of the octagon pretty pendentives in the form of shells support the dome. The marble mimber and sultan's loge are of admirable workmanship, as are the inlaid ivory panels of the door. Over the mihrab are tiles with inscriptions; these must be a subsequent addition, for they appear to be from the very latest Iznik period or perhaps even from the 18C potteries of Tekfur Saray. In the mosque garden there is the attractive open türbe of the founder with a marble sarcophagus. The pious foundation, whose date is given in calligraphic inscriptions over the garden gates, originally included a mektep and a hamam, but these have perished.

**From Silivri Kapísí to Yeni Mevlevihané Kapísí** (distance c 900m). All of the original 15 towers are still standing in the stretch of wall between these two gates, but neither they nor the walls themselves are as well-preserved as those closer to the Marmara. Between the fifth and seventh towers there is a curious indentation in the wall; this is known as the *Sigma* because its shape resembles the uncial form of that Greek letter, which is like the letter C. Just beyond the Sigma is the *Third Military Gate*, now walled up. Over this little gate there once stood a statue of Theodosius II, builder of these walls; this did not disappear until the 14C. The second tower of the inner wall bears an inscription of Leo III and Constantine V, and on the tenth tower is one with the names of Leo IV (775–80), Constantine VI (780–97), and the Empress Eirene (797–802). Two of the towers in the outer wall, the first before the Sigma and the second beyond it, bear inscriptions of John VIII, dated respectively 1439 and 1438.

*Yeni Mevlevihane Kapísí* takes its Turkish name from a tekke of Mevlevi dervishes that once stood outside the gate. In Byzantium it was called the Gate of Rhegium, and sometimes also the Gate of the Reds, after the circus faction that built it. The gateway is remarkable for the number of inscriptions preserved upon it. One inscription

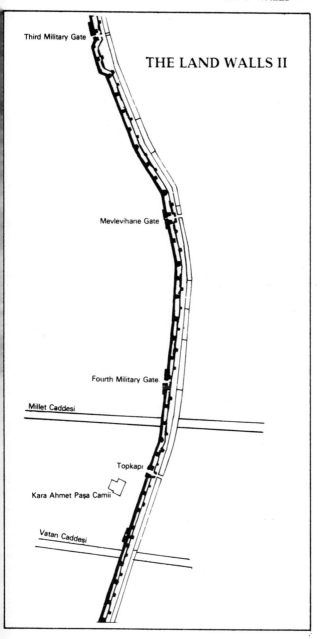

Third Military Gate

# THE LAND WALLS II

Mevlevihane Gate

Fourth Military Gate

Millet Caddesi

Topkapı

Kara Ahmet Paşa Camii

Vatan Caddesi

mentions the Red faction and is, undoubtedly, of 447, when the final phase of the Theodosian walls was completed by Constantine, Prefect of the East. This great feat is commemorated in two inscriptions on the S corbel of the outer gate, one in Greek and the other in Latin. The Greek inscription merely gives the facts; the Latin one is more boastful, reading: 'By the command of Theodosius, Constantine erected these strong walls in less than two months. Scarcely could Pallas herself have built so strong a citadel in so short a span'. There is also an inscription on the lintel of the outer gate recording a restoration by Justin II (565–78), his wife Sophia, and Narses. Narses was a eunuch who succeeded Belisarius as commander of the Byzantine army, and was the last Byzantine Exarch of Italy before its conquest by the Lombards. Another inscription bears the names of Basil II (976–1025) and Constantine VIII (1025–28).

**From Yeni Mevlevihane Kapísí to Top Kapí** (distance c 900m). The stretch between these two gates forms the centre of the long arc of walls extending from the Marmara to the Golden Horn. All but one of the 15 towers in the inner wall are still standing, along with all 14 towers of the protichisma. The seventh tower of the inner wall bears the names of Leo III and Constantine V, along with this inscription: 'Oh Christ, God, preserve thy city undisturbed and free from war. Conquer the wrath of our enemies'. Between the ninth and tenth towers the inner wall is pierced by the *Fourth Military Gate*, now closed up. On the first tower of the protichisma N of this gate there is an inscription mentioning a certain Georgius. This is believed to have been removed from a nearby church and placed in the walls during the restoration by John VIII in 1438–39, evidence that many buildings near the walls were torn down to strengthen them against the impending siege by the Turks.

A short distance to the N of the Fourth Military Gate the walls have been breached to permit the passage of Millet Cd. Some 300m down Millet Cd and on the right is a minor monument, perhaps of interest only to Byzantinists; this is the tiny Byzantine church known locally as *Monastir Mescidi*, located just inside the entrance to a vast bus depot. Its Byzantine name and history are unknown; various identifications have been proposed, but none is at all convincing. The church is of the very simplest form: a long rectangular chamber ending at the E with the usual three projecting apses, and preceded at the W by a small narthex; a date between the 13 and 14C seems most likely.

Opposite Monastir Mescidi on the N side of Millet Cd is an equally insignificant little mosque called *Kürekçibaşí Camii*, founded by one Ahmet Bey during the reign of Süleyman the Magnificent. The mosque is rectangular in form and has a wooden roof. It once had a fine porch, of which only the columns now remain; they are Byzantine, with crosses on the shaft and interesting Byzantine capitals.

After starting back along Millet Cd, take the first right onto Topkapí Cd. At the end of this street on the left there is another small mosque, which is of little interest except for its great age. This is *Beyazit Ağa Camii*, which dates from the reign of the Conqueror. It is of the same type as Kürekçibaşí Camii; that is, rectangular with a wooden roof, and it appears to be built on top of an ancient cistern.

Just opposite the end of Topkapí Cd is a very impressive mosque complex a short distance inside the Theodosian walls; this is *Kara Ahmet Paşa Camii** (Pl 4,7), one of the loveliest and most masterful of Sinan's works. Sinan built this mosque complex in 1554 for Kara Ahmet Paşa, who at that time served as Grand Vezir under Süleyman the Magnificent.

EXTERIOR. One enters through a gate in the S wall of the complex, passing into a spacious and charming courtyard shaded by plane trees. The court is formed by the cells of the medrese; to the left stands the large dershane with pretty shell-shaped pendentives under the dome; beside it a passage leads to the lavatories. The porch of the mosque has unusually wide and attractive arches supporting its five domes. Over the niches of the porch there are some exceptional tiles, decorated, predominantly, in apple-green and vivid yellow in the old cuerda seca technique. They are the latest recorded examples of the second period of the Iznik potteries, the only other important examples being those in the türbe of the Şehzade and the fine series of panels in the mosque of Selim I. A few more of these panels, but with blue and white inscriptions, will be found inside the mosque on the E wall. The marble revetment around the entrance portal evidently belongs to a restoration carried out in 1896; fortunately, though very Empire in style, it is restrained and does not clash badly with the rest.

INTERIOR. The internal plan of the mosque is a hexagon inscribed in a rectangle. The four semidomes lie along the diagonals of the building and each rests on two small conches; six great columns support the arches, and there are galleries on three sides. The proportions of the building are unusually fine, as are many of the details; for example, the polychrome voussoirs of the arches and the elegant mihrab and mimber. The wooden ceilings under the W galleries, painted with elaborate arabesques in rich reds, dark blue, gold and black, are most original features. This is perhaps the most extensive and best-preserved example of this kind of painting in the city; it is singularly rich and beautiful. Unfortunately, the ceiling on the left has recently been spoiled by an attempt at restoration, but the one on the right still retains its sombre brilliance.

Precincts. Outside the courtyard wall, towards the W, is the türbe of the founder, a simple octagonal building; unfortunately it is ruined inside. Beyond it stands the large double mektep, of a very interesting design: a long rectangular building with a wooden roof. It is still in use as a primary school, one of the very few Ottoman mekteps that continues to serve its original purpose.

*Top Kapí*, the Cannon Gate, was known in Byzantium as the Gate of St. Romanus, because of its proximity to a church of that name. Its Turkish name stems from the siege in 1453 when the gate faced the largest cannon in the Turkish arsenal, the famous Urban. This enormous weapon was named after the Hungarian engineer who made it for Mehmet II; it was 8m long, 20cm in diameter, and could fire a 1200-pound cannon ball a distance of 1·6km. This cannon caused considerable damage during the final days of the siege, which was principally directed against the stretch of walls between the Sixth and Seventh Hills. Inside the gateway some of the stone cannon balls fired by Urban, and other Turkish cannon, during the final siege, are suspended.

A short distance outside Top Kapí there is an unusual and interesting mosque that is well worth a detour. This is approached by taking Topkapí Davut Paşa Cd, the road that leads off from the gate; it stands about 500m along on the left. This is **•Takkeci Ibrahim Ağa Camii** (Pl 4,7), recognisable immediately by its unique wooden porch and dome.

HISTORY. The mosque was founded in 1592 by a certain Ibrahim Ağa, who was a maker of the felt hats called takke, the most distinctive of which were the tall conical headdresses worn by the dervishes. (In Turkish, a maker of such hats would be called a takkeci.) Takkeci Ibrahim Ağa Camii is the only ancient wooden mosque in the city to have retained its porch and dome, spared by its remote location outside the walls from the many fires that destroyed or badly damaged all of the other structures of its type that once stood in the city.

EXTERIOR. A stone wall with grilles and the remains of a fine sebil at the corner surrounds a very dirty and unkempt yard; one can scarcely call it a garden. The deeply projecting tiled roof of the porch is supported by a double row of wooden pillars. Since the porch extends halfway round both sides of the mosque, the pillars give the effect of a little copse of trees, the more so since the paint has long since worn off. The roof itself has three dashing gables along the facade; a very quaint and pretty arrangement. On the right rises the fine minaret with a beautiful stalactited şerefe. Handsome but rather heavy inscriptions adorn the spaces above the door and windows.

INTERIOR. Within, a wooden balcony runs around the W wall and half of the side walls; it has a cornice that preserves the original arabesque painting, such as that just seen at Kara Ahmet Paşa Camii. The ceiling is of wood painted dark green and in the centre is a wooden dome on an octagonal cornice. Here one sees how greatly the dome adds to the charm of the interior, and what a disaster it is when these ceilings are reconstructed flat. Two rows of windows admit light; the tiny one over the mihrab preserves some ancient and brilliant stained glass. Beneath the upper row of windows the walls are revetted, entirely, with tiles of the greatest Iznik period in large panels with vases of leaves and flowers. These are celebrated, and are as fine as those seen on the previous itinerary at Ramazan Efendi Camii.

**Top Kapí to Edirne Kapísí** (distance c 1250m).

The stretch of fortifications between these two gates was known in Byzantium as the Mesoteichion. This part of the walls was the most vulnerable in the whole defence system, since here the fortifications descend into the valley of the Lycus, which entered the city midway between the two gates. During the last siege the defenders on the Mesoteichion were at a serious disadvantage, being below the level of the Turkish guns on either side of the valley. For that reason, the walls in the Lycus valley are the most badly damaged in the whole length of the fortifications, and most of the defence towers are mere piles of rubble or great shapeless hulks of masonry. It was this section of the walls that was finally breached by the Turks on the morning of 29 May 1453. The final charge was led by a giant Janissary named Hasan, who fought his way onto one of the towers of the outer wall. Hasan himself was slain, but his companions then forced their way across the peribolos and over the inner wall into the city, and within hours Constantinople had fallen to the Turks.

The course of the ancient river Lycus is today marked by the broad new Vatan Cd, which breaches the walls midway between Top Kapí and Edirne Kapísí. Just inside the walls between this breach and the Fifth Military Gate, about 400m to the N, is the area called Sulukule. Since late Byzantine times this has been the Gypsy quarter of the city, and, despite frequent attempts by the authorities to evict them, the Gypsies still live there, in ramshackle wooden houses built right up against the Theodosian walls.

The section of walls in the area that is now called Sulukule was originally known as the Murus Bacchatureus; according to tradition this is where Constantine XI had his command post during the last siege. He was last seen there just before the walls were breached, fighting valiantly beside his cousins Theophilus

Palaeologus and Don Francisco of Toledo and his faithful comrade John Dalmata, none of whom survived. The *Fifth Military Gate* is known in Turkish as Hücum Kapísí, the Gate of the Assault, preserving the memory of that last battle. On the outer lintel of the gate there is an inscription recording a repair by one Pusaeus, dated to the 5C. On the eighth tower of the protichisma there is an inscription of John VIII dated 1433 and another by one Manuel Iagari, in the reign of Constantine XI (1449–53). The latter inscription is the latest record of a repair to the walls, and it was probably placed there at the time of the preparations for the final siege in 1453.

*Edirne Kapísí* stands at the peak of the Sixth Hill and is thus at the highest point in the old city, 77m above sea-level. This gate has preserved in Turkish form one of its ancient names, Porta Adrianopoleos, as from here the main road to Adrianople began, the modern Edirne. It was also known in Byzantium as the Gate of Charisius, or sometimes as the Porta Polyandriou, the Gate of the Cemetery. This latter name came from the large necropolis outside the walls in this area; this still exists with large Turkish, Greek, and Armenian burial-grounds, the latter two probably dating from Byzantine times. Three ancient funerary steles from this necropolis can still be seen set into the courtyard wall of the Greek *church of St. George*, which stands just inside the walls near the gate. It was through Edirne Kapísí that Mehmet II made his triumphal entry after his capture of Constantinople, early in the afternoon of 29 May 1453, and a plaque on the S side of the gate commemorates that historic event.

Just inside Edirne Kapísí, to the S, stands the splendid **\*Mihrimah Sultan Camii** (Pl 4,6), one of the great imperial mosques of Istanbul. Built on the peak of the Sixth Hill, it adorns the view from all parts of the old city and is one of the most prominent landmarks on the skyline of Stamboul.

HISTORY. Mihrimah Camii is one of the architectural masterpieces of Sinan, built by him for the Princess Mihrimah, the favourite daughter of Süleyman the Magnificent. The külliye was built between 1562 and 1565 and includes, besides the mosque, a medrese, mektep, türbe, double hamam, and a long row of shops in the substructure of the terrace on which it was built. Unfortunately, the complex has been very severely damaged by earthquakes at least twice, in 1766 and 1894. Each time the mosque itself was restored, but the attendant buildings were for the most part neglected; in recent years so me not altogether satisfactory, reconstruction has been carried out.

EXTERIOR. From the exterior the building is strong and dominant, as befits its position at the highest point of the city. The square of the dome base with its multi-windowed tympana, identical on all sides, is given solidity and boldness by the four great weight-towers at the corners, prolongations of the piers that support the dome arches. Above this square rises the dome itself on a circular drum pierced by windows.

The mosque is approached from the main street through a gate giving access to a short flight of steps leading up to the terrace. On the right is the great courtyard, around three sides of which are the porticoes and cells of the medrese. The W side, which stands opposite the Theodosian walls with only a narrow road between, has only had its portico restored, and it is difficult to be sure how many cells there would have been along this side and whether the dershane had stood there, as one might expect. In the centre of the courtyard there is an attractive şadírvan. The mosque is preceded by an imposing porch of seven domed bays supported by eight marble and granite columns. This was originally preceded by another porch, doubtless with a

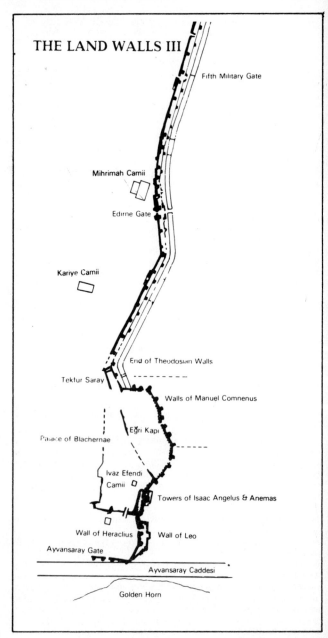

THE LAND WALLS III

Fifth Military Gate

Mihrimah Camii

Edirne Gate

Kariye Camii

End of Theodosian Walls

Tektur Saray

Walls of Manuel Comnenus

Eğri Kapı

Palace of Blachernae

Ivaz Efendi Camii

Towers of Isaac Angelus & Anemas

Wall of Heraclius

Wall of Leo

Ayvansaray Gate

Ayvansaray Caddesi

Golden Horn

sloping wooden roof supported on 12 columns, the bases of which may be seen on the ground. This type of double porch was a favourite of Sinan's; he used it in an earlier mosque built for Mihrimah (see Iskele Camii, Rte 20) and in many others.

INTERIOR. The central area of the interior is square, covered by a great dome 20m in diameter and 37m high under the crown, resting on smooth pendentives. To N and S high triple arcades supported on granite columns open into side aisles with galleries above; each of these has three domed bays, reaching only to the springing of the dome arches. The tympana of all four dome arches are filled with three rows of windows, flooding the mosque with light.

Unfortunately, the interior stencil decoration is modern, insipid in colour and characterless in design. The mimber, however, is a fine original work of white marble with a beautiful medallion perforated like an iron grille. The voussoirs of the gallery arches are fretted polychrome of verd antique and Proconnesian marble. Altogether Mihrimah Camii is one of the very finest mosques in the city and must be counted as one of Sinan's masterpieces.

PRECINCTS. To the S of the mosque is a small graveyard, at the end of which stands an unusually large sibyan mektebi with a central dome flanked by two cradle-vaults. Beyond this, and entered through the mosque, is the ruined türbe of the Grand Vezir Semiz Ali Paşa, Mihrimah's son-in-law. (Mihrimah herself is buried in her father's türbe at the Süleymaniye.) Ali Paşa's türbe is like only one other built by Sinan, that of Pertev Paşa at Eyüp (see below, Rte 17). It is rectangular, more than twice as long as it is wide; its roof has fallen in but one can see that it was originally covered by a large dome and two cradle-vaults. The türbe contains a large number of sarcophagi of members of Princess Mihrimah's family, many of them children.

On the NE side of the mosque, entered from the main street, are the remains of the double hamam of the foundation. The camekan of the women's bath is a complete ruin, while that on the men's side now has a wooden roof supported by wooden columns; originally both undoubtedly had masonry domes. The soğukluk and the hararet of both sides are still structurally intact, though in poor condition and mostly stripped of their marble fittings. There is nothing unusual about the plan of this hamam: the eyvans of the hararet have semidomes; the domes of the cells are on simple pendentives; and the entrance is, as so often, off-centre through one of the cells. This must once have been an elegant example of a Sinan bath, and it is urgent that it should be restored before it is too late. At the corner of the hamam there is a simple but effective çeşme.

**From Edirne Kapísí to Tekfur Saray** (distance c 650m). The Theodosian walls continue on for about 600m beyond Edirne Kapísí, at which point they give way to a stretch of walls constructed in later times. The inner wall in this stretch is well-preserved and has nine towers that are more or less intact. At the very end of the existing Theodosian walls, just next to its last tower, are the remains of a small postern that played a fateful role in the final hours of the last siege. This is the *Porta Xylokerkou*, the Gate of the Wooden Circus, named after a hippodrome that once stood outside the walls in this area. At the climax of the last battle on 29 May 1453 this gate was left open and unguarded for a few moments, and it was through here that the

Janissaries first made their way into the city. And it was from the tower beside the Porta Xylokerkou, the very last bastion on the long line of the Theodosian walls, that the Turkish ensign first waved over Constantinople.

Just beyond this gate there stands one of the most remarkable buildings remaining from the days of Byzantium. It is known in Turkish as *Tekfur Saray (Pl 5,3), the Palace of the Sovereign, but it is better known in English as the **Palace of the Porphyrogenitus**. The palace was probably built in the latter part of the 13C or early in the 14C and served as one of the imperial residences during the last two centuries of Byzantium; it was perhaps an annexe of the nearby Palace of Blachernae. It is a large three-storeyed building wedged in between the inner and outer fortifications of the last stretch of the Theodosian walls. On the ground floor an arcade, with four wide arches, opens onto the courtyard, which is overlooked on the first floor by five large windows. The top floor, which projects above the walls, has windows on all sides, seven overlooking the courtyard, a curious bow-like apse on the opposite side, and a window with the remains of a balcony to the E. The roof and all of the floors have disappeared. The whole palace, but especially the facade on the court, is elaborately decorated with geometrical designs in red brick and white marble, so typical of the later period of Byzantine architecture; compare the facades of St. Saviour in Chora and St. Theodore, both of the 14C.

HISTORY. Its close proximity to the walls caused the palace to be badly damaged in the last siege, but after the Conquest it was repaired and used for a variety of purposes. During the 16–17C it served as an imperial menagerie, particularly for larger and tamer animals such as elephants and giraffes. (The latter particularly amazed European travellers to the city.) Before the end of the 17C the animals were moved elsewhere and the palace served for a while as a brothel. But it was soon redeemed from this misuse, for in 1719 the famous Tekfur Saray pottery was set up here. This pottery produced a new kind of Turkish tiles, the so-called Tekfur Saray type, inferior to those of Iznik and beginning to show European influence, but nevertheless quite charming. The project, however, was short-lived, and by the second half of the 18C the palace was in full decline and eventually lost its roof and floors. During the first half of the 19C Tekfur Saray served as a poorhouse for Jews and in the present century it housed a bottle works before being abandoned altogether; today it is a mere shell. In recent years the palace has been restored to a very slight extent, but a much more thorough programme of restoration and maintenance is called for.

**From Tekfur Saray to Eğri Kapı** (distance c 220m). Just beyond Tekfur Saray the Theodosian walls come to an abrupt end and the fortifications are continued by walls of later construction. There has been much discussion about the original course of the Theodosian walls from Tekfur Saray down to the Golden Horn. It would appear that they turned almost due N at Tekfur Saray and from there followed a more-or-less straight line down to the Horn, whereas the present walls are bent in an arc farther out into Thrace. Stretches of what are undoubtedly the original Theodosian walls can be seen at Tekfur Saray and also along Mumhane Cd, which can be reached by turning right in the little square beyond the palace and then taking the first left. The ruined walls along this street are quite impressive and picturesque; like so many other ruins in town they are inhabited by squatters.

The present stretch of walls from Tekfur Saray to the Golden Horn is quite different from the Theodosian fortifications. It is a single bulwark without a moat; to make up for this deficiency it is thicker and more massive than the main Theodosian wall, and its towers are stronger, higher and placed closer together. The part of it that encloses the western bulge between Tekfur Saray and the Blachernae terrace can best be seen by following the street just inside the wall and walking along the garden paths of the intervening houses.

**From Eğri Kapí to the Golden Horn** (distance c 650m). The first part of this section of the walls was built by the Emperor Manuel Comnenus (1143–80). This wall begins just beyond Tekfur Saray, where it starts westward almost at right angles to the last fragment of the Theodosian wall, then turning N at the third tower. The wall of Manuel Comnenus is an admirably constructed fortification consisting of high arches closed on the outer face; it contains nine towers and one public gate, now called Eğri Kapí.

Most authorities identify Eğri Kapí with the ancient Gate of the Kaligaria. It was here that Constantine XI Dragases was last seen alive by his friend George Phrantzes, who would later write a history of the fall of Byzantium. On the night of 28 May 1453 the Emperor, accompanied by Phrantzes, stopped briefly at the Palace of Blachernae after returning from his last visit to Haghia Sophia. According to Phrantzes, Constantine assembled the members of his household and said goodbye to each of them in turn, asking their forgiveness for any unkindness he might ever have shown them. 'Who could describe the tears and groans in the palace?' Phrantzes wrote, 'Even a man of wood or stone could not help weeping'. The Emperor then left the Palace and rode with Phrantzes down to the Gate of the Kaligaria. They dismounted there and Phrantzes waited while Constantine ascended one of the towers nearby, whence he could hear the Turkish army preparing for the final assault. Soon after he returned and mounted his horse once again. Phrantzes then said goodbye to Constantine for the last time and watched as the Emperor rode off to his command post on the Murus Bacchatureus, never to be seen again.

Eğri Kapí, the Crooked Gate, is so called because the narrow lane that leaves the city here must detour around a türbe that stands almost directly in front of the portal. This is the supposed *tomb of Hazret Hafíz*, a companion of the Prophet, who, according to tradition, was killed on this spot during the first Arab siege of the city in 674–78. Several sainted Arab heroes of that campaign are buried in the vicinity, all having been dispatched to Paradise by the defenders on the walls of Byzantium. The burial-place of Hazret Hafíz was only 'discovered' in the 18C by the Chief Black Eunuch Beşir Ağa, who thereupon built this türbe.

From Eğri Kapí continue along the path just inside the walls to see the remainder of the wall of Manuel Comnenus, which ends at the third tower past the gate. The rest of this section of wall, from the third tower to where it joins the retaining wall of the Blachernae terrace, appears to be of later construction. The workmanship here is much inferior to that in the wall of Manuel Comnenus; this can clearly be seen where the two join without bonding, just beyond the third tower from Eğri Kapí. This section is guarded by four towers, all square and also much inferior to those in the previous section. The wall of Manuel Comnenus bears no dated inscriptions; the later northern one has three: one dated 1188 by Isaac II Angelus; another 1317 by Andronicus II Palaeologus; and the third 1441 by John VIII Palaeologus. There is also in this northern section a postern, now walled up, which is thought to be the ancient Gyrolimne Gate. This was an entrance to the Palace of Blachernae, whose outer retaining wall and two towers continue the line of fortifications in this area.

The fortification from the N corner of the Blachernae terrace to the Golden Horn consists of two parallel walls joined at their two ends to form a kind of citadel. The inner wall was built by the Emperor Heraclius in 627 in an attempt to strengthen the defences in this area; for the city was at that time being attacked by both the Avars and the Persians. The three hexagonal defence towers in this short stretch of wall are perhaps the finest in the whole system. In 813, when the city was threatened by Krum of the Bulgars, Leo V decided to strengthen the defences in this vulnerable area by building an outer wall with four small towers, a fortification thinner than the older one behind it and much inferior in construction. These walls were pierced by a single entryway, the *Gate of the Blachernae*; that part of the gate which passed through the wall of Leo has now collapsed, but it is still open through the Heraclian wall, passing between the first and second towers.

The *citadel* between the walls of Leo and Heraclius is quite fascinating. The ground is covered with rubble that has fallen from the walls and towers, among which there has developed a little hamlet of squatters who have built their hovels from the debris. At one end of the citadel there is a small Moslem graveyard that contains the graves of Ebu Şeybet ül-Hudri and Hamd ül-Ensari, two other martyred companions of the Prophet. In the centre of the citadel one finds the ancient ayazma of St. Basil, now half choked with debris and garbage. Despite the ruination and the squalour, it is still very picturesque.

At the northern end of the citadel the walls of Leo and Heraclius come together and link up with the sea-walls along the Golden Horn. One can leave the citadel through the Gate of the Blachernae. There turn left on Toklu Dede Sk to walk down to the main road along the Golden Horn, ending a long stroll along the ancient land walls of Byzantium.

# 17 Up the Golden Horn to Eyüp

The Golden Horn is a scimitar-shaped inlet of the Bosphorus, joining the strait just before it flows into the Marmara. The modern English name for the inlet is a direct translation of its ancient Greek name, Chrysokeras, the linguistic derivation of which is obscure. The Horn (in Turkish, Haliç) is some 7·5km long; at its broadest part, near Kasím Paşa, it is 750m in width; and it reaches a maximum depth of 35m where it joins the Bosphorus to flow into the Sea of Marmara.

Eyüp, a village some 4·5km up the Golden Horn from the Galata Bridge, is the site of one of the most sacred shrines in the Moslem world (see below). This shrine was established at the time of the Conquest, and it has been an extremely popular place of pilgrimage ever since. During Ottoman times numerous great men and women of the Empire arranged to be buried there in splendid türbes, many of which were the centres of extensive pious foundations. As a result, Eyüp is a veritable outdoor museum of Ottoman architecture, particularly of sepulchral monuments. Many other Ottomans of lower station chose to be buried on the hill above the shrine, which became one of the most extensive cemeteries in the Turkish world. Until half a century ago Eyüp had the reputation of being wildly romantic and picturesque. Surrounded on two sides by high hills covered with groves of cypress trees and turbaned tombstones, commanding magnificent views of both shores of the Golden Horn, it was a peaceful backwater devoted to death and religion. Since then the uncontrolled development of industry has badly polluted the Golden Horn and turned both its shores into squalid slums. But Eyüp itself, because of its sacrosanct status as a religious shrine, has been spared from this decay, and it has retained most of its unique character and charm.

APPROACHES. The Golden Horn Ferries leave from the upstream side of the Galata Bridge. The various ferries make several stops on both banks of the Golden Horn on their way up to Eyüp, but the only place worth breaking the journey is at Kasím Paşa, the first stop on the left bank, where there are several sights, of some interest, in the area.

*Kasím Paşa.* Kasím Paşa is the site of the once-famous Ottoman Naval Arsenal (in Turkish, Tershane). In the 16–17C the Arsenal made a great impression on foreign travellers, for it could accommodate 120 ships at one time. This was one of the factors responsible for the rise of the Ottoman Empire as a great sea-power, for the powerful Turkish fleets that swept the Mediterranean were built and maintained here, in a shipyard that had no equal anywhere in the world during that period. During the decline of the Ottoman Empire the Arsenal became more and more neglected, so that in the last century of its existence the Turkish fleet was completely ineffective as a military force. Today the old Arsenal is little more than a repair yard for freighters, ferry-boats, and the few liners of the Turkish Maritime Lines.

At the water's edge not far beyond the ferry-landing there is a pretty little Ottoman palace of the mid-19C; this is on the grounds of a Turkish Navy base, and is used as the headquarters of the naval commandant in charge. Farther up the Horn there is another little Ottoman palace called Aynalí Kavak. The first palace on this site was built early in the 18C by Ahmet III, but the present building dates to the mid-19C. The earlier palace was the site, in 1779, of the signing of the Treaty of Aynalí Kavak, ending a war between Russia and the Ottoman Empire. The palace of Aynalí Kavak has recently been restored and is now open to the public.

*The Ok Meydaní.* On the upper slopes of the hill above are the remains of the Ok Meydaní, or Archery Field, where the sultans loved to practise their skill at bowmanship. On the field there are still a number of marble columns commemorating prodigious shots by various sultans; there is also a namazgah, an outdoor place of prayer, where the sultans performed their devotions while practising their archery.

The principal monument in the vicinity of Kasím Paşa is *Piyali Paşa Camii (Pl 6,2), one of the most interesting and enigmatic of the classical mosques. The mosque is some 1·6km straight up the valley along Bahriye Cd, the valley that leads inland from the left of the ferry-station. One finds the mosque nestling in the hills above the Golden Horn, in a quiet and secluded backwater, surrounded by a picturesque grove of cypresses and plane trees.

HISTORY. The mosque was completed in 1573 by an unknown follower of Sinan. Piyali Paşa, the founder, began life as a Christian, the son of a Croatian shoemaker; he was taken up in the devşirme, educated in the Palace School, and eventually rose to the rank of Grand Admiral. While in command of the Ottoman fleet he terrorised the eastern Mediterranean, raiding as far as the coast of southern Italy, and captured a large number of Aegean isles, including Chios.

He was a favourite of Selim II, and capped his career by marrying one of the Sultan's daughters, Hace Guheri Mülük Sultan.

EXTERIOR. Piyale Paşa Camii is unique in the classical period in more than one respect. In the first place, it is the only classical mosque to revert to the Ulu Cami or multi-domed type common in the Selcuk and early Ottoman periods. Its six ample and equal domes in two rows of three each are supported by two great red granite columns. Thus far the plan follows the earlier type, but all else is different. Round three sides of the building there is a deep porch whose vaults are supported by stout rectangular pillars. Above the side porches are galleries with sloping roofs supported on small columns, while in front of the main western porch there was another lower porch with 22 columns. Unfortunately, the roofs of this and the upper galleries on the sides have vanished, but from old prints and photographs of the mosque one can see how fascinating this unique arrangement was. The founder's türbe behind the mosque also had a colonnaded porch, but this too has gone. In the centre of the W wall there is a small balcony supported on six columns; behind this rises the single minaret, which is thus in the very unusual position of being in the middle of the W facade. The entrance portals are to the right and left of the balcony.

INTERIOR. The mosque is lighted by numerous windows, many of the upper ones are round, *oeils-de-boeuf*. Between the second and third tier of windows a wide frieze of faience has inscriptions from the Kuran in white on a blue ground; these are from the hand of the famous calligrapher Karahisarí, who wrote the inscriptions in the Süleymaniye. The mihrab is also a very beautiful work, with Iznik tiles of the best period. The whole interior, though in poor repair, is not only unusual but exceptionally charming.

On the ferry ride from Kasím Paşa to Eyüp one sees high up in the hills to the right an enormous cemetery. This is the principal Jewish cemetery in Istanbul, in which the oldest gravestones go back to the end of the 15C. To the left here one now sees the great line of the Byzantine land-walls as they march down to the Golden Horn. Then, after passing under the suspension bridge that carries the new ring road around the city, the ferry steams into the landing at Eyüp.

**Eyüp** (off Pl 4,2). The shrine at Eyüp is some 500m inland from the ferry landing, approached along Camii Kabir Cd. Eyüp is the holiest Moslem shrine in Istanbul; indeed, after Mecca and Jerusalem, it is perhaps the third most sacred place of pilgrimage in the Islamic world.

HISTORY. The shrine is famous as the reputed burial-place of Eyüp (Job) Ensari, the friend and standard-bearer of the Prophet Muhammed. Long after the Prophet's death Eyüp is said to have been among the leaders of the first Arab siege of Constantinople in the years 674–78, when he was killed and buried somewhere outside the walls of the city. According to tradition, the tomb of Eyüp was miraculously discovered by the Şeyh-ül Islam Akşemsettin during the Turkish siege in 1453, after which the Conqueror built a shrine on the site. This legend, although repeated in countless guidebooks to the city, is probably apocryphal, because the tomb is known to have been a sacred place in the Byzantine period. Several Arab historians note that it was made a condition of peace after the first Arab siege that the tomb should be preserved. An Arab traveller during the reign of Manuel I Comnenus (1143–80) mentions it as still existing in his day, while another traveller, Zakariya al-Kazwini (c 1203–83) relates that 'this tomb is now venerated among them [the Byzantines] and they open it when they pray for rain in time of drought, and rain is granted them'. If the tomb was still visible in the 13C, it seems unlikely that it should have

*Eyüp is the most sacred Moslem shrine in Istanbul. Eyüp Ensari, standard-bearer of the Prophet Muhammed, is reputed to have died here during the Arab siege of Constantinople in 674–678.*

disappeared so completely before the Turkish Conquest. Probably the Conqueror restored the shrine or rebuilt it on a grander scale.

The külliye as a whole, originally including the türbe, mosque, medrese, han, hamam, imaret, and market, was originally built by the Conqueror in 1458. Here on their accession to the throne the sultans were girded with the sword of Osman, the eponymous founder of the Ottoman (in Turkish, Osmanli) dynasty, a ceremony equivalent to coronation. By the end of the 18C the mosque had fallen into ruins, perhaps a victim of the great earthquake of 1766 that had destroyed the Conqueror's own mosque. In 1798 Selim III ordered that the remains of the building be torn down and a new mosque built in its place, a project that was completed in 1800. The mosque that is seen today dates from that time, except for the minarets, which were erected by Ahmet III early in the 18C.

EXTERIOR. The mosque is approached through an exceptionally picturesque outer courtyard: the two great gateways with their undulating baroque forms, the huge old plane trees in whose hollows live lame storks and in whose branches beautiful grey herons build their nests in spring, the flocks of pampered pigeons being fed by the pilgrims. It is the gayest and most delightful courtyard in Istanbul. From here one enters the inner court, shaded by venerable plane trees and with an unusually tall and stately colonnade along three sides.

INTERIOR. In plan the mosque is an octagon inscribed in a rectangle. In spite of its late date the mosque is singularly attractive, with its pale honey-coloured stone, the decorations picked out in gold, the elegant chandelier hanging from the centre of the dome, and the magnificent turquoise carpet that covers the entire floor.

*The Türbe.* The side of the building opposite the mosque is a blank wall, most of it covered with panels of tiles without an overall pattern and of many different periods, some of them of great individual beauty. A door in the wall leads to the vestibule of the türbe of Eyüp Ensari, an octagonal building, three sides of which project into the vestibule. The latter is itself sheathed in tiles, many of them of the best Iznik period. The türbe is sumptuously decorated, though with work largely of the baroque period.

*Precincts.* According to Evliya Çelebi, the medrese of the külliye formed the courtyard of the mosque; this was evidently swept away during the rebuilding in 1798–1800. Apparently the imaret was not included in that rebuilding, for it is a total ruin. But of the hamam the soğukluk and hararet still remain and are in use; they have the elaborate and attractive dome structure typical of the early period, along with handsome marble floors. The original camekan has completely disappeared and been replaced by a rather makeshift one largely of wood. (In the Victoria and Albert Museum, London, there is a very fine panel of 24 Iznik tiles of c 1570 from this hamam, very probably from the demolished camekan.)

On the hill above the mosque is the great cemetery of Eyüp, the last resting-place of many notables from Ottoman times. At the top of the hill, above the cemetery, there is a café known as the *Teahouse of Pierre Loti*; this is named after the French novelist who frequented it during his stay in Istanbul in 1876. The café commands a superb view of the Golden Horn, particularly in late afternoon and early twilight.

From the Teahouse of Pierre Loti there is a good view of the upper reaches of the Golden Horn and of the two little streams that flow into it at its northern extremity. These are Alibey Suyu on the W and Kağíthane Suyu on the E, the ancient Barbyzes and Cydaris, respectively. These streams are separated at their mouth by the promontory known in Turkish as *Sivri Tepe*, the Semistra of the Greeks. According to Dionysius of Byzantium, it was on this hill that Io, daughter of Inachus, who had fled here pursued by the gadfly of jealous Hera, gave birth to Cereossa. According to one version of the myth, Byzas, the eponymous founder of Byzantium, was the son of Poseidon and Cereossa.

During Ottoman times the two streams that fed the Golden Horn were known in English as the Sweet Waters of Europe. For centuries the meadows and banks of the Sweet Waters were the site of royal palaces, mansions, gardens and pavilions, and were a favourite holiday resort for the ordinary people of Istanbul. But today the area is a squalid industrial slum of the worst sort, the Sweet Waters are a sewer, and only a few pathetic ruins remain of the pleasure domes that graced its shores in Ottoman times. (A project is now under way to clean up the Golden Horn and to create a park and promenade along its shores.)

Leaving Eyüp Camii by the N gate, one finds oneself in a narrow street that leads down to the Golden Horn. Most of the left side of this street is occupied by the enormous **külliye of Mihrişah Valide Sultan**, mother of Selim III. Built in 1791, this is one of the largest and most elaborate of all the baroque complexes; it includes the türbe of the foundress, together with a mektep, an imaret, and a splendid sebil and çeşme. The türbe is round, but the undulating facade turns it into a polygon, with the various faces separated by slender columns of red or dark grey marble. The entrance is in a little courtyard filled with tombstones and trees; the columned portico of the mektep runs along one side. Farther along the street another monumental gateway leads into the vast main courtyard, which is filled with more tombstones and surrounded on three sides by the porticoes of the huge imaret. This is the only imaret in Istanbul that still fulfils its original function as a soup kitchen for the poor of the city: some 500 people are served free food daily at 11 o'clock, and are allowed to take away with them enough for their evening meal. In leaving the imaret do not fail to notice the magnificent sebil at the end of the garden on the street side.

Continuing toward the water, one passes between the two buildings of a little külliye founded in 1839 by Hüsref Paşa, with the founder's türbe on the right and the library on the left. They are both in Empire style; but the domes of the library reading-rooms contain a good example of that Italianate comic opera painted decoration of garlands, draperies and columns, so distressing when it occurs in classical buildings, but quite appropriate here.

At the end of the street at the water's edge there is a pleasant little teahouse overlooking the Golden Horn. This is probably the teahouse that Pierre Loti frequently visited during his years in Istanbul, rather than the much publicised one in the cemetery above Eyüp. From the terrace of the teahouse, looking downstream, there is a good view of the neo-classical *türbe of Sultan Mehmet V Reşat*, who died in 1918. Mehmet V was the penultimate ruler of the Ottoman Empire; oddly enough, he was the only one of all the sultans to be buried in the holy precincts of Eyüp and the last to be interred in his own country. The last Sultan, Mehmet VI, died in exile and was buried abroad, as was Abdül Mecit (II), who held only the title of Caliph. It is a rather heavy building, the interior revetted in modern Kütahya tiles predominantly of an overly vivid green.

Taking the street that runs parallel to the Golden Horn, one soon comes to a crossroads where several classical türbes stand. The finest and most elaborate of these is that of *Ferhat Paşa*, octagonal, with a richly decorated cornice and polychrome voussoirs and window-frames.

Farther up the street, that leads back toward Eyüp Camii, two classical türbes of great simplicity face one another. The one on the left is the *türbe of Sokollu Mehmet Paşa*, built by Sinan in c 1572; it forms part of a small külliye. Elegant and well-proportioned, it is severely plain. The interior contains some interesting stained glass, partly ancient and partly a modern imitation, but very well done; alternate windows are predominantly blue and green. A little colonnade attaches the türbe to the dershane of the külliye's very fine medrese. Notice the handsome identical doorways of the two buildings; the only difference is that the rich polychrome work of the türbe is in verd antique, while that of the dershane in red conglomerate marble. The dershane also has stained glass windows; these are of modern manufacture and not as good as those in the türbe. The dome is supported on squinches of very bold stalactites. The opposite door leads into the medrese courtyard; this is long and narrow, with 10 domes on the long sides of its colonnade, only three at the ends. Recently the building has been well restored and is now used as a children's clinic; it is pretty and charming, with a delightful, well-kept garden. In the little garden of the türbe the family and descendants of Sokollu Mehmet Paşa are buried. Just beyond the graveyard there is a building in the same style as the dershane; this is the dar-ül kura, the school for the study of the Kuran. This little complex as a whole is certainly one of Sinan's most attractive works.

The türbe across the street from that of Sokollu Mehmet Paşa is that of *Siyavuş Paşa*. This is again austere, but adorned within by inscriptions and pendentives in excellent Iznik tiles. This türbe is also by Sinan. Siyavuş Paşa died in 1601, outliving Sinan by a dozen years; he seems to have had Sinan build this türbe originally for some of his children who died young, and was finally buried there himself.

Alongside the türbe of Siyavuş Paşa a picturesque alley leads back toward Eyüp Camii through a forest of tombstones. Halfway along this alley is another türbe by Sinan, built for *Pertev Paşa* in 1572–73. This türbe is of a very unusual design, rectangular in plan, and looking more like a house than a tomb; unfortunately it is now in ruins. It was originally divided into two equal areas each covered with a dome exquisitely painted, but these were destroyed through neglect. Inside the türbe there are still to be seen some charming marble sarcophagi of Pertev Paşa and his family.

We have now come full circle back to the N gate of the courtyard of Eyüp Camii. Crossing the court and taking the inner of the two roads parallel to the Golden Horn, one soon comes to the second group of buildings that make Eyüp illustrious.

The first of these, *Kízíl Mescit*, is perhaps hardly worth a visit, though it has been reasonably well restored in recent years. Built in 1581 by Kiremitçi Süleyman Çelebi, it is of the simplest type, a rectangular room of stone and brick with a tiled roof and a brick minaret.

A little farther along on the opposite side of the street stands the *mosque of Silahi Mehmet Bey*, dating to c 1490. This mosque is also of the simplest type, but with an unusual and fascinating minaret. This is hexagonal in shape, built of stone and brick; instead of the usual balcony it has a sort of lantern with six windows and a tall conical cap. There are in the city three or four other minarets with this lantern arrangement but this is much the most striking and pretty.

Opposite Silahi Mehmet Bey Camii is the grandest and most interesting mosque in Eyüp, the **\*Mosque of Zal Mahmut Paşa**, a mature but unique work of Sinan.

HISTORY. The date of construction of the mosque is unknown; that usually given, 1551, is at least 20 years too early, and a date in the mid-1570s seems most likely. Zal was a rather unsavoury character; when in 1553 Süleyman decided to execute his son Mustafa it was Zal who finally strangled him. Later he married the Princess Şah Sultan, sister of Selim II, as a reward, it was said, for having smoothed that prince's path to the throne by the elimination of his brother. Little is known of Zal's subsequent career, except that one night in 1580 he and his wife died.

EXTERIOR. A fine view of the S facade of the building may be had from the garden of Silahi Camii, which is a little higher. With its four tiers of windows and its great height and squareness it looks more like a palace than a mosque. The N facade is even more towering, for the mosque is built on a slope and supported on vaulted substructures in which rooms for the lower medrese have been made. The building is constructed of alternate courses of brick and stone.

INTERIOR. A handsome porch of five bays gives access to the interior. This is a vast rectangular room; the massive dome arches spring on the E from supports in the wall itself, on the W from thick and rather stubby pillars some distance in from the W wall. Round three sides of the mosque a rather heavy arcade supports a gallery; some of the arches are of the ogive type. The walls, which rise in a rectangle to the height of the dome drum, are pierced with many windows, so that despite the width of the galleries the mosque is full of light. The leaves of the main entrance door are fine inlaid work in wood, as are the mimber and müezzin's pew in carved marble. The only other decoration that survives is some excellent faience in the mihrab. It is possible that some tile work has perished, for Evliya Çelebi writes that 'architectural ornaments and decorations are nowhere lavished in so prodigal a way as here, in this the finest of all the mosques in the Empire built by vezirs'. The mosque was for many years in a state of near ruin, but recently it has been very well restored. The general effect of the interior is perhaps a little heavy, but nonetheless grand and impressive; there is no other mosque quite like it.

PRECINCTS. The complex includes two medreses; like the mosque itself, these are built of brick and stone, one around three sides of the main courtyard, the other on a lower level to the N, enclosing two sides of the türbe garden. They are both extremely picturesque and irregular in design. In the upper medrese most of the S side consists of a building without a portico, which looks rather like an imaret and may perhaps have served as one. The dershane is not in the centre of the W wall, but has been shifted to near the N end, and the last arches of the portico on this side are smaller than the others. There is no obvious reason for any of these abnormalities, but they have a certain charm, enhanced by the ogive arches of the arcade. At the NE corner a long flight of steps leads down to the garden of the türbe, two sides of which are partly enclosed by the lower medrese. It is an octagonal building of the usual type, within which are the catafalques of Zal Mahmut Paşa and his wife.

A door in the E wall of the türbe garden leads to another külliye of a very different type, one of the most delightful of the smaller baroque complexes. It consists of an elaborate türbe and mektep, with a sebil on the street and a çeşme in the garden. It was built at the end of the 18C by Şah Sultan, a sister of Selim III. The undulating facades of the türbe and the amusing turned-back staircase of the mektep are very charming.

Return to the inner street, where there are two buildings that are worth at least a glance. First is the small *mosque of Cezri Kasím Paşa*, erected in 1515. It has a pretty porch with four handsome antique columns of red granite, and the balcony of the minaret is supported on an unusual zigzag corbel. Most of the tile decoration inside the mosque is of late date and of little merit, but near the mihrab there is a very interesting one dated 1726 and signed 'Mehmet, son of Osman of Iznik.' This is a very fine panel showing the Kaaba at Mecca with much interesting detail, including several large tents in the background; it is one of the earliest products of the kilns at Tekfur Saray.

A little farther down the street is the *mosque of the Defterdar* (Lord High Treasurer) *Mahmut Efendi*; it is also ancient in foundation but wholly rebuilt in the 18C, and of little intrinsic interest. In the garden is the founder's curious open türbe, with a dome supported on arches with scalloped soffits.

A short stroll down the Golden Horn road brings one back within the ancient Byzantine walls of the city. Here one can turn left off the main road and walk down to the pier at Ayvansaray, to take a ferry back to the Galata Bridge.

# 18  Pera and Galata

This Rte begins at Taksim Square, the centre of the modern town. The modern name for the area around Taksim is Beyoğlu, but in Ottoman times it was known as Pera, when it was the quarter in which most of the Europeans and many of the Christian minorities in the city resided. After a brief detour to the N of Taksim, the itinerary proceeds from there along Istiklal Cd, the old Grand Rue de Pera, continuing as far as Tünel, named after the underground funicular railway that goes down to the vicinity of the Galata Bridge. From Tünel the itinerary follows a meandering course down through the back streets of Galata to the Golden Horn, and then through the port quarter at the confluence of the Horn and the Bosphorus. There are no major monuments in Pera and only a few in Galata, but both quarters are quite fascinating and colourful, very different in their character and atmosphere from the old Turkish neighbourhoods on the other side of the Golden Horn.

HISTORY. The historic origins of Pera and Galata are as remote as those of Constantinople itself. From very early times there had been settlements along the northern shores of the Golden Horn; Byzas himself is said to have erected a temple there to the hero Amphiaraus. The most important of these communities, Sykai, the Figtrees, was located on the present site of Galata. As early as the 5C AD, this was included as the VIIIth Region of Constantinople itself, under the name of Regio Sycaena; it had churches, a forum, public baths, a theatre, a harbour, and was surrounded by a defence-wall. In 528 Justinian restored its theatre and defence-walls, grandiloquently renaming it Justinianae, a name which soon fell out of use and was forgotten. Toward the end of the same century Tiberius II (578–82) is said to have built a fortress at the confluence of the Golden Horn and the Bosphorus, from which a chain could be stretched to the opposite shore to close the Horn to enemy shipping. The name Sykai seems to have continued in use until the 9C, when the name Galata began to supplant it, at first for a small district only, later for the whole region. The derivation of the name Galata is unknown, though that of Pera is quite straightforward. In Greek 'pera' means 'beyond', at first in the general sense of 'on the other side of the Golden Horn', later restricted to medieval Galata, and still later to the heights above.

The town of Galata took its present form chiefly under the Genoese. After the reconquest of Constantinople from the Latins in 1261, the Byzantine emperors granted the district to the Genoese as a semi-independent colony with its own Podesta, or Governor, appointed annually by the senate of Genoa. Although the Genoese were expressly forbidden to fortify the colony, they did so almost immediately and went on expanding its area and fortifications for more than a hundred years. Sections of these walls with a few towers and one postern are still in existence and will be seen on the present itinerary. After the Turkish Conquest of 1453 the outer walls of Galata were partially destroyed, as the district became the general European quarter of the city. Here the foreign merchants had their houses and shops and the ambassadors of the European powers also built their palatial embassies here. When the Sephardic Jews in Spain were expelled by Ferdinand and Isabella in 1492, Beyazit II invited them to live in the Ottoman Empire and many settled in Galata. Early in the following century a large number of Moorish refugees settled there as well, joining the large number of Greeks and Armenians who had arrived from Anatolia in the century after the Conquest, giving Galata the polyglot flavour that it retained until very recent times.

As time went on the confines of Galata became too crowded for the tastes of the foreign ambassadors and richer merchants, who began to move out, beyond the medieval walls, to the hills and vineyards above. Here the foreign powers built enormous mansions surrounded by spacious gardens; all of them standing

*A street in Galata, with the recently restored Galata Tower.
(Ergun Cagatay)*

along the road that would later be known as the Grand Rue de Pera. Nevertheless, the region must have remained rural until well into the 18C; for in that period one often sees references to 'les vignes of Pera'. But as Pera became more and more built up, it fell a prey like the rest of the city to the endemic fires that ravaged it periodically. Two especially devastating ones, in 1831 and 1871, destroyed nearly everything built before those dates. Hence the dearth of anything of much historic or architectural interest in modern Beyoğlu.

Before beginning the main itinerary, a detour to the N of Taksim Square takes in two museums of some interest. Both museums are approached by walking up Cumhuriyet Cd, the broad avenue that leads off to the N from Taksim Square. A walk of some 900m brings one past Taksim Park, then the entrance to the Hilton Hotel, and finally past Radioevi, the edifice that houses Radio Istanbul. The first street on the right after Radioevi, makes a sharp bend to the left behind the Harbiye Military Barracks; then about 300m farther along it passes, on the right, the Sporve Sergi Sarayi, an indoor sports arena and exhibition hall where some of the performances of the Istanbul Festival are held. Beyond that on the left is the *Askeri Müze, the Military Museum.

ADMISSION. The Military Museum is open 9–12 every day except Mon and Tues.

The Military Museum has an extensive and interesting collection of exhibits from all periods of Ottoman military history. Among the more interesting exhibits are the beautiful cannon captured by the Turks in their campaigns in Europe and the Middle East. The fascinating miniature Janissary costumes are exact replicas of the varied and colourful uniforms worn by the various members of that elite army corps. There are also some links of the huge chain that the Byzantines stretched across the Golden Horn to close it to enemy shipping; and the huge imperial tent in which the sultans lived when on campaign is also on display. Also of interest is the Mehter Band, which plays Ottoman military marches outside the museum from 3–4 every day except Mon and Tues. The uniforms worn by the band members are exact copies of those worn by Ottoman military musicians, as are the instruments they play. Many of the marches played by the band were composed by Donizetti Paşa, the elder brother of Gaetano Donizetti, who served as imperial bandmaster in the reigns of Mahmut II and Abdül Mecit I.

The second museum in the area is the **Atatürk Müzesi**. This is approached by continuing along Cumhuriyet Cd past the Harbiye Military Barracks (where Atatürk served as a cadet in 1899–1901) and then bearing left on Halaskargazi Cd. The museum is a short distance along on the left, in an old house at 25 Halaskargazi Cd.

ADMISSION. The Atatürk Müzesi is open 9–12, 1:30–5:30 every day except the fifteenth of the month.

The Atatürk Museum is housed in the old mansion where Atatürk lived in 1919, just before he went off to Anatolia to organise the Turkish Nationalist movement, an effort that eventually gave rise to the present Turkish Republic. On exhibition are a number of personal effects and papers of Atatürk, the Father of modern Turkey.

At the eastern end of Taksim Square is the handsome glass-walled building that houses the *Istanbul Opera House*, the site of many of the musical and theatrical performances connected with the Istanbul Festival. In a small park near the western end of the square is the

*Monument of Independence*, with life-sized representations of
Atatürk and other leaders of the Turkish Nationalist movement; this
group was done in 1928 by the Italian sculptor Canonica. At the
beginning of Istiklal Cd on the right is the pretty little octagonal
building that has given its name to the square and the surrounding
neighbourhood: this is the *taksim*, or water-distribution centre, built
in 1732 by Sultan Mahmut I. Here the waters from the reservoirs in the
Belgrad Forest are distributed to the various quarters of the modern
town. Just beyond this, after the first street leading off Istiklal Cd to
the right, is the old French Consulate (not to be confused with the old
French Embassy, which is farther down the avenue); it is a building
with a rather quaint courtyard originally constructed by the French in
1719 for those suffering from the plague. S of the square, off to the left
of Istiklal Cd, is the large Greek Orthodox church of *Aya Triada*, the
Holy Trinity, founded in the late 19C.

The first stretch of Istiklal Cd, from Taksim Square to Galatasaray
Square (c 600m), is a succession of shops interspersed with several
cinemas and theatres. Halfway down the avenue on the right there is
a small mosque, Ağa Camii; this was built early in the present century
and is of no interest. The last street on the right before Galatasaray
Square is Called Şahne Sk, the Street of the Theatre, which leads
downhill through the **Galatasaray fish-market**. This is the heart of
what remains of old Pera, an extraordinarily picturesque, lively and
colourful quarter, a veritable labyrinth lined with the stalls and
barrows of fishmongers and greengrocers, with numerous kerbside
pubs and subterranean taverns.

Galatasaray Square takes its name from the *Galatasaray Lycée*, whose ornate
entryway is at the near left corner of the avenue. Although the present Lycée
buildings date only to 1908, Galatasaray is a venerable and distinguished
institution. It was founded by Beyazit II toward the end of the 15C as a school for
the imperial pages, ancillary to the one in Topkapí Sarayí. After a somewhat
chequered career, it was reorganised in 1868 under Sultan Abdül Aziz as a
modern lycée on the French model, with the instruction partly in Turkish, partly
in French. After the University of Istanbul, it is the oldest Turkish institution of
learning in the city; and over the past century it has produced a large number of
the statesmen and intellectuals who have shaped modern Turkey.

The street leading off to the right from Galatasaray Square, Hamal-
başí Cd, goes past the southern boundary of the fish market. At the
first intersection on the left is the main entrance to the *old British
Embassy*. (This is now officially the British Consulate, for all the
foreign embassies were relocated in Ankara after that became the
capital of the Turkish Republic in 1923; nevertheless, this and the
other palatial old ambassadorial residences are still referred to as
embassies.) The British Embassy is a very handsome building in the
Italian Renaissance style; it was built in 1845 by Sir Charles Barry, the
architect of the Houses of Parliament in London. At the rear of the
Embassy there is a magnificent and very English garden.

The embassies in this part of old Pera, on or near the Grand Rue, belong to those
powers that have had legations here since the early centuries of the Ottoman
Empire. Though most of these buildings are relatively modern, the embassies
themselves—especially those of Venice, France, Britain, Holland, Sweden and
Russia—are of some historical interest. They were established more or less
where they are now in the course of the 16–18C, generally by grants of land
bestowed by the sultans, and each formed the centre of its 'Nation', as it was
called; that is, of the community of resident merchants and officials of the various
countries. These embassies came to exert a growing influence on the Ottoman
Empire as its powers declined, and collectively they dominated the life of Pera

until the establishment of the Turkish Republic. Near the embassies various churches were established, more or less under their protection, and some of these survive in a modern form. They are all situated on the left side of Istiklal Cd between Galatasaray Square and Tünel, some of them standing next to the old ministries to whose 'Nation' they once ministered.

Just before the first turning to the left off Istiklal Cd one comes to a large church at the rear of a courtyard below street level. This is the Franciscan church of *St. Anthony of Padua*, the largest Roman Catholic sanctuary in the city. The first church of St. Anthony was established on this site in 1725; the present building dates only from 1913, but it is a good example of Italian neo-Gothic architecture in red brick.

Taking the second turning on the left after St. Anthony's, one sees on the right the *Maison de France*; it is situated in a fine French garden with views of the Bosphorus and the Marmara. France was the first European nation to establish formal diplomatic relations with the Ottoman Empire, beginning with the envoys sent by François I to Süleyman in 1525; however the present building dates only from soon after the fire of 1831. (It was on this site that the great Turkish astronomer Takiuddin built his observatory in 1570.) The chapel connected with the embassy, that of St. Louis of the French, is the oldest in foundation of the Latin churches along the Grand Rue de Pera, dating from 1581; though the present structure also postdates the fire of 1831.

Among the masses celebrated here every Sunday there is one in the Chaldean rite. St. Louis is the local house of worship for the Chaldean Church, an 18C offshoot of the ancient Nestorian Church that is in union with Rome. The members of this Church in Istanbul are all from the Hakkiâri region in the far SE corner of Turkey, descendants of the ancient Chaldean and Assyrian peoples; parts of their mass are still sung in Aramaic, the language of Christ.

Continuing along the left side of Istiklal Cd one comes next to the *Dutch Embassy*, a very pretty building that looks rather like a small French château. The present building was designed by the Fossati brothers and completed in 1855; the lower structure, visible from the garden, goes back two centuries or more. The original Dutch Embassy, built in 1612, was burned twice, but parts of the substructure of the earlier buildings were preserved and incorporated into the present Embassy.

The first turning on the left beyond the Embassy brings one to the *Dutch Chapel*, whose entrance is a short way along on the left. Since 1857 this building has housed the Union Church of Istanbul, an English-speaking congregation from many lands. The chapel dates from the late 17C or the early 18C, although the original church must go back to the founding of the Dutch Embassy. The basement rooms of the chapel, now used as a Sunday school, have in the past served as a prison. The building is basically a single massive barrel vault of heavy masonry; the brickwork of the facade, newly exposed to view, is particularly fine.

A short way below the Dutch Chapel on the right is the former *Spanish Embassy*, no longer functioning, with only the embassy chapel remaining in use. This chapel, dedicated to Our Lady of the Seven Sorrows, was originally founded in 1670; the present church dates from 1871.

At the bottom of the street is a small square flanked by two large old buildings. The one to the left, at the top of the square, is the former

French Tribunal of Justice, a 19C structure in which much of the legal affairs of the European 'Nations' was handled in late Ottoman times. The handsome old building on the right side of the square is the *Palazzo di Venezia*, now the Italian Embassy. The present building is believed to date from c 1695, though the Venetian Embassy was established here long before that. In Ottoman times this was the residence of the Venetian *bailo*, the ambassador of the Serene Republic and one of the most powerful of the foreign legates in the city. The Palazzo is large and imposing, its facade covered with ivy and surrounded by a typically Italian garden. We learn from his 'Memoirs' that Giacomo Casanova was a guest here in the summer of 1744; in his three months in the city this great lover did not make a single conquest but was himself seduced by one Ismail Efendi.

Returning to Istiklal Cd, one comes next to the Franciscan church of *St. Mary Draperis*, down a flight of steps from the street level. The first church on this site was built in 1678 and the present structure dates from 1789. The parish itself, however, is a very ancient one, dating from the beginning of 1453, when the Franciscans built a church near the present site of Sirkeci Station. After the Conquest the Franciscans were forced to leave Constantinople, settling first in Galata and then here in Pera. The Franciscans still preserve in the church a miraculous icon of the Virgin, which they claim to inherit from their first church in Constantinople.

Just beyond this church is the *Russian Embassy*; this was built in 1837 by the Fossati brothers, supplanting an older embassy of Russia farther down the Grand Rue de Pera. The Fossati brothers, who were of Italian Swiss origin, had been in Moscow for several years as official architects of Czar Nicholas I, who sent them to Istanbul to build his new embassy in Pera. Here they remained for 20 years or so as official architects for the Sultan, restoring Haghia Sophia in 1847–49 and building several other structures, including the Russian and Dutch Embassies and the church of SS. Peter and Paul in Galata.

After going down a steep street to the left beyond the Russian Embassy and then turning around a corner to the left, one comes to the *Crimean Memorial Church*, by far the largest and most handsome of the western churches in the city. This was built between 1858 and 1868 under the aegis of Lord Stratford de Redcliffe, known to the Turks as Büyük Elçi, or the Great Ambassador, because of the enormous influence he exerted on Turkish affairs during his three terms as Great Britain's Ambassador to the Ottoman Empire during the period 1810–56. The church was designed by C.E. Street, the architect of the London Law Courts; it is built in the neo-Gothic style with a cavernous porch, like the Law Courts themselves. Inside the church there are some interesting old photographs and newspaper clippings showing the laying of the cornerstone of the church on 19 October 1858 by the Büyük Elçi himself.

Returning once again to Istiklal Cd, one comes next to the last of the old embassies on the avenue. This is the *Embassy of Sweden*, established here in its present building towards the end of the 17C; the ambassadorial mansion is perhaps the most handsome of all those that still stand along what was once the Grand Rue de Pera. The huge old building that stands directly across the avenue is thought to have been the Russian Embassy before the Fossatis built the new one farther up the street in 1837. This edifice, which is now given over to various shops and ateliers, appears to date from the 18C. The building is precious in Turkish culture as having been for many years the residence of Aliye Berger-Boronai (1903–74), whom many consider to have been the greatest painter produced by Turkey in modern times.

This brings one to the end of Istiklal Cd. Just ahead, where the avenue turns sharply left, is the entrance to *Tünel*, the underground funicular railway, which in 80 seconds reaches the bottom of the hill near the Galata Bridge. Tünel was built by French engineers in 1875 and was one of the first underground railways in the world.

The street turning off to the left, downhill, just before the Tünel terminal is known as Galip Dede Cd. A short way down the street on the left side there is an early 19C sebil founded by one Halil Efendi. A gate beside the sebil leads to a large courtyard with a garden to the right and a picturesque graveyard to the left. Just to the left of the entrance is the *türbe of Galip Dede*, after whom the street outside is named. Galip Dede was a Mevlevi dervish and one of the most celebrated mystic poets in Turkey in the 17C; during the latter years of his life he was the şeyh of the Galata Mevlevi Tekkesi, which still stands at the far end of the courtyard.

This tekke was originally built by Iskender Paşa in c 1492, and is thus the oldest surviving dervish monastery in the city. The present building, however, dates only from 1796; it was restored in the mid-19C and again in the 1970s. This is the famous tekke of the whirling dervishes, described by so many travellers to Istanbul in the 19C. The dancing room of the tekke has been superbly restored, so too has the latticed loge from which the sultan observed the ceremonies.

At the back of the tekke graveyard is the tombstone of the famous Count Bonneval, known in Turkish as Kumbaraci Ahmet Paşa. Bonneval was a French officer who enrolled in the Ottoman army in the reign of Mahmut I and was made Commandant of the Corps of Artillery. He became a Moslem, changed his name to Kumbaraci (the Bombardier) Osman Ahmet, and spent the remainder of his life in the Ottoman service, dying in Istanbul in 1747. A French contemporary of Bonneval wrote of him that he was 'a man of great talent for war, intelligent, eloquent with charm and grace, very proud, a lavish spender, extremely debauched, and a great plunderer'.

Continuing down Galip Dede Cd for another 250m brings one to the **\*\*Galata Tower** (Pl 7,5),the most prominent landmark on this side of the Golden Horn and one of the most historic monuments in the city.

HISTORY. The Galata Tower was the apex of the Genoese fortifications of medieval Galata. Originally known as the Tower of Christ, it was built in 1348 in connection with the first expansion of the Genoese colony. The first fortified area, walled in as early as 1304, was a long, narrow rectangle along the Golden Horn between where the two bridges now begin. In order to defend themselves more adequately on the side of the heights above Galata, the Genoese added a triangular wedge with the Tower of Christ as its highest point. Later still, in 1387 and 1397, they took successive areas to the NW, and finally, in 1446, they enclosed the eastern slope of the hill leading down to the Bosphorus. The final defence system consisted of six walled enceints, with the outer wall bordered by a moat, a short stretch of which can still be seen beside the Galata Tower. Bits and pieces of the walls and towers still exist here and there around Galata; the best-preserved section is just below the Galata Tower. Until the late 1960s the Tower was used as a fire observation post, but then it was restored and converted into a tourist attraction, with a modern restaurant and night club on its upper level. From there one commands a magnificent view of the city and its surrounding waters.

In the little square beside the Tower, fixed against the remnants of the barbican, is a famous street fountain. In its present form it dates from 1732, but it was originally constructed just after the Conquest. Its founder was Bereketzade Hací Ali Ağa, the first Turkish governor of the citadel of Galata. The fountain originally stood near Bereket-zade's mosque, which was located a short distance away from the tower, but it was moved to its present site in 1950 when that was demolished. Unfortunately, this charming rococo fountain has suffered badly from being painted.

Behind the tower a steep and winding street, Galata Kulesi Sk, leads downhill towards the Golden Horn. A short distance down the street on the left is the entrance to one of the three surviving medieval Latin churches in Galata. This is the *church of SS. Peter and Paul*, which, with its Dominican convent, was founded in the late 15C by the Genoese. Later it was taken under the protection of France and became the French parochial church in Galata; in more recent times it has been the parish church of the local Maltese community, and several of their tombstones are built into the courtyard wall. The present church dates only from 1841 and is a work of the Fossati brothers. The most treasured possession of the church is a painting of the Virgin which the Dominicans claim to be the famous icon of the Hodegetria, the fabled protectress of Byzantium, which pious tradition attributes to St. Luke. At the rear of the monastery there is a fairly well-preserved stretch of the ancient Genoese walls with three defence towers still standing.

Round the corner in the next alley to the right is the *Han of St. Peter*, built in 1771 by the Comte de Saint Priest as the 'lodging-place and bank of the French Nation', as one reads in his bequest. In a house on this site the French poet André Chénier was born, on 30 October 1762. He is one of the very few to be honoured in this city by a plaque on his birthplace; next to this plaque are the arms of the Comte de Saint Priest and of the Bourbons.

At the end of Galata Kulesi Sk a flight of steps leads down to the main avenue in this area, Bankalar Cd, known until recent years by the more ancient name of Voyvoda Cd. (Voyvoda was the name by which Ottoman governors were known in the Balkans.) The building just to the left of the steps is the ancient *Podestat*, the mansion of the Podesta, the Genoese governor of Galata. The building was originally erected in 1316, and it retained its original appearance until the widening of the avenue in recent years.

Crossing Bankalar Cd, continue downhill on the street directly opposite, Perşembe Pazar Sk. In this street there are some very picturesque old houses and hans which used to be identified as Byzantine or Genoese, although in fact they are typical Turkish houses of the 18C. The most handsome is at the first turning on the right, dated by an inscription to 1735–36. The general structure is completely characteristic of Turkish buildings of that period, with the masonry in alternate courses of brick and stone and the pointed arches of the windows. It has three storeys, the upper ones projecting in zigzags held up by corbels, with two zigzags in Perşembe Pazar Sk and four in the alley to the right. Inside is a small courtyard with a staircase leading to the upper floors. The rooms are small but picturesquely vaulted, mostly with cradle vaults, and they each look out two ways through the zigzags. This is a fine little building and one hopes that it will be preserved; there are several other such buildings in this street, similar in structure and date, but none so elegant.

The next turning on the right soon brings one to a very unusual building ending in a tall square tower with a pyramidal roof, known locally as ***Arap Camii** (Pl 6,8), another of the surviving medieval Latin churches of Galata.

HISTORY. There are many baseless legends concerning the origin and history of this church, but the evidence indicates that it was constructed by the Dominicans during the years 1323–37 and dedicated to St. Dominic. It seems to have taken the place of, or included, a chapel of St. Paul, by whose name the church was popularly known. Early in the 16C it was converted into a mosque and given over to the colony of Moorish refugees who had settled in Galata; hence its Turkish name, the Mosque of the Arabs.

INTERIOR. The building has been partially burned and restored several times; on one occasion it was considerably widened by moving the left-hand wall several metres to the N. Nevertheless, it remains a rather typical medieval Latin church, originally Gothic: a long hall ending in three rectangular apses, and with a belfry (now the minaret) at the E end. The flat wooden roof and the rather pretty wooden galleries date only from a restoration in 1913–19. At that time also the original floor was uncovered and large quantities of medieval Genoese tombstones came to light, some of them dating to 1347, the year when the Black Death first struck Constantinople; these are now in the Archaeological Museum (see above, Rte 4B). On the N side of the building there is a large and unkempt but not unattractive courtyard with a şadírvan.

After continuing in the same direction on the street that passes Arap Camii, take the second turning on the right and then the second turning on the left. This brings one onto Yaník Kapí Sk, the Street of the Burnt Gate, which takes its name from the *ancient portal* about 100m ahead. This is the only surviving city gate of medieval Galata; it once led from the fourth enceint to the fifth. Above the archway of the gate there is a bronze tablet emblazoned with the Cross of St. George, symbol of Genoa the Superb, between a pair of escutcheons bearing the heraldic arms of the noble houses of Doria and De Merude.

After passing through the archway take the next left, this soon leads out to the main highway paralleling the Golden Horn. On the seashore off to the right, just beside the Atatürk Bridge, is the handsome mosque known as ***Azap Kapí Camii** (Pl 6,8), the most important Ottoman monument in Galata.

HISTORY. The mosque was founded by the Grand Vezir Sokollu Mehmet Paşa, and it was built by Sinan in 1577–78. During late Ottoman times the mosque was abandoned and fell into serious disrepair. When the present Atatürk Bridge was being designed, in 1942, there was talk of demolishing the mosque, until wiser heads prevailed and succeeded in having it preserved and restored. It is now in excellent condition and is once again serving as a house of worship.

EXTERIOR. While Azap Kapí Camii hardly equals Sokollu Mehmet Paşa's slightly earlier mosque near the Hippodrome, it is nevertheless a fine and interesting building. Like Rüstem Paşa Camii across the Golden Horn, it is raised on a high basement in which there were once vaulted shops; the entrance, now rather squeezed by the approach to the bridge, is by staircases under the enclosed porch. The minaret is unusual both in position and structure. First of all, it is on the left or N side instead of the S; this is doubtless because the sea at that time came up very close to the S wall and the ground would not have been firm enough to support a minaret. Furthermore, it is detached from the building and placed on a solid foundation of its own, connected with the mosque above porch level by a picturesque arch; this contains a communicating passage so that it can be entered from the porch.

INTERIOR. Internally the plan is an octagon inscribed in a nearly square rectangle. The dome is supported by eight small semidomes, those in the axes slightly larger than those in the diagonals, while the eastern semidome covers a rectangular projecting apse for the mihrab, with narrow galleries on three sides. The mihrab and minber are very fine work in carved marble. It appears that the interior was once decorated with fine Iznik tiles, like that of Sokollu Mehmet Paşa's other mosque, but these have been replaced by modern Kütahya tiles. This detracts considerably from the appearance of the interior; nevertheless, this is among the more interesting and important of Sinan's buildings.

Just to the N of the mosque stands the *Azap Kapí fountain*, one of the most famous in the city. This baroque structure was founded in 1732–33 by Saliha Valide Hatun, mother of Mahmut I; it consists of a projecting sebil with three grilled windows flanked by two large and magnificent çeşmes. The facades of the çeşmes and sebil are entirely covered with floral decorations in low relief and with a little dome. For many years in almost total ruins, it has recently been conserved although unfortunately the fluted drum of the dome has been restored in concrete. It is one of the most attractive of the early 18C baroque fountains in the city.

Walking back on the avenue between the two bridges, about halfway along on the right is an ancient and imposing building with nine domes. This is the *Galata Bedesten* (Pl 6,8), a covered market built by Mehmet II soon after the Conquest. A nearly square structure, its nine equal domes are supported by four great rectangular piers, and around the outside is a series of vaulted shops. Several authorities have claimed that the building in its present form dates from the 17–18C; however, both the form of the structure and the masonry in brick and rubble are quite obviously typical products of the 15C. One has only to compare it to the Old Bedesten in the Kapalí Çarşí, a construction of the Conqueror, to be convinced that it too is from that period.

Just beside the Bedesten, but entered from the next turning to the E, is a handsome and unusual *han*. This was built by Sinan for the Grand Vezir Rüstem Paşa shortly before 1550. The date of construction is fixed by the French scholar Petrus Gyllius, who says that the han was built on the foundations of the Latin church of St. Michael; this was still standing when Gyllius arrived in the city in 1544, but had been pulled down before he left in 1550 to make way for Rüstem Paşa's new building. The han is in two storeys with a long, narrow courtyard; from the centre of this a stairway leads to the upper floor, in an arrangement as picturesque as it is unique. The lower arcade of the courtyard has round arches, while those of the gallery are of the ogive type. This fine and unusual building has been badly treated and is now in a sad state of dilapidation and squalour.

Continuing in the same direction, one passes the lower terminal of the underground funicular railway, and a short way farther along one arrives in Karaköy, the great square at the end of the Galata Bridge. The area along the shore beside the bridge is extremely lively, colourful and picturesque, with fishermen hawking their catch from boats along the shore, and with ferries and water-taxis criss-crossing the Golden Horn in all directions.

From the upstream side of the Galata Bridge the shore road, Rihtim Cd, leads past the large ferry-terminal and towards the docks along the lower Bosphorus. Cross Rihtim Cd and walk along its left side for about 200m, then turn left and left again at the next corner, after which one finds, on the right, the entrance to *Yer Alti Camii*, the Underground Mosque, one of the strangest and most fascinating monuments in the city.

HISTORY. The mosque is housed in the low, vaulted cellar or keep of a Byzantine tower or castle, which some scholars have identified with the ancient Castle of Galata, originally constructed by the Emperor Tiberius II (578–82). This was the place where one end of the famous chain that closed the mouth of the Golden Horn in times of siege was fastened; the other end was fixed somewhere along Saray Point, and the chain was kept afloat by buoys.

INTERIOR. Descending into the mosque, one finds oneself in a maze of dark, narrow passages between a forest of squat pillars supporting low vaults; six rows of nine each, or 54 in all. Toward the rear of the mosque are two large chambers separated from the rest of the interior by grilles. These are the tombs of two sainted martyrs, Abu Sufyan and Amiri Wahibi, both of whom died in the first Arab siege of Constantinople in 674–78. The site of their graves was revealed in a dream to a Nakşibendi dervish one night in 1640. When Murat IV learned of this he had the graves opened and the saints reinterred in a shrine on the site; later, in 1757, the whole dungeon was converted into a mosque by Köse Mustafa Paşa, who was Grand Vezir under three sultans: Mahmut I, Osman III, and Mustafa III.

Walking away from the Bosphorus to the main avenue, Kemeraltı Cd, on the far side is a church with a tall tower. This is the church of *St. Benoit*, founded by the Benedictines in 1427; later it became the royal chapel of the French ambassadors to the Ottoman Empire, several of whom are buried there. After being in the hands of the Jesuits for several centuries, it was given, on the temporary dissolution of that order in 1773, to the Lazarists, to whom it still belongs. In 1804 they established a school next to the church; this is still in operation and continues to be one of the best foreign lycées in the city. Of the original 15C church, only the tower remains, with the rest of the building dating from two later reconstructions: the nave and S aisle in 1732, and the N aisle in 1871.

Turning right on Kemeraltı Cd, one soon sees on the right a fine new church built of gleaming white stone. This is the Armenian church of *Surp Kirkor Lusavoriç*, St. Gregory the Illuminator, erected in 1960 after the original church near the site had been demolished to widen the avenue. The new church is interesting as a replica of the famous church of St. Gregory at Echmiadzin, in Russian Armenia, a 7C sanctuary which is one of the masterpieces of medieval Armenian architecture. The church that was demolished was a 19C structure of no great architectural interest, but it did contain some unusual tiles from the Tekfur Saray kilns; these have been transferred to the crypt of the present church.

The quarter between Kemeraltı Cd and the Bosphorus, in this area, is a labyrinth of narrow, winding streets in which it is impractical to give specific directions. By wandering through the neighbourhood behind St. Gregory visitors will come upon three Greek churches of some interest. These are the churches of *St. John the Baptist, St. Nicholas*, and *the Panaghia* (the Blessed Virgin): all three of these are 19C structures, but they were founded in the 15–16C.

The most interesting of these is the church of the Panaghia, which is enclosed within a high courtyard wall. Notice over the main gate to the courtyard the curious emblem beside the name of the church: a cross with the Turkish star and crescent in the upper right-hand quadrant. This is the symbol of the Turkish

Orthodox Church; this sect was founded in 1922 by a dissident Greek priest from Anatolia known as Papa Eftim, who took his parishioners with him in a schism with the Greek Orthodox Church. In the half-century from that time until his death, Papa Eftim, who styled himself Patriarch Efthemios I, engaged in a running battle with the Ecumenical Patriarchate, in the course of which he won temporary control, on several occasions, of the neighbouring churches of St. John and St. Nicholas. At the moment his son and successor, Efthemios II, seems to have control only of the church of the Panaghia, and his congregation has dwindled to a handful of old people. The mass there is particularly interesting; it is said in Turkish rather than Greek, as Turkish is the language of the Karamanlí, the Anatolian Greeks who lost their mother language during the long centuries of Turkish occupation. The church's most treasured possession is an icon of the Hodegetria known as the Black Virgin, which is believed to have been brought from Kaffa in the Crimea in the late 15C.

Continuing along Kemeraltí Cd and crossing to the left side, one soon comes to a street called Hendek Sk, the Street of the Moat. The name stems from the fact that the street follows the course of the moat that once extended around the walls of medieval Galata. In fact, a fragment of the medieval fortifications still survives in the structure of the coffeehouse at the street corner. This was part of a tower that formed the junction between the walls running along the Bosphorus and those coming down from the heights above.

At this point one has reached the outer bounds of what was once medieval Galata, but the present itinerary will continue a little farther to visit a few monuments in Tophane, the district just beyond.

Just across the avenue at this point stands the mosque complex of **Kílíç Ali Paşa**, one of the most imposing monuments on the European shore of the lower Bosphorus.

HISTORY. This mosque complex was built by Sinan, in 1580, for Kílíç Ali Paşa, one of the great admirals in Ottoman history. Born in Calabria of Italian parents, he was captured in his youth by Algerian pirates and spent 14 years as a galley slave. After regaining his freedom he entered Süleyman's service as a bucca-neer, becoming a Moslem and changing his name to Uluç Ali. He distinguished himself in several naval engagements, and as a reward for this he was made an admiral and was also given the post of Governor of Algiers. He was one of the few officers to serve with distinction at the disastrous Ottoman defeat at the battle of Lepanto in 1571. As a result of this Selim II appointed him Kaptan Paşa, the chief of command of the entire Ottoman navy, and renamed him Kílíç Ali, or Ali the Sword.

While serving as Governor of Algiers Kílíç Ali Paşa came into contact with Miguel Cervantes, who had been enslaved there after his capture at the battle of Lepanto. Five years after being brought to Algiers Cervantes managed to escape, but he was recaptured and brought before Kílíç Ali Paşa. Ali Paşa was apparently impressed with Cervantes, for he released him from captivity and gave him enough money to return to Spain. Cervantes paid tribute to the kindness of Ali Paşa in Chapter 32 of 'Don Quixote', where 'The captive relates his life and adventures'.

The climax of Ali Paşa's career came in 1573, when he recaptured Tunis from Don John of Austria. Seven years later he retired to Istanbul, when he decided to build his mosque complex. When Ali Paşa asked permission from Murat III to build his mosque, so the story goes, the Sultan sarcastically suggested that he construct it on the sea, since that was the Kaptan Paşa's domain. Ali Paşa proceeded to do just that, and commissioned Sinan to build him a mosque on land he had filled-in along the shore of the Bosphorus in Tophane.

EXTERIOR. Although Sinan had been deeply impressed and inspired by Haghia Sophia, he had always avoided any kind of direct imitation of that edifice. Now in his old age—he was over 90 when he designed the mosque—he designed a near replica of the Great Church. It is one of his least successful buildings, perhaps because the greatly reduced proportions make the building seem heavy and squat.

The mosque is preceded by a very picturesque double porch. The outer porch has a deeply sloping penthouse roof, supported by 12 columns on the W facade and three on each side, all with lozenge capitals. In the centre of this porch is a monumental marble portal, and there are bronze grilles between the columns. The inner porch is of the usual type, with five domed bays supported by columns capped with stalactite capitals. Above the entrance portal is the historical inscription giving the date of foundation of the mosque, and above this is a text from the Kuran in a fascinating calligraphy, set in a curious projecting marble frame, triangular in shape and adorned with stalactites.

INTERIOR. Sinan's main departures from the plan of Haghia Sophia are these: the provision of only two columns instead of four between each of the piers to N and S, and the suppression of the exedrae at the E and W ends. Both of these departures seem to have been dictated by the reduced scale; had the original disposition been retained the building would certainly have been even heavier and darker. Nevertheless, the absence of the exedrae deprives the mosque of what in Haghia Sophia is one of its main beauties. The mihrab is in a square projecting apse, where there are some Iznik tiles of the best period. At the W there is a kind of pseudo-narthex of five cross-vaulted bays separated from the prayer area by four rectangular pillars.

*Precinct.* The külliye of Kílíç Ali Paşa Camii is extensive, including a medrese, a hamam, and the türbe of the founder, who died in 1587. (The 19C historian von Hammer thus describes Ali Paşa's death: 'Although ninety years of age, he had not been able to renounce the pleasures of the harem, and he died in the arms of a concubine'.) The türbe is in the pretty graveyard behind the mosque; it is a plain but elegant octagonal building with alternately one or two windows in each facade, in two tiers. The medrese, opposite the SE corner of the mosque, is almost square; like the mosque itself, it is a little squat and shut in. This structure is probably not by Sinan, since it does not appear in the 'Tezkere', the list of his works; it is now used as a clinic. The hamam, which is a single bath, is just in front of the medrese. The plan is unique among the extant hamams of Sinan. From the vast camekan, doors lead into two separate soğukluks situated on either side of the hararet, each consisting of three domed rooms of different sizes. From the soğukluk on the right, the only one now being used for its original purpose, a passage leads off to the lavatories; the rooms in the opposite soğukluk are used as semi-private bathing cubicles. The hararet itself, instead of having the usual cruciform plan, is hexagonal, with open bathing places in four of its six arched recesses, the other two giving access from the two soğukluks. The plan of the bath is an interesting variation on the standard one, and broadly similar to one or two of the older hamams at Bursa, the first Ottoman capital.

Across the street N of Kílíç Ali Paşa Camii is one of the most famous of the baroque street fountains in the city, the *Tophane Çeşmesi*. Built in 1732 by Mahmut I, it has marble walls completely covered with floral designs and arabesques carved in low relief, which were originally painted and gilded. Its charming domed and widely-over-hanging roof was lacking for many years but has recently been restored.

Directly across the avenue from Kílíç Ali Paşa Camii is a little mosque known as *Karabaş Mescidi*. The mosque was founded in 1530 by Karabaş Mustafa Ağa, who served as Chief Black Eunuch during the reign of Süleyman the Magnificent. It is rectangular in plan with a hipped wooden roof. The building was restored in 1962 and is once again in use.

Across the side street from Karabaş Mescidi is the building from which the whole district takes its name; this is **Tophane**, the Cannon House (Pl 9,5), which was once the principal military foundry in the Ottoman Empire.

HISTORY. The original Ottoman foundry was built on this site by Mehmet II soon after the Conquest. It was extended and improved by Beyazit II, but then demolished by Süleyman the Magnificent, who replaced it with a larger and more modern establishment in preparation for his campaigns of conquest. Süleyman's foundry has long since disappeared; the present structure was built by Selim III in 1803, doubtless in connection with his own attempt to reform and modernise the Ottoman army.

EXTERIOR. The foundry is a large rectangular building of brick and stone, with eight great domes supported by three lofty piers. Some years ago a project was begun to restore the building, but sadly it was abandoned halfway through. At present the military are occupying the building and it is closed to the public. Beyond the foundry itself, along the height overlooking the street, one sees a series of ruined substructures, walls and domes; these once formed part of the general complex of Tophane, which included extensive barracks for the artillerymen. Across the street there is a small kiosk in the Empire style that was also part of the Tophane complex; this was built by Abdül Aziz as a pavilion from which he could review parades of his artillery troops.

Beyond the Kiosk is *Nusretiye Camii*, the Mosque of Victory. This was built between 1822 and 1826 by Mahmut II; it was completed just after the Sultan's extermination of the Janissaries, and its name commemorates that event. The architect was Kirkor Balyan, the founder of the large family of Armenian architects who served the sultans through most of the 19C and who built many of the mosques and palaces that one sees today along the shores of the Bosphorus. Kirkor Balyan had studied in Paris and his mosque shows a curious blend of baroque and Empire motifs, highly un-Turkish, but not without charm. In building the mosque he abandoned the traditional arrangement of a monumental courtyard and substituted an elaborate series of palace-like apartments in two storeys; these form the western facade of the building, a feature which became a characteristic of all the Balyan mosques. Notice the bulbous weight-towers, the jutting dome arches, and the overly-slender minarets (they were so slender that they fell down soon after construction and had to be re-erected). Observe also the ornate bronze grilles and inside the abundance of marble garlands in the Empire style. Do not fail to look closely at the mimber, a marvellous baroque creation.

Not far beyond the Nusretiye, on the heights above, one sees the dome and minaret of *Cihangir Camii*. The present mosque, which was built for Abdül Hamit II in 1890, is of no interest whatsoever. However, it occupies the site of a mosque built in 1553 by Sinan for Süleyman the Magnificent. The mosque was dedicated to Prince Cihangir, Süleyman's hunchback son, who died in that year of heartbreak, it is said, because of the Sultan's execution of his beloved half-brother, Prince Mustafa. Sinan's mosque was burned down in

1720, as were several other mosques erected successively on the site before the present building.

# 19   The Bosphorus

This Rte begins at the docks on the Stamboul shore of the Golden Horn, just downstream from the Galata Bridge, where the various ferries begin their journeys up the Bosphorus. These ferries have a wide variety of itineraries, crossing back and forth between the continents on their way up the strait, so the timetables should be carefully consulted before going aboard. This itinerary is an idealised one, describing the European shore of the Bosphorus from the Golden Horn to the Black Sea, and then returning along the Asian shore to the Sea of Marmara. In this description the distances of all points will be given in km from the Galata Bridge.

Since antiquity travellers have praised the beauties of the **\*\*Bosphorus** and its verdant shores, for this historic strait is one of the loveliest and most dramatic sights in the world.

HISTORY. The Bosphorus derives its name from the myth of Io, a priestess of Hera who was seduced by Zeus. Zeus transformed Io into a heifer to conceal her from his jealous wife, but Hera was not deceived and sent a gadfly to torment Io. Pursued by the gadfly, Io plunged into the strait that separates Europe from Asia, and thenceforth it was known as the Bosphorus, or the Ford of the Cow. The Bosphorus also appears in Greek mythology in the legend of Jason and the Argonauts, who travelled up the strait to the Black Sea, the ancient Euxine, in their quest for the Golden Fleece. Many places on the Bosphorus are associated with the adventures of the Argonauts on their way up the strait, an heroic voyage which represents the expansion of the Ionian Greeks along the shores of the Euxine at the beginning of the first millennium BC.

The Bosphorus first appears in Greek literature in the 'Histories' of Herodotus, where he describes the bridge of boats Darius constructed in 512 BC to transport his army across the strait in his campaign against the Scythians. From that time onward it played an important and even decisive role in the history of the city founded at its southern extremity in 667 BC; for as Gyllius eloquently points out, the Bosphorus is 'the first creator of Byzantium, greater and more important than Byzas, the founder of the City'. And he later sums up the predominant importance of this 'Strait that surpasses all straits', by the epigram: 'The Bosphorus with one key opens and closes two worlds, two seas'.

TOPOGRAPHY AND OCEANOGRAPHY. The Bosphorus is a strait some 30km long, running in the general direction NNE to SSW, and varying greatly in width from about 700m at its narrowest to over 3·5km at its widest. Its average depth at the centre of the channel is between 50m and 75m, but at one point it reaches a depth of over 100m. The predominant surface current flows at a rate of 3–5km per hour from the Black Sea to the Marmara, but, because of the sinuosity of the channel, eddies producing strong reverse currents flow along most of the indentations of the shore. A very strong wind may reverse the main surface current and make it flow toward the Black Sea, in which case the counter-eddies also change their direction. At a depth of about 40m there is a sub-surface current, called *kanal* in Turkish, which flows from the Marmara to the Black Sea. Its waters, however, are for the most part prevented from entering the Black Sea by a threshold just beyond the mouth of the Bosphorus; these lower waters, denser and more saline than the fluid above them, are turned back by the threshold, mingle with the upper waters, and are driven back toward the Marmara with the surface current. The lower current is so strong, under certain conditions, that if fishing nets are lowered into it, it may pull the boats toward the Black Sea against the surface current.

Both shores of the Bosphorus are indented with frequent bays and harbours, and in general it will be found that an indentation on one shore corresponds to a cape or promontory on the other. Most of the bays are at the mouths of valleys reaching back into the hills on either side, and a great many of these have streams that flow into the Bosphorus. Almost all of these are insignificant, only the so-called Sweet Waters of Asia has any claim to be called a river, and this is quite small. Both shores are lined with hills, none of them very high, the most imposing being Büyük Çamlıca (262m) and Yuşa Tepesi (201m), both on the Asian side. Nevertheless, especially on the upper Bosphorus, the hills often seem very high because of the way in which they come down in precipitous cliffs into the sea. In spite of the almost continuous line of villages and the frequent forest fires, both sides of the Bosphorus are well-wooded, especially with cypresses, umbrella-pines, plane trees, horse chestnuts, terebinths, and judas trees. The pink blossoms of the judas trees in spring, mingled with the mauve flowers of the wisteria and the red and white candles of the chestnuts, give the Bosphorus at that season an even more superlative beauty.

**From the Galata Bridge to Kabataş** (c 2km). After leaving the ferry landing there is a superb view of the old city and then of the massed houses in Galata above the confluence of the Golden Horn and the Bosphorus. Then the ferry steams by the docks on the European shore of the lower Bosphorus, and passes in turn Kílíç Ali Paşa Camii, Nusretiye Camii, and then Cihangir Camii on the heights above, before heading into the landing at Kabataş.

**Kabataş** (2km). In Byzantium this settlement was known as Argyropolis, the Town of Silver, since it stood opposite Chrysopolis (modern Usküdar), the City of Gold. According to Greek tradition, it was here that St. Andrew the Apostle landed and annointed St. Stachys, his first successor.

There are a number of interesting Ottoman monuments in the immediate vicinity of the ferry-landing in Kabataş. The most important of these is *Molla Çelebi Camii*, which stands on the shore a short distance downstream from the ferry-landing. This elegant mosque was built by Sinan in 1561–6; the founder was Molla Mehmet Efendi, Chief Justice in the reign of Süleyman the Magnificent. The building is hexagonal in plan, covered by a dome supported by pillars engaged in the walls. Between these pillars to N and S there are four small semidomes, with another small semidome covering the rectangular projecting apse in which stands the mihrab.

Between the mosque and the ferry station stands the *street fountain of Hekimoglu Ali Paşa*, who founded the baroque mosque on the slopes of the Seventh Hill. The fountain, which dates from 1732, is a beautifully carved work in white marble, with çeşmes on its two faces; unfortunately, it has lost its quaint overhanging roof.

Directly across the highway there is one of the most beautiful of the baroque sebils in the city; this was built in 1787 by Koca Yusuf Paşa, who served as Grand Vezir under Abdül Hamit I. It has a magnificent çeşme in the centre, flanked by the two grilled windows of the sebil. The whole of the sebil is elaborately carved and decorated with encrustations of various marbles, with a long calligraphic inscription forming a frieze above the windows. The sebil now serves as a café, pleasantly embowered in a copse of trees.

The mosque on the seashore some 300m upstream from the Kabataş ferry landing is *Dolmabahçe Camii*. This was founded by the Valide Sultan Bezmialem, mother of Abdül Mecit I, and was completed in 1853 by Nikoğos Balyan. On the opposite side of the avenue is Midhat Paşa Stadium, the largest sports arena in Istanbul.

**From Kabataş to Beşiktaş** (distance c 1km). After leaving Kabataş the ferry steams by the gleaming marble facade of **Dolmabahçe Palace** (Pl 7,8), the principal imperial residence in the late years of the Ottoman Empire. Unfortunately, the palace is not generally open to the public, although special tours are occasionally arranged. (Check with the Bureau of Tourism for information.)

HISTORY. Shortly after the Conquest Mehmet II laid out a royal garden on this site, and early in his reign Selim I built a kiosk on the seashore here. A century later Ahmet I extended the royal gardens by filling in the small harbour in front of it, a project that was continued by his son, Osman II. As Evliya Çelebi describes this effort: 'By order of Sultan Osman II all ships of the fleet, along with all merchant ships at that time in the harbour of Constantinople, were obliged to load with stones; these were dropped into the sea so that a space of 400 yards along the shore of the Bosphorus became dry land, and thenceforth it was called Dolmabahçe, or "the filled-in garden".'

The present palace was commissioned by Abdül Mecit I (1839–61), who decided that Topkapí Sarayí was too confining and immured in the past to be a suitable residence for a reforming sultan like himself. The chief architect was Nikoğos Balyan, who in collaboration with his father Karabet completed construction of the palace in 1853. Essentially, the palace consists of a vast throne room in the centre, impressive by its mere size and height and by the richness of its décor, flanked by lower wings on either side, in which, among other things to be seen, are an incredible crystal staircase and an alabaster bathroom. Dolmabahçe Palace served as the imperial residence for all of the later Ottoman sultans save Abdül Hamit II, who preferred his own palace of Yíldíz a little farther up the Bosphorus. Atatürk also used it as his presidential residence when he was in Istanbul, and it was here that he died, on 10 November 1938. The palace is now used occasionally to entertain royal or official visitors or for very grand official parties.

**Beşiktaş** (c 3km). The ferry-landing at Beşiktaş is a short distance beyond the Palace of Dolmabahçe. Various explanations have been advanced for the name Beşiktaş, or Cradle Stone, the most probable being that it is a Turkish adaptation of the Greek name, Diplokionion, the Twin Columns, from two lofty columns of Theban granite that stood near the shore. In Byzantine times there was a famous church of St. Mamas here, as well as a port, a royal kiosk, and a hippodrome. These have all vanished without a trace, but there are still several Ottoman monuments of some interest in the vicinity.

The ferry-station is surrounded by a pleasant park, in the centre of which there is a *statue of Hayrettin Paşa*, the famous Ottoman admiral, known in the West as Barbarossa. The statue, a vivid and lively work by the Turkish sculptor Zühtü Müridoğlu, was erected in 1946 on the third centenary of Barbarossa's death. *Barbarossa's türbe* is at the far left-hand corner of the park, directly opposite his statue. This is one of the earliest works of Sinan, dated by an inscription over the door to AD 1541–42. The structure is octagonal in plan, with two rows of windows. The upper row of windows has recently been filled in with stained glass; and the dome has been rather well repainted with white arabesques on a rust-coloured ground. Three catafalques occupy the centre of the türbe, and in the little garden outside there is a cluster of handsome sarcophagi in each of which are planted purple irises.

Across the avenue from Barbarossa's türbe there is a brick and stone *mosque*, another work of Sinan; this was founded by Sinan Paşa, Ottoman admiral and brother of the Grand Vezir Rüstem Paşa. Inscriptions on the şadírvan and over the entrance portal give the date of completion as 1555–56, two years after the death of its founder. The mosque is interesting architecturally, though not particularly attractive. Its plan is essentially a copy of the ancient Üç Şerefeli Camii, built in Edirne in 1447. Its central dome rests on six arches, one incorporated in the E wall, the others supported by four hexagonal pillars, two on the W, one each to N and S; beyond the latter are side aisles each with two domed bays. Thus far the plan is almost like that of Üç Şerefeli, but while there the western piers are incorporated into the W wall, here Sinan has added a sort of narthex of five bays, four with domes, the central one cross-vaulted. The proportions are not very good and the interior seems squat and heavy.

The same indeed is true of the courtyard, where the porticoes are not domed but have steeply-sloping penthouse roofs, with the cells of the medrese occupying three sides. Sinan seems to have been less happy when he was more or less copying an older building; as in Kílíç Ali Paşa Camii, a miniature copy of Haghia Sophia, and in the present mosque, a miniature copy of Üç Şerefeli Camii. These are among his least successful buildings.

There are also two museums in Beşiktaş, both of them along the coastal road in the direction of Dolmabahçe. The first is the *Maritime Museum* (open 10–12, 1:30–5 every day except Mon); the prize exhibit is the map of America made in the first half of the 16C by Piri Reis, the Turkish cartographer. Also of interest here are the great imperial caiques used in Ottoman times to row the Sultan to his seaside palaces along the Bosphorus.

A short distance beyond, on the same side of the road, is the *Güzel Sanatlar Müzesi*, the Museum of Fine Arts (open 10–4:30 every day except Mon and Tues) which exhibits modern Turkish paintings and sculpture.

**From Beşiktaş to Ortaköy** (distance c 2·2km). About 500m beyond Beşiktaş the ferry passes the ruined shell of the *Palace of Çirağan*.

Çirağan was built during the reign of Abdül Aziz and was completed in 1874; the Sultan died there on 4 June 1876, five days after he had been deposed. His death was officially declared to be a suicide, but the suspicious circumstances suggested to many of his contemporaries that he had been murdered. His nephew and successor, Murat V, was so mentally disturbed at the time of his accession that he proved unable to rule, whereupon he was deposed in favour of his brother, Abdül Hamit II. For the next three decades Murat and his family were kept as virtual prisoners in Çirağan, living in conditions of almost unbelievable squalour and degradation. Murat died there in 1905, after which the palace was abandoned for a few years. Then, after the Constitution of 1908, Çirağan was restored and used for a time to house the new Turkish Parliament. The last act in the tragedy of this ill-starred palace occurred one night in January 1910, when Çirağan was totally gutted in a disastrous fire, leaving only the blackened shell that is seen today. There are plans to rebuild the palace and convert it into a luxury hotel.

A short distance beyond Çirağan is the entrance to Yíldíz Park and its palaces and kiosks. Just beside the entrance is *Mecidiye Camii*, built by Abdül Mecit in 1848–49; it has a very quaint but ugly minaret in the pseudo-Gothic style. The various buildings at Yíldíz were constructed at various dates in the 19C from the reign of Mahmut II to that of Abdül Hamit II, but most of them are by the latter, who preferred this more secluded palace to Dolmabahçe and the other imperial residences on the Bosphorus. They have no interest as architecture, though some of the kiosks are attractive in their setting, particularly the Şale Köşkü and the Malta Köşkü; these have been restored and are now open to the public. At the NW corner of the gardens, just outside the enclosure, is the ugly Hamidiye Camii, built in 1886 by Abdül Hamit II. A pleasant hour or two can be spent wandering here in the gardens and the park, which has many fine old trees and magnificent views of the Bosphorus.

A few yards beyond the entrance to Yíldíz Park a steep but short street leads to the very picturesque *shrine of Yahya Efendi*, a foster-brother of Süleyman the Magnificent, whom his mother nursed as an infant. Yahya Efendi died in 1570, and so the little külliye, which is a work of Sinan, must date to about that time. The külliye originally included Yahya Efendi's türbe and an associated medrese, but these have been enveloped by various wooden structures of the 19C and it is difficult to see what remains of the medrese, but at least its dershane appears to be intact. The türbe communicates by a large grilled opening to a small wooden mosque with a baroque wooden dome. The various buildings are picturesque, but the surroundings are even more so: topsy-turvy old tombstones lie scattered among a lovely copse of trees, through which one catches occasional glimpses of the Bosphorus. This is one of the most popular religious shrines in the city, and it is always thronged with pious people at their devotions.

**Ortaköy** (5·2km). In Byzantine times this village was called Ayios (St.) Phocas, after a church of that saint which stood there. There is still a modern Greek church of St. Phocas in the village, along with a very old synagogue.

On the main street in Ortaköy there is an ancient *hamam* that appears to have been wholly overlooked by writers in modern times. This was built by Sinan for Hüsrev Kethüda, who served as steward for the Grand Vezir Sokollu Mehmet Paşa; unfortunately there is no inscription to date the hamam. As so often happens, the facade on the street has been hidden by a modern stucco house-front built against it. The interior of the hamam, which is a double bath, is curious and unlike any other by Sinan. From a camekan of the usual form (though confused by a modern gallery), one enters a rather large soğukluk consisting of a central area in two unequal bays each covered by a cradle-vault; at one end are the lavatories, at the other a bathing-cubicle. From the central area the hararet is entered. This, instead of being the usual large domed cruciform room, consists of four domed areas of almost equal size. The first two of these communicate with each other by a wide arch. Here, instead of the central göbektaşí, there is a raised marble sofa or podium against one wall, with domed bathing cubicles leading from it.

There is also at Ortaköy a very striking mosque on a promontory at the water's edge. This was built in 1854 for Abdül Mecit I; the architect was Nikoğos Balyan, the builder of the palace and mosque at Dolmabahçe. But the mosque here is a much better building than those; although the style as usual is hopelessly mixed, there is a genuinely baroque verve and movement in the undulating walls of the tympana between the great dome arches.

**From Ortaköy to Arnavutköy** (distance c 2·3km). Just beyond Ortaköy the ferry passes under the new Bosphorus Bridge, which was opened in 1973. This is the fourth longest suspension bridge in the world, 1074m in length between the two great piers, and with its roadway 64m above the water. *Kuruçeşme* (6·5km), the next village on the European shore, is a once-pretty hamlet, disfigured by the coal, sand and gravel depots that line its waterfront. Then the ferry

rounds a point and approaches *Arnavutköy (7·5km), a very picturesque and lively village nestling in one of the most colourful harbours on
the Bosphorus.

The interior of Arnavutköy, the Albanian Village, is also quite
charming and picturesque, particularly if one takes the back streets
and lanes and climbs the slopes of the hills and valleys on which they
are perched. The village, like most others along the Bosphorus, still
has a large and very lively Greek community.

On the highest hill above Arnavutköy, in a superb position, are the
buildings of Robert College, an American coeducational lycée,
founded in 1871 as the American College for Girls. This was the first
modern lycée of its kind in Turkey and produced many women who
played a leading part in the life of their country, the most famous
being the writer Halide Edib Adívar. In 1971, on the occasion of its
centenary, the American College for Girls was amalgamated with the
boys' lycée of the old Robert College, a little farther up the Bosphorus,
with the new institution taking the latter name and occupying the site
above Arnavutköy. From the grounds of the school there is a superb
view of this part of the Bosphorus and its shores.

**Arnavutköy to Bebek** (distance c 2km). The point that separates
Arnavutköy harbour from the bay of Bebek, the next village on the
European shore, is called Akinti Burnu, the Cape of the Current. This
is the deepest part of the Bosphorus, which here reaches a depth of
some 100m at the centre of the strait; as a result, the current is
extremely powerful, making it very difficult for rowboats and sailing
vessels to round the point.

**Bebek** (c 9·5km). After rounding Akinti Burnu the ferry enters
**Bebek Bay**, one of the most beautiful havens on the Bosphorus. Lush
rolling hills with groves of umbrella pines and cypresses rise up to
form a verdant background to the bay, a green frieze of trees between
the blues of sea and sky. As the ferry approaches the landing it passes
the Egyptian Embassy, built in the late 19C. On the water's edge just
past the ferry landing there is a little mosque built in 1913 by
Kemalettin Bey, a leader of the neoclassical school of Turkish
architecture. Like most of Kemalettin Bey's buildings, it is a little
lifeless and dull, although the setting is quite pretty. The village itself
was once the most beautiful on the Bosphorus, but it has been
somewhat spoiled by high-rise apartments and luxury restaurants.
Nothing can detract from its superb setting however, and the
promenade along the shore on either side of the ferry-landing takes
one along a beautiful part of the strait.

On the hill between Bebek and Rumeli Hisarí, the next village on
the European shore, stand the buildings of *Bogaziçi Universitesi*, the
University of the Bosphorus. This new Turkish university was established in 1971, occupying the buildings and grounds of the old Robert
College.

Robert College, which in its time was the finest institution of higher education in
Turkey, was founded in 1863 by Cyrus Hamlin, an American missionary who
had baked bread and washed clothes for Florence Nightingale's hospital in
Üsküdar. The College was named after Christopher Robert, an American
philanthropist who provided the initial funds to build and run the institution.
During the 108 years of its existence the College had among its staff and
ex-students a number of important men, including several who played a leading
role in the cultural and political life of Turkey, as well as Greece and Bulgaria.

*The mighty fortress of Rumeli Hisarí, built in 1452,
effectively cut off Constantinople from the Black Sea in
preparation for the first Turkish siege in 1453. (Şemsi Güner)*

The site of the University is superb, and its lovely terrace commands a
stunning view of this incredibly beautiful stretch of the Bosphorus.
Just below the terrace there is an attractive old house that once
belonged to Tevfik Fikret (1867–1915), for many years professor of
Turkish Literature at Robert College. The house is called *Aşiyan*, or
the Nest, and it has been converted into a museum to exhibit
memorabilia of Tevfik Fikret. (Aşiyan is open 10–4:30 every day
except Fri.) Fikret was one of the leading poets of his time, an idealist
and utopian socialist who was convinced that the salvation of Turkey
lay in its youth.

**Rumeli Hisari** (c 10·5km). After leaving Bebek Bay the ferry passes
the point below Aşiyan; this brings one into the narrowest part of the
Bosphorus, about 700m. The ferry then passes directly under the
walls of **Rumeli Hisari**, the magnificent fortress that dominates the
strait. The romantic medieval fortress, brooding over the turquoise
water of the Bosphorus, provides one of the most extraordinary
sights in the city, and exceeds in beauty even the stretch between
Arnavutköy and Bebek. Then the ferry lands at the **village of
**Rumeli Hisari**, a very picturesque hamlet nestling under the walls
of the fortress.

HISTORY. It was here at the narrowest part of the Bosphorus that Darius chose to
cross the strait in his campaign against the Scythians in 512 BC. This crossing
was accomplished on a bridge of boats designed by Mandrocles of Samos. While

his army, estimated to be 700,000 strong, crossed the strait, the Great King watched from a stone throne cut into a cliff on the European shore. This throne, which was located about where the N tower of the fortress now stands, was later flanked by two columns raised to commemorate the historic crossing; these were still standing in early Byzantine times.

Soon after he succeeded to the throne for the third and final time in 1451, Mehmet II began preparations for the long-awaited siege of Constantinople. His first step was to cut off the city from its sources of grain on the shores of the Black Sea; to do this he decided to build a fortress on the European shore of the middle Bosphorus, directly across from Anadolu Hisari, the fortress constructed on the Asian shore by Beyazit I in the late 14C. He demanded from Constantine XI Dragases a plot of land on which to build his fortress, and the Emperor was powerless to disagree. The young Sultan himself selected the site, drew the general plan of the fortress, and hired 1000 artisans and 2000 labourers for the task, which began in April 1452. The Sultan entrusted the construction of each of the three main towers of the fortress to one of his chief vezirs: the N tower to Saruca Paşa, the sea-tower to Halil Paşa, his Grand Vezir, and the S one to Zaganos Paşa. The three of them strove to complete their task with the greatest speed and efficiency, while the Sultan himself assumed the overall supervision of the project. As a result the project was completed early in August 1452, less than four months after it had been started. The castle was then garrisoned with a force of Janissaries, whose bombardiers trained their huge cannon on the strait, warning foreign captains not to try and get through to Constantinople from the Black Sea. One Venetian captain made the attempt, but his boat was sunk by the Turkish artillery, and then he and his surviving crewmen were impaled. As a result, Constantinople was cut off from the Black Sea, a factor that contributed to its eventual capture by the Turks in 1453. After the Conquest the fortress lost its military importance and it became a mere garrison post and prison, particularly for foreign ambassadors and prisoners of war. Rumeli Hisari was very well restored in 1953, in connection with the 500th anniversary of the Conquest of Constantinople, and today it is used for performances associated with the Istanbul Festival.

ADMISSION. Rumeli Hisari is open 9:30–5 every day except Mon, and also when performances are being held.

*The Fortress.* The fortress spans a steep valley with two tall towers on opposite hills and a third at the bottom of the valley at the water's edge, where there is a sea gate protected by a barbican. A curtain wall, defended by three smaller towers, joins the three major ones, forming an irregular figure some 250m long by 125m broad at its maximum. The N tower, built by Zaganos Paşa, was used as a prison in Ottoman times; this is open to the public, and includes a small museum showing objects used by the Janissaries. The area inside the fortress has been made into a charming park, and the circular cistern on which once stood a small mosque (part of the minaret has been left to mark its position) has been converted into the acting area of a Greek-type theatre. Performances of theatre and folk-dancing are given here in summer months.

*From Rumeli Hisari to Emirgan* (c 2km). From Rumeli Hisari onwards the shores of the Bosphorus, even on the European side, become more and more rural, a succession of picturesque villages following one another with wider and wider spaces of open country between. The next village after Rumeli Hisari is *Balta Liman* (c 12km), the Port of the Axe; this is named after the Turkish admiral Balta Oğlu, who constructed here the Turkish fleet that participated in the siege of Constantinople in 1453. During that siege Balta Oğlu was unable to get his ships into the Golden Horn because of the chain stretched across its mouth, so one night he put them all on greased rollers and had them transported overland from Dolmabahçe to the Horn, a feat that contributed significantly to the final Turkish victory. The tree-

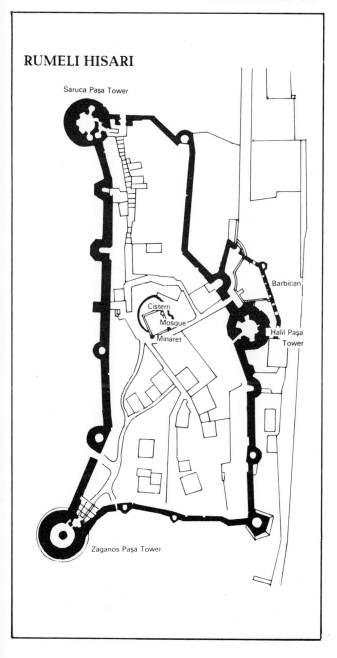

# RUMELI HISARI

Saruca Paşa Tower

Barbican

Cistern
Mosque
Minaret

Halil Paşa
Tower

Zaganos Paşa Tower

lined valley that leads inland from Balta Liman is one of the widest and prettiest along the Bosphorus.

**Emirgan** (c 12·5km). The village of Emirgan is named after the Persian prince Emirgune, who in 1638 surrendered the Persian city of Erivan to Murat IV without a fight. Emirgune later became the Sultan's favourite in drinking and debauchery, and was rewarded with the gift of a palace in this village. On the left side of the shore road, not far from the ferry station, there are the remains of a handsome old *yalí*, or seaside mansion. This is believed to stand on the site of the palace erected by Murat IV for Emirgune; parts of the structure may go back to that time, but most of it dates to the 19C, when a new or at least rebuilt mansion was erected by a Şerif of Mecca named Abdullah Paşa. The village square is very picturesque, with outdoor cafés and teahouses shaded by giant plane trees. Beside the square stands a baroque mosque, partly of wood, built in 1781–82 by Abdül Hamit I. It consists of a large rectangular room, almost square, but curiously assymetrical, and its décor is quite elegant in its baroque way. Just above the village are the famous tulip gardens of Emirgan, which are at their most glorious during the annual Tulip Festival in April.

**Istinye** (c 13km). Beyond Emirgan comes the deep indentation of the bay of Istinye. Petrus Gyllius, in his authoritative work on the topography of the strait, written c 1550, writes of Istinye that 'after the Golden Horn it must be acknowledged the largest bay and the safest port of the entire Bosphorus, rich as this is in bays and ports'. Today Istinye shelters the principal shipyard on the Bosphorus, and it is filled with floating drydocks where large ships are reconditioned. The Turkish name Istinye is a corruption of the Greek Sosthenion; according to one version of the legend Jason and the Argonauts erected a statue here, in thanksgiving (in Greek, *sosthenion*) for aid given by a winged genius of the place against their enemy on the opposite shore, King Amycus, ruler of the savage Bebryces (see Beykoz, below).

**Yeniköy** (c 13·5km). *Yeniköy was known in Byzantium as Neapolis, its name having the same meaning in Greek and Turkish: New Town. This is a serene and pretty little village with some handsome yalís on the sea, most of them dating from the late 19C. There is still a substantial community of Greeks resident in the village; their parish church, dedicated to St. George, has an old graveyard in which three Ecumenical Patriarchs of the Greek Orthodox Church are buried. At the northern extremity of the village is the summer residence of the old embassy of Austria-Hungary. Beyond that is the hamlet of *Kalender*, named after the mendicant order of dervishes who had a tekke there in Ottoman times. A little way past Kalender the beautiful grounds of the German summer embassy begin.

**Tarabya** (c 17km). **Tarabya once vied with Bebek in its claim to be the most beautiful village on the Bosphorus, and for centuries it has been celebrated for its crescent-shaped azure bay. But now, while still lovely, it is suffering from the same ravages of tourism that are spoiling Bebek, with the proliferation of expensive restaurants and the erection of a luxury hotel. The village retains, in a slightly modified form, its old Greek name, Therapeia (cure, healing): this name was apparently given to it by the Patriarch Atticus (406–25), because of its salubrious atmosphere. The ancient name of the village was Pharmakeus, the Poisoner, based on the legend that Medea, in her pursuit of Jason, there threw away the poison that she had intended to kill Jason with. The shore road beyond Tarabya is lined with the summer embassies of several European powers; among these, France and Britain have the loveliest gardens.

**From Tarabya to Büyükdere** (c 2km). Beyond Tarabya the shore curves almost directly westward to Kireçburnu, a small cluster of houses and fish restaurants at a bend in the Bosphorus. This was known in Byzantium as Kledai tou Pontou, the Keys of the Pontus; here for the first time on the journey up the strait one can see directly into the Black Sea.

**Büyükdere** (c 19km). The big village of Büyükdere stands at the N end of a large bay. Its Turkish name means Large Valley, while in Byzantium it was known as Kalos Agros, the Beautiful Meadow. It is indeed a very lovely and fertile valley with fine old trees through which a road leads into the *Belgrad Forest.*

The forest takes its name from the village of Belgrad that once stood in its midst. This was founded by Süleyman the Magnificent after his conquest of Belgrad in 1521, when he transported a number of the inhabitants of that city and settled them here to look after the reservoirs and aqueducts with which the forest abounds. The village of Belgrad became a popular summer retreat for European residents of Istanbul in the Ottoman period, particularly in times of plague. Lady Mary Wortley Montagu lived there during her stay in Istanbul, 1716–18, and in the letters which she later published her encomiums made the village famous. The village was abandoned in late Ottoman times and now only a few foundations remain.

The aqueducts and reservoirs that are scattered here and there throughout the Belgrad Forest are very impressive indeed. Many of these were built for Süleyman the Magnificent by Sinan during the period 1554–65, some of them replacing or restoring Byzantine works. The nearest aqueduct to Büyükdere is at the top of the hill along the road leading inland from the Bosphorus. This grand structure was founded by Mahmut I and completed in 1732, and conveys the waters from his reservoir and several others to the distribution centre in Taksim Square. Sultan Mahmut's reservoir (in Turkish, *bend*) is deeper in the Belgrad Forest; this is a magnificent structure, with a great dam of Proconnesian marble. Two aqueducts of Sinan are on the main road near the village of Burgaz. The first is known in Turkish as *Eğrikemer*, or the Bent Aqueduct, because it consists of two sections that meet in an obtuse angle; this has a total length of 342m. This aqueduct seems to have been built originally by Andronicus I Comnenus (1183–85); it was in ruins when Gyllius saw it in c 1550, and Sinan appears to have rebuilt it almost completely. Sinan's second aqueduct in this vicinity is past Pirgoz; this is *Uzunkemer*, the Long Aqueduct; it is 716m in length and strides across the valley in a most Roman fashion. There are two other aqueducts of Sinan far up the Sweet Waters of Europe, but these are very hard to find.

*Sarıyer* (22km). Sarıyer is the largest village on the European shore of the upper Bosphorus, a very lively place inhabited largely by fishermen and their families. The most picturesque part of the village is on the shore behind the mosque, where there is a small port for the fishermen who work in the upper Bosphorus and the Black Sea. The *fish-market is particularly colourful, and on the pier are a number of good restaurants where one can dine on the day's catch, with a splendid view of the Asian shore of the upper Bosphorus. There are more fish restaurants along the shore in Yeni Mahalle, which adjoins Sarıyer just to the N.

In the main square in Sarıyer are public taxis that one can take to the beach resort at *Kilyos*, a village on the Black Sea (c 15km). The first part of this ride commands a magnificent view of the upper Bosphorus, and there are places where almost the full length of the strait from the Black Sea to the Sea of

*Tarabya has for centuries been celebrated for its crescent-shaped azure bay. Across the strait is the Asian shore of the upper Bosphorus.*

Marmara can be seen. Approaching Kilyos there is a good view of the Black Sea coast and the long sandy beach that extends for miles along the shore of Thrace. As the village is reached one sees on the left three large ruined towers; these are known in Turkish as suterazi, and were water-control points for the aqueduct that once brought water to the town. The town itself perches on a promontory above the sea; at the highest point there are the substantial ruins of a Genoese fortress dating from the 14–15C. Unfortunately, this area is occupied by the military and is off-limits to the public.

**Saríyer to Rumeli Kavağí** (3km). Saríyer and Yeni Mahalle constitute the last heavily settled area on the European shore of the Bosphorus, for above them there are only the two tiny fishing villages of Rumeli Kavağí and Rumeli Fener. The coast road runs only as far as Rumeli Kavağí, from where a new highway runs inland, with one branch going to Kilyos and the other to Rumeli Fener, which is at the very beginning of the Bosphorus. This road is sometimes closed, because the upper Bosphorus is in a military zone, so inquiries should be made before setting out. The ferry goes only as far as Rumeli Kavağí, so that

those wishing to explore the upper Bosphorus must hire a motor boat (in Turkish, *sandal*) there or in Saríyer.

About midway between Saríyer and Rumeli Kavaǧí on the coast road one sees on the right the turbe of a Moslem saint known as *Telli Baba.* This is one of the most popular Moslem religious shrines in the city, and it is much frequented by women who pray to the saint for a husband. Those who are successful return to give thanks to the saint, usually fastening on his tomb strands of gold wire. The tomb looks very much like the simple little churches of the Greek countryside, and it is quite probable that this was in earlier days a Christian shrine, sacred to the Greek fishermen who made up most of the population along the Bosphorus.

**Rumeli Kavaǧí** (c 25km). *Rumeli Kavaǧí consists of a small cluster of houses around the ferry-landing, on either side of which there are excellent and inexpensive fish-restaurants. The view from these restaurants and the pier is superb, including the whole of the upper Bosphorus up to the Black Sea. On the Asian shore directly opposite are the ruins of a medieval fortress (see below), which, together with a castle on the European side, made up the principal Byzantine defences and customs control points on the upper Bosphorus. Of the European castle only a few scattered ruins remain; these are on the hill above Rumeli Kavaği and are known locally as *Kara Taş,* or Black Stone. The batteries below the castles on either side are relatively modern Turkish works; they were built in 1783 by Toussaint and strengthened in 1794 by Monnier, two French military engineers in the Ottoman service.

HISTORY. The villages of Rumeli and Anadolu Kavaği are probably to be identified with the ancient Serapion and Hieron, respectively. These were the Byzantine toll and customs control points, and a chain was strung between them to prevent ships from passing to and from the Euxine without paying their fees. Both of these posts were guarded by fortresses on the hills above; that on the European side was built by Manuel I Comnenus (1143–80) and called the Castle of the Incorporeal Saints, while the one on the Asian side, founded at some time early in the dynasty of the Palaeologues, was called the Castle of Hieron. In the 14C the Genoese seized both fortresses from the Byzantines, after which they collected the tolls and customs fees from shipping in the Bosphorus, further contributing to the decline of the Byzantine Empire. Mehmet II captured both fortresses in 1452; they then fell into ruins in the peaceful centuries after the Conquest.

**The European Shore of the Upper Bosphorus**. An excursion by boat along the shores of the upper Bosphorus is one of great delight, for both shores are wild, rugged and desolate, but extremely beautiful. Now for the first time on the Bosphorus one finds sandy beaches hidden away in secluded coves; grey herons haunt the cliffs, black cormorants dive into the limpid water, and schools of dolphins often gambol by. The scene is still much as it was when the Greeks first settled these shores some 3000 years ago. This was probably when the myth of Jason and the Argonauts was first formulated, a product of the Greek imagination speculating on the unknown world stretching out beyond the Bosphorus. Consequently, many features of the upper Bosphorus have associations with the mythical voyage of the Argo, and a number of these were identified by Gyllius in his pioneering work on the topography of the strait, adding further interest to this excursion.

Just beyond Rumeli Kavaği and still accessible by the public road is Altín Kum, or Golden Sands, the first of the sandy beaches, with a restaurant under a pleasant grove of acacia trees. Beyond this point one sails along for 2 or 3km below precipitous cliffs sparsely covered with shrubs, a region which obviously has never been inhabited and probably never will be. At length a wide but shallow harbour called *Büyük Liman* is reached, anciently called the Harbour of the Ephesians. On the shore are the ruins of a number of buildings, including a hamam; the beach is sandy and the valley behind is wooded and attractive, making this a pleasant place to stop for a swim and picnic.

Another km or so farther on is a strangely shaped and craggy point; in Turkish this has the appropriate name of Garipçe, which means strange or curious. There is a fairly well-preserved *Ottoman fortress* here; this was built in 1773 for Mustafa III by the Baron de Tott, another French military engineer in the Turkish service.

HISTORY. The ancient name of this place was Gyropolis, the Place of Vultures. It received its name through its association with the myth of King Phineus, the blind old prophet who was the son-in-law of Boreas, god of the North Wind. It seems that Phineus was tormented by the Harpies, two winged monsters who, every time a meal was set before the King, would swoop down upon it, snatch away most of the food, and render what was left inedible. As a result, Phineus had almost wasted away by the time the Argonauts arrived on their journey up the Bosphorus in quest of the Golden Fleece. Among them were Zetes and Calais, the winged sons of Boreas, who took pity on their brother-in-law, King Phineus, flying up into the air to chase away the Harpies for ever. In return the grateful Phineus advised the Argonauts about the rest of their journey, particularly on how to avoid the baleful Symplegades. These were two huge rocks at the mouth of the Bosphorus, which were supposed to clash together with great violence, thus making it extremely perilous for ships to enter or leave the strait. Phineus told the Argonauts to let loose a dove which would fly between the Symplegades; if it was caught they were to give up their journey, but if it got through safely they were to wait till the rocks opened again and then row their hardest. They did so, the clashing rocks just shaved off the tail feathers of the dove and the Argo got safely through, with only some slight damage to its stern-works.

The *Symplegades*, the Clashing Rocks, were also called Cyanean, the Blue Rocks, and Gyllius identified two of them, one on either side of the Bosphorus. The European one, which in Turkish is known as *Öreke Taşí*, or the Midwife's Stool, is a striking feature at the very mouth of the Bosphorus, some 100m offshore from *Rumeli Feneri*, the Lighthouse of Rumeli (the European province of the Ottoman Empire). There is a tiny fishing village here and the remains of a fort built in 1769 by a Greek engineer. This huge rock, which is now joined to the shore by a concrete mole, is about 20m high and something less than 200m long, divided by deep fissures into several parts. On the highest plateau of the rock are the remains of the so-called *Pillar of Pompey*.

This is not really a column base but an ancient altar, decorated with a garlanded ram's head and other reliefs now much worn; it once had a Latin inscription, no longer legible, the transcription and interpretation of which is debated. Certainly neither altar nor column had anything to do with Pompey, and it is not known who first gave it this misleading name: it was after the time of Gyllius, however, since he does not mention it. He thought that the altar was probably a remnant of the shrine to Apollo which Dionysius of Byzantium says the Romans erected on one of the Cyanean rocks. The column itself, with its Corinthian capital, toppled down in April 1680 and had utterly disappeared by 1800.

**The Asian Shore of the Upper Bosphorus**. The Asian shore of the upper Bosphorus is very imperfectly known and seems to have been rarely visited even by the few travellers who write about it. The only safe guide is Gyllius, for he alone appears to have explored the region in detail. Even his account, however, is not altogether free from difficulties, for he never gives the Turkish names of places in this region, perhaps because in his time they did not have any. Nevertheless, there are four places in his narrative that can be identified with certainty: the River Rhebas, the Promontarium Ancyraeum, the Promontarium Coracium, and the Fanum Jovis; and from these the others can be worked out. The Rhebas still retains a version of its ancient name—*Riva Deresi*—it is a river that flows into the Black Sea about 4km beyond the mouth of the Bosphorus. Just beyond it is the great table-like rocky islet that Gyllius calls Colonean, but which is known today as *Eşek Adasí*, Donkey Island. Riva is very attractive and picturesque, with its 14C Genoese castle at the end of a long sandy beach, a fine place to swim and picnic.

The Ancyraean Cape is *Yum Burnu*, Cape of Good Omen, which is just at the mouth of the Bosphorus. In the time of Gyllius it was called Cape Psomion, but anciently it was known as Ancyraean, the Cape of the Anchor, taking its name from the legend that it was here that Jason took on a stone anchor for the Argo. The reef or rock that has the best claim to be the Asian Symplegades stands immediately under the southern cliff face of Yum Burnu.

The bay to the S of Yum Burnu is now called *Kabakoz Limaní*, the Harbour of the Wild Walnuts. In Gyllius' time it was known as the Bay of Haghios Sideros (that is, St. Anchor: the half-remembered story of the Argonautic anchor had given rise in the minds of the medieval Greeks to an apocryphal holy man). On the S this bay is bounded by a point not named by Gyllius but nowadays called *Anadolu Feneri Burnu*, after the lighthouse (in Turkish, *fener*) on the promontory above. Below the lighthouse the village of *Anadolu Feneri* clings perilously to the cliff. Just S of this is the bay that Gyllius calls Ampelodes; this is now known as *Çakal Limaní*, the Bay of Jackals, fringed by savage and rocky precipices. The next promontory beyond this, unnamed by Gyllius, is now called *Poyraz*. (In Turkish, Poyraz is the fierce NE wind that howls down the Bosphorus from the Black Sea in winter; its Greek name is Boreas, the Greek god of the wind from that corner of the compass.) On Poyraz Burnu, just opposite Garipçe, is a *fortress* built in 1773 by Baron de Tott for Mustafa III, a twin of the fortress across the strait; there is also a small village on the cape. The long sandy beach to the S is now known as *Poyraz Limaní*; the Greeks of Gyllius' time called it Dios Sacra, 'because', as he writes, 'I suppose, there was once an altar here either of Jove or of Neptune, the other Jove'. This is one of the most pleasant spots on the Asian shore of the Bosphorus to swim and spend a leisurely afternoon. This bay is bounded on the S by *Fil Burnu*, Elephant Point; Gyllius writes that in his time it was called Coracium. The long stretch of concave coast is now called *Keçili Limaní*, the Harbour of the Goats, but it is so rugged and precipitous that it can hardly be called a harbour.

One now comes to the place that Gyllius called the Fane of Jove, by which he meant the temple of Zeus Ourios, Zeus of the Favouring Winds. In the temple there was a Hieron, or sacred precinct, where there were shrines of the Twelve Gods. Keçili Limaní is bounded on the S by a cape still known by a version of its ancient name, *Yoros Burnu*, doubtless from Ourios. According to one version of the myth, this shrine was founded by Jason on his return from Colchis with the Golden Fleece. In Byzantine times the name Hieron applied to the toll and customs station on the Asian shore at this point, which was guarded by the huge *\*fortress* on the hill above. This fortress is often called 'the Genoese Castle'; but, like the fortress above Rumeli Kavağí, it is actually Byzantine in foundation, although the Genoese may have repaired or rebuilt it, to a certain extent, when they took control of it in the mid-14C. The Byzantine origin of the fortress is evidenced by various Greek inscriptions that are found on its walls. One of these contains the imperial motto of the Palaeologus dynasty, a cross with the letter B (the first letter of Basileus, or King) repeated in all four quadrants, meaning 'King of Kings, who Kings it over Kings'. Gyllius rather oddly describes this fortress as small, though in fact it is the largest on the Bosphorus, almost twice the area of Rumeli Hisarí. However, Gyllius referred only to the citadel itself; this was probably the only part still inhabited in his day. Unfortunately, the fortress is now occupied by the military and is off-limits to the public.

**Anadolu Kavağí** (c 25km). Below the fortress to the S is the village of Anadolu Kavağí, the first settlement of any size on the Asian shore of the upper Bosphorus, and the last stop of the Bosphorus ferry on this

side. The fortifications here, like those at Rumeli Kavağí, were built in
1783 by Toussaint and increased in 1794 by Monnier. To the S of the
village, above the caves of Macar and Sütlüce, is the hill known as
Yuşa Tepesi, the Hill of Joshua, though the Joshua in question seems
not to have been Judge of Israel but a local Moslem saint. The hill is
over 200m high, the second highest on the Bosphorus after Büyük
Çamlíca. Anciently it was called the Bed of Hercules, but in modern
times it has been known to Europeans as the Giant's Grave. On top of
the hill there is a huge filled-in pit some 18m long, which local
tradition holds to be the grave of a giant.

**From Anadolu Kavağí to Beykoz** (c 7km). Opposite Büyükdere the
coast forms a long shallow bay with rather dangerous sandbanks in
the sea and a rugged and inhospitable coast line. At *Selvi Burnu*,
Poplar Point, somewhat disfigured now by the oil installations of
Socony, the coast turns E to the charming valley of the *Tokat Deresi*.
Here the Conqueror built a royal kiosk, as did Süleyman the
Magnificent, at a later date. Gyllius described the later building as a
'royal villa shaded by woods of various trees, especially planes'; he
goes on to mention the landing stairs, 'by which the King, crossing the
shallow shore of the sea, disembarks into his gardens'. It is from these
landing stairs that the place gets its modern name. *Hünkar Iskelesi*,
the Emperor's Landing-Place, which in turn gave its name to the
historic peace treaty signed here in October 1833 between Russia and
the Ottoman Empire. The little palace that now stands on the site was
built in the mid-19C for Abdül Mecit I by the Armenian architect
Sarkis Balyan; it serves as a hospital.

**Beykoz** (18km). The large village of *Beykoz, Prince's Walnut, is still
extremely pretty despite the existence of several factories and depots
nearby. In addition to some large and handsome houses in pretty
gardens, the village also has a quite extraordinary *fountain* in the
main square. This beautiful fountain was built in 1746 by one Ishak
Ağa, Inspector of Customs; it forms a domed and columned loggia,
and is quite unlike any other çeşme in the city.

Gyllius was at pains to show that Beykoz was the home of the savage King
Amycus, ruler of the barbarous people known as the Bebryces. When strangers
landed on this coast Amycus forced them to box with him. Amycus and his
opponent both wore the nail-studded gloves known as the cestus, but since
Amycus, the mighty son of Poseidon, was the best boxer in the world, he always
killed his man. However, when the Argonauts landed, Amycus challenged
Polydeuces (in Latin, Pollux), who turned out to be an even greater boxer than
he, and the King finally met his death. On the spot where King Amycus was
killed an *insana laurus*, an insane bay-tree, grew.
　From Beykoz a road leads inland from the Bosphorus. One branch of this road
leads to the Black Sea beach resort of **Şile** (c 80km), where there is a
magnificent beach of white sand that stretches westward for miles from the
village. (There are several hotels in the village and along the beach, the best of
which is the Kumbaba, superbly situated in among the dunes.) The village itself,
the ancient Calpe, is quite picturesque, perched on a rocky promontory high
above the sea, with the ruins of a 14C Genoese castle clinging to a craggy islet in
the little harbour.
　Another branch of the road from Beykoz leads to *Polonezköy*, the Polish
Village (c 25km). This pretty little village was founded in the mid-19C by Polish
refugees led by Prince Adam Czartoryski, who received a grant of land from
Abdül Mecit I as a reward for having commanded a detachment of Polish
soldiers in the Ottoman army during the Crimean War. Their descendants
remain there to this day, many of them having married with other Christian
minorities in Istanbul. Their village, together with their Roman Catholic church
and the well-tended fields and orchards around it, appears to have been

transplanted from 19C eastern Europe, a serene little oasis in the barrenness of the surrounding region. Rooms with full board can be rented in the village, which is renowned for its good Polish cooking, and horses are available for riding.

**Beykoz to Kanlíca** (c 5km). S of Beykoz the ferry passes *Incir Köyü*, Figtree Village; one sees here the charming valley of Sultaniye Deresi, where Beyazit II laid out extensive gardens. A little farther on is *Paşabahçe*, the Paşa's Garden, named after the palace and gardens established here by Hezarpare Ahmet Paşa, Grand Vezir under Murat IV. The village mosque is an undistinguished structure built in 1763 by Mustafa III. On the seashore is the *Paşabahçe glass factory*, world famous for its fine crystal and glassware; guided tours of the factory can be arranged, and there is an outlet shop in the entrance lobby.

The next village is *Çubuklu*, a pleasant hamlet in a verdant setting. In Byzantium this was known as Eirenaion, or Peaceful, and it had a very famous monastery founded in 420 by St. Alexander for his order of Akoimetai, the Unsleeping, who prayed in relays throughout the day and night. Half a century later a branch of this order was installed in the newly founded monastery of St. John of Studius in Constantinople, where they became renowned for their piety and scholarship. The appearance of the village has been spoiled by the installation of petroleum tanks, but behind it there is still a very beautiful and fruitful valley.

On the hill above the village is the *palace of the Khedive of Egypt* (the Khedive was the hereditary Viceroy of Egypt under Ottoman rule); its distinctive tower is one of the most conspicuous landmarks on this part of the Bosphorus. The palace was built in 1900 by Abbas Hilmi Paşa, the last Khedive; for such a late date it has considerable charm. Its western facade overlooking the Bosphorus is semicircular, with a handsome marble-columned porch and a grand semicircular hall within. The tower room and the charming loggia on the roof command a panoramic view of the whole of the middle Bosphorus and its shores. The palace has recently been restored and is now a luxury hotel.

**Kanlíca** (c 13km). Kanlíca has been famous for its delicious yogurt since at least as far back as the mid-17C, when Evliya Çelebi praised it as being the best in Istanbul. The local yogurt is served in several little restaurants around the very attractive square beside the ferry-landing, where the tables are set out on the shore under the shade of venerable plane-trees. On the far side of the square there is a mosque which is a minor work of Sinan; an inscription over the entrance portal records that it was founded in 1559–60 by the Vezir Iskender Paşa. It is of the very simplest type, with a wooden porch and a flat wooden roof; but both porch and roof are clearly modern reconstructions. According to Evliya Çelebi, it originally had a wooden dome, which would have made it much more attractive. The founder's türbe is nearby.

**Kanlíca to Anadolu Hisarí** (distance c 2km). Between Kanlíca and Anadolu Hisarí there are the remains of the most historic yalí on the Bosphorus; the seaside *mansion of Amcazade Hüseyin Paşa*, who founded the külliye in Şehzadebaşí. Hüseyin Paşa, the fourth member of the illustrious Köprülü family to serve as Grand Vezir, is thought to have built this yalí in 1698, the year in which he represented Mustafa II in the negotiations between the European powers and the Ottoman

Empire at Carlowitz (c 100km NW of Belgrad). The final articles of the Peace of Carlowitz were signed in this yalí on 26 January 1699, a treaty which historians consider to be the turning-point in the Ottoman penetration of Europe. All that remains of the original house is the wreck of a once very beautiful room built out on piles over the sea, and one hopes that this will be preserved.

**Anadolu Hisarí** (11km). The ferry-landing in Anadolu Hisarí has the most beautiful ✦✦ setting of any on the Bosphorus. It is at the mouth of Göksü Deresi, the Sky Stream, one of the two little rivers which in late Ottoman times Europeans called the Sweet Waters of Asia; the second of these rivers, Küçüksu, is a few hundred metres to the S. Just beside the ferry-station, to the N, is the fortress of ✦✦**Anadolu Hisarí**, one of the most romantic sights on the Bosphorus, a medieval castle which well deserves its Turkish name: *Güzelce*, the Beautiful One. The fortress was built c 1390 by Sultan Beyazit I, the Thunderbolt, who ended his life in ignominious captivity after his catastrophic defeat by Tamerlane at the battle of Ankara in 1401. It was rebuilt and perhaps extended by Mehmet II in 1452, when he was constructing the great fortress of Rumeli Hisarí across the Bosphorus. The fortress is a small one, consisting of a keep and its surrounding wall together with an outer wall or barbican guarded by three towers. Parts of the barbican have been demolished, but the rest of the fortress is in fairly

*The Palace of Küçüksu on the shore of the Bosphorus was built in 1856–57 by Sultan Abdül Mecit I and is a charming example of Turkish rococo architecture. (Sedat Pakay)*

good condition. One authority has suggested, on the basis both of historical sources and methods of construction, that only the keep and its wall were built by Beyazit I, and that the barbican and towers were added in 1452 by the Conqueror.

**Küçüksu** (10·5km). The ferry-landing at Küçüksu is just S of the *Sweet Waters of Asia, a lovely meadow which in Ottoman times was a favourite resort of the *beau monde*. The people of Istanbul still come here on summer weekends and holidays, to picnic in the meadows (now partially occupied by a football stadium) or to swim at the artificial sand beach slightly N of the ferry-station.

The principal adornment of the Sweet Waters of Asia is the *Palace of Küçüksu*, which stands on the shore midway between the two streams. This little rococo palace, erected on the site of several earlier imperial pleasure domes, was built in 1856–57 for Abdül Mecit I by Nikoğos Balyan. From this time it was used by the Ottoman sultans when they and their entourage came to enjoy a holiday at the Sweet Waters of Asia. Unfortunately, it is not open to the public, and is now used only for occasional state ceremonies.

On the seashore near the palace is the baroque *fountain of the Valide Sultan Mihrişah*, built in 1796. It is square with upturned eaves and colonettes set in its corners, with the spigots and their basins framed in round arches. The situation of the fountain is extremely picturesque, and has been a favourite subject for painters.

Just to the S of the ferry-landing in Küçüksu stands the largest and grandest seaside mansion on the Bosphorus, the **Kíbríslí Yalísí**. (The name of the yalí stems from the fact that one of its owners, Mustafa Emin Paşa, was the Ottoman governor of Cyprus, which in Turkish is called Kíbrís.) Built originally in c 1760 but added to and redecorated later, its facade on the Bosphorus is over 60m long, mostly of one storey but with two in the central section. The rooms are arranged symmetrically around three great halls. The eastern hall is the most beautiful; it is paved in marble, with a central marble fountain and the vaulted ceiling is decorated with exquisite mouldings and painted panels of bowls of flowers. To the N and S slender wooden columns with Corinthian capitals divide the central space from two bays, one looking directly out to sea, the other providing the entrance from the garden. Four superbly proportioned rooms open from this hall, two overlooking the Bosphorus and the other two opening into the garden. Farther to the E is an enormous ballroom and a charming greenhouse with a pebble-mosaic and a great marble pool with a curious fountain. The harem occupied the western wing of the house and was the oldest part of it; unfortunately it was demolished in 1970.

A short distance beyond the Kíbríslí Yalísí is the **Kírmízí Yalí**, or the Red Yalí. This is the best-preserved seaside mansion on the Bosphorus and its exterior is the most beautiful of all the yalís. The yalí was built c 1790 by the Ostrorogs, a noble French-Polish family that had connections with the Ottoman Empire since the 16C. The last of the line, Count Jean Ostrorog, died in the yalí in 1975.

**From Kandilli to Beylerbey** (c 3km). The next ferry stop after Küçüksu is *Kandilli*, where the waters of the Bosphorus rush past the point with such speed that the Turks call this the Devil's Current. The ferry then stops at the adjacent hamlet of *Vaniköy*, which consists of little more than a line of seaside mansions between the shore road and the Bosphorus. On the hill above Kandilli there is a large girls' lycée. This was formerly the *palace of Adile Sultan*, sister of Abdül Aziz; it was built in 1856 and has a superb view of the lower reaches of the Bosphorus. Above Vaniköy is the tower of the *Istanbul Rasathane*, an astronomical observatory and meteorological station. The Rasathane has a small but very interesting exhibition of the antique astronomical instruments used by the 16C Turkish astronomer Takiuddin.

The large and imposing building on the shore S of Vaniköy is the *Kuleli Naval Officers' Training College*. The original military training school and barracks here were built c 1800 by Selim III, as part of his attempted reform of the Ottoman armed forces. The present structure dates from an extensive rebuilding and enlargement by Abdül Mecit I, completed in 1860. The older building served as a military hospital in 1855–56, during the Crimean War, and was one of two medical institutions which at that time were under the supervision of Florence Nightingale, the other and larger one being the Selimiye Barracks in Üsküdar.

It was more-or-less on this site that the Empress Theodora, wife of Justinian the Great, established her famous home for reformed prostitutes; the institution was called Metanoia, or Repentance. Procopius, the court chronicler, writes in his 'Secret History' that some of the women 'threw themselves from the parapets at night and thus freed themselves from an undesired salvation'.

The ferry then stops at Çengelköy (c 8·5km), the Village of the Hooks. According to Evliya Çelebi, the village took its name from the fact that shortly after the Conquest Mehmet II found a store of Byzantine anchors there. The village is exceptionally pretty and has a very picturesque square on the sea, shaded by plane trees and graced by a baroque fountain. There are two good restaurants on the square where one can dine while gazing down the Bosphorus at the majestic skyline of the old city.

Immediately after leaving Çengelköy the ferry passes the handsome *Sadullah Paşa Yalísí*. This early 19C building is, unfortunately, no longer inhabited and it is beginning to fall into serious disrepair. Hopefully, it will be restored, for it is one of the few remaining yalís from that early period.

The ferry soon passes *Beylerbey Palace*, named after the village just beyond it. The palace, in much the same style as Dolmabahçe, was completed in 1865 by Sarkis Balyan. From the sea it looks very attractive; it has two little marble pavilions at either end of the quay and is bordered by lovely gardens. The palace was built principally as a residence for visiting royalty and heads of state, among whom were the Empress Eugenie of France, the Emperor Franz Joseph of Austria, the Shah Nasireddin of Persia, and King Edward VIII of England (when he was still Prince of Wales). The former Sultan Abdül Hamit II lived out the last years of his life here after his return from exile in Thessalonika in 1913; he died in 1918. When unoccupied the palace is occasionally open to the public.

**Beylerbey** (7km). Beylerbey was known in Byzantium as Chrysokeramos, or the Golden Tiles, apparently because it had a church with gilded roof tiles. When Gyllius visited the village he saw the ruins of a palace built by Justinian, but not a trace of this survives. Next to the little port there is a mosque known as *Beylerbey Camii*; this was built in 1778 by Mehmet Tahir for Abdül Hamit I. It is an attractive example of the baroque style, its dome arches arranged in an octagon, vigorously emphasised within and without, its mihrab in a projecting apse, richly decorated with an assortment of tiles of various periods from the 16–18C. The mimber and Kuran kürsü are unusually elegant and beautiful works, both of them of wood inlaid with ivory. It has two minarets, the second one added later by Mahmut II. The lower part of each minaret consists of a base of square cross-section above which there is a bulbous foot, rather like a flattened bell-jar and from which rises the fluted shaft, with a single şerefe and a bulbous stone crown with a tall horned alem, or crescent-like symbol. This is the first appearance of this type of minaret which, particularly its bulbous foot, became a characteristic feature in mosques of the late 18C and the 19C.

**From Beylerbey to Üsküdar** (c 6km). After leaving Beylerbey the ferry once again passes under the Bosphorus Bridge, after which it stops at *Kuzguncuk* (c 5km). This quiet little village takes its name from Kuzgun Baba, a Turkish holy man who lived there in the time of the Conqueror. Near the ferry-landing is a handsome yalí with a rounded facade on the Bosphorus.

From Kuzguncuk the ferry heads down along the last stretch of the Asian shore of the lower Bosphorus. The shore here has been ruined by the intrusion of modern apartments, factories and depots of various kinds, but the hills above are still beautiful. The tallest of these is Büyük Çamlíca (262m), which is included in the next itinerary. Finally the ferry pulls in to the landing at **Üsküdar**, ending the voyage down the Asian shore of the Bosphorus.

# 20 Üsküdar and Kadíköy

Visitors to Istanbul sometimes forget that an important part of the city is located in Asia. The most interesting of these Anatolian suburbs from the point of view of historical monuments is **Üsküdar**, which lies directly opposite the mouth of the Golden Horn. Adjoining Üsküdar to the S is **Kadíköy**, which in antiquity was the more important of the two towns, but now has virtually no historical monuments of importance. Nevertheless, there are one or two minor sights to see at Kadíköy, and there are a number of pleasant walks.

APPROACHES. Passenger ferries leave for Üsküdar both from the Galata Bridge and from the ferry station downstream from the bridge on the right bank of the Golden Horn. There is also a car-ferry to Üsküdar, from Kabataş, on the Bosphorus. Ferries to Kadíköy leave from the Galata Bridge and also from the large maritime terminal, downstream from the bridge on the left bank of the Golden Horn, where it meets the Bosphorus. One can also get to both places by bus or dolmuş, via the Bosphorus Bridge, from Taksim and other transportation centres in the city.

HISTORY. Üsküdar used to be known as Chrysopolis, the City of Gold. In antiquity Chrysopolis was a suburb of the neighbouring and more important town of Chalcedon, the modern Kadíköy. According to tradition, both towns were founded early in the 7C BC, shortly before the founding of Byzantium. Chrysopolis, because of its fine natural harbour and its strategic position at the head of the strait, began to develop rapidly and later surpassed Chalcedon in size and importance. The town became the starting-place for the great Roman roads that lead from Byzantium into Asia, and it was a convenient mustering-place for military and commercial expeditions into Anatolia. Throughout the Byzantine period both Chrysopolis and Chalcedon were suburbs of Constantinople and thus had much the same history as the capital. Their sites were not

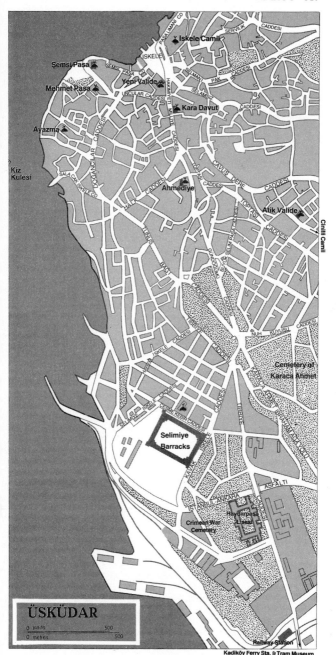

İskele Camii

Şemsi Paşa

Mehmet Paşa

Yeni Valide

Kara Davut

Ayazma

Kız Kulesi

Ahmediye

Atik Valide

Chilili Camii

Cemetery of Karaca Ahmet

Selimiye Barracks

Crimean War Cemetery

Haydarpaşa Lisesi

Railway Station

Kadıköy Ferry Sta. & Tram Museum

## ÜSKÜDAR

0 yards     500

0 metres     500

well suited for defence, however, and on several occasions they were occupied
and destroyed by invading armies while Constantinople remained safe behind
its great walls. For this reason there are no monuments from the Byzantine
period remaining there. Both towns were taken by the Turks in the mid-14C,
more than a hundred years before the fall of Constantinople. Chalcedon came to
be called Kadíköy, the City of the Judge, for it was the headquarters for the Chief
Justice of the Anatolian provinces of the Ottoman Empire. Chrysopolis came to
be called Üsküdar, a corruption of Scutari, the name by which the town was
known in the latter Byzantine period and by which foreign residents continued
to call it until quite recent times. This name dates from the 12C and derives from
the imperial palace of Scutarion, which was at the point of land opposite the
Maiden's Tower (see below). This has completely vanished, as have all other
traces of Byzantine Chrysopolis and Chalcedon.

During the Ottoman period several members of the royal family, particularly
the Valide Sultans, adorned Üsküdar with splendid mosques and pious foundations, most of which are still to be seen. Many great and wealthy Osmanlís built
their mosques, palaces and mansions there, preferring the quieter and more
serene environment of Üsküdar to the tumult of Stamboul. Until fairly recently
Üsküdar had a charmingly rustic atmosphere reminiscent of old Ottoman days.
Traces of this still remain, although uncontrolled urban development is fast
destroying old Üsküdar.

The focal point of Üsküdar is Iskele Meydaní, the great square beside
the ferry-landing. In Ottoman times this was known as Doğancílar
Meydaní, the Square of the Falconers, and old prints show it as an
extremely colourful and picturesque spot. This was the rallying-place
for the Sürre-i-Hümayun, the Sacred Caravan that each year departed for Mecca and Medina with its long train of pilgrims and its sacred
white camel bearing gifts from the Sultan to the Şerif of Mecca. Today
the square is just a vast traffic circle and has lost all of its former
oriental charm; nevertheless, it is still an exhilarating place, swept by
sea-breezes from the Bosphorus and the Marmara, commanding a
superb view of the imperial city across the strait.

The ferry-landing is dominated on the left by a stately mosque on a
high terrace; this is *Iskele Camii, taking its name from the ferry-
landing (in Turkish, *iskele*). This mosque was built in 1547–48 by
Sinan for Mihrimah Sultan, daughter of Süleyman the Magnificent.
The exterior is very imposing because of its dominating position high
above the square and its great double porch, a curious projection from
the porch covers a charming fountain. The interior is perhaps less
satisfactory, for the central dome is supported by three instead of the
usual two or four semidomes; this gives the mosque a rather truncated
appearance, which is not improved by the universal gloom. Perhaps it
was the darkness of the interior here that made Mihrimah insist on
floods of light when, in 1562, she commissioned Sinan to build her
mosque near Edirne Kapí.

The medrese of the külliye is to the N, a pretty building of the
rectangular type, now used as a clinic. The primary school is behind
the mosque, built on sharply rising ground so that it has very
picturesque supporting arches; it has recently been restored and is
now a children's library. On leaving the mosque terrace one finds at
the foot of the steps the very handsome baroque *fountain of Ahmet
III*, dated 1726.

Passing the fountain and entering the main avenue of Üsküdar, one
soon comes, on the left, to a supermarket housed in the remains of an
ancient hamam. The owner calls it *Sinan Hamam Çarşísí*, thus
ascribing the bath to Sinan; this is probably not so, though it certainly
dates from his time. It was a double bath, but the main entrance
chambers were destroyed when the street was widened.

A little farther on there is an ancient and curious *mosque* built by

Nişancí Kara Davut Paşa toward the end of the 15C. It is a broad
shallow room divided into three sections by arches, each section
having a dome, an arrangement unique in Istanbul.

Across the street and opening into the square is the large complex
called *Yeni Valide Camii*; this was built in 1708–10 by Ahmet III, who
dedicated it to his mother, the Valide Gülnus Emetullah. At the corner
is the Valide's charming open türbe, looking like a large aviary, and
next to it a grand sebil. On entering the gate from the square one sees
a very attractive facade, a later addition, which is the entrance to the
imperial loge. The mosque itself was built in the very last phase of the
classical period, and just before the baroque influence had come to
enliven it. In plan it is a variant of the octagon-in-a-square theme,
decorated with inferior tiles of late date. Walking through the outer
courtyard, one comes to the main gate, over which is the mektep.
Outside the gate stands the large imaret with a çeşme at the corner;
this is of later date than the rest of the külliye and is fully in the
baroque style.

*Sinan's Şemsi Paşa Camii stands at the confluence of the
Bosphorus and the Sea of Marmara. (Sedat Pakay)*

Take the street opposite the main gate of the mosque and turn left,
then right, past some tobacco factories, to reach the precincts of
**Şemsi Paşa Camii**. This is one of the most delightful of the smaller

mosque complexes in the city, built of glittering white stone and standing in a very picturesque location right at the water's edge. Built by Sinan for the Vezir Şemsi Paşa in 1580, the mosque is of the simplest type: a square room covered by a dome with conches as squinches. Şemsi Paşa's türbe opens into the mosque itself, from which it is divided by a green grille, a most unusual and pretty feature. The well-proportioned medrese forms two sides of the courtyard, while the third side consists of a wall with grilled windows opening directly onto the quay and the Bosphorus. The külliye has been beautifully restored in recent years.

The walk along this quay to the S is very pleasant; at its end turn and walk halfway up a low hill to an ancient mosque. This is *Rum* (the Greek) *Mehmet Paşa Camii*, built in 1471. In its present state, part badly restored, part left dilapidated, it is not a very attractive building, but it has some interesting and unusual features. Of all the early mosques this is the most Byzantine in external appearance: the high cylindrical drum of the dome; the exterior cornice following the curve of the round-arched windows; the square dome base broken by the projection of the great dome arches. These and several other features suggest a strong Byzantine influence, which is undoubtedly due to the fact that Mehmet Paşa was a Greek who became one of the Conqueror's vezirs. Internally the mosque has a central dome with smooth pendentives and one semidome to the E, like Atik Ali Paşa Camii; but here the side chambers are completely cut off from the central area. Behind the mosque is Mehmet Paşa's gaunt türbe.

If one leaves the mosque complex by the back gate and follows the winding street outside, keeping firmly to the right, before long an imposing baroque mosque known as *Ayazma Camii* is reached. Built in 1760–61 by Mustafa III and dedicated to his mother, it is one of the more successful of the baroque mosques, especially on the exterior. A handsome entrance portal opens onto a courtyard from which a pretty flight of semicircular steps leads up to the mosque porch; on the left is a large cistern and beyond that an elaborate two-storeyed colonnade gives access to the imperial loge. The upper structure is also diversified with little domes and turrets, and many windows give light to the interior. The interior, as in many of the baroque mosques, is less successful, though the grey marble gallery along the entrance wall, supported by slender columns, is effective. At the back of the mosque there is a picturesque graveyard with some interesting old tombstones.

Leaving by the S gate and following the street to the E, one comes to a wider street, Doğancílar Cd, with two pretty baroque çeşmes at the intersection; turning right here, at the end of the street, one finds a türbe. This severely plain tomb was built by Sinan for Hací Mehmet Paşa, who died in 1559. It stands on an octagonal terrace covered with tombstones and overshadowed by a dying terebinth tree.

The wide street just ahead leads downhill past a little park; the third turning on the right followed by the first on the left leads to an elaborate and delightful külliye, the **\*Ahmediye mosque and medrese**. Built in 1722 by Eminzade Hací Ahmet Paşa, Comptroller of the Arsenal under Ahmet III, it is perhaps the last building complex in the classical style, though verging toward the baroque. Roughly square in layout, it has the porticoes and cells of the medrese along two sides; the library, one entrance portal, and the mosque occupy a third side, while the fourth has the main gate complex with the dershane above and a graveyard alongside. The whole plan is, however, very irregular because of the alignment of the surrounding streets and the slope of the ground. The dome of the little mosque is supported by scallop-shell squinches and has a finely-carved mimber and Kuran kürsü. The library and the dershane over the two gates are the most attractive features of the complex and show great ingenuity of design. The whole külliye ranks with those of Amcazade Hüseyin Paşa and Bayram Paşa as being among the most charming and inventive in the city. Unfortunately, though partially restored some years ago, it is now quite dilapidated.

At the SE corner of the courtyard a stairway under the dershane leads to the street below. A short, narrow street opposite the outer gate leads to a wider avenue, Toptaşí Cd, the Avenue of the Cannon Ball. Turn right here and follow the avenue for about 600m, as it winds uphill through a pleasantly rural and picturesque neighbourhood. Toward the top of the hill and somewhat toward the left is **Atik Valide Camii**, the great mosque complex that dominates the skyline of Üsküdar.

HISTORY. The great külliye of Atik Valide Camii was built by Sinan, in 1583, for the Sultan Valide Nur Banu, wife of Selim II and mother of Murat III. This is the most splendid and extensive of all Sinan's constructions in Istanbul with the sole exception of the Süleymaniye. In addition to the mosque itself, the külliye consists of a medrese, a hospital, an imaret, a school for reading the Kuran, a caravansaray, and a hamam. All of these buildings are still in existence and most are in good condition, though several now form part of a prison and cannot be visited. Altogether this is certainly one of the half-dozen most impressive monuments of Ottoman architecture in the whole of Turkey.

EXTERIOR. The precinct is entered by an alley beside the graveyard behind the mosque. This is one of the most beautiful of all the mosque courtyards in the city, a grandly proportioned cloister with domed porticoes supported on marble columns; in the centre are the şadírvan and a copse of ancient plane trees and cypresses. The mosque is entered through an elaborate double porch, the outer one with a penthouse roof, the inner domed and with handsome tiled inscriptions over the windows.

INTERIOR. Inside is a wide rectangular room with a central dome supported by a hexagonal arrangement of pillars and columns; to the N and S there are side aisles, each with two domed bays. The aisles were added at a later date, and although, when closely examined, the arrangement leads to certain anomalies, the general impression is very attractive. There are galleries around three sides of the room, and the wooden ceilings under some of them preserve that rich painting typical of the period: floral and arabesque designs in black, red and gold. The mihrab is in a square projecting apse entirely revetted in magnificent tiles of the best Iznik period; notice also the window frames of deep red conglomerate marble with shutters richly inlaid with mother-of-pearl. The mihrab and mimber are fine works in carved marble.

*Precincts.* The medrese of the complex stands at a lower level than the mosque and is entered by a staircase in the W wall of the courtyard. Its own courtyard is almost as pretty as that of the mosque itself; it is oddly irregular: there are five domed bays to the S but only three to the N. The dershane is in the centre of the W side in the axis of the mosque, though at an obtuse angle to it, and it projects out over the street below, which passes under it through an archway. Leaving the medrese by the gate in the S side, one can walk around the building and pass under this picturesque arch. At the next corner beyond it stands the large hospital, also highly irregular in plan but quite as attractive as the other buildings. These various irregularities are partly due to the alignment of the surrounding streets and the varying level of the terrain, but Sinan may also have decided to utilise these features to give variety and liveliness to his design.

The other buildings of the külliye are either part of the prison or are in a half-ruined condition. The double hamam has lost its two large entrance chambers and the rest is used as a carpenter's shop, while the caravansaray is partly incorporated into the prison, partly used as a storehouse. It is to be hoped that the prison will be relocated and the complex restored to its original condition, for this is one of the most interesting and important monuments in the city.

The street to the E of Atik Valide Camii leads after a walk of about 1km to *Çinili Cami*, the Tiled Mosque. This small complex was built in 1640 by the Valide Sultan Kösem, mother of Murat IV and Crazy Ibrahim. The mosque, in a pretty garden filled with flowers and trees, is small and simple: a square room covered by a dome. The mosque is decorated both on the facade and in the interior by a revetment of tiles; these date from just after the best period but they are still quite fine, chiefly pale blue and turquoise on a white ground. The mimber of white marble has its own carving very prettily picked out in gold, red and green,

*Kíz Kulesi, the Maiden's Tower, was originally a 12C Byzantine fortress. The present structure dates from the 18C.*

and its conical roof is tiled. The porch of the mosque is a baroque addition, as is the minaret, of which the şerefe has a corbel of very pretty folded-back acanthus leaves, unique in the city. In the courtyard there is a very fine şadírvan with a huge witch's cap for a roof, and a tiny triangular shaped medrese, sloping headlong downhill. Just outside the precinct is a handsome mektep, and not far off there is a large hamam, both of which are part of the külliye.

The street outside the mosque, Çavuş Dere Cd, winds downhill toward the centre of Üsküdar, and in about 1·5km it reaches Iskele Meydaní, where this itinerary began.

**Environs of Üsküdar**. There are several interesting and pleasant excursions in the vicinity of Üsküdar. These places can easily be reached by bus or taxi from Iskele Meydaní, or, if one has the time and energy one can stroll to them through the town, for none is at any great distance.

*The Maiden's Tower*. One of the most familiar sights in Istanbul is perhaps the one least visited. This is Kíz Kulesi, the Maiden's Tower, which stands on a tiny islet a few hundred metres off Üsküdar. It can be reached by hiring a boat at the ferry landing in Üsküdar.

The Turkish name of the islet is derived from a legend concerning a princess who was confined there by her father to protect her from the fate foretold by a dire prophecy: that she would die from the bite of a serpent. However, the princess was eventually bitten by the serpent, which had been smuggled out to the islet, and she died instantly. (The Turks are very attached to this legend, associating it with virtually every tower or castle along their coasts.) In English the place is usually called Leander's Tower, in the mistaken notion that Leander drowned there in his attempt to swim the strait to see his lover Hero, although this legendary tragedy should be located near Abydos in the Hellespont. According to Nicetas Choniates, the Emperor Manuel I Comnenus built a small fortress on the islet, using it to attach one end of the great chain which he stretched across the mouth of the Bosphorus, fastening the other end at a tower just below the acropolis. Since then the islet has served as the site of a lighthouse, semaphore station, quarantine post, customs control point, and a home for retired naval officers. At present it is used as an inspection station by the Turkish Navy; the present quaint structure dates from the 18C, and is one of the most distinctive landmarks in the city.

*Büyük Çamlíca*. Büyük Çamlíca is the tallest peak in the vicinity of Istanbul, 267m above sea-level, distinguished by the tall television antenna and weather light at its summit.

APPROACHES. Büyük Çamlíca is about 4km E of Iskele Meydaní, and is approached by the main highway leaving Üsküdar in that direction. Bus 9 goes directly from Iskele Meydaní to the peak; buses Nos 11, 11A, and 11B go from the square to Kísíklí, from where it is a pleasant stroll to the summit. Those driving to Büyük Çamlíca from the Bosphorus Bridge should take the Kísíklí exit after reaching the Asian side, after which the way is signposted.

Büyük Çamlíca, the Great Place of Pines, is the taller of the twin peaks of Mount Bulgurlu, a few m higher than Küçük Çamlíca. For centuries the Great Çamlíca, as it is called in English, has been famous for its view. In the morning, when the sun is still easterly, one has a panoramic sight of the whole city and its surrounding waters: the Bosphorus almost as far as the Black Sea; the Marmara with the Princes' Isles (see below), and beyond that the great snow-covered ridge of Ulu Dağ, the Bithynian Mount Olympus. Toward evening the sun sets almost directly behind Stamboul, and its domes and minarets are silhouetted against the flaming western sky like a splendid stage drop. Other delightful walks may be taken over the hills to the N of Çamlíca and down through any of the numerous valleys to the little villages along the Asian shore of the lower Bosphorus. These hills and valleys are particularly beautiful in spring, when the whole area is red-pink with blossoming judas trees and one is serenaded by nightingales.

*Cemetery (Mezarlík) of Karaca Ahmet.* The area is famous for the walk to the vast Turkish cemetery of Karaca Ahmet, which covers the hills to the SW of Üsküdar toward Kadíköy.

*The cemetery of Karaca Ahmet is the oldest and largest Moslem burial-ground in Istanbul. (Sedat Pakay)*

APPROACHES. The nearest part of the cemetery is c 1·2km from Iskele Meydaní. To get there start off along the main street that leads off from the far right-hand corner of Iskele Meydaní (facing away from the sea); the first stretch of the street is called Hakimiyeti Milliye Cd, but about halfway along it becomes Gündöğümü Cd. This latter street brings one to the main entrance to the cemetery, beside which there is a mosque and a türbe.

HISTORY. According to tradition, the cemetery was founded here at the time of the Turkish conquest of the surrounding area, in the mid-14C; however, the tombstone bearing the most ancient date is of AH 927, or AD 1521. The cemetery is named after Karaca Ahmet, a sainted warrior from the time of Orhon Gazi (1326–59), who was killed and buried here at the time of the Turkish conquest of Chrysopolis and Chalcedon. As so often happens, Karaca Ahmet's grave was miraculously discovered in later times, revealed in a dream to a dervish. A türbe was then erected to house the saint's remains (the present structure is a modern one, dating to the 19C), and alongside it a monument in the form of a cupola was built to honour his favourite horse, whose skeleton was also found on the spot. (Simple peasants often worship before the horse's tomb, thinking that it too is the türbe of a holy man.) As time went on many of the famous men and women of the Ottoman Empire chose to be buried here, so that eventually it became the largest cemetery in Turkey, and perhaps in all of the Islamic world.

After passing through the gate it is possible to walk for hours through this haunting and exceptionally picturesque burial-ground, with acre after acre thick with cypress trees and with serried but topsy-turvy ranks of tombstones. Many of the older tombstones are beautifully designed and carved, usually bearing calligraphic obituary inscriptions: besides giving the name, dates, and circumstances of the deceased's life, there is often an epitaph. Some of these epitaphs are poetic and often moving, but others are sometimes irreverent and amusing, such as this inscription on a roadside tomb: 'Passerby, spare me your prayers, but please don't steal my tombstone'. The stones are topped by representations of the headdresses of the deceased, which indicate their sex and station in life. The older tombstones of the men are surmounted with large stone turbans, whose variety exhibit the full range of the Ottoman civil, military and religious hierarchies. The later tombstones are far less picturesque, since the turban was banned by Mahmut II in 1828, and replaced by the fez, which was, in turn, banned by Atatürk in 1925. Some of the older tombstones of the women are crowned with archaic oriental hats and draped with shawls, with the face of the stone decorated with floral reliefs, in which every blossom signifies a child that the deceased bore. The oldest and quaintest of these tombstones are to be found in the area toward Haydarpaşa, the district along the coast between Üsküdar and Kadíköy.

*Selimiye Barracks and Mosque.* The most prominent monument in Haydarpaşa is the enormous four-towered structure between the Karaca Ahmet Cemetery and the Marmara. This is the Selimiye Barracks, known in Turkish as Kíşla, famous in English history as the site of Florence Nightingale's hospital during the Crimean War.

HISTORY. The barracks owe their name to the fact that the original military residence hall here, a wooden structure, was built by Selim III in 1799 to house the men of his New Army, the modern force with which he hoped to replace the Janissaries. But these barracks burned down in 1808, shortly after Selim had been deposed and killed in a Janissary insurrection. New stone barracks were erected on the site by Mahmut II in 1828, within two years after he finally destroyed the Janissaries. This building had only a single wing; the other three wings were added by Abdül Mecit I in the period 1842–53. During the Crimean War the barracks served as a British military hospital; during the first months of its operation conditions there were so bad that the death toll reached the appalling rate of more than 20 per cent of the patients admitted. In October 1854 Florence Nightingale organised a party of 38 nurses, mostly from various religious orders, for service in the Crimean War. When her party arrived in Istanbul the following month she took charge of the medical services at the barracks in Scutari, as it was then called, and also at the other military hospital at Kuleli on the Bosphorus. Before she left Istanbul, in the summer of 1856, shortly after the end of hostilities, the death rate at the two hospitals under her charge in the city had dropped to 2 per cent. After the war the Selimiye barracks was once again used to house Turkish soldiers, a function it still performs today. In recent years it has also been used to house political prisoners. Consequently, it is not normally open to the public, but permission to visit Florence Nightingale's former quarters can sometimes be obtained by applying to the officer in charge.

*The Barracks.* The Selimiye is among the most enormous barracks ever constructed. The barracks are raised on a basement where the ground slopes sharply down to the Marmara; very imposing when seen from Stamboul, they are the most prominent landmark on the Asian shore of the city. They consist of four enormous wings, each of three storeys, surrounding a vast quadrangular parade ground; at the corners there are five-storeyed towers with tall turrets above, the one to the NE rising above the chambers where Florence Nightingale lived when she was directing the hospital here. One of the downstairs rooms in this tower has been converted into a museum in her honour by the Turkish Nurses Association. On the wall is a romanticised picture of 'The Lady of the Lamp', depicting her making her late night rounds through the teeming wards of the hospital. There are also, on exhibition, some pamphlets on military nursing written by Florence Nightingale, along with battle scenes from the Crimean War.

*The Selimiye Mosque.* Opposite the main entrance to the barracks is the Selimiye Camii, the mosque that Selim III built for the men of his new army. Constructed in 1803–04, it is the last and one of the most handsome of the baroque mosques. Not only are its proportions and details most attractive, but it is placed in an exceptionally lovely garden shaded by three of the finest old plane trees in the city. The interior of the mosque is a little stark, though of impressive proportions. The western gallery, the mihrab, and the mimber are all of highly polished grey marble and give the place a certain charm.

*The Crimean War Cemetery.*The large building to the S of the Selimiye barracks is the Haydarpaşa Lisesi, and tucked in between this school and a grain elevator by the sea is the Crimean War Cemetery. There is no sign to identify the cemetery and the gate is usually locked; but if one stands by the entrance the caretaker will emerge to open the gate. The cemetery is very well maintained and landscaped, a contrast to the romantic disarray and decay in the Karaca Ahmet burial-ground; it has been kept up by the British since the Crimean War. Many of the graves here are the last resting-places of British soldiers who died in the nearby Selimiye barracks, and several of Florence Nightingale's nurses are interred here. Also buried here are British soldiers who fell at Gallipoli and others who died in the Middle East during World War II, along with British and other civilians who have died in Istanbul during the past century. The principal funerary monument is an obelisk of grey Aberdeen granite, with, in several languages, an inscription paying tribute to the dead by Queen Victoria. There is also a plaque dedicated by Queen Elizabeth II, honouring the pioneering nursing work done by Florence Nightingale and her staff in Scutari during the Crimean War.

The main road from Haydarpaşa S to Kadíköy runs past the front of the Haydarpaşa Lisesi and then behind the huge building that houses the Haydarpaşa railway station, the terminus for the trains that cross Turkey to its eastern and southern borders and beyond. After passing the station the road runs along the shore to the Kadíköy ferry-station. From there it is just a short walk to the only place of interest in Kadíköy, the *Tram Museum.* This is approached by walking along the main avenue inland from the ferry-landing, Söğütlü Cd, and continuing as far as Kuşdili Cd, which is to the right at the first major intersection. There, underneath a metal shed, at the Kuşdili Tramvay Deposu is the Tram Museum. This is an absolutely delightful museum, and helps make up for Kadíköy's total lack of historical monuments. A wonderful assortment of Istanbul trams, and other vehicles once used in the city's public transport, are arranged around the shed.Some of the trams are drawn by sculptured horses and inside are models of the occupants: a conductor wearing a fez, passengers wearing turbans and antique Ottoman costumes, and a lady from the Saray accompanied by a black eunuch. The museum includes some of the first cars in Tünel. Also on display are old photographs of Taksim and Eminönü, the two main transportation centres in Istanbul, all of them showing the quaint old trams which used to be such an integral part of the life of Istanbul, until their final disappearance during the 1960s.

After leaving the Tram Museum one can return to the Kadíköy ferry-station and take a boat back to the Galata Bridge. Or, if there is time, one can continue to walk along the shore S of the ferry-station, where there are several pleasant seaside promenades. Some of the neighbourhoods S of Kadíköy, particularly *Moda, Kalamíş and Fenerbahçe*, have long been famous as summer resorts. There are places to swim, along with outdoor restaurants and cafes by the sea.

# 21  The Princes' Isles

The most famous of all the beauty spots in the vicinity of Istanbul are the **Princes' Isles** (Atlas 16), the little suburban archipelago just off the Asian coast of the Marmara. The group consists of nine islands, all but four of them tiny. The nearest is some 15km from the Galata Bridge, the farthest about 30km, though in spirit they seem at a far greater remove than that, they are so different in atmosphere and appearance from the rest of the city.

APPROACHES. There are scheduled passenger ferries to the four largest and most populous of the islands, the closest of which is Kínalí, followed by Burgaz, then Heybeli, and finally Büyükada, the largest in the archipelago. Some of the ferries stop at all four of these islands in turn, beginning with Kínalí, in which case it can take at least 90 minutes to reach Büyükada, but express boats to Büyükada make the journey in about an hour. In summer months there are occasional ferries stopping at Kaşik and Sedef, for in other seasons these tiny islets have virtually no residents. Tavşan and Sivri are totally uninhabited, while the only residents on Yassí are the staff at the military installation there.

HISTORY. In the medieval Byzantine period the archipelago was known as Papadonisia, the Isles of the Monks, from the many monasteries that had been established there. These monasteries became famous because of the many emperors and empresses of Byzantium who were shut up there after losing their thrones, along with numerous ecumenical patriarchs deposed in the frequent religious controversies that divided the Greek Orthodox Church. According to the Byzantine chronicler Cedrenus, the Emperor Justin II in 569 built himself a palace and a monastery on the largest of the isles. This island was called Megale, or the Great Island, but soon after the royal palace was built it became known as Prinkipo, the Isle of the Prince. Later, the entire archipelago came to be called the Princes' Isles.

Throughout the Byzantine period and until the last century of Ottoman rule there were mainly monks and nuns, in various monasteries and convents, living on the islands, together with a small number of fishermen and their families living in the port-villages on the four larger islands. However, all this changed in 1846, when a regular passenger ferry-service was established between Istanbul and the four largest isles. This brought a large influx of summer visitors who built fine houses on the four islands, and many of them eventually settled in as year-round residents. These were largely well-off Greeks, but included substantial numbers of Armenians, Jews, resident foreigners, and a few wealthy Ottoman families. The ferries also brought crowds of people on weekend holidays in the summer months, particularly to Büyükada, resulting in the construction of large numbers of hotels, restaurants, cafés and bathing establishments. The rapid development of tourism in recent years has, to a certain extent, spoiled the natural beauty of Büyükada, particularly in the town and along the northern shore of the island. However, the hilly interior and its southern coast are relatively untouched; large parts of the other islands are also unspoiled. Motor vehicles are not permitted on the islands, and the only public transport is provided by phaetons, picturesque horse-drawn vehicles which can be hired at the ferry-landings. The absence of automotive traffic has done much to preserve the natural beauty of the isles, making them sybaritic retreats from the crowded and polluted metropolis on their western horizon.

*Kínalí.* The ferry calls first at **Kínalí**, which is some 15km from the
Galata Bridge by sea. The island takes its Turkish name (Henna-Red)
from the colour of the sandstone cliffs that plunge into the sea at its
eastern end. The island has for centuries been inhabited principally
by Armenians, and today they still make up most of its population.

HISTORY. The Greeks have always called the island Proti, since it is the nearest
in the archipelago to the city. In Byzantine times there were two monasteries on
the island, one of them dedicated to the Panaghia (the Virgin) and the other to
the Transfiguration, there was also a convent of unknown name. All three of
these establishments housed royal exiles at one time or another. The first was
Michael I, who was banished to Proti in 813 after he had lost his throne to Leo V,
the Armenian. Michael took the cowl, as the monk Anastios, and spent the
remaining 27 years in the monastery of the Panaghia. The next imperial arrival
on Proti was none other than the deposed Leo V. Leo did not survive, his
butchered corpse was sewn up in a leather sack and thrown into the boat that
carried his family off into exile on Proti, where they were confined to the
monastery of the Transfiguration. Leo's remains were buried there. In the
following century a new batch of imperial exiles arrived on Proti. On 17
December 944 Romanus I was deposed by his two sons, Stephen and Constantine, who then shipped their father off into exile in the monastery of the
Panaghia on Proti. But then on 27 January of the following year Stephen and
Constantine were themselves deposed and sent off to join their father. In 970 a
convent on Proti received the deposed Empress Theophano, widow of Romanus
II and Nicephorus II. Theophano had been banished by John I Tzimisces, the
new emperor and her former lover, with whom she had conspired to kill her
second husband so that John could usurp the throne; apparently he wanted her
safely confined to a nunnery so that she could not do the same to him. The last
imperial exile on the island was Romanus IV Diogenes, who was deposed and
banished from the capital after his disastrous defeat by the Selcuk Turks at the
battle of Manzikirt in 1071. He spent his last years at the monastery of the
Panaghia, after having been blinded so that he could never conspire to regain
the throne.

Kínalí is a rather bare and barren isle, but it has a few sandy coves
where one can picnic and swim, and it has fine views from the
summits of its three bare hills: Çínar Tepesi, Teşvekiye Tepesi, and
Monastir Tepesi. Otherwise there is little to do on the island, which
has no hotels and restaurants.

Almost nothing remains of the two Byzantine monasteries on the
island and the medieval nunnery has vanished without a trace. The
modern Greek church of the Panaghia, which can be seen to the left of
the ferry-landing, a few streets in, is believed to stand on, or near, the
site of the Byzantine monastery of the same name. Around the church,
and also in a nearby park, there are architectural fragments that
almost certainly belonged to the medieval monastery.

The second street to the S of the church, Kínalí Firín Sk, leads
inland past a Byzantine cistern thought to have supplied water to the
monastery of the Panaghia.

It was undoubtedly from here that the British Admiral Duckworth obtained
water for his fleet when he anchored off Kínalí, during his show of force against
Istanbul. While watering his fleet Duckworth learned that a party of Turkish
troops had taken refuge at the Monastery of the Transfiguration, which was just
a short distance outside the town to the SW. He thereupon ordered a bombardment which utterly destroyed the monastery, which had probably been in
existence for a thousand years.

One block beyond the cistern the street leads to a path which heads
out into the countryside. A short way along, on the left, is the modern
Monastery of the Transfiguration; this was founded in the mid-19C by
Simon Sinosoğlu to replace the Byzantine structure destroyed by
Duckworth. A bust of Sinosoğlu stands beside the church, which has a

superb iconostasis of dark wood and some fine icons. All that remains of the Byzantine monastery that stood on this site are a few fragments, the most notable of which is a large Byzantine capital.

The path passes between Monastir Tepesi (to the S) and Teşvekiye Tepesi (to the N), after which it turns right to pass between Teşvekiye Tepesi (to the E) and Çinar Tepesi (to the W). From either of these two hills, both are 115m, there is an excellent and unobstructed view of the two tiny isles to the SW: Sivri (to the right) and Yassí (to the left).

*Sivri and Yassí.* In Byzantium Sivri was known as Oxya and Yassí as Plate: the Turkish and Greek names are descriptive and mean the same thing in each case: the first meaning Pointed and the second Flat. Sivri is nothing more than a tall craggy reef rising to a height of 90m, taller than any of the Seven Hills of Constantinople. Because of its remoteness and barreness this and its flat neighbour Yassí have been used for centuries solely as places of exile and imprisonment. During the last century of Ottoman rule Sivri was used on several occasions to dispose of the street dogs of Istanbul, who were rounded up in their thousands and left to starve and tear each other to pieces. Yassí formerly boasted what Murray's 'Handbook' of 1892 describes as 'a dilapidated Anglo-Saxon castle' built by Sir Henry Bulwer, English ambassador to the Sublime Porte and brother of the novelist Bulwer-Lytton; here he is popularly supposed to have engaged in nameless orgies. Some remains of this castle were still visible until 1960, but it has been largely engulfed in the buildings erected for the trial of the deposed Turkish Prime Minister, Adnan Menderes, and 14 of his associates. After a lengthy trial they were all convicted and sentenced to death, but 12 of the sentences were commuted to life imprisonment and only Menderes and two of his former ministers suffered the death penalty. They were hanged on the night of 16–17 September 1961 on the island of Imralí, farther W in the Marmara. Since then Yassí has been used occasionally as a place of detention for political prisoners, and as such it is off-limits to the public, as is Sivri because of its proximity.

**Burgaz.** The second large island at which the ferry stops is Burgaz, some 4km from Kínalí by sea. This island, which is inhabited principally by Greeks, is one of the most pleasant in the archipelago; it is as beautiful as the two larger and more popular isles to its E, Heybeli and Büyükada, but it has fortunately escaped virtually all of the ravages of uncontrolled development and tourism.

HISTORY. In antiquity the island was known as Panormas, but in Byzantine times it was called Antigone, and it is still known by this name by its Greek inhabitants. Burgaz, its Turkish name, is a corruption of pyrgos, the Greek word for tower; this stemmed from the fact that there was a watch-tower atop the summit of the island, a landmark which continued to be noted by travellers as late as the early 19C. During Byzantine times the island had a large monastery dedicated to the Transfiguration, but it is not known to have housed any imperial exiles. The only famous personage exiled on Antigone during the Byzantine period was St. Methodius, who was imprisoned there in 822 by Michael II because of his support for icon veneration, which the Emperor detested. Methodius was confined to a dungeon for seven years; he was finally set free by the Emperor Theophilus, who succeeded to the throne in 829. In 842 Methodius was made Patriarch of Constantinople, and in his brief term he proved to be one of the most distinguished men who ever held that office. After the death of Methodius in 846 he was recognized as a saint in the Greek Orthodox Church; and a shrine was built over the dungeon on Antigone by the Empress Theodora, widow of Theophilus. Later, a church dedicated to St. John the Baptist was built around the shrine, fragments of which can still be seen today.

The town of Burgaz is the prettiest in the isles, with white and pastel houses ringing a crescent bay. There is a pleasant marble square next to the ferry-landing, and two good restaurants where one can dine beside the sea. There are no hotels, but the owner of the Yordan Restaurant runs a pension that is open from May through September.

The most prominent landmark in town is the high dome of the

Greek church of *St. John the Baptist*. This is a modern structure, but it stands on the site of the Byzantine church of the same name that was built over the shrine dedicated to St. Methodius. According to tradition, the shrine occupies the dungeon where the saint was imprisoned for seven years; it is approached by entering the narthex and passing between the two columns on the left, from where a stairway leads down into the subterranean chamber.

One block beyond the church on Çayír Sk one finds the *former home of Sait Faik* (1907–54), the famous Turkish writer. The house is now a museum, exhibiting memorabilia of Sait Faik. The house is open to the public on Tues to Fri from 9–12 and 2–5, and on Sat from 9–1.

At the S end of the village the second road in from the seashore leads to a path that runs around the southern side of the island. This leads up the slopes of the heavily wooded Christos Tepesi, the highest peak on the island (170m). There one finds the modern Greek *church of Haghios Christos*, surrounded by some impressive architectural fragments from a large medieval sanctuary, which is probably the monastery of the Transfiguration. According to tradition, this was founded by the Emperor Basil I (867–86), and it appears to have stood until 1720 when it was probably demolished by the Turkish authorities.

From the N side of the village a paved road leads out to the northern and western sides of the island. Just as the road leaves the village it passes on the right a monastery dedicated to St. George, beside which there is a café pleasantly situated by the sea.

A narrow strait, less than 1km wide, separates Burgaz from Heybeli, the next island-stop on the ferry. On the way across the ferry passes the tiny islet of Kaşík, or Spoon, a name vaguely suggested by its topography. Its Greek name is Pitta and it is the smallest of the nine islands in the archipelago, too minute to support a monastery. In recent years a number of villas have been built on the islet, and in summer months there is a motor launch which makes a few trips a day there from Burgaz.

**Heybeli**. Heybeli is perhaps the most beautiful of all the Princes' Isles, although many would argue in favour of its neighbour, Büyükada. The village is a pretty cluster of white-washed stone houses and pastel-hued villas on the eastern side of the island.

HISTORY. The island has always been known to the Greeks as Halki, a name bestowed upon it in antiquity because of its copper-mines, long ago exhausted. Its general outline as seen from the sea, two symmetric hills separated by a rounded valley, is responsible for its Turkish name, which derives from heybes, or saddle-bag. In Byzantine times there were two monasteries on the island. One of these was the monastery of the Holy Trinity, founded in 857 by the Patriarch Photius. This monastery, which has vanished without a trace, is believed to have stood on Ümit Tepesi, the northernmost of the hills on Heybeli, which is now surmounted by the impressive buildings of the Greek Orthodox School of Theology, founded in 1841. According to tradition, the original monastery on this site was founded in 857 by the Patriarch Photius, one of the intellectual giants in Byzantine history. It was he who was principally responsible for the schism which took place in 867 between the Greek Orthodox Church and the Latin Church of Rome, a split which has not yet been repaired. Photius, who was twice Patriarch of Constantinople, was deposed by Michael III in 886 and exiled to the monastery he had founded on Halki, where he died four years later. This monastery continued in existence until the construction of the present School of Theology, which is also dedicated to the Holy Trinity. This school operated until 1971, when it was closed by an act of the Turkish Parliament. However the establishment itself continues to function as a scholarly institution, for its library has a particularly rich collection of Byzantine manuscripts.

The second of the two Byzantine monasteries on Halki stood on the western slope of Değirmen Tepesi, the more westerly of the two peaks that flank the village across from Ümit Tepesi. This monastery, which was dedicated to the Panaghia Theotokou, the Mother of God, was founded by John VIII Palaeologus (1425–48), and was the last monastic establishment to be founded in the Byzantine Empire. The original monastery was destroyed by fire in 1672; it was rebuilt but then wrecked in the anti-Greek riots in 1821. The monastery was abandoned at that time, but in 1833 the building was restored and converted into a Greek commercial school; this continued in operation until 1916, when it was converted into an orphanage. In 1942 the building and grounds were taken over by the Turkish government, and from that time on it has been part of the Turkish Naval Academy. The only part of the original Byzantine structure that seems to have survived is the church of the Panaghia Kamariotissa, which served as the monastery chapel. This was founded some time between 1427 and 1439 by Maria Comnena, third wife of John VIII Palaeologus and the last Empress of Byzantium. This church remained in the hands of the Greek community until 1942, when it too was taken over by the Turkish government.

ACCOMODATION. The Panorama Hotel near the N end of the port is open during summer months only. There are a number of restaurants in the village, most of them along the sea-front, and there is also one at Çam Limaní, the large cove on the NW coast of the island.

To the left of the ferry-landing are the buildings and grounds of the Turkish Naval Academy. Anchored offshore from the Academy is the 'Savarona', an American-built boat acquired by the Turkish government in the 1920s; it served as Atatürk's private yacht during the latter years of his life and is now used by the commandant of the Naval Academy.

A paved road leads around the coast of Heybeli, with a branch road cutting across the waist of the island. Phaetons can be hired near the ferry-station; to go all the way around the island tell the driver Büyük (Grand) Tour, or to circle only the northern half say Küçük (Small) Tour.

The most interesting spot on the island is at the intersection of the coast road and the road leading across the waist of the island. To the right of the intersection are the buildings and grounds of the inland branch of the Turkish Naval Academy, where the monastery of the Panghia Theotokou once stood. Normally civilians are not permitted on the grounds of the Academy,but sometimes the officer in charge will allow one to see the church of the *Panaghia Kamariotissa*, the former chapel of the monastery. The chapel is an extremely interesting building, tiny, and of the quatrefoil or tetraconch type; that is, with a central dome surrounded by four semidomes over exedrae, three of which project from the outside of the building, with the fourth being contained within the narthex. This is the only Byzantine church, of the tetraconch type,that has survived in the city.

Buried in the courtyard of the church are seven Patriarchs of Constantinople. Four of them died violently in the 17–18C. The most famous of these is the celebrated Cyril Lucaris, six times Patriarch of Constantinople and once of Alexandria. His final downfall and death came as the result of a truly Byzantine conspiracy. Cyril had some years before been secretly converted to Calvinism and was hoping to take the entire Greek Orthodox Church with him into that faith. The Holy Synod eventually learned of his intentions, however, and did all in their power to oppose him. Some of the Greek bishops even resorted to a secret alliance with the Jesuits in Galata, who were themselves hoping to bring the weak and divided Orthodox Church under the power of Rome. This group of conspirators let it be known to the secret agents of Sultan Murat IV that Cyril was plotting with the Russians to enable them to take Constantinople. When the Sultan learned of this he immediately gave orders to his mutes to do away with Cyril, who died by the bowstring on 25 June 1638, after which his body was flung into the Bosphorus. His corpse was washed ashore several days later, and was then taken secretly to Halki for burial at the church of the Panaghia

Kameriotissa. Thus ended the remarkable career of the man whom Pope Urban had called 'the son of darkness and the athlete of Hell'.

On the hillside, above the entrance to the Naval Academy, there is a very interesting old graveyard. The most striking sepulchral monument there is a large statue of an angel holding the imperial Russian coat-of-arms, which, like that of Byzantium, is inscribed with the figure of a double-headed eagle. (The angel once also held a cross, but this was destroyed during some anti-Christian riot.) This is a memorial to the three hundred or so Russian soldiers who died in the nearby monastery, imprisoned there after having been captured in the Russo-Turkish war in 1828. Only the names of the officers are inscribed on the monument.

The most interesting tombstone in the cemetery is that of Edward Barton, the second ambassador from Queen Elizabeth I to the Sublime Porte. The tomb is inscribed with Barton's coat of arms and a long inscription in Latin. There are many mistakes in the inscription, but it seems to be intended to read something like this: 'TO EDWARD BARTON/ THE ILLUSTRIOUS AND SERENE/AMBASSADOR OF/THE QUEEN OF THE ENGLISH/A MAN MOST PREEMINENT/WHO ON HIS RETURN FROM/THE WAR IN HUNGARY/ WHITHER HE HAD ACCOMPANIED/THE INVINCIBLE EMPEROR/OF THE TURKS/DIED IN THE 35TH YEAR OF HIS AGE/AND OF OUR SALVATION 1597/THE 15TH DAY OF SEPTEMBER'. The Emperor to whom the inscription refers was Sultan Mehmet III.

**Büyükada**. The ferry finally stops at Büyükada, the Greek Prinkipo, the largest and most populous of the Princes' Isles. When people visit the islands they nearly always come here; it is the the summer resort *par excellence.*

HISTORY. During Byzantine times there were at least four monasteries and a convent on Prinkipo. The convent sheltered several imperial exiles during the medieval period. It had originally been founded by the Emperor Justinian in the mid-6C, but it was completely rebuilt and considerably enlarged in the last years of the 8C by the Empress Eirene, one of the very few women to rule Byzantium in her own right. In 797 Eirene usurped the throne from her son, Constantine VI, whom she mutilated so badly that he died a few days later. The Emperor left behind a young daughter, the Princess Euphrosyne, whom Eirene banished to her convent on Prinkipo so that she could not contest the throne. In 802 Eirene was herself deposed and exiled to Lesbos, where she died shortly afterwards. Her body was then taken to Prinkipo to be buried in the garden of her convent. Euphrosyne remained in the convent on Prinkipo for 26 years, while five emperors in turn succeeded one another on the throne of Byzantium. The last of these ephemeral emperors, Michael II, the Stammerer, suddenly grew tired of his old wife, the Empress Thecla, in the year 829. Rumour reached him of the pretty princess-nun who had been locked up all these years on Prinkipo. So he sent for her, and after banishing Thecla to the convent on Prinkipo married Euphrosyne. Later that same year Michael died and was succeeded by his son Theophilus. The new Emperor showed himself a loyal son, for he restored his mother Thecla to the palace and sent Euphrosyne back to her convent on Prinkipo.

Two centuries later, in 1041, this same convent sheltered for a time the amorous Empress Zoë after she had been exiled by her adopted son, Michael V, the Caulker. She was freed from the monastery a few weeks later however, when the people of Constantinople deposed Michael and raised Zoë and her sister Theodora to the throne, where they ruled in their own right for a few months before being succeeded by Constantine IX, whom Zoë married.

Anna Delasena, mother of the future Alexius I Comnenus, was imprisoned in the convent for a few months in 1060, before being allowed to return to the capital. In 1115 the Empress Eirene, wife of Alexius I, entered the convent voluntarily so that she could be near her husband, who was suffering a slow and painful death in one of the monasteries on Prinkipo. He died there in 1118.

In 1204 Prinkipo was occupied by the Venetians, who pillaged the convent and the monasteries, severely damaging all of them. In 1302 the Venetians raided the island and carried all the monks and nuns off into captivity, forcing Andronicus II to empty the imperial treasury to ransom them. That was the last historic incident involving the monasteries and convent on Prinkipo, of which only fragments remain.

The island consists of two large hills separated in the middle by a broad valley, so that the road around it makes a figure eight. There are phaetons for hire in the main square, and here again one asks for Büyük Tour for a ride all the way around the island or Küçük Tour to go around the northern half only. One should really take the Grand Tour, for the southern end of the island is almost totally unspoiled and in places it is extraordinarily beautiful. But the best way to tour the island is on foot, for one can then wander off on pathways up into the hills or down to the sea, where there are secluded coves, ideal for picnicking and swimming.

Before leaving the village stroll for a while around the town to look at some of the beautiful old Büyükada houses. One house of interest is at 55 Çankaya Cd; this is the *former residence of Izzet Paşa*, head of the secret police during the reign of Abdül Hamit II. Leon Trotsky lived here during the first years of his exile on Büyükada (1929–33), and it was here that he began to write his monumental 'History of the Russian Revolution'. Another very interesting house is on an unnamed street in the back of town; this is the *mansion of the Papal Nuncio*, the representative of the Vatican in Istanbul. The most notable of the Papal legates who lived here was Angelo Giuseppe Roncali, the future Pope John XXIII, who was Nuncio in Istanbul from 1934 to 1944. Across the street from the Nuncio's palace is the crumbling konak of the Şakirs, one of the most distinguished families in the last years of the Ottoman Empire. This was the birthplace of Aliye Berger-Boronai, one of the greatest Turkish painters in modern times.

Both of the island's hills are surmounted by monasteries. The one on Isa Tepesi, the Hill of Christ, is dedicated to the *Transfiguration*. Virtually nothing is known of the history or date of foundation of this monastery, other than that it was restored in 1597; the present buildings date from the 19C. It is well worth climbing the hill to see the monastery, for it is in a very picturesque location in the midst of a pine forest.

Yüce Tepe, the southern hill, is also thickly forested; it rises to an altitude of 202m, the highest in the archipelago. The picturesque **monastery of \*St. George** stands in a beautiful clearing at the top of the hill.

HISTORY. There is evidence that there was a monastery on this site as early as the 12C, though most of the present structure is modern. The monastery is known locally as Ayios Yorgios Coudonas, St. George of the Bells. One version of the legend that explains the foundation of the monastery has it that a shepherd was grazing his flock on the hill when he heard the sound of bells coming from under the ground. When he dug down he found an icon of St. George, which he and the other islanders enshrined on the spot.

The present structure consists of six separate chapels on three levels, the older sanctuaries being on the lower levels. On the ground floor is the caretaker's house and a chapel of St. George, built early in the present century. A flight of stairs leads down to the first level below. Just beside the steps is a chapel of the Blacherniotissa, Our Lady of Blachernae. Beyond that is a shrine of St. Haralambos, and past that is another chapel of St. George. Small iron rings set into the floor of these chapels were for controlling the madmen who were brought here in the hope of being cured, for in Byzantine times the monastic complex included an insane asylum. The room at the bottom of the stairs is a tiny shrine with an ayazma, a sacred spring. Beyond the ayazma one comes to the final chapel, dedicateted to the Twelve Apostles.

The building to the W of the church is a hostel for those who come to visit the monastery on the feast days of the several saints who have sanctuaries here. The most important of these festival days is that of St. George, 23 April, when hundreds of pious Greeks flock to visit the church. On that day the small café to the E of the church provides food and drink for those who visit the shrine, in a setting of incomparable beauty.

From the summit of Yüce Tepe one has an excellent view of the two tiny islets beyond Büyükada, *Sedef Adasi*, or Mother-of-Pearl Island (to the E), and *Tavşan Adasi*, Rabbit Island (to the S). In Byzantine times Sedef was known as Terebinthos and Tavşan was called Nyandros. Tiny as they are, both islets were the sites of religious establishments in Byzantium, with a monastery on Terebinthos and a convent on Nyandros. Both of them were founded in the mid-9C by the famous Patriarch Ignatius. Ignatius was the oldest son of Michael I, who reigned from 811 until 813, when he was deposed and exiled to Proti. At that time Ignatius was castrated so that he could never succeed to the throne. When he came of age he became a monk and his piety and learning soon made him a leader in the monastic community. In 842, the first year in the reign of Michael III, the Sot, his mother Theodora ruled as Regent, a position which allowed her to appoint Ignatius Patriarch of Constantinople. However, when Michael came of age he dismissed Ignatius, who had been critical of the scandalous behaviour of the Emperor and his court. Ignatius was then exiled to his monastery on Terebinthos for a time, before being dragged from one prison to another, continually humiliated and subjected to inhuman tortures. Widespread public indignation at this treatment of the saintly Ignatius finally forced Michael to allow him to return to his monastery on Terebinthos. When Basil I murdered Michael and usurped the throne in 867 he immediately restored Ignatius as Patriarch of Constantinople, dismissing Photius, who had been appointed by his predecessor. Ignatius served as Patriarch until his death in 877, after which his remains were brought back for burial in his monastery on Terebinthos.

Both Sedef and Tavşan can be reached by boats hired at the port in Büyükada. Sedef now has a colony of summer villas, but Tavşan is uninhabited. On Tavşan there are still some scattered ruins of the convent founded by the Patriarch Ignatius.

What little remains of the famous convent founded by the Empress Eirene is to be seen in the district called Maden; the site is on the E coast of the island near the Villa Rifat Pension. The scattered ruins there are known locally as *Kamares*, which in Turkish means the Arches, because until recent years there were a few arches of the convent still standing. Now there are only some overgrown foundation walls and fragments of architectural members scattered in the fields between the shore road and the sea.

# INDEX

Topographical names are printed in **bold** type, names of persons in *italics*, and other entries in ordinary type.

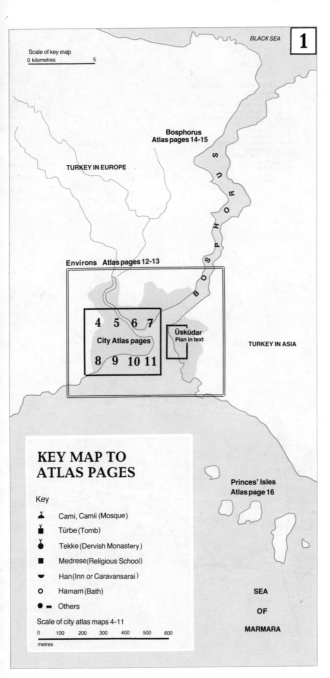

BLACK SEA

**1**

Scale of key map
0 kilometres — 5

Bosphorus
Atlas pages 14-15

TURKEY IN EUROPE

Environs  Atlas pages 12-13

| 4 | 5 | 6 | 7 |

City Atlas pages

| 8 | 9 | 10 | 11 |

Üsküdar
Plan in text

TURKEY IN ASIA

# KEY MAP TO
# ATLAS PAGES

Key

☖ Cami, Camii (Mosque)

⚰ Türbe (Tomb)

◉ Tekke (Dervish Monastery)

■ Medrese (Religious School)

▼ Han (Inn or Caravansarai)

○ Hamam (Bath)

● ▬ Others

Princes' Isles
Atlas page 16

Scale of city atlas maps 4-11

0    100   200   300   400   500   600

metres

SEA

OF

MARMARA

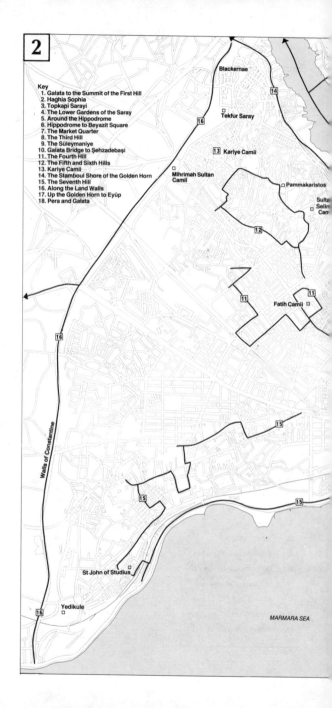

**2**

Key
1. Galata to the Summit of the First Hill
2. Haghia Sophia
3. Topkapi Sarayi
4. The Lower Gardens of the Saray
5. Around the Hippodrome
6. Hippodrome to Beyazit Square
7. The Market Quarter
8. The Third Hill
9. The Süleymaniye
10. Galata Bridge to Şehzadebaşi
11. The Fourth Hill
12. The Fifth and Sixth Hills
13. Kariye Camii
14. The Stamboul Shore of the Golden Horn
15. The Seventh Hill
16. Along the Land Walls
17. Up the Golden Horn to Eyüp
18. Pera and Galata

Blackernae

14

Tekfur Saray

16

13 Kariye Camii

Mihrimah Sultan
Camii

Pammakaristos

Sulta
Selin
Cam

12

11

11

Fatih Camii

16

Walls of Constantine

15

15

15

St John of Studius

16

Yedikule

MARMARA SEA

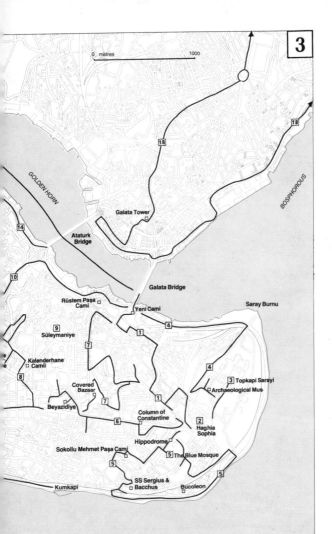

## PLAN OF ROUTES

3

0 metres 1000

GOLDEN HORN

BOSPHORUS

18

18

Galata Tower

Ataturk Bridge

14

10

Galata Bridge

Rüstem Paşa Cami

Yeni Cami

Saray Burnu

9 Süleymaniye

7

1

4

4

3 Topkapı Sarayı

Archaeological Mus

Kalenderhane Camii

8

7

Covered Bazaar

Beyazidiye

7

1

Column of Constantine

6

2 Haghia Sophia

Hippodrome

Sokollu Mehmet Paşa Cami

5

5 The Blue Mosque

5

SS Sergius & Bacchus

Bucoleon

5

Kumkapi

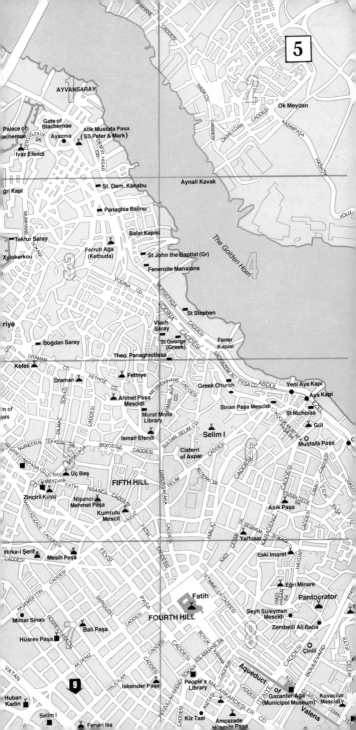

5

AYVANSARAY

Ok Meydan

Palace of Blachernae
Gate of Blachernae
Ayazma
Atik Mustafa Paşa (SS Peter & Mark)
İvaz Efendi

gri Kapi

Aynali Kavak

St. Dem. Kanabu

Panaghia Balinu

Tekfur Saray

The Golden Horn

Balat Kapisi

Xylokerkou

Ferruh Aga (Kethuda)

St John the Baptist (Gr)

Feneroite Mansions

St Stephen

riye

Vlach Saray

St George (Greek)

Fener Kapisi

Boğdan Saray

Theo. Panaghiotissa

Kefeli

Fethiye

Draman

Greek Church

Yeni Aya Kapi

Aya Kapi

n of
os

Ahmet Paşa Mescidi

Sinan Paşa Mescidi

St Nicholas

Murat Molla Library

Gül

İsmail Efendi

Selim I

Mustafa Paşa

Cistern of Aspar

Üç Baş

FIFTH HILL

Aşik Paşa

Zincirli Kuyu

Nişanci Mehmet Paşa

Kumrulu Mescit

Yarhisar

Eski İmaret

Hirka-i Şerif

Mesih Paşa

Eğri Minare

Pantocrator

Fatih

Şeyh Süleyman Mescidi

FOURTH HILL

Zembelli Ali Baba

Mimar Sinan

Çinili

Bali Paşa

Hüsrev Paşa

Aqueduct of

9

İskender Paşa

People's Library

Gazanfer Aga (Municipal Museum)

Kovacilar Mescidi

Huban Kadin

Selim I

Kiz Tasi

Fenari İsa

Amcazade Hüseyin Paşa

Valens

Spor ve Sergi Sarayı
Askeri Müze
(Military Museum)

Military
Barracks

Radioevi

Hilton Hotel

ELMADAG CADDESI

ASKEROCAĞI CD.

BEYOGLU

TAKSIM PARK

TAKSIM
SQUARE

French Consulate

Aya Triada

Opera House

Ağa

TAKSIM

Fish Market

British
Consulate

GALATASARAY
SQUARE

Galatasaray Lycée

St.Anthony

Dutch
Embassy

Maison de France

Chapel

Cihangir v

Mary Draperis

Russian
Embassy

Pal.di Venezia

Swedish
Embassy

NEL

Hafi
Efendi

Crimean
Memorial Ch

Cannon House

Karabaş
Mescidi

Nusretiye

Kiliç Ali Paşa

Galata
Tower

SS Peter
& Paul

Sta

Yer Altı

Ferry Terminal

The Bosphorus

Galata Bridge

**11**

**8**

MILLET
Monastir Mescidi
TATİPAŞA BAHRİYE NEZARETİ CADDESİ

MEVLEVİHANE
CADDESİ
Yeni Mevlevihane Kapısı
MEYDANCİK CADDESİ
MİMARKASIM CADDESİ
YAYLA CADDESİ
AHMET VEFİK PAŞA CADDESİ

Cistern of
St Mocius
*Alti Mermer*

CEVDET PAŞA

SİLİVRİKAPI
Silivri Kapisi
SEVENTH HILL
HEKİMOĞLU ALİ PAŞA CADDESİ
Zoodochus Pege
SEVRİKAPI BALIKLİ CD
SEVTNİZAM CD.
İbrahim Paşa
Hekimoğlu
Ali Paşa
Davu
Ramazan Efendi
İsa
Me

Koca Mustafa
Paşa
Sancaktar
Mescidi
Sulu Monastir
Ağa
Crypt
(SS Karpos & Papylos)
St George

Belgrad Kapisi
MERHABA CADDESİ

SS Constantine & Helena
Narlı Kapi
Imrahor
(St John of Studius)

Yediküle Kapısı
Golden Gate
Yediküle
Gate of Christ

KENNEDY

Marble Tower

HALICILAR CADDESI

İskender Paşa

People's Library

MACARKARDEŞLER

Aqueduct

of

Gazanf

(Municipa

**5**

Huban Kadin

Selim I

Fenari Isa (Constantine Lips)

Kiz Tasi

Amcazade Hüseyin Paşa

St Polyeuktos

Kovacılar Mescidi

**9**

Burmali

Şehzade

Belidiye

Şehzadebaşı

Şeyh-ul Islam Ankaravi Mehmet Efendi

Kale T

MILLET

Selçuk Hatun

Murat Paşa

CADDESI

HÜSREY SOKAĞI

HORPOR

BOSTAN

ATATÜRK

SELIM PAŞA SOKAĞI

Büyük Taş

Valide Sultan

AKSARAY SQUARE

Laleli

ORDU

GENÇTÜRK

FETHI BEY CD

HABIR

FETHIYE

HARIKZEDELER SOKAĞI

Ragıp Paş Library

seki Hürrem

Bayram Paşa

Column of Arcadius

PAŞA

CADDESI

HASEKI

Ebu Bekir Paşa Mektebi

INKILAP CADDESI

SAIT

SAIR HAŞMET SOK

CADDES

Bodrum

EFENDI SK

MESIH

PAŞA

CERRAH

Cerrah Paşa

LANGA

CADDESI

KÜÇÜK

KUÇÜK LANGA CADDESI

AZIMKAR SOKAĞI

HAYRIYE

MUSTAFA

KEMAL

TÜCCARI

LALELI

SOKAĞI

NISNA

MOLLA

KEMAL

LANGA HISARI SOKAĞI

ALIŞAN

NAMIK

CADDESI

KENNEDY

5

6

Sea of Marmara

7

8

Yer Altı

Ferry Terminal

Galata Bridge

1

2

SARAY BURNU

KÖŞKU CADDESI

KENNEDY CADDESI

Sirkeci Station

Goth's Column

DES

BİNBE MAL CADDESI

ANKARA CADDESI

EBUSSUUT CADDESI

TAYAHATUN SOKAGI

Çinili Köşkü

Gülhane Park

Topkapi Sarayi

Sublime Porte

Mus. of the Ancient Orient

Beşir Ağa

Archaeological Museum

Çağaloğlu

Alay Köşkü

4

ALEMDAR CADDESI

Haghia Eirene

FIRST HILL

Zeynep Sultan

Soğuk Kuyu

ÇEŞME SOKAGI

CADDES

Yerebatan Saray

Haghia Sophia

YEREBATAN CADDESI

Ahmet III Fountain

DIVAN YOLU

Firuz Ağa

AYASOFYA MEYDANI

BABIHUMAYUN CADDESI

PAŞA CADDESI

İSHAK

birdirek

Augustaeum

Roxelana

Atmeydanı

MİMAR MEHMET

KABASAKAL SOKAGI

KUTLUGUN SOKAGI

Hippodrome Park

Sultan Ahmet I

AK BIYIK CADDESI

Byzantine sea walls

sea walls

Mosiac Museum

İncili Köşkü

TAVUKHANE S.K.

CANKURTARAN CADDESI

OKRUSU

AK BIYIK MEYDANI

SOFYA CADDESI

Pal. of Bucoleon

ÜÇÜNCÜ SOKAGI

Stable Gate

ergius & Bacchus

Lighthouse

Byzantine sea walls

6

MARMARA

7

8

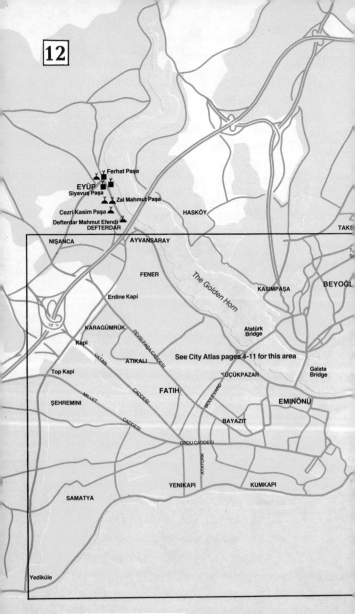

## 12

Ferhat Paşa

EYÜP
Siyavuş Paşa
Zal Mahmut Paşa

Cezri Kasim Paşa
Defterdar Mahmut Efendi
DEFTERDAR

HASKÖY

TAKS

NIŞANCA

AYVANSARAY

FENER

The Golden Horn

KASIMPAŞA

BEYOĞL

Erdine Kapi

KARAGÜMRÜK

FEVSIPAŞA CADDESI

Atatürk
Bridge

Kapi

VATAN

See City Atlas pages 4-11 for this area

Top Kapi

ATIKALI

CADDESI

FATIH

KÜÇÜKPAZAR

Galata
Bridge

ŞEHREMINI

MILLET

CADDESI

BAYAZIT

BOULEVARD

EMINÖNÜ

ORDU CADDESI

SAMATYA

YENIKAPI

ATATÜRK

KUMKAPI

Yediküle

## ISTANBUL
## Environs

0 metres    500    1000    1500

*Sea of Marmara*

Bay

Kandilli

AKINTI
BURNU

American Coll. for Girls ∎    Arnavutköy    **13**

Vaniköy    ∎ Istanbul
Rasathane

Kuruçeşme

Kuleli Naval
∎ College

Sadullah Paşa Yalisí ∎
Çengelköy

Hamidiye ⚓

Şale Köşkü ∎    Malta Köşkü ∎

Yildiz Park

Shrine ⚱    Abdül Mecit I ⚱
⚲ Mecidiye    Ortaköy    Beylerbey
BEŞIKTAŞ
Askeri Müse    ● Palace of Çirağan    Bosphorous
(Military Museum)    Bridge
Fine Arts    Beylerbey Palace ∎
Museum    Maritime
Museum
at Paşa    Beşiktas
ium    ● Dolmabahçe Palace
○
Yusuf    ● Dolmabahçe    **The Bosphorus**    Kuzguncuk
∎ Kabataş
olla Çelebi

BÜYÜK ▲
CAMLÍCA

ÜSKÜDAR

See large scale plan

SELIMIYE

HAYDARPASA

KADIKÖY    ∎ Tram Mus

MODA

KALAM IŞ

FENERBAHCE

14

BELGRAD FOREST

Sultan Mahmut's
Reservoir

Long Aqueduct

)(

Burgaz

)( Bent Aqueduct

TURKEY IN EUROPE

)(

)(

Alibey Suyu

Kağıthane Suyu

The Golden Horn

See larger scale
Envi

ISTANBUL

Sea of Marmara

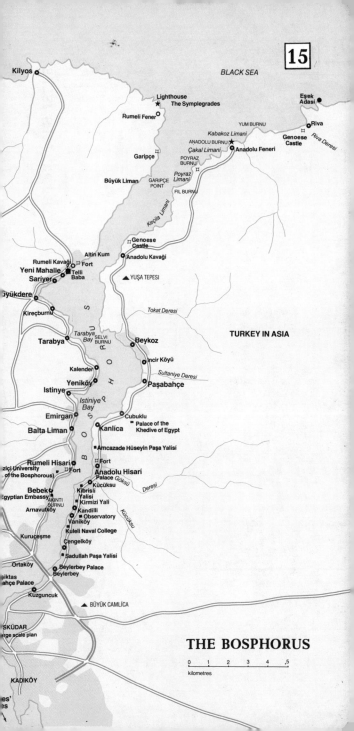

**THE BOSPHORUS**

15

BLACK SEA

Kilyos

Lighthouse
The Symplegrades

Eşek Adası

Rumeli Feneri

Riva

YUM BURNU

Kabakoz Limani

ANADOLU BURNU

Genoese Castle

Riva Deresi

Garipçe

Çakal Limani

POYRAZ BURNU

Anadolu Feneri

Büyük Liman

GARIPÇE POINT

Poyraz Limani

FIL BURNU

Keçila Limani

Genoese Castle

Altin Kum

Anadolu Kavaği

Rumeli Kavaği

Fort

Yeni Mahalle

Telli Baba

Sariyer

YUŞA TEPESI

üyükdere

TURKEY IN ASIA

Kireçburnu

Tokat Deresi

Tarabya Bay

SELVI BURNU

Tarabya

Beykoz

Incir Köyü

Kalender

Sultaniye Deresi

Yeniköy

Paşabahçe

Istinye

Istinye Bay

Emirgan

Cubuklu
Palace of the Khedive of Egypt

Balta Liman

Kanlica

Amcazade Hüseyin Paşa Yalisi

Fort

zİçi University
(of the Bosphorous)

Rumeli Hisari

Fort

Anadolu Hisari
Palace Göksü

Bebek

Küçüksu

Egyptian Embassy

Kibrisli Yalisi

AKINTI BURNU

Kirmizi Yali

Deresi

Arnavutköy

Kandilli

Observatory

Yaniköy

Kuleli Naval College

Kuruçeşme

Cengelköy

Ortaköy

Sadullah Paşa Yalisi

Beylerbey Palace

şiktas
ahçe Palace

Beylerbey

Küzguncuk

BÜYÜK CAMLICA

SKÜDAR
arge scale plan

KADIKÖY

es'
es

0  1  2  3  4  .5
kilometres

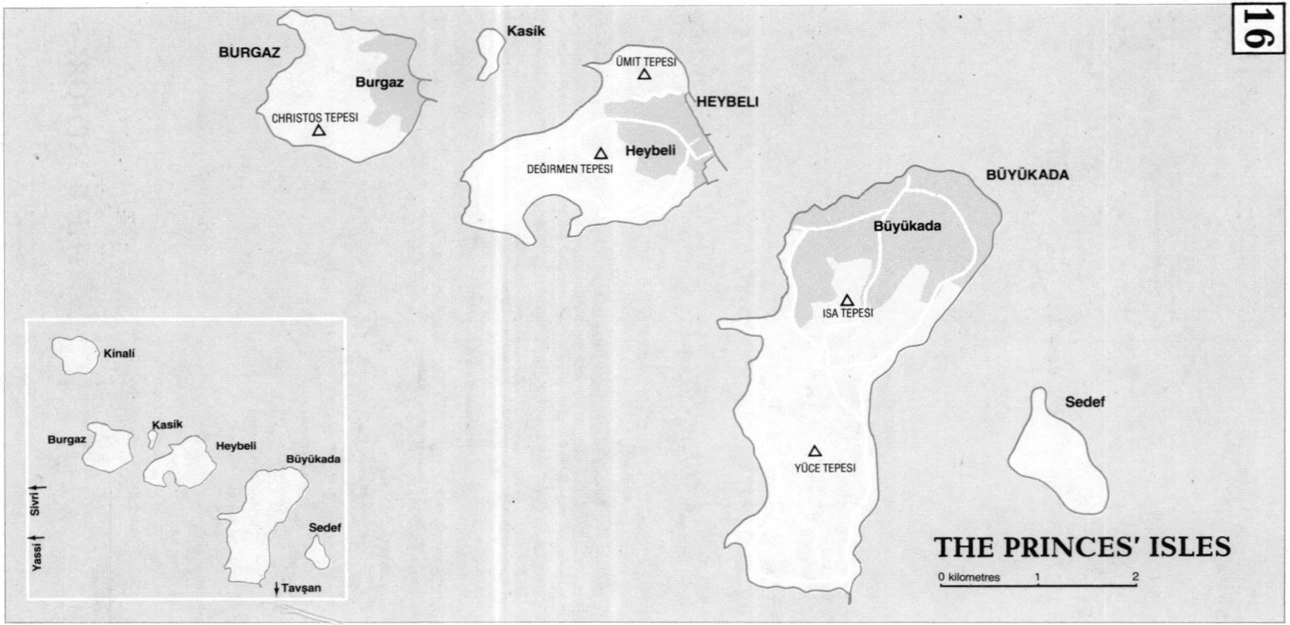

# THE PRINCES' ISLES

0 kilometres 1 2

**BÜYÜKADA**

Büyükada

ISA TEPESI

YÜCE TEPESI

Sedef

**HEYBELİ**

Ümit Tepesi

Heybeli

DEĞİRMEN TEPESI

Kasik

**BURGAZ**

Burgaz

CHRISTOS TEPESI

Kinali

Burgaz

Kasik

Heybeli

Büyükada

Sedef

Tavşan

Sivri

Yassi

16